PHYSIOLOGICAL PSYCHOLOGY

Dr. Sherly Williams E

Dr. Razeena Karim L

INDIA • SINGAPORE • MALAYSIA

Notion Press

Old No. 38, New No. 6
McNichols Road, Chetpet
Chennai - 600 031

First Published by Notion Press 2018
Copyright © Sherly Williams E & Razeena Karim L 2018
All Rights Reserved.

ISBN 978-1-64324-265-1

Dedicated to Our Beloved Parents

William Fernandez & Elsie Williams
And
Dr. M A Karim & Laila Beevi

CONTENTS

Brain and Behaviour   **1–34**

❖   Neuroscience – Techniques in neurophysiology – CT SCAN – Magnetic Resonance Imaging (MRI) – fMRI – Positron Emission Tomography (PET) – rCBF – EEG – Lesioning and stimulation – The Neuron – Function and type of neuron – Saltatory propagation – Nerve fibre – Nerve impulse – Action potential – All or none law – Synapse – Synaptic transmission – Properties of a synapse – Central Nervous System – Brain – Forebrain – Mid brain – Hind brain – Ventricles of brain – Functions of major parts of brain – Spinal cord – Anatomy of reflex – Physiology of reflex – The Reflex action – Blood brain barrier – Peripheral nervous system (PNS) – Autonomous Nervous System (ANS) – Sympathetic Nervous System (SNS) – Para Sympathetic Nervous System (PSNS) – Emergency theory – Para Sympathetic Nervous System effect (PNS effect) – Polygraph – Neurotransmitters and drug action – Neuropeptides – Psycho Active drugs – Types of drugs – Asymmetry in Human brain – The theory of localization – Wernicke's and Broca's area

Biological basis of Sensory Processes   **35–93**

❖   Visual system – Hue, saturation, and brightness – Structure of eye – The retina – Functioning of eye – Visual pathways – Visual defects – Myopia (short sight) – Hyperopia (Long sight) – Astigmatism – Presbyopia – Transduction in the retina – Theories of colour vision – Auditory system – Ear – Coding of auditory information – Theories of audition – The Resonance or Place Theory – The Frequency Theory – Volley theory – Nature of sound – Intensity of sound – Loudness – Pitch – Frequency – Ultrasound – Infra sound – Amplitude – Receptor organs – Chemoreceptor – Gustatory receptors – Taste bud – Taste papillae – Taste reception – Neural pathway of coding for taste – Olfactory system – Olfactory receptors – Mechanism of olfactory coding and perception – Categorisation of odours – Interaction of olfaction and taste – Olfactory disorders – Cutaneous system – Ruffini's end organ (skin stretch) – End-bulbs of Krause (Cold) – Meissner's corpuscle (changes in texture, slow vibrations) – Pacinian corpuscle (deep pressure, fast vibrations) – Merkel's disc (sustained touch and pressure) – Free nerve endings – Thermoreceptor – Nociceptors – Proprioception - kinesthetics – Applications – NEURAL CODING – Types of pain – Stimulation produced analgesia (SPA) – Ascending and Descending Pain Suppression Mechanism

PREFACE

Physiological Psychology is the study of the physiological basis of how we think, connecting the physical operation of the brain with what we actually say and do. It is thus concerned with sensation, sleep, emotion, motivation, memory, learning, nerve cells, brain structures and components and how all this leads to speech and action. It is also, of course, important to understand how we take in information from our five senses.

Physiological Psychology covers the general area of 'brain and behaviour' which is a modular subject in many university courses. Most psychologist would agree that physiological psychology has developed rapidly in recent years and also the expanded use of physiological ideas have spread to many areas of psychology which were not common before. This text attempts to prepare students to understand physiological concepts in other specialized fields that they will encounter in their higher studies. The biology departments in many colleges lack a psychologist just as the psychology department often has no physiological psychologist. A prescribed text book will go a long way in helping the students to study and master this subject.

This book is intended to be a text book for psychology undergraduate college students. This book is organised in four chapters. The first chapter covers the area under Brain and Behaviour which includes Techniques in neurophysiology, the Neuron and its functions, Central Nervous System, Autonomous Nervous System (ANS), Sympathetic Nervous System (SNS), Para Sympathetic Nervous System (PSNS), Neurotransmitters and Drug Action. Second chapter deals with Biological basis of Sensory Processes including Visual system, Auditory system, Gustatory system, Olfactory system and Cutaneous system. The third chapter contains Physiological basis of Sleep, Eating, Drinking and Sexual behaviour. The last chapter covers the area of Emotion, Learning and Memory.

The text book is presented in a way so that it serves as an adequate reference book for any psychology students having physiological psychology in the degree level. It covers majority of the topics under the syllabi of various universities. With these features, we sincerely hope that this book would serve as a valuable text for the students.

As teachers handling physiological psychology for UG psychology students who are from multidisciplinary background, it came to the notice that the students are finding it difficult to understand the subject. This motivated us to write a book on the subject, which can be understood by the under graduate students.

We are glad to express our gratitude to the Principal Dr. Vincent B Netto, Manager Rev Fr. Anil Jose and Pro manager Rev Fr. Roldon Jacob of Fatima Mata National College (Autonomous) for their support and encouragement. We are also expressing our sincere gratitude to our former Principal Dr. Sr. Soosamma Kavumpurath for her support and guidance. The help and support provided by all the teaching faculty and non teaching members of the Department of Zoology needs special mention. The help rendered by the research scholars under the first author are acknowledged.

Suggestions for further improvement of this book are cordially invited and shall be incorporated in future revised editions.

We extend our sincere thanks to Notion Publishers for bringing out this book in the present form.

– Authors

ABBREVIATIONS

5-HIAA	–	5-hydroxyindoleacetic acid
5-HT	–	5- Hydroxytryptamine
ACE	–	Angiotensin-Converting Enzyme
Ach	–	Acetyl Choline
ACTH	–	Adrenocorticotropic hormone
ADH	–	Adenosine Diphosphate
AMP	–	Adenosine Mono Phosphate
AMPA	–	α – amino-3-hydroxy-5-methyl-4-isoxazolepropionic acid
AMPAR	–	α – amino-3-hydroxy-5-methyl-4-isoxazolepropionic acid receptor
ANS	–	Autonomous Nervous System
APC	–	Anterior Piriform Cortex
ARAS	–	Ascending Reticular Activating System
ARC	–	Activity Regulated Cytoskeleton Associated Protein
ARP	–	Agouti Related Protein
ATPase	–	Adenosine Triphosphatase
AVP	–	Arginine Vasopressin
BBB	–	Blood–Brain Barrier
BBS	–	Bardet–Biedl syndrome
BMI	–	Body Mass Index
BMR	–	Basal Metabolic Rate
BP	–	Blood Pressure
C –terminal	–	Carboxy terminal
cAMP	–	Cyclic Adenosine Monophosphate
CART	–	Cocaine- and Amphetamine Regulated Transcript
CCK	–	Cholecystokinin
CF	–	Characteristic Frequency

CN	–	Caudate Nucleus
CNS	–	Central Nervous System
CO_2	–	Carbondioxide
COPD	–	Obstructive Pulmonary Disease
CORT	–	Corticosterone
CPAP	–	Continuous Positive Airway Pressure
CRF	–	Corticotrophin-Releasing Factor
CRH	–	Corticotropin-Releasing Hormone
CRT	–	Cathode Ray Tube
CSA	–	Central Sleep Apnea
CSF	–	Cerebrospinal Fluid
CT	–	Computed Tomography
DA	–	Dopamine
DDD	–	Degenerative Disc Disease
DNA	–	Deoxyribonucleic Acid
DR	–	Dorsal Raphe
DSIP	–	Delta Sleep Inducing Peptide
DSM-IV	–	Diagnostic and Statistical Manual of Mental Disorders -IV edition
DWI	–	Diffusion-Weighted Imaging
EBA	-	Extrastriate Body Area
EC	–	Enriched condition
EEG	–	Electroencephalogram
EMR	–	Electromagnetic Radiation
FDA	–	Food and Drug Administration
fMRI	–	Functional Magnetic Resonance Imaging
FMSF	–	False Memory Syndrome Foundation
FNE	–	Free Nerve Ending
FSH	–	Follicle-Stimulating Hormone
FTG	–	Gigantocellular Tegmental Field
GABA	–	Gamma Amino Butyric Acid
GCs	–	Glucocorticoids
GI	–	Gastro Intestine
GIP	–	Gastric Inhibitory Peptide
GPCR	–	G protein coupled reactions
G-protein	–	Guanine Nucleotide binding Protein
GSR	–	Galvanic Skin Response
HCl	–	Hydrochloric Acid
HPA	–	Hypothalamic–Pituitary–Adrenal Axis

Hz	–	Hertz
IBS	–	Irritable Bowel Syndrome
IC	–	Impoverished Condition
ICD-10-CM	–	International Classification of Diseases, 10th Revision,Clinical Modification
ICD-9-CM	–	International Classification of Diseases, 9th Revision,Clinical Modification
ICSH	–	Interstitial Cell-Stimulating Hormone
IQ	–	Intelligent Quotient
IR	–	Infra Red Radiation
LC	–	Locus Coeruleus
LC-NE	–	Locus Coeruleus-noradrenergic
LGN	–	Lateral Geniculate Nucleus
LH	–	Leutinizing Hormone
LSD	–	Lysergic Acid Diethylamide
LTD	–	Long-Term Depression
LTP	–	Long-Term Potentiation
M1	–	Primary Motor Cortex
MAO	–	Monoamine Oxidase
MCH	–	Melanin Concentrating Hormone
MEG	–	Magnetoencephalography
MHPG	–	3-Methoxy-4-HydroxyPhenylGlycol
MR	–	Mineralocorticoid Receptor
MRI	–	Magnetic Resonance Imaging
N3	–	Slow-wave sleep
NaCl	–	Sodium Chloride
NE	–	Norepinephrine
NINDS	–	Neurological Disorders and Stroke
NMDA	–	N-methyl D-aspartate
NMDAR	–	N-methyl D-aspartate Receptors
NPY	–	Neuropeptide Y
NREM	–	Non- Rapid Eye Movement Sleep
NRG	–	Nucleus Reticularis Gigantocellularis
NRM	–	Nucleus Raphe Magnus
NST	–	Nucleus of Solitary Tract
OA	–	Opiate Analgesia
OCD	–	Obsessive compulsive disorder
OR	–	Olfactory Receptor
OSA	–	Obstructive Sleep Apnea
OVLT	–	Organum Vasculosum of the Lamina Terminalis

PAD	–	Peripheral Artery Disease
PAG	–	Periaqueductal Gray
PCPA	–	Parachlorophenylalanine
PET	–	Positron Emission Tomography
PFC	–	Prefrontal cortex
PGO	–	Ponto-geniculo-occipital waves
PKA	–	Protein kinase A
PLR	–	Pupillary Light Reflex
PMC	–	Pre-Motor Cortex
PNE	–	Primary Nocturnal Enuresis
PNS	–	Peripheral Nervous System
PNS effect	–	Parasympathetic Nervous System effect
POMC	–	Pro-Opiomelanocortin
PPA	–	Parahippocampal Gyrus
PPC	–	Posterior Piriform Cortex
PS	–	Paradoxical Sleep
PSD-95	–	Post Synaptic Density protein 95
PSNS	–	Para Sympathetic Nervous System
PTSD	–	Post Traumatic Stress Disorder
PWS	–	Prader–Willi Syndrome
PYY	–	Peptide Tyrosine Tyrosine
RAAS	-	Renin–Angiotensin–Aldosterone System
RAS	–	Reticular Activating System
RAWM	–	Radial Arm Water Maze
rCBF	–	Regional Cerebral Blood Flow
REM	–	Rapid Eye Movement Sleep
RLS	–	Restless Leg Syndrome
RN	–	Raphe Nuclei
RNA	–	Ribonucleic Acid
SAD	–	Seasonal Affective Disorder
SCN	–	Suprachiasmatic Nuclei
SDB	–	Sleep-Disorder Breathing
SFO	–	Subfornical Organ
SIDS	–	Sudden infant death syndrome
SNE	–	Secondary Nocturnal Enuresis
SNRIs	–	Selective norepinephrine reuptake inhibitors
SNS	–	Sympathetic Nervous System
SPA	–	Stimulation Produced Analgesia

SSRIs	–	Serotonin Reuptake Inhibitors
TBI	–	Traumatic Brain Injury
TENS	–	Transcutaneous Electrical Nerve Stimulation
THC	–	Tetrahydrocannabinol
THP	–	Tetra Hydro Papaveroline
TMS	–	Transcranial Magnetic Stimulation
TRAAK	–	TWIK Related Arachidonic acid Activated K+ channel
TREK	–	TWIK RElated K+ channels
TRF	–	Thyrotropic hormone-Release Factor
TRP	–	Transient Receptor Potential
TRPM8	–	Transient Receptor Potential Cation Channel Subfamily M Member 8
TRPV1	–	The Transient Receptor Potential Cation Channel Subfamily V Member 1
TTH	–	Thyrotropic hormone
UR	–	Unconditioned Response
US	–	Unconditioned Stimulus
VIP	–	Vasoactive Intestinal Polypeptide
VMH	–	Ventromedial Hypothalamus
WGTA	–	Wisconsin General Testing Apparatus
α MSH	–	α Melanocyte Stimilating Hormone.

INTRODUCTION

Psychology is the science of behaviour and mind including conscious and unconscious phenomena, as well as thought. It is an academic discipline of immense scope and diverse interests that, when taken together, seek an understanding of the emergent properties of brains, and all the variety of epiphenomena they manifest. Psychology has been described as a "hub science" with psychological findings linking to research and perspectives from the social sciences, natural sciences, medicine, humanities, and philosophy. One of the greatest challenges that we face today is to understand how the brain and in doing so, understand ourselves as well. There are different types of psychology, such as cognitive, forensic, social, and developmental psychology. A person with a condition that affects their mental health may benefit from assessment and treatment with a psychologist. Psychologists attempt to understand the role of mental functions in individual and social behaviour, while also exploring the physiological and biological processes that underlie cognitive functions and behaviours. A psychologist may offer treatment that focuses on behavioural adaptations. Psychologists explore behaviour and mental processes, including perception, cognition, attention, emotion (affect), intelligence, phenomenology, motivation (conation), brain functioning, and personality. This extends to interaction between people, such as interpersonal relationships, including psychological resilience, family resilience, and other areas. A psychiatrist is a medical doctor who is more likely to focus on medical management of mental health issues.

There are different types of psychology that serve different purposes. Clinical psychology integrates science, theory, and practice in order to understand, predict and relieve problems with adjustment, disability, and discomfort. It promotes adaption, adjustment, and personal development. Cognitive psychology investigates internal mental processes, such as problem solving, memory, learning, and language. It looks at how people think, perceive, communicate, remember, and learn. It is closely related to neuroscience, philosophy, and linguistics. Developmental psychology is the scientific study of systematic psychological changes that a person experiences over the life span, often referred to as human development. Evolutionary psychology looks at how human behaviour, for example language, has been affected by psychological adjustments during evolution. Forensic psychology involves applying psychology to criminal investigation and the law. Health psychology is also called behavioural medicine or medical psychology. Neuropsychology looks at the structure and function of the brain in relation to behaviours and psychological processes. A neuropsychology may be involved if a condition involves lesions in the brain, and assessments that involve recording electrical activity in the brain. Occupational or organizational psychology involved in assessing and making recommendations about the performance of people at work and in training. Social psychology uses scientific methods to understand how social influences impact human behaviour. It seeks to explain how feelings, behaviour, and thoughts are influenced by the actual, imagined or implied presence of other people.

Physiological psychology is the branch of psychology that concerns with the relation between nervous system and behaviour. This field of psychology takes an empirical and practical approach when studying the brain and human behaviour. In this area of research, the focus of attention is on the functions of the brain and spinal cord, sense organ, muscles and glands. Physiological psychology can uncover many truths about human behaviour. Physiological psychology studies concerned with the brain cells, structures, components, and chemical interactions that are involved in order to produce actions. Physiological psychologists believe that the mind is a function performed by the brain. Study of human brain functions has helped us gain some insight into the nature of human consciousness, which appears to be related to the language functions of the brain. The physiological approach to psychology focuses on our biological make up, and the events that occur in our bodies which cause our behaviour. Mainly, therefore, physiological psychology will focus on the brain, but it will also include study of the nervous system, and hormones. The approach has revealed that a number of areas of the brain have specific functions.

BRAIN AND BEHAVIOUR

Behaviour results from neural and chemical systems working together in the brain. Everything that goes on in the mind, the way we see, feel, remember and act, is constrained by the way the brain works. Mind, brain and behaviour focuses on the workings of the individual from a psychological perspective. It includes the details of neural components, constituting the brain, operation of sensory system, underlying interaction with the external environment and the cognitive processes that constructs the internal world experienced by the individual. Careful consideration will be given to the nature of the internal world and the importance of its relationship to the external world.

NEUROSCIENCE

Neuroscience is the study of the brain and behaviour and it is a science and a practice. Neuroscience comprises the neuroanatomy, neurophysiology, brain functions and related physiological aspects. Neurobiological data provides physical evidence for a theoretical approach to the investigation of cognition. Behavioural neuroscience deals with the study of behaviour and its physiological correlation in the brain with the goal of understanding the neural mechanism. Neuroscientists studies on the behavioural mechanism techniques ranging from recording of activity in single neuron to imaging activity in the human brain. Psychological physiology is the branch of psychology concerned with the relationship with the physical functioning of the organism and its behaviour. It is a subdivision of behavioural neuroscience that studies the neural mechanism of perception and behaviour.

TECHNIQUES IN NEUROPHYSIOLOGY

Neurophysiology, the precursor to modern neuroscience allowed us to learn a great deal about brain function. Techniques in neurophysiology help to track temporal dynamics of brain function, its effective connectivity, excitability and plasticity. It is a tool for basic research and for clinical diagnostics purposes. A number of brain imaging techniques are available to investigate the function of brain.

Brain imaging techniques allow doctors and researchers to view activity or problems within the human brain, without invasive neurosurgery. There are a number of accepted, safe imaging techniques in use today in research facilities and hospitals throughout the world. Neuroimaging falls into two broad categories: structural imaging and functional imaging.

Structural imaging, which deals with the structure of the brain and the diagnosis of large-scale intracranial disease (such as a tumor), as well as injury. Functional imaging, which is used to diagnose metabolic diseases and lesions on a finer scale (such as Alzheimer's disease), and also for neurological and cognitive-psychology research. Functional imaging allows the brain's information processing to be visualized directly, because activity in the involved area of the brain increases metabolism and "lights up" on the scan.

CT SCAN

Computed tomography (CT) scanning builds up a picture of the brain based on the differential absorption of X-rays. During a CT scan the subject lies on a table that slides in and out of a hollow, cylindrical apparatus. An X-rays source rides on a ring around the inside of the tube, with its beam aimed at the subjects head. After passing through the head, the beam is sampled by one of the many detectors that line the machine's circumference. Images made using X-rays depend on the absorption of the beam by the tissue it passes through. Bone and hard tissue absorb X-rays well, air and water absorb very little and soft tissue is somewhere in between. Thus, CT scans reveal the gross features of the brain but do not resolve its structure well.

MAGNETIC RESONANCE IMAGING (MRI)

Magnetic resonance imaging (MRI) (Fig -1) and functional magnetic resonance imaging (fMRI) scans are the form of neural imaging most directly useful to the field of psychology. An MRI uses strong magnetic fields to align spinning atomic nuclei (usually hydrogen protons) within body tissues, then disturbs the axis of rotation of these nuclei and observes the radio frequency signal generated as the nuclei return to their baseline status. Through this process, an MRI creates an image of the brain structure. MRI scans are noninvasive, pose little health risk, and can be used on infants and in utero, providing a consistent mode of imaging across the development spectrum. One disadvantage is that the patient has to hold still for long periods of time in a noisy, cramped space while the imaging is performed.

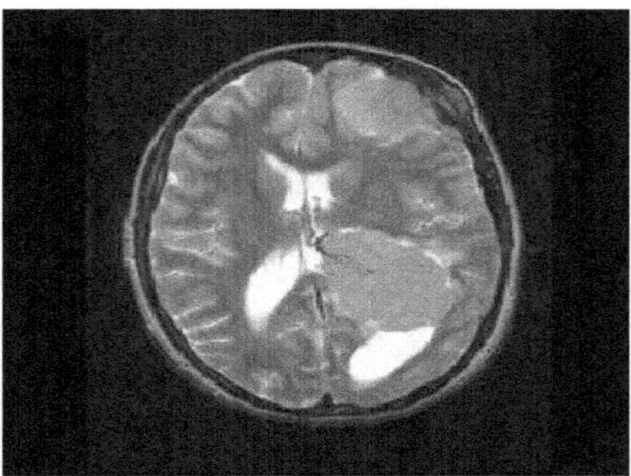

(Fig -1) MRI brain scan (in the axial plane—that is, slicing from front-to-back and side-to-side through the head) showing a brain tumor at the bottom right.

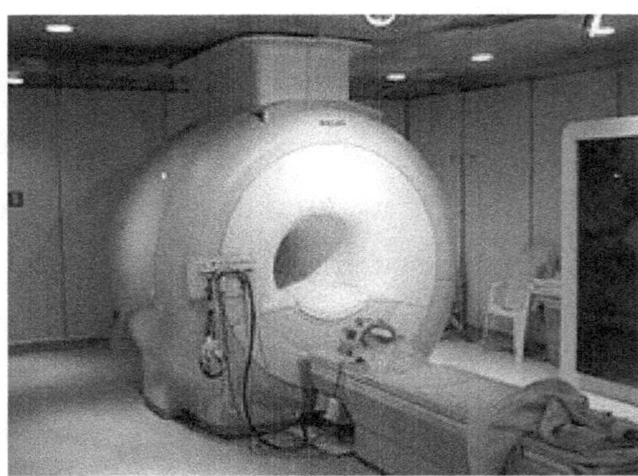

fMRI

Functional magnetic resonance imaging, or fMRI, (Fig -2) is a technique for measuring brain activity. It works by detecting the changes in blood oxygenation and flow that occur in response to neural activity – when a brain area is more active it consumes more oxygen and to meet this increased demand blood flow increases to the active area. fMRI can be used to produce activation maps showing which parts of the brain are involved in a particular mental process.

The fMRI is a series of MRIs that measures both the structure and the functional activity of the brain through computer adaptation of multiple images. Specifically, the fMRI measures signal changes in the brain that are due to changing neural activity. In an fMRI, a patient can perform mental tasks and the area of action can be detected through blood flow from one part of the brain to another by taking pictures less than a second apart and showing where the brain "lights up". For example, when a person processes visual information, blood rushes to the back of the brain, which is where the occipital lobe is located. fMRIs make it possible to show when things happen, how brain areas change with experience, and which brain areas work together. They have been used to study a wide range of psychological phenomena, including the neural activity of telling a lie, the differences between novices and experts when playing a musical instrument, and what happens inside our heads when we dream.

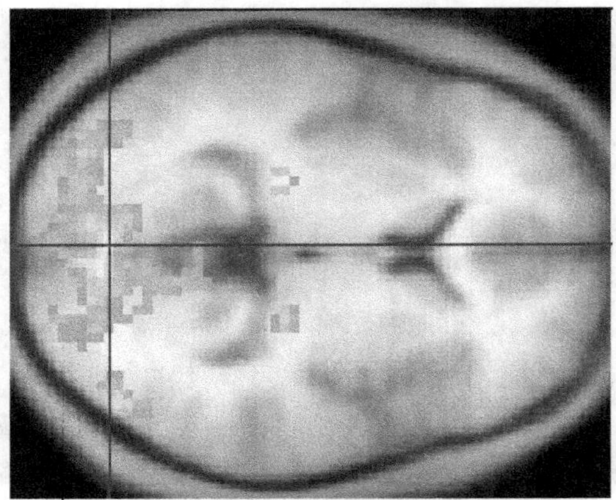

(Fig -2) An fMRI scan showing regions of activation including the primary visual cortex.

POSITRON EMISSION TOMOGRAPHY (PET)

Positron Emission Tomography (PET) uses trace amounts of short-lived radioactive material to map functional processes in the brain. When the material undergoes radioactive decay a positron is emitted, which can be picked up by the detector. Areas of high radioactivity are associated with brain activity. Positron emission tomography (PET) scans (Fig -3) measure levels of the sugar glucose in the brain in order to illustrate where neural firing is taking place. This works because active neurons use glucose as fuel. As part of the scan, a tracer substance attached to radioactive isotopes is injected into the blood. When parts of the brain become active, blood (which contains the tracer) is sent to deliver oxygen. This creates visible spots, which are then picked up by detectors and used to create a video image of the brain while performing a particular task. However, with PET scans, we can only locate generalized areas of brain activity and not specific locations. In addition, PET scans are costly and invasive, making their use limited. However, they can be used in some forms of medical diagnosis, including for Alzheimer's.

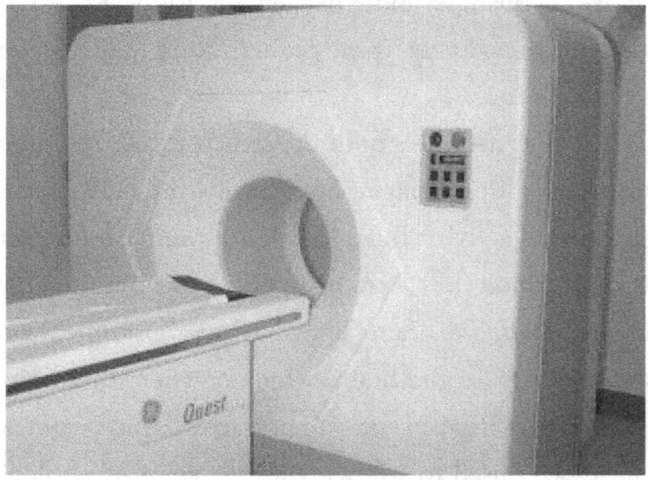

(Fig -3) This is a view of the PET scanner from the outside; the radiation detectors are under the covering panel.

RCBF

rCBF is a type of PET scan that also measures more and less active brain regions based on radioactive substances transported through blood flow. Patients inhale a small amount of radioactive gas such as xenon, which the blood carries to the brain.

Patients sit under devices resembling hair dryers that cover your head. These "caps" have sensors that measure the radioactivity transported to the brain, identifying the more active areas of the brain. Similar to PET scans, rCBF does not measure neuronal activity but only changes in blood-flow activity.

EEG

Electroencephalography (EEG) is the measurement of the electrical activity of the brain by recording from electrodes placed on the scalp. The resulting traces are known as an electroencephalogram (EEG) and represent an electrical signal from a large number of neurons. EEGs are frequently used in experimentation because the process is non-invasive to the research subject. The EEG is capable of detecting changes in electrical activity in the brain on a millisecond-level. It is one of the few techniques available that has such high temporal resolution. Electroencephalography (EEG) is used to show brain activity in certain psychological states, such as alertness or drowsiness. It is useful in the diagnosis of seizures and other medical problems that involve an overabundance or lack of activity in certain parts of the brain.

To prepare for an EEG, electrodes are placed on the face and scalp. After placing each electrode in the right position, the electrical potential of each electrode can be measured. According to a person's state (waking, sleeping, etc.), both the frequency and the form of the EEG signal (Fig -4) differ. Patients who suffer from epilepsy show an increase of the amplitude of firing visible on the EEG record. The disadvantage of EEG is that the electric conductivity—and therefore the measured electrical potentials—may vary widely from person to person and also over time, due to the natural conductivities of other tissues such as brain matter, blood, and bones. Because of this, it is sometimes unclear exactly which region of the brain is emitting a signal.

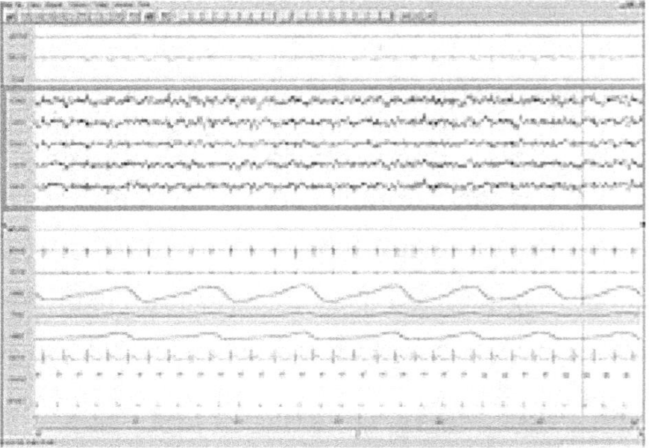

(Fig -4) EEG record during sleep

LESIONING AND STIMULATION

In lesioning, the part of the brain is removed and comparison is made between performance before and after the lesion and consequent deficits are noted. This branch of neuropsychology sounds brutal, but is often carried out when brain surgery is required (e.g. to remove parts of the brain where epileptic seizures are known to originate). Lesion studies have informed our understanding, of which brain regions can be removed with minimal consequence for the patient.

Stimulation involves feeding a signal (chemical or electrical) into some part of a neural circuit and measuring its consequences. Invasive stimulation involves surgery and is often carried out as part of a procedure to assess which regions of the brain it might be least disruptive to lesion. For example, it is very important to leave brain regions associated with language processing intact so that surgery does not totally impair a person's ability to communicate.

Non-invasive stimulation in the form of transcranial magnetic stimulation (TMS) is a relatively recent development in the experimental neurosciences. A coil is held up to the head of healthy participants, positioned directly over the part of the brain which is intended to be temporarily stimulated, and causes neurons on the surface of the brain (nearest the coil) to discharge, effectively temporarily lesioning that brain region. This technique allows experimenters to conduct lesion-like studies on large number of participants.

THE NEURON

Human nervous system is equipped with sense and responds to continuous change within the body and its external environment. A human body must react to various external and internal stimuli. The nervous system can regulate 1000 of activities simultaneously. It monitors and controls most body processes from automatic function such as breathing to activities that involve motor coordination, learning and thought. The brain and the spinal cord, and nerves that emerge from them and connect them to the rest of the body, make up the human nervous system.

The nervous system is composed of only two main types of the cells- neurons and cells that support neurons, which are called glial cells. Neuron is the basic structural and functional unit of the nervous system (Fig -5). They are specialized to respond to physical and chemical stimuli, to conducts electrochemical signals, and to release chemicals that regulate various body processes.

Neuron consists of a cell body from which a number of process lead to another neuron or effector organs. It has a nucleus that contains the chromosomes which constitute the genetic information. The nucleus is large and spherical contain a nucleolus. It has other standard cellular components, the organelles like mitochondria, golgi bodies, lysosomes, endoplasmic reticulum, neurofibrils. The cell centre is absent in a mature neuron, this organelle is concerned with cell division and because of its absence the nerve cell cannot do cell division or replace themselves.

Nissle bodies and neurofibrils are two unique bodies present in the neuron. The nissle bodies are granules of RNA and are regarded as site of protein synthesis. The neurofibrils are reticulate network corresponds to microtubules in other cells.

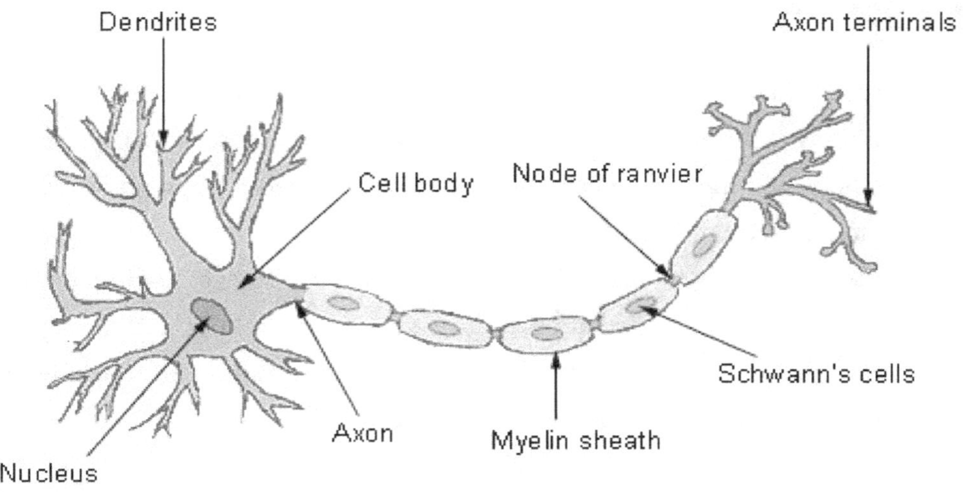

(Fig -5)- Structure of a neuron

In the bipolar neurons, there are two types of extensions extended out from cell body namely dendrites and axons. The dendrites are branched extension of neurons that receive signals and conduct them towards the cell body. Dendrites are afferent processes since it carry impulse towards the cell body and sensory in function. Whereas, axons are unbranched extensions of neuron that conducts signals away from the cell body to other cells, hence it is motor in function. Axons are thus called efferent processes. Some human axon can reach in length of over 3 feet. The axon is mad up of central core of protoplasm known as axoplasm. The axons of some neurons are enclosed in a fatty insulating layer called the myelin sheath and a membrane called neurilemma. Neurilemma is a transparent nucleated membrane which is also known as sheath of Schwann cells. During embryonic development the myelin sheath is formed by the spiral twisting of the plasma membrane of the Schwann cell around an axon.

An axon with myelin sheath are called myelinated. Axon without a myelin sheath are said to be unmyelinated. Myelin sheath protects the myelinated neurons and speeds the rate of nerve impulse transmitted. Schwann cells, a type of glial cells, form myelin by wrapping themselves around the axon. Myelin sheath is interrupted at regular intervals along the myelinated neurons. This interrupted regions or nodes are called nodes of ranvier. Saltatory conduction (from the Latin *saltare*, to hop or leap) is the propagation of action potentials along myelinated axons from one node of Ranvier to the next node, increasing the conduction velocity of action potentials. The uninsulated nodes of Ranvier are the only places along the axon where ions are exchanged across the axon membrane, regenerating the action potential between regions of the axon that are insulated by myelin. The terminal part of the axon is devoid of myelin and neurilemma and provided with number of fine branches known as telodendria. Telodendria bears knob like expansion called terminal buttons.

In central nervous system or CNS, myelinated neurons form white matter and unmyelinated neurons forms grey matter. Most neurons in the peripheral nervous system are myelinated. Activitiy of neurons are supported by a type of cells called glial cells (the word glial comes from a greek word that means glue). Glial cells nourish the neurons, remove their waste and defend against infection. Glial cells also provide a supporting framework for all the nervous system tissue. Individual neurons organised in to tissues are called nerves.

FUNCTION AND TYPE OF NEURON

Based on the functional status, neurons are classified in to three types. They are sensory or receptor neurons, motor or effector neurons and interneurons or internuncial nerons. Sensory neurons gather information from the sensory receptors and transmit this impulse to the central nervous system (brain and spinal cord). Motor neurons transmit information from the central nervous system to the muscles, glands and other organs (effectors). Interneurons are found entirely within the CNS. They act as a link between sensory and motor neurons. They processes and integrate incoming sensory information, and relay outgoing motor information. Thus it acts as an integration centre. According to the number of processes arising from cell body, neurons are classified in to unipolar, bipolar and multi polar (Fig -6).

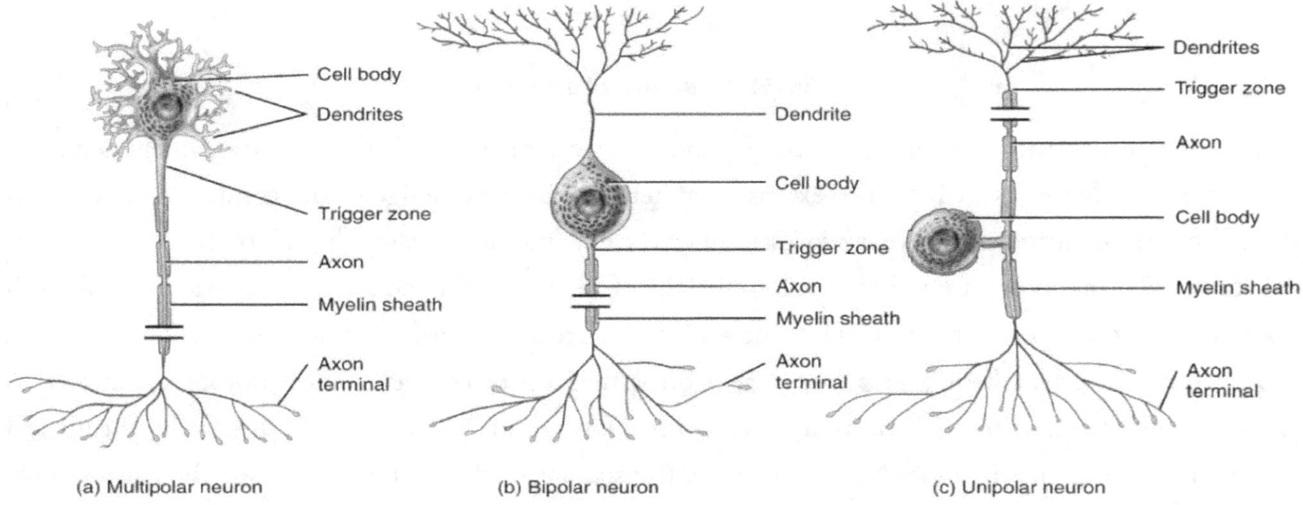

(Fig -6) Neurons - classification

Unipolar neurons are characterized by the presence of just one process arising from cell body. The unipolar neurons of vertebrates are modified cells with two extensions from the cell body. During the early stages of development the extensions migrate to one side of the cell body and fuse to form a single extension. The unipolar neurons of the vertebrates are confined to the dorsal root ganglia of the spinal nerves. They are sensory neurons conduct impulses from skin receptors to the spinal cord. The bipolar neuron possess two extensions. One of the extensions is a dendrite while other is an axon. In vertebrate the dendrite of bipolar neuron is branched and axon is unbranched. They are confined to the retinal layers of the eye. In the case of multipolar neurons, numerous extensions arise from the cell body. In vertebrates there are several short and branched extensions called dendrites and one long unbranched extension called axon. Majority of vertebrate come under this category.

SALTATORY PROPAGATION

Saltatory conduction (Fig -7) is the propagation of action potentials along myelinated axons from one node of ranvier to next node. In myelinated nerve fibre, the myelin coat provide an electrical insulation to the fibre and ions cannot easily pass through. The unmyelinated nodes of Ranvier that occur between the myelinated internode facilitate the leaping of action potential from one node to another because of the momentary reversal of polarity at this region.

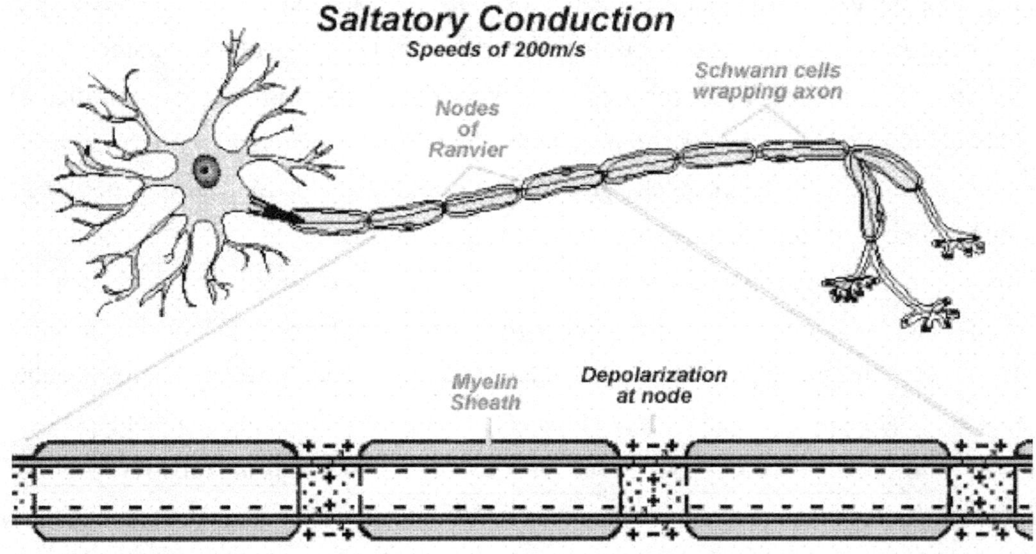

(Fig -7) Saltatory Conduction

NERVE FIBRE

Individual neurons are organised in to tissues called nerves. Hundreds of individual neurons are grouped in to nerve bundles and surrounded by a connective tissue. A nerve is thus an association of individual nerve fibres. Some of the nerve fibres transmit messages from the peripheral receptors to CNS. These are sensory nerve fibres. Others carry messages from CNS to the effectors. These are motor nerve fibres. Some nerve trunks are composed of sensory fibres, some are composed of motor fibres and others contain a mixture of both motor and sensory fibres, which are called as mixed nerves. In a nerve trunk, the individual fibres are surrounded by thin envelop of connective tissue known as endoneurium, each bundle of nerve fibres are enclosed by a sheath of connective tissue sheath called epineurium. Neurons and their processes are formed by the non nervous glial cells.

NERVE IMPULSE

A message carried along a neuron is called nerve impulse, with which the nerve cells communicate one another. Nerve impulse is electro-chemical phenomenon which involves electrical signals. Hence the impulse was considered to be an electric current and the nerve was compared to an electric conductor.

There is an electrical difference between the inside of the axon and its surroundings, like a tiny battery. When the nerve is activated, there is sudden change in the voltage across the wall of the axon, caused by the movement of ions in and out of the neuron. In a resting neuron, the nerve cell membrane bears an electrical charge like the two charges of a battery. Normally the external surface is positively charged and inner surface is negatively charged. If two minute electrodes are kept one on either side of the membrane and connected to a very sensitive galvanometer, the needle of galvanometer move indicating the flow of current. This is because the fact that the membrane has potential energy in the form of a differential charge on its two sides. This differential charge across the membrane is the resting potential. This resting potential accounts to about 70 millivolts. It is represented as -70mv.

The resting potential is due to the differential distribution of ions on the two sides of membrane. The cell membrane is selectively permeable and it allows the inward diffusion of potassium ions (K^+) across the membrane. Hence the potassium ions accumulate inside the cell. The organic molecules present in the neuroplasm are negatively charged. These molecules more than counterbalance the positively charged potassium ions gives the negative charge inside. On the other hand sodium ions (Na^+) are kept outside the cell and the positive charge outside is due to this sodium ions. The resting membrane potential are established by the Na^+/ K^+ - ATPase (sodium- potassium pump) which transport 2 potassium ions and 3 sodium ions outside at the cost of 1 ATP molecule.

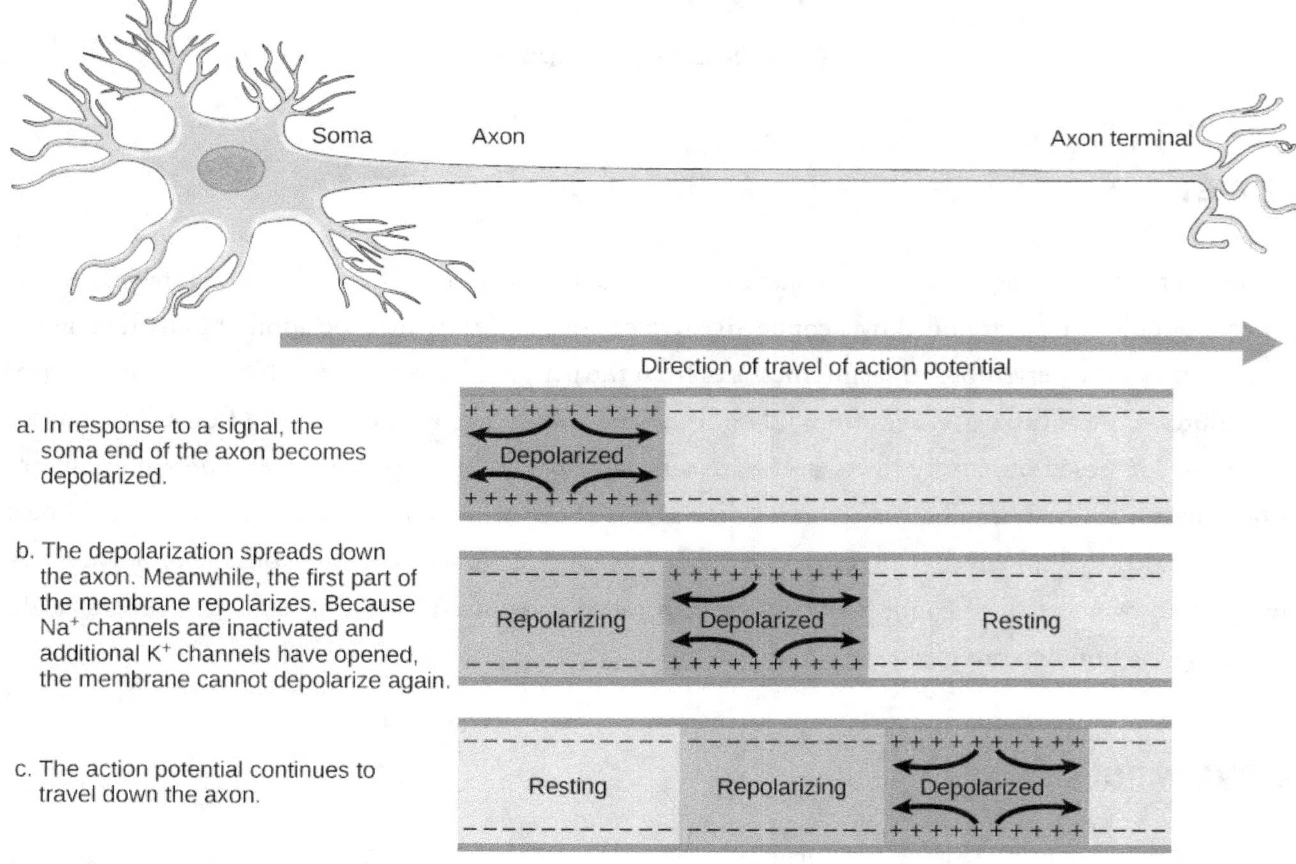

(Fig -8) Action Potential

ACTION POTENTIAL

Plasma membrane of the neuron separates extracellular space from intracellular space. Sodium ions are found in high concentration outside the cell where as potassium ions are found in high concentration inside of the cell. Voltage gated sodium channel, sodium potassium ATPase pump and voltage gated potassium channels are found embedded in the plasma membrane of a neuron. To initiate an action potential a stimulus causes a wave of positive charge to reach voltage gated sodium channels on the neuron membrane. The increase in the positive charge causes the voltage gated sodium channel to open. Positive charged sodium ions flood in to the neuron following their concentration gradient. This causes the inside the membrane near the open channel to become more positive charge. This is the depolarisation of the cell membrane. This may be called as rising phase (Fig -8).

The build up of positive charge on the inside of the membrane eventually causes the voltage gated sodium channels to close, at the same time voltage gated potassium channels open, since they open only when the inside of the membrane is at its maximum positive charge. Positively charged potassium ions flow rapidly out of the neuron, following their concentration gradient. This decreases the level of positive charge on the inside surface of the neuron. The return of membrane to resting level of negative charge is repolarisation. This may be called falling phase. Once the region of the membrane has been fully repolarised, the potassium channels close. A sodium potassium pump uses ATP energy to restore the concentration gradient of sodium and potassium. This is the recovery phase of the neuron leading to resting status. This process is repeated over and over again in successive series of adjacent regions and thus the action potential propagate down the neuron like a wave.

ALL OR NONE LAW

All or none law was first described in 1871 by physiologist Henry Pickering Bowdicth. The all or none law is a principle states that, for eliciting an impulse in a neuron a minimum threshold level of stimulus is required. If a stimulus is above that threshold level the nerve fibre will elicit an impulse and travels at a maximum speed irrespective of the intensity of the stimulus.

SYNAPSE

Synapse is the junction between two nerve cells, consisting of a minute gap across which impulses are pass by diffusion of a neurotransmitter. Sir Charles Sherrington (1861–1954) was the first person who applied the functional term synapse to the junctional point between two neurons. The physiological importance of the synapse for the transmission of nerve impulse was established by Mc Lennan in 1963. At the point of synapse the neurons are in the close proximity but they are not anatomically continuous. The synaptic junction is formed by two neurons (Fig -9). The neuron which contributes the axon involved in the synapse is the presynaptic neuron. The neuron that provides dendritic site in the synaptic area is the post synaptic neuron. Impulse that reaches the synapse through pre synaptic neuron is carried along the post synaptic neuron.

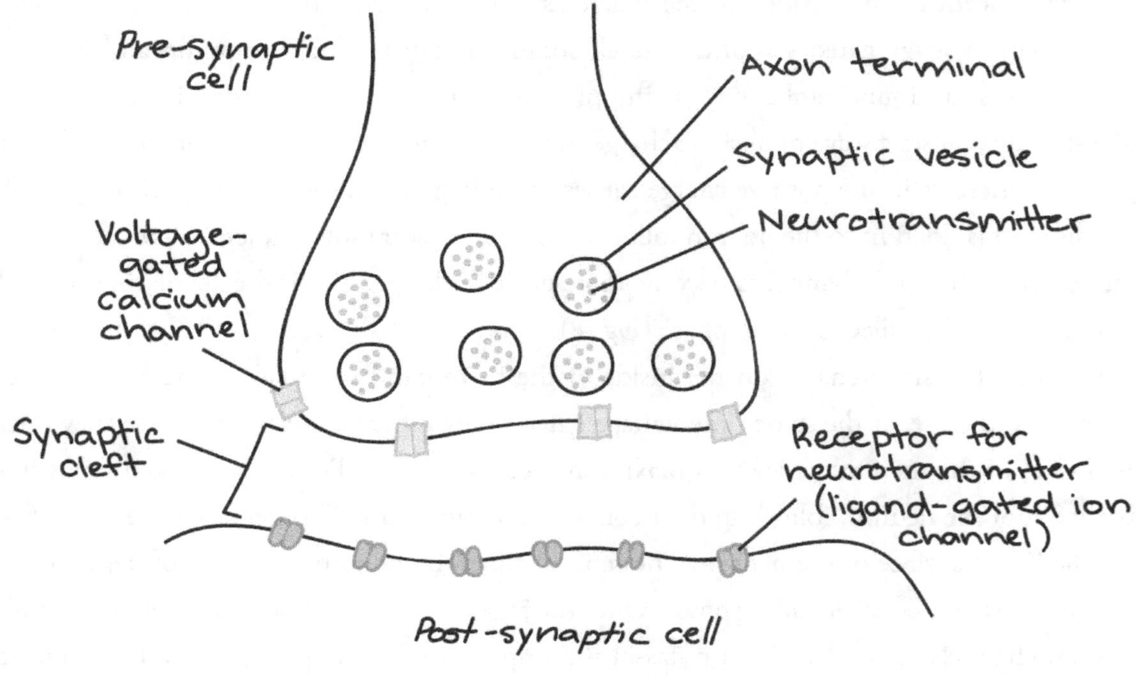

(Fig -9) - Synapse

Electron microscopic studies revealed that in a synapse the axon terminal of a neuron may be connected with the dendrite of the cell body or even sometimes the axon of one more neuron. Hence such synapses are known as axon-dendrite or axon-cell body or axon-axon type. The axon terminals end in knob like structures called the synaptic knob or synaptic button of 1–5 μ. It encloses numerous small membrane bounded bubble like vesicle called the synaptic vesicle, which are the source of chemical substances involved in the transmission of impulses across the synapse. The transmitter substance or neuro hormones are usually in the form of acetylcholine or norepinephrine. The synaptic knob also contain mitochondria that provide energy for the synthesis and release of the chemical substances of the synaptic vesicle.

In the region of synapse there is a gap between the pre-synaptic and post-synaptic neuron. It is called as synaptic cleft. The membrane covering the pre-synaptic knob is pre-synaptic membrane and the membrane covering the post-synaptic knob is called post-synaptic or sub-synaptic membrane. The time taken for the impulse to generate across the synaptic cleft is termed as synaptic delay and it is about 0.6 milliseconds.

SYNAPTIC TRANSMISSION

There are basically two different types of synaptic transmissions namely electrical and chemical. Synapses that operate on the basis of electrical transmission are characterised by the presence of tight junctions.

Electrical resistance between the two membranes are made as low as possible along these junctions. The depolarisation wave in the synaptic membrane spreads across the synapse and a potential difference is noticeable in the post synaptic membrane. There is no indication of any increased polarisation in the pre-synaptic membrane during post synaptic depolarisation. Hence there is only a one directional flow of depolarisation. This is described as a rectifier action, the synaptic membrane acting as a rectifier of positive current from pre synaptic to post synaptic and producing resistance to flow in the opposite direction.

Chemical transmission is mainly carried out by the involvement of chemical agents such as neurotransmitters. During this transmission, the pre-synaptic potential on reaching a synapse, activate synaptic vesicles and leads in to its rupturing, thereby releases transmitter substances. The molecules of these transmitter substances diffuse across the synaptic gap to combine with a special receptor located on the sub synaptic membrane. This will results in changes in polarity along the sub synaptic membrane and thus set up a new action potential. This passes along the post synaptic neuron to the next synapse were also the same process repeated. The transmitter substance acetylcholine (ACh) in the presence of an enzyme known as Cholineacetylase and it is hydrolysed by acetylcholine esterase. Acetylcholine esterase splits acetyl choline in to choline and acetate. Due to the action of this enzyme acetylcholine remains only for a short period. The synaptic transmission will continue as long as there is adequate supply of oxygen and ATP (Adenosine Tri Phosphate). In the absence of this, synapse may undergo the process of fatigue. The synaptic fatigue is also caused due to the deficiency of transmitter substance.

PROPERTIES OF A SYNAPSE

1. One way transmission- the synaptic transmission is always from pre synaptic to post synaptic neuron and hence it is one way.
2. Synaptic delay – transmission of impulse across the synapse requires a delay because some time period is required for the discharge of transmitter substance from synaptic vesicle. The time taken for synaptic delay is 0.3 to 10 milliseconds.
3. Fatigue – repeated stimulation at a rapid rate of the presynaptic neuron produces a corresponding rate of discharge from post synaptic neuron. But this is gradually become less and less called fatigue, which is due to the exhaustion of transmitter substances.
4. Summation- a single action potential in the pre synaptic neuron may not result in the release of sufficient transmitter substances for the production of action potential in the post synaptic neurons. A series of action potentials in the presynaptic knob within a short time period results in the release of sufficient quantity of transmitter and this may evoke single action potential in the post synaptic neuron. This adding up of a number of presynaptic impulses to elicit an impulse in post synaptic neuron is called temporal summation. A number pre synaptic neuron may be associated with post synaptic neuron, hence all the presynaptic neuron together produce an action potential in the post synaptic neuron. This is called spatial summation.

5. Inhibition- inhibitory neurons may also exists along the sensory neuron among the presynaptic neuron. Such inhibitory neurons concerned with the production of non transmitter substance such as Gamma Amino Butyric Acid (GABA).

6. Repetitive discharge- a single action potential along the presynaptic neuron may result in a series of action potential in the post synaptic neuron. The impulse multiplied at the synapse. The transmitter substances can evoke a series of action potential until it is broken down by the enzyme.

CENTRAL NERVOUS SYSTEM

The nervous system which is made up of neurons exerts rapid control over bodily activities by controlling nerve impulses. Nervous system coordinates the bodily activity in many ways. It receives information from the external environment through receptors or sense organs. The information conducted to brain and then different parts of the body, which stimulates or inhibit the activities of the muscles or glands.

Nervous system also regulates the internal environment of the body through controlling visceral organs. Nervous system is well developed in mammals especially in man. It consists of central nervous system (CNS), peripheral nervous system (PNS) and Autonomous nervous system (ANS). The central nervous system is with the brain and spinal cord. The PNS consists of nerves from brain and spinal cord, that link brain and spinal cord with different parts of the body. ANS consist of special system of nerve fibres and ganglia that controls involuntary activities.

It is a system consists of brain and spinal cord, which is a concentration of neurons or nerve cells. There are two differentially coloured region in the CNS is called as grey and white matter. The grey matter represents area where cell bodies of neurons present. The white matter mainly consists of nerve fibres and white colour is due to the presence of myelin sheath. The brain and spinal cord are covered by three protective covering called Meninges. The inner membrane is piamater, the middle is arachnoid and the outer is duramater. The space between each layer is filled with a fluid called cerebrospinal fluid. The Meninges along with fluid protect the brain and spinal cord against mechanical injury and shock.

BRAIN

The brain is present in the cranial cavity well protected by the bones of the cranium. The human brain may be divided in to forebrain, midbrain and hind brain (Fig -10).

FOREBRAIN

It is the anterior division of the brain. It consists of cerebrum, thalamus and hypothalamus. Cerebrum is the most prominent and largest part of the brain. The cerebrum is divided in to right and left halves by a mid dorsal tissue. These halves are called as cerebral hemispheres. There is a tough band of nerve fibres at the bottom of the fissure which holds the cerebral hemispheres tighter. This band is called corpus callosum. Each hemisphere is further divided in to four lobes by deep grooves or fissures. The lobes are frontal, parietal, occipital and temporal. The surface of each lobe is divided into a number of irregular folds like convolutions called gyri by shallow grooves called sulci. Thus the surface area of cerebrum is greatly increased. The peripheral part of the brain is called as cerebral cortex. It is made of grey matter and contains millions of nerve cell bodies. Beneath the grey matter of the cerebellum is the white matter and made of nerve fibres.

Several nerve centres are located in the cerebral cortex. They are broadly divided in to sensory, motor, and association areas. The surface areas are concerned with the receptors and interpretations of the sense of vision, hearing, smell, taste and skin sensation.

Visual area is located in occipital lobes and auditory area is in the temporal lobes. Sensation of smell and taste are also interpreted in the temporal lobes. Sensory area in the parietal lobe is concerned with skin sensation such as pain, touch and temperature. Motor area is present at the posterior part of the frontal lobe control voluntary movements. The involuntary movements are controlled by premotor areas in the frontal lobe. The association area present in the frontal lobes are the seat of memory, imagination, thought, intelligence and emotions.

Thalamus and hypothalamus form the posterior part of the forebrain. They are almost hidden by the cerebrum. The thalamus is placed laterally and hypothalamus ventrally. The thalamus is concerned with the passage of sensory messages to the brain and relay of motor messages from the brain.

Hypothalamus consists of many groups of nerve cell bodies scattered in the whole matter. It contain higher nerve centre that control the body temperature, hunger, thirst and water balance. Hypothalamus also contains neurosecretory cells producing neuro hormones which control secretions of anterior pituitary hormones.

MID BRAIN

It is very small and inconspicuous in man. It contains groups of nerve cells scattered in the white matter. The midbrain comprises the tectum, tegmentum, the cerebral aqueduct, and the cerebral peduncles, as well as several nuclei and fasciculi. Caudally the midbrain adjoins the metencephalon. Rostrally it adjoins the diencephalon. Tectum is a region of the brain, specifically the dorsal part of the midbrain responsible for auditory and visual reflexes. The tegmentum (from Latin for "covering") is a general area within the brainstem. It forms the floor of the midbrain. It is a multisynaptic network of neurons that is involved in many subconscious homeostatic and reflexive pathways. It is a motor center that relays inhibitory signals to the thalamus and basal nuclei preventing unwanted body movement. The cerebral aqueduct, also known as the aqueductus mesencephali, mesencephalic duct, sylvian aqueduct or the aqueduct of Sylvius is within the mesencephalon (or midbrain), contains cerebrospinal fluid (CSF), and connects the third ventricle in the diencephalon to the fourth ventricle within the region of the mesencephalon and metencephalon, located dorsal to the pons and ventral to the cerebellum. The cerebral peduncles are structures at the front of the midbrain which arise from the front of the pons and contain the large ascending (sensory) and descending (motor) nerve tracts that run to and from the cerebrum from the pons. The cerebral peduncles are located on either side of the midbrain and are the frontmost part of the midbrain, and act as the connectors between the rest of the midbrain and the thalamic nuclei and thus the cerebrum. As a whole, the cerebral peduncles assists in refining motor movements, learning of new motor skills, and converting proprioceptive information into balance and posture maintenance.

HIND BRAIN

It is the posterior part of the brain and consists of cerebellum, pons varoli and medulla oblongata. Cerebellum lies on the back of medulla oblongata. Like cerebrum, cerebellum is much folded and divisible in to outer cerebellar cortex of grey matter and an inner medulla of white matter. The chief function of the cerebellum is to coordinate the motor impulses arising from the cerebral cortex to control the muscular activities of the body. It is also responsible for the maintenance of the poster and equilibrium.

Pons varoli and medulla oblongata form the brain stem on which the cerebellum rests. The pons acts as a bridge of nerve fibres connecting the cerebrum above, cerebellum behind and medulla oblongata below. It also connects the right and left lobes of the cerebellum. Medulla oblongata is the lower part of the brain stem that continues posteriorly as the spinal cord.

VENTRICLES OF BRAIN

The hollow, tubular distorted cavities of the brain are called ventricles. The cavities of cerebral hemispheres are the lateral ventricles. The thalamus and the hypothalamus form the posterior part of the forebrain. Third ventricle lies between the thalami of two sides. Between the cerebellar hemispheres above pons and medulla lies the fourth ventricle. The hollow part of the inconspicuous midbrain is called cerebral aqueduct. Fourth ventricle is continued with cerebral aqueduct which in turn continuous with third ventricle. Third ventricle connected with lateral ventricles in front through the Foramen of Monro and behind with the fourth ventricle by a narrow canal called iter or aquaeductus Sylvii.

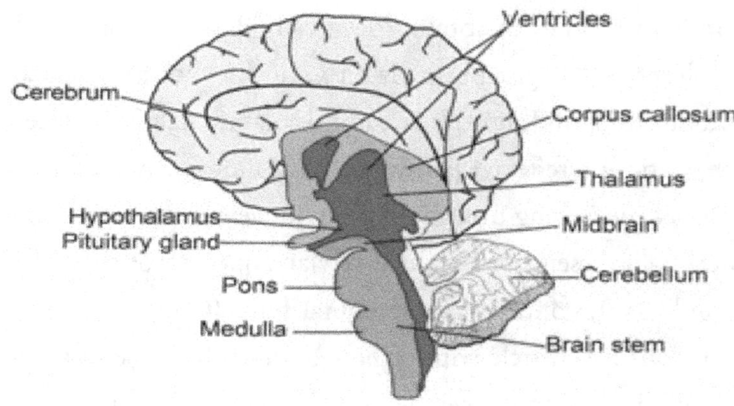

(Fig - 10) Structure of Brain

FUNCTIONS OF MAJOR PARTS OF BRAIN

Cerebral Cortex- It is the highest seat of integrating centres of the human brain. Excitations originating in the receptors and that are carried to the cerebral cortex through cranial and spinal nerves. The cerebral cortex can connect any part of the brain with any other part at least indirectly.

Cerebral cortex undergoes greater development in man than in any lower animal. The cerebral hemispheres and cortex covering have expanded in size and area. This increase in size of the cortex has resulted in a thickening that forms several layers of cells and synaptic connection. The cortex expansion has occurred in the limited cranial capacity, as a result the cortex has developed folds to increase its area within the limited volume and hence much of the cortex is buried in the sulci. The cortex is also divided in to frontal, temporal, occipital and parietal lobe. The thickness of the cortex is caused by six well defined cortical layers.

Meninges-The CNS is surrounded by three layers of connective tissue called Meninges.

Cerebrospinal Fluid-Brain and Spinal cord are surrounded by this fluid. This fluid cushions the brain and spinal cord.

Neuroglia-supporting cells are collectively called as neuroglia or glial cells. They produce myelin sheath for axons; they are mobile and can absorb damaged cells.

Corpus striatum-locate in the wall of cerebral hemispheres, it regulates the sequence and timing of movements, certain facial expressions in emotions and controls sequential acts such as swinging the arms for balance while walking.

Hypothalamus- It contains many centres that are sensitive to conditions in the fluid internal environment of the blood and cerebrospinal fluid (the extracellular tissue fluid of brain and spinal cord). The neurons of these centres acts as receptors and are stimulated by changes in fluid salt content, osmotic pressure, chemical composition. Such condition is called "need condition of the tissue".

SPINAL CORD

Spinal cord lies in the neural canal of the vertebral column (Fig -11). It is a slender cylindrical column continuous with the brain stem and extends up to the level of the second lumbar vertebra, terminally it tapers as filum terminale. The spinal cord contains a central canal internally which is filled with cerebrospinal fluid. The central canal is surrounded by grey matter and white matter outer to it. The grey matter penetrates in to white matter at certain regions in the form of horns. Depending up on the location they are called dorsal horns, ventral and lateral horns of grey matter. Spinal nerves emerge from the lateral sides of the spinal cord. The horns serves as the pathway for the motor impulses from brain to effector organs and for sensory impulses from receptor organs to brain. It also acts as a reflex centre that initiates spontaneous and local reflexes.

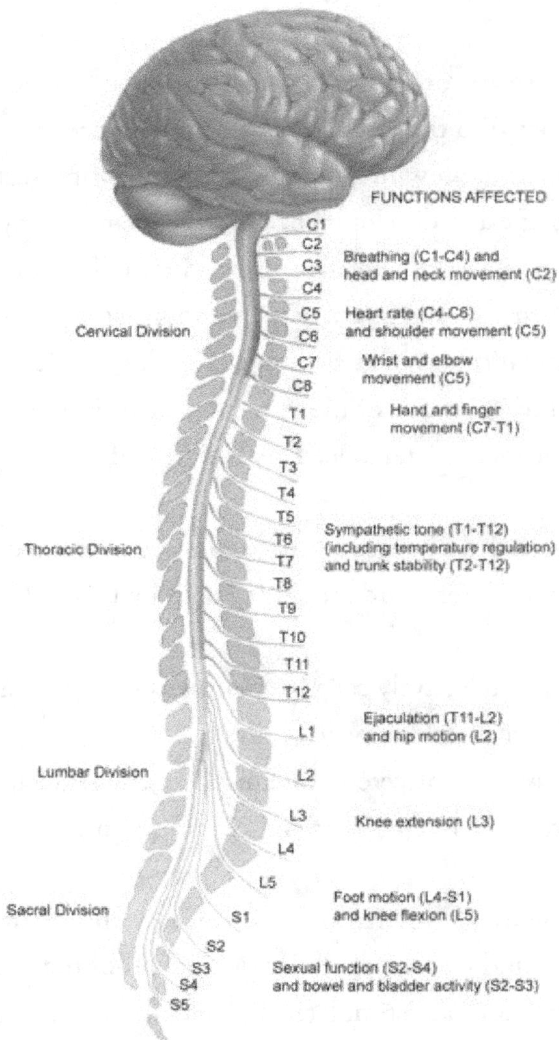

(Fig -11) - TS of spinal cord

ANATOMY OF REFLEX

Reflex may include pathways in the cranial nerves and synapses in the brain or they may involve spinal nerves and spinal cord. Spinal nerves are attached to the spinal cord by two routes- dorsal routes and ventral routes. Spinal nerve divided in to dorsal ramus and ventral ramus. Spinal cord is connected to receptors and effectors by way of dorsal root, ventral root and ramus. Dorsal root containing incoming sensory neurons and ventral root containing outgoing motor neurons. Spinal cord has H shaped grey matter which is surrounded by white matter. This H shaped grey matter includes dorsal horn and ventral horn. The white matter divided in to three areas on either side of the cord. The dorsal funiculus is the area between mid line and dorsal root, the ventral funiculus is the area between mid line and ventral root, the lateral funiculus is the area between dorsal and ventral root.

PHYSIOLOGY OF REFLEX

Stimulation of receptor will give rise to generator potential, the potential that will initiate a spike potential in the sensory or afferent nerve fibre. Sensory neurons reach the spinal nerve by way of dorsal or ventral ramus, it will then enter the spinal cord by way of dorsal root, and synapse with association neuron in the grey matter. The association neuron carry the excitation to the motor neuron, which in turn carry the excitation to the striated muscle effectors via ventral root and then via dorsal or ventral rami.

THE REFLEX ACTION

When movements occur without necessarily, the intervention of the brain, they are called reflex action or spinal reflexes, eg: if the knee is hit lightly just below the knee cap, the knee jerks. This is due to a spinal reflex. Similarly, if the finger is accidently pricked by a needle, the hand is suddenly withdrawn. In all these reactions, the sensation of pain is perceived by several pain receptors in the skin which send impulses by the dorsal, sensory roots, to the spinal cord. The sensory neuron synapse with an interneuron in the grey matter and finally the impulse is transmitted by the ventral, motor neuron, to the muscle which contracts, resulting in the withdrawal of the finger or hand as the case may and this entire reaction occur in the fraction of a second (Fig -12).

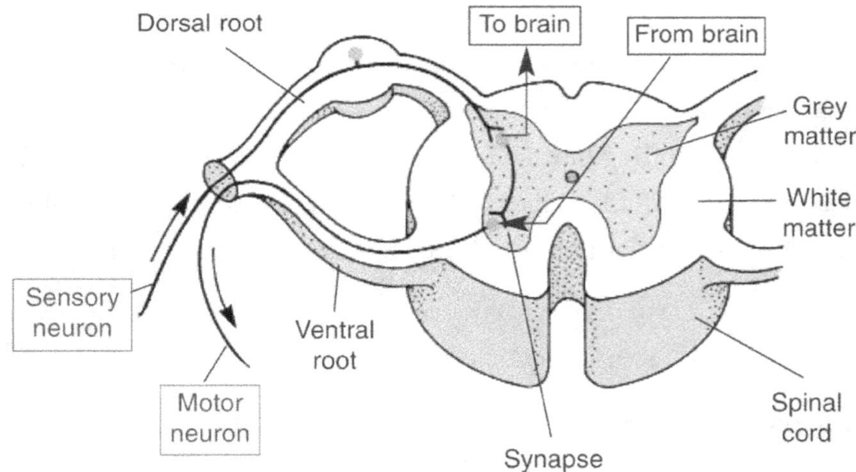

(Fig -12) Reflex action

Meninges: CNS contain not only nerve cell but also specialized tissues to provide nutrients, oxygen and protection. Dura matter is a tough fibrous covering which covers the brain and spinal cord. Arachnoid matter is a thin fragile layer of connective tissue contains many blood vessels and nourishes the CNS. Pia matter adheres closely to the brain and spinal cord. The space between the pia matter and arachnoid matter encloses the cerebrospinal fluid

Cerebrospinal fluid: Brain and spinal cord are surrounded with the cerebrospinal fluid. It is also found in the ventricles and spinal canals. This fluid minimizes the damage to the brain and it is similar to the other extracellular fluid.

BLOOD BRAIN BARRIER

The blood–brain barrier (BBB) is a highly selective semipermeable membrane barrier that separates the circulating blood from the brain and extracellular fluid in the central nervous system (CNS). The blood–brain barrier is formed by brain endothelial cells and it allows the passage of water, some gases, and lipid-soluble molecules by passive diffusion, as well as the selective transport of molecules such as glucose and amino acids that are crucial to neural function. Furthermore, it prevents the entry of lipophilic potential neurotoxins by way of an active transport mechanism mediated by P-glycoprotein. Astrocytes have been claimed to be necessary to create the blood–brain barrier. A few regions in the brain, including the circumventricular organs, do not have a blood–brain barrier.

The blood–brain barrier occurs along all capillaries and consists of tight junctions around the capillaries that do not exist in normal circulation. Endothelial cells restrict the diffusion of microscopic objects (e.g., bacteria) and large or hydrophilic molecules into the cerebrospinal fluid (CSF), while allowing the diffusion of hydrophobic molecules (O_2, CO_2, hormones). Cells of the barrier actively transport metabolic products such as glucose across the barrier with specific proteins. This barrier also includes a thick basement membrane and astrocytic endfeet. The blood–brain barrier is composed of high-density cells restricting passage of substances from the bloodstream much more than do the endothelial cells in capillaries elsewhere in the body. Astrocyte cell projections called astrocytic feet (also known as "glia limitans") surround the endothelial cells of the BBB, providing biochemical support to those cells. The BBB is distinct from the quite similar blood–cerebrospinal fluid barrier, which is a function of the choroidal cells of the choroid plexus, and from the blood–retinal barrier, which can be considered a part of the whole realm of such barriers.

PERIPHERAL NERVOUS SYSTEM (PNS)

This includes cranial and spinal nerves. Each nerve consists of bundle of nerve fibers covered over, by a sheath of connective tissue. Depending on the direction of propagation of nerve impulse neurons may be classified in to afferent and efferent neurons. Afferent neurons and fibers conduct impulse from the peripheral tissue and organs towards CNS, hence they are also called as sensory neurons or sensory nerve fibers. Efferent neurons and its fibers carry impulses from CNS and effector organs such as muscles and glands and they are also known as motor neurons or fibers. Nerves are of two types depending on the function. If the nerve contain only sensory nerve fibres called sensory nerve or afferent nerve. Some nerve contain only motor nerve fibres called motor nerves or efferent nerves. Some nerves inclues both motor and sensory nerves called mixed nerves.

There are 31 pairs of spinal nerves in man. Each nerve is mixed nerve and it is connected to the spinal cord by two branches called ventral and dorsal roots. Cell bodies of motor fibres are located in the ventral horn of the grey matter of spinal cord. The dorsal spinal nerve root contains only sensory nerve fibres and is connected to the dorsal horn of grey matter of spinal cord. There are 12 pairs of cranial nerves in man (Table 1). They arise from different parts of the brain.

(Table-1): The cranial nerves, the organ innervated, the type of fibre and the function of the twelve cranial nerve of man

No.	Cranial nerve	Organ Innervated	Type of fibre	Function
1.	Olfactory	Olfactory mucous membrane	Sensory	Smell
2	Optic	Retina	Sensory	Vision
3	Oculomotor	Four of the six eye muscle	Motor	Eye movement
4.	Trochlear	Superior oblique eye muscle	Motor	Eye movement
5.	Trigeminal	Skin and mucous membrane of the head	Sensory	Sensation
6.	Adducens	Rectus eye muscle	Motor	Eye movement
7.	Facial	Muscle of the face, neck,salivary glands, taste buds	Sensory, Motor	Movement,saliva secretion, taste
8.	Auditory	Internal ear	Sensory	Equillibrium, hearing
9.	Glossopharyngeal	Pharynx, tongue, salivary gland, pharyngeal muscles	Sensory, Motor	Taste, sensation,saliva secretion, swallowing
10	Vagus	Pharynx, larynx, trachea, oesophagus, thoracic and abdominal viscera	Sensory, Motor	Visceral reflexes
11	Accessory	Thoracic and abdominal viscera	Sensory, Motor	Visceral reflexes, movement
12	Hypoglossal	Muscle of the tongue	Motor	movement

AUTONOMOUS NERVOUS SYSTEM (ANS)

It is a special system of motor nerve fibres and ganglia that innervate the visceral organs and coordinate their activities. This system is connected to the CNS through spinal nerves and cranial nerves and control involuntarily by nerve centres located in the brain. An important peculiarity of ANS is that the effector organs are connected by two motor neurons. The motor nerve fibre emerges from the brain and spinal cord and entering into the autonomic ganglia are called pre ganglionic fibres. The axons of nerve cells from an autonomic ganglia emerge as post ganglionic fibres. ANS is composed of sympathetic and para sympathetic parts (Fig -13). Each system consists of pre and post ganglionic fibres. The pre ganglionic nerve fibre of sympathetic nervous system (SNS) emerges from thoracic and lumbar regions of spinal cord and constituted thoracic – lumbar outflow. The para sympathetic nerve fibres of autonomous nervous system emerges from brain and sacral region forms cranio – sacral outflow.

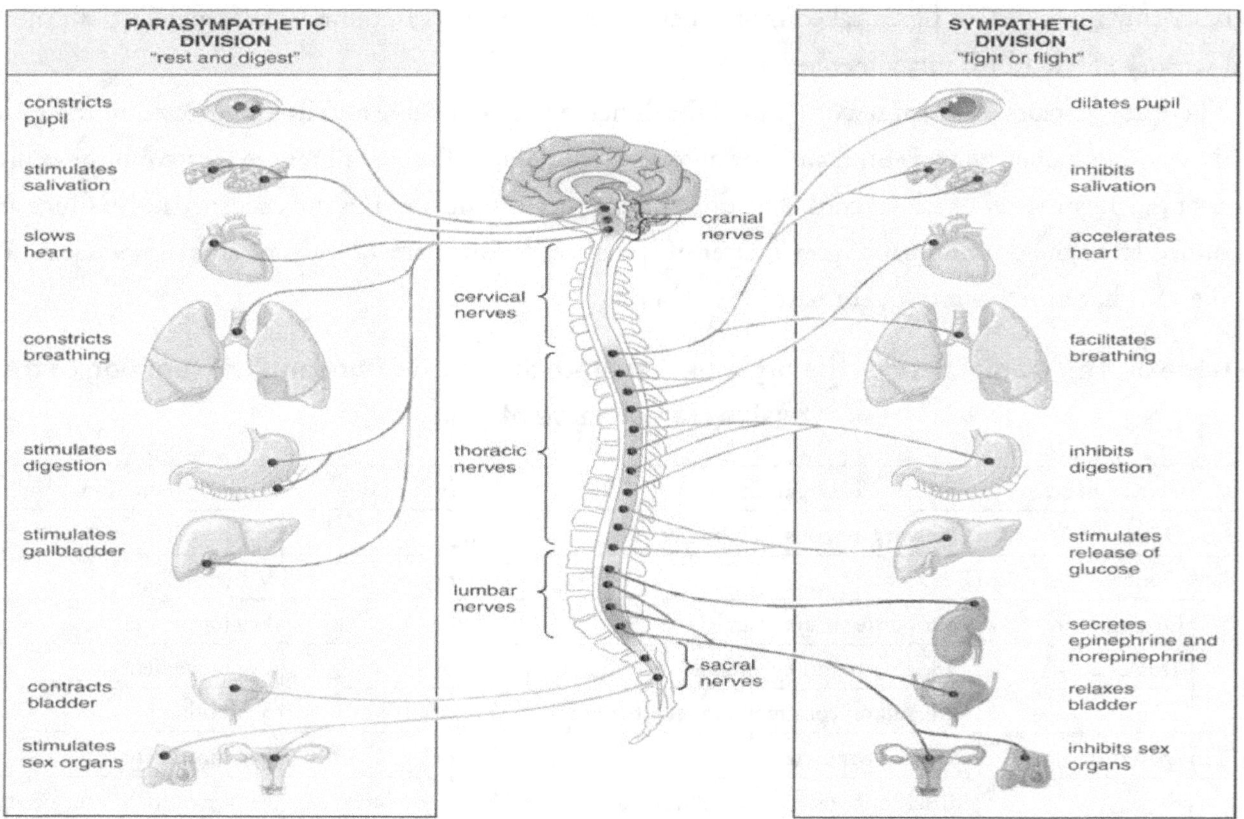

(Fig -13) Symapthetic and parasympathetic nervous system

SYMPATHETIC NERVOUS SYSTEM (SNS)

It consists of two lateral chains of ganglia one on either side of the vertebral column. It coordinates a large number of body organs. The pre ganglionic nerve fibres are axons of nerve cells in lateral horns of grey matter and come out through ventral spinal root. The post ganglionic nerve fibres are axon cells in the ganglia and innervate different organs. Some pre ganglionic fibres pass through lateral ganglia without terminating there but emerge from the ganglia and end in isolated ganglia called collateral ganglia. Post ganglionic nerve fibres are mostly adrenergic because they release the neurotransmitter adrenaline.

PARA SYMPATHETIC NERVOUS SYSTEM (PSNS)

It consist of para sympathetic ganglia situated very close to the peripheral tissues and pre and post ganglionic fibres. Pre ganglionic fibres emerge from mid brain, brain stem as well as from sacral parts of spinal cord. Pre ganglionic fibres are connected to III, VII, IX, X cranial nerves and lateral pons of sacral region. Post ganglionic fibres are very short and not prominent. They are cholinergic as they discharge acetylcholine for the transmission of impulse. The two division of ANS is antagonistic in function. The sympathetic side generally accelerates the bodily activities on stimulation. Eg – increases heart rate, constrict blood vessel, raises blood pressure and dilate pupil etc. whereas para sympathetic nervous system on stimulation decreases heart rate, dilate blood vessel, lowers blood pressure and constrict pupil. Thus a balance between the actions of two helps to maintain a constancy in the internal environment of the body. Sympathetic nervous system acts on emergency where as para sympathetic nervous system acts on reflex reactions or involuntary actions.

EMERGENCY THEORY

This theory was put forward by Cannon based on the reactions of sympathetic nervous system. SNS mobilize the animal for fighting an emergency. The theory predicts the effect of SNS on visceral structures. According to this theory contraction and relaxation of arteries, high rate diversion of blood from digestive system to somatic muscles, rise in the rate of heart beat and BP, high rate of breathing, increased sweating and contraction or shutting off sphincter for digestion and digestive contraction are enhanced by the release of epinephrine and nor epinephrine into the blood stream by the adrenal glands. These hormones will help in spreading the reactions of sympathetic nervous system widely.

PARA SYMPATHETIC NERVOUS SYSTEM EFFECT (PNS effect)

It can be predicted from emergency theory. The Parasympathetic Nervous System effect is exactly opposite to Sympathetic Nervous System. Thus the PNS effect slows down the heart rate, respiration, diverte blood from somatic area to digestive system, increase digestive functions. PNS effect can also be predicted from body reactions during sleep. During sleep digestive rate is high, heart rate is low, breathing deep and sweat inhibited.

POLYGRAPH

The functioning of autonomous nervous system in human body is measured with the polygraph. It is an instrument that measures bodily changes that results from parasympathetic and sympathetic nervous reactions and records them on a moving paper plate. Three measurement are mostly used, they are depth and rate of breathing (pneumograph), heart rate and BP (Sphygmomanometer), palmer sweating (galvanic skin response or GSR). All the above three activities increased by Sympathetic Nervous System activity and vice versa by Parasympathetic Nervous System activity. Sympathetic Nervous System reactions and Parasympathetic Nervous System counter reactions are going on all the times in our body. However a sudden increase in the Sympathetic Nervous System activity results in an emotional state which can be indicated by polygraph.

NEUROTRANSMITTERS AND DRUG ACTION

Neurotransmitters are also known as chemical messengers, which are endogenous chemicals that enable neurotransmission. They transmit signals across a chemical synapse, such as a neuromuscular junction, from one neuron to another neuron, muscle cells or gland cells. Neurotransmitters are released from synaptic vesicles of synapses in to the synaptic cleft, where they are received by neurotransmitter receptors on the target cells (Fig -14). Many neurotransmitters are synthesised from simple precursors such as amino acid which are readily available from the diet and only a small number of biosynthetic steps required for conversion. Neurotransmitters play a major role in shaping everyday life and functions (Table – 2). The exact number of these messengers are unknown but more than 100 numbers have been identified.

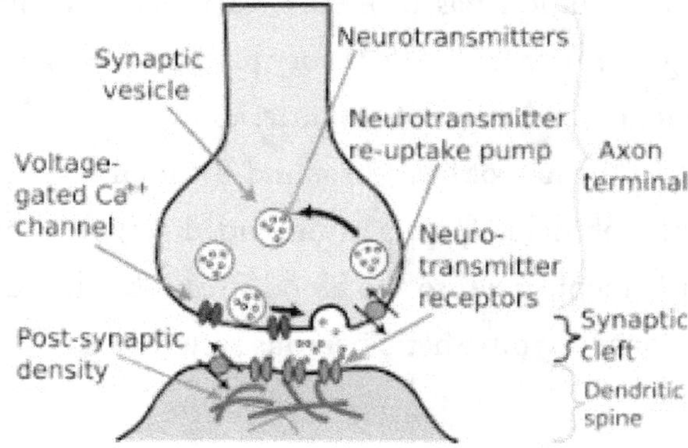

(Fig -14) Neurotransmission

Neurotransmittors comprises two major groups namely small molecule rapidly acting transmitters and large molecule of neuropeptides of slow activity. The small molecule rapidly acting transmitters are the ones that cause most of the acute responses of nervous system, such as transmission of sensory signals to and inside the brain and motor signals back to the muscles. On the other hand the neuropeptides usually cause more prolonged action such as long term changes in number of receptors, closure of ion channels, and possibly even long term changes in number of synapses.

The small molecule type of transmitters are synthesised in the cytosol of pre synaptic terminal and they are absorbed by active transport in to transmitter vesicles in the terminal. At each time an action potential reaches the pre synaptic terminal, a few vesicles at a time release their contents in to synaptic cleft, usually within a millisecond. Also the subsequent action of small molecule transmitter on the post synaptic receptors occurs within milliseconds. The effects of this transmitter substance are either to increase or to decrease conductance through ion channels. The vesicles that store and release small molecule transmitters are continually recycled that is used over and over again. For example Acetylcholine splits in to Acetate and Choline by the enzyme Acetylcholine esterase and Acetyl choline is recycled from Acetate and Choline by the enzyme Choline acetylase. They fused with the synaptic membrane and open it to release their transmitters. The vesicle membrane at first simply becomes part of the synaptic membrane but within seconds to minutes the vesicle portion of the membrane navigate back to the inside of pre synaptic terminal and pinches off to form a new vesicle. It still contains appropriate new transmitter substance inside the vesicle.

Acetylcholine is a typical small molecule transmitter that obeys the above principles of synthesis and release. It is synthesized in the pre synaptic terminal from Acetyl Co enzyme A. Then it is transmitted to specific vesicle. When the vesicle later release acetyl choline unite the synaptic cleft, it rapidly split again in to choline and acetate by the enzyme choline esterase, which is bound to the proteoglycan reticulum that fills the space of synaptic cleft. Then the vesicles are recycled and choline also is actively transported back in to the terminal to be used again for the synthesis of new Ach.

(Table-2): Types of Neurotransmitters, their location and function

Name	Location	Function
Acetylcholine	1. Pyramidal cells of cortex 2. Neurons of basal ganglia 3. Motor neurons of skeletal muscle 4. Pre ganglionic neurons of ANS 5. Post ganglionoic neurons of PSNS and SNS	Inhibitory effect at peripheral nerve endings inhibit heart rate by vagus nerve
Nor epinephrine	1. Neurons of brain stem and hypothalamus 2. Locus of cerulus in the Pons 3. Neurons of post ganglion neuron	Excitatory and Inhibitory
Dopamine	1. Neurons of Substantia Nigra	Inhibitory
Glycine	1. Synapse in the spinal cord	Inhibitory
GABA	1. Nerve terminals in spinal cord 2. Cerebellum 3. Basal ganglia 4. Many areas of cortex	Inhibitory
Glutamate	1. Pre synaptic terminal 2. Many areas of cortex	
Serotonin	1. Median raphe of the brain stem	Inhibitor of pain Control mood Cause sleep

NEUROPEPTIDES

They are not synthesise in the cytosol of the pre synaptic terminals but they are synthesized as an integral part of large protein molecule by the ribosomes in the neural cell body. The protein molecules are immediately transported to Endoplasmic reticulum of the cell body. Endoplasmic reticulum and Golgi bodies function together and enzymatically split the original protein in to smaller fragments and there by release neuro peptides. The golgi body convert the neuropeptide in to minute transmitter vesicle that are released in to the cytoplasm. Then it transported to tips of nerve fibres by axonal streaming of axon cytoplasm. These vesicles release their transmitter in response to action potential.

The productions of neuropeptides are labourious. They usually cause much more prolonged action such as closure of calcium pores, change in metabolic machinery cells, alternations in excretory/inhibitory receptors etc.

PSYCHO ACTIVE DRUGS

Psycho active drug, psycho pharmaceuticals is a chemical substance that changes brain function and results in alternations in perception, mood, consciousness or behaviour. These substances may be used medically, recreationally to improve performance or alter one's consciousness. Some psycho active drugs have therapeutical value are generally prescribed by physicians and other health care practitioners. It include anaesthetic, analgesic, anticonvulsant and antiparkinsonian drug as well as meditations used to treat neuropsychiatric disorders such as anti depressants, anxiolytics, antipsychotic and stimulant meditations.

Psycho active substances bring about subjective changes in counsciouness and mood that the user may find Euphoria or a sense of relaxation. Substances which are both rewarding and positively reinforcing have the potential to induce a state of addiction- compulsive drug use. Sustained use of some substances may produce physical or psychological dependence associated with psychological withdrawal state repectively.

Central nervous system shows high rate of metabolism hence they are more sensitive to drugs than any other cells of the body. The effects of various drugs on central nervous system vary, some drugs may stimulate the CNS activity, some prevents sleep when they affect the cortex. Other drugs may depress the cortex causing drowsiness, unconsciousness or coma. Some other drugs are selective in their effects, interfering with the perception of pain or may leads to the arousal of the sympathetic nervous system. Some drugs disorganise CNS activity causing hallucination. Stimulants increase the metabolic rate of CNS cells and increase their excitability. Some stimulants affect the entire nervous system where others affect the selected areas of brain. The effects of drugs have three stages. The first stage involves stimulation, the second stage is the CNS effect and the final stage is the addiction with withdrawal symptoms.

TYPES OF DRUGS

Lysergic acid diethylamide (LSD)

LSD is a stimulant and also a psychogenic drug that produce delusions and hallucinations. It is used mainly as a recreational drug and for spiritual medicines. LSD is typically either swallowed or held under tongue. It is sensitive to oxygen, ultraviolent light and chlorine. It is odourless, crystalline and white in colour, 20 to 30 micrograms can produce an effect. LSD can cause physical effects like dilation of pupil, decreasing the appetite, nausea, numbness, weakness, elevated blood sugar, increased heart rate, jaw clenching, perspiration, saliva production, mucous productions and tremors.

Caffeine

It is a mild cortical stimulant of the methylxanthine class present in coffee, coco and some soft drinks. It is bitter, white crystalline purine, methylxanthine alkaloid, chemically related to adenine and guanine bases of Deoxyribonucleic acid (DNA) and Ribonucleic acid (RNA). It is found in seeds, nuts or leaves of number of plants native of South America and East Asia. The most well known source of caffeine is the coffee bean, a misnomer for the seed of coffee plants. The effect on the user depends on the tolerance. The tolerance may increase with the habitual usage. Small doses improve the performance of persons. However doses if exceeds individual tolerance level can result in indigestion, nervousness and sleeplessness.

Nicotine

Nicotine is a potent parasympathomimetic stimulant and an alkaloid found in tobacco (*Nicotiana tabacum*) plants. Nicotine functions as an antiherbivore chemical was widely used as an insecticide in the past. Nicotine is highly addictive, act as stimulant,leads to increased SNS activity. This results in heart rate, peripheral vasoconstriction, release of blood glucose form liver and muscles. The intensity of it depends on habitual use. Inhaling enables the nicotine to reach the blood stream through the lungs. Nicotine and pyridine content of the tobacco smoke contain carcinogens in the form of 'tars'. Excess smoking leads to tremors of extremity, palpitation, tachycardia, high BP, watering of eyes and loss of appetite, coronary heart diseases, abnormal and excessive proliferation of bronchial cells leads to bronchitis.

Benzedrine or Amphetamine

It belongs to phenylalanine class. Benzedrine is the trade name and the Amphetamine is common name. It is a kind of drug that affects SNS leads to the peripheral vasoconstriction. For this reason it is used in nasal decongestion. It helps in the shrinking of mucous tissue by constricting the blood vessels to increase the size of nasal passages for easy breathing when they are clogged by cold. It is also a cerebral stimulant and has been widely used by military personals, night truck drivers, athletes etc. Its toxic side effect leads to deafness and nervous disorders. The stimulant effect of amphetamines and its derivatives are used for treatment in psychotic depression. At therapeutical doses, amphetamine causes emotional and cognitive effects such as euphoria, change in desire for sex, increased wakefulness and increased cognitive control. It induces physical effects such as decreased reaction time, fatigue resistance and increased muscle strength. Larger doses of amphetamine may impair cognitive function and induce rapid muscle breakdown. Very high doses can result in psychosis (delusions and paranoia) which rarely occurs at therapeutic doses even during long term use.

Cocaine

Cocaine also known as coke, is a strong stimulant mostly used as recreational drug. It is commonly snorted, inhale as smoke or as a solution injected in to the vein. It is a drug obtaining from coca shrubs. Cocaine is used medically as local anaesthetic for mucous tissue. It is a powerful CNS stimulant that causes mood swings from kick euphoria to depression. Habitual use of cocaine leads to insomnia, weight loss, sensory hallucination, Alzheimer's etc. Its use also increases the risk of stroke, myocardial infarction, lung problems, blood infections and sudden cardiac death. Peruvian Indians chew coco leaves to alleviate symptoms of hunger and fatigue from hard work at high altitudes. Cocaine acts by inhibiting the reuptake of serotonine, norepinephrine and dopamine results in greater concentration of these three neurotransmitters in the brain. It can easily cross the blood –brain barrier and may lead to the breakdown of the barrier.

Opium (Heroine)

It is the dried latex extract of opium poppy (*Papaver somniferum*). Its active ingredient is morphine, which is processed chemically to produce heroine and other synthetic opoids for medical use and for illegal drug trade. The latex also contains non-analgesic alkaloids such as papaverine and noscapine. The action of the drug is narcotic. The addiction of drug results within three weeks of daily usage. It is also used as analgesic in surgery. Withdrawal symptoms for the addict are severe, including vomiting, incessant yawning, sweating and sometimes collapse and death.

Marijuana

It comes from the leaf of the plant Indian Hemp (*Cannabis sativa*), that grows wild over most of the country. The main psychoactive part of this plant is tetrahydrocannabinol (THC). The leaves are dried, crumpled and made in to cigarettes by users in the same way that the tobacco leaves are made in to cigarettes. The upper leaves of the plants are stronger. Cannabis is often used for mental and physical effects such as "high" or "stoned" feeling, a general change in perception, euphoria and an increase in appetite. Inhaling the smoke from one or two marijuana cigarettes is enough to make the user "high". Onset of effect is within minutes when smoked, and about 30 to 60 minutes when cooked and eaten. The initial sensations are euphoria and floating feelings. The effect of marijuana depends on its most active ingredient THC. Short term use increases the risk of both minor and major adverse effects. Common side effects include dizziness, feeling tried, vomiting and hallucination.

Alcohol

Also known by its chemical name ethanol (ethyl alcohol), is a psychoactive drug contained in alcoholic beverages such as beer, wine, and distilled spirit. It is one of the oldest and most common recreational substances causing the characteristic effect of alcohol intoxication. It is usually produced by the effect of living organism in yeast on the sugar contained in grapes or grain through fermentation. The unit of measurement of alcohol is "proof". Two hundred proof is pure ethyl alcohol, 100 proof is half alcohol, 86 proof is scotch. The effect of alcohol on the CNS depends on the concentration of alcohol in the blood and the tissue fluid. Blood alcohol content depends on the rate of intake, rate of elimination, and size of the individual. Alcoholism leads to depression, coma, delirium, increased sociability, euphoria, sedation, manner. It has also been suggested that weak acids, such as B_1 and generalised depression of CNS function. Alcoholism shows behaviour like hypomania, mania and hostility. One of the compound that result from the breakdown of alcohol by the liver is acetaldehyde. When acetaldehyde is in excess it interferes with dopamine, a neurotransmitter. Thus dopamine combined with the acetaldehyde to form a compound called tetrahydropapaveroline (THP) which is a highly addictive.

Cortical Localization in brain

The cerebral cortex, or outer cell layer of the brain, is divided into a mosaic of discrete areas with different functions: specific regions control vision, sensory and motor function, hearing, and language. The cerebral cortex is divided into many different areas, each of which is closely associated with specific mental and behavioural functions (Fig -15). This division of the cortex is based on differences in detailed microscopic structure, anatomical connections, and functional properties (what it does) among different areas.

The idea that different parts of the brain do different things is called localization of function. The modern cognitive neuro science development was derived from this idea comes from psudoscience phrenology created by Franz Joseph Gall. Accoridng to this assumption of pherenology the different regions in ones brain have different functions and very well associated with different behaviours. But the cerebral cortex is now subdivided in a very different way. According to many data, the cerebral cortex is divided into a hierarchy of three kinds of areas: primary sensory areas at the bottom, sensory association areas, and higher order association areas at the top. Information from each sense (eyes, ears, etc.) reaches the cerebral cortex first and most directly at its own specialized areas called its primary sensory cortex (or area), each sense has its own area. The visual pathway from the eyes projects (makes connections) most directly to the primary visual cortex on the occipital lobe at the back of the brain. The auditory pathway from the ear projects most directly to the primary auditory cortex on the top edge of the temporal lobe, located under the temple pieces of a pair of glasses. The somatosensory (soma = body) or touch pathways project most directly to the primary somatosensory cortex on the front edge of the parietal lobe. The most direct pathways from the cortex to motor neurons in spinal cord arise from the primary motor cortex.

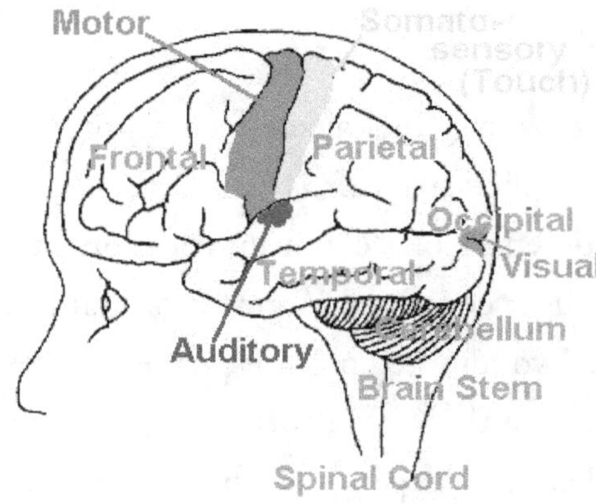

(Fig -15) Left cerebral hemisphere, showing the sulci and the major primary areas.

Cortical Mapping

- ❖ The mapping system devised by Brodmann has very widespread use.
- ❖ He divided the cortex of each hemisphere into 52 areas **(Table-3).**

(Table-3): Different areas in the brain, their location and other names

Lobe	Number	Location	Other names
Frontal	4	Precentral gyrus, paracentral lobule	Primary motor area
	6	Superior and middle frontal gyri, precentral gyrus	Premotor area, supplementary motor area
	8	Superior and middle frontal gyri	Inferior portion = frontal eye field
	44, 45	Opercular and triangular parts of inferior frontal gyrus	Broca's area
Parietal	3, 1, 2	Postcentral gyrus, paracentral lobule	Primary somatosensory area; S1
	5, 7	Superior parietal lobule	Somatosensory association area
	39	Inferior parietal lobule	Angular gyrus
	40	Inferior parietal lobule	Supramarginal gyrus
Occipital	17	Banks of calcarine sulcus	Primary visual area; V1
	18, 19	Surrounding 17	Visual association area; V2, V3, V4, V5
Temporal	41	Superior temporal gyrus	Primary auditory area; A1
	42	Superior temporal gyrus	Auditory association area; A2
	22	Superior temporal gyrus	Wernicke's area

ASYMMETRY IN HUMAN BRAIN

The right and left hemisphere of human brain shows structural and anatomical difference. Geschwind and Levitsky (1968) made a post-mortem examination of hundred adult human brain free of significant brain disease. They observed that a section of left temporal lobe was larger than a corresponding section on the right of in 65% of the cases, while the right lobe section was larger in 11% of cases. According to LeMay (1976), the CT scan observations of 223 cases found that the left occipital region was usually wider than the right and the right frontal region was wider than the left, the differences more pronounced among right handed than in left handed individuals. Witelson and Pallie (1973), in a sample of fourteen neonatal ranging in age from 1 day to 3 months old and sixteen adult human brains, found a hemispherical asymmetry at the temporal lobe in both groups.

THE THEORY OF LOCALIZATION

The theory of localization refers to the idea that different parts of the brain are responsible for specific behaviours, or that certain functions are localized to certain areas in the brain. For example, damage to the Broca's area, or that part of the brain that is involved in language expression, will render a person unable to communicate even when he is perfectly capable of understanding language.

Theories of localization first gained scientific credence in the 1860s with Paul Broca's discovery that damage to a specific part of the brain—the left frontal lobe—was associated with speech impairment. Other discoveries followed: in 1874, Carl Wernicke identified the part of the brain responsible for receptive speech (the upper rear part of the left temporal lobe, known as Wernicke's area), and in 1870 Gustav Fritsch and J. L. Hitzig found that stimulating different parts of the cerebral cortex produced movement in different areas of the body. By the beginning of the twentieth century, detailed maps were available showing the functions of the different areas of the brain. Currently there are two major theories of brain cognitive function. The first is the theory of modularity, this theory supports functional specialization, suggesting that brain has different modules having different functions. The second is the distributive processing theory, it proposes that brain is more interactive and its regions are functionally interconnected rather than specialized. The cognitive theory of distributed processing suggests that brain areas are highly interconnected and process information in a distributive manner. Human cognition involves interactions between the brain regions responsible for processes sensory information such as vision, audition and other mediating areas like prefrontal cortex.

The modularity of mind theory indicates that distinct neurological regions called modules are defined by their functional roles in cognition. One of the fundamental believes of domain specificity and the theory of modularity suggests that it is a consequences of natural selection and is a feature of our cognitive architecture. There are cortical anatomical difference from persons to persons. Areas representing modularity in the brain are as follows.

Fusiform phase area – it is well knowm example for functional specialization specifically for phase perception

- ❖ Visual area V4 V5 – specifically for perception of colour and vision motion.
- ❖ Frontal lobes – this controls process involve in the coordination, planning and organising action towards individual goals such as behaviour, language, reasoning etc. More specifically it was found to be the pre frontal cortex. The dorsolateral, ventrolateral and anterior cingulate regions within the prefrontal cortex are proposed to work together in different cognitive tasks.

❖ Right and left hemispheres – corpus callosum is the area of brain bringing both right and left hemispheres of brain. Left hemisphere is dedicated to language, right hemisphere involved in more creative activity like drawing.

❖ Parahippocampal place area- located in the parahippocampal gyrus (PPA) helps in encoding the geometry of local environment.

❖ Extrastriate body area- located in the lateral occipito temporal cortex. The extrastriate body area (EBA) is a sub part of the extrastriate visual cortex involved in the visual perception of human body and body parts, akin in its respective domain to the fusiform face area, involved in the perception of human faces.

Not all researchers have agreed with theories of localization, however an influential conflicting view is the equipotential theory, which asserts that all areas of the brain are equally active in overall mental functioning. According to this theory, the effects of damage to the brain are determined by the extent rather than the location of the damage. Early exponents of this view—including Goldstein and Lashley—believed that basic motor and sensory functions are localized, but that higher mental functions are not. There is still controversy between adherents of the localization and equipotential theories of brain function. Some experts advocate a combination of the two theories, while others search for new alternatives, such as that proposed by J. Hughlings Jackson in 1973. Jackson claimed that the most basic skills were localized but that most complex mental functions combined these so extensively that the whole brain was actually involved in most types of behaviour.

WERNICKE'S AND BROCA'S AREA

Wernicke's area is classically located in the posterior section of the superior temporal gyrus (STG) in the (most commonly) left cerebral hemisphere. This area encircles the auditory cortex on the lateral sulcus (the part of the brain where the temporal lobe and parietal lobe meet). This area is neuroanatomically described as the posterior part of Brodmann area 22. Broca's area is now typically defined in terms of the pars opercularis and pars triangularis of the inferior frontal gyrus, represented in Brodmann's cytoarchitectonic map as areas 44 and 45 of the dominant hemisphere. Broca's area plays a significant role in language comprehension. Wernicke's area is involved in the comprehension or understanding of written and spoken language.

Broca's discovery of localization of the centre for expressive language gave rise to the frantic search for the localization of other psychological and intellectual function. It is observed that in some patients disorders of language associated with lesions of parts of the brain, some others have no language problems but autopsy revealed the presence of lesion.

Wernicke proposed a theory of language representation in the brain. His basic assumption was that different aspects of language function were supported by different areas of the brain. According to him individuals with expressive language disorder were able to speak but did not to be sensible. These patients also have the problem of understanding what was said to them. Although their deficit gave them the appearance of having a learning problem, they were perfectly able to hear and discriminate individual sounds.

An examination of such brain revealed the presence of a lesion in the area around the first temporal gyrus. Wernicke postulated that the lesion in this area were responsible for deficits in receptive- language function, since there were no detectable lesions in the Broca's area of these patients. He also concluded that same lesion is also responsible for the deficit in language expression. The proposed area- first temporal gyrus contained auditory memories for words. These word memories are necessary for not only auditory comprehension but also for word articulation carried out in Broca's area.

The expressive- language deficit of Wernicke's patients was not caused by impairment of Broca's area but by inadequate input from Wernicks area. The different areas of language functions of brain centres were connected each other by neural pathways. Linguistic information is transmitted across these pathways.

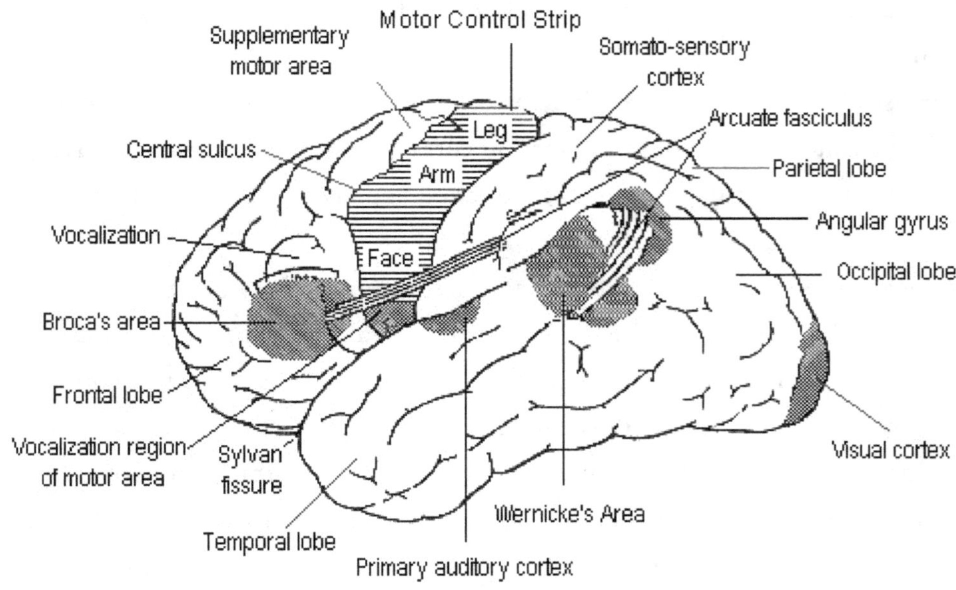

(Fig- 16) Picture of the typical placement of Broca's area and Wernicke's area relative to various landmarks of cortical anatomy and physiology

Brocas area is considered as a centre containing motor representation of words and Wernicke'sarea contained auditory pictures of words. A lesion to the centre where motor word representations are stored will cause Broca's aphasia with disturbance in spontaneous speech and repetition. A lesion to the auditory word representation centre will lead to Wernicke's aphasia causes severe deficit of comprehension with preserved expressive language abilities. Interruption of connection between Wernicke'sand Broca's area leads to conduction aphasia with severe impairment of repetition. Aphasia means partial or total loss of the ability to articulate ideas due to brain damage. Broca's aphasia sometime called disfluent aphasia or agrammatic aphasia. It is named after Pierre-Paul Broca (1824–1880), a French surgeon and anthropologist who first described the syndrome and its association with injuries to a specific region of the brain. Agrammatism typically involves laboured speech and a lack of use of syntax in speech production and comprehension.

An example for agrammatic speech

Ah … Monday … ah, Dad and Paul Haney [himself] and Dad … hospital. Two .. .ah, doctors … and ah … thirty minutes .. .and yes … ah … hospital. And, er, Wednesday … nine o'clock. And er Thursday, ten o'clock …doctors. Two doctors … and ah … teeth. Yeah, … fine.

Wernicke's aphasia is sometimes called sensory aphasia or fluent aphasia. The speech of a Wernicke's patient is often a normally-intoned stream of grammatical markers, pronouns, prepositions, articles and auxiliaries, with difficulty in recalling correct content words, especially nouns (anomia). Words may be meaningless neologisms (paraphasia). Wernicke's patients seem to suffer from much greater disorders of thought than Broca's patients, who often seem able to reason much as before their stroke, but are simply unable to express themselves fluently. However, their non-fluency causes them much frustration, and they are said to be unhappier than Wernicke's patients, who are often blissfully unaware that nothing they say makes any sense at all, and whose higher-level thinking processes are often as haphazard as their language is.

Wernicke's area is related to the parietal lobe association cortex, where cross-modality integration is performed, and is adjacent to the auditory association cortex. Thus Wenicke's aphasia is sometimes called a "receptive" aphasia, by distinction with the "production" aphasia of the motor-system-related Broca's syndrome.

Based on Wernicke's model, Lichtheim described the relationship between Broca's and Wernick's area. Broca's area is designated as 'M' is called Motor word representative centre. Where as Wernicke'sarea is designated as 'A' is called Auditory word centre. Both the centres are connected to a common centre called 'B' is the concept centre. The Broca's and Wernicke's are also connected each other directly through a nervous pathway. Interruption of the B-M connection leads to transcortical motor aphasia, which is similar to Broca's aphasia but with excellent preservation of repeating ability. Disruption of Motor output leads to severe articulation impairment known as dysarthria. Dysarthria is a motor speech disorder resulting from neurological injury of the motor component of the motor-speech system. Interruption of A- B connection leads to transcortical sensory aphasia with severe comprehension deficit, but preserved repetition and fluent production. Disruption of auditory input leads to impairment of comprehension known as pure word deafness.

BIOLOGICAL BASIS OF SENSORY PROCESSES

Sensation is a process by which neutral impulses are created by stimulation of sensory neurons that result in awareness of conditions inside or outside the body. Perception refers to the elaboration and interpretation of these sensory experiences. It is governed with our past and present experiences. We have five sense organs through which we acquire information. These include eye, ear, skin, nose and tongue. We have mainly two functions of our senses: survival and sensuality. If we could not see any colours or the beauty of flowers or the pictures on our television or the traffic lights, our life would become dull and risky. Colours do not really exist "out there" in objects rather our world of colour is a product of sensory and perceptual processes of brain. We derive sensual pleasure in breathing fresh air, enjoying tasty food, good music or feeling relaxed by gently touching a cat or dog. Our senses do more than just making contact with our external world. They add to happiness, variety and satisfaction in life.

Sensation can be explained as the process by which one form of energy is converted into another form. For example light is converted into neural impulses by which we code sensory events in our system that can be processed by our brain. The sensory systems process information reaching to the brain. The motor systems process information going out of the brain to muscles and glands.

VISUAL SYSTEM

The visual system is the part of the central nervous system which gives organisms the ability to process visual detail, as well as enabling the formation of several non-image photo response functions (Fig-17). It detects and interprets information from visible light to build a representation of the surrounding environment. The visual system carries out a number of complex tasks, including the reception of light and the formation of monocular representations; the buildup of a nuclear binocular perception from a pair of two dimensional projections; the identification and categorization of visual objects; assessing distances to and between objects; and guiding body movements in relation to the objects seen. The psychological process of visual information is known as visual perception, a lack of which is called blindness. Non-image forming visual functions, independent of visual perception, include the pupillary light reflex (PLR) and circadian photoentrainment. Human vision is one of the most complex visual systems among animals. The main sensory organ of the visual system is the eye, which takes in the physical stimuli of light rays and transduces them into electrical and chemical signals that can be interpreted by the brain to construct physical images.

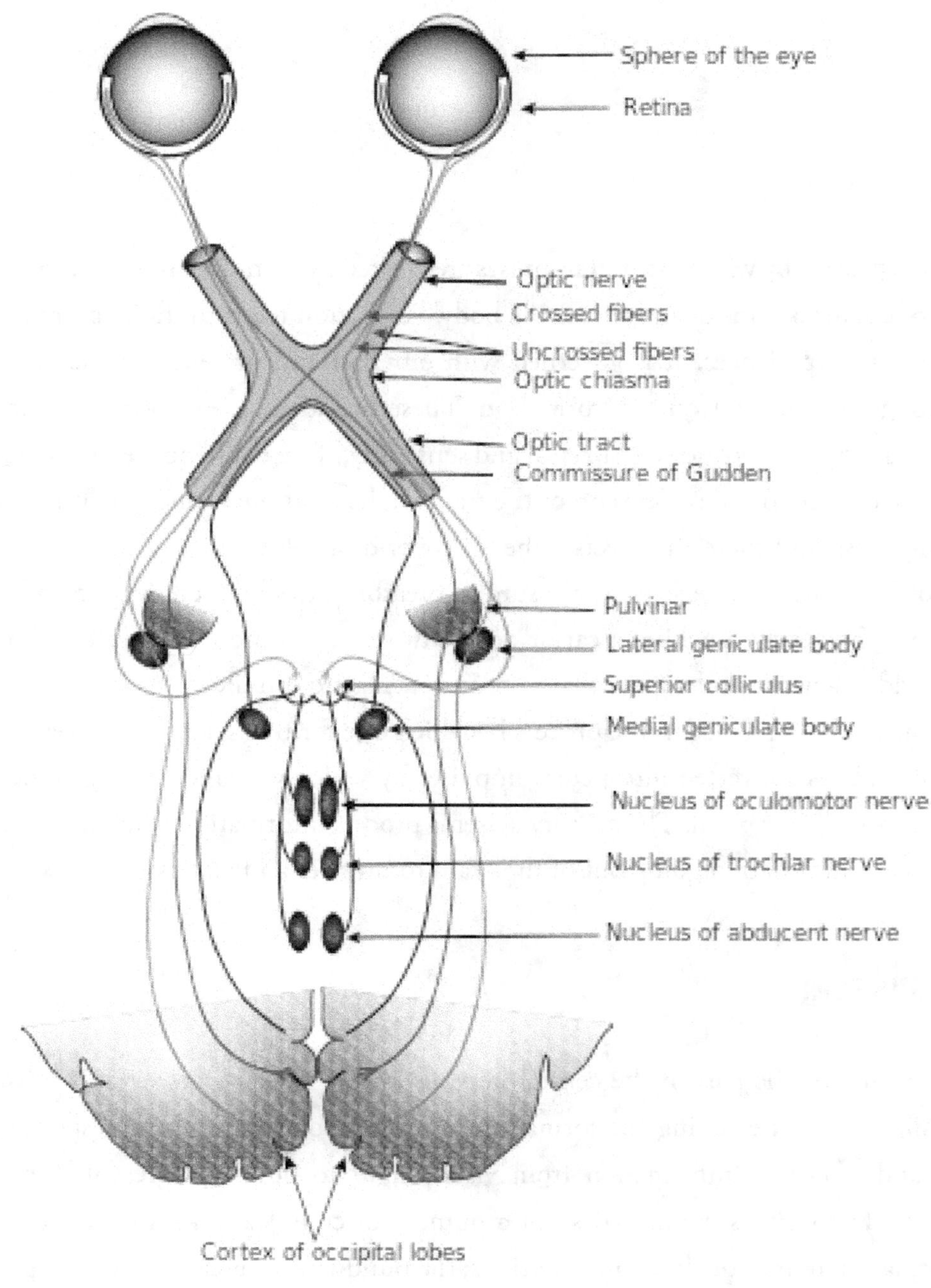

(Fig -17) Visual system anatomy

HUE, SATURATION, AND BRIGHTNESS

Hue is one of the main properties (called colour appearance parameters) of a colour, defined technically (in the CIECAM02 model), as "the degree to which a stimulus can be described as similar to or different from stimuli that are described as red, green, blue, and yellow"(the unique hues). Orange and violet (purple) are the other hues, for a total of six, as in the rainbow: red, orange, yellow, green, blue, violet. The other colour appearance parameters are colourfulness, chroma, saturation, lightness, and brightness. Usually, colours with the same hue are distinguished with adjectives referring to their lightness and/or colourfulness, such as with "light blue", "pastel blue", "vivid blue". Exceptions include brown, which is a dark orange, and pink, a light red with reduced chroma. In painting colour theory, a hue refers to a pure colour—one without tint or shade (added white or black pigment, respectively). A hue is an element of the colour wheel. Hues are first processed in the brain in areas in the extended V4 called globs. Hue is the the property of light by which the colour of an object is classified as red, blue, green, or yellow in reference to the spectrum.

Saturation is a colour term commonly used by imaging experts. Saturation is usually one property of three when to determine a certain colour and measured as percentage value. Saturation defines a range from pure (100%) to gray (0%) at a constant lightness level. A pure colour is fully saturated. From the perceptional point of view saturation influences the grade of purity or vividness of an image. A desaturated image is said to be dull, less colourful or washed out but can also make the impression of being softer. Although a number of different methods can be used to characterize a combination of wavelengths, it turns out that all of them use either 3 or 4 parameters. This is not an accident, since this small number of parameters is related to the way the eye perceives colour. The simplest triplet of parameters are called hue, saturation and intensity (brightness). Hue, saturation, and brightness are aspects of colour in the red, green, and blue (RGB) scheme. These terms are most often used in reference to the colour of each pixel in a cathode ray tube (CRT) display. All possible colours can be specified according to hue, saturation, and brightness (also called brilliance), just as colours can be represented in terms of the R, G, and B components.

If we break up a beam of light into each of its component wavelengths and if we plot the intensity of each component as a function of wavelength, then, loosely speaking, the hue is the peak of this plot – the wavelength (or relatively small band of wavelengths) which has the greatest intensity. The hue is generally the single word that we would use to describe a composite colour. Hue values range from about 440 nm for violet, 450 nm for blue, up to about 700 nm for red light. The names associated with different hues follow the spectral decomposition of a rainbow: red, orange, yellow, green, blue, and violet. These descriptive colours are associated with ranges of wavelengths rather than with unique values, and some people can see colours outside of this conventional range of wavelengths (ultra-violet with a wavelength shorter than violet or infra-red with a wavelength longer than red).

Most sources of visible light contain energy over a band of wavelengths. Hues are colours and what hue we see is dependent on the wavelength of light being reflected or produced. Hue is the wavelength within the visible-light spectrum at which the energy output from a source is greatest. This is shown as the peak of the curves (Fig -18) in the accompanying graph of intensity versus wavelength. In this example, all three colours have the same hue, with a wavelength slightly longer than 500 nanometers, in the yellow-green portion of the spectrum.

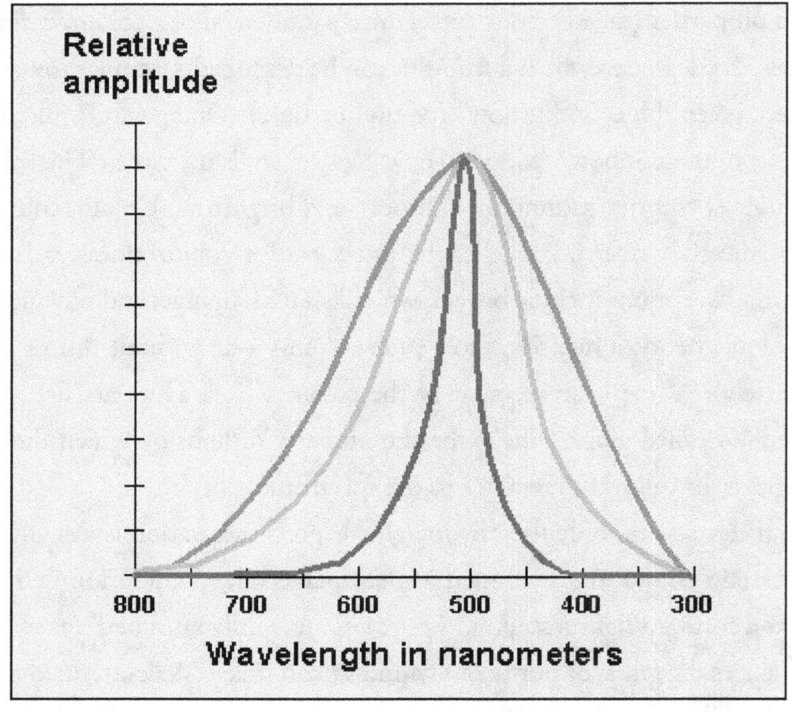

(Fig -18) Graph showing hue, saturation and Intensity

The saturation of a beam of light is related to the width of the plot of intensity vs. wavelength described above. A completely saturated beam would have only one wavelength and would be called monochromatic, which a completely unsaturated beam would contain all wavelengths in equal proportion and would appear white. A completely saturated beam therefore has a very narrow intensity distribution function (possibly consisting of only one non-zero value in the limit), while a completely unsaturated beam has a very wide distribution function, possibly consisting of a constant value over most or all of the visible spectrum. Saturation is an expression for the relative bandwidth of the visible output from a light source. In the diagram, the saturation is represented by the steepness of the slopes of the curves. Here, the red curve represents a colour having low saturation, the green curve represents a colour having greater saturation, and the blue curve represents a colour with fairly high saturation. As saturation increases, colours appear more "pure." As saturation decreases, colours appear more "washed-out."

The intensity is related to the strength of the light beam. Intensity is very tricky to specify because the apparent brightness and the actual brightness can differ significantly. Loosely speaking, intensity is related to the total power in the light beam as measured by some objective instrument (such as a photographic light meter), but the perceived brightness of a light (or lightness of a surface) is strongly influenced by lots of other factors and cannot always be specified objectively.

Brightness is a relative expression of the intensity of the energy output of a visible light source. It can be expressed as a total energy value (different for each of the curves in the diagram), or as the amplitude at the wavelength where the intensity is greatest (identical for all three curves). In the RGB colour model, the amplitudes of red, green, and blue for a particular colour can each range from 0 to 100 percent of full brilliance. These levels are represented by the range of decimal numbers from 0 to 255, or hexadecimal numbers from 00 to FF.

These parameters are often not independent of each other. For example, the intensity and hue of a standard light bulb are related through the black-body relationships – decreasing the output intensity of a black body also shifts the hue towards longer wavelengths. The hue, saturation and brightness of a light beam are often specified using a three-dimensional colour tree, as shown below (Fig -19). The vertical axis of the tree specifies the intensity of the beam, from nothing at the bottom (that is, black) through gray to some maximum value at the top corresponding to the brightest possible white. At each level of the tree (which corresponds to a given lightness or brightness), we draw a circle whose circumference shows the various pure, fully saturated, monochromatic colours of the rainbow in wavelength order from red to violet. The points on a radius line from the centre of the tree to some point on the circumference represent different unsaturated colours formed by mixing some amount of white from the center of the tree with some amount of the colour at the end point of the line.

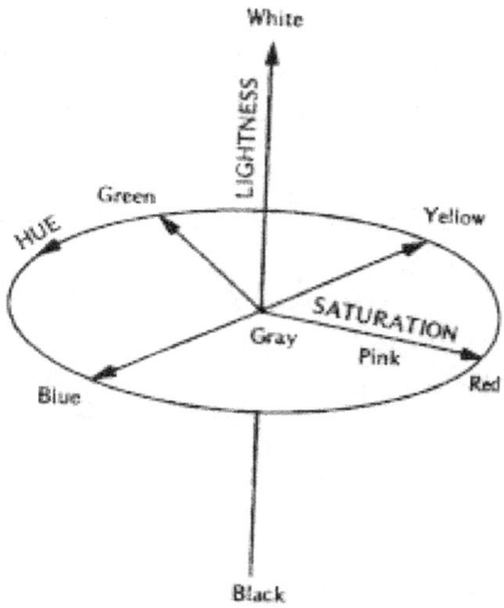

(Fig -19) Three dimensional tree showing hue, saturation and Intensity

STRUCTURE OF EYE

The eye has three main layers: the sclera, which includes the cornea; the choroid, which includes the pupil, iris, and lens; and the retina, which includes receptor cells called rods and cones (Fig -20). The human visual system is capable of complex colour perception, which is initiated by cones in the retina and completed by impulse integration in the brain. Depth perception is our ability to see in three dimensions and relies on both binocular (two-eye) and monocular (one-eye) cues. The front most layer of the eye is the cornea. It is a tough, clear covering, bathed in tears, very painful when scratched. We blink in order to keep the cornea moist. The cornea refracts light, so it is the first stage in the process of focusing the visual image.

The transparent liquid behind the cornea, called the aqueous humour, also refracts light and helps bring the image of the outside world closer to a focus. Behind the chamber containing the aqueous humour is the iris, the coloured part of the eye. The colour of the iris and thus the eye is determined by the amount of pigment contained in them. Albinos, who lack pigment, have pink iris.

The iris has a complex internal structure, including a set of muscles all its own. The muscles allow the iris to change the size of the hole in the middle of the iris, called the pupil. Pupil size changes to compensate for changing levels of light: this is the pupillary reflex. If you are in a brightly lit room, your pupil will shrink or constrict; if you are in a dimly lit room, your pupils will enlarge or dilate. The fully dilated pupil has 17 times greater area than the fully constricted pupil. Muscles in the iris are controlled by the brain stem, so the pupillary reflex works only as long as the brain stem is alive. Doctors check the pupillary response of unconscious people brought into an Emergency Room. If the pupil is fixed and dilated, wide open and unresponsive to light, the patient is dead. Immediately behind the iris is the lens. Shaped like a magnifying glass, it refracts light even more than the cornea and aqueous humor. It plays a primary role in focusing the visual image on the back of the eye. The lens is not rigid; it can be bulged and flattened somewhat. The lens changes its shape when pulled by fibers called the suspensory ligaments attached to the ciliary muscles. Focusing on near objects requires bulging the lens and it is due to strain in ciliary muscles. We can relax ciliary muscles when looking at something far away.

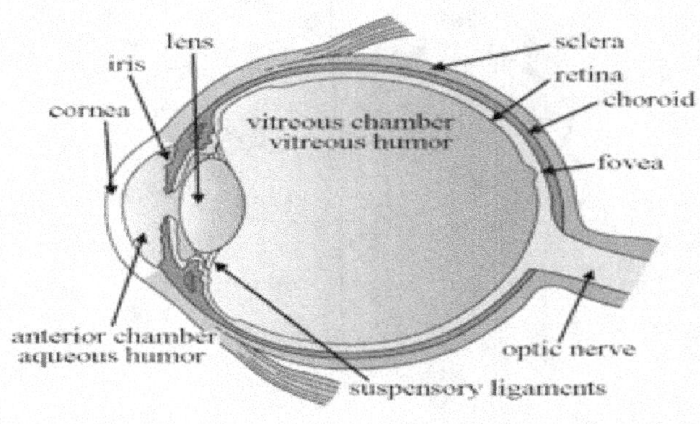

(Fig -20) – Structure of eye

THE RETINA

The retina consists of many layers of nerve cells. It is like a secondary brain that does complicated processing on the visual image before passing information on to the brain. The rods and cones are photoreceptor cells of the eye (Fig -21). Before arriving at the photoreceptors, light passes through the blood vessels and several layers of nerve cells. Cones are the cone-shaped cells at the bottom; rods are the rod-shaped cells next to them. Rods and cones consist of layer upon layer of folded cell membranes. Each layer contains light-sensitive chemicals. When light strikes the chemicals, it stimulates a chemical reaction, generating a tiny electrochemical current that influences nerve cells near the receptors. Although rods and cones both use layers of chemicals that react to light, they use different chemicals, so they respond differently to light. Cones are specialized for colour vision. They are called chromatic receptors, where as rods are specialised for black and white vision. They are called achromatic (no colour) receptors. Rods have greater sensitivity to light and cones have greater keenness (ability to pick out details). As rods are more sensitive to light, they are the receptors we use at night.

When light is not present, the rods and cones build up their supplies of photosensitive chemicals-a process called dark adaptation. This makes our eyes much more sensitive to light. The rod receptors become more and more light sensitive for 30 minutes after being deprived of high light levels. When rods are fully dark adapted, they are 10,000 times more sensitive than they are when they are bleached by strong light. This is why dark adaptation has such a noticeable effect in places like movie theatres. People coming in from bright daylight stumble around in darkness, while people who have been sitting in the theater for a long time can see clearly, because their eyes are adjusted to the darkness and more sensitive to light.

Rods and cones differ in their placement within the eye. Cones are concentrated in the centre of the retina in an area called the fovea. In the fovea centralis (centre of the fovea) there are no rod receptors at all but closely packed with approximately 50,000 cones. It is in the fovea where the central part of the image falls when we look at a object. Near the fovea, blood vessels and other structures are less numerous, so it is easier for the light to get through. The area outside the fovea is called the periphery of the retina. As there are more rods in the periphery, and rods are more sensitive to light than cones, one can see a faint star in the night sky more clearly if one does not look directly at it.

As a rule, however, rod-based vision is not very good at picking out details. That is why night vision lacks detail: it is predominantly rod vision. Because cones are far more numerous in the fovea, acuity of vision is much greater in the centre of the field of vision compared to the periphery. Cells in the periphery of the retina are very sensitive to movement. Movements in the periphery trigger an eye movement that centres the stimulus on the fovea where it can be given more detailed analysis.

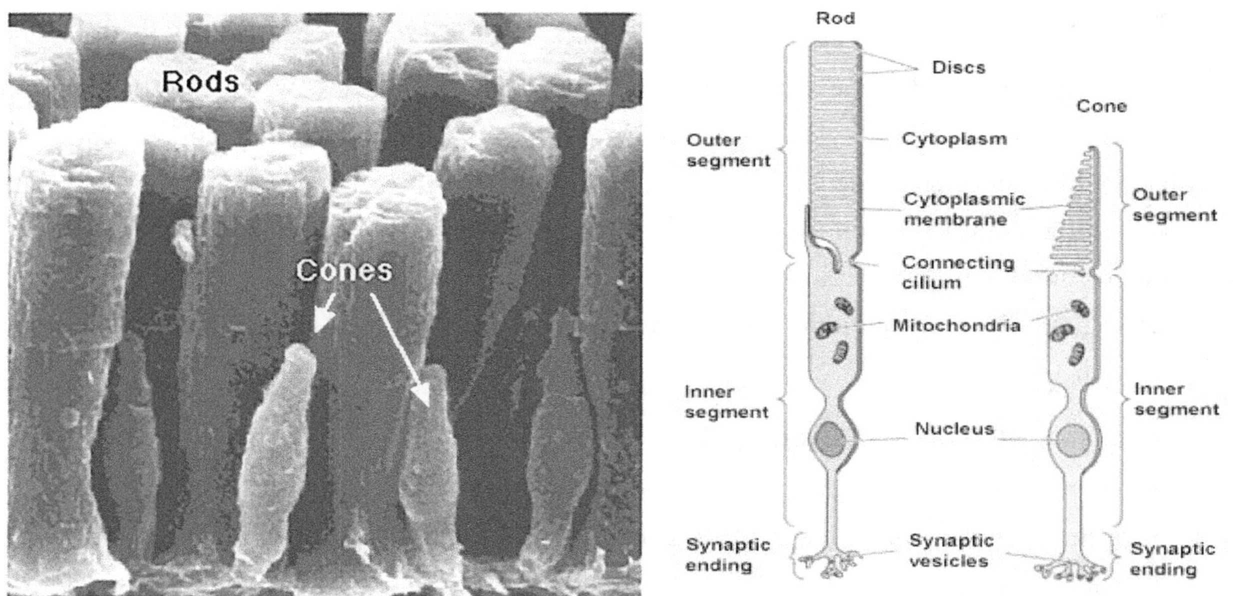

(Fig -21) Structure of Rodes and Cones in eye

FUNCTIONING OF EYE

Light enters the eye through an opening in the centre of the iris called the pupil. The light is focused by the cornea and lens and projected on to the retina. Light from the top left of the visual scene reaches the bottom right of the retina and vice versa so the visual image on the retina is upside down and reversed. The centre of the retina is called the macula and this is the most sensitive part of the retina used for vision. The most accurate region of visual analysis takes place within the macula at the fovea. Rods and cones contain chemicals that release energy when struck by light (photopigments). They consist of a derivative of vitamin A called 11-cis-retinal, which is stable in the dark, but is converted to all-trans-retinal by light. Rods and cones connect to the bipolar cells, which receive support from the horizontal cells and the amacrine cells. Amacrine cells are the interneuron in the retina. In turn the bipolar cells induce action potentials in the ganglion cells. Magnocellular (M) cells and Parvocellular (P) cells are two types of ganglion cells. Magnocellular (M) are large and are found mainly in the periphery of the retina, and so get their input mainly from rods. They are thus sensitive to light and movement, but not to colour. Parvocellular (P) cells are smaller, and are found mainly in the fovea. They get their input mainly from cones and so are sensitive to colour and fine detail. The axons of both M and P cells form the optic nerve, which leaves the retina at the optic disc or blind spot where there are no receptors. The human retina contains around 120 million rods and 6 million cones. In the macula only a few cones converge upon each ganglion cell so visual acuity is enhanced. In the periphery, many rods converge upon each ganglion cell so sensitivity is reduced. The receptive fields of the ganglion cells converge to form the receptive fields at the next neural level and so on.

In the 1930's Hartline discovered that the retina contains 3 types of ganglion cells:

- ❖ On cells: these respond when a light strikes the retina.
- ❖ Off cells: these respond when the light is removed.
- ❖ On/off cells: these respond briefly when the light is on and also again briefly when the light is switched off.

In the 1950's Kuffler recorded the activity of retinal ganglion cells and discovered that their receptive fields are in the form of a central region surrounded by a concentric circle. Stimulation of the centre or the surround had different effects depending upon the type of the cell:

- ❖ On-centre: Light falling on the centre of the receptive field stimulates the cell, but light falling in the surround inhibits the cell.
- ❖ Off-centre: Light falling on the surround stimulates the cell but light falling on the centre inhibits the cell.

At rest all ganglion cells fire spontaneously at a low rate, but when light falls across their receptive fields 'on cells' signal an increase in illumination, 'off cells' signal a decrease.

Receptive fields overlap which ensures that a small spot of light will excite or inhibit many ganglion cells - this is how we determine shapes.

It also ensures that the visual system is primed to perceive edges - even where none actually exist.

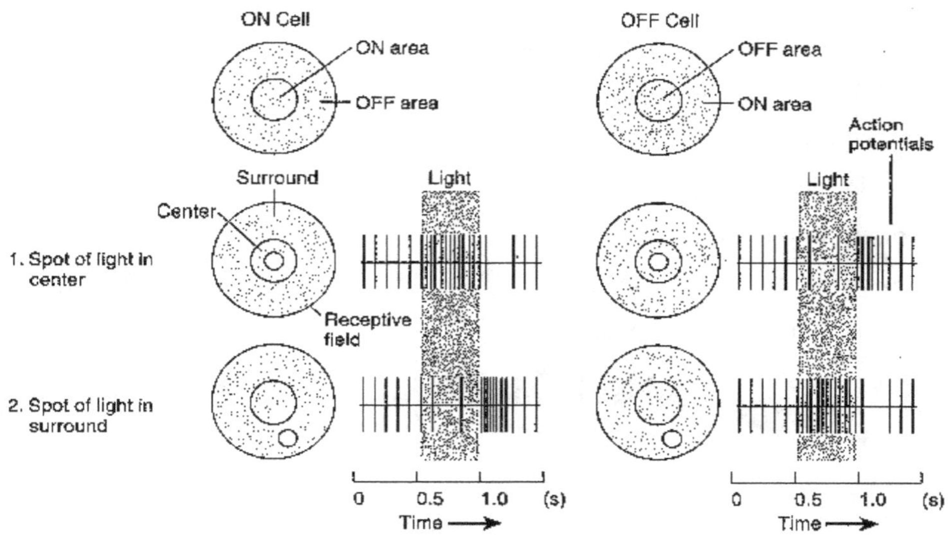

(Fig -22) On /off centre diagram

VISUAL PATHWAYS

Visual pathway starts when the photoreceptors in the retina receives the information. The retina projects to four subcortical regions in the brain (Fig -23): 1) the Lateral Geniculate Nucleus,(LGN), the major subcortical center relaying visual information to the primary visual cortex; 2) the superior colliculus, which control orienting eye movements; 3) the hypothalamus, which regulate the circadian rhythms; and 4) the pretectum, which control the pupillary light reflex. The Lateral Geniculate nucleus (LGN) in the thalamus is the major target of the retinal ganglion cells. It receives inputs from both eyes and relays these messages to the primary visual cortex via the optic radiation. The optic nerves from both eyes meet at the optic chiasmata. Here fibres from both visual fields in each eye cross over to be represented in opposite hemispheres. All the P ganglion cell axons and some of the M ganglion cell axons project to the lateral geniculate nucleus (LGN). The LGN then sends projections to the visual (striate) cortex. This pathway is called the geniculostriate system. Remaining M ganglion cell axons connect to the superior colliculus (of the tectum) then to part of the thalamus called the pulvinar, and then on to visual regions in temporal and parietal cortices. This pathway is called the tectopulvinar system. The main components of the visual pathway can be summarised as follows.

A. Retina
    1. Retina regions
    2. Retina layers and cell types.
B. Optic nerve and optic chiasm.
C. Superior Colliculus.

D. Lateral geniculate nucleus (of the thalamus).

E. Optic radiations and projections to the 1° visual cortex.

    1. magnocellular/parvocellular projections.

    2. Column Organization of the 1° visual cortex.

        a. ocular dominance columns.

        b. orientation columns.

        c. colour blobs.

F. Inputs to higher-order visual cortical areas.

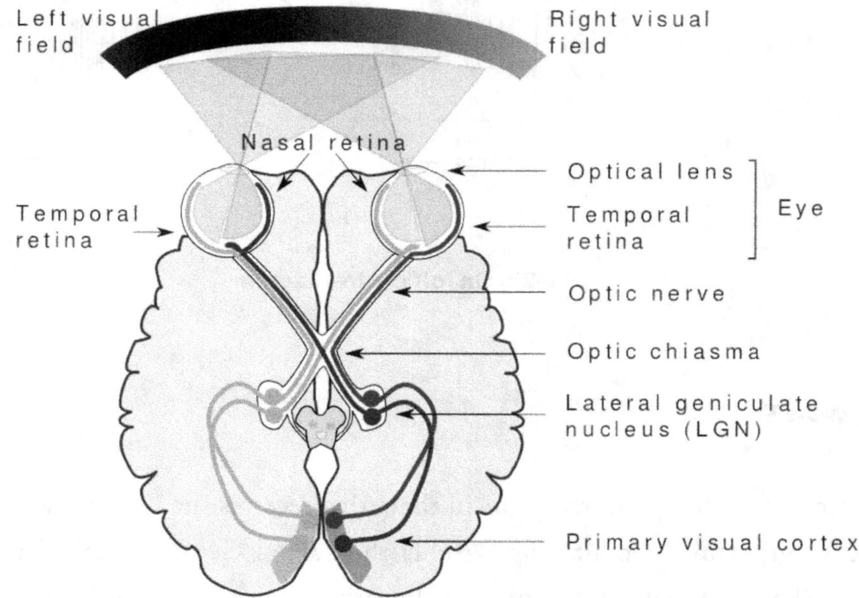

(Fig -23) Sub cortical regions in the brain

The human eye can be compared to a camera which gathers, focuses, and transmits light through a lens to create an image of the environment. In a camera, the image is created on film where as in the eye, the image is created on the retina. The lens of the eye bends, or refracts, light that enters the eye. The cornea, which is a clear, transparent covering in the front portion of the eye also contributes to focusing light on the retina. Nerve fibres extending back from the retina's nerve cells come together behind the retina to form the optic nerve which connects the eye with the brain. The optic nerve transmits messages from the eye to the brain. Like a camera, the human eye controls the amount of light that enters the eye through the lens under various lighting conditions.

Visual acuity is the sharpness of vision determined by a person's ability to discriminate fine details, and is calculated by using specially devised tests and charts. One chart that is commonly used for measuring visual acuity is the Snellen chart, which contains letters of the alphabet arranged by line, with each line of letters from the bottom up increasing in size. The letters on the lowest line are the smallest letters on the chart, and the letter at the top is the largest. The character on the bottom line represents 20/20 vision; the single large letter at the top represents 20/200, the designation of legal blindness. When the Snellen chart is used, visual acuity is generally calculated with a person seated 20 feet away from the chart. A person who has normal visual acuity has 20/20 vision. This means that at 20 feet the person can see the line of letters that people with normal sight see from 20 feet.

VISUAL DEFECTS

Most often people need to wear eye glasses to correct blurred or distorted vision caused by imperfections in the eyes' focusing mechanism. These imperfections, which occur because light entering the eye is not brought into sharp focus on the retina, are known as common errors of refraction or refractive errors. Refractive errors occur as a result of irregularities in the shape of the cornea, the actual size or shape of the eyeball itself, or the focusing capacity of the lens.

MYOPIA (SHORT SIGHT)

Myopia is an eyesight problem mainly caused by the eye being "too long", meaning the distance between the cornea and the retina is too great. In such cases, the image forms just in front of the retina, which means a myopic has trouble seeing things far away, but not close up. Myopia can be corrected by means of a divergent lens, i.e. a lens that is thinner in the center and thicker at the edges. This lens, also called a negative or concave lens, is designed to refocus the image on the retina and restore good eyesight (Fig -24a).

HYPEROPIA (LONG SIGHT)

Hyperopia is mainly caused by the eye being "too short", meaning the distance between the cornea and the retina is not great enough. In such cases, the image formed is just behind the retina. Clear vision can only be achieved using forced accommodation which can be demanding in the long term. Hyperopia is corrected by using a convergent lens (thin at the edge and thicker at the centre). This lens, also known as a positive or convex lens, is designed to refocus the image on the retina and restore near vision (Fig -24b).

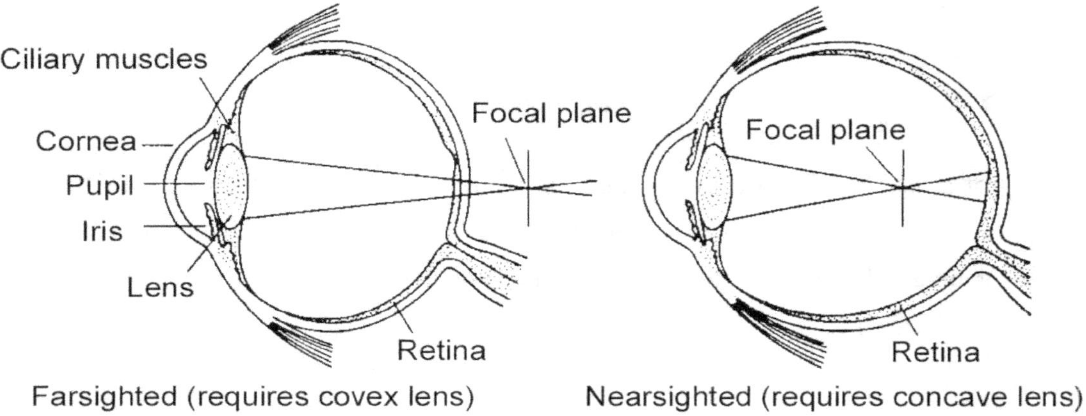

(Fig -24a) and (Fig -24b) : Long sight and short sight

ASTIGMATISM

Astigmatism is an eyesight problem mainly caused by "incorrect curvature of the cornea", i.e. the cornea is slightly oval in shape instead of being spherical.

Astigmatism is described in terms of :

- ❖ module (difference in curvatures)
- ❖ axis (orientation of curvatures)

Astigmatics have inaccurate near and far vision, their peripheral vision is unclear and they cannot clearly distinguish certain shapes and details or see contrasts clearly between horizontal, vertical or oblique lines. Astigmatism may be combined with other eyesight problems such as myopia, hypermetropia or presbyopia. Astigmatism is very common among young children and can have a negative impact on academic success since it causes confusion between letters and number. Astigmatism is corrected by means of a toric lens (curved and of varying thickness at the edges). This lens is designed to compensate the defect of the cornea and correct the axis of the astigmatism. The difference in thickness at the edge of the lens is therefore greater the stronger the astigmatism (Fig -25).

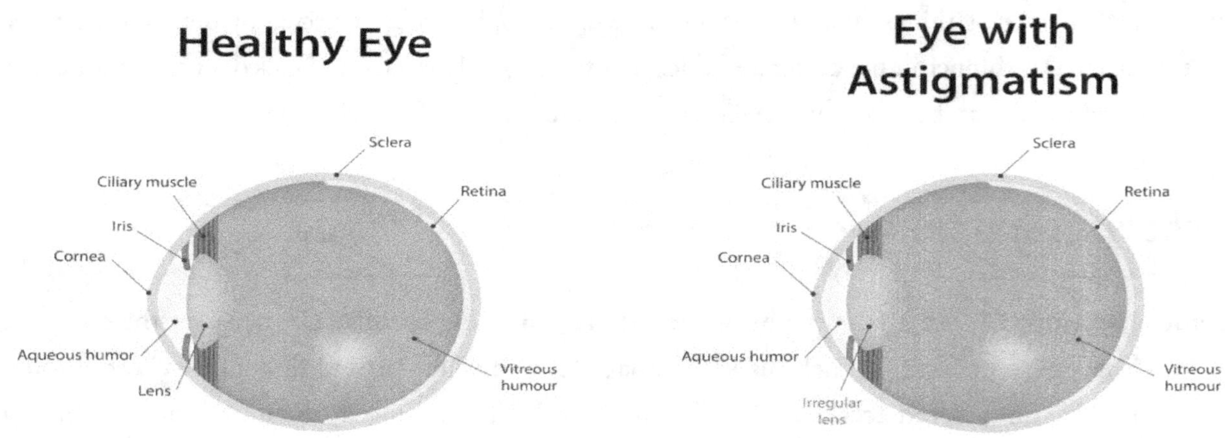

(Fig -25) Normal eye and Astigmatic Eye

PRESBYOPIA

Presbyopia is not a visual defect but a natural change in vision which affects everyone. Over time the crystalline lens loses some of its suppleness and therefore its ability to bulge out and focus. The effects of this change are generally felt around the age of 40. Like a badly adjusted camera, the eye no longer focuses the image correctly(Fig -26).

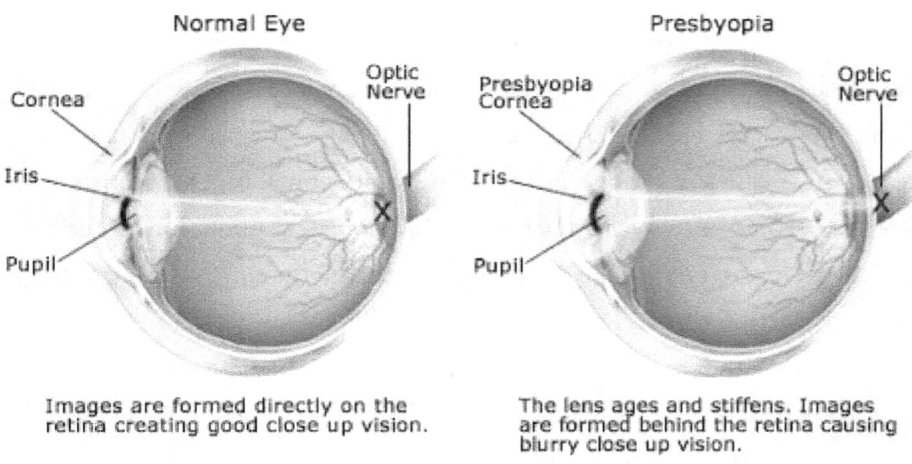

(Fig -26)Presbyopia of the eye.

TRANSDUCTION IN THE RETINA

The retina is the most important part of our eye (it is often referred to as the brain of the eye). Transduction may be defined as a kind of water filtration process. The rods and cones are the site of transduction of light into a neural signal. Both rods and cones contain photopigments, which are pigments that undergo a chemical change when they absorb light. In vertebrates, the main photopigment, rhodopsin, has two main parts: an opsin, which is a membrane protein (in the form of a cluster of α-helices that span the membrane); and retinal, a molecule that absorbs light. When light hits a photoreceptor, it causes a shape change in the retinal, altering its structure from a bent (cis) form of the molecule to its linear (trans) isomer. This isomerization of retinal activates the rhodopsin, starting a cascade of events that ends with the closing of Na^+ channels in the membrane of the photoreceptor. There are three types of cones (with different photopsins) that differ in the wavelength to which they are most responsive. Some cones are maximally responsive to short light waves of 420 nm; they are called S cones ("S" for "short"). Other cones (M cones, for "medium") respond maximally to waves of 530 nm. A third group (L cones, or "long" cones) responds maximally to light of longer wavelengths at 560 nm. With only one type of cone, colour vision would not be possible; a two-cone (dichromatic) system has limitations. Primates use a three-cone (trichromatic) system, resulting in full colour vision. Visual signals leave the cones and rods, travel to the bipolar cells, and then to ganglion cells. A large degree of processing of visual information occurs in the retina itself, before visual information is sent to the brain.

Photoreceptors in the retina continuously undergo refresher activity. That is, they are always slightly active even when not stimulated by light. In neurons that exhibit tonic activity, the absence of stimuli maintains a firing rate at an equilibrium; while some stimuli increase firing rate from the baseline, other stimuli decrease firing rate. In the absence of light, the bipolar neurons that connect rods and cones to ganglion cells are continuously and actively inhibited by the rods and cones. Exposure of the retina to light hyperpolarizes the rods and cones, removing the inhibition of their bipolar cells. The now-active bipolar cells in turn stimulate the ganglion cells, which send action potentials along their axons (which leave the eye as the optic nerve). Thus, the visual system relies on change in retinal activity, rather than the absence or presence of activity, to encode visual signals for the brain. Sometimes horizontal cells carry signals from one rod or cone to other photoreceptors and to several bipolar cells. When a rod or cone stimulates a horizontal cell, the horizontal cell inhibits more-distant photoreceptors and bipolar cells, creating lateral inhibition. This inhibition sharpens edges and enhances contrast in the images by making regions receiving light appear lighter and dark surroundings appear darker. Amacrine cells can distribute information from one bipolar cell to many ganglion cells.

For centuries scientists wondered how humans perceived colour. The scientific study of colour vision began with a classic 1666 experiment by Isaac Newton. He was fascinated by glass prisms he obtained at the Stourbridge Fair, an international trade exposition. Newton performed a simple but original experiment. Positioning a lens in front of the prism, he recombined the rainbow of colours, focusing them back onto a single spot. To his surprise, this mix of colours produced a white light "not at all sensibly differing from the direct light of the sun." He tried recombining only parts of the coloured light by moving a slotted board in front of the prism. He found that if he allowed a band of yellow to project on the wall, and next to it a band of red, he saw a third colour—orange—where they mixed. This third colour was always an intermediate colour that appeared between the other two on the rainbow.

THEORIES OF COLOUR VISION

In 1802, Thomas Young proposed that all human vision occurred through the combination of sensitivity to red, green, and blue. This theory, modified by Hermann von Helmholtz in 1852, came to be known as the Young-Helmholtz or trichromatic (three-colour) theory of colour vision. The basic idea was that the eye responded to three primary colours, and combining the three primary colours of additive colour mixing formed all the other colours. The finding that there are three types of colour-sensitive cone receptors in the retina supported the three-colour theory. One set of receptors is sensitive to long wavelengths such as red, one to medium wavelengths such as green, and one is sensitive to short wavelengths such as blue. So there is some truth to the three-colour theory. However, other aspects of colour vision cannot be accounted for by the trichromatic theory. For example, there is the phenomenon of colour after images. If you stare at a red dot, then move your gaze to a white wall, you will see a green dot as an afterimage. If you stare at a green dot, you will see a red afterimage. The same thing happens with yellow and blue.

Based on the existence of colour afterimages, Ewald Hering proposed the opponent process theory of colour vision in 1878. He suggested that colour vision occurred in three channels where "opposite" colours (called complementary colours) are in a form of competition. For example, red and green are complementary colours.

When you stare at something red, your redness detectors are worn out or fatigued. Their opponents, the green receptors, gain the upper hand, and you see a green afterimage after staring at a red dot. The modern form of this theory assumes there are three basic channels for vision. One channel is the red/green channel; another is the yellow/blue channel. A third channel, the black/white or brightness/darkness channel, may also provide information relevant to colour vision, but that is a complex issue being debated among researchers.

The yellow/blue channel may seem odd, because there are no yellow-sensitive cones in the retina. Yellow light stimulates a combination of long-wavelength (red-sensitive) and medium wavelength (green-sensitive) cones. If there is more activity in blue receptors (compared to red plus green receptors) the brain interprets this as blue. If there is more red plus green activity (as compared to blue) the brain interprets this as yellow. The result is a yellow/blue channel. Yellow and blue act as opponent processes just like red and green. If you stare at a blue image, you get a yellow afterimage; if you stare at a yellow dot, you get a blue afterimage.

Colour-blind people usually are missing one or more cone types: red-sensitive, green-sensitive, or blue sensitive. The result is a disorder in one or both colour channels. The most common type of colourblindness is red/green colourblindness. Genetic studies show this type of colour-blindness is usually caused by a defective gene on the X chromosome. If this gene is defective, women (having two X chromosomes) are "protected" by a duplicate copy of the gene on the other X chromosome. Males (having one X and one Y chromosome) do not have the extra copy, so red/green colourblindness is about 20 times more common in men than in women.

A person with no colour-sensitive pigments, therefore no colour vision, is called amonochromat (one-colour person). To such a person, the world looks like a black-and-white TV picture. Colours are shades of gray. A person with a defect in one channel-either the red/green or yellow/blue channel-is called a dichromat. Both colours in a channel are affected, so if the person cannot distinguish red that same person cannot distinguish green. A person who cannot see blue as a distinct colour will also not see yellow as a distinct colour. People with normal colour vision use all three channels (black/ white, red/green, and yellow/blue) and are called trichromats. (subtractive colour mixing).

For nearly a century, scientists argued about whether the trichromatic theory or the opponent process theory explained colour vision. As it turned out, both theories were partly right. The trichromatic theory was upheld by the discovery of the three types of cones. The opponent-process theory was upheld by the discovery of red/green and yellow/blue pathways. However, neither theory fully explains human colour perception. A series of demonstrations by Edwin Land, inventor of instant colour photography, made this clear in the 1950s.

AUDITORY SYSTEM

The auditory system works to hear, perceive, and store sounds. It includes the structures and processes responsible for hearing. The human auditory system allows the body to collect and interpret sound waves into meaningful messages. The main sensory organ responsible for the ability to hear is the ear, which can be broken down into the outer ear, middle ear, and inner ear. The inner ear contains the receptor cells necessary for both hearing and equilibrium maintenance. While the eye responds to electromagnetic radiation, the ear responds to pressure waves in the air. Sound energy consists of alternating waves of compressed and decompressed air. Sound requires a substance to pass through—a medium *to compress*. There can be no sound of space ships blowing up in outer space, because sound cannot pass through a vacuum. Sound travels only through air, water, or other materials. The denser the medium, the faster sound travels. Sound goes 1,100 feet per second in the air, 4,900 feet per second in water, 20,000 feet per second in steel. That is why you can detect a train from very far away by putting your ear directly to a rail. Not only is the vibration from a train strong; it travels quickly for a long distance because it is propagated in the rails, a dense medium.

EAR

The ear is the main sensory organ of the auditory system. It performs the first processing of sound and houses all of the sensory receptors required for hearing. The ear's three divisions (outer, middle, and inner) have specialized functions that combine to allow us to hear (Fig -27).

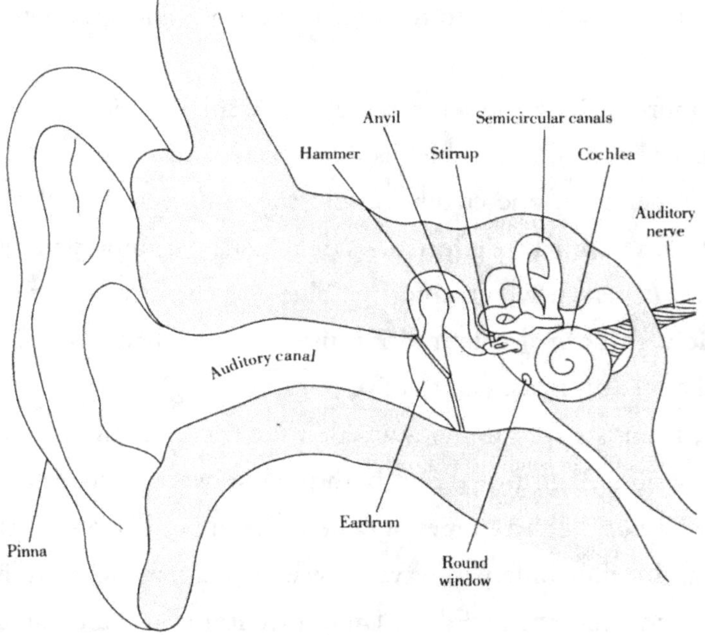

(Fig -27) Structure of Ear

Sound is initially collected by the outer ear. It includes the pinna, the ear canal, and the most superficial layer of the ear drum, the tympanic membrane. This is the visible, fleshy part of the ear. The outer ear is shaped like a funnel, which helps to collect sound. The outer ear's main task is to collect sound energy and amplify sound pressure. The pinna, the fold of cartilage that surrounds the ear canal, reflects and attenuates sound waves, which helps the brain to determine the location of the sound. The sound waves enter the ear canal, which amplifies the sound into the ear drum. Once the wave has vibrated the tympanic membrane, sound enters the middle ear.

The middle ear is an air-filled tympanic cavity that transmits sound energy from the ear canal to the cochlea in the inner ear. This is accomplished by a series of three bones called ossicles (Fig-28) in the middle ear namely malleus, the incus, and the stapes. The malleus ("hammer") is connected to the mobile portion of the ear drum. It senses sound vibrations and transfers them on to the incus. The incus ("anvil") is the bridge between the malleus and the stapes. The stapes ("stirrup") transfers the vibrations from the incus to the oval window, the portion of the inner ear to which it is connected. The ossicles increase the force of vibrations of the tympanic membrane 20–30 times before passing them on to the inner ear. Therefore the middle ear is an amplifying system. In order for the eardrum to move freely and painlessly, the air pressure inside the middle ear should be the same as it is outside. This is accomplished naturally in the body by venting the middle ear to the outside world through a small tube, the Eustachian tube, which runs from the middle ear to the back of the throat. The Eustachian tube opens to equalize middle ear pressure.

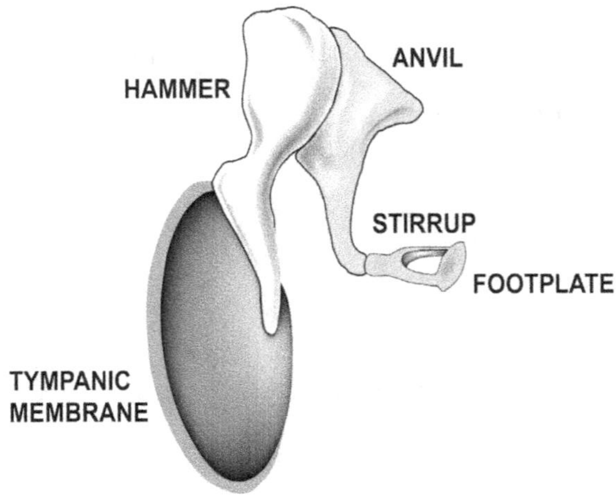

(Fig -28) : Bones in the Ear

The inner ear lies beyond the ossicles. Just as the eardrum between the middle and outer ear the oval window is the boundary between the middle and inner ear. The inner ear is filled with fluid and enclosed in some of the hardest bone of the skull. The main organ of the inner ear is the cochlea, a snail-shaped structure. The cochlea is a transducer, which means it is a system for converting energy from one form into another. The cochlea transduces mechanical vibrations of sound into nerve impulses. Throughout its entire length the cochlea is divided into several parallel channels filled with fluid. The function of the cochlea is to transform mechanical sound waves into electrical or neural signals for use in the brain. The basilar membrane is a thin sheet of tissue that runs the length of the cochlea. It is surrounded by channels of fluid where travelling waves occur. Along the basilar membrane is an elaborate structure called the Organ of Corti. Within the cochlea there are three fluid-filled spaces: the tympanic canal, the vestibular canal, and the middle canal. Fluid movement within these canals stimulates hair cells of the organ of Corti. These hair cells transform the fluid waves into electrical impulses using cilia, a specializedtype of mechanosensor.

Hearing begins with pressure waves hitting the auditory canal and ends when the brain perceives sounds. Sound reception occurs at the ears, where the pinna collects, reflects, attenuates, or amplifies sound waves. These waves travel along the auditory canal until they reach the ear drum, which vibrates in response to the change in pressure caused by the waves. The vibrations of the ear drum cause oscillations in the three bones in the middle ear, the last of which make the fluid in the cochlea in motion. The cochlea separates sounds according to their place on the frequency spectrum. Hair cells in the cochlea perform the transduction of these sound waves into afferent electrical impulses. Auditory nerve fibers connected to the hair cells form the spiral ganglion, which transmits the electrical signals along the auditory nerve and eventually on to the brain stem. The brain responds to these separate frequencies and composes a complete sound from them. Humans are able to hear a wide variety of sound frequencies, from approximately 20 to 20,000 Hz. Our ability to judge or estimate where a sound originates, called sound localization, is dependent on the hearing ability of each ear and the exact quality of the sound. Since each ear lies on an opposite side of the head, a sound reaches the closest ear first, and the sound's amplitude will be larger (and therefore louder) in that ear. Much of the brain's ability to localize sound depends on these interaural (between-the-ears) differences in sound intensity and timing. Bushy neurons can resolve time differences as small as ten milliseconds, or approximately the time it takes for sound to pass one ear and reach the other.

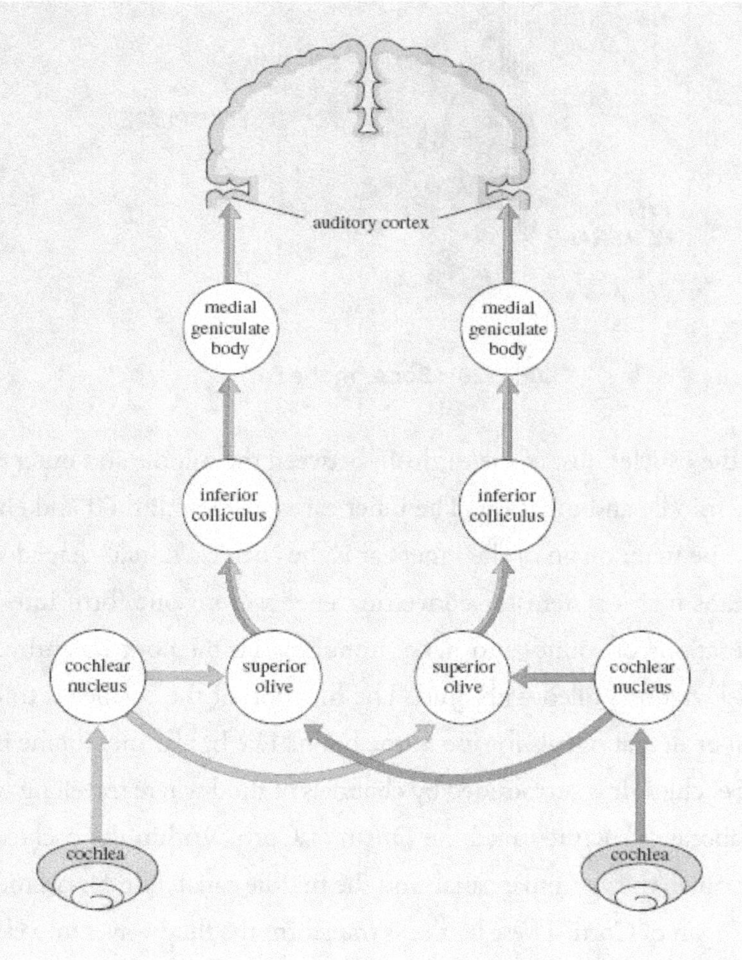

(Fig -29) Auditory pathway

The Fig -29 above clearly shows the schematic representation of auditory pathway. The major structures of the auditory pathway are (1) the receptors in the cochlea of the ear, (2) the cochlear nucleus of the medulla, (3) the olivary complex of the medulla, (4) the inferior colliculus of the mid brian, (5) the medial geniculate nucleus of the thalamus and finally (6) area of the temporal lobe of the neocortex. Within the brainstem almost all fibres of the auditory nerve synapse on cells of the cochlear nucleus. The Auditory pathway once they leave the cochlear nucleus, most of the axons of the cochlear nucleus cells cross over to the opposite side (contralateral side) of the brain. This means that most of the auditory information processed by each half of the brain comes from the ear on the other side of the head. This is in contrast to that found in the visual system, where ganglion cell fibres either cross or stay on the same side of the brain in equal proportions. Both crossed and uncrossed fibres from the cochlear nuclei synapse in the area of the brainstem called the superior olivary complex. This is the first place in the ascending pathway to receive information from both ears. Neural impulses are transmitted from the superior olivary complex to the inferior colliculus through and/or around the lateral lemniscus (some fibres synapse in the lateral lemniscus but most travel through it to the inferior colliculus), from there to the medial geniculate body and finally to the auditory cortex. The auditory system transmits information from the cochlea to the auditory cortex. Another system follows a similar path, but in reverse, from the cortex to the cochlear nuclei. This is the descending auditory pathway. In general, the descending pathway may be regarded as exercising an inhibitory function by means of a sort of negative feedback. It may also determine which ascending impulses are to be blocked and which are allowed to pass to other centres in the brain. The olivocochlear bundle, which arises from the olivary complex, is involved in sharpening or otherwise modifying the analysis that is made in the cochlea. The auditory system transmits information from the cochlea to the auditory cortex (Fig -30).

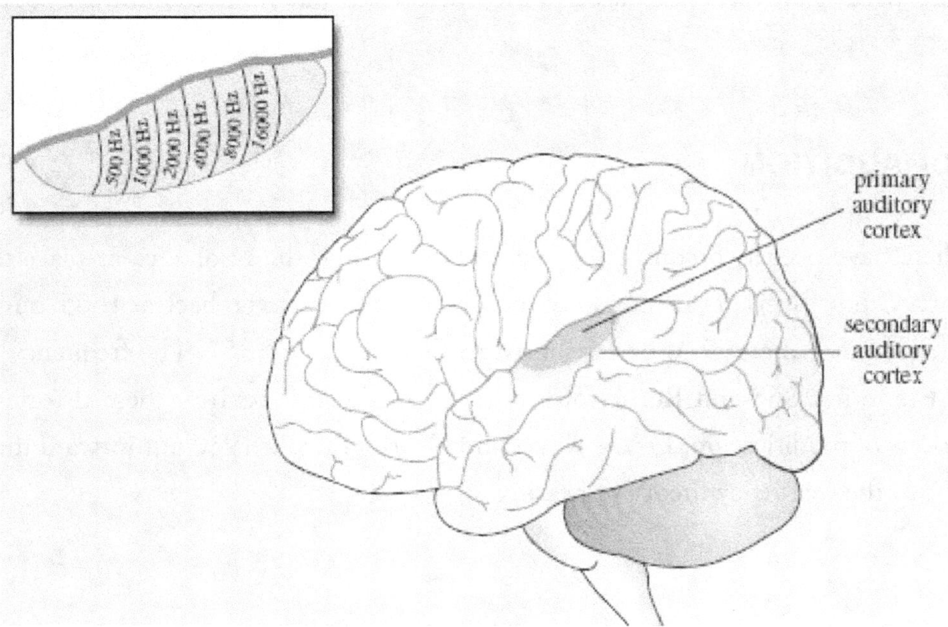

(Fig -30)The primary auditory cortex in humans

CODING OF AUDITORY INFORMATION

Information about sound intensity is coded for in two ways: the firing rates of neurons and the number of neurons active. These two mechanisms of coding signal intensity are found throughout the auditory pathway and are believed to be the neural correlates of perceived loudness. The tonotopic organisation of the auditory nerve is also preserved throughout the auditory pathway; there are tonotopic maps within each of the auditory nerve relay nuclei, the medial geniculate nucleus and the auditory cortex. Conversion from frequency to position that originates on the basilar membrane is maintained all the way up to the auditory cortex. One source of information about sound frequency is therefore derived from tonotopic maps; the location of active neurons in the auditory nuclei and in the cortex is an indication of the frequency of a sound. Phase locking as a means of frequency coding is also present in centres further along the pathway.

There are, in fact, two distinct pathways that occur in the Central Auditory Nervous System:

1. The 'what' pathway which is monaural and receives information from only one ear. This pathway is concerned with the spectral (frequency) and temporal (time) features of a sound and is hardly concerned with the spatial aspects. It focuses mainly on identifying and classifying different types of sound.
2. The 'where' pathway which is binaural and receives information from both ears. It is involved in the localisation of a sound stimulus.

Despite the apparent dichotomy of these two processing pathways, the same types of acoustic cues may be important for the analysis that occurs in each. For example, spectral information is used in the 'where' pathway for determining a sound's elevation; and temporal information, used for our perception of frequency in the 'what' pathway, is also used in the 'where' pathway for determining a sound's horizontal location.

THEORIES OF AUDITION

Historically, there have been two competing theories of hearing, the resonance or place theory and the frequency theory. Crude forms of the resonance theory can be found as far back as 1605, but the beginning of the modern resonance theory can be attributed to Helmholtz in 1857. The frequency theory can be dated back to Rinne in 1865 and Rutherford in 1880. In the 20th century these theories underwent a continuous process of modification. Ernest Wever and Charles Bray in 1930 put forward the volley theory as a supplement to the frequency theory of hearing.

THE RESONANCE OR PLACE THEORY

The Place theory, in its most modern form, states that the inner ear acts as a tuned resonator which extracts a spectral representation of the incoming sounds which it passes via the auditory nerve to the brainstem and the auditory cortex. This process involves a tuned resonating membrane, the basilar membrane, with frequency place-mapping. In other words, each position on the basilar membrane is associated with a particular characteristic frequency (CF). A tone of 500Hz, for example, would stimulate most strongly that part of the basilar membrane which has a characteristic frequency of 500Hz. Further, this mapping of frequency to place is linearly related to frequency with CF gradually decreasing as one moves from the oval window to the apex of the cochlea. This kind of frequency to place mapping is called tonotopic mapping and systems with this characteristic are said to display tonotopicity. The place encoded frequency pattern is passed to the brainstem and thence to the auditory cortex, both of which also display tonotopicity. A major premise of the place theories is that the frequency analysis is carried out in the inner ear creating a neural spectrogram that is transmitted to the brain.

THE FREQUENCY THEORY

Early forms of the frequency theory were sometimes referred to as telephone theories and assumed that the auditory nerve passed complete time domain representations of the incoming acoustic signal to the brain in a manner analogous to the way the waveform of a speech sound is transformed into fluctuating voltages in a telephone line. This theory assumes that a complete time domain representation of the incoming waveform is directly encoded in the pattern of firings of the auditory nerve. This theory, in this simple form, assumes that the auditory nerve can fire at rates of 20 to 20,000 times per second. This is a necessary assumption if the theory is to be able to account for the frequency range of human hearing, 20–20,000 Hz. A major premise of the frequency theories is that the frequency analysis is not carried out in the inner ear, but that a time domain representation is transmitted to the brain and the frequency analysis is carried out in the brain.

VOLLEY THEORY

Volley theory states that groups of neurons of the auditory system respond to a sound by firing action potentials slightly out of phase with one another so that when combined, a greater frequency of sound can be encoded and sent to the brain to be analyzed. The theory was proposed by Ernest Wever and Charles Bray in 1930 as a supplement to the frequency theory of hearing. It was later discovered that this only occurs in response to sounds that are about 500 Hz to 5000 Hz.

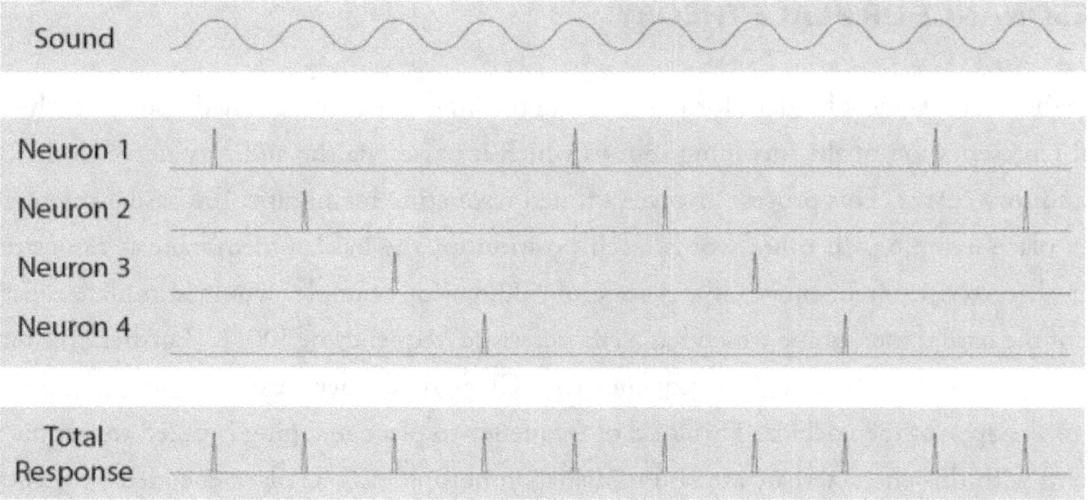

(Fig -31)Volley Theory of Hearing demonstrated by four neuronsfiring at a phase-locked frequency to the sound stimulus. The total response corresponds with the stimulus.

NATURE OF SOUND

Sound is a variation in pressure. It is a longitudinal wave in which the particles oscillate to and fro in the same direction of wave propagation. Sound cannot be transmitted through vacuum and it requires at least a medium of solid, liquid or gas for the transmission. Sound represents a longitudinal wave of wavelength (λ) and frequency (f) which is transmitted by pressure (density) changes with speed of sound (υ) in transmitting media (Fig -32). Relation between the speed of sound υ, frequency f and wavelength λ. Wave length depend on speed of sound.

$$\upsilon = \lambda.f$$

(Fig -32) longitudinal propagation of sound

INTENSITY OF SOUND

Intensity is the rate at which a wave's energy flows through a given area. It depends on amplitude of the wave and distance from the sound source. It is measured in decibels (dB). For example when a sound wave carries a large amount of energy, the molecules of the medium move a greater distance as the wave pass by, and the sound has greater amplitude.

LOUDNESS

Loudness is subjective to interpretation. It is a physical response for the intensity of sound. A sound wave with a higher amplitude and energy is perceived as a higher sound. A sound wave with lower amplitude and energy is perceived as softer sound. Loudness depends on factors like frequency and amplitude.

PITCH

It is the measure of how high or low a sound is perceived to be. It depends on the frenquency of wave, low frequency gives low pitch and high frequency give high pitch.

FREQUENCY

The number of vibrations occur per second in a sound wave. It is measured in Hertz (Hz). A frequency of 50Hz means 50 vibrations per second. We hear sounds with frequencies that are between 20Hz and 20000Hz.

ULTRASOUND

Ultrasound is sound waves with frequencies higher than the upper audible limit of human hearing. Ultrasound is no different from 'normal' (audible) sound in its physical properties, except in that humans cannot hear it. This limit varies from person to person and is approximately 20 kilohertz (20,000 hertz) in healthy, young adults. Ultrasound devices operate with frequencies from 20 kHz up to several gigahertz. Ultrasound is used in many different fields. Ultrasonic devices are used to detect objects and measure distances. Ultrasound imaging or sonography is often used in medicine. In the nondestructive testing of products and structures, ultrasound is used to detect invisible flaws. Industrially, ultrasound is used for cleaning, mixing, and to accelerate chemical processes. Animals such as bats and porpoises use ultrasound for locating prey and obstacles. Scientist are also studying ultrasound using graphene diaphragms as a method of communication. An ultrasonic level or sensing system requires no contact with the target. For many processes in the medical, pharmaceutical, military and general industries this is an advantage over inline sensors that may contaminate the liquids inside a vessel or tube or that may be clogged by the product.

INFRA SOUND

Infrared radiation is electromagnetic radiation (EMR) with longer wavelengths than those of visible light, and is therefore invisible to the human eye. It is sometimes called infrared light. It extends from the nominal red edge of the visible spectrum at 700 nanometers (frequency 430 THz), to 1 millimeter (300 GHz). Most of the thermal radiation emitted by objects near room temperature is infrared. Like all EMR, IR carries radiant energy, and behaves both like a wave and like its quantum particle, the photon.

Infrared was discovered in 1800 by astronomer Sir William Herschel, who discovered a type of invisible radiation in the spectrum lower in energy than red light, by means of its effect on a thermometer. Slightly more than half of the total energy from the Sun was eventually found to arrive on Earth in the form of infrared. The balance between absorbed and emitted infrared radiation has a critical effect on earth's climate.

Infrared radiation is emitted or absorbed by molecules when they change their rotational-vibrational movements. It excites vibrational modes in a molecule through a change in the dipole moment, making it a useful frequency range for study of these energy states for molecules of the proper symmetry. Infrared spectroscopy examines absorption and transmission of photons in the infrared range. Infrared radiation is used in industrial, scientific, and medical applications. Night-vision devices using active near-infrared illumination allow people or animals to be observed without the observer being detected. Infrared astronomy uses sensor-equipped telescopes to penetrate dusty regions of space such as molecular clouds, detect objects such as planets, and to view highly red-shifted objects from the early days of the universe. Infrared thermal-imaging cameras are used to detect heat loss in insulated systems, to observe changing blood flow in the skin, and to detect overheating of electrical apparatus.

AMPLITUDE

Amplitude may be defined as the maximum displacement of distance moved by a point on vibrating body or wave measured from its equilibrium position. Loudness depends on the amplitude of sound waves. The larger the amplitude the more energy the sound waves contain therefore louder the sound.

RECEPTOR ORGANS

Traditional classification of five sense organs is sight, smell, taste, touch and hearing. Each of the five senses consists of organs with specialized cellular structures that have receptors for specific stimuli. These cells have link to nervous system and thus to the brain. Sense organs or receptors are specialized organs that have information about both the external and internal environment of an animal. Each sense organ contains different types of receptors namely general and special. General receptors are found throughout the body because they are present in skin, visceral organs, muscles and joints. Special receptors include chemoreceptors or chemical receptors found in mouth and nose, photoreceptors or light receptors found in the eyes and mechanoreceptors found in ears.

CHEMORECEPTOR

Chemoreceptor is also known as chemosensor, a specialised sensory receptor cells which responds to chemical substance and generate biological signal. This signal may be in the form of an action potential if the chemoreceptor is a neuron or in the form of a neurotransmitter if it is a specialized sensory receptor cell like taste bud in a taste receptor. There are two main class of chemoreceptor namely direct and distance. Distance chemoreceptors are olfactory receptor neurons in olfactory system. Olfaction includes ability to detect the chemicals in the gaseous state. In vertrebrates, Olfactory system detects odours and pheromones in the nasal cavity. There are two anatomicaly distinct organs within the olfactory system, the main olfactory epithelium and the vomeronasal organ. Both the system can detect odour and pheromones. Olfaction in invertebrates differ from olfaction in vertrebrates. Taste receptors in the gustatory system are an example for direct chemoreceptor system.

GUSTATORY RECEPTORS

Gustatory or taste receptors respond to chemicals in liquid state. These receptors are located in or near the mouth, have a moderate sensitivity and they respond to relatively non volatile substance such as sugars and salts. Substances come in direct contact with the sensory cells and dissolve in a liquid on the surface of sensory epithelium is sensed by the receptors. Hence the chemorecptors of this type are also known as contact receptors. In man, the taste receptors are called as the taste buds.

TASTE BUD

Taste bud contains taste receptor cells arranged in barrel shaped clusters on the surface of tongue, are also known as gustatory cells (Fig -33). Each taste bud has ten to fifty sensory cells. These cells form a capsule that is shape like a flower bud. At the tip of the capsule there is a pore works as a fluid filled funnel called taste pores. This funnel contains thin finger shaped sensory cell extensions called taste hairs. Taste buds are found on the upper surface of the tongue, soft palate, upper oesophagus, the cheek and epiglottis. These structures are involved in detecting the five elements of tastes, salty, sour, bitter, sweet and umami (Fig -34).

Saltiness is a taste produced primarily by the presence of sodium ions. Other ions of the alkali metal group also taste salty. The saltiness of substance is relative to sodium chloride, which has an index of 1. Potassium, as potassium chloride is the principle ingredient in salt substitutes and has an saltiness index of 0.6.

Sourness is the taste that detects acidity. The sourness of substance is rated relative to dilute hydrochloric acid which has a sourness index of 1. By comparison, tartaric acid has a sourness index of 0.1, citric acid an index of 0.46, and carbonic acis an index of 0.06. The mechanism for detecting sour taste is similar to that which detects salt taste. Hydrogen ion channel detect the concentration of hydronium ions that are formed from acids and water. Hydrogen ions are capable of permeating the amiloride- sensitive channels, but this is not the only mechanism involved in detecting the quality of sourness. Hydrogen ions also inhibit the potassium channel, which normally functions to hyperpolarised cell. By a combination of direct intake of hydrogen ions and inhibition of the hyperpolarising channel, sourness causes the taste fire in this specific manner. It has also been suggested that weak acids, such as CO_2 which is converted in to the bicarbonate ion by the enzyme carbonic anhydrase,to mediate weak acid transport. The most common food group that contains naturally sour foods is the fruit, with examples such as the lemon,grape,orange, and sometimes the melon.

Sweetness, usually regarded as a pleasurable sensation, is produced by the presence of sugars, some proteins and a few other substances. Sweetness is often connected to aldehydes and ketones, which contain a carbonyl group. Sweetness is detected by a variety of G protein coupled receptors found on the taste buds. At least two different variants of the "sweetness receptors" need to be activated for the brain to register sweetness. The compounds which the brain senses as sweet are thus compounds that can bind with varying bond strength to two different sweetness receptors. These receptors are T1R2+3 (heterodimer) and T1R3 (homodimer), which are shown to be accountable for all sweet sensing in humans and animals. Taste detection thresholds for sweet substances are rated relative to sucrose, which has an index of 1. The average human detection threshold for sucrose is 10 millimoles per litre. For lactose it is 30 millimoles per litre, with a sweetness index of 0.3.

Umami has been described as savory, and characteristic of cooked meats and broths, recently recognised as the fifth basic taste since the cloning of a specific amino acid taste receptor. Savory taste is exemplified by the non salty sensations evoked by some free amino acids such as monosodium glutamate.

Taste buds sensitive to sweetness and saltiness are concentrated at the tip of the tongue. Those for sourness are mostly confined to the sides and those for bitterness are at the back ofthe tongue. The number of taste buds are substantially more in earlier stages of life. In general, the number of taste buds decline with age. The taste buds themselves are in a constant process of renewal, with taste cell formed at the periphery of the bud gradually migrate in to the centre. The majority of taste buds are estimated to have a functional life span of 9 to 10 days. The fine hair like projections of taste receptor cell extending in to this pore. Food dissolve in saliva comes in contact with taste receptors. Each taste bud contains 30 to 100 taste receptor cells. They are long, thin, oriented perpendicular to the surface of the tongue. Taste receptors cells send information detected by clusters of various receptors and ion channels to the gustatory areas of the brain via the seventh, nineth and eighth cranial nerves.

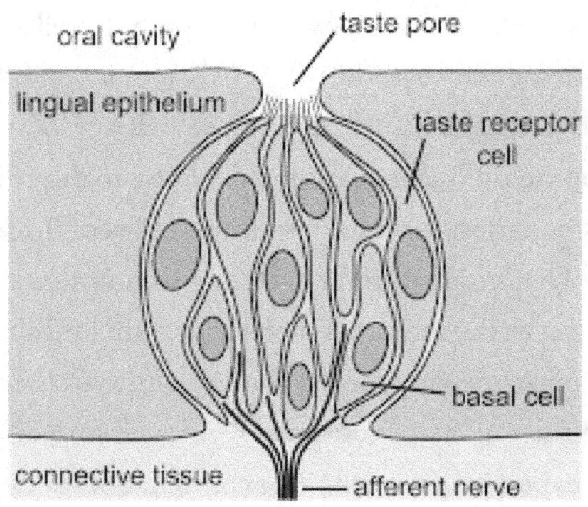

(Fig -33)Taste bud

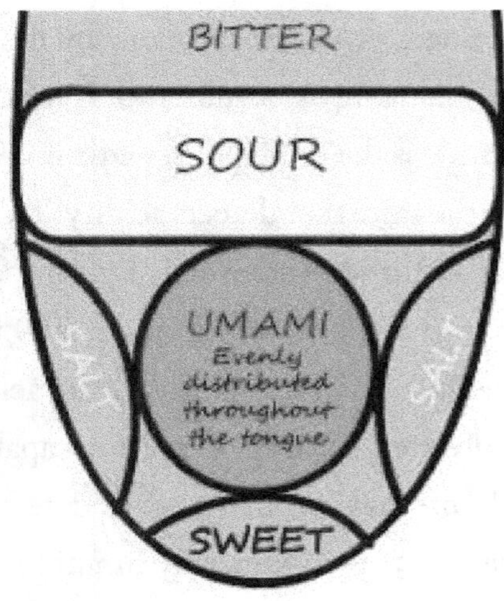

(Fig -34)-Tongue map

TASTE PAPILLAE

Taste system consists of three types of taste papillae on which taste buds are located. Fungiform papillae, which are mushroom shaped structures are located towards the front of the tongue. Each fungiform papillae usually contain 3 to 5 taste buds. Circumvallate papillae are located towards the back of the tongue. Each circumvallate papillae contain more than 100 taste buds. The ridges and grooves are located along the sides of the tongue are foliate papillae. It also contains more than 100 taste buds. A fourth type of papillae called filliform papillae also present but does not contain any taste buds.

TASTE RECEPTION

The sense of taste affords an animal ability to evaluate what it eats and drinks. This evaluation promotes the ingestion of nutritious substance and prevents consumption of potential poisons or toxins. Humans have a taste preference that is why they choose certain type of food in preference to others. When stimuli enter the oral cavity they bind to the taste cell membrane receptors, pass through the specific channels or active ion channels. Once taste signals are transmitted to the brain several efferent neural pathways are activated that are important to digestive function. These processes trigger the taste cell to release neurotransmitter sending a signal to the brain. The way in which different types of stimuli generate taste responses is not still fully understand. Sweet and bitter taste are thought to operate by way of specific G protein coupled reactions (GPCR), T_1R, T_2R respectively. T_1R GPCR for sweet taste has shown to have multiple binding sites used by sugars, artificial sweet taste antagonists. Bitter taste can be elicited by a far great number, and more diverse set of compounds than sweet taste. The great variety of bitter compounds indicates that no single receptor could be responsible to all bitter compounds.

Salt taste reception studies have pointed the presence of cation channels. As the concentration in the oral cavity increases cations flow in to salt receptor cells, resulting in depolariazation and eventually the release of neurotransmitters.

The reception of sour taste was originally linked to the concentration of hydrogen ions. However there is no direct relationship between pH, titrable acidity and sour taste. Solutions of organic acids at the same pH elicit differing sour taste responses. It is obvious that undissociated acid play a role in sour taste, but the mechanism is unclear.

NEURAL PATHWAY OF CODING FOR TASTE

A single afferent neuron with all its receptor endings makes a sensory unit. When stimulated, this is the portion of body that leads to activity in a particular afferent neuron is called the receptive field of that neuron. Afferent neurons enter the CNS, diverge and synapse upon many interneurons. These afferent neurons are called sensory or ascending pathways and specific ascending pathways if they carry information about a single type of stimulus. The ascending pathways reach the cerebral cortex on the side opposite to where their sensory receptors are located. Specific ascending pathways that transmit information from somatic receptors and taste buds go to somatosensory cortex (parietal lobe), the ones from eyes go to visual cortex (occipital lobe), and the ones from ears go to auditory cortex (temporal lobe).

Taste physiologists Sue Kinnamon (Colourado State University, Fort Collins, Colourado, United States) explains the two theories of taste-coding. In the 'labelled-line' model, sweet-sensitive cells, for example, are hooked up to sweet-sensitive nerve fibres that go to the brain and code sweet. If you stimulate that pathway, says Kinnamon, 'you should elicit the appropriate behavioural response without any input from other cell types'. In the 'cross-fibre' model, the pattern of activity over many receptors codes taste. This model predicts that taste receptor cells are broadly tuned, responding to many tastants. Support for this theory, says Kinnamon, comes from electrical recordings from receptor cells and from nerves innervating the taste buds that show that one cell can respond to more than one taste quality.

The gustatory pathway begins with the sensory cranial nerves emerging from the mouth regions (Fig -35). The chorda tympani branch of the seventh (facial) cranial nerves carries information from the front two-third of the tongue and the ninth cranial nerve (glossopharngeal) carries taste information from the back one-third. The tenth (vagus) cranial nerves carries taste information from other areas of the mouth. All the nerve fibres converge at the level of the medulla in the nucleus called tractus solitarius. The next synapse is in the parabranchial nucleus of the pons. Fibres then ascend through the thalamus to two regions of the frontal cortex- anterior insular cortex and an area of the somatosensory cortex near to the place where sensory information from the tongue is delivered. Offshoots of the gustatory pathway lead to the hypothalamus and limbic system, where the information is used as the path of the overall regulation of eating and drinking.

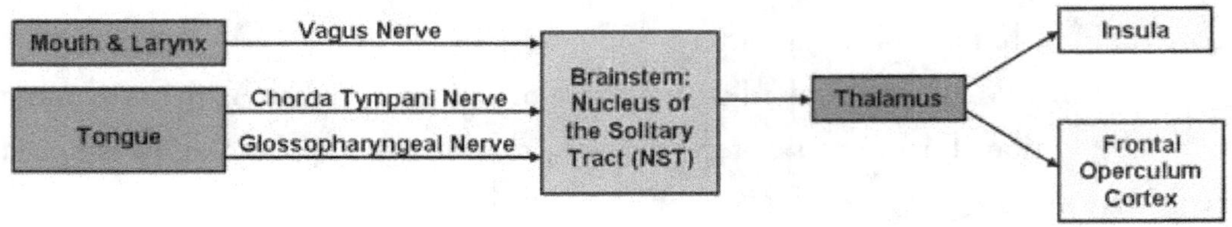

(Fig-35) gustatory pathway

Transduction occurs when different taste substance cause a change in the flow of ions across the membrane of a taste cell. Transduction refers to the conversion of sensory information into neural form. In the case of taste, this occurs at the receptor sites located on the tips of the taste cells when they are stimulated by taste molecules. Specifically, it is the result of taste substances affecting the flow of ions across the membrane of a taste cell. Different types of substances affect the taste cell membrane in different ways. Bitter and sweet substances bind to receptor sites. Sour substances contain hydrogen ions that block channels in the membrane. Salty substances become sodium ions that flow through membrane channels directly into the cell. Each of these affect the cell's electrical charge by changing the flow of ions across its membrane. For example, a rise in the level of calcium ions inside the cell leads to the release of neurotransmitter molecules across the synapses of the taste buds, in turn, causing spike potentials to travel along the taste nerves.

Electrical signal generated in the taste cell are transmitted in three path ways namely the chorda tymphani, glossopharngeal and the vagus. These three nerves make connection with the brain stem in the nucleus of solitary tract (NST) before going on to thalamus and then to two regions of the frontal lobe-the insula and the frontal operculum cortex.

All of our taste sensation can be described as a combination of the four basic tastes. Our experience of taste depend on our internal state (things always taste better when you are hungry). Familiar foods generally taste better than unfamiliar food. People have different sensitivity to certain tastes based on the genes. Our sensation of taste also depends heavily on smell and texture.

OLFACTORY SYSTEM

The scientific world is still not very much interested in the olfactory organ. There are various possible explanations for this. Scents and associated olfactory sensations are not nearly as easy to measure or map as stimuli and observations based on light and sound: after all, a scent has no wavelength or other easily measurable property. Moreover, olfactory sensations are triggered by chemical substances of very different kinds, which are difficult to group under a single common denominator. Our knowledge of the operation of the sense of smell is so poor that we do not know exactly what properties of chemical substances cause the sensations. Strictly speaking, we don't even know whether chemical characteristics of substances are responsible for olfactory sensations, or whether, to mention just one possibility, the shape of the molecule is responsible (the key-lock principle or the so-called stereochemical theory). A researcher has expressed this uncertainty as follows: "It is still impossible to predict with any degree of accuracy whether a chemical compound will have a smell, and if so, what qualitative properties that smell will have."

Odours can interact with their environment in all kinds of ways before we perceive them. This means that the experimental area and the equipment used must be odour-free, and that the researcher must be very familiar with the doses used. Only in the second half of the twentieth century have researchers developed good "olfactometers"–apparatus for administering carefully calculated quantities of odours. Research is further complicated by the fact that people display wide differences both in their sensitivity to smells and in their appreciation of smells. All kinds of diseases or congenital defects may underlie these differences, but even among normal, healthy people the sense of smell varies enormously. The range of smells on offer also varies from country to country and village to village. As a result, it is possible for people to lose their ability to distinguish certain smells to a greater or lesser extent through conditioning; members of a particular culture, for example, may develop extreme sensitivity to certain (say, dangerous) smells.

The olfactory system is the most thoroughly studied component of the chemosensory triad and processes information about the identity, concentration, and quality of a wide range of chemical stimuli. The olfactory system, or sense of smell, is the part of the sensory system used for smelling (olfaction). Most mammals and reptiles have a main olfactory system and an accessory olfactory system. The olfactory system is thus unique among the sensory systems in that it does not entail a thalamic relay en route to the primary cortical region that processes the sensory information. The main olfactory system detects airborne substances, while the accessory system senses fluid-phase stimuli. The sense of smell - like the sense of taste - is part of the chemosensory system, or the chemical senses. The ability to smell comes from specialized sensory cells, called olfactory sensory neurons, which are found in a small patch of tissue high inside the nose. These cells connect directly to the brain. The chemicals themselves which activate the olfactory system, generally at very low concentrations, are called odourants.

OLFACTORY RECEPTORS

Olfactory receptors are the organs of smell detect chemicals in gaseous state. They are organs of high sensitivity and specificity responding to chemicals that are volatile. The gaseous molecules of such chemicals can be carried some distance through the air from their point of origin to the sense organ. Hence the chemoreceptor concerned with smell are distance chemoreceptors. Activated olfactory receptors are the initial player in a signal transduction cascade which ultimately produces a nerve impulse which is transmitted to the brain. These receptors are members of the class A rhodopsin like family of G protein-coupled receptors (GPCRs).

In vertebates olfactory receptors are situated inside the nasal cavities and consists of olfactory epithelium (Fig -36). The epithelium composed of olfactory cells and supporting cells. The olfactory cells are considered to be the actual receptor cells. The terminal surface of these radiate fine filaments of cilia which are concerned with olfaction. The supporting cells are providing with microvilli of unknown function. The nerves emerging from the base of the olfactory cells form the olfactory nerves. The fine filaments found on the olfactory cells are concerned with the detection of odours. Humans can identify hundreds of substances by their odours. It is believed that all odours are made up of combiantions of seven primary odours. They are camphoraceous, musky, floral, pepperminty, pungent,ethereal and putrid. Odouriferous molecules of certain configuration and fit in to the same type of receptor.

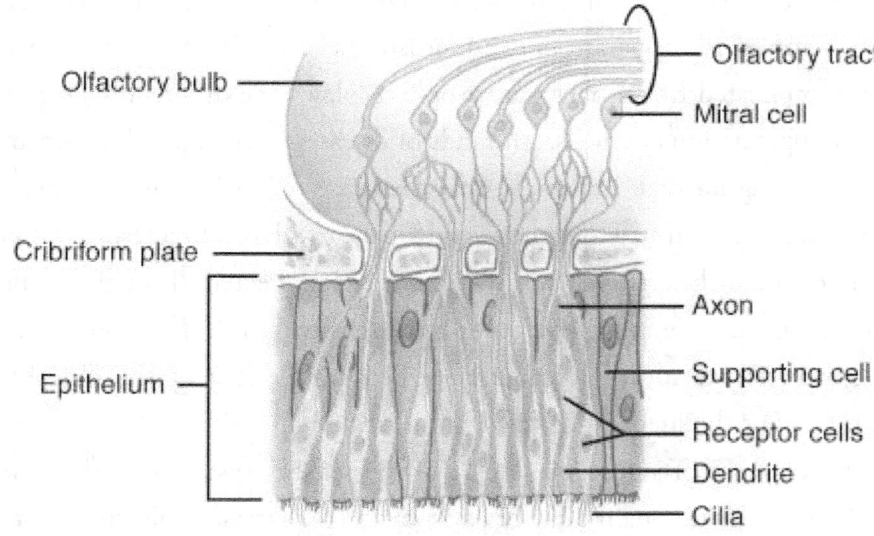

(Fig -36) olfactory epithelium

Olfactory sensory neurons project axon to the brain within the olfactory nerve. This axon pass to the olfactory bulb through the cibriform plate which in turn projects olfactory information in to olfactory cortex. The axon from the olfactory receptors converge in to outer layer of olfactory bulb within small structures called glomeruli. Mitral cells located in the inner layer of olfactory bulb form the synapse with axon of the sensory nuerons within glomeruli and send information about the odour to the parts of the olfactory sytem, where multiple signals may be processed to form a synthised olfactory perception. The mitral cells leave the olfactory bulb in the lateral olfactory tract which synapse five regions of the cerebrum- the anterior olfactory nucelus, the olfactory tubercles, the amygdala, the piriformcortex and entorhinal cortex. The entorhinal cortex with amygdala involves in emotional and autonomic response to odour. The odour informaiton is stored in long term memory and had long connection with emotional memory. The anterior olfactory nucleus project via the anterior commissor, to the contralateral olfactory bulb. The piriform cortex has two major divisions with the anatomically distinct organisations and functions. The anterior piriform cortex (APC) is better associated with determining the chemical sturcture of the odourant molecule where as the posterior piriform cortex (PPC) is best known for its strong role in categorising odours. The piriform cortex projects in to a number of thalamic and hypothalamic nuclei, the hippocampus, amygdala and orbitoprofundal cortex. But its function is unknown.

MECHANISM OF OLFACTORY CODING AND PERCEPTION

Olfactory mucosa located high inside the nasal cavity is the site of olfactory transduction. Olfactory mucosa contain olfactory receptor neurons. The mucus of nasal passage contains mucoploysaccharides, salts, enzymes and antibodies. They are highly important, as the olfactory nuerons provide the direct passage for infections to pass to the brain. Olfacotry receptor neurons have cilia, with olfacory receptor proteins. Rather than binding specific ligands like most receptors, olfactory receptors display affinity for a range of odour molecules, and conversely a single odourant molecule may bind to a number of olfactory receptors with varying affinities. When the odourant molecule passes throught the nasal passage, dissolve in the mucuos lining and it is detected by olfacotry receptors on the dendrties of the olfactory sensory neurons. This may occur by diffusion or by binding of odourant to odourant binding protien. After the binding of odourant molecules to receptor, the activated receptor will send a signal to glomeruli. Each glomerulus receive signals from multiple receptors that detect similar odourant features. All the signals from glomeruli will then send to the brain, where the combination of glomeruli activation will encode differnt chemical features of the odourant. The brain will then essentailly put the pieces of activation pattern back together in order to identify and perceive the odour. Odourant that are similar in structure activate similar pattern of glomeruli which lead to a similar perception in the brain. Once the odourant has bound to the odour receptor, the receptor undergoes structural changes and it binds and activates the olfactory-type G protein on the inside of the olfactory receptor neuron. The G protein (Golf and/or Gs) in turn activates Adenylyl cyclase which converts ATP into cyclic AMP (cAMP). The cAMP opens cyclic nucleotide-gated ion channels which allow calcium and sodium ions to enter into the cell, depolarizing the olfactory receptor neuron and beginning an action potential which carries the information to the brain and brain will detect the smell.

CATEGORISATION OF ODOURS

The sense of smell gives rise to the perception of odours, mediated by the olfactory nerve. The olfactory receptor (OR) cells are neurons present in the olfactory epithelium, a small patch of tissue at the back of the nasal cavity. There are millions of olfactory receptor neurons that act as sensory signaling cells. Each neuron has cilia in direct contact with air. The olfactory nerve is considered the smell mediator, the axon connects the brain to the external air. Odourous molecules act as a chemical stimulus. The primary sequences of thousands of olfactory receptors are known from the genomes of more than a dozen organisms: they are seven-helix transmembrane proteins, but there are no known structures of any olfactory receptors.

The widest range of odours consists of organic compounds, although some simple compounds not containing carbon, such as hydrogen sulfide and ammonia, are also odourants. The perception of an odour effect is a two-step process. First, there is the physiological part; the detection of stimuli by receptors in the nose. The second part is that the stimuli are processed by the region of the human brain which is responsible for olfaction. Because of this, an objective and analytical measure of odour is impossible. While odour feelings are very personal perceptions, individual reactions are related to gender, age, state of health, and personal history.

Common odours that people are used to, such as their own body odour, are less noticeable to individuals than external or uncommon odours. This is due to habituation; after continuous odour exposure, the sense of smell fatigues quickly, but recovers rapidly after the stimulus is removed. Odours can change due to environmental conditions, for example odours tend to be more distinguishable in cool dry air.

Habituation affects the ability to distinguish odours after continuous exposure. The sensitivity and ability to discriminate odours diminishes with exposure, and the brain tends to ignore continuous stimulus and focus on differences and changes in a particular sensation. When odourants are mixed, the conditioned odourant is blocked out because of habituation. This depends on the strength of the odourants in the mixture which can change perception and processing of an odour. This process helps classify similar odours as well as adjust sensitivity to differences in complex stimuli.

For most untrained people, the process of smelling gives little information concerning the specific ingredients of an odour. Their smell perception primarily offers information related to the emotional impact. Experienced people, however, such as flavourists and perfumers, can pick out individual chemicals in complex mixes through smell alone.

Odour perception is a primal sense. The sense of smell enables pleasure, can subconsciously warn of danger, help locate mates, find food, or detect predators. Human's remarkable sense of smell is just as good as many animals and can distinguish a diversity of odours- approximately 10,000 scents.

Different categorizations of primary odours are as follows.

1. Musky – perfumes/aftershave
2. Putrid – rotten eggs
3. Pungent – vinegar
4. Camphoraceous – mothballs
5. Ethereal – dry cleaning fluid
6. Floral – roses
7. Pepperminty – mint gum

INTERACTION OF OLFACTION AND TASTE

Olfaction, taste, trigeminal receptors together contribute to flavour. The human tongue can distinguish only four distinct qualities of taste while the nose can distinguish among the 100 of substance, even in minute quantities. It is during exhalation that the olfaction contribution to flavour occurs, in contrast that of proper smell, which occurs during the inhalation phase. Both taste and odour stimuli are molecules taken in from the environment. Humans have about 350 olfactory receptor subtypes that work in various combinations to allow us to sense about 10,000 different odours.

Humans detect taste using receptors called taste buds. Each of these receptors is specially adapted to determine one type of taste sensation. Recent evidence suggests that taste receptors are uniformly distributed across the tongue. The senses of smell and taste combine at the back of the throat. When you taste something before you smell it, the smell lingers internally up to the nose causing you to smell it. Both smell and taste use chemoreceptors, which essentially mean they are both sensing the chemical environment. This chemoreception in regards to taste, occurs via the presence of specialized taste receptors within the mouth that are referred to as taste cells and are bundled together to form taste buds.

In addition to the activation of the taste receptors, there are similar receptors within the nose that coordinates with activation of the taste receptors. When you eat something, you can tell the difference between sweet and bitter. It is the sense of smell that is used to distinguish the difference. Although humans commonly distinguish taste as one sense and smell as another, they work together to create the perception of flavour. A person's perception of flavour is reduced if he or she has congested nasal passages.

OLFACTORY DISORDERS

Olfactory dysfunction can be quantitative or qualitative. Quantitative smell disorders refer to disorders in which there is complete or partial loss of olfaction. Quantitative smell disorders includes:

❖ Anosmia- the complete loss of olfaction.

❖ Hyposmia - the partial loss of olfaction are the two disorders classified as quantitative because they can be measured.

Qualitative smell disorders can't be measured and refer to disorders in which there is alternation or distortion in the perception of smell. Qualitative disorders include :

- ❖ Dysosmia- The term dysosmia refers to a qualitative olfaction disorder of distorted sense of smell caused by medical/mental situations and include both parosmia and phantosmia.
- ❖ Parosmia- Parosmia refers to a distortion in the perception of an odourant. Odourants smell different from what one remembers. A more specific term, cacosmia, refers to an unpleasant perception of an odourant due to nasosinusal or pharyngeal infection
- ❖ Phantosmia- Phantosmia refers to the perception of an odour when there is no actual odourant present. When a phantom smell lasts less than a few seconds, the term olfactory hallucination can be used.

Olfactory dysfunction including anosmia, hyposmia, and dysosmia can be either bilateral or unilateral on either nostril. Anosmia only on the left nostril would be termed unilateral left anosmia while bilateral anosmia would be termed total anosmia.

The causes of dysosmia are not yet clear, there are two general theories that describe the etiology: the peripheral and central theories. In parosmia, the peripheral theory refers to the inability to form a complete picture of an odourant due to the loss of functioning olfactory receptor neurons. The central theory refers to integrative centers in the brain forming a distorted odour. In phantosmia, the peripheral theory refers to neurons emitting abnormal signals to the brain or the loss of inhibitory cells that are normally present in normal functioning. The central theory for phantosmia is described as an area of hyper-functioning brain cells that generate the odour perception. Evidence to support these theories include findings that for the majority of individuals with distortions, there is a loss of sensitivity to smell that accompanies it and the distortions are worse at the time of the decreased sensitivity. It has been reported in parosmia cases that patients can identify triggering stimuli. Common triggers include gasoline, tobacco, coffee, perfume, fruits and chocolate.

The cause of dysosmia has not been determined but there have been clinical associations with the neurological disorder. They are upper respiratory tract infection (urtis), nasal and paranasal sinus disease, toxic chemical exposure, neurological abnormalities, head trauma, nasal surgery, tumors on the frontal lobe or olfactory bulb and epilepsy. Psychiatric causes for smell distortion can exist in schizophrenia, alcoholic psychosis, depression, and olfactory reference syndrome.

CUTANEOUS SYSTEM

The cutaneous receptors are the types of sensory receptor found in the dermis or epidermis. They are a part of the somatosensory system. Cutaneous receptors (Fig -37) include cutaneous mechanoreceptors, nociceptors (pain) and thermoreceptors (temperature). The cutaneous senses are traditionally thought to comprise four recognized submodalities that relay tactile, thermal, painful and pruritic (itch) information to the central nervous system, but there is growing evidence for the presence of a fifth modality that conveys positive affective (pleasant) properties of touch. Cutaneous sensory channels can be further classified as serving predominantly either discriminative or affective functions. Receptor types of the skin can sense the modalities touch, pressure, vibration, temperature and pain. The modalities and their receptors are partly overlapping, and are innervated by different kinds of fiber types (Table-4).

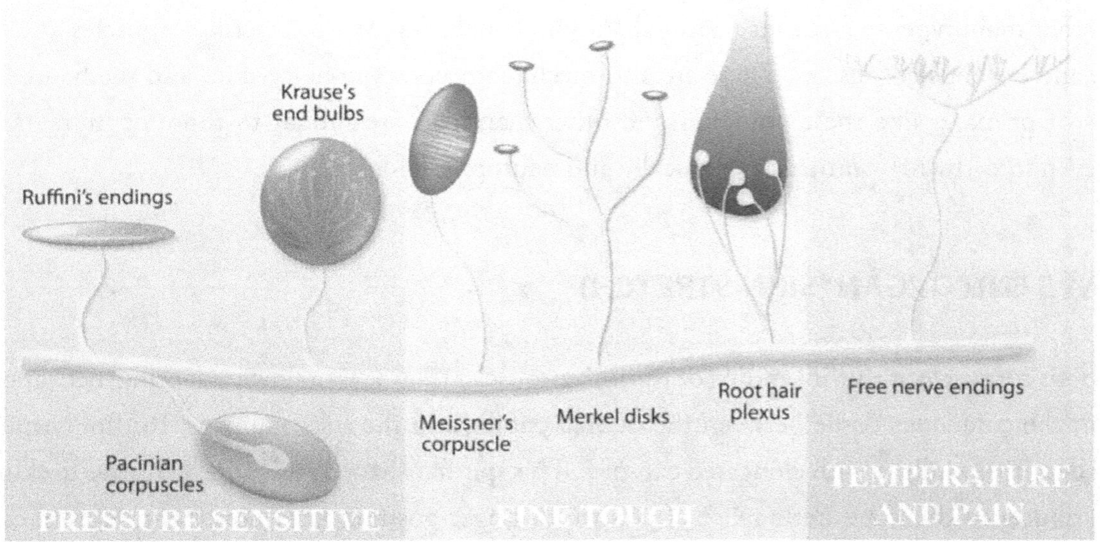

(Fig -37) Cutaneous Receptors

(Table-4): Cutaneous receptors, Types and Fibre type

Modality	Type	Fibre type
Touch	Rapidly adapting cutaneous mechanoreceptors (Meissner corpuscle end-organs, Pacinian corpuscle end-organs, hair follicle receptors, some free nerve endings)	Type II sensory fiber (group Aβ)
Touch and pressure	Slowly adapting cutaneous mechanoreceptors (Merkel and Ruffini corpuscle end-organs, some free nerve endings)	Aβ fibers (Merkel and Ruffini's), Aδ fibers (A delta fiber, alpha delta fiber) (free nerve endings)
Vibration	Meissners and Pacinian corpuscle end-organs	Aβ fibers
Temperature	Thermoreceptors	Aδ fibers (cold receptors) C fibers (warmth receptors)
Pain and Itch	Free nerve ending nociceptors	Aδ fibers (Nociceptors of neospinothalamic tract) C fibers (Nociceptors of paleospinothalamic tract)

The sensory receptors in the skin are:
- ❖ Cutaneous mechanoreceptors
  - ➢ Ruffini's end organ (skin stretch)
  - ➢ End-bulbs of Krause (Cold)
  - ➢ Meissner's corpuscle (changes in texture, slow vibrations)
  - ➢ Pacinian corpuscle (deep pressure, fast vibrations)
  - ➢ Merkel's disc (sustained touch and pressure)
  - ➢ Free nerve endings
- ❖ Thermoreceptor

- ❖ Nociceptors
- ❖ Chemoreceptors

A mechanoreceptor is a sensory receptor that responds to mechanical pressure or distortion. Normally there are four main types in glabrous mammalian skin: lamellar corpuscles, tactile corpuscles, merkel nerve endings, and bulbous corpuscles. There are also mechanoreceptors in hairy skin, and the hair cells in the receptors of primates like rhesus monkeysand other mammals are similar to those of humans and also studied even in early 20th century anatomically and neurophysiologically.

RUFFINI'S END ORGAN (SKIN STRETCH)

The Bulbous corpuscle or Ruffini ending or Ruffini corpuscles (Fig-38) is a slowly adapting mechanoreceptor located in the cutaneous tissue between the dermal papilla and the subcutaneous. Ruffini corpuscles are enlarged dendritic endings with elongated capsules. This spindle-shaped receptor is sensitive to skin stretch, and contributes to the kinesthetic sense of control of finger position and movement. Ruffini corpuscles respond to sustained pressure and show very little adaptation. Ruffinian endings are located in the deep layers of the skin, and register mechanical deformation within joints, more specifically angle change, with a specificity of up to 2.75 degrees, as well as continuous pressure states. They also act as thermoreceptors that respond for a long time, so in case of deep burn there will be no pain as these receptors will be burned off. Classically regarded as a thermoreceptor, the Ruffinian endings/corpuscle is not actually a thermoreceptor but is rather a mechanoreceptor.

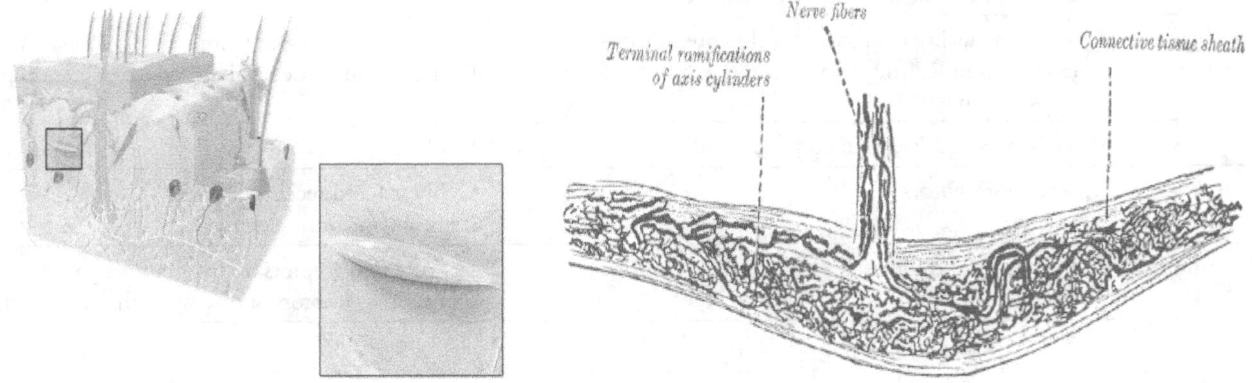

(Fig 38) Ruffini Corpuscle

END-BULBS OF KRAUSE (COLD)

The bulboid corpuscles (end-bulbs of Krause) (Fig-39) are cutaneous receptors in the human body. The end-bulbs of Krause were named after the German anatomist Wilhelm Krause. The end-bulbs of Krause are thermoreceptors, sensing cold temperatures. They are minute cylindrical or oval bodies, consisting of a capsule formed by the expansion of the connective-tissue sheath of a medullated fiber, and containing a soft semifluid core in which the axis-cylinder terminates either in a bulbous extremity or in a coiled-up plexiform mass.

End-bulbs are found in the conjunctiva of the eye (where they are spheroidal in shape in humans, but cylindrical in most other animals), in the mucous membrane of the lips and tongue, and in the epineurium of nerve trunks.

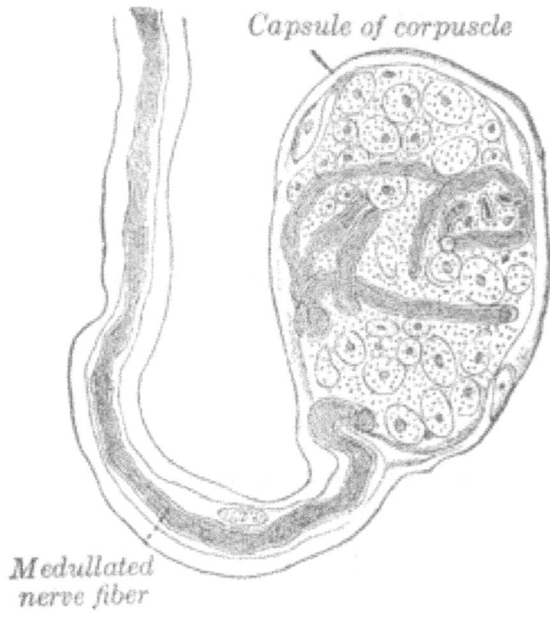

(Fig -39) End bulbs of Krause

MEISSNER'S CORPUSCLE (CHANGES IN TEXTURE, SLOW VIBRATIONS)

Tactile corpuscles (or Meissner's corpuscles; discovered by anatomist Georg Meissner (1829–1905) (Fig -40) and Rudolf Wagner are a type of mechanoreceptor. They are a type of nerve ending in the skin that is responsible for sensitivity to light touch. In particular, they have their highest sensitivity (lowest threshold) when sensing vibrations between 10 and 50 Hertz. They are rapidly adaptive receptors. They are most concentrated in thick hairless skin, especially at the finger pads.

Tactile corpuscles are encapsulated unmyelinated nerve endings, which consist of flattened supportive cells arranged as horizontal lamellae surrounded by a connective tissue capsule. The corpuscle is 30–140 μm in length and 40–60 μm in diameter. Tactile corpuscles are rapidly adapting mechanoreceptors. They are sensitive to shape and textural changes in exploratory and discriminatory touch. Their acute sensitivity provides the neural basis for reading Braille text. Because of their superficial location in the dermis, these corpuscles are particularly sensitive to touch and vibrations, but for the same reasons, they are limited in their detection because they can only signal that something is touching the skin.

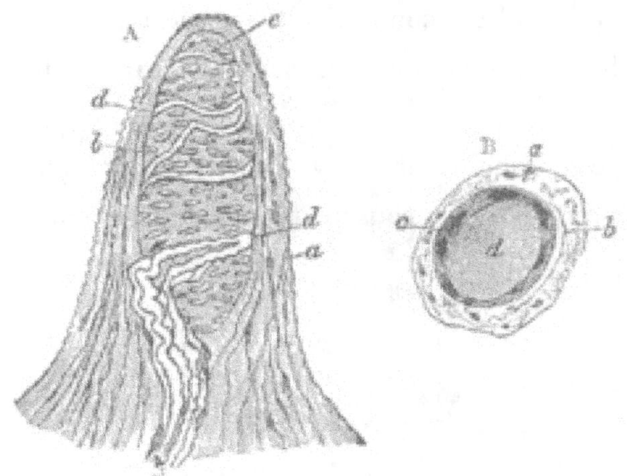

(Fig -40)Papilla of the hand, magnified 350 times.

A. Side view of a papilla of the hand.

  a. Cortical layer.

  b. Tactile corpuscle.

  c. Small nerve of the papilla, with neurolemma.

  d. Its two nervous fibers running with spiral coils around the tactile corpuscle.

  e. Apparent termination of one of these fibers.

B. A tactile papilla seen from above so as to show its transverse section.

  a. Cortical layer.

  b. Nerve fiber.

  c. Outer layer of the tactile body, with nuclei.

  d. Clear interior substance.

PACINIAN CORPUSCLE (DEEP PRESSURE, FAST VIBRATIONS)

Lamellar corpuscles, or Pacinian corpuscles, are one of the four major types of mechanoreceptor cell in mammalian skin (Fig -41). They are nerve endings in the skin responsible for sensitivity to vibration and pressure. They respond only to sudden disturbances and are especially sensitive to vibration. The vibrational role may be used to detect surface texture, e.g., roughness and smoothness. Lamellar corpuscles are also found in the pancreas, where they detect vibration and possibly very low frequency sounds. Lamellar corpuscles act as very rapidly adapting mechanoreceptors. Lamellar corpuscles are larger and fewer in number than Meissner's corpuscle, Merkel cells and Ruffini's corpuscles. The Lamellar corpuscle is approximately oval-cylindrical-shaped and 1 mm in length. The entire corpuscle is wrapped by a layer of connective tissue. Its capsule consists of 20 to 60 concentric lamellae including fibroblasts and fibrous connective tissue (mainly Type IV and Type II collagen network), separated by gelatinous material, more than 92% of which is water. Any deformation in the corpuscle causes action potentials to be generated by opening pressure-sensitive sodium ion channels in the axon membrane. This allows sodium ions to influx, creating a receptor potential.

These corpuscles are especially susceptible to vibrations, which they can sense even centimeters away. Their optimal sensitivity is 250 Hz, and this is the frequency range generated upon fingertips by textures made of features smaller than 1 μm. Lamellar corpuscles cause action potentials when the skin is rapidly indented but not when the pressure is steady, due to the layers of connective tissue that cover the nerve ending. It is thought that they respond to high-velocity changes in joint position.

Lamellar corpuscles sense stimuli due to the deformation of their lamellae, which press on the membrane of the sensory neuron and causes it to bend or stretch. When the lamellae are deformed, due to either pressure or release of pressure, a generator potential is created as it physically deforms the plasma membrane of the receptive area of the neuron, making it "leak" Na+ ions. If this potential reaches a certain threshold, nerve impulses or action potentials are formed by pressure-sensitive sodium channels at the first node of Ranvier, the first node of the myelinated section of the neurite inside the capsule. This impulse is now transferred along the axon with the use of sodium channels and sodium/potassium pumps in the axon membrane.

Once the receptive area of the neurite is depolarized, it will depolarize the first node of Ranvier; however, as it is a rapidly adapting fibre, this does not carry on indefinitely, and the signal propagation ceases. This is a graded response, meaning that the greater the deformation, the greater the generator potential. Action potentials are formed when the skin is rapidly distorted but not when pressure is continuous because of the mechanical filtering of the stimulus in the lamellar structure. The frequencies of the impulses decrease quickly and soon stop due to the relaxation of the inner layers of connective tissue that cover the nerve ending. This adaptation is useful, as it stops the nervous system from being overloaded with unnecessary information such as the pressure exerted by clothing.

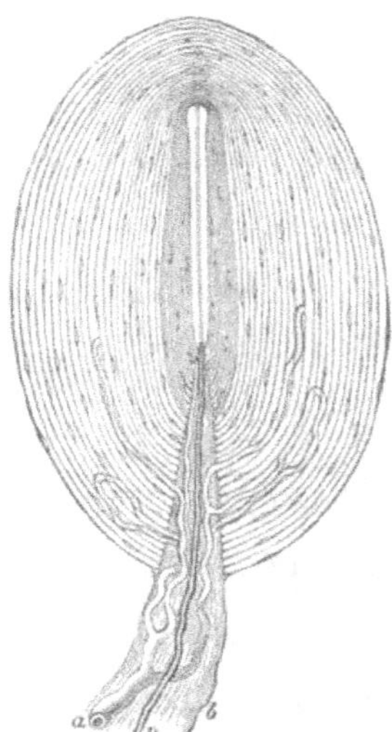

(Fig -41) Lamellar corpuscle, with its system of capsules and central cavity.
a. Arterial twig, ending in capillaries, which form loops in some of the intercapsular spaces,
and one penetrates to the central capsule.
b. The fibrous tissue of the stalk.
n. Nerve tube advancing to the central capsule, there losing its white matter and stretching along the axis to the opposite end, where it ends by a tuberculated enlargement.

MERKEL'S DISC (SUSTAINED TOUCH AND PRESSURE)

Merkel nerve endings are mechanoreceptors, a type of sensory receptor, that are found in the basal epidermis and hair follicles (Fig -42). They are nerve endings and provide information on mechanical pressure, position, and deep static touch features, such as shapes and edges. Merkel cells in the basal epidermis of the skin store serotonin which they release to associated nerve endings in response to pressure. Each ending consists of a Merkel cell in close apposition with an enlarged nerve terminal. This is sometimes referred to as a Merkel cell–neurite complex, or a Merkel disk receptor.

In humans, Merkel cells along with Meissner's corpuscles occur in the superficial skin layers, and are most densely clustered beneath the ridges of the highly sensitive fingertips which make up fingerprints, and less so in the palms and forearm. In hairy skin, Merkel nerve endings are clustered into specialized epithelial structures called "touch domes" or "hair disks". Merkel receptors are also located in the mammary glands. Wherever they are found, the epithelium is arranged to optimize the transfer of pressure to the ending.

Merkel cells provide information on pressure, position, and deep static touch features such as shapes and edges. They are tactile sensors in mechanotransduction. They encode surface features of touched objects into a perception, but also have to do with proprioception. Merkel cells transduce tactile stimuli/ mechanical forces into excitatory signals, which trigger vesicular serotonin release; they have also been called a "serotonergic synapse". They have similar functions as the enterochromaffin cell, the mechanosensory cell in the GI epithelium, which synthesizes 95% of the body's total setrotonin.

Merkel nerve endings are classified as slowly adapting, which respond only to the onset and offset of mechanical deflection. In mammals, electrical recordings from single afferent nerve fibres have shown that the responses of Merkel nerve endings are characterized by a vigorous response to the onset of a mechanical ramp stimulus (dynamic), and then continued firing during the plateau phase (static). Firing during the static phase can continue for more than 30 minutes. The inter-spike intervals during sustained firing are irregular, in contrast to the highly regular pattern of inter-spike intervals obtained from slowly adapting type II mechanoreceptors.

Merkel nerve endings are the most sensitive of the four main types of mechanoreceptors to vibrations at low frequencies, around 5 to 15 Hz. Merkel nerve endings are extremely sensitive to tissue displacement, and may respond to displacements of less than 1 µm. If the skin is touched in two separate points within a single receptive field, the person will be unable to feel the two separate points. If the two points touched span more than a single receptive field then both will be felt. The size of mechanoreceptors' receptive fields in a given area determines the degree to which detailed stimuli can be resolved: the smaller and more densely clustered the receptive fields, the higher the resolution. Type I afferent fibres have smaller receptive fields than type II fibres. Several studies indicate that type I fibres mediate high resolution tactile discrimination, and are responsible for the ability of our finger tips to feel fine detailed surface patterns (e.g. for reading Braille). Merkel Discs have small receptive fields which allow for them to detect fine spatial separation. They also have two point discrimination.

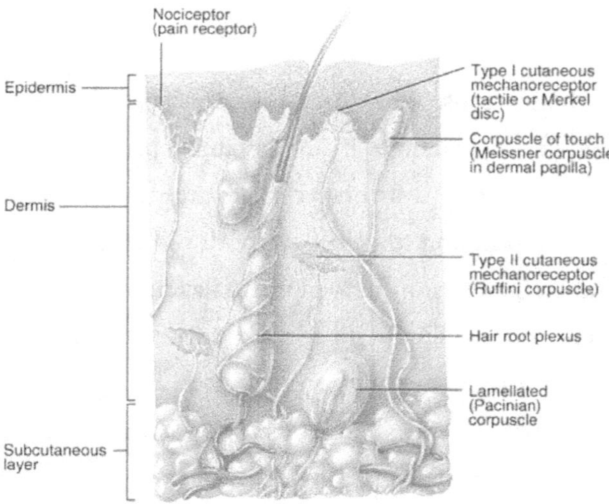

(Fig -42) Merkel's disc

FREE NERVE ENDINGS

A free nerve ending (FNE) or bare nerve ending (Fig-43), is an unspecialized, afferent nerve fibre ending of a sensory neuron. They function as cutaneous nociceptors and are essentially used by vertebrates to detect pain. Free nerve endings are unencapsulated and have no complex sensory structures. They are the most common type of nerve ending, and are most frequently found in the skin. They mostly resemble the fine roots of a plant. They penetrate the dermis and end in the stratum granulosum. FNEs infiltrate the middle layers of the dermis and surround hair follicles.

Free nerve endings have different rates of adaptation, stimulus modalities, and fibre types. Different types of FNE can be rapidly adapting, intermediate adapting, or slowly adapting. A delta type II fibres are fast-adapting while A delta type I and C fibres are slowly adapting.

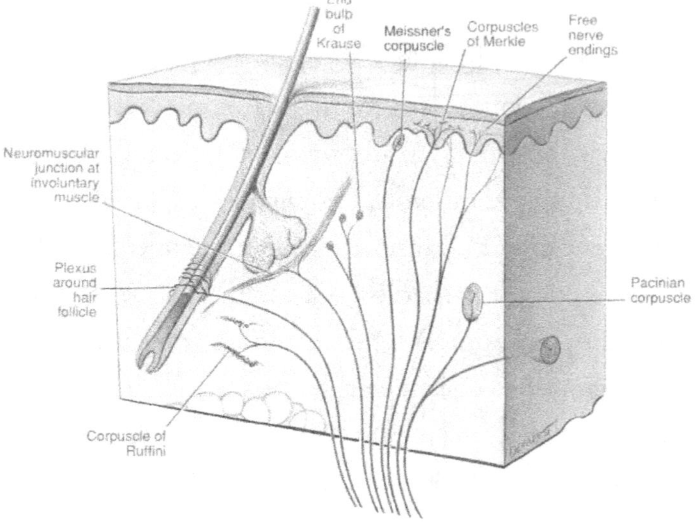

(Fig -43) Free Nerve endings

THERMORECEPTOR

A thermoreceptor is a non-specialised sense receptor, or more accurately the receptive portion of a sensory neuron, that codes absolute and relative changes in temperature, primarily within the innocuous range. In the mammalian peripheral nervous system, warmth receptors are thought to be unmyelinated C-fibres (low conduction velocity), while those responding to cold have both C-fibres and thinly myelinated A delta fibres (faster conduction velocity). The adequate stimulus for a warm receptor is warming, which results in an increase in their action potential discharge rate. Cooling results in a decrease in warm receptor discharge rate. For cold receptors their firing rate increases during cooling and decreases during warming. Some cold receptors also respond with a brief action potential discharge to high temperatures, i.e. typically above 45°C, and this is known as a paradoxical response to heat. The mechanism responsible for this behaviour has not been determined.

In humans, temperature sensation enters the spinal cord along the axons of Lissauer's tract that synapse on second order neurons in grey matter of the dorsal horn. The axons of these second order neurons then decussate, joining the spinothalamic tract as they ascend to neurons in the ventral posterolateral nucleus of the thalamus. Thermoreceptors are 'free' non-specialized endings; the mechanism of activation in response to temperature changes is not completely understood.

Warm and cold receptors play a part in sensing innocuous environmental temperature. Temperatures likely to damage an organism are sensed by sub-categories of nociceptors that may respond to noxious cold, noxious heat or more than one noxious stimulus modality hence they are polymodal. The nerve endings of sensory neurons that respond preferentially to cooling are found in moderate density in the skin but also occur in relatively high spatial density in the cornea, tongue, bladder, and facial skin.

The transduction of temperature in cold receptors are mediated in part by the Transient receptor potential cation channel subfamily M member 8 (TRPM8). TRPM8 channel passes a mixed inward cationic (predominantly carried by Na^+ ions although the channel is also permeable to Ca^{2+}) current of a magnitude that is inversely proportional to temperature. The channel is sensitive over a temperature range spanning about 10–35°C. TRPM8 can also be activated by the binding of an extracellular ligand. Since the TRPM8 is expressed in neurons whose physiological role is to signal cooling, menthol applied to various bodily surfaces evokes a sensation of cooling. The feeling of freshness associated with the activation of cold receptors by menthol, particularly those in facial areas with axons in the trigeminal (V) nerve, accounts for its use in numerous toiletries including toothpaste, shaving lotions, facial creams and the like.

Another molecular component of cold transduction is the temperature dependence of so-called leak channels which pass an outward current carried by potassium ions. Some leak channels derive from the family of two-pore (2P) domain potassium channels. Amongst the various members of the 2P-domain channels, some close quite promptly at temperatures less than about 28°C (e.g. TRAAK, TREK). Temperature also modulates the activity of the Na^+/K^+-ATPase. The Na^+/K^+-ATPase is a P-type pump that extrudes $3Na^+$ ions in exchange for $2K^+$ ions for each hydrolytic cleavage of ATP. This results in a net movement of positive charge out of the cell, i.e. a hyperpolarizing current. The magnitude of this current is proportional to the rate of pump activity.

NOCICEPTORS

A nociceptor is a type of receptor at the end of a sensory neuron's axon that responds to damaging or potentially damaging stimuli by sending "possible threat" signals to the spinal cord and the brain. If the brain thinks the threat is credible, it creates the sensation of pain to direct attention to the body part, so the threat can hopefully be mediated. This process is called nociception.

In mammals, nociceptors are found in any area of the body that can sense noxious stimuli. External nociceptors are found in tissue such as the skin (cutaneous nociceptors), the corneas, and the mucosa. Internal nociceptors are found in a variety of organs, such as the muscles, the joints, the bladder, the gut, and the digestive tract. The cell bodies of these neurons are located in either the dorsal root ganglia or the trigeminal ganglia. The trigeminal ganglia are specialized nerves for the face, whereas the dorsal root ganglia are associated with the rest of the body. The axons extend into the peripheral nervous system and terminate in branches to form receptive fields.

The peripheral terminal of the mature nociceptor is where the noxious stimuli are detected and transduced into electrical energy. When the electrical energy reaches a threshold value, an action potential is induced and driven towards the central nervous system (CNS). This leads to the train of events that allows for the conscious awareness of pain. The sensory specificity of nociceptors is established by the high threshold only to particular features of stimuli. Only when the high threshold has been reached by either chemical, thermal, or mechanical environments are the nociceptors triggered. The majority of nociceptors are classified by which of the environmental modalities they respond to. Some nociceptors respond to more than one of these modalities and are consequently designated polymodal. Other nociceptors respond to none of these modalities (although they may respond to stimulation under conditions of inflammation) and are referred to as sleeping or silent.

Thermal nociceptors are activated by noxious heat or cold at various temperatures. There are specific nociceptor transducers that are responsible for how and if the specific nerve ending responds to the thermal stimulus. The first to be discovered was The transient receptor potential cation channel subfamily V member 1 (TRPV1), and it has a threshold that coincides with the heat pain temperature of 42 °C. Other temperature in the warm–hot range is mediated by more than one TRP channel. Each of these channels express a particular C-terminal domain that corresponds to the warm–hot sensitivity. The interactions between all these channels and how the temperature level is determined to be above the pain threshold are unknown at this time. The cool stimuli are sensed by TRPM8 channels. Its C-terminal domain differs from the heat sensitive TRPs. Although this channel corresponds to cool stimuli, it is still unknown whether it also contributes in the detection of intense cold. An interesting finding related to cold stimuli is that tactile sensibility and motor function deteriorate while pain perception persists.

Mechanical nociceptors respond to excess pressure or mechanical deformation. They also respond to incisions that break the skin surface. The reaction to the stimulus is processed as pain by the cortex, just like chemical and thermal responses.

Chemical nociceptors have TRP channels that respond to a wide variety of spices. The one that sees the most response and is very widely tested is capsaicin. Other chemical stimulants are environmental irritants like acrolein, a World War I chemical weapon and a component of cigarette smoke. Apart from these external stimulants, chemical nociceptors have the capacity to detect endogenous ligands, and certain fatty acid amines that arise from changes in internal tissues. Like in thermal nociceptors, TRPV1 can detect chemicals like capsaicin and spider toxins.

PROPRIOCEPTION - KINESTHETICS

Proprioception, from Latin proprius, meaning "one's own" and perception, is the sense of the relative position of neighbouring parts of the body. Unlike the exteroceptive senses by which we perceive the outside world, and interoceptive senses, by which we perceive the pain and movement of internal organs, proprioception is a third distinct sensory modality that provides feedback solely on the status of the body internally. It is the sense that indicates whether the body is moving with required effort, as well as where the various parts of the body are located in relation to each other.

Kinesthesia is another term that is often used interchangeably with proprioception, though use of the term "kinesthesia" can place a greater emphasis on motion. Some differentiate the kinesthetic sense from proprioception by excluding the sense of equilibrium or balance from kinesthesia. An inner ear infection, for example, might degrade the sense of balance. This would degrade the proprioceptive sense, but not the kinesthetic sense. The affected individual would be able to walk, but only by using the sense of sight to maintain balance; the person would be unable to walk with eyes closed.

Proprioception and kinesthesia are seen as interrelated and there is considerable disagreement regarding the definition of these terms. Some of this difficulty stems from Sherrington's original description of joint position sense (or the ability to determine exactly where a particular body part is in space) and kinesthesia (or the sensation that the body part has moved) under a more general heading of proprioception. Clinical aspects of proprioception are measured in tests that measure a subject's ability to detect predetermined position. The initiation of proprioception is the activation of a proprioreceptor in the periphery. The proprioceptive sense is believed to be composed of information from sensory neurons located in the inner ear (motion and orientation) and in the stretch receptors located in the muscles and the joint-supporting ligaments (stance). There are specific nerve receptors for this form of perception termed "proprioreceptors," just as there are specific receptors for pressure, light, temperature, sound, and other sensory experiences. Proprioreceptors are sometimes known as adequate stimuli receptors. Although it was known that finger kinesthesia relies on skin sensation, recent research has found that kinesthesia-based haptic perception relies strongly on the forces experienced during touch. In humans, a distinction is made between conscious proprioception and unconscious proprioception. Conscious proprioception is communicated by the posterior column-medial lemniscus pathway to the cerebrum. Unconscious proprioception is communicated primarily via the dorsal spinocerebellar tract, to the cerebellum. Such an unconscious reaction is seen in the human proprioceptive reflex. This remarkable proprioceptive reflex

(Law of Righting), in the event that the body tilts in any direction, will cock the head back to level the eyes against the horizon. This is seen even in infants as soon as they gain control of their neck muscles. This control comes from the cerebellum, the part of the brain affecting balance.

Neurophysiological studies in monkeys show that activity of neurons in primary cortex (MI), pre-motor cortex (PMC), and cerebellum varies systematically with the direction of reaching movements. These neurons exhibit preferred direction tuning, where the level of neural activity is highest when movements are made in the preferred direction (PD), and gets progressively lower as movements are made at increasing degrees of offset from the PD. Motor control is central to executive functions of the nervous system. It guarantees that planned actions are efficiently translated into appropriate limb displacements. A striking feature of this translation from 'ideas of motion' to 'mechanical motion' is the paradoxical contrast between the apparent easiness with which movements are performed on the one hand, and the complexity of Newtonian dynamics and the existence of multiple levels of redundancy on the other. A common method to address this issue is to record NCs (Normal Controls) in vivo, e.g. using single-unit recordings in the primary motor cortex (M1) and spinal cord of behaving animals (monkeys), and to perform a correlation analysis in order to reveal preferential relationships between discharge rates and parameters of motor behaviour like direction of movement, velocity, joint torques. This method has revealed a large repertoire of discharge patterns as well as a large repertoire of correlations that were thought to reflect sometimes kinematic (direction, velocity), sometimes dynamic (forces) representations of motor acts.

Proprioceptive senses generated as a result of our own actions They include the senses of position and movement of our limbs and trunk, the sense of effort, the sense of force, and the sense of heaviness. Receptors involved in proprioception are located in skin, muscles, and joints. Information about limb position and movement is not generated by individual receptors, but by populations of afferents. Afferent signals generated during a movement are processed to code for endpoint position of a limb. The afferent input is referred to a central body map to determine the location of the limbs in space. Experimental phantom limbs, produced by blocking peripheral nerves, have shown that motor areas in the brain are able to generate conscious sensations of limb displacement and movement in the absence of any sensory input. In the normal limb tendon organs and possibly also muscle spindles contribute to the senses of force and heaviness. Exercise can disturb proprioception, and this has implications for musculoskeletal injuries. Proprioceptive senses, particularly of limb position and movement, deteriorate with age and are associated with an increased risk of falls in the elderly. The more recent information available on proprioception has given a better understanding of the mechanisms underlying these senses as well as providing new insight into a range of clinical conditions.

The equilibrium sense, generally associated with balance, provides feedback about the positions and movements of our heads and bodies in space. The other system—the kinesthetic sense—tells us about the orientation of different parts of our bodies in relation to each other. While the kinesthetic information needed by the brain comes from joints and muscle fibers throughout the body, the receptors for equilibrium are located in the semicircular canals and vestibular sacs of the inner ear. (The equilibrium sense is also called the vestibular sense, and the relevant parts of the inner ear are sometimes called the vestibular system or apparatus).

APPLICATIONS

Law enforcement

Proprioception is tested by American police officers using the field sobriety test, wherein the subject is required to touch his or her nose with eyes closed. People with normal proprioception may make an error of no more than 20 millimeters. People suffering from impaired proprioception (a symptom of moderate to severe alcohol intoxication) fail this test due to difficulty locating their limbs in space relative to their noses.

Diagnosis

There are several relatively specific tests of the subject's ability to propriorecept. These tests are used in the diagnosis of neurological disorders. They include the visual and tactile placing reflexes.

Learning new skills

Proprioception is what allows someone to learn to walk in complete darkness without losing balance. During the learning of any new skill, sport, or art, it is usually necessary to become familiar with some proprioceptive tasks specific to that activity.

Training

The proprioceptive sense can be sharpened through study of many disciplines. The Alexander Technique uses the study of movement to enhance kinesthetic judgment of effort and location. Standing on a wobble board or balance board is often used to retrain or increase proprioception abilities, particularly as physical therapy for ankle or knee injuries. Standing on one leg (storkstanding) and various other body-position challenges are also used in such disciplines as Yoga or Wing Chun. There are even specific devices designed for proprioception training, such as the exercise ball, which works on balancing the abdominal and back muscles.

Impairment

It has been seen that temporary loss or impairment of proprioception may happen periodically during growth, mostly during adolescence. Growth that might also influence this would be large increases or drops in body weight/size due to fluctuations of fat (liposuction, rapid fat loss, rapid fat gain) and muscle content (body building, anabolic steroids, catabolisis/starvation). It can also occur in those that gain new levels of flexibility, stretching, and contortion. A limb's being in a new range of motion never experienced (or at least, not for a long time since youth perhaps) can disrupt one's sense of location of that limb. Possible experiences include suddenly feeling that feet or legs are missing from one's mental self-image; needing to look down at one's limbs to be sure they are still there; and falling down while walking, especially when attention is focused upon something other than the act of walking. Proprioception is occasionally impaired spontaneously, especially when one is tired. One's body may appear too large or too small, or parts of the body may appear distorted in size. Similar effects can sometimes occur during epilepsy or migraine auras. These effects are presumed to arise from abnormal stimulation of the part of the parietal cortex of the brain involved with integrating information from different parts of the body.

Vestibular system

Awareness of body balance and movement are monitored by the vestibular system. The vestibular sense contributes to our ability to maintain balance and body posture. The vestibular organs are fluid-filled and have hair cells, similar to the ones found in the auditory system, which respond to movement of the head and gravitational forces. When these hair cells are stimulated, they send signals to the brain via the vestibular nerve. Although we may not be consciously aware of our vestibular system's sensory information under normal circumstances, its importance is apparent when we experience motion sickness and/or dizziness related to infections of the inner ear . The sensation of body rotation arises in the three semicircular canals in the inner ear. Movement of fluid in the canals stimulates hair cells, which send messages to the brain about speed and direction of body rotation. Gravitation and movement sensations are produced by movement of two vestibular sacs in each ear that lie between the semicircular canal and the cochlea. Both sacs are filled with millions of tiny crystals that bend hair cells when moved. In turn, impulses giving a sense of position are sent to the brain. (Motion sickness originates from excessive stimulation of the vestibular organs).

The semicircular canals are three pretzel-like curved tubes arranged at angles roughly perpendicular to each other, with the two vestibular sacs located at their base. Both the canals and sacs contain fluid and tiny hair cells, which act as receptors. When a person's head moves, the fluid disturbs the hair cells, which stimulate a branch of the auditory nerve, signaling the brain to make adjustments in the eyes and body. A movement at any given angle will have its primary effect on one of the three canals. Overstimulation from extreme movements will produce dizziness and nausea. Our sense of body position when we are at rest is provided by the vestibular sacs, which contain small crystals called otoliths (literally, "ear stones") that exert pressure on the hair cells. In their normal position, the otoliths inform our brains that we are standing or sitting upright. When the head is tilted, the position of the otoliths changes, and the signal sent to the brain changes accordingly. The neural connections of the vestibular system lead to the cerebellum, the eye muscles, and a part of the autonomic nervous system involved in digestion (which accounts for the link between dizziness and nausea).

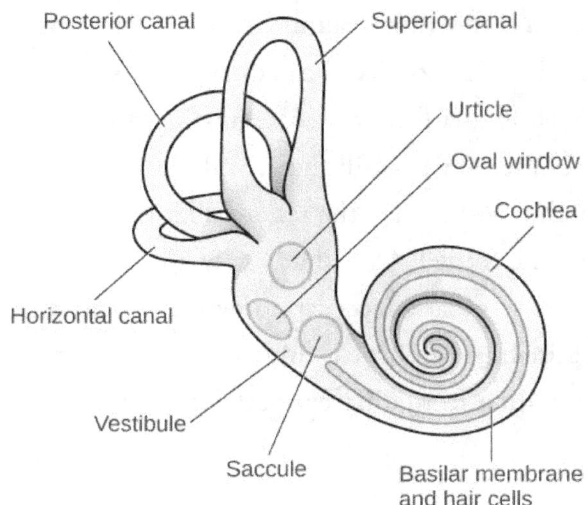

(Fig -44) Major sensory organs of the vestibular system

The major sensory organs of the vestibular system are located next to the cochlea in the inner ear (Fig-44). These include the utricle, saccule, and the three semicircular canals (posterior, superior, and horizontal.

NEURAL CODING

Neural coding is a neuroscience-related field concerned with how sensory and other information is represented in the brain by networks of neurons. The main goal of studying neural coding is to characterize the relationship between the stimulus and the individual or ensemble neuronal responses and the relationship among electrical activity of the neurons. Neurons are remarkable among the cells of the body in their ability to propagate signals rapidly over large distances. They do this by generating characteristic electrical pulses called action potentials or, more simply, spikes that can travel down nerve fibers. Sensory neurons change their activities by firing sequences of action potentials in various temporal patterns, with the presence of external sensory stimuli, such as light,sound, taste, smell and touch. It is known that information about the stimulus is encoded in this pattern of action potentials and transmitted into and around the brain. Although action potentials can vary somewhat in duration, amplitude and shape,they are typically treated as identical stereotyped events in neural coding studies. The study of neural coding involves measuring and characterizing how stimulus attributes, such as light or sound intensity, or motor actions, such as the direction of an arm movement, are represented by neuron action potentials or spikes. In order to describe and analyze neuronal firing, statistical methods and methods of probability theory and stochastic point processes have been widely applied. The link between stimulus and response can be studied from two opposite points of view. Neural encoding refers to the map from stimulus to response. The main focus is to understand how neurons respond to a wide variety of stimuli, and to accurately construct models that attempt to predict responses to other stimuli. Neural decoding refers to the reverse map, from response to stimulus, and the challenge is to reconstruct a stimulus, or certain aspects of that stimulus, from the spike sequences it evokes.

Paradoxical cold

Paradoxical cold, specifically is when you increase the temperature or decrease the temperature to a certain point (depending on species) at which you feel the opposing sensation to the temperature. ie. contact with an object approximately 50 degrees will evoke some cold receptors to be activated, yielding a feeling of coldness. This situation is also the same for warm receptors and cold temperatures except not as evident due to the fact that warm receptors are non-myelinated.

Pain

Pain is a distressing feeling often caused by intense or damaging stimuli. The International Association for the Study of Pain's widely used definition defines pain as "an unpleasant sensory and emotional experience associated with actual or potential tissue damage, or described in terms of such damage". It is the feeling common to such experiences as stubbing a toe, burning a finger, putting iodine on a cut, and bumping the "funny bone". Pain motivates us to withdraw from damaging or potentially damaging situations, protect the damaged body part while it heals, and avoid those situations in the future. It is initiated by stimulation of nociceptors in the peripheral nervous system, or by damage to or malfunction of the peripheral or central nervous systems. Most pain resolves promptly once the painful stimulus is removed and the body has healed, but sometimes pain persists despite removal of the stimulus and apparent healing of the body; and sometimes pain arises in the absence of any detectable stimulus, damage or pathology.

Pain can be classed according to its location in the body, as in headache, low backpain and pelvic pain; or according to the body system involved, i.e., myofascial pain (emanating from skeletal muscles or the fibrous sheath surrounding them), rheumatic (emanating from the joints and surrounding tissue), causalgia ("burning" pain in the skin of the arms or, sometimes, legs; thought to be the product of peripheral nerve damage), neuropathic pain (caused by damage to or malfunction of any part of the nervoussystem), or vascular (pain from blood vessels).

TYPES OF PAIN

Chronic pain

Chronic pain usually falls into one of two categories:
- ❖ Nociceptive pain arises from various kinds of trouble in tissues, reported to the brain by the nervous system. This is the type of pain everyone is most familiar with, everything from bee stings and burns and toe stubs to repetitive strain injury, nausea, tumours, and inflammatory arthritis. Nociceptive pain typically changes with movement, position, and load.

❖ Neuropathic pain arises from damage to the nervous system itself, central or peripheral, either from disease, injury, or pinching. The simplest neuropathies are mechanical insults, like hitting your funny bone or sciatica, but this is a big category: anything that damages neurons, from multiple sclerosis to chemotherapy to alcoholism to phantom limb pain. It's often stabbing, electrical, or burning, but nearly any quality of pain is possible. Unfortunately, it's also more likely to lead to chronic pain: nerves don't heal well.

Psychogenic pain

Psychogenic pain, also called psychalgia or somatoform pain, is a sensation of pain caused, increased, or prolonged by mental, emotional, or behavioural factors. Headache, back pain, and stomach pain are sometimes diagnosed as psychogenic. Sufferers are often stigmatized, because both medical professionals and the general public tend to think that pain from a psychological source is not "real". However, specialists consider that it is no less actual or hurtful than pain from any other source. People with long term pain frequently display psychological disturbance, with elevated scores on the Minnesota Multiphasic Personality Inventory scales of hysteria, depression and hypochondriasis (the "neurotic triad"). Some investigators have argued that it is this neuroticism that causes acute injuries to turn chronic, but clinical evidence points the other way, to chronic pain causing neuroticism. When long term pain is relieved by therapeutic intervention, scores on the neurotic triad and anxiety fall, often to normal levels. Self-esteem, often low in chronic pain patients, also shows striking improvement once pain has resolved.

Phantom pain

Phantom pain is the sensation of pain from a part of the body that has been lost or from which the brain no longer receives physical signals. It is a type of neuropathic pain. Phantom limb pain is a common experience of amputees. One study found that eight days after amputation, 72 per cent of patients had phantom limb pain, and six months later, 65 percent reported it. Some experience continuous pain that varies in intensity or quality; others experience several bouts a day, or it may occur only once every week or two. It is described as shooting, crushing, burning or cramping. If the pain is continuous for a long period, parts of the intact body may become sensitized, so that touching them evokes pain in the phantom limb, or phantom limb pain may accompany urination or defecation. Local anaesthetic injections into the nerves or sensitive areas of the stump may relieve pain for days, weeks or, sometimes permanently, despite the drug wearing off in a matter of hours; and small injections of hypertonic saline into the soft tissue between vertebrae produces local pain that radiates into the phantom limb for ten minutes or so and may be followed by hours, weeks or even longer of partial or total relief from phantom pain. Vigorous vibration or electrical stimulation of the stump, or current from electrodes surgically implanted on to the spinal cord all produce relief in some patients. Paraplegia, the loss of sensation and voluntary motor control after serious spinal cord damage, may be accompanied by root ("girdle") pain at the level of the spinal cord damage, visceral pain evoked by a filling bladder or bowel, or, in five to ten per cent of paraplegics, phantom body pain in areas of complete sensory loss. Phantom body pain is initially described as burning or tingling but may evolve into severe crushing or pinching pain, fire running down the legs, or a knife twisting in the flesh. Onset may be immediate or may not occur until years after the disabling injury. Surgical treatment rarely provides lasting relief.

Pain asymbolia

Pain asymbolia is the pain may be experienced as a sensation devoid of any unpleasantness and this happens in a syndrome called pain asymbolia or pain dissociation, caused by conditions like lobotomy, cingulotomy or morphine analgesia. Typically, such patients report that they have pain but are not bothered by it, they recognize the sensation of pain but are mostly or completely immune to suffering from it.

Insensitivity to pain

The ability to experience pain is essential for protection from injury, and recognition of the presence of injury. Episodic analgesia may occur under special circumstances, such as in the excitement of sport or war: a soldier on the battlefield may feel no pain for many hours from a traumatic amputation or other severe injury.

However, insensitivity to pain may also be acquired following conditions such as spinalcord injury, diabetes mellitus, or more rarely leprosy. A small number of people suffer from congenital analgesia ("congenital insensitivity to pain"), a genetic defect that puts these individuals at constant risk from the consequences of unrecognized injury or illness. Children with this condition suffer carelessly repeated damage to their tongue,eyes, joints, skin, and muscles. They may attain adulthood, but have a shortened life expectancy.

Pain receptor

Pain receptors are any one of the many free nerve endings throughout the body that warn of potentially harmful changes in the environment, such as excessive pressure or temperature. The free nerve endings constituting most of the pain receptors are located chiefly in the epidermis and in the epithelial covering of certain mucous membranes. They also appear in the stratified squamous epithelium of the cornea, in the root sheaths and the papillae of the hairs, and around the bodies of sudoriferous glands. The terminal ends of pain receptors consist of unmyelinated nerve fibers that often anastomose into small knobs between the epithelial cells. Any kind of stimulus, if it is intense enough, can stimulate the pain receptors in the skin and the mucosa, but only radical changes in pressure and certain chemicals can stimulate the pain receptors in the viscera. Referred pain results only from stimulation of pain receptors located in deep structures, such as the viscera, the joints, and the skeletal muscles, and never from pain receptors in the skin.

Pain Codes

According to ICD-10-CM manual pain codes as follows

Pain of Unspecified Site

Sometimes the radiology department or imaging center will receive a requisition that simply states "Pain" without specifying the location of the pain. This constitutes poor documentation, and the department or facility should ask the ordering physician to provide a more specific clinical history, such as pain in knee joint, flank pain, precordial pain, etc.

In a 2004 letter to the American College of Radiology, the AHA Central Office™ stated that it is acceptable to assign the code for pain of the site that is being imaged when the requisition does not indicate the location of the pain. For example, if the clinical history for a hand x-ray simply states "Pain," it is appropriate to code hand pain. However, keep in mind that this guidance was issued for ICD-9-CM, not ICD-10-CM.

The ICD-10-CM Index indicates that pain NOS is reported with code R52 (Pain, unspecified). However, reimbursement for this vague code is likely to be problematic.

Abdominal Pain

ICD-10-CM contains over 30 different codes in category R10 for various types of abdominal and pelvic pain. In addition to the codes for pain in the various parts of the abdomen, there are codes for:

Acute abdomen (R10.0): This is sudden, severe abdominal pain, often accompanied by rigidity of the abdomen. Patients with this type of pain are likely to have a condition that requires surgery, such as acute appendicitis, a penetrating duodenal ulcer, or peritonitis.

Abdominal tenderness (R10.81-): Tenderness is abnormal sensitivity to touch. While pain is a symptom that the patient reports, tenderness is a reaction that the physician observes while examining the patient's abdomen.

Rebound abdominal tenderness (R10.82-): Tenderness is discomfort that occurs when the examiner presses on the abdomen. Rebound tenderness, on the other hand, occurs when the examiner releases the pressure. It is a sign of peritonitis.

Colic (R10.83): Colic is pain that comes in waves. It is associated with contractions of smooth muscles, like those in the intestine or the ureter.

The flank is the side of the patient's torso below the ribs. Flank pain can be a sign of kidney stones. In the ICD-10-CM Index, the entry for "Pain, flank" shows a note to "see Pain, abdominal." You must code flank pain as unspecified abdominal pain (R10.9) unless the physician provides additional information about the location of the pain, such as whether it is in the upper or lower portion of the abdomen.

Pelvic pain is classified to code R10.2 (Pelvic and perineal pain). It also includes perineal pain, which is pain in the area between a man's anus and scrotum, or a woman's anus and vulva.

Here's an example of code assignment for abdominal pain in ICD-10-CM: The emergency physician orders an ultrasound exam of the abdomen in a patient who has right upper quadrant abdominal pain. The exam does not reveal any cause for the pain. The code assignment is R10.11 (Right upper quadrant pain).

Chest Pain

The ICD-10-CM Index refers you to the code for angina (I20.9) when the patient's chest pain is described as "ischemic." However, other types of chest pain are reported with codes from category *R07 (Pain in throat and chest)*. There is an exception for post-thoracotomy pain, which we'll discuss later.

ICD-10-CM contains codes for the following types of chest pain:

Chest pain on breathing (R07.1): This type of pain can be a sign of pulmonary embolism.

Precordial pain (R07.2): This is pain in the precordium, which includes the lower chest and epigastric area.

Pleurodynia (R07.81): Spasms of pain in the intercostal muscles, which can be a sign of pleurisy (inflammationof the pleural membranes).

Intercostal pain (R07.82): This is pain originating in the intercostal nerves, which run between pairs of adjacent ribs.

Other chest pain (R07.89): Includes chest wall pain as well as chest pain described as a typical, musculoskeletal, or non-cardiac.

Category G89 Codes

Category G89 includes codes for acute pain, chronic pain, and neoplasm-related pain, as well as codes for two pain syndromes. In order for you to assign these codes, the physician must document that the pain is acute, chronic, or neoplasm-related.

The ICD-10-CM guidelines state that if the cause of the pain is known, you should assign a code for the underlying diagnosis, not the pain code. However, if the purpose of the encounter is to manage the pain rather than the underlying condition, then you should assign a pain code and sequence it first.

For example, a patient is referred to an interventional radiologist for a facet joint injection. The clinical history is chronic low back pain due to degenerative disc disease (DDD) of the thoracic spine with radiculopathy. Because this encounter is for pain control rather than to evaluate or treat the DDD, you should code the pain first. The primary diagnosis is G89.29 (Other chronic pain), and the secondary diagnosis is M51.14 (Intervertebral disc disorders with radiculopathy, thoracic region).

In another example, an interventional radiologist performs kyphoplasty on a patient who has chronic back pain due to an osteoporotic compression fracture of the thoracic spine. Because this encounter is to treat the vertebral compression fracture, you should code only the compression fracture. The code assignment is M80.08- [Age-related osteoporosis with current pathological fracture, vertebra(e)].

The ICD-10-CM guidelines also state you can assign the G89 codes in conjunction with codes from other categories and chapters to provide more detail about acute or chronic pain or neoplasm-related pain. For example, you can assign a G89 code to indicate that the pain is acute or chronic. You should assign the site-specific pain code first unless the purpose of the encounter is pain management, in which case the G89 code is first.

For example, a patient is referred for ankle x-rays for chronic right ankle pain. The exam does not reveal any findings to explain the pain. In this case you need to assign two codes—one for the ankle pain and one from category G89 to indicate that the pain is chronic. Since the purpose of the encounter is not pain management, the site-specific pain code is listed first. The primary diagnosis is M25.571 (Pain in right ankle). Code G89.29 (Other chronic pain) is assigned as a secondary diagnosis.

Trauma Pain

Category G89 contains codes for acute (G89.11) and chronic (G89.21) pain due to trauma. You should not assign these codes if a cause for the pain (i.e., a specific injury) has been identified, except in the unlikely event that the purpose of the encounter is pain management. Also, the physician must document the pain as acute or chronic in order to use these codes.

Postoperative Pain

Category G89 contains four codes for acute and chronic post-thoracotomy pain (G89.12, G89.22) and other postprocedural pain (G89.18, G89.28). The ICD-10-CM guidelines state that you should not code "routine or expected postoperative pain immediately after surgery." Additionally, in order to assign these codes, the physician must document that the patient's pain is a complication of the surgery.

If the patient is experiencing pain associated with a specific postoperative complication, such as painful wire sutures, the primary diagnosis is the complication. You can assign a code from category G89 as a secondary diagnosis, if appropriate, to identify whether the pain is acute or chronic.

Neoplasm-Related Pain

Pain caused by a benign or malignant neoplasm in any part of the body is reported with code G89.3 [Neoplasm related pain (acute) (chronic)]. The neoplasm is coded separately. If the purpose of the encounter is pain control, then the pain code should be listed first. Otherwise, the neoplasm is coded first. The ICD-10-CM guidelines state that it is not necessary to assign a site-specific pain code together with G89.3.

For example, a patient is referred for CT of the abdomen with clinical history of "Cancer of the head of the pancreas with increasing cancer pain." The purpose of the encounter is to evaluate the cancer, not manage the pain, so the cancer is coded first. The primary diagnosis is C25.0 (Malignant neoplasm of head of pancreas). Code G89.3 [Neoplasm related pain (acute) (chronic)] is listed as a secondary diagnosis.

Central Pain Syndrome and Chronic Pain Syndrome

Category G89 contains two codes for pain syndromes. Radiology coders will seldom use these codes, but it is important to understand the difference between them:

Central pain syndrome is defined by the National Institute of Neurological Disorders and Stroke (NINDS) as "a neurological condition caused by damage to or dysfunction of the central nervous system." Central pain syndrome can occur as a result of stroke, multiple sclerosis, neoplasm, epilepsy, CNS trauma, or Parkinson's disease. Patients with central pain syndrome may experience localized pain, burning, and/or numbness in specific parts of the body, or throughout the body. ICD-10-CM classifies central pain syndrome to code G89.0 (Central pain syndrome).

Chronic pain syndrome is chronic pain associated with significant psychosocial dysfunction. The psychosocial problems may include depression, drug dependence, complaints that are out of proportion to the physical findings, anxiety, and other manifestations. Chronic pain syndrome is not synonymous with chronic pain. You should code this condition only when the physician specifically documents it. Chronic pain syndrome is reported with code G89.4 (Chronic pain syndrome).

Melzack-wall theory

The gate control theory of pain asserts that non-painful input closes the "gates" to painful input, which prevents pain sensation from traveling to the central nervous system. Therefore, stimulation by non-noxious input is able to suppress pain. First proposed in 1965 by Ronald Melzack and Patrick Wall, the theory offers a physiological explanation for the previously observed effect of psychology on pain perception. Combining early concepts derived from the specificity theory and the peripheral pattern theory, the gate control theory is considered to be one of the most influential theories of pain because it provided a neural basis which reconciled the specificity and pattern theories and ultimately revolutionized pain research.

Although there are some important observations that the gate control theory cannot explain adequately it remains the theory of pain that most accurately accounts for the physical and psychological aspects of pain perception.

The authors proposed that both thin (pain) and large diameter (touch, pressure, vibration) nerve fibers carry information from the site of injury to two destinations in the dorsal horn of the spinal cord: transmission cells that carry the pain signal up to the brain, and inhibitory interneurons that impede transmission cell activity. Activity in both thin and large diameter fibers *excites* transmission cells. Thin fiber activity impedes the inhibitory cells (tending to allow the transmission cell to fire) and large diameter fiber activity *excites* the inhibitory cells (tending to inhibit transmission cell activity). So, the more large fiber (touch, pressure, vibration) activity relative to thin fiber activity at the inhibitory cell, the less pain is felt.

Gate control theory asserts that activation of nerves which do not transmit pain signals, called nonnociceptive fibers, can interfere with signals from pain fibers, thereby inhibiting pain. Afferent pain-receptive nerves, those that bring signals to the brain, comprise at least two kinds of fibers - a fast, relatively thick, myelinated "Aδ" fiber that carries messages quickly with intense pain, and a small, unmyelinated, slow "C" fiber that carries the longer-term throbbing and chronic pain. Large-diameter Aβ fibers are non nociceptive (do not transmit pain stimuli) and inhibit the effects of firing by Aδ and C fibers.

The peripheral nervous system has centers at which pain stimuli can be regulated. Some areas in the dorsal horn of the spinal cord that are involved in receiving pain stimuli from Aδ and C fibers, called laminae, also receive input from Aβ fibers. The non nociceptive fibers indirectly inhibit the effects of the pain fibers, 'closing a gate' to the transmission of their stimuli. In other parts of the laminae, pain fibers also inhibit the effects of nonnociceptive fibers, 'opening the gate'.

The presynaptic inhibition of the dorsal nerve endings can occur through specific types of $GABA_A$ receptors (not through the α1 $GABA_A$ receptor and not through the activation of glycine receptors which are also absent from these types of terminals). Thus certain $GABA_A$ receptor subtypes but not glycine receptors can presynaptically regulate nociception and pain transmission.

An inhibitory connection may exist with Aβ and C fibers, which may form a synapse on the same projection neuron. The same neurons may also form synapses with an inhibitory interneuron that also synapses on the projection neuron, reducing the chance that the latter will fire and transmit pain stimuli to the brain. The inhibitory interneuron fires spontaneously. The C fiber's synapse would inhibit the inhibitory interneuron, indirectly increasing the projection neuron's chance of firing. The Aβ fiber, on the other hand, forms an *excitatory* connection with the inhibitory interneuron, thus *decreasing* the projection neuron's chance of firing (like the C fiber, the Aβ fiber also has an excitatory connection on the projection neuron itself). Thus, depending on the relative rates of firing of C and Aβ fibers, the firing of the nonnociceptive fiber may inhibit the firing of the projection neuron and the transmission of pain stimuli.

Gate control theory thus explains how stimulus that activates only nonnociceptive nerves can inhibit pain. The pain seems to be lessened when the area is rubbed because activation of nonnociceptive fibers inhibits the firing of nociceptive ones in the laminae. In transcutaneous electrical nerve stimulation (TENS), nonnociceptive fibers are selectively stimulated with electrodes in order to produce this effect and thereby lessen pain.

One area of the brain involved in reduction of pain sensation is the periaqueductal gray matter that surrounds the third ventricle and the cerebral aqueduct of the ventricular system. Stimulation of this area produces analgesia (but not total numbing) by activating descending pathways that directly and indirectly inhibit nociceptors in the laminae of the spinal cord. Descending pathways also activate opioid receptor-containing parts of the spinal cord.

Afferent pathways interfere with each other constructively, so that the brain can control the degree of pain that is perceived, based on which pain stimuli are to be ignored to pursue potential gains. The brain determines which stimuli are profitable to ignore over time. Thus, the brain controls the perception of pain quite directly, and can be "trained" to turn off forms of pain that are not "useful". This understanding led Melzack to assert that pain is in the brain.

When it was first proposed in 1965, the theory was met with considerable skepticism. Despite having to undergo several modifications, its basic conception remains unchanged

Pain suppression and management

Pain is interpreted and perceived in the brain. Pain is modulated by two primary types of drugs that work on the brain: analgesics and anesthetics. The term analgesic refers to a drug that relieves pain without loss of consciousness. The term central anesthesia refers to a drug that depresses the CNS. It is characterized by the absence of all perception of sensory modalities, including loss of consciousness without loss of vital functions.

Opiate Analgesia (OA)

The most effective clinically used drugs for producing temporary analgesia and relief from pain are the opioid family, which includes morphine, and heroin. There are currently no other effective pain therapeutic alternatives to opiates. Several side effects resulting from opiate use include tolerance and drug dependence (addiction). In general, these drugs modulate the incoming pain information in the spinal and central sites, as well as relieve pain temporarily, and are also known as opiate producing analgesia(OA). Opiate antagonist is a drug that antagonizes the opioid effects, such as naloxone or maltroxone, etc. They are competitive antagonists of opiate receptors. The brain has a neuronal circuit and endogenous substances to modulate pain.

Endogenous Opioids

Opioidergic neurotransmission is found throughout the brain and spinal cord and appears to influence many CNS functions, including nociception, cardiovascular functions, thermoregulation, respiration, neuroendocrine functions, neuroimmune functions, food intake, sexual activity, aggressive locomotor behaviour as well as learning and memory. Opioids exert marked effects on mood and motivation and produce euphoria.

Three classes of opioid receptors have been identified: μ-mu, δ-delta and κ-kappa. All three classes are widely distributed in the brain. The genes encoding each one of them have been cloned and found to be members of the G protein receptors. Moreover, three major classes of endogenous opioid peptides that interact with the above opiate receptors have been recognized in the CNS: β-endorphins, enkephalins and the dynorphins. These three opioid peptides are derived from a large protein precursor by three different genes: the proopiomelanocortin (POMC) gene, the proenkephalin gene and the prodynorphin gene. The opioid peptides modulate nociceptive input in two ways: 1) block neurotransmitter release by inhibiting Ca^{2+} influx into the presynaptic terminal, or 2) open potassium channels, which hyperpolarizes neurons and inhibits spike activity. They act on various receptors in the brain and spinal cord. Enkephalins are considered the putative ligands for the δ receptors, β endorphins for the μ-receptors, and dynorphins for the κ receptors. The various types of opioid receptors are distributed differently within the central and peripheral nervous system. There is evidence for functional differences in these receptors in various structures. This explains why many unwanted side effects occur following opiate treatments. For example, mu (μ) receptors are widespread in the brain stem parabrachial nuclei, a respiratory center and inhibition of these neurons elicits respiratory depression.

Central or peripheral terminals of nociceptive afferent fibers contain opiate receptors where exogenous and endogenous opioids could act to modulate the ability to transmit nociceptive information. Moreover, high densities of opiate receptors are found in periaqueductal gray (PAG), nucleus raphe magnus (NRM), and dorsal raphe (DR) in the rostral ventral medulla, in the spinal cord, caudate nucleus (CN), septal nucleus, hypothalamus, habenula and hippocampus. Systemically administered opioids at analgesic doses activate spinal and supraspinal mechanisms via μ, δ, and κ type opioid receptors and modulate pain signals.

STIMULATION PRODUCED ANALGESIA (SPA)

Evidence for an intrinsic analgesia system was demonstrated by intracranial electrical stimulation of certain discrete brain sites. These areas are the periaqueductal gray (PAG) and nucleus raphe magnus (NRM), dorsal raphe (DR), caudate nucleus (CN), septal nucleus (Spt) and other nuclei. Such stimulation inhibits pain, (i.e., producing analgesia without behavioural suppression), while the touch, pressure and temperature sensation remain intact. SPA is more pronounced and lasts a longer time after stimulation in humans than in experimental animals. Moreover, during SPA, the subjects still respond to nonpainful stimuli such as touch and temperature within the circumscribed area of analgesia. The most effective CNS sites for SPA are the PAG and the raphe nuclei (RN). Electrical stimulation of PAG or NRM inhibits spinal thalamic cells, (i.e. spinal neurons that project monosynaptically to the thalamus) in laminae I, II and V so that the noxious information from the nociceptors are modulated at the spinal cord level. PAG has neuronal connections to NRM.

The action of the PAG most likely occurs by activation of the descending pathway from NRM and probably also by activation of ascending connections acting on higher subcortical levels of the CNS. Moreover, electrical stimulation of PAG or NRM produces behavioural analgesia. Stimulation produced analgesia (SPA) elicits release of endorphin and is blocked by the opiate antagonist naloxone.

During PAG and/or RN stimulation, serotonin (5-HT) is also released from ascending and descending axons in subcortical nuclei, in spinal trigeminal nuclei and in the spinal cord. This release of 5-HT modulates pain transmission by inhibiting incoming sensory activity. Depletion of 5-HT by electrical lesion of the raphe nuclei or by a neurotoxic lesion produced by local injection of a chemical agent like parachlorophenylalanine (PCPA) results in blocking the ability of both opiate (intracranial and systemic) and electrical stimulation to produce analgesia. To verify whether the electrical stimulation produced analgesia via the release of opiate and serotonin, the area was locally microinjected with morphine or 5-HT. These microinjections indeed produce analgesia. These procedures also provide a method of identifying brain regions associated with pain suppression and help to produce a map of pain centers. The most effective method of producing opiate analgesia (OA) is by intracerebral injection of morphine into the PAG.

The PAG and RN and other brain structures where analgesia is produced are also rich in opiate receptors. Intracerebral opioid administration produced analgesia and SPA can be blocked by either systemic or by local microinjections of naloxone, the morphine antagonist, into the PAG or RN. Therefore, it has been suggested that the two (OA and SPA) operate by a common mechanism.

If OA and SPA act through the same intrinsic system, then the hypothesis that opiates activate a pain-suppression mechanism is more likely. In fact, present evidence indicates that microinjections of an opiate into the PAG activate an efferent brainstem system that suppresses pain transmission at segmental (spinal cord) levels. These observations indicate that analgesia elicited from the PAG requires a descending pathway to the spinal cord.

ASCENDING AND DESCENDING PAIN SUPPRESSION MECHANISM

The primary ascending pain fibers (the A δ and C fibers) reach the dorsal horn of the spinal cord from peripheral sites to innervate the nociceptor neurons in Rexed laminae I & II. Cells from Rexed lamina II make synaptic connections in Rexed layers IV to VII. Cells, especially in laminae I and VII of the dorsal horn, give rise to ascending spinothalamic tracts. At the spinal level, opiate receptors are located at the presynaptic ends of the nocineurons and at the interneural level layers IV to VII in the dorsal horn. Activation of opiate receptors at the interneuronal level produces hyperpolarization of the neurons, which result in the inhibition of firing and the release of substance P, a neurotransmitter involved in pain transmission, thereby blocking pain transmission. The circuit that consists of the periaqueductal gray (PAG) matter in the upper brain stem, the locus coeruleus (LC), the nucleus raphe magnus (NRM) and the nucleus reticularis gigantocellularis (Rgc) contributes to the descending pain suppression pathway, which inhibits incoming pain information at the spinal cord level.

As mentioned previously, opioids interact with the opiate receptors at different CNS levels. These opiate receptors are the normal target sites for neurotransmitters and endogenous opiates such as the endorphins and enkephalins. As a result of binding at the receptor in subcortical sites, secondary changes which lead to a change in the electrophysiological properties of these neurons and modulation of the ascending pain information.

Chapter 3

PHYSIOLOGY AND MOTIVATION

The motivated behaviour is a function of the amount of activity in certain excitatory centers of the hypothalamus. According to Pardee, R. L, 1990 motivation is the reason for people's actions, desires, and needs. Motivation is also one's direction to behaviour, or what causes a person to want to repeat a behaviour. Motivation can be conceived of as a cycle in which thoughts influence behaviours, behaviours drive performance, performance affects thoughts, and the cycle begins again. Each stage of the cycle is composed of many dimensions including attitudes, beliefs, intentions, effort, and withdrawal which can all affect the motivation that an individual experiences. Most psychological theories hold that motivation exists purely within the individual, but socio-cultural theories express motivation as an outcome of participation in actions and activities within the cultural context of social groups. In psychology, a motive is generally defined as a state of physiological or psychological arousal which influences how we behave. For example, a physiological arousal, such as hunger or thirst, motivates us to eat or get something to drink.

According to psychologists motives are of three types - Biological motives, social motives and personal motives. Whenever a need arises the organism is driven to fulfil that want or need. If there is no need in the organism, there will be no behaviour. For example, Horse and water. Horse does not drink water unless it has thirst or if it is not motivated. Unlike the external stimuli, the motives are limited. The behaviour to fulfil such needs is mechanical and alike in all the organisms. Hunger is a motive which stimulates the organism to have food. We develop hunger when the food that was taken earlier is exhausted. The need for food drives us to go in search of food and to have it. Here the hunger motive not only initiated the action, but also continued until the goal (having food) is reached. The motives are powerful forces. They do not allow us to stop our action or behaviour until the need is satisfied. Hence, they are called the 'dynamos' of behaviour.

TYPES OF MOTIVES:

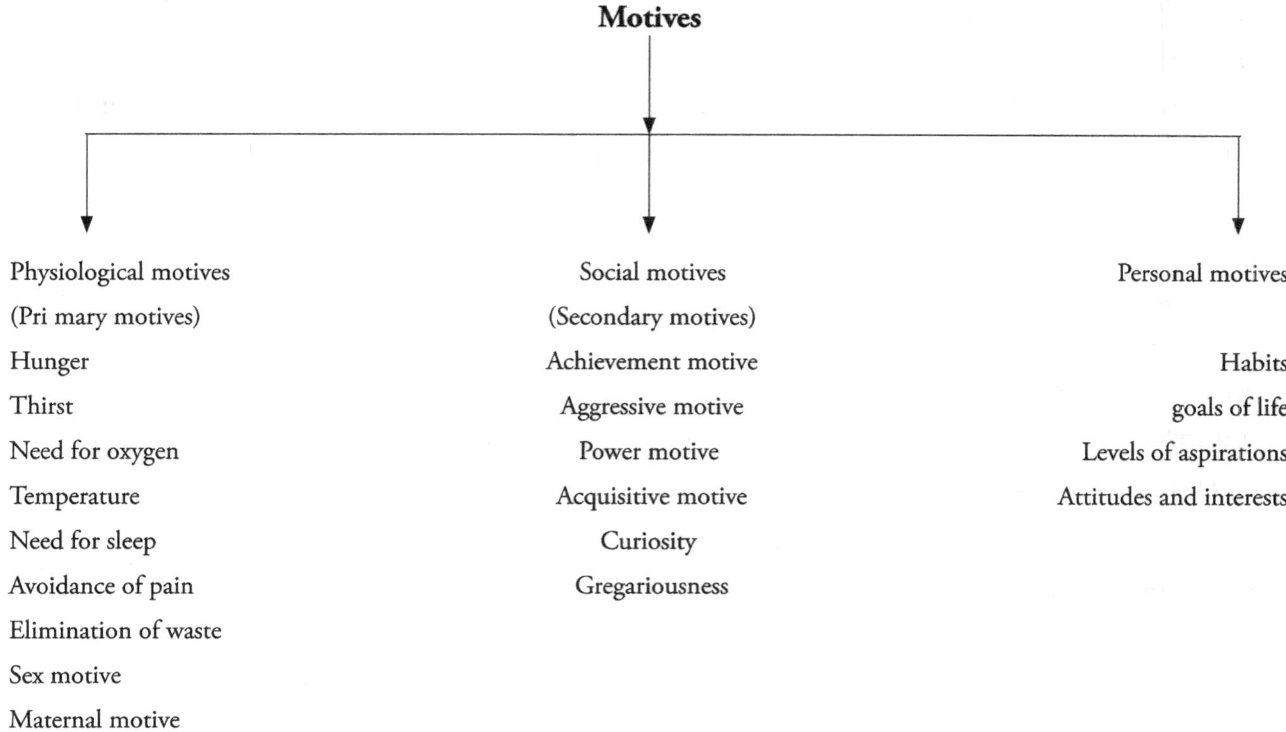

BIOLOGICAL MOTIVATION AND HOMEOSTASIS

Biological motives are called as physiological motives. These motives are essential for the survival of the organism. Such motives are triggered when there is imbalancement in the body. The body always tends to maintain a state of equilibrium called "Homeostasis"- in many of its internal physiological processes. This balance is very essential for the normal life. Homeostasis helps to maintain internal physiological processes at optimal levels. The nutritional level, fluid level, temperature level, etc., are maintained at certain optimal level or homeostasis levels. When there is some variation in these levels the individual is motivated for restoring the state of equilibrium.

I) PHYSIOLOGICAL MOTIVES:

a. Hunger motive:

We eat to live. The food we take is digested and nutritional substances are absorbed. The biochemical processes get their energy from the food in order to sustain life. When these substances are exhausted, some imbalancement exists. We develop hunger motive in order to maintain homeostasis. This is indicated by contraction of stomach muscles causing some pain or discomfort called hunger pangs. Psychologists have demonstrated this phenomenon by experiments.

b. Thirst motive:

In our daily life regularly we take fluids in the form of water and other beverages. These fluids are essential for our body tissues for normal functioning. When the water level in the body decreases we develop motive to drink water. Usually thirst motive is indicated by dryness of mouth. Experiments by psychologists have shown that just dried mouth getting wetted is not enough. We need to drink sufficient quantity of water to satiate our thirst.

c. Need for oxygen:

Our body needs oxygen continuously. We get it through continuous respiration. Oxygen is necessary for the purification of blood. We cannot survive without regular supply of oxygen. Lack of oxygen supply may lead to serious consequences like damage to brain or death.

d. Motive for regulation of body temperature:

Maintenance of normal body temperature (98.6°F or 37.0°C) is necessary. Rise or fall in the body temperature causes many problems. There are some automatic mechanisms to regulate body temperature, like sweating when the temperature rises above normal or, shivering when it falls below normal. These changes motivate us to take necessary steps. For example, opening of windows, put on fans, take cool drinks, remove clothes, etc., when the temperature increases to above normal level; and closing doors and windows, wear sweaters, take hot beverages when temperature falls down. In this way we try to regulate the body temperature.

e. Need for sleep:

Sleep is an essential process for normal functioning of body and mind. When our body and mind are tired they need rest for rejuvenation of energy. It is observed that there is excess accumulation of a toxin called 'Lactic acid' when tired. After sleep it disappears and the person becomes active. Sleep deprivation also leads to psychological problems like confusion, inability to concentrate, droopy eyelids, muscle tremors, etc.

f. Need for avoidance of pain:

No organism can continue to bear pain. Whenever we experience pain we try to avoid it. We are motivated to escape from painful stimulus. For example, when we are under hot sun we go to shade. When something is pinching we avoid it.

g. Drive for elimination of waste:

Our body cannot bear anything excess or anything waste. Excess water is sent out in the form of urine or sweat. So also digested food particles after absorption of nutritional substances are sent out in the form of stools. We experience discomfort until these wastes are eliminated.

h. Sex motive:

This is a biological motive, arises in the organism as a result of secretion of sex hormones-like androgens and estrogens. Sex need is not essential for the survival of the individual, but it is essential for the survival of the species. However, fulfillment of the sex need is not like satisfying hunger or thirst. The society and the law exercise certain codes of conduct. Human being has to adhere to these rules. Usually this need is fulfilled through marriage.

i. Maternal drive:

This is an instinct or an inborn tendency. Every normal woman aspires to become a mother. Motivation, Emotion and Attitudinal Processes learnt from related studies that, this is a most powerful drive. That is why in many cases the women who cannot bear children of their own, will sublimate that motive and satisfy it through socially acceptable ways, like working in orphan schools, baby sittings or adopting other's children.

II) SOCIAL MOTIVES:

Physiological motives discussed above pertain to both animals as well as human beings, but the social motives are specific only to human beings. These are called social motives, because they are learnt in social groups as a result of interaction with the family and society. That is why their strength differs from one individual to another. Many social motives are recognised by psychologists. Some of the common social motives are:

a. Achievement motive:

Achievement motivation refers to a desire to achieve some goal. This motive is developed in the individual who has seen some people in the society attaining high success, reaching high positions and standards. He/she develops a concern to do better, to improve performance. David C Mc Clelland who conducted a longitudinal study on characteristics of high and low achievers found that the high achievers choose and perform better at challenging tasks, prefers personal responsibility, seeks and utilizes feedback about the performance standard, having innovative ideas to improve performance.

On the other hand, low achievers do not accept challenges, puts on average standards and accepts failures easily. Parents must try to inculcate leadership qualities in children for better achievement in their future life. They must allow children to take decisions independently, and guide them for higher achievement from the childhood, so that the children develop high achievement motivation.

b. Aggressive motive:

It is a motive to react aggressively when faced frustrations. Frustration may occur when a person is obstructed from reaching a goal or when he is insulted by others. Even in a fearful and dangerous do or die situation the individual may resort to aggressive behaviour. Individual expresses such behaviour to overcome opposition forcefully, which may be physical or verbal aggression.

c. Power motive:

People with power motive will be concerned with having an impact on others. They try to influence people by their reputation. They expect people to bow their heads and obey their instructions. Usually people with high power motive choose jobs, where they can exert their powers. They want people as followers. They expect high prestige and recognition from others. For example, a person may aspire to go for jobs like Police Officer, Politician, Deputy Commissioner, etc.

d. Acquisitive motive:

This motive directs the individual for the acquisition of material property. It may be money or other property. This motive arises as we come across different people who have earned a lot of money and leading a good life. It is a human tendency to acquire all those things which appear attractive to him.

e. Curiosity motive:

This is otherwise called stimulus and exploration motive. Curiosity is a tendency to explore and know new things. We see people indulge in a travelling to look at new places, new things and new developments taking place outside their environment. People want to extend their knowledge and experiences by exploring new things. Curiosity motive will be very powerful during childhood. That is why they do not accept any toy or other articles unless they examine them from different angles, even at the cost of spoiling or breaking the objects.

f. Gregariousness:

This is also known as affiliation need. Gregariousness is a tendency to associate oneself with other members of the group or same species. The individual will be interested in establishing, maintaining and repairing friendly relationships and will be interested in participating in group activities. Individual will conform to social norms, morals and other ethical codes of the groups in which he/she is interested. To the greater extent gregariousness is developed because many of the needs like basic needs, safety and security needs are fulfilled. In addition to the above there are some other social motives like need for self-esteem, social approval, self-actualization, autonomy, master motive, combat, defense, abasement, etc.

III) PERSONAL MOTIVES:

In addition to the above said physiological and social motives, there are some other motives which are allied with both of the above said motives. These are highly personalized and very much individualized motives. The most important among them are:

a. Force of habits:

We see different people having formed different habits like chewing tobacco, smoking, alcohol consumption, etc. There may be good habits also like regular exercising, reading newspapers, prayers, meditations, etc. Once these habits are formed, they act as drivers and compel the person to perform the act. The specialty of habits is that, they motivate the individual to indulge in that action automatically.

b. Goals of life:

Every normal individual will have some goals in the life. They may be related to education, occupation, income, sports, acquisition of property, public service, social service, etc. Once a goal is set, he will be motivated to fulfil that goal. The goals people set, depend upon various factors like knowledge, information, guidance, support, personality, facilities available, aspirations, family and social background, etc.

c. Levels of aspirations:

Aspiration is aspiring to achieve or to get something or a goal. But such achievement depends upon the level of motivation the individual has. Every individual will have a goal in his life and strive to reach that goal. But the effort to attain that goal varies from one individual to another. The amount of satisfaction he gains depends upon his level of aspiration.

For example, if a student is expecting 80% of marks in examination, gets only 75%, he may be unhappy. On the other hand, a student expecting failure may feel very happy if he gets just 35% passing marks, because, the student with high level of aspiration works hard, whereas the student with low level may not. Hence, always higher level of aspiration is advisable. However, it should be on par with his abilities also. Because, if an individual aspires for higher level of achievement without possessing required ability, he will have to face frustration and disappointment.

d. Attitudes and interests:

Our attitudes and interests determine our motivation. These are specific to individual. For example, a person within the family, may have positive attitude towards family planning and all others having negative attitudes. So also, interests differ from one individual to another. Example, interest in sports, T.V, etc. Whenever we have a positive attitude, we will have motivation to attain. In negative attitude, we will be motivated to avoid. If a person is interested in music, he will be motivated to learn it. In this way, our personal motives determine our behaviour.

UNCONSCIOUS MOTIVATION:

Sigmund Freud, the famous psychologist has explained elaborately about unconscious motivation. According to him, there are certain motives of which we are unaware, because they operate from our unconscious. These motives or desires which are repressed by our conscious remain in our unconscious and will be influencing our behaviour. Our irrational behaviour, the slip of tongue, slip of pen, amnesia, multiple personality, somnambulism, etc., are some examples of such behaviours for which we do not have answers apparently. These motives can be delineated only by psychoanalysis. Many times psychosomatic disorders like paralysis, headaches, gastric ulcers, etc., also may be due to unconscious motivation.

Physiological basis of sleep

Knowledge about the physiological basis of sleep has increased rapidly over the last few years. It is now recognized to be a highly complex and heterogeneous state, which is intimately connected to the state of wakefulness. The functions of sleep are still uncertain, but NREM and REM sleep almost certainly have different functions. Sleep is in many ways, a vulnerable state, due to reduced awareness and responsiveness to the environment. Wakefulness may also have important biochemical influence on neuron which are compensated by the influence of sleep. During wakefulness neuronal glucose utilization is more rapid, this process is reversed during sleep so that glucose can be available for neuronal activity and to enable normal metabolic function during the next episode of wakefulness. Sleep has been considered to be a restorative or a recovery phase or to prepare an organism physiologically for the next phase of wakefulness. Sleep also have an important effects on the immune system and is itself influenced by cytokines which are an integral component of immunity. Energy is conserved during sleep, but it is only between 100 and 200 calories per night and is probably of little significance.

Stages of sleep

Sleep is actually an active physiological state. During sleep metabolism generally slows down but all major organs and regulatory system continue to function. In fact sleep can be categorized in to two distinct types namely Rapid Eye Movement (REM) Sleep and Non-REM (NREM) sleep (Table-5). Changes in the brain activity that take place during sleep can be measured by using an electroencephalogram (EEG). NREM sleep is characterized by a reduction in the physiological activity. As sleep gets deeper breathing and heart rate slows down and blood pressure drops.

Type of brain wave recorded during sleep

1. Alpha waves occur during the period of relaxation while still awake. Brain waves become slower, increased amplitude and become more synchronous
2. Beta waves associated with day today wakefulness, highest in frequency, lowest in amplitude and more desynchronous than the other waves
3. Theta waves recorded during first of sleep, slower in frequency, greater in amplitude than alpha waves
4. Delta waves slowest and highest amplitude brain waves occur during deep sleep

Non- Rapid Eye Movement (NREM) Sleep

NREM sleep phase consist of four stages:

Stage 1: is the time of drowsiness or transition from being awake to fall in asleep. It occurs mostly in the beginning of sleep with slow eye movements. This state is sometime referred to as relaxed wakefulness. Brain waves and muscle activity begin to slow down during the stage. The sleeper loses some muscle tone and most consciousness of the external environment. People in the stage 1 sleep may experienced sudden muscle jerk, preceded by a falling sensation. The stage 1 NREM is characterized by slow breathing, regular but slower heart beat and lowered brain temperature. EEG of the stage 1 shows small irregular alpha waves and the theta waves appears. People aroused from this stage often believe that have been fully awake.

Stage 2: This is period of sleep during which no eye movement occurs and dreaming is very rare. The brain waves become slower with occasional burst of rapid waves called sleep spindles, coupled with spontaneous period of muscle tone mixed with periods of muscle relaxation. The heart rate slows and body temperature decreases.

Stage 3 and 4: stage 3 and 4 together called slow wave sleep. Stage 3 was formerly the transition stage between stage 3 and stage 4. This slow wave sleep is characterized by the presence of slow brain waves called delta waves interspersed with smaller, faster waves. Dreaming is more common in this stage than any other stage in NREM sleep. This is also the stage during which parasomnias most commonly occur. Parasomnias are a category of sleep disorders that involve abnormal movements, behaviours, emotions, perceptions, and dream that occur while falling asleep, sleeping, between sleep stages, or during arousal from sleep. Most parasomnias are dissociated sleep states which are partial arousal during the the transitions between wakefulness and NREM sleep or wakefulness and REM sleep. During this stage of sleep blood pressure falls, breathing slows, body temperature drops and body become immobile. Sleep is deeper with no eye movements and decreased muscle activity, though muscle retian their ability to function, it is most difficult to awakened during slow wave sleep. People who are awakened this stages of sleep may feel groggy or disorientated for several minutes after they wake up. It is also during the stage that some children experienced bed wetting, night terrors or sleep walking.

Rapid Eye Movement (REM)

REM sleep is an active period of sleep marked by intense brain activity. Brain waves are fast and desynchronized, similar to those in the waking state. Breathing becomes more rapid, irregular and shallow,eye moves rapidly in various directions and limb muscles become temporarily paralyzed. Heart rate increased and blood pressure rises. This also is the sleep stage in which most dreams occur. Although the role of each of these states plays in overall health is uncertain, having the right balance between them is believed to be important for obtaining restful, restorative sleep and for promoting processes such as memory, mood, and ability to concentrate. The REM phase is also known as paradoxical sleep (PS) and sometimes desynchronized sleep because of physiological similarities to waking states, including rapid, low-voltage desynchronized brain waves. Electrical and chemical activity regulating this phase seems to originate in the brain stem and is characterized most notably by an abundance of the neurotransmitter acetylcholine, combined with a nearly complete absence of monoamine neurotransmitters histamine, serotonin, and norepinephrine.

(Table-5): Physiological Changes During NREM and REM sleep

Physiological Process	NREM	REM
Brain activity	Decreases from wakefulness	Increases in motor and sensory areas, while other areas are similar to NREM
Heart rate	Slows from wakefulness	Increases and varies compared to NREM
Blood Pressure	Decreases from wakefulness	Increased (up to 30 percent) and varies from NREM
Sympathetic nerve activity	Decreases from wakefulness	Increases significantly from wakefulness
Muscle tone	Similar to wakefulness	Absent
Blood flow to brain	Decreases from wakefulness	Increases form NREM depending on brain region
Respiration	Decreases from wakefulness	Increases and varies from NREM, but may show brief stoppage, coughing suppressed
Airway resistance	Increased from wakefulness	Increases and varies from wakefulness
Body temperature	Is regulated at lower set point than wakefulness, shivering initiated at tower temperature than during wakefulness	Is not regulated, no shivering or sweating, temperature drifts toward that of the local environment
Sexual arousal	Occurs infrequently	Greater than NREM

NEURAL MECHANISM

Stimulation of hypothalamic site influences sleep pattern. The posterior hypothalamus controls the maintenance of behavioural arousal. Anterior hypothalamus and posterior portion of telencephalon where collection of nuclei are formed. It shows opposite action of posterior hypothalamus. Raphe nuclei control slow wave sleep. The region of reticular formation in the lower pons-locus coeruleus controls the maintenance of REM sleep. Gigantocellular tegmental field (FTG) located in the pons near to the locus coeruleus increase the firing rate during REM sleep. FTG and coeruleus are jointly involved in the process of REM sleep.

Biochemistry of sleep

Serotonin in the raphe nuclei induces the onset of slow wave sleep. Delta sleep inducing peptide (DSIP) initiates slow wave sleep. The sleep promoting factor's' in the brain induces the EEG signs of sleep. Nor adrenergic neurons are rich in locus coerulus produce noradrenaline which plays a significant role in REM sleep. It has an inhibitory response. It decreases REM sleep because the activity in the locus coerulus is depressed during the REM sleep.

Functions of sleep

Sleep deprived animals suffered impairment in organ functioning and weight loss. Deprivation also produced enlarged adrenal gland and stomach ulcers indicating a stress reaction. Sleep allow the animal to conserve its energy stores for periods of the day for activity. A sleep wake cycle is a strategy for survival. REM deprivation in human produces pronounced psychological effects like irritability, ravenous appetite, increased oral behaviour and oral symbolism in the subjects thinking. REM sleep is a necessary element of one's sleep. It serves as a 'safety value' that allows a great deal of neural activity to occur in the brain without any behavioural consequences. REM sleep serves to maintain the mechanism necessary for conjugate eye movement. Conjugate eye movement refers to motor coordination of the eyes that allows for bilateral fixation on a single object. Human depth vision is better subsequent to REM sleep and that eye movements during the REM sleep are more vigorous. Thus REM serves as a significant function in adulthood. REM sleep during infancy play a major role in brain development and serve as an important sign in the developmental processs.

The neocortex receives increased activation from the brain stem during REM sleep and interprets the neural signals syntheticaly in termas if information already stored in the memory. The result of the synthesis is the content of dream. REM sleep serves to allow a kind of reverse learning or dampening down of cortical circuits so as to prevent them from being overloaded during waking hours. REM sleep and the imagery of dreams are random firing of neurons needed for a daily cleansing of cortical system.

Sleep and arousal

Behavioural arousal decreases as EEG frequency decreases. High frequency EEG(β) signs coincide with alert wakefullness (eye open). Moderate frequency (α) coincides with relaxed wakefullness (eye closed) and low frequency (δ) with sleep. At fairly regular intervals during sleep, the EEG changes from delta frequencies to higher frequencies without any increase in the behavioural arousal. These periods are REM and individuals awakened at the time frequently report experiences of dreaming. The remaining period-slow wave sleep, in which delta EEG frequencies are observed. The physiological basis of changes in arousal level showed that stimulation of the reticular formation could produce EEG desynchronisation common to wakefulness. The input from the reticular formation to the entire neocortex may underlie the maintenance of arousal. Both the reticular formation and the posterior hypothalamus are involved in arousal. Nightmares may awaken the individual from sleep and often remembered vividly,while night terrors are always unaware the next morning of what has occurred.

Circadian Rythms

It is the cycling of rest and activity during a 24 hr period and is accomplished by the suprachiasmatic nuclei (SCN) in the anterior portion of the hypothalamus. These nuclei receive information regarding the peroid of a day via optic pathways from the retina and thalamus. The active behaviour of human being's is a vast system of cycles and epicycles (longest –extending through life, shortest – in seconds). A circadian rhythm is any biological process that displays an endogenous, entrainable oscillation of about 24 hours. These 24-hour rhythms are driven by a circadian clock, and they have been widely observed in plants, animals, fungi, and cyanobacteria. The term circadian comes from the Latin *circa*, meaning "around" (or "approximately"), and *diēm*, meaning "day". The formal study of biological temporal rhythms, such as daily, tidal, weekly, seasonal, and annual rhythms, is called chronobiology. Processes with 24-hour oscillations are more generally called diurnal rhythms; strictly speaking, they should not be called circadian rhythms unless their endogenous nature is confirmed.

Although circadian rhythms are endogenous ("built-in", self-sustained), they are adjusted (entrained) to the local environment by external cues called zeitgebers (from German, "time giver"), which include light, temperature and redox cycles. In medical science, an abnormal circadian rhythm in humans is known as circadian rhythm disorder.

Diurnality

Diurnality is a form of plant or animal behaviour characterized by activity during the day, with a period of sleeping, or other inactivity, at night. The common adjective used for daytime activity is "diurnal". The timing of activity by an animal depends on a variety of environmental factors such as the temperature, the ability to gather food by sight, the risk of predation, and the time of year. Diurnality is a cycle of activity within a twenty-four-hour period; cyclic activities called circadian rhythms are endogenous cycles not dependent on external cues or environmental factors. Animals active at dawn or dusk are crepuscular, those active at night are nocturnal, and animals active at sporadic times during both night and day are cathemeral.

SLEEP DISORDERS

1. Narcolepsy (Disorder of Excessive Somnolence)

Periodic attacks of sleep during wakeful hours, accompanied by sudden weakness of the body and temporary paralysis. They experience 5–35 minutes sleep attack unpredictability and emotional/stressful experiences. It is a kind of neural defect and appears to be an inheritance pattern across generations. The narcoleptic individuals begin their nocturnal sleep in REM sleep (instead of slow wave sleep). They are in REM sleep during their day time sleep attacks. The exact cause of narcolepsy is unknown with potentially several causes. In up to 10% of cases there is a family history of the disorder. Often those affected have low levels of the neuropeptide orexin which may be due to an autoimmune disorder. Trauma, infections, toxins, or psychological stress may also play a role. Diagnosis is typically based on the symptoms and sleep studies, after ruling out other potential causes. Excessive daytime sleepiness can also be caused by other sleep disorders such as sleep apnea, major depressive disorder, anemia, heart failure, drinking alcohol, and not getting enough sleep. The condition often begins in childhood. Men and women are affected equally. Untreated narcolepsy increases the risk of motor vehicle collisions and falls. The term narcolepsy is from the French *narcolepsie*. The French term was first used in 1880 by Jean-Baptiste-Édouard Gélineau. The classic symptoms of the disorder, often referred to as the "tetrad of narcolepsy,"are cataplexy, sleep paralysis, hypnagogic hallucinations, and excessive daytime sleepiness. Cataplexy is an episodic loss of muscle function, ranging from slight weakness such as limpness at the neck or knees, sagging facial muscles, weakness at the knees often referred to as "knee buckling", or inability to speak clearly, to a complete body collapse. Sleep paralysis is the temporary inability to talk or move when waking (or less often, when falling asleep). It may last a few seconds to minutes. This is often frightening but is not dangerous. Hypnagogic hallucinations are vivid, often frightening, dream like experiences that occur while dozing or falling asleep. Hypnopompic hallucinations refer to the same sensations while awakening from sleep. These hallucinations may manifest in the form of visual or auditory sensations.

2. Insomnia (inability to fall asleep)

Insomnia, also known as sleeplessness, is a sleep disorder where people have trouble sleeping. They may have difficulty falling asleep, or staying asleep as long as desired. Insomnia is typically followed by daytime sleepiness, low energy, irritability, and a depressed mood. It may result in an increased risk of motor vehicle collisions, as well as problems focusing and learning. Insomnia can be short term, lasting for days or weeks, or long term, lasting more than a month. Insomnia can occur independently or as a result of another problem. Conditions that can result in insomnia include psychological stress, chronic pain, heart failure, hyperthyroidism, heartburn, restless leg syndrome, menopause, certain medications, and drugs such as caffeine, nicotine, and alcohol. Other risk factors include working night shifts and sleep apnea. Diagnosis is based on sleep habits and an examination to look for underlying causes. A sleep study may be done to look for underlying sleep disorders. Screening may be done with two questions: "do you experience difficulty sleeping?" and "do you have difficulty falling or staying asleep?"

Sleep hygiene and lifestyle changes are typically the first treatment for insomnia. Sleep hygiene includes a consistent bedtime, exposure to sunlight, a quiet and dark room, and regular exercise. Cognitive behavioural therapy may be added to this. While sleeping pills may help, they are associated with injuries, dementia, and addiction. Medications are not recommended for more than four or five weeks. The effectiveness and safety of alternative medicine is unclear. Between 10% and 30% of adults have insomnia at any given point in time and up to half of people have insomnia in a given year. About 6% of people have insomnia that is not due to another problem and lasts for more than a month. People over the age of 65 are affected more often than younger people. Females are more often affected than males. Symptoms of insomnia are difficulty falling asleep, including difficulty finding a comfortable sleeping position, waking during the night and being unable to return to sleep, feeling unrefreshed upon waking, daytime sleepiness, irritability or anxiety.

3. Somnambulism (Sleep walking)

Sleepwalking, also known as somnambulism or noctambulism, is a phenomenon of combined sleep and wakefulness. It is classified as a sleep disorder belonging to the parasomnia family. It occurs during slow wave sleep stage, in a state of low consciousness, with performance of activities that are usually performed during a state of full consciousness. These activities include sitting up in bed, walking to a bathroom, and cleaning, or as hazardous as cooking, driving, violent gestures, grabbing at hallucinated objects etc. Although sleepwalking cases generally consist of simple, repeated behaviours, there are occasionally reports of people performing complex behaviours while asleep, although their legitimacy is often disputed. Sleepwalkers often have little or no memory of the incident, as their consciousness has altered into a state in which it is harder to recall memories. Although their eyes are open, their expression is dim and glazed over. This may last from 30 seconds to 30 minutes. Sleepwalking occurs during slow-wave sleep (N3) of non-rapid eye movement sleep (NREM sleep) cycles. It typically occurs within the first third of the night when slow-wave sleep is most prominent. Usually, it will occur once in a night, if at all. Symptoms of sleep walking include glassy-eyed stare/blank expression, disorientation consequent to awakening, meaningless talk and amnesia.

In the study "sleepwalking and sleep terrors in prepubera children", it was found that, if a child had another sleep disorder such as restless leg syndrome (RLS) or sleep-disorder breathing (SDB), there was a greater chance of sleepwalking. The study found that children with chronic parasomnias may often also present SDB or, to a lesser extent, RLS. Furthermore, the disappearance of the parasomnias after the treatment of the SDB or RLS periodic limb movement syndrome suggests that the latter may trigger the former. The high frequency of SDB in family members of children with parasomnia provided additional evidence that SDB may manifest as parasomnias in children. Children with parasomnias are not systematically monitored during sleep, although past studies have suggested that patients with sleep terrors or sleepwalking have an elevated level of brief EEG arousals. When children receive polysomnographies, discrete patterns (e.g., nasal flow limitation, abnormal respiratory effort, bursts of high or slow EEG frequencies) should be sought; apneas are rarely found in children. Children's respiration during sleep should be monitored with nasal cannula/pressure transducer system and/or esophageal manometry, which are more sensitive than the thermistors or thermocouples currently used in many laboratories. The clear, prompt improvement of severe parasomnia in children who are treated for SDB, as defined here, provides important evidence that subtle SDB can have substantial health-related significance. Also noteworthy is the report of familial presence of parasomnia. Studies of twin cohorts and families with sleep terror and sleepwalking suggest genetic involvement of parasomnias. RLS and SDB have been shown to have familial recurrence. RLS has been shown to have genetic involvement.

In some cases, sleepwalking in adults may be a symptom of a psychological disorder. One study suggests higher levels of dissociation in adult sleepwalkers, since test subjects scored unusually high on the hysteria portion of the "Crown-Crisp Experiential Index". Another suggested that "A higher incidence (of sleepwalking events) has been reported in patients with schizophrenia, hysteria and anxiety neuroses". Also, patients with migraine headaches or Tourette Syndrome are 4–6 times more likely to sleepwalk.

There may be a genetic component to sleepwalking. One study found that sleepwalking occurred in 45% of children who have one parent who sleepwalked, and in 60% of children if both parents sleepwalked. Thus, heritable factors may predispose an individual to sleepwalking, but expression of the behaviour may also be influenced by environmental factors. Sleepwalking may be inherited as an autosomal dominant disorder with reduced penetrance.

Medications, primarily in four classes—benzodiazepine receptor agonists and other GABA (Gamma Amino Butyric Acid) modulators, antidepressants and other serotonergic agents, antipsychotics, and β-blockers— have been associated with sleepwalking. The best evidence of medications causing sleepwalking is for Zolpidem and sodium oxybate—all other reports are based on associations noted in case reports. A number of conditions, such as Parkinson's Disease, are thought to trigger sleepwalking in people without a previous history of sleepwalking.

Three common diagnostic systems that are generally used for sleepwalking disorders are International Classification of Diagnoses, the International Classification of Sleep Disorders and the Diagnostic and Statistical Manual. Polysomnography is the only accurate measure of sleepwalking. Other measures commonly used include self-report, parent, partner or house-mate report.

4. Enuresis (Nocturnal Bedwetting)

Nocturnal enuresis, also called bedwetting, is involuntary urination while asleep after the age at which bladder control usually occurs. Bedwetting in children and adults can result in emotional stress.

Complications can include urinary tract infections. Most bedwetting is a developmental delay—not an emotional problem or physical illness. Only a small percentage (5% to 10%) of bedwetting cases are caused by specific medical situations. Bedwetting is frequently associated with a family history of the condition. Nocturnal enuresis is considered primary (PNE) when a child has not yet had a prolonged period of being dry. Secondary nocturnal enuresis (SNE) is when a child or adult begins wetting again after having stayed dry. Treatments range from behavioural-based options such as bedwetting alarms, to medication such as hormone replacement, and even surgery such as urethral enlargement. Since most bedwetting is simply a developmental delay, most treatment plans aim to protect or improve self-esteem. Treatment guidelines recommend that the physician counsel the parents, warning about psychological damage caused by pressure, shaming, or punishment for a condition children cannot control. Bedwetting is the most common childhood complaint. Most girls stay dry by age six and most boys stay dry by age seven. By ten years old, 95% of children are dry at night. Studies place adult bedwetting rates at between 0.5% and 2.3%. Psychologists may use a definition from the American Psychiatric Association's DSM-IV (Diagnostic and Statistical Manual), defining nocturnal enuresis as repeated urination into bed or clothes, occurring twice per week or more for at least three consecutive months in a child of at least 5 years of age and not due to either a drug side effect or a medical condition. Even if the case does not meet these criteria, the DSM-IV definition allows psychologists to diagnose nocturnal enuresis if the wetting causes the patient clinically significant distress.

5. Sleep apnea (Failure to Breathe) in infants

Sleep apnea, also spelled sleep apnoea, is a sleep disorder characterized by pauses in breathing or periods of shallow breathing during sleep. Each pause can last for a few seconds to a few minutes and they happen many times at night. In the most common form, this follows loud snoring. There may be a choking or snorting sound as breathing resumes. As it disrupts normal sleep, those affected may experience sleepiness or feel tired during the day. In children it may cause problems in school, or hyperactivity.

There are three forms of sleep apnea: obstructive (OSA), central (CSA), and a combination of the two called mixed. OSA is the most common form. Risk factors for OSA include being overweight, a family history of the condition, allergies, a small airway, and enlarged tonsils. In OSA, breathing is interrupted by a blockage of airflow, while in CSA breathing stops due to a lack of effort to breathe. People with sleep apnea may not be aware they have it. In many cases it is first observed by a family member. Sleep apnea is often diagnosed with an overnight sleep study.

Treatment may include lifestyle changes, mouthpieces, breathing devices, and surgery. Lifestyle changes may include avoiding alcohol, losing weight, stopping smoking, and sleeping on one's side. Breathing devices include the use of a CPAP (Continuous Positive Airway Pressure) machine. Without treatment sleep apnea may increase the risk of heart attack, stroke, diabetes, heart failure, irregular heartbeat, obesity, and motor vehicle collisions.

OSA affects 1 to 6% of adults and 2% of children. It affects males about twice as often as females. While people at any age can be affected it occurs most commonly among those 55 to 60 years old. Central sleep apnea affects less than 1% of people. Sudden infant death syndrome (SIDS) occurs as a result of sleep apnea in infants. Sleep apnea in adults is a form of insomnia, the person awakens suddenly from sleeping as a result of increased level of Co_2 in the blood.

6. SADS (Seasonal Affective Disorder)

Seasonal affective disorder (SAD), also known as winter depression, summer depression, summer time sadness, or seasonal depression. It is a mood disorder in which people who have normal mental health throughout most of the year experience depressive symptoms in the winter or summer. Sleeping for more than normal and finding it hard to get up in the morning. Craving for carbohydrates and gaining weight. Lack of sunlight might stop the working of hypothalamus properly which inturn causes melatonin production-makes you feel sleepy, production of serotonin- affects mood, appetite and sleep, affects circadian rythms-causing disturbances in sleep and wake cycle. Treatment includes light therapy, talk therapy and antidepressant medication.

7. Restless Legs syndrome

Those who suffer from this syndrome have uncomfortable feelings in the legs. The sensory manifestations of RLS include intense disagreeable feeling which are described as burning, aching, cramping or itching sensations. These sensations occurs mostly between knees and ankles causing an intense urge to move the limbs to relieve these feelings. Most of the movements in the early stages are noted in the evening through to the early hours of the morning. Sometimes it occurs due to the deficiency of iron in the body.

8. Sleep Hypoventilation

The people who have breathing muscles that are weak or under excessive load from severe lung disorders or obesity may not breathe strongly enough during sleep. With no treatment, this can lead to breathing and heart failure during the day. Devices to help breathing during sleep will work in treating this. This treatment is called non-invasive positive pressure ventilation. Many people with this condition also frequently stop breathing altogether for short periods of time during sleep (obstructive sleep apnea), resulting in many partial awakenings during the night, which leads to continual sleepiness during the day. The disease puts strain on the heart, which eventually may lead to the symptoms such as heart failure, leg swelling and various other related symptoms. The most effective treatment is weight loss, but it is often possible to relieve the symptoms by nocturnal ventilation with CPAP or related methods.

9. Snoring

Snoring is the vibration of respiratory structures and the resulting sound due to obstructed air movement during breathing while sleeping. In some cases, the sound may be soft, but in most cases, it can be loud and unpleasant. Snoring during sleep may be a sign, or first alarm, of obstructive sleep apnea (OSA). Snoring is known to cause sleep deprivation to snorers and those around them, as well as daytime drowsiness, irritability, lack of focus and decreased libido. It has also been suggested that it can cause significant psychological and social damage to sufferers. Snoring is a common problem. It affects up to 40% of men and 20% of women on a regular basis. It gets worst with age and weight gain. Someone who snores can disturb their partner's sleep. This can cause distress for both of them. As well, many regular snorers also have obstructive sleep apnoea. It can be caused by throat weakness, causing the throat to close during sleep, mispositioned jaw, often caused by tension in the muscles, obesity that has caused fat to gather in and around the throat, obstruction in the nasal passageway, obstructive sleep apnea, sleep deprivation, relaxants such as alcohol or other drugs relaxing throat muscles and sleeping on one's back, which may result in the tongue dropping to the back of the mouth.

10. Bruxism

This involves grinding of the teeth during sleep. It is quite common. If not treated, it can cause permanent damage to the teeth. Sometimes it causes jaw discomfort. But often the people who have it aren't aware of anything. If they use dental guards they can protect their teeth. It is an oral parafunctional activity; i.e., it is unrelated to normal function such as eating or talking. Bruxism is a common behaviour; reports of prevalence range from 8–31% in the general population. Several symptoms are commonly associated with bruxism, including hypersensitive teeth, aching jaw muscles, headaches, tooth wear, and damage to dental restorations (e.g. crowns and fillings) to teeth. But symptoms may be minimal, without patient awareness of the condition. There are two main types of bruxism: one occurs during sleep (sleep bruxism) and one during wakefulness (awake bruxism). Dental damage may be similar in both types, but the symptoms of sleep bruxism tend to be worse on waking and improve during the course of the day, and the symptoms of awake bruxism may not be present at all on waking, and then worsen over the day. The causes of bruxism are not completely understood, but probably involve multiple factors. Awake bruxism is more common in females, whereas males and females are affected in equal proportions by sleep bruxism. Awake bruxism is thought to have different causes from sleep bruxism, several treatments are in use, although there is little evidence of robust efficacy for any particular treatment.

PHYSIOLOGICAL BASIS OF EATING

Eating is ingesting food to provide for all humans and animals nutritional needs, particularly for energy and growth. All creatures must eat in order to survive: carnivores eat other animals, herbivores eat plants, and omnivores consume a mixture of both. Eating is an activity of daily living.

People commonly have two or three meals a day at regular times. Snacks of smaller amounts may be consumed between meals. Having three well-balanced meals (thus 1/2 of the plate with vegetables, 1/4 protein food as meat, and 1/4 carbohydrates as pasta, rice, ...) will then account to some 1800–2000 kcal; which is the average requirement for a regular person. The issue of healthy eating has long been an important concern to individuals and cultures. Among other practices, fasting, dieting, and vegetarianism are all techniques employed by individuals and encouraged by societies to increase longevity and health. Some religions promote vegetarianism, considering it wrong to consume animals. Leading nutritionists believe that instead of indulging oneself in three large meals each day, it is much healthier and easier on the metabolism to eat five smaller meals each day (e.g. better digestion, easier on the lower intestine to deposit wastes) whereas larger meals are tougher on the digestive tract.

Emotional eating is "the tendency to eat in response to negative emotions". Empirical studies have indicated that anxiety leads to decreased food consumption in people with normal weight and increased food consumption in the obese.

FEEDING CENTERS IN BRAIN

Feeding center is a group of cells in the lateral hypothalamus that when stimulated cause a sensation of hunger. The lateral hypothalamus or lateral hypothalamic area is a part of the hypothalamus is concerned with hunger. Damage to this area can cause reduced food intake. Stimulating the lateral hypothalamus (LH) causes a desire to eat, while stimulating the Ventromedial Hypothalamus (VMH) causes a desire to stop eating. Hence Lateral Hypothalalmus is known as hunger centre and the Ventromedial Hypothalamus is known as the satiety centre.

THE DUAL CENTER HYPOTHESIS

Hypothalamus controls body temperature, hunger, thirst, fatigue, sleep and circadium rhythms. It is a part of limbic system located below the thalamus. It is responsible for certain metabolic processes and other activities of brain. Hypothalamus contain two centers responsible for physiological mechanisms of feeding, one responsible for hunger and the other for satiety. This hypothesis came to be known as the dual center hypothesis or dual control theory of feeding. Eating behaviour is regulated by a body, peripheral to the Central Nervous System (CNS). There are two signals generated from the brain for feeding- they are hunger and satiety. It is a homeostatic drive.VMH is brain satiety centre whereas LH is the hunger centre.

The stomach exhibits peristaltic movements. Normally when the stomach is empty it produces vigorous peristaltic movements and it signals to the hunger centre of CNS, the feel of hunger is given by LH centre. When the stomach is filled with food, the stomach wall stretches, the stretching activity activates stretch receptors of stomach wall. This stretching of stomach will be given to the CNS giving the feeling of satiety by VMH centre. The two areas of brain are involved with the control of eating hence feeding is under the control of dual mechanism by the brain.

Hunger signals arising from factors such as lowering of blood glucose level or an empty stomach will stimulate LH. The activity within the LH gave rise the hunger, inhibit activity in the VMH and send a signal to higher areas of brain giving rise to feeling of hunger which enhance the attractiveness of food relative stimuli. This motivated the search of food leading to consumption. The ingested food undergo digestion and nutrients began to enter the blood stream. This resulting in diminishing of hunger signals and strengthening of satiety center signal. When these reached sufficient intensity, they will overcome the weakening inhibition of VMH by the LH, and the VMH switched on resulting in the feeling of fullness or satiety. Satiety inhibits further feeding.

Researchers used two sources of evidence to construct the dual center hypothesis, in which they conduct experiment in the brain of a laboratory rat. The electrode could be used to create a lesion, or small area of destruction, around the tip of the electrode. Alternatively, the electrode could be implanted permanently and used to stimulate the region of brain surrounding the electrode tip. The results which led to the dual center hypothesis:

❖ **Lateral Hypothalamus** (LH)

➤ *Lesioning*: Leads to Aphagia (lack of eating). The rat no longer seemed interested in food, would refuse to eat, and would waste away unless force-fed.

➤ *Stimulation*: A rat that had just finished consuming a meal, apparently satisfied, would return to the food and resume eating.

Taken together, these two findings suggested to researchers that the lateral hypothalamus functions as a hunger center. That is, when the LH turns on, the individual feels hungry and becomes motivated to seek out and consume food.

❖ **Ventromedial Hypothalamus** (VMH)

➤ *Lesioning*: Leads to Hyperphagia (over-eating). After recovery from the surgery, the rat would begin to eat more than it had before, and rapidly gained weight until it weighed perhaps two to three times its normal weight of around 500 grams (male rat).

➤ *Stimulation*: A hungry rat in the midst of a meal would drop the food pellet and ignore the food for a couple of minutes following a brief burst of stimulation of the VMH.

These two pieces of evidence suggested to researchers that the VMH might function as a satiety center. When activated, the satiety center would produce that feeling of having had perhaps too much. More than the mere absence of hunger, this would be a drive to avoid any further consumption of food, even if it continued to taste good.

The changes in eating habits of a VMH leisoned rat, commonly observed in two distinct stages. Dynamic stage is the first stage lasting 4 to 12 weeks. During this period the animal consumes more food than a normal unleisoned animal and weight gain is also increased. Second phase is a static stage, in which food consumption is still higher for maintaining the gained body weight. VMH leisoned animals are very much particular in selecting highly palatable, sweet tasting food. They are also more emotional in their responses to environmental stress. The anatomical locus of VMH concerned as feeding center is ventral noradrenergic bundle or VNA bundle. Leisoning of this region can produce hyperphagia effect.

HUMAN DIGESTIVE SYSTEM

Human digestive tract includes a receiving organ, a region of conduction and storage, a region of internal trituration and early digestion, a region of water absorption and faeces formation.

The receiving organ is mouth- the ducts of the salivary glands open in to the mouth cavity. The region of conduction and storage is oesophagus. The stomach is the region of internal trituration and early digestion. The region of stomach in to which oesophagus opens is called cardiac stomach followed by fundus and the posterior part of the stomach opens in to intestine is called pyloric region. The wall of stomach is composed of circular, longitudinal and diagonal muscles. The internal lining of the stomach or mucosa contains gastric glands. The region of final digestion and absorption is the small intestine. It has two parts, duodenum is very short, the bile duct and pancreatic duct open in to it. The reminder of the small intestine is highly coiled and vascular and is concerned with absorption of digested food. The epithelial lining of the intestine is provided with several finger like projection called villi, which increases the surface area for absorption. The region of water absorption and faeces formation is the large intestine or colon. Colon leads to rectum which opens out by anus.

DIGESTIVE GLANDS

Digestive gland associated with digestive system of man are salivary glands, gastric glands, liver, pancreas and glands of small intestine. The gland secretes digestive juice containing enzymes.

Salivary glands: There are three major pairs of salivary glands namely Parotid, Sublingual and Sub maxillary. The Parotid gland lie below and in front of ears. The Sublingual glands lies beneath the tongue and submaxillary found beneath the angle of lower jaw. The collective secretion of these glands is salivia. About 1200–1500ml of saliva is generally secreted by a man in 24 hrs. It is a moistening fluid that contain mucin. Mucin lubricates food. Saliva contains salivary amylase and lingual lipase. The activity of salivary gland is under nervous control and is stimulated by thought, smell or taste of food.

Gastric glands: Small tubular glands opens on the inner surface of the stomach. The gastric gland composed of mucous cells or goblet cells secrete mucous, chief cells secrete enzymes and parietal cell which secrete Hydrochloric acid (HCl). The secretion of gastric gland is known as gastric juice. Normal amount of gastric juice produced in man is 400–800 ml/meal. Gastric juice consists of watery enzyme such as pepsin and gastric lipase, mucin and HCl. The secretion of gastric juice is under the control of both nervous and hormonal factors. Presence of food in stomach exert a chemical effect and stimulated to produce a hormone called gastrin, it stimulate secretion of gastric juice particularly HCl. The thoroughly mixed partly digested form of food called chyme leaves stomach and enters duodenum followed by the production of gastric juice stopped. Fats present in the chyme stimulates the tissue of duodenum to produce a hormone called enterogastrin which inhibits the activity of gastric glands.

Pamcreas: It is both exocrine and endocrine in function. Exocrine portion of gland is concerned with production of pancreatic juice. Endocrine part of the gland is known as Islets of langerhans. Pancreas lies between stomach and duodenum. Pancreatic juice passes along the pancretic duct which joins the duodenum along with the bile duct from the liver. Islets of Langerhans secrete hormones insulin and glucagon. Pancreatic juice contain pancreatic amylase. Pancreatic lipase and proteases. Two important proteases are trypisnogen and chymotrypsinogen. Trypsinogen is activated by an intestinal enzyme called enterokinase which convert trpsinogen to trypsin which in turn converts chymotrypsinogen to active form of chymotrypsin. Production of pancreatic juice is under hormonal control.

Liver: Liver is the largest gland in the body. It store and filter blood, secreting bile and bringing out metabolic reactions. Approximately 750ml bile is produced by a human liver daily. Bile is yellowish or greenish alkaline fluid. Being alkaline it helps digestion by neutralizing acid chyme. Release of bile in to the duodenum is under the hormonal control. The presence of fat in the chyme passes in to the duodenum causes the duodenal tissue to produce a hormone called cholecystokinin (CCK).

Intestinal glands: The wall of small intestine contains millions of tiny glands called intestinal glands. The glands of Brunner in the duodenum secrete mucin and the crypts of Lieberkuhn secrete variety of digestive enzymes. The secretion of intestinal gland called intestinal juice or succus entericus. This secretion is highly alkaline. The intestinal juice contains enterokinase, proteases, carbohydrases, lipases, maltases, lactases, sucrose and nucleases.

NERVOUS AND HORMONAL CONTROL AND DIGESTIVE ACTIVITY

The gastrointestinal activities have both hormonal and neural control. There is an intrinsic system of nerves which extends from oesophagus to anus. The system is fully confined within the walls of guts called enteric nervous system. There are two nerve plexus- the outer one lying between the circular and longitudinal muscles of the gut wall is called myenteric plexus or aurobach plexus. The inner one lying in the submucosa is called submucosal plexus or messiners plexus. The submucosal plexus control the gastrointestinal secretion while the myenteric plexus regulated the intestinal movement.

Branches of nerves from sympathetic and parasympathetic system constitute extrinsic innervations either inhibit or activate gastrointestinal activity. A number of gastro intestinal hormones also control the gastrointestinal function. Gastrin produced by G cells from the gastric mucosa stimulate the secretion of gastric juice and gastric motility. The enterogastrin produced by the tissues of duodenum inhibit gastric secretion. CCK and pancreozymin are secreted by duodenum. CCK promotes the contraction of gall bladder and relaxation of sphincter valves at the cystic duct effectively helps in the release of bile in to small intestine. Pancerozyme promotes the secretion of pancreatic juice secreted by S cells of duodenum, increases the secretion of bicarbonates by the pancreas and make the pancreatic juice watery and alkaline. The gastric inhibitory peptide or GIP produced by the K cells of the mucosa of duodenum and jejunum inhibits gastric secretion and mobility and stimulate Beta cells of pancreas to produce insulin.

Vasoactive intestinal polypeptide (VIP) is a neuro transmitter produced by vaso motor nerve fibres in the gastro intestinal tract. It promotes the secretion of electrolyte and water in the intestine, stimulates the regulation of intestinal smooth muscles. It also inhibits hydrochloric acid secretion. Two specific hormones enterocrinin and neocrinin produced by the tissues of intestinal tract stimulate the activities of intestinal glands. Villikinin secreted by duodenum stimulates motility of Villi. Motilin secreted by the cells of duodenal mucosa causes contraction of intestinal smooth muscles and regulate interdigestive motility and preparing the intestine to the next meal. Neurotensin secreted by motor neurons of the enteric nervous system causes inhibition of gastrointestinal motivation. Stomatostatin, the growth hormone released to the intestinal lumen inhibits the secretion of many gastrointestinal hormones.

Eating signals

Eating is ingestion of food with energy to allow for growth. Empirical studies have indicated that anxiety has decreased the food consumption in the people with normal weight and increased food consumption in obese. There are many physiological mechanisms to control starting and stopping a meal called as on and off eating signals.

The control of food intake is a physiologically complex, motivated behavioural system(Fig - 45). Hormones such as CCK, Bombesin (Gastrin releasing peptide hormone), Neurotensin (found in enteroendocrine cells of small intestine), Anorectin (reduce food intake), calcitonin (calcium regulation), enterostatin (inhibit fat intake), Leptin (satiety hormone made by adipose cells), corticotrophin (releasing hormone have shown to suppress food intake), ghrelin (from gastro Intestinal tract is a stimulant of hunger) etc found to control this processes. There are numerous signals given off that initiate signals. The feeling of hunger could be triggered by the thought and smell of food, the sight of a plate, or hearing someone talk about food. The signals from the stomach are initiate by the release by the peptide hormone ghrelin, that increases appetite by signalling to the brain. The body starts to take nutrients from long term reservoirs during the time interval between the meals. When the gluscoe levels of the cell drops (glucoprivation), the body starts to produce the feeling of hunger. The body also stimulate eating by dectecting a drop in cellular lipid level (lipoprivation). Both brain and liver moniter the level of metabolic fuels. The brain checks for glucoprivation on its side of blood-brain barrier while the liver monitors the rest of the body for both lipoprivation and glucoprivation.

There are short term signals of satiety that arise from head, the stomach, the intestine and the liver. The long term signals of satiety comes from adipose tissue. The stomach contain recceptors to allow us to know when we are full. The intestine also contain receptors that send satiety signals to brain. The hormone CCK is secreted by duodenum controls the rate of emptying of the stomach, thus this hormone is said to be a satiety signal to the brain. Long term satiety comes from fat stored in adipose tissue. Adipose tissue secretes the hormone leptin which supresses appetite. Increased level of leptin reduces food intake. During hunger leptin decreses which causes the release of ghrelin, which initiates hunger. When leptin level rises they bind receptors in ARC (protein), suppress the release of NPY (Neuropeptide Y), which prevent appetite by the production of orexin that binds LH.

There are two peptides in the hypothalamus that produce hunger. They are melanin concentrating hormone (MCH) and orexin. MCH play a greater role in hunger and oraxin play a role in controlling relationship between eating and sleeping. Other peptide of hypothalamus that induce eating is Agouti Related Protein (ARP). Saitety in the hypothalamus is stimulated by leptin. It taget the receptors on arcuate nucleus and supresses the secretion of MCH and orexin. The arcuate nucleus also contain two more peptides that suppress hunger. The first one is Cocaine- and Amphetamine Regulated Transcript (CART), the second is α MSH (α Melanocyte Stimilating Hormone).

The two neurotransmitters namely adrenalin and serotonin from the medial hypothalamus play an important role in eating behaviour. Noradrenaline stimulated intake of carbohydrate and serotonin inhibit it. Electrical stimulation of areas like amygdala,hippocampus, thalamus and frontal cortex also enhance eating.

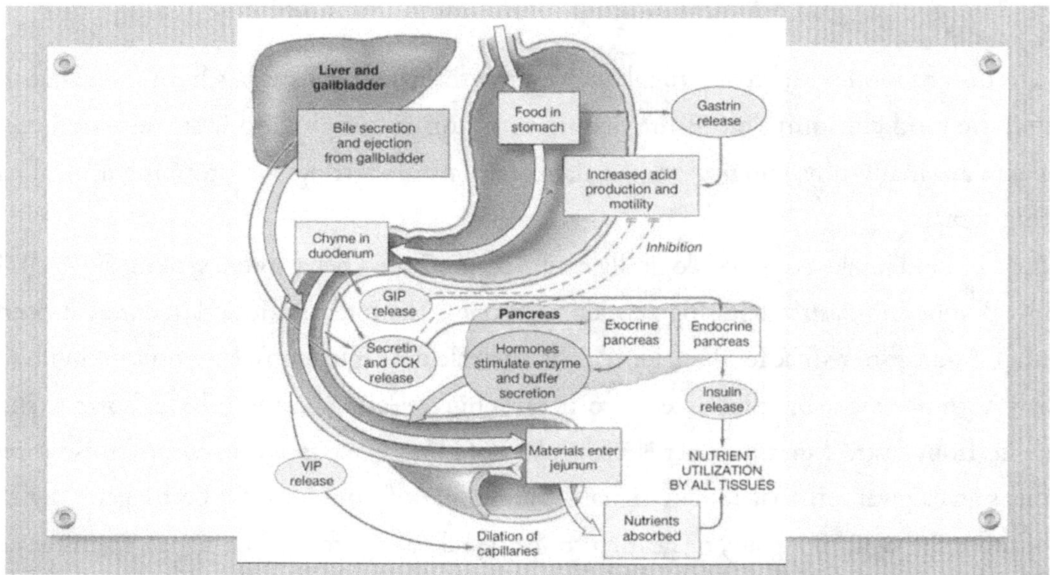

(Fig - 45) Human digestive system showing the production site of hormones

REGULATION OF FOOD INTAKE

In the brain there are mechanisms to control hunger, appetite and motivation. Hunger is a homeostatic drive. There are two signals generated from brain for hunger and satiety. This hunger signal regulated and working on the basis of different hypothesis and it can be called as set point theories.

1. Lipostatic hypothesis- According to this hypothesis, adipose tissue produces a humoral signal that is proportional to the amount of fat and act on hypothalamus to decrease food intake and increase energy out put. Hormone Leptin act on hypothalamus in this way. The end product of fat metabolism is fatty acid and glycerol. The fat or lipid is stored in adipose tissue mostly lying beneath the skin. The body fat is normally maintained at a relatively constant level. Everyone's body has a set point for body fat and deviation from the set point leads to compensatory adjustments in food intake.

2. Gut peptide hypothesis- Gastrointestinal hormone like GrP (Gastrin Releasing Peptide), Glucagons and CCK inhibit food intake. The food entering the gastrointestinal tract triggers the release of these hormones, which act on brain to produce satiety. The brain contains both CCK-A and CCK-B receptors. CCK is a peptide hormone of the gastro intestinal system responsible for stimulating the digestion of fat and protein. It synthesise and secreted by enteroendocrine cells of duodenum, and causes the release of digestive enzymes, bile etc. It also acts as a hunger suppressant.

3. Glucostatic hypothesis- According to this theory the appetite depends on blood glucose level. When the concentration of glucose falls low enough, the hunger centres in the hypothalamus stimulated and individual feels hungry. An increase in the blood glucose concentration results in increased feeling of satiety.

4. Thermostatic hypothesis- According to this hypothesis, a decrease in body temperature below a given set point stimulates appetite, where as an increase above the set point inhibits appetite.

OBESITY

Overweight and obesity are defined as abnormal or excessive fat accumulation that may impair health (Fig - 46). Body mass index (BMI) is a simple index of weight-for-height that is commonly used to classify overweight and obesity in adults. It is defined as a person's weight in kilograms divided by the square of his height in meters (kg/m^2).

$$BMI = m/h^2$$

where m and h are the subject's weight and height respectively.

For most adults, a BMI of:
- ❖ 18.5 to 24.9 means you're a healthy weight
- ❖ 25 to 29.9 means you're overweight
- ❖ 30 to 39.9 means you're obese
- ❖ 40 or above means you're severely obese

(Table-6):Body Mass Index and its classification

BMI (kg/m^2)		Classification
from	up to	
	18.5	underweight
18.5	25.0	normal weight
25.0	30.0	overweight
30.0	35.0	class I obesity
35.0	40.0	class II obesity
40.0		class III obesity

BMI (Table-6) provides the most useful population-level measure of overweight and obesity as it is the same for both sexes and for all ages of adults. However, it should be considered a rough guide because it may not correspond to the same degree of fatness in different individuals. For children, age needs to be considered when defining overweight and obesity.

Worldwide obesity has nearly tripled since 1975. In 2016, more than 1.9 billion adults, 18 years and older, were overweight. Of these over 650 million were obese. 39% of adults aged 18 years and over were overweight in 2016, and 13% were obese. Most of the world's population live in countries were overweight and obesity kills more people than underweight. 41 million children under the age of 5 were overweight or obese in 2016. Over 340 million children and adolescences aged 5–19 were overweight or obese in 2016. Obesity is preventable.

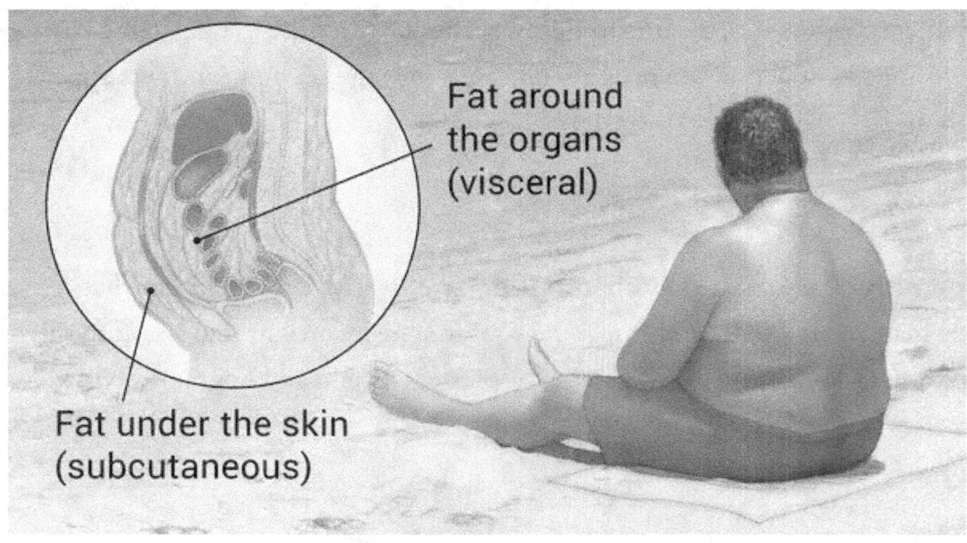

(Fig - 46) Human obesity

Obesity is most commonly caused by a combination of excessive dietary calories, lack of physical activity, and genetic susceptibility, although a few cases are caused primarily by genes, endocrine disorders, medications or psychiatric illness. Evidence to support the view that some obese people eat little yet gain weight due to a slow metabolism. Average obese people have a greater energy expenditure than their thin counterparts due to the energy required to maintain an increased body mass. The primary treatment for obesity is dieting and physical exercise. To supplement this, or in case of failure, anti-obesity drugs may be taken to reduce appetite or inhibit fat absorption. In severe cases, surgery is performed or an intragastric balloon is placed to reduce stomach volume and/or bowel length, leading to earlier satiation and reduced ability to absorb nutrients from food.

Obesity is a leading preventable cause of death worldwide, with increasing prevalence in adults and children, and authorities view it as one of the most serious public health problems of the 21st century. Obesity is stigmatized in the modern Western world,   though it has been perceived as a symbol of wealth and fertility at other times in history, and still is in many parts of Africa.

Effects of obesity on health

Excessive body weight is associated with various diseases and conditions, particularly cardiovascular diseases, diabetes mellitus type 2, obstructive sleep apnea, certain types of cancer, osteoarthritis and asthma. As a result, obesity has been found to reduce life expectancy.

MORTALITY

Obesity is one of the leading preventable causes of death worldwide. A number of reviews have found that mortality risk is lowest at a BMI of 20–25 kg/m in non-smokers and at 24–27 kg/m^2 in current smokers, with risk increasing along with changes in either direction. This appears to apply in at least four continents. In contrast, a 2013 review found that grade 1 obesity (BMI 30–35) was not associated with higher mortality than normal weight, and that overweight (BMI 25–30) was associated with "lower" mortality than was normal weight (BMI 18.5–25). Other evidence suggests that the association of BMI and waist circumference with mortality is U- or J-shaped, while the association between waist-to-hip ratio and waist-to-height ratio with mortality is more positive. In Asians the risk of negative health effects begins to increase between 22–25 kg/m^2. A BMI above 32 kg/m^2 has been associated with a doubled mortality rate among women over a 16-year period. In the United States, obesity is estimated to cause 111,909 to 365,000 deaths per year, while 1 million (7.7%) of deaths in Europe are attributed to excess weight. On average, obesity reduces life expectancy by six to seven years, a BMI of 30–35 kg/m^2 reduces life expectancy by two to four years, while severe obesity (BMI > 40 kg/m^2) reduces life expectancy by ten years.

Although the negative health consequences of obesity in the general population are well supported by the available evidence, health outcomes in certain subgroups seem to be improved at an increased BMI, a phenomenon known as the obesity survival paradox. The paradox was first described in 1999 in overweight and obese people undergoing hemodialysis, and has subsequently been found in those with heart failure and peripheral artery disease (PAD).

In people with heart failure, those with a BMI between 30.0 and 34.9 had lower mortality than those with a normal weight. This has been attributed to the fact that people often lose weight as they become progressively more ill. Similar findings have been made in other types of heart disease. People with class I obesity and heart disease do not have greater rates of further heart problems than people of normal weight who also have heart disease. In people with greater degrees of obesity, however, the risk of further cardiovascular events is increased. Even after cardiac bypass surgery, no increase in mortality is seen in the overweight and obese. One study found that the improved survival could be explained by the more aggressive treatment obese people receive after a cardiac event. Another found that if one takes into account chronic obstructive pulmonary disease(COPD) in those with PAD, the benefit of obesity no longer exists.

MORBIDITY

Morbidity is the departure from a state of physical or psychological well-being, resulting from disease, illness, injury, or sickness, specially where the affected individual is aware of his or her condition. Obesity is one considered as a main cause of morbidity. Obesity and its repercussions constitute an important source of morbidity, impaired quality of life and its complications can have a major bearing on life expectancy. Obesity increases the risk of many physical and mental conditions (Fig - 47). These comorbidities are most commonly shown in metabolic syndrome, a combination of medical disorders which includes diabetes mellitus type 2, high blood pressure, high blood cholesterol, and high triglyceride levels.

Complications are either directly caused by obesity or indirectly related through mechanisms sharing a common cause such as a poor diet or a sedentary lifestyle. The strength of the link between obesity and specific conditions varies. One of the strongest is the link with type 2 diabetes. Excess body fat underlies 64% of cases of diabetes in men and 77% of cases in women.

Health consequences fall into two broad categories: those attributable to the effects of increased fat mass (such as osteoarthritis, obstructive sleep apnea, social stigmatization) and those due to the increased number of fat cells (diabetes, cancer, cardiovascular disease, non-alcoholic fatty liver disease). Increases in body fat alter the body's response to insulin, potentially leading to insulin resistance. Increased fat also creates a proinflammatory state, and a prothrombotic state.

(Fig – 47) Obesity-associated morbidity

CAUSES OF OBESITY

Consuming too many calories: These days people are eating much more food than in previous generations. This used to be the case just in developed nations - however, the trend has spread worldwide. The energy value of food is measured in units called calories. The average physically active man needs about 2,500 calories a day to maintain a healthy weight, and the average physically active woman needs about 2,000 calories a day. Most of the increased food consumption has consisted of carbohydrates (sugars). Increased consumption of sweetened drinks has contributed significantly to the raised carbohydrate intake of most young American adults over the last three decades. The consumption of fast-foods has tripled over the same period.

Various other factors are also said to have contributed to increased calorie and carbohydrate intake. The amount of calories may sound high, but it can be easy to reach if you eat certain types of food. For example, eating a large takeaway hamburger, fries and a milkshake can contribute a total of 1,500 calories – and that's just one meal. Another problem is that many people are not physically active, so lots of the calories they consume end up being stored in their body as fat.

Leading a sedentary lifestyle: With the arrival of televisions, computers, video games, remote controls, washing machines, dish washers and other modern convenience devices, people are commonly leading a much more sedentary lifestyle compared to their parents and grand parents. Some decades ago shopping consisted of walking down the road to the high street where one could find the grocers, bakers, banks, etc. As large out-of-town supermarkets and shopping malls started to appear, people moved from using their feet to driving their cars to get their provisions. In some countries, such as the USA, dependence on the car has become so strong that many people will drive even if their destination is only half-a-mile away. The less you move around the fewer calories you burn. However, this is not only a question of calories. Physical activity has an effect on how your hormones work, and hormones have an effect on how your body deals with food. Several studies have shown that physical activity has a beneficial effect on your insulin levels - keeping them stable. Unstable insulin levels are closely associated with weight gain.

Children who have a television in their bedroom are much more likely to be obese or overweight than kids who do not, researchers from the Pennington Biomedical Research Center in Baton Rouge, LA, reported in the *American Journal of Preventive Medicine* (December 2012 issue). The Department of Health recommends that adults do at least 150 minutes (two-and-a-half hours) of moderate-intensity aerobic activity, such as cycling or fast walking, every week. This doesn't need to be done all in one go, but can be broken down into smaller periods. For example, you could exercise for 30 minutes a day for five days a week.

Poor diet: Obesity doesn't happen overnight. It develops gradually over time, as a result of poor diet and lifestyle choices, such as eating large amounts of processed or fast food that is high in fat and sugar. Drinking too much alcohol contains a lot of calories, and people who drink heavily are often overweight. Eating out a lot and may be tempted to have a starter or dessert in a restaurant, and the food can be higher in fat and sugar. You may be encouraged to eat too much if your friends or relatives are also eating large portions. Drinking too many sugary drinks including soft drinks and fruit juice. If you have low self-esteem or feel depressed, you may eat to make yourself feel better. Unhealthy eating habits tend to run in families. You may learn bad eating habits from your parents when you're young and continue them into adulthood.

Genetics: Like many other medical conditions, obesity is the result of an interplay between genetic and environmental factors. Polymorphisms in various genes controlling appetite and metabolism predispose to obesity when sufficient food energy is present. As of 2006, more than 41 of these sites on the human genome have been linked to the development of obesity when a favourable environment is present. People with two copies of the FTO gene (fat mass and obesity associated gene) have been found on average to weigh 3–4 kg more and have a 1.67-fold greater risk of obesity compared with those without the risk allele. Obesity is a major feature in several syndromes, such as Prader–Willi syndrome, Bardet–Biedl syndrome, Cohen syndrome, and MOMO syndrome (The term "non-syndromic obesity" is sometimes used to exclude these conditions). Prader–Willi syndrome (PWS) is a genetic disorder due to loss of function of specific genes. In newborns symptoms include weak muscles, poor feeding, and slow development. Bardet–Biedl syndrome (BBS) is a ciliopathic human genetic disorder that produces many effects and affects many body systems. It is characterized principally by obesity. Cohen syndrome is caused by gene mutation, has several characteristics such as obesity, mental retardation and craniofacial dysmorphism. MOMO syndrome is an extremely rare genetic disorder which belongs to the overgrowth syndromes and has been diagnosed in only seven cases around the world, and occurs in 1 in 100 million births.

Studies that have focused on inheritance patterns rather than on specific genes have found that 80% of the offspring of two obese parents were also obese, in contrast to less than 10% of the offspring of two parents who were of normal weight. Different people exposed to the same environment have different risks of obesity due to their underlying genetics.

The thrifty gene hypothesis postulates that, due to dietary scarcity during human evolution, people are prone to obesity. Their ability to take advantage of rare periods of abundance by storing energy as fat would be advantageous during times of varying food availability, and individuals with greater adipose reserves would be more likely to survive famine. This tendency to store fat, however, would be maladaptive in societies with stable food supplies. This theory has received various criticisms, and other evolutionarily-based theories such as the drifty gene hypothesis and the thrifty phenotype hypothesis have also been proposed.

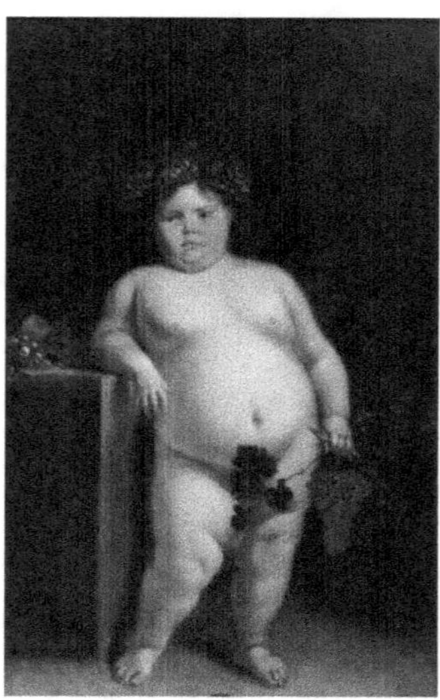

(Fig – 48)A 1680 paintingby Juan Carreno de Miranda of a girl presumed to have Prader–Willi syndrome

MEDICAL AND PSYCHIATRIC ILLNESS

In some cases, underlying medical conditions may contribute to weight gain. These include an underactive thyroid gland (hypothyroidism) – where your thyroid gland doesn't produce enough hormones. Cushing's syndrome – a rare disorder that causes the over-production of steroid hormones. However, if conditions such as these are properly diagnosed and treated, they should pose less of a barrier to weight loss. Certain medicines, including some corticosteroids, medications for epilepsy and diabetes, and some medications used to treat mental illness – including antidepressants and medicines for schizophrenia – can contribute to weight gain. Weight gain can sometimes be a side effect of stopping smoking.

Obesity is not regarded as a psychiatric disorder, and therefore is not listed in the DSM-IVR (Diagnostic and Statistical Manual of Mental Disorders -IV edition) as a psychiatric illness. The risk of overweight and obesity is higher in patients with psychiatric disorders than in persons without psychiatric disorders. Certain medications may cause weight gain or changes in body composition; these include insulin, sulfonylureas, thiazolidinediones, a typical antipsychotics, antidepressants, steroids, certain anticonvulsants (phenytoin and valproate), pizotifen, and some forms of hormonal contraception.

NOT SLEEPING ENOUGH

Research has suggested that if you do not sleep enough your risk of becoming obese doubles. Research was carried out at Warwick Medical School at the University of Warwick. The risk applies to both adults and children. Various research studies clearly showed that sleep deprivation significantly increased obesity risk in both groups.

SOCIAL DETERMINANTS

While genetic influences are important to understanding obesity, they cannot explain the current dramatic increase seen within specific countries or globally. Though it is accepted that energy consumption in excess of energy expenditure leads to obesity on an individual basis, the cause of the shifts in these two factors on the societal scale is much debated. There are a number of theories as to the cause but most believe it is a combination of various factors.

The correlation between social class and BMI varies globally. A review in 1989 found that in developed countries women of a high social class were less likely to be obese. No significant differences were seen among men of different social classes. In the developing world, women, men, and children from high social classes had greater rates of obesity. An update of this review carried out in 2007 found the same relationships, but they were weaker. The decrease in strength of correlation was felt to be due to the effects of globalization. Among developed countries, levels of adult obesity, and percentage of teenage children who are overweight, are correlated with income inequality. A similar relationship is seen among US states: more adults, even in higher social classes, are obese in more unequal states.

Many explanations have been put forth for associations between BMI and social class. It is thought that in developed countries, the wealthy are able to afford more nutritious food, they are under greater social pressure to remain slim, and have more opportunities along with greater expectations for physical fitness. In undeveloped countries the ability to afford food, high energy expenditure with physical labour, and cultural values favouring a larger body size are believed to contribute to the observed patterns. Attitudes toward body weight held by people in one's life may also play a role in obesity. A correlation in BMI changes over time has been found among friends, siblings, and spouses. Stress and perceived low social status appear to increase risk of obesity. Smoking has a significant effect on an individual's weight. Those who quit smoking gain an average of 4.4 kilograms (9.7 lb) for men and 5.0 kilograms (11.0 lb) for women over ten years. Malnutrition in early life is believed to play a role in the rising rates of obesity in the developing world. Endocrine changes that occur during periods of malnutrition may promote the storage of fat once more food energy becomes available. Consistent with cognitive epidemiological data, numerous studies confirm that obesity is associated with cognitive deficits. Whether obesity causes cognitive deficits, or vice versa is unclear at present.

GUT BACTERIA

The study of the effect of infectious agents on metabolism is still in its early stages. Gut flora has been shown to differ between lean and obese humans. There is an indication that gut flora in obese and lean individuals can affect the metabolic potential. This apparent alteration of the metabolic potential is believed to confer a greater capacity to harvest energy contributing to obesity. Whether these differences are the direct cause or the result of obesity has yet to be determined unequivocally. An association between viruses and obesity has been found in humans and several different animal species. The amount that these associations may have contributed to the rising rate of obesity is yet to be determined.

PATHOPHYSIOLOGY

Flier summarizes the many possible pathophysiological mechanisms involved in the development and maintenance of obesity. This field of research had been almost unapproached until leptin was discovered in 1994. Since this discovery, many other hormonal mechanisms have been elucidated that participate in the regulation of appetite and food intake, storage patterns of adipose tissue, and development of insulin resistance. Since leptin's discovery, ghrelin, insulin, orexin, PYY 3–36, cholecystokinin, adiponectin, as well as many other mediators have been studied. The adipokines are mediators produced by adipose tissue; their action is thought to modify many obesity-related diseases. Leptin and ghrelin are considered to be complementary in their influence on appetite, with ghrelin produced by the stomach modulating short-term appetitive control (i.e. to eat when the stomach is empty and to stop when the stomach is stretched). Leptin is produced by adipose tissue to signal fat storage reserves in the body, and mediates long-term appetitive controls (i.e. to eat more when fat storages are low and less when fat storages are high). Although administration of leptin may be effective in a small subset of obese individuals who are leptin deficient, most obese individuals are thought to be leptin resistant and have been found to have high levels of leptin. This resistance is thought to explain in part why administration of leptin has not been shown to be effective in suppressing appetite in most obese people. While leptin and ghrelin are produced peripherally, they control appetite through their actions on the central nervous system. In particular, they and other appetite related hormones act on the hypothalamus, a region of the brain central to the regulation of food intake and energy expenditure. There are several circuits within the hypothalamus that contribute to its role in integrating appetite, the melanocortin pathway being the most well understood. The circuit begins with an area of the hypothalamus, the arcuate nucleus, that has outputs to the lateral hypothalamus (LH) and ventromedial hypothalamus (VMH), the brain's feeding and satiety centers, respectively. The arcuate nucleus contains two distinct groups of neurons. The first group coexpresses neuropeptide Y (NPY) and agouti-related peptide (AgRP) and has stimulatory inputs to the LH and inhibitory inputs to the VMH. The second group coexpresses pro-opiomelanocortin (POMC) and cocaine- and amphetamine regulated transcript (CART) and has stimulatory inputs to the VMH and inhibitory inputs to the LH. Consequently, NPY/AgRP neurons stimulate feeding and inhibit satiety, while POMC/CART neurons stimulate satiety and inhibit feeding. Both groups of arcuate nucleus neurons are regulated in part by leptin. Leptin inhibits the NPY/AgRP group while stimulating the POMC/CART group. Thus a deficiency in leptin signaling, either via leptin deficiency or leptin resistance, leads to overfeeding and may account for some genetic and acquired forms of obesity.

MANAGEMENT

The main treatment for obesity consists of dieting and physical exercise. Diet programs may produce weight loss over the short term, but keeping this weight off can be a problem and often requires making exercise and a lower calorie diet a permanent part of a person's lifestyle. Success rates of long-term weight loss maintenance are low and range from 2–20%. In a more structured setting, however, 67% of people who lost greater than 10% of their body mass maintained or continued to lose weight one year later. An average maintained weight loss of more than 3 kg (6.6 lb) or 3% of total body mass could be sustained for five years. Some studies have found significant benefits in mortality in certain populations with weight loss. In a prospective study of obese women with weight related diseases, intentional weight loss of any amount was associated with a 20% reduction in mortality. In obese women without obesity related illnesses a weight loss of greater than 9 kg (20 lb) was associated with a 25% reduction in mortality. A recent review concluded that certain subgroups such as those with type 2 diabetes and women show long term benefits in all cause mortality, while outcomes for men do not seem to be improved with weight loss. The most effective treatment for obesity is bariatric surgery; however, due to its cost and the risk of complications, researchers are searching for other effective yet less invasive treatments.

DIETING

Diets to promote weight loss are generally divided into four categories: low-fat, low carbohydrate, low-calorie, and very low calorie. A meta-analysis of six randomized controlled trials found no difference between three of the main diet types (low calorie, low carbohydrate, and low fat), with a 2–4 kilogram (4.4–8.8 lb) weight loss in all studies. At two years these three methods resulted in similar weight loss irrespective of the macronutrients emphasized. Very low calorie diets provide 200–800 kcal/day, maintaining protein intake but limiting calories from both fat and carbohydrates. They subject the body to starvation and produce an average weekly weight loss of 1.5–2.5 kilograms (3.3– 5.5 lb). These diets are not recommended for general use as they are associated with adverse side effects such as loss of lean muscle mass, increased risks of gout, and electrolyte imbalances. People attempting these diets must be monitored closely by a physician to prevent complications.

EXERCISE

With use, muscles consume energy derived from both fat and glycogen. Due to the large size of leg muscles, walking, running, and cycling are the most effective means of exercise to reduce body fat. Exercise affects macronutrient balance. During moderate exercise, equivalent to a brisk walk, there is a shift to greater use of fat as a fuel. To maintain health the American Heart Association recommends a minimum of 30 minutes of moderate exercise at least 5 days a week.

A meta-analysis of 43 randomized controlled trials by the Cochrane Collaboration found that exercising alone led to limited weight loss. In combination with diet, however, it resulted in a 1 kilogram weight loss over dieting alone. A 1.5 kilogram loss was observed with a greater degree of exercise. Even though exercise as carried out in the general population has only modest effects, a dose response curve is found, and very intense exercise can lead to substantial weight loss. During 20 weeks of basic military training with no dietary restriction, obese military recruits lost 12.5 kg. High levels of physical activity seem to be necessary to maintain weight loss. A pedometer appears useful for motivation. Over an average of 18-weeks of use physical activity increased by 27% resulting in a 0.38 decreased in BMI.

WEIGHT LOSS PROGRAMS

Weight loss programs often promote lifestyle changes and diet modification. This may involve eating smaller meals, cutting down on certain types of food, and making a conscious effort to exercise more. These programs also enable people to connect with a group of others who are attempting to lose weight, in the hopes that participants will form mutually motivating and encouraging relationships. A number of such popular programs exist, including Weight Watchers, Overeaters Anonymous, and Jenny Craig. These appear to provide modest weight loss (2.9 kg,6.4 lb) over dieting on one's own (0.2 kg, 0.4 lb) over a two year period. Internetbased programs appear to be ineffective. The Chinese government has introduced a number of "fat farms" where obese children go for reinforced exercise, and has passed a law which requires students to exercise or play sports for an hour a day at school.

MEDICATION

The two most commonly used medications to treat obesity: orlistat (Xenical) and sibutramine (Meridia). Only two anti-obesity medications are currently approved by the FDA for long term use. One is orlistat (Xenical), which reduces intestinal fat absorption by inhibiting pancreatic lipase; the other is sibutramine (Meridia), which acts in the brain to inhibit deactivation of the neurotransmitters norepinephrine, serotonin, and dopamine (very similar to some anti-depressants), therefore decreasing appetite. Rimonabant (Acomplia), a third drug, works via a specific blockade of the endocannabinoid system. It has been developed from the knowledge that cannabis smokers often experience hunger, which is often referred to as "the munchies". It had been approved in Europe for the treatment of obesity but has not received approvalin the United States or Canada due to safety concerns. European Medicines Agency in October 2008 recommended the suspension of the sale of rimonabant as the risk seem to be greater than the benefits. Weight loss with these drugs are modest. Over the longer term, average weight loss on orlistat is 2.9 kg (6.4 lb), sibutramine is 4.2 kg (9.3 lb) and rimonabant is 4.7 kg(10.4 lb).

Orlistat and rimonabant lead to a reduced incidence of diabetes, and all three drugs have some effect on cholesterol. However, there is little information on how these drugs affect the longer-term complications or outcomes of obesity. In 2010 the FDA noted concerns that sibutramine increases the risk of heart attacks and strokes in patients with a history of cardiovascular disease. There are a number of less commonly used medications. Some are only approved for short term use, others are used off-label, and still others are used illegally. Most areappetite suppressants that act on one or more neurotransmitters. Phendimetrazine (Bontril), diethylpropion (Tenuate), and phentermine (Adipex-P) are approved by the FDA for short term use, while bupropion (Wellbutrin), topiramate (Topamax), and zonisamide (Zonegran) are sometimes used off-label. The usefulness of certain drugs depends upon the comorbities present. Metformin (Glucophage) is preferred in overweight diabetes, as it may lead to mild weight loss in comparison to sulfonylureas or insulin. The thiazolidinediones, on the other hand, may cause weight gain, but decrease central obesity. Diabetes also achieve modest weight loss with fluoxetine (Prozac), orlistat and sibutramine over 12–57 weeks. Preliminary evidence has however found higher number of cardiovascular events in people taking sibutramine verses control (11.4% vs. 10.0%). The long-term health benefits of these treatments remain unclear. Fenfluramine and dexfenfluramine were withdrawn from the market in 1997, while ephedrine (found in the traditional Chinese herbal medicine *má huáng* made from the *Ephedra sinica*) was removed from the market in 2004. Dexamphetamines are not approved by the FDA for the treatment of obesity due to concerns regarding addiction. The use of these drugs is not recommended due to potential side effects. However, people do occasionally use these drugs illegally.

SURGERY

Bariatric surgery ("weight loss surgery") is the use of surgical intervention in the treatment of obesity. As every operation may have complications, surgery is only recommended for severely obese people (BMI > 40) who have failed to lose weight following dietary modification and pharmacological treatment. Weight loss surgery relies on various principles: the two most common approaches are reducing the volume of the stomach (e.g. by adjustable gastric banding and vertical banded gastroplasty), which produces an earlier sense of satiation, and reducing the length of bowel that comes into contact with food (gastric bypass surgery), which directly reduces absorption. Band surgery is reversible, while bowel shortening operations are not. Some procedures can be performed laparoscopically. Complications from,weight loss surgery are frequent. Surgery for severe obesity is associated with long-term weight loss and decreased overall mortality. One study found a weight loss of between 14% and 25% (depending on the type of procedure performed) at 10 years, and a 29% reduction in all cause mortality when compared to standard weight loss measures. A marked decrease in the risk of diabetes mellitus, cardiovascular disease and cancer has also been found after bariatric surgery. Marked weight loss occurs during the first few months after surgery, and the loss is sustained in the long term. In one study there was an unexplained increase in deaths from accidents and suicide, but this did not outweigh the benefit in terms of disease prevention. When the two main techniques are compared, gastric bypass procedures are found to lead to 30% more weight loss than banding procedures one year after surgery. The effects of liposuction on obesity are less well determined. A treatment involving the placement of an intragastric balloon via gastroscopy has shown promise. One type of balloon lead to a weight loss of 5.7 BMI units over 6 months or 14.7 kg (32.4 lb). Regaining lost weight is common after removal, however, and 4.2% of people were intolerant of the device.

SPECIFIC HUNGER

A type of hunger that is satisfied by specific dietary requirements, such as vitamins and minerals. Many animals vary their food intake according to the nutritive value of the products of digestion. A variety of mechanisms are involved in this type of regulation. The simplest mechanism is the direct detection of the substance in the food, as is the case with sodium. In a free natural environment there are few complete foodstuffs for any particular species. Animals are therefore faced with the task of identifying and ingesting a variety of foods which will constitute a nutritionally complete diet. In addition, they must be able to identify and discriminate those foods which may be safely ingested from among poisonous or inedible foods. The task of obtaining adequate foods may sometimes be further complicated by physiological imbalances or disorders which make it necessary to obtain greater than normal amounts of some nutrient in order to maintain the homeostatic balance and metabolic integrity of the internal environment. Animals can detect sodium in the diet in two main ways. First, sodium salt (NaCl) is a primary aspect of taste in most vertebrates. Secondly, sodium has profound effects upon the body fluids, and its presence there can be directly detected. Sodium appetite appears to be innate, but many animals are adapt at learning and remembering the location of sources of sodium. There are many vitamins and minerals that animals are not able to detect, either by taste or by their levels in the blood. Nevertheless, deficient animals develop strong preferences for foods containing the missing substances. Rats (*Rattus norvegicus*) deficient in thiamine show an immediate marked preference for a novel food, even when that food is thiamine deficient. The preference is short lived. If consumption of a novel food is followed by recovery from the dietary deficiency, however, then the rat rapidly learns to prefer the novel food. Such rapid learning on the basis of the physiological consequences of ingestion enables the rat to exploit new sources of food, and to find out which contains the required ingredients. The effects of a vitamin-deficient diet have much in common with poison avoidance. Vitamin-deficient rats are reluctant to eat familiar food, and show a more than normal interest in novel foods. The aversion to previously familiar food persists even after the animals have recovered from the deficiency. Rats that become sick after eating poisoned food also show an aversion to familiar food and an interest in novel foods. There is very little strong evidence for specific appetite in humans. However, it has been demonstrated that humans have the ability to taste calcium, and indirect evidence supports the idea that patients on kidney dialysis who develop hypocalcemia prefer cheese with greater amounts of calcium added. Exercise also increases the preference for salt. Addison's disease is known to induce a specific craving for sodium, although other diseases causing hyponatremia may not induce the same response. Extreme sodium depletion in human volunteers has been demonstrated to increase the desire for high-salt foods.

PHYSIOLOGICAL BASIS OF DRINKING

Thirst is the motivation to find and consume water. Thirst is the craving for fluids, resulting in the basic instinct of animals to drink. It is an essential mechanism involved in fluid balance. It arises from a lack of fluids and/or an increase in the concentration of certain osmolites, such as salt. If the water volume of the body falls below a certain threshold or the osmolite concentration becomes too high, the brain signals thirst. Thirst motivates water seeking and consumption by both positive and negative valence mechanisms. Thirst positively reinforces drinking behaviour by magnifying the rewarding sensory properties of water: a glass of water tastes wonderful when you are thirsty, but much less so when you are sated. At the same time, thirst negatively reinforces drinking behaviour by virtue of the fact that thirst itself is an unpleasant state, and thus animals are motivated to consume water in order to eliminate this aversive feeling. These two motivational mechanisms act in unison to promote drinking behaviour.

Two kinds of dehydration trigger thirst. All water in the body is present either inside or outside of cells, and the loss of water from these two compartments triggers different behavioural responses. Intracellular dehydration refers to the loss of water from inside cells and is typically caused by an increase in blood osmolality, which draws water out of cells by osmosis and causes them to shrink. By contrast, extracellular dehydration refers to a decrease in the total blood volume, such as occurs during bleeding. Intracellular dehydration can be corrected by drinking water alone, extracellular dehydration requires consumption of both water and salt in order to regenerate the blood at its correct osmolality. For this reason extracellular dehydration triggers not only thirst but also salt appetite.

OSMETRIC AND HYPOVOLEMIC THIRST

There are mainly two kinds of thirsts reported, Osmotic thirst or osmometric thirst. and Hypovolemic thirst.

Osmetric thirst or cellular dehydration thirst

The increase in interstitial fluid solute concentration causes water to migrate from the cells of the body, through their membranes, to the extracellular compartment, by osmosis, thus causing cellular dehydration. It is the thirst resulting from eating salty foods. Eating salty food causes sodium ions to spread through the blood and extracellular fluid of the cell. The higher concentration of solutes outside the cell results in osmotic pressure, drawing water from the cell to the extracellular fluid. Perspiration and excretion of urine from the body increase the salt concentration in the extracellular fluid. Certain neurons detect the loss of water and trigger osmotic thirst to help restore the body to the normal state. The brain detects osmotic pressure from receptors around the third ventricle. The OVLT (Organum Vasculosum Laminae Terminalis) and the subfornical organ detect osmotic pressure and salt content. Receptors in the periphery, including the stomach, which detect high levels of sodium. Receptors in the OVLT, subfornical organ, stomach and elsewhere relay information to areas of the hypothalamus including the supraoptic nucleus and paraventricular nucleus. Both control the rate at which the posterior pituitary releases vasopressin. Receptors also relay information to the lateral preoptic area which controls drinking. When osmotic thirst is triggered, water that you drink has to be absorbed through the digestive system. To inhibit thirst, the body monitors swallowing and detects the water contents of the stomach and intestines.

Hypovolemic thirst

It is the thirst resulting from loss of fluids due to bleeding or sweating. It is associated with low volume of body fluids. Triggered by the release of the hormones vasopressin and angiotensin II, which constrict blood vessels to compensate for a drop in blood pressure. Angiotensin II stimulates neurons in areas adjoining the third ventricle. Neurons in the third ventricle send axons to the hypothalamus where angiotensin II is also released as a neurotransmitter. Animals with osmotic thirst have a preference for pure water. Animals with hypovolemic thirst have a preference for slightly salty water as pure water dilutes body fluids and changes osmotic pressure.

There are many different receptors for sensing decreased volume or an increased osmolite concentration. The control of the concentration and volume of the body fluids equally clearly a matter of cooperation between internal and external mechanisms of homeostasis between hormonal regulation and drinking behaviour, and is associated particularly with the supraoptic region. Certain cells in this region acts as osmoreceptors, stimulating the release of ADH when the blood becomes too concentrarted, autonomic afferents carrying information about blood volume from stretch receptors in the venous circulation also appear to contribute to the control of ADH by hypothalamus. Other information that is relevant to the regulation of water balance comes from the receptors in the subfrontal region, just above the hypothalamus, they respond to hormone angiotensin

Renin-angiotensin system

Hypovolemia leads to activation of the renin- angiotensin system (RAS) (Fig - 49)and a decrease in atrial natriuretic peptide. These mechanisms, along their other functions, contribute to elicit thirst, by affecting the subfornical organ. For instance, angiotensin II, activated in RAS, is a powerful dipsogen (ie it stimulates thirst) which acts via the subfornical organ. The renin–angiotensin system (RAS) or the renin–angiotensin–aldosterone system (RAAS) is a hormone system that regulates blood pressure and fluid balance. When renal blood flow is reduced, juxtaglomerular cells in the kidneys convert the precursor – prorenin, already present in the blood into renin and secrete it directly into the circulation. Plasma renin then carries out the conversion of angiotensinogen, released by the liver, to angiotensin I. Angiotensin I is subsequently converted to angiotensin II by the angiotensin-converting enzyme (ACE) found in the lungs. Angiotensin II is a potent vasoconstrictive peptide that causes blood vessels to narrow, resulting in increased blood pressure. Angiotensin II also stimulates the secretion of the hormone aldosterone from the adrenal cortex. Aldosterone causes the renal tubules to increase the reabsorption of sodium and water into the blood, while at the same time causing the excretion of potassium (to maintain electrolyte balance). This increases the volume of extracellular fluid in the body, which also increases blood pressure.

If the RAS is abnormally active, blood pressure will be too high. There are many drugs that interrupt different steps in this system to lower blood pressure. These drugs are one of the primary ways to control high blood pressure, heart failure, kidney failure, and harmful effects of diabetes.

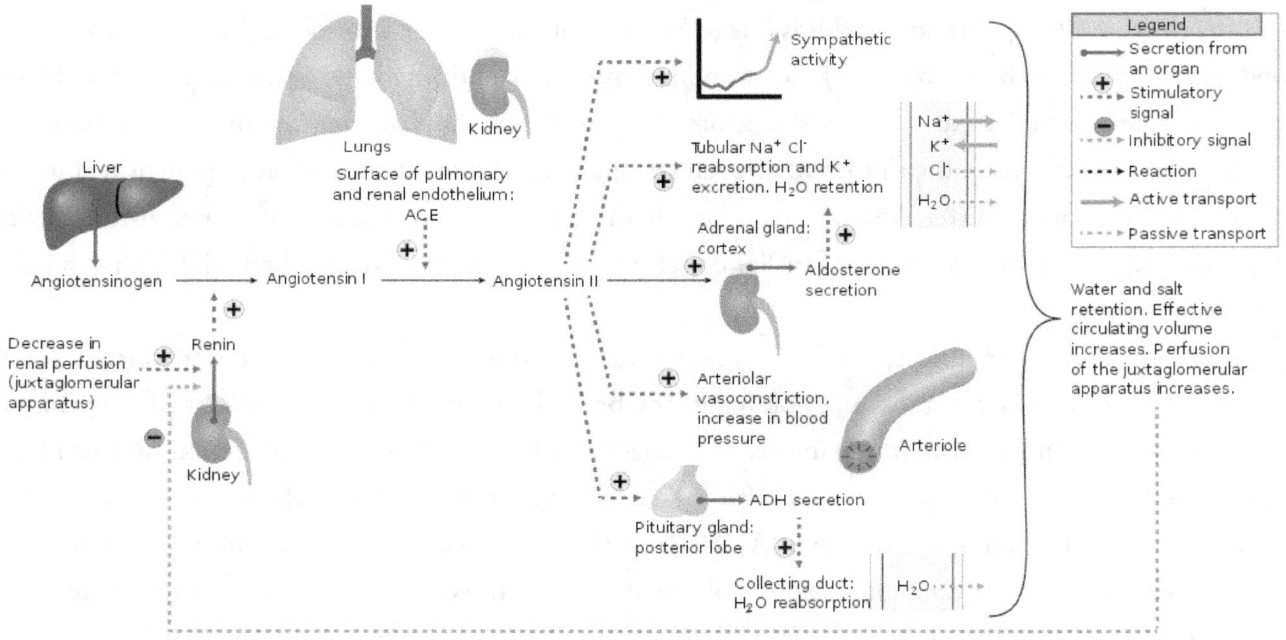

(Fig - 49) Renin angiotensin- aldosterone system

INCREASED OSMOLITE CONCENTRATION

An increase in osmotic pressure, e.g. after eating a salty meal activates osmoreceptors. There are osmoreceptors already in the central nervous system, more specifically in the hypothalamus, notably in two circumventricular organs that lack an effective blood-brain barrier, the organum vasculosum of the lamina terminalis (OVLT) and the subfornical organ (SFO). However, although located in the same parts of the brain, these osmoreceptors that evoke thirst are distinct from the neighbouring osmoreceptors in the OVLT and SFO that evoke arginine vasopressin release to decrease fluid output. In addition, there are visceral osmoreceptors. These project to the area postrema and nucleus tractus solitarii inthe brain. Because sodium is also lost from the plasma in hypovolemia, the body's need for salt proportionately increases in addition to thirst in such cases. This is also a result of the renin-angiotensin system activation. For adults over age 50, the body's thirst sensation diminishes and continues diminishing with age, causing many to suffer symptoms of dehydration. The area postrema and nucleus tractus solitarius signal, by 5-HT (5-hydroxytryptamine receptors), to lateral parabrachial nucleus, which in turn signal to median preoptic nucleus. In addition, the area postrema and nucleus tractus solitarius also signal directly to subfornical organ. Thus, the median preoptic nucleus and subfornical organ receive signals of both decreased volume and increased osmolite concentration. They signal to higher integrative centers, where ultimately the conscious craving arises. However, the true neuroscience of this conscious craving is not fully clear.

REGULATING DRINKING BEHAVIOUR

Thirst is a conscious sensation that results in a desire to drink. Although all normal humans experience thirst, science can offer no precise definition of this phenomenon because it involves numerous physiological responses to a change in internal fluid status, complex patterns of central nervous system function, and psychological motivation. Three factors are typically recognized as components of thirst: a body water deficit, brain integration of central and peripheral nerve messages relating to the need for water, and an urge to drink. In laboratory experiments, thirst is measured empirically with subjective perceptual scales (for example, ranging from "not thirsty at all" to "very, very thirsty") and drinking behaviour is quantified by observing the timing and volume of fluid consumed. Psychologists classify thirst as a drive, a basic compelling urge that motivates action. Other human drives involve a lack of nutrients (for example, glucose, sodium), oxygen, or sleep; these are satiated by eating, breathing, and sleeping. Clark Hull published a major, relevant theory describing the nature of human drives in 1943. He observed that learned habits, in addition to the thirst drive, influence drinking strongly. If a behaviour reduces thirst, that behaviour is reinforced and learned as a habit. Irrelevant behaviours (for example, sneezing, grooming) provide no reinforcement, have no effect on drinking, and do not become habits. Further, Hull realized that external incentives, such as the qualities or quantity of a fluid, also influence fluid consumption. On a hot summer day, for example, a cold beverage is more attractive than a cup of hot tea. Yet when chilled to a very low temperature, a cold beverage becomes an aversive stimulus to drinking behaviour. Physiologists have popularized the term alliesthesia (from Greek root words referring to altered sensation) to describe the fact that the sensation of thirst may have either pleasant or unpleasant qualities, depending on the intensity of the stimulus and the state of the person.

Numerous investigations have verified that thirst and drinking behaviour are complex entities. For example, drinking behaviour (that is, the timing and the amount of fluid consumed) is not linearly related to the intensity of perceived thirst. Nor should we infer that individuals experience thirst simply because they drink. These facts indicate that thirst and drinking behaviour are distinct entities that influence each other and are influenced by numerous internal and external factors.

Physiological Components of Thirst

Thirst is often viewed by physiologists and physicians as a central nervous system mechanism that regulates the body's water and minerals. The significance of the thirst drive is emphasized by three facts: 50 to 70 percent of adult body weight is water, the average adult ingests and loses 2.5 liters of water each day, and body weight is regulated within 0.2 percent from one day to the next. Clearly, water is essential to life and the body responds in a manner that ensures survival.

In 1954, Edward Adolph and colleagues proposed a multiple-factor theory of thirst that has not been refuted to date. This theory states that no single mechanism can account for all drinking behaviour and that multiple mechanisms, sometimes with identical functions, act concurrently.

Among these, thirst appears to be regulated primarily by evaluation of changes in the concentration of extracellular fluid, measured as the osmolality of blood plasma. Osmolality is a measurement that describes the concentration of all dissolved solids in a solution, that is, dissolved substances per unit of solvent. In research and clinical laboratories, the unit for osmolality of blood is Osm/kg or osmoles per kilogram of water. Below a certain threshold level of plasma osmolality, thirst is absent. Above this threshold, a strong desire to drink appears in response to an increase of 2 to 3 percent in the level of dissolved substances in blood. The brain's thirst center lies deep within the brain, in an area known as the hypothalamus. This anatomical site contains cells that respond to changes in the concentration of body fluids. When the thirst center is stimulated by an increased concentration of blood (that is, dehydration), thirst and fluid consumption increase. As the brain senses the concentration of blood, it allows a minor loss of body water before stimulating the drive to drink. This phenomenon has been named voluntary dehydration. Specifically, several research studies since the 1930s have observed that adults and children replace only 34 to 87 percent of the water lost as sweat, by drinking during exercise or labour in hot environments. The resulting dehydration is due to the fact that thirst is not perceived until a 1 to 2 percent body weight loss occurs. Inter individual differences, resulting in great voluntary dehydration in some individuals, have caused them to be named reluctant drinkers. Reduced extracellular fluid volume, including blood volume, also increases thirst. Experiments (for example, reducing blood volume without altering blood concentration) have demonstrated that volume-sensitive receptors in the heart and blood vessels likely regulate drinking behaviour by increasing the secretion of hormones. Osmolality-sensitive nerves in the mouth, throat, and stomach also play a role in abating thirst. As fluid passes through the mouth and upper gastrointestinal tract, the sense of dryness decreases. When this fluid fills the stomach, stretch receptors sense an increase in gastric fullness and the thirst drive diminishes.

As dehydration causes the body's extracellular fluid to become more concentrated, the fluid inside cells moves outward, resulting in intracellular dehydration and cell shrinkage, and the hormone arginine vasopressin (AVP, also known as the antidiuretic hormone) is released from the brain. AVP serves two purposes: to reduce urine output at the kidneys and to enhance thirst; both serve to restore normal fluid balance. Other hormones influence fluid-mineral balance directly and thirst indirectly. Renin, angiotensin II, and aldosterone are noteworthy examples. As dehydration reduces circulating blood volume, blood pressure decreases and renin is secreted from blood vessels inside the kidneys. Renin activates the hormone angiotensin II, which subsequently stimulates the release of aldosterone from the adrenal glands. Both angiotensin II and aldosterone increase blood pressure and enhance the retention of sodium and water; these effects indirectly reduce the intensity of thirst. Angiotensin II also affects thirst directly. When injected into sensitive areas of the brain, it causes a rapid increase in water consumption that is followed by a slower increase in sodium chloride consumption and water retention by the kidneys.

HOST FACTORS

Repeated training sessions in cool or hot environments alter fluid consumption in four ways. First, physical training increases the secretion of the hormone AVP, which stimulates drinking and body water retention. Second, exercise-heat acclimation (that is, adaptations due to exercise in a hot environment over eight days) increases the volume of fluid consumed and the number of times that adults drink during exercise. Third, frequent rest periods, in the midst of labour or exercise, will increase fluid replacement time and enhance fluid consumption. Humans tend to drink less when they are preoccupied or are performing physical or mental tasks. Fourth, learned behaviours can enhance fluid consumption when thirst is absent. This phenomenon is widely appreciated among military personnel and athletes who are trained to consume water at regular intervals, whether they are thirsty or not. Several research groups have reported that chronological age influences thirst and drinking behaviour. Elderly men experience a blunted thirst drive and reduced fluid intake, perhaps due to their brains' reduced ability to sense changes in plasma osmolality or blood volume. Further, elderly individuals experience a decrease in the ability of their kidneys to conserve water. This suggests that the elderly are predisposed to dehydration when illness increases water loss (that is, vomiting, diarrhea) or when physical incapacity prevents access to water.

Fluid and Environmental Characteristics

Many fluid characteristics stimulate or enhance drinking, during or after exposure to a hot environment. Fluid temperature (consumption is greatest at 14 to 16°C, reduced above 37°C), turbidity, sweetness, fruit flavourings (for example, cherry, grape, orange, lemon), addition of citric acid which imparts a citrus flavour, and addition of sodium chloride or other minerals are examples. These components enhance palatability and increase fluid consumption. The addition of a small amount of salt (sodium chloride), besides enhancing palatability, may result in thirst and increased drinking, due to the specific action of sodium on fluid movements. An increased sodium concentration outside of cells causes water to leave cells via osmosis. The resulting cellular dehydration is an important stimulus for drinking. Increased beverage carbonation tends to reduce the palatability of a fluid as well as the volume of fluid consumed, without an increase in thirst. In addition, intakes of food and water are closely related. During 24-hour observations of fluid intake, most studies report that the majority of fluid (69 to 78 percent) is consumed during meals. The foregoing characteristics, therefore, tend to reduce the magnitude of voluntary dehydration. Conversely, fluid characteristics may influence drinking behaviour negatively, regardless of the intensity of thirst. Experiments conducted during mild prolonged exercise have shown that the following qualities are perceived as undesirable: nausea, bloating, an objectionable feeling in the mouth, excessive viscosity, and excessive sweetness. Exercise and high ambient temperature may independently alter an individual's perception of fluid palatability. For example, drinking behaviour increases when air temperature exceeds 25°C. Fluid consumption can also be enhanced by changing the shape of a fluid container, proximity of fluid containers to the drinker, volume of fluid that is available, and time allowed for drinking. Societal customs may influence fluid consumption, as evidenced by cross-cultural differences in beverage preferences. Even rituals, such as accepting the friendly offer of a beverage in a social setting, may enhance fluid intake beyond that driven by physiological cues. These factors usually involve learned habits. Similarly, when people repeatedly drink fluids with initially unfamiliar flavours, the palatability of the fluids is enhanced.

There are two magnitudes of thirst altering factors. The Factors that influences to increase the thirst are increased concentration of blood, decreased blood volume, decreased blood pressure, mouth and throat dryness and increased angiotensin II. Whereas the factors that decreased the thirst includes decreased concentration of blood, increased blood volume, increased blood pressure,increased stomach fullness and decreased angiotensin II.

Clinical disturbances in thirst

Clinically, thirst and increased intake of fluid may mean a normally functioning thirst mechanism responding to dehydration or they may indicate an abnormality of the thirst mechanism itself which results in excessive drinking. In addition, when water is freely available and intake does not match water losses, it must be supposed that there is some disturbance in thirst or in the signals generating it. Diminished or absent thirst results in progressive dehydration. When drinking exceeds water losses, there will be progressive accumulation of fluid and possibly water intoxication if the water is not accompanied by appropriate solute. It is not difficult to recognise the more extreme forms of excessive thirst. In diabetes insipidus insatiable thirst so dominates the patient's existence that his daily routine is centered on his need for water and his sleep is disturbed. However, in most cases of diabetes insipidus the increased drinking is the response of a normally functioning thirst mechanism to urinary loss of body fluid. Actual disturbances of the thirst mechanisms leading to excessive drinking are not necessarily as obvious as the sometimes dramatic polydipsia of diabetes insipidus. Intake of water may not, in fact, be greater than normal, but drinking of even small amounts of water is inappropriate if the intake exceeds the fluid loss. Therefore, in the diagnosis of clinical thirst it is not enough to measure only the amount of water drunk. It is also necessary to assess any trend in the overall fluid balance by noting any obvious disproportion between intake and urine volume and by looking for evidence of clinical oedema. Disturbances in thirst may be classified as follows:

1. **Symptomatic thirst**: This includes all those cases where thirst results from the loss of body water or electrolytes. Notable examples occur in severe vomiting (e.g., pyloric stenosis), severe diarrhoea (e.g., cholera), true diabetes insipidus (i.e., where there is a failure to release antidiuretic hormone, ADH), nephrogenic diabetes insipidus, diabetes mellitus, certain forms of chronic renal failure, sodium depletion, potassium depletion and hypercalcemia. In all these cases the thirst mechanism is functioning normally, and polydipsia is a physiological response to dehydration.

2. **Pathological thirst**: The patient is thirsty despite the fact that the body is normally hydrated or even overhydrated. The thirst mechanism is therefore directly and inappropriately activated. Examples of pathological thirst are as follows: primary polydipsia caused by continued irritation of the thirst neurones by tumor, trauma, inflammation, compulsive water drinking, stimulation of neural thirst systems by high plasma renin concentrations, possible direct stimulation of centers in hypercalcemia or in hypokalemia, and drinking during the onset of oedema in congestive heart failure. Thirst in oedematous states is interesting because it implies that the mechanisms that control water intake are being provided with misleading information about the fluid status of the body. Oedema fluid represents an excess of intake over loss, and though the kidneys are at fault in not excreting sufficient water and electrolyte, the continuing intake indicates inappropriate activation of thirst mechanisms. It has been reported that patients with congestive heart failure sometimes show intense thirst. In most cases of pathological thirst, it must be recognized that the body fluids are often normal, that thirst does not indicate a need for water and that continuing excessive intake may be harmful leading to complications such as oedema and water intoxication.

3. **Hypodipsia**: In the absence of thirst the kidney's capacity for water conservation is easily exceeded resulting in hypertonic dehydration. If, as is usually the case, the pathological process affects the supraopticohypophyseal system as well as the thirst centers, the accompanying diabetes insipidus exacerbates the dehydration and makes the clinical management extremely difficult. The cause of the hypodipsia is usually a slowly growing tumor (e.g., craniopharyngioma, ectopic pinealoma or germinoma, glioma), SchUller-Christian disease or trauma. Several derangements of thirst and ADH secretion that can cause abnormalities of water metabolism have been described. Where the ADH secreting mechanism is functioning normally, chronic dehydration and hypernatremia resulting from inadequate water intake can be satisfactorily dealt with by insisting that the patient drinks enough water. When hypodipsia complicates classical diabetes insipidus or ADI-I reset, the problem is more difficult but chlorpropamide has been found useful because it has the dual action of improving renal concentrating ability and augmenting drinking behaviour. Chlorpropamide is a sulfonyl urea and stimulates insulin secretion. There is indirect evidence that sulfonyl ureas increase 3', 5'-adenosine monophosphate (cyclic AMP) and this may be the basis of their antidiuretic action. It is also conceivable that enhanced thirst is in some way related to cyclic AMP. The f3-adrenergic agent isoproterenol is a potent dipsogen and the effects of f3-adrenergic stimulation are cyclic AMP mediated. However, the role if any of cyclic AMP in the control of water intake is unknown.

PHYSIOLOGICAL BASIS OF SEXUAL BEHAVIOUR

Human sexuality, is a general term referring to various sexually related aspects of human life, including physical and psychological development, and behaviours, attitudes, and social customs associated with the individual's sense of gender, relationships, sexual activity, mate selection, and reproduction. Sexuality permeates many areas of human life and culture, thereby setting humans apart from other members of the animal kingdom, in which the objective of sexuality is more often confined to reproduction. Human sexual behaviour or human sexual practices or human sexual activities refers to the manner in which humans experience and express their sexuality. It encompasses a wide range of activities, such as strategies to find or attract partners (mating and display behaviour), interactions between individuals, physical or emotional intimacy, and sexual contact.

History

In Europe and the United States, the scientific study of human sexuality began in the late 19th century during the Victorian Age, a time of repressive sexual norms. German psychiatrist Richard von Krafft-Ebing focused on what he considered to be the psychopathological problems of sex. Viennese physician Sigmund Freud, founder of psychoanalysis, considered sexuality central to his psychoanalytic theory. Havelock Ellis, an English physician, collected a wealth of information on sexuality from case histories, medical research, and anthropological reports. The first work in his series studies in the Psychology of Sex was published in 1896. His scientific objectivity foreshadowed modern sexology. Early in the 20th century, German physician Magnus Hirshfeld founded the first sex-research institute in Germany. He conducted the first large-scale sex survey, collecting data from 10,000 men and women. He also initiated the first journal for publishing the results of sex studies, and started a marriage-counseling service. Most of his materials were destroyed by the Nazis during World War II (1939–1945). In the early 1930s, American anthropologist Margaret Mead and British anthropologist Bronislaw Malinowski began collecting data on sexual behaviour in other cultures. The most noted scientific studies of sexuality in the 20th century are those of American biologist Alfred Charles Kinsey and his colleagues and those of William H. Masters and Virginia Johnson. Kinsey began interviewing people about their sexual histories in 1938, and with his colleagues he published Sexual Behaviour in the Human Male (1948) and Sexual Behaviour in the Human Female (1953), based mostly on interviews with 5300 white men and 5940 white women. Masters and Johnson began their clinical studies of the physiology of sexual response and sexual dysfunctions in the 1950s. These observations were published in Human Sexual Response (1966) and Human Sexual Inadequacy (1970), among others. The AIDS crisis has prompted a number of contemporary surveys of sex, including the National Health and Social Life Survey, the results of which were published in the book Sex In America (1994). As in any area of science, particularly relatively new and sensitive areas such as sex research, these studies have been criticized, on the basis of their findings and methodologies, but each study brings us closer to a fuller understanding of human sexuality.

Definition of sex

Sex is the fundamental distinction, found in most species of animals and plants, based on the type of gametes produced by the individual and the category to which the individual fits on the basis of that criterion is also called gender. The sex can be determined on the basis of chromosomal method by the presence of XX female of XY male genotype in somatic cells without regard to phenotypic manifestations, is also called as genetic sex. There is another method of sex determination through phenotypic manifestations of endocrine influence such as development of sex and genital organs. Gonadal sex is determined on the basis of the gonadal tissue present (ovarian or testicular).

Human Sexual Characteristics

Sexual characteristics are divided into two types. Primary sexual characteristics are directly related to reproduction and include the sex organs (genitalia). Secondary sexual characteristics are attributes other than the sex organs that generally distinguish one sex from the other but are not essential to reproduction, such as the larger breasts characteristic of women and the facial hair and deeper voices characteristic of men.

There are two periods of marked sexual differentiation in human life. The first occurs prenatally and the second occurs at puberty. Although adult women and men may differ greatly in genital appearance and secondary sexual characteristics, they are almost identical during prenatal development. When an egg and a sperm unite during fertilization, they each bring to the new cell half the number of chromosomes (thread like structures that contain genetic material) present in other cells. From fertilization to about the first six weeks of development, male and female embryos differ only in the pair of sex chromosomes they have in each cell—two X chromosomes (XX) in females and one X and one Y chromosome (XY) in males. At this stage, both male and female embryos have undifferentiated gonads (ovaries or testes), two sets of ducts (one set capable of developing into male internal organs and the other into female organs), and undifferentiated external genital folds and swellings.

Prenatal Sexual Development

About six weeks after conception, if a Y chromosome is present in the embryo's cells (as it is in normal males), a gene on the chromosome directs the undifferentiated gonads to become testes. If the Y chromosome is not present (as in normal females), the undifferentiated gonads will become ovaries. These androgens stimulate development of the one set of the genital ducts into the epididymes, vas deferens, and ejaculatory duct. The presence of androgens also stimulates development of the penis and the scrotum. The testes later descend into the scrotum. Males also produce a substance that inhibits the development of the second set of ducts into female organs. In the absence of such hormonal stimulation, female structures develop. Prenatal hormones also play a role in the sexual differentiation of the brain. For example, prenatal hormones direct the development of sex differences in some cells and the neural pathways in the hypothalamus (the part of the brain that controls the endocrine system). Beginning at puberty, based on prenatal sexual differentiation, the hypothalamus directs either the cyclic secretion of sex hormones that controls the female menstrual cycle or the relatively continuous production of male sex hormones. Other brain differences may be related to differences in sexual and aggressive behaviour or in cognitive and perceptual characteristics. Most of the research on sexual differentiation of the brain has been performed with animals or with biased human samples, and there is much debate about the nature and behavioural relevance of these differences in humans.

Postnatal Sexual Development

After birth, the process of sex-role socialization begins immediately. There may be small, physiologically-based differences present at birth that lead girls and boys to perceive the world or behave in slightly different ways. There are also well-documented differences in the ways that boys and girls are treated from birth onward. The behavioural differences between the sexes, such as differences in toy and play preference and in the degree of aggressive behaviour, are most likely the product of complex interactions between the way that the child perceives the world and the ways that parents, siblings, and others react to the child. The messages about appropriate behaviour for girls and boys intensify differences between the sexes as the child grows older. As the first bodily changes of puberty begin, sometime from the age of 8 to the age of 12, the child may become self-conscious and more private. Because preadolescents tend to play with others of their own sex, it is not at all uncommon that early sexual exploration and experience may happen with other members of the same sex.

Sexual orientation

Sexual orientation may become a question during puberty or adolescence. The term sexual orientation refers to a person's erotic, romantic, or affectional attraction to the other sex, the same sex, or both. A person who is attracted to the other sex is labeled heterosexual, or sometimes straight. A person attracted to the same sex is labeled homosexual. The word gay may be used to describe homosexuals and is most often applied to men, whereas the term lesbian is applied to homosexual women. A person who is attracted to both men and women is labeled bisexual. A trans sexual is a person whose sense of self is not consistent with his or her anatomical sex—for example, a person whose sense of self is female but who has male genitals. Homosexuality is not synonymous with transsexuality. Homosexual men's sense of self is male and lesbian women's sense of self is female.

Physiology of sex

Understanding the processes and underlying mechanisms of sexual arousal and orgasm is important to help people become more familiar with their bodies and their sexual responses and to assist in the diagnosis and treatment of sexual dysfunctions. Nevertheless, it was not until the work of American gynecologist William H. Masters and American psychologist Virginia Johnson that detailed labouratory studies were conducted on the physiological aspects of sexual arousal and orgasm in a large number of men and women. Based on data from 312 men and 382 women and observations from more than 10,000 cycles of sexual arousal and orgasm, Masters and Johnson described the human sexual response cycle in four stages: excitement, plateau, orgasm, and resolution.

Sexual Response Cycle

Excitement -The excitement stage of sexual arousal is characterized by increased blood flow to blood vessels (vasocongestion), which causes tissues to swell. Both women and men may develop "sex flush" during this or later stages of the sexual response cycle, although this reaction appears to be more common among women. Sex flush usually starts on the upper abdomen and spreads to the chest. In addition, pulse rate and blood pressure increase during the excitement phase.

- ❖ Plateau – During the plateau stage, vasocongestion peaks and the processes begun in the excitement stage continue until sufficient tension is built up for orgasm to occur. Breathing rate, pulse rate, and blood pressure increase.

- ❖ Orgasm – Orgasm, or climax, is an intense and usually pleasurable sensation that occurs at the peak of sexual arousal and is followed by a drop in sexual tension. Not all sexual arousal leads to orgasm, and individuals require different conditions and different types and amounts of stimulation in order to have an orgasm. Orgasm consists of a series of rhythmic contractions in the genital region and pelvic organs. Breathing rate, pulse rate, and blood pressure increase dramatically during orgasm.

- ❖ Resolution – During resolution, the processes of the excitement and plateau stages reverse, and the bodies of both women and men return to the unaroused state. The muscle contractions that occurred during orgasm lead to a reduction in muscular tension and release of blood from the engorged tissues. Resolution generally takes from 15 to 30 minutes, but it may take longer, especially if orgasm has not occurred.

Sexual Behaviours

The reason why and how humans and other animals engage in the 3C's – courting, copulating and cohabitating has not been well studied. Still it is seen that all sexual/reproductive behaviourhave 4 stages in their completion. They are Sexual Attraction, Appetitive Behaviour, Copulation, and Post Copulatory Behaviour.

- ❖ Sexual Attraction – Sexual attraction is the first step in bringing the male and female together. Physical attributes, pheromones/hormonal action, postures, gestures, eye contact, verbal/ non verbal communication etc., are seen to initiate this stage. Once mutually attracted, the pair may progress to the second stage of appetitive behaviours.

- ❖ Appetitive Behaviour – These behaviours establish, maintain, or promote sexual interaction. The female mammal that engages in such behaviour is said to be Proceptive. Male behaviours usually consist of staying near the female. If both exhibit such behaviour they may progress to the next stage of mating.

- ❖ Copulation – Also termed as Coitus. It refers to the act that sexual species engage in to provide the male's semen to the female. There occurs the insertion of the male genitalia into the female genitalia. This behaviour of insertion is reffered to as Intromission. After copulation they will not mate again for some period of time, which is called Refractory period.
- ❖ Post Copulatory Behaviour – These behaviours are varied across species and not so expressed in humans. Parental behaviours like egg laying, incubation, feeding squabs etc., are seen in other animals.

Brain and sexual behaviour

The brain is the structure that translates the nerve impulses from the skin into pleasurable sensations. It controls nerves and muscles used during sexual behaviour. The brain regulates the release of hormones, which are believed to be the physiological origin of sexual desire. The cerebral cortex, which is the outer layer of the brain that allows for thinking and reasoning, is believed to be the origin of sexual thoughts and fantasies. Beneath the cortex is the limbic system, which consists of the amygdala, hippocampus, cingulate gyrus, and septal area. These structures are where emotions and feelings are believed to originate, and are important for sexual behaviour.

The hypothalamus is the most important part of the brain for sexual functioning. This is the small area at the base of the brain consisting of several groups of nerve-cell bodies that receives input from the limbic system. Studies with lab animals have shown that destruction of certain areas of the hypothalamus causes complete elimination of sexual behaviour. One of the reasons for the importance of the hypothalamus is its relation to the pituitary gland, which secretes the hormones that are produced in the hypothalamus.

Hormones and sexual behaviour

Sex Hormone, is any of the several chemical substances that affect the development and functioning of the reproductive system in vertebrates, or animals with a backbone. The sex hormones are divided into three major groups: gonadotropins, gonadal hormones, and lactogens. Gonadotropins stimulate the gonads, which are sperm- or egg-producing organs. The male gonads are the testes, which produce sperm, and the female gonads are the ovaries, which produce eggs. Gonadotropins are secreted by the pituitary gland, which is located in the center of the brain and is controlled by an area of the brain known as the hypothalamus. Gonadotropins, such as the leutinizing hormone (LH) and the follicle-stimulating hormone (FSH) in females and the interstitial cell-stimulating hormone (ICSH) in males, control the development and functions of the ovaries and testes, including menstruation and sperm production. Gonadal hormones such as estrogen, progesterone, and testosterone are secreted primarily by the testes and ovaries, placenta (the sac of nutritive tissue that supports and protects the fetus), and adrenal glands. Their chief function is to regulate the development of the secondary sex characteristics such as deepening of the voice in males and distribution of body hair. The third group, the lactogens, are secreted by the pituitary gland and are necessary for the secretion of milk in the mammary glands of mammals. They are also believed to affect maternal behaviour patterns. Sex hormones regulate the development of sexual organs, sexual behaviour, reproduction, and pregnancy. Another gonadotropin called luteinizing hormone regulates the production of eggs in women and the production of the male sex hormone testosterone. Testosterone regulates changes in the male body during puberty, influences sexual behaviour, and plays a role in growth. The female sex hormones, called estrogens, regulate female sexual development and behaviour as well as some aspects of pregnancy. Progesterone, a female hormone secreted in the ovaries, regulates menstruation and stimulates lactation in humans and other mammals. The hormonal theory of sexuality holds that, just as exposure to certain hormones plays a role in foetal sex differentiation, such exposure also influences the sexual orientation that emerges later in the adult. Foetal hormones may be seen as the primary determiner of adult sexual orientation, or a co-factor with genes and /or environmental and social conditions.

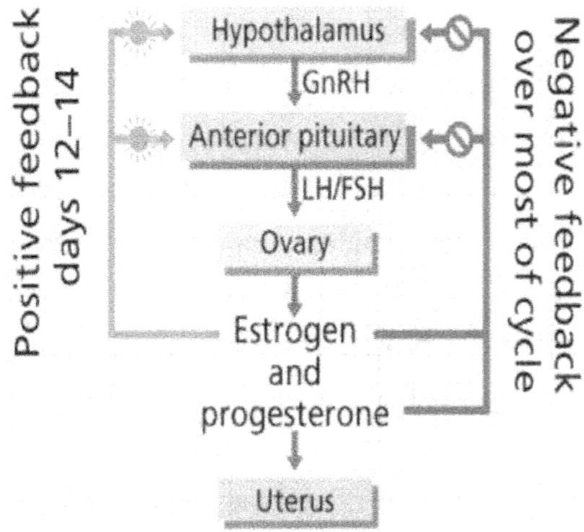

(Fig - 50) Hormonal control of female reproductive functions

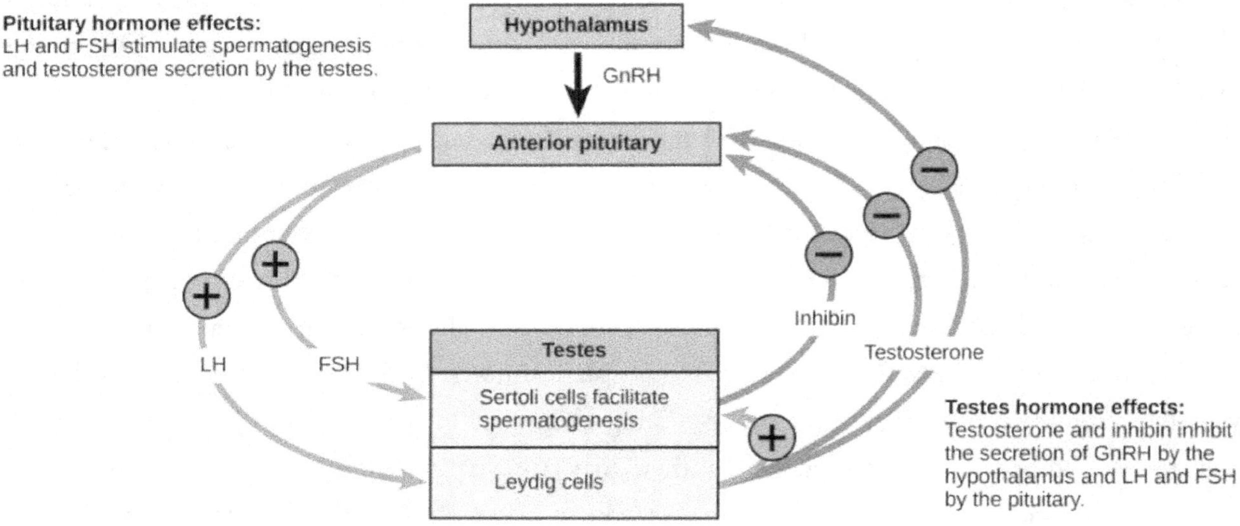

(Fig - 51) Hormonal control of Male Reproductive functions

External cues

Animals use a variety of visual, auditory, and chemical signals throughout courtship and mating. Some are important for identification—firefly species, for example, are remarkably similar, and during courtship, each species sends out a unique pattern of flashes to signal its identity to potential mates. Frogs use a vocal morse code for species recognition, and birds sing different kinds of songs to announce their species identity. Visual cues often help animals locate each other in habitats with dense vegetation. The black and white markings of pandas, for instance, help individuals stand out in the thick bamboo forests where they live. Audio cues are also used to help animals find each other. The very low sounds of a male elephant, inaudible to human ears, are a beckoning call that females can hear up to 4.8 km away. Chorusing bullfrogs, bugling elk, and warbling songbirds build a fence of sound that warns off competing males, while enticing females to check out the territory. Recently, there has been huge interest in studying human behavioural cues that could be useful for developing an interactive and adaptive human-machine system. Unintentional human gestures such as making an eye rub, a chin rest, a lip touch, a nose itch, a head scratch, an ear scratch, and a finger lock have been found conveying some useful information in specific context. Some researchers have tried to extract such gestures in a specific context of educational applications. Chemical cues called pheromones bring together individuals that are separated by miles. A male silk moth, for example, can detect the female's invitational pheromones at a distance of up to 11 km. Many fish species, highly sensitive to chemicals in the water, secrete pheromones to locate mating partners. Pheromones can also indicate fertility to a prospective mate. The female giraffe secretes pheromones in her urine that are detected by the male. These pheromones announce her fertility and signal the correct timing for courtship and mating.

Other studies have suggested that people might be using odour cues associated with the immune system to select mates who are not closely related to themselves. Using a brain imaging technique, Swedish researchers have shown that homosexual and heterosexual males' brains respond differently to two odours that may be involved in sexual arousal, and that the homosexual men respond in the same way as heterosexual women, though it could not be determined whether this was cause or effect. The study was expanded to include homosexual women; the results were consistent with previous findings meaning that homosexual women were not as responsive to male identified odours, while their response to female cues was similar to heterosexual males. In 2008, it was found using functional magnetic resonance imaging that the right orbitofrontal cortex, right fusiform cortex, and right hypothalamus respond to airborne natural human sexual sweat. Courtship and mating behaviours are often triggered by physiological changes set in motion by changes in the environment. For instance, longer daylight hours, warmer temperatures, or other environmental cues in the spring may trigger multiple hormonal fluctuations. These varying hormone levels may produce territoriality in males or nesting behaviour in females. Brain and sexual behaviour recent research in brain function suggests that there may be sexual differences in both brain anatomy and brain function. One study indicated that men and women may use their brains differently while thinking. Researchers used functional magnetic resonance imaging to observe which parts of the brain were activated as groups of men and women tried to determine whether sets of nonsense words rhymed. Men used only Broca's area in this task, whereas women used Broca's area plus an area on the right side of the brain. A number of sections of the brain have been reported to be sexually dimorphic; that is, they vary between men and women. There have also been reports of variations in brain structure corresponding to sexual orientation. In 1990, Swaab and Hofman reported a difference in the size of the suprachiasmatic nucleus between homosexual and heterosexual men. In 1992, Allen and Gorski reported a difference related to sexual orientation in the size of the anterior commissure. In some cultures sexual activity is considered acceptable only within marriage, although extramarital sex still takes place within such cultures. Some sexual activities are illegal either universally or in some countries, and some are considered against the norms of a society. Forexample, sexual activity with a minor is a criminal offense in many jurisdictions, as is sexual abuse of individuals in general. Human sexual behaviour, like many other kinds of activity engaged in by human beings, is generally governed by social rules that are culturally specific and vary widely. These social rules are referred to as sexual morality (what can and can not be done by society's rules) and sexual norms (what is and is not expected). People commonly display sexual interest in other people via body language, although the precise form and degree vary by culture, era, and sex. Some of the cues to signal interest include exaggerated gestures and movement, echoing and mirroring, room encompassing glances, leg crossing, the pointing knee, hair tossing or touching, head tilt, rotation of the pelvis, showing wrists, adjusting clothes, laughing and smiling, eye contact, touching, playfulness, and proximity. Humans also demonstrate physiological cues when sexually aroused such as pupil dilation.

PHYSIOLOGY OF EMOTION AND COGNITION

Emotion is any conscious experience characterized by intense mental activity and a certain degree of pleasure or displeasure. It is often intertwined with mood, temperament, personality, disposition, and motivation. In some theories, cognition is an important aspect of emotion.

Emotions are complex. "Emotions can be defined as a positive or negative experience that is associated with a particular pattern of physiological activity." Emotions produce different physiological, behavioural and cognitive changes. The original role of emotions was to motivate adaptive behaviours that in the past would have contributed to the survival of humans. Emotions are responses to significant internal and external events.

According to some theories, they are states of feeling that result in physical and psychological changes that influence our behaviour. The physiology of emotion is closely linked to arousal of the nervous system with various states and strengths of arousal relating, apparently, to particular emotions. Emotion is also linked to behavioural tendency. Extroverted people are more likely to be social and express their emotions, while introverted people are more likely to be more socially withdrawn and conceal their emotions. Emotion is often the driving force behind motivation, positive or negative. According to other theories, emotions are not causal forces but simply syndromes of components, which might include motivation, feeling, behaviour, and physiological changes, but no one of these components is the emotion. Nor is the emotion an entity that causes these components.

Emotions involve different components, such as subjective experience, cognitive processes, expressive behaviour, psychophysiological changes, and instrumental behaviour. More recently, emotion is said to consist of all the components. The different components of emotion are categorized somewhat differently depending on the academic discipline. In psychology and philosophy, emotion typically includes a subjective, conscious experience characterized primarily by psychophysiological expressions, biological reactions, and mental states. A similar multicomponential description of emotion is found in sociology. For example, Peggy Thoits described emotions as involving physiological components, cultural or emotional labels (anger, surprise, etc.), expressive body actions, and the appraisal of situations and contexts.

Research on emotion has increased significantly over the past two decades with many fields contributing including psychology, neuroscience, endocrinology, medicine, history, sociology, and computer science. The numerous theories that attempt to explain the origin, neurobiology, experience, and function of emotions have only fostered more intense research on this topic. Current areas of research in the concept of emotion include the development of materials that stimulate and elicit emotion. In addition PET scans and fMRI scans help study the affective processes in the brain.

Cognitive neuroscience is the scientific field that is concerned with the study of the biological processes and aspects that underlie cognition, with a specific focus on the neural connections in the brain which are involved in mental processes. It addresses the questions of how cognitive activities are affected or controlled by neural circuits in the brain. Cognitive neuroscience is a branch of both neuroscience and psychology, overlapping with disciplines such as behavioural neuroscience, cognitive psychology, physiological psychology and affective neuroscience. Cognitive neuroscience relies upon theories in cognitive science coupled with evidence from neurobiology, and computational modeling. Parts of the brain play an important role in this field. Neurons play the most vital role, since the main point is to establish an understanding of cognition from a neural perspective, along with the different lobes of the cerebral cortex. Methods employed in cognitive neuroscience include experimental procedures from psychophysics and cognitive psychology, functional neuroimaging, electrophysiology, cognitive genomics, and behavioural genetics.

Studies of patients with cognitive deficits due to brain lesions constitute an important aspect of cognitive neuroscience. The damages in lesioned brains provide a comparable basis with regards to healthy and fully functioning brains. These damages change the neural circuits in the brain and cause it to malfunction during basic cognitive processes, such as memory or learning. With the damage, we can compare how the healthy neural circuits are functioning, and possibly draw conclusions about the basis of the affected cognitive processes. Also, cognitive abilities based on brain development are studied and examined under the subfield of developmental cognitive neuroscience. This shows brain development over time, analyzing differences and concocting possible reasons for those differences. The term "cognition" refers to all processes by which the sensory input is transformed, reduced, elaborated, stored, recovered, and used.

NEURAL BASIS OF EMOTION

Limbic system controls the expression of emotion was first introduced by Papez. The limbic system consists of an inter-connected series of structures bordering the thalamus, and includes the amygdala, hippocampus, septum, fornix, olfactory bulb, mammillary body and cingulated cortex. Papez view was that the expression of emotion was due to actions of limbic structures on the hypothalamus, and the experience of emotion through projections to cortical sites. There has been major progress in elucidating the neural basis of the emotions and of emotional feelings. As a result of extensive animal and human studies, the best understood emotion is fear.

FEAR AND RAGE

Fear relative to external circumstances is triggered by the amygdala, two sets of subcortical nuclei located in the depth of each temporal lobe. The amygdala receive signals related to a certain situation, for example, a visually represented threat such as a looming shadow or an auditorily represented threat such as a high-pitched scream. When those signals have a suitable configuration, an appropriate context, and reach a workable threshold, i.e. when they are emotionally-competent, they activate nuclei in the hypothalamus and in the sector of the brain stem known as the periaqueductal gray. Working together those brain sites execute the requisite emotional actions — release of cortisol into the bloodstream, adjustment of heart rate, respiratory rate, degree of gut contraction, and fear-specific behaviours such as changes in facial expression and posture, and freezing in place or running away from danger. The ensemble of these actions constitutes the emotional state of fear. Thus, included in the emotional state are specific behaviours aimed at protecting the integrity of the individual, e.g. running away or freezing in place, and also a preparation of the organism meant to allow it to carry out those protective behaviours. When the situation is best handled by a flight response, the emotional state ensures that sources of energy are available in the blood stream and adjusts cardiac and respiratory functions so that they meet the metabolic needs ahead. The emotional state even provides for analgesia to offset the pain that might result from potential injuries. In situations best dealt with by staying in place as inconspicuously as possible, the preparatory actions are radically different since no muscular effort will be needed and, immobility is instead the desired goal. The selection of fleeing or freezing responses is made automatically although humans may override the natural selection and decide for one of the other option. This fine-tuned mechanism calls for the engagement of different cellular columns of the periaqueductal gray.

Fear caused by internal events, for example, the extreme pain associated with myocardial infarction or the development of acidosis associated with CO_2 inhalation, is probably triggered by chemoreceptors located subcortically, namely in the brain stem. The emotion program of disgust is another good example of protection of the organism's integrity. Disgust is triggered from a small region of the anterior insular cortex when certain stimuli are present, for instance, the sight of decomposing food or body waste, as well as tastes or odours from decomposing organic matter. The sight of body-boundary violations, as in a wound with blood, also causes disgust. The actions that constitute disgust include a typical facial expression and, for example, the rapid expulsion of the potentially offending food.

In the social emotion of contempt there is a rejection of certain behaviours or ideas rather than an expulsion of toxic substances or their tell-tale signs. Contempt can be seen as a biological metaphor for disgust. Significantly, we refer to actions that cause moral revulsion as "disgusting," and the repertoire of facial expressions that accompanies a contemptuous judgment is similar to that of disgust. The advantages of contempt are apparent: the rejection of behaviours deemed dangerous to individuals or groups, and the social isolation of those who produce such behaviours.

Compassion is another emotion, whose trigger region is located in the ventral and medial sector of the prefrontal cortex. When this region is activated by the sight of others facing a predicament, for example, an accident resulting in physical injury, facial expressions and even gestures meant to help the victims are rapidly deployed.

Rage is a feeling of intense, violent, or growing anger. It is sometimes associated with the fight-or-flight response, and is often activated in response to being in the presence of a threat. Rage can sometimes lead to a state of mind where the individual experiencing it believes they can do, and often is capable of doing, things that may normally seem physically impossible. Those experiencing rage usually feel the effects of high adrenaline levels in the body. This increase in adrenal output raises the physical strength and endurance levels of the person and sharpens their senses, while dulling the sensation of pain. High levels of adrenaline actually impair memory. Temporal perspective is also affected, people in a rage have described experiencing events in slow-motion. Time dilation occurs due to the individual becoming hyper aware of the hind brain (the seat of fight or flight). Rational thought and reasoning would inhibit an individual from acting rapidly upon impulse. An older explanation of this "time dilation" effect is that instead of actually slowing our perception of time, high levels of adrenaline increase our ability to recall specific minutiae of an event after it occurs. Since humans gauge time based on the number of things they can remember, high-adrenaline events such as those experienced during periods of rage seem to unfold more slowly. It is safe to assume that there is truth in both theories.

A person in a state of rage may also lose much of their capacity for rational thought and reasoning, and may act, usually violently, on their impulses to the point that they may attack until they themselves have been incapacitated or the source of their rage has been destroyed. A person in rage may also experience tunnel vision, muffled hearing, increased heart rate, and hyperventilation. Their vision may also become "rose-tinted" (hence "seeing red"). They often focus only on the source of their anger. The large amounts of adrenaline and oxygen in the bloodstream may cause a person's extremities to shake. Psychiatrists consider rage to be at one end of the spectrum of anger, and annoyance to be at the other side.

In 1995, rage was hypothesized to occur when oxytocin, vasopressin, and corticotropin-releasing hormone are rapidly released from the hypothalamus. This results in the pituitary gland producing and releasing large amounts of the adrenocorticotropic hormone, which causes the adrenal cortex to release corticosteroids. This chain reaction occurs when faced with a threatening situation.

AGGRESSION

Aggression is overt, often harmful, social interaction with the intention of inflicting damage or other unpleasantness upon another individual. It may occur either in retaliation or without provocation. In humans, frustration due to blocked goals can cause aggression. Human aggression can be classified into direct and indirect aggression, whilst the first is characterized by physical or verbal behaviour intended to cause harm to someone, the second one is characterized by a behaviour intended to harm social relations of an individual or a group.

Aggression can take a variety of forms, which may be expressed physically, or communicated verbally or non-verbally: including anti-predator aggression, defensive aggression (fear-induced), predatory aggression, dominance aggression, inter-male aggression, resident-intruder aggression, maternal aggression, species-specific aggression, sex-related aggression, territorial aggression, isolation-induced aggression, irritable aggression, and brain-stimulation-induced aggression (hypothalamus). There are two subtypes of human aggression: (1) controlled-instrumental subtype (purposeful or goal-oriented); and (2) reactive-impulsive subtype (often elicits uncontrollable actions that are inappropriate or undesirable). Aggression differs from what is commonly called assertiveness, although the terms are often used interchangeably among laypeople as in phrases such as "an aggressive salesperson".

The operative definition of aggression may be affected by moral or political views. Examples are the axiomatic moral view called the non-aggression principle and the political rules governing the behaviour of one country toward another. Likewise in competitive sports, or in the workplace, some forms of aggression may be sanctioned and others not. Aggressive behaviours are associated with adjustment problems and several psychopathological symptoms such as Antisocial Personality Disorder, Borderline Personality Disorder, and Intermittent Explosive Disorder.

Biological approaches conceptualize aggression as an internal energy released by external stimuli, a product of evolution through natural selection, part of genetics, a product of hormonal fluctuations. Psychological approaches conceptualize aggression as a destructive instinct, a response to frustration, an affect excited by a negative stimulus, a result of observed learning of society and diversified reinforcement, a resultant of variables that affect personal and situational environments.

In mammals, the hypothalamus and periaqueductal gray of the midbrain are critical areas of aggression. These brain areas control the expression of both behavioural and autonomic components of aggression including vocalization. Electrical stimulation of the hypothalamus causes aggressive behaviour and the hypothalamus has receptors that help determine aggression levels based on their interactions with serotonin and vasopressin. These midbrain areas have direct connections with both the brainstem nuclei controlling these functions, and with structures such as the amygdala and prefrontal cortex.

The broad area of the cortex known as the prefrontal cortex (PFC) is crucial for self-control and inhibition of impulses, including inhibition of aggression and emotions. Reduced activity of the prefrontal cortex, in particular its medial and orbitofrontal portions, has been associated with violent and antisocial aggression.

The role of the chemicals in the brain, particularly neurotransmitters, in aggression has also been examined. This varies depending on the pathway, the context and other factors such as gender. A deficit in serotonin has been theorized to have a primary role in causing impulsivity and aggression. Nevertheless, low levels of serotonin transmission may explain a vulnerability to impulsiveness, potential aggression, and may have an effect through interactions with other neurochemical systems. These include dopamine systems which are generally associated with attention and motivation toward rewards, and operate at various levels. Norepinephrine, also known as noradrenaline, may influence aggression responses both directly and indirectly through the hormonal system, the sympathetic nervous system or the central nervous system (including the brain). It appears to have different effects depending on the type of triggering stimulus, for example social isolation/rank versus shock/chemical agitation which appears not to have a linear relationship with aggression. Similarly, GABA, although associated with inhibitory functions at many CNS synapses, sometimes shows a positive correlation with aggression, including when potentiated by alcohol.

The hormonal neuropeptides vasopressin and oxytocin play a key role in complex social behaviours in many mammals such as regulating attachment, social recognition, and aggression. Vasopressin has been implicated in male-typical social behaviours which includes aggression. Oxytocin may have a particular role in regulating female bonds with offspring and mates, including the use of protective aggression.

In human, aggressive behaviour has been associated with abnormalities in three principal regulatory systems in the body serotonin systems, catecholamine systems, and the hypothalamic–pituitary–adrenal axis. Abnormalities in these systems also are known to be induced by stress, either severe, acute stress or chronic low-grade stress.

THE NEURAL BASIS OF FEELINGS

Recent progress in the elucidation of the neural basis of feelings has been just as remarkable. Historically, it was thought that emotion would occur when a causative object first triggered a feeling state as a result of which the body would be aroused emotionally. Feeling states elicited by a situation produced bodily manifestations, in the face and in the viscera. Late in the nineteenth century William James proposed to invert this sequence, as outlined in his 1884 paper: "Our natural way of thinking" about these emotions is that the mental perception of some fact excites the mental affection called the emotion, and that this latter state of mind gives rise to the bodily expression. Each emotion is a collection of bodily actions so well differentiated that the overall perception of the particular action program of a given emotion yields a distinct pattern. There were early attacks on this position and claims that the body engagement was not differentiated enough to generate distinct feelings. It was said that the body component consisted of a non-specific arousal state, no different for fear than for sadness or happiness. Current evidence suggests, however, that the body state associated with each kind of emotion is distinctive and capable of supporting distinctive representations of emotion even if those representations are probably transformed by subcortical stations charged with transmitting signals from the body to cerebral cortex. Once it was possible to conceive of emotions-proper and feelings of emotion as distinctive components of a functional sequence, and once the mechanisms behind the triggering and execution of emotions gained clarity, the search for a physiological platform for feelings of emotion turned to somato-sensing brain regions. At the level of the cerebral cortex the insula offered itself as a main candidate and indeed a large number of studies have shown that numerous emotional feeling states, positive as well as negative, simple or complicated, activate the insular cortex. The fact that the insula is the main cortical target of signals hailing from the body's interior — the viscera and the internal milieu — is likely the reason for this differential activity. But the neural basis of feeling states is not to be found only at the level of the cerebral cortex. The complete destruction of the insula in both cerebral hemispheres does not abolish feelings, indicating that the feeling process probably begins at the level of the brain stem in nuclei which bring together at any moment information about the ongoing state of the body and can elabourate on that information. It has been suggested that the brainstem provides the most basic level of feelings — primordial feelings — whose modification would give rise to emotional feelings.

In brief, feelings of emotions are the perceptions of the action program that constitutes an emotion as it unfolds together with the salient representation of the causative object and with thoughts related to the situation. Organisms with simple brains need not perceive the unfolding of an emotional program for the emotional behaviour to be effective. In organisms with complex brains, however, and with elaborate consciousness and memory, aspects of the feeling process are recorded and can be used for future planning and for optimized decision-making. In other words, feelings play a practical role in adaptive behaviour and extend the advantages of emotions to the realm of conscious behaviour. Feelings are not a useless reflection of the emotion process. Although the brain devices required to process emotions and feelings are put in place by the genome early in development, individual experience and learning introduce variations in the performance of emotions. As a consequence there is a subtle customization that makes an individual's expressive patterns distinctive, in spite of their basic stereotypy. We laugh and cry with partially distinctive expressions. The fact that the emotional competence of objects and situations varies from individual to individual further undermines the possibility of genetic determinism. We all generate fear responses to a number of comparable situations, but each of us has learned to fear certain objects and situations that others will not. Different individuals exhibit different degrees of emotional regulation. Over the course of biological evolution, emotions have allowed organisms to cope with threats originating within the body or in the environment and to take advantage of opportunities related to nutrition or mating. Emotional action programs increase survival by delivering an advantageous standard response to particular circumstances in the absence of thinking and deliberation. For species with limited cognitive abilities this is a spectacular advantage. For humans the advantages vary with the circumstances. A rapid and comprehensive response can be beneficial, although on numerous occasions suppressing emotions and substituting a deliberated response constitutes the best response. But deliberated responses depend not only on an accumulation of factual knowledge and on the exercise of logic, but also on the past experience of emotional feelings relative to prior objects and situations.

NEURAL BASIS OF PLEASURE

Pleasure is a broad class of mental states that humans and other animals experience as positive, enjoyable, or worth seeking. It includes more specific mental states such as happiness, entertainment, enjoyment, ecstasy, and euphoria. The early psychological concept of pleasure, the pleasure principle, describes it as a positive feedback mechanism, motivating the organism to recreate in the future the situation which it has just found pleasurable and to avoid situations that have caused pain in the past.

The experience of pleasure is subjective and different individuals will experience different kinds and amounts of pleasure in the same situation. Many pleasurable experiences are associated with satisfying basic biological drives, such as eating, exercise, hygiene, and sex. The appreciation of cultural artifacts and activities such as art, music, dancing, and literature is often pleasurable.

Pleasure centers or "hedonic hotspots" are a set of brain structures within the reward system that are directly responsible for mediating the "liking" or pleasure component of an intrinsic reward, as opposed to brain structures that activate in correlation with or as a consequence of the perception of pleasure. Various compartments within the nucleus accumbens, ventral pallidum, and parabrachial nucleus have been identified as pleasure centers which respond to a variety of pleasurable stimuli. The orbitofrontal cortex and insular cortex likely contain hedonic hotspots as well. The anterior cingulate cortex, ventral tegmental area, and amygdala have also been observed to activate in functional neuroimaging studies in response to pleasurable stimuli, but these structures do not necessarily contain hedonic hotspots.

The simultaneous activation of every hedonic hotspot within the reward system is believed to be necessary for generating the sensation of an intense euphoria. Pleasure is considered to be one of the core dimensions of emotion. It can be described as the positive evaluation that forms the basis for several more elabourate evaluations such as "agreeable" or "nice". As such, pleasure is an affect and not an emotion, as it forms one component of several different emotions. Pleasure is sometimes subdivided into fundamental pleasures that are closely related to survival (food, sex, and social belonging) and higher-order pleasures (e.g., viewing art and altruism). The clinical condition of being unable to experience pleasure from usually enjoyable activities is called anhedonia. An active aversion to obtaining pleasure is called hedonophobia.

Pleasure is often regarded as a bipolar construct, meaning that the two ends of the spectrum from pleasant to unpleasant are mutually exclusive. Some lines of research suggest that people do experience pleasant and unpleasant feelings at the same time, giving rise to so-called mixed feelings. The degree to which something or someone is experienced as pleasurable not only depends on its objective attributes (appearance, sound, taste, texture, etc.), but on beliefs about its history, about the circumstances of its creation, about its rarity, fame, or price, and on other non-intrinsic attributes, such as the social status or identity it conveys.

FRONTAL LOBE

The frontal lobes (Fig – 52) are considered as our emotional control center and home to our personality. There is no other part of the brain where lesions can cause such a wide variety of symptoms. The frontal lobes are involved in motor function, problem solving, spontaneity, memory, language, initiation, judgement, impulse control, social and sexual behaviour. The frontal lobes are extremely vulnerable to injury due to their location at the front of the cranium, proximity to the sphenoid wing and their large size. MRI studies have shown that the frontal area is the most common region of injury following mild to moderate traumatic brain injury. There are important asymmetrical differences in the frontal lobes. The left frontal lobe is involved in controlling language related movement, whereas the right frontal lobe plays a role in non-verbal abilities. Some researchers emphasize that this rule is not absolute and that with many people, both lobes are involved in nearly all behaviour.

Disturbance of motor function is typically characterized by loss of fine movements and strength of the arms, hands and fingers. Complex chains of motor movement also seem to be controlled by the frontal lobes. Patients with frontal lobe damage exhibit little spontaneous facial expression, which points to the role of the frontal lobes in facial expression. Broca's Aphasia, or difficulty in speaking, has also been associated with frontal damage.

An interesting phenomenon of frontal lobe damage is the insignificant effect it can have on traditional IQ testing. Researchers believe that this may have to do with IQ tests typically assessing convergent rather than divergent thinking. Frontal lobe damage seems to have an impact on divergent thinking, or flexibility and problem solving ability. There is also evidence showing lingering interference with attention and memory even after good recovery from a TBI(Traumatic Brain Injury). Another area often associated with frontal damage is that of "behavioural sponteneity", found that individual with frontal damage displayed fewer spontaneous facial movements, spoke fewer words (left frontal lesions) or excessively (right frontal lesions).

One of the most common characteristics of frontal lobe damage is difficulty in interpreting feedback from the environment. Perseverating on a response, risk taking, and non-compliance with rules and impaired associated learning (using external cues to help guide behaviour) are a few examples of this type of deficit. The frontal lobes are also thought to play a part in our spatial orientation, including our body's orientation in space. One of the most common effects of frontal damage can be a dramatic change in social behaviour. A person's personality can undergo significant changes after an injury to the frontal lobes, especially when both lobes are involved. There are some differences in the left versus right frontal lobes in this area. Left frontal damage usually manifests as pseudodepression and right frontal damage as pseudopsychopathic.

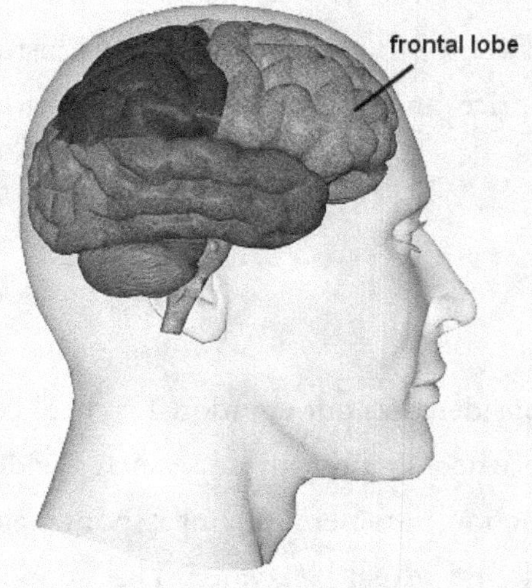

(Fig – 52) : structure of brain showing frontal lobe

Sexual behaviour can also be effected by frontal lesions. Orbital frontal damage can introduce abnormal sexual behaviour, while dorolateral lesions may reduce sexual interest. Some common tests for frontal lobe function are Wisconsin Card Sorting (response inhibition), Finger Tapping (motor skills), Token Test (language skills). The limbic system, which is the area of the brain involved in emotion and memory. It includes the hypothalamus, thalamus, amygdala, and the hippocampus. The hypothalamus plays a role in the activation of the sympathetic nervous system that is a part of any given emotional reaction. The thalamus serves as a sensory relay center whose neurons project to both the amygdala and the higher cortical regions for further processing. The amygdala plays a role in processing emotional information and sending that information on to cortical structures. The hippocampus integrates emotional experience with cognition.

Anatomy of emotion

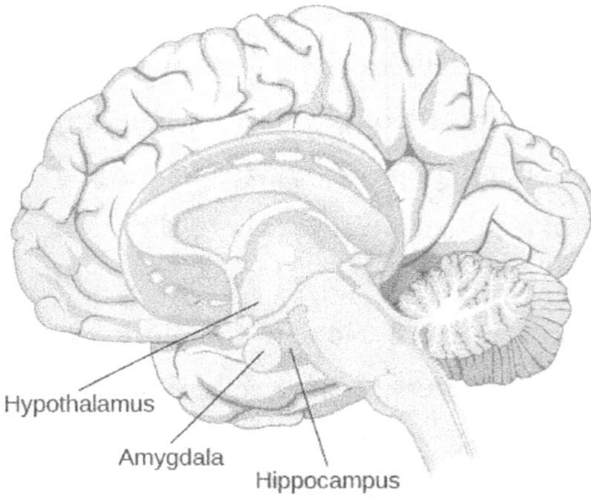

(Fig – 53) The limbic system, which includes the hypothalamus, thalamus, amygdala, and the hippocampus, is involved in mediating emotional response and memory.

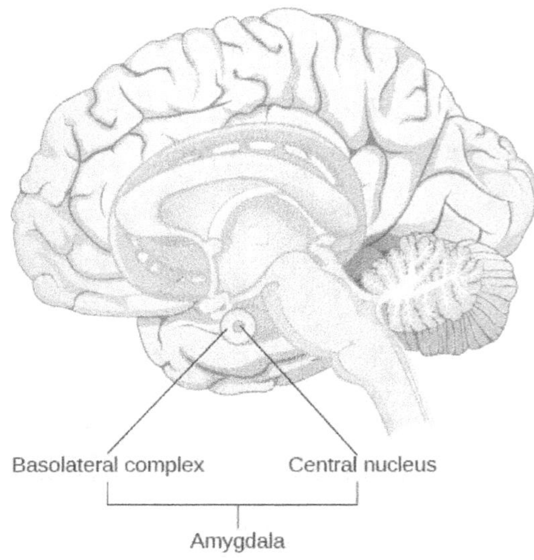

(Fig – 54) The anatomy of the basolateral complex and central nucleus of the amygdala are illustrated in this diagram

HYPOTHALAMUS

The hypothalamus is a small but important part of the brain. It contains several small nuclei with a variety of functions. It plays an important role in the nervous system as well as in the endocrine system. It is linked to another small and vital gland called the pituitary gland. The hypothalamus is located below the thalamus and right above the brain stem. It forms the anterior part of the diencephalon. All vertebrate brains contain a hypothalamus. In humans, it is roughly the size of an almond. The hypothalamus is vital for living as it plays a very important role. It controls certain metabolic processes and other activities of the Autonomic Nervous System. It synthesizes and secretes neurohormones, often called hypothalamic-releasing hormones. These hypothalamic releasing hormones control and regulate the secretion of pituitary hormones. The hypothalamus contains a large number of nuclei and fiber tracts. The cells in the two major nuclei secrete vasopressin (ADH, antidiuretic hormone), oxytocin, and CRH (corticotropin releasing hormone). The two major nuclei are the supraoptic and paraventricular nuclei. ADH and oxytocin are then transported down the axons from cells in the supraoptic and paraventricular nuclei through the infundibulum to the neurohypophysis (posterior pituitary), where they are released into the blood stream. This pathway is termed the supraopticohypophysial tract. Damage to the anterior hypothalamus blocks the production of ADH. This leads to a condition where the kidney fails to conserve water and the condition is called diabetes insipidus. CRH is released by the paraventricular nuclei and taken up by the portal system where it has action on the anterior lobe of the pituitary.

Lesions of the hypothalamic nuclei interfere with several vegetative functions and some of the so-called motivated behaviours, like thermal regulation, sexuality, combativeness, hunger and thirst. The hypothalamus is also believed to play a role in emotion. Specifically, its lateral parts seem to be involved with pleasure and rage, while the median part is like to be involved with aversion, displeasure and a tendency to uncontrollable and loud laughing. However, in general terms, the hypothalamus has more to do with the expression (symptomatic manifestations) of emotions than with the genesis of the affective states. When the physical symptoms of emotion appear, the threat they pose returns, via hypothalamus, to the limbic centers and, thence, to the pre-frontal nuclei, increasing anxiety. This negative feed-back mechanism can be so strong as to generate a situation of panic.

THALAMUS

The thalamus is a small structure within the brain located just above the brain stem between the cerebral cortex and the midbrain and has extensive nerve connections to both. The main function of the thalamus is to relay motor and sensory signals to the cerebral cortex. It also regulates sleep, alertness and wakefulness. Also located in the diencephalon, are the epithalamus and the perithalamus which contain regions called the zona incerta and the reticulate nucleus. These are distinct from the thalamus proper. The thalamus lies at the top of the brain stem near the centre of the brain from where nerve fibres project out towards the cerebral cortex. The thalamus is supplied with blood by four branches of the posterior cerebral artery, namely the polar artery, paramedian thalamic-subthalamic arteries, thalamogeniculate arteries and the posterior choroidal arteries.

Lesion or stimulation of the medial dorsal and anterior nuclei of the thalamus are associated with changes in emotional reactivity. However, the importance of these nuclei on the regulation of emotional behaviour, is not due to the thalamus itself, but to the connections of these nuclei with other limbic system structures. The medial dorsal nucleus makes connections with cortical zones of the pre-frontal area and with the hypothalamus.

AMYGDALA

The amygdala has received a great deal of attention from researchers interested in understanding the biological basis for emotions, especially fear and rage. The amygdala is composed of various subnuclei, including the basolateral complex and the central nucleus. The basolateral complex has dense connections with a variety of sensory areas of the brain. It is critical for classical conditioning and for attaching emotional value to learning processes and memory. The central nucleus plays a role in attention, and it has connections with the hypothalamus and various brainstem areas to regulate the autonomic nervous and endocrine system's activity.

Animal research has demonstrated that there is increased activation of the amygdala in rat pups that have odour cues paired with electrical shock when their mother is absent. This leads to an aversion to the odour cue that suggests the rats learned to fear the odour cue. Interestingly, when the mother was present, the rats actually showed a preference for the odour cue despite its association with an electrical shock. This preference was associated with no increases in amygdala activation. This suggests a differential effect on the amygdala by the *context* (the presence or absence of the mother) determined whether the pups learned to fear the odour or to be attracted to it .

Research studies conducted in rats showed that negative early life experiences could alter the function of the amygdala and result in adolescent patterns of behaviour that mimic human mood disorders. In this study, rat pups received either abusive or normal treatment during postnatal days 8–12. There were two forms of abusive treatment. The first form of abusive treatment had an insufficient bedding condition. The mother rat had insufficient bedding material in her cage to build a proper nest that resulted in her spending more time away from her pups trying to construct a nest and less times nursing her pups. The second form of abusive treatment had an associative learning task that involved pairing odours and an electrical stimulus in the absence of the mother, as described above. The control group was in a cage with sufficient bedding and was left undisturbed with their mothers during the same time period. The rat pups that experienced abuse were much more likely to exhibit depressive-like symptoms during adolescence when compared to controls. These depressive-like behaviours were associated with increased activation of the amygdala.

Human research also suggests a relationship between the amygdala and psychological disorders of mood or anxiety. Changes in amygdala structure and function have been demonstrated in adolescence who are either at-risk or have been diagnosed with various mood and/or anxiety disorders. It has also been suggested that functional differences in the amygdala could serve as a biomarker to differentiate individuals suffering from bipolar disorder from those suffering from major depressive disorder.

HIPPOCAMPUS

The hippocampus is also involved in emotional processing. Like the amygdala, research has demonstrated that hippocampal structure and function are linked to a variety of mood and anxiety disorders. Individuals suffering from posttraumatic stress disorder (PTSD) show marked reductions in the volume of several parts of the hippocampus, which may result from decreased levels of neurogenesis and dendritic branching (the generation of new neurons and the generation of new dendrites in existing neurons, respectively). While it is impossible to make a causal claim with correlational research like this, studies have demonstrated behavioural improvements and hippocampal volume increases following either pharmacological or cognitive-behavioural therapy in individuals suffering from PTSD.

MONOAMINERGIC SYSTEMS (SEROTONIN, NOREPINEPHRINE, DOPAMINE) AND EMOTIONS

The neural circuits and brain structures involved in emotions are modulated by a myriad of chemical neurotransmitters. The ascending monoamine systems have received considerable attention over the past several decades. These include the serotonin, norepinephrine, and dopamine systems. Prior to the discovery of neurotransmitters, researchers believed that a major ascending neural system was responsible for arousal of forebrain (epithalamus, thalamus, subthalamus) and telencephalon (cerebral cortex, basal ganglia and associated structures like the nucleus basilis of Meynert and the nucleus accumbens). This neural system used to be called the ascending reticular activating system, before the monoamines were characterized. It is believed that a balance among these systems (as well as other neurotransmitters) is necessary for normal emotional states and arousal. Over the last three decades, the neurochemical basis of this ascending system was described and receptors identified.

RETICULAR ACTIVATING SYSTEM

The reticular formation (Fig – 55) is a set of interconnected nuclei that are located throughout the brainstem. The reticular formation is not anatomically well defined because it includes neurons located in diverse parts of the brain. The neurons of the reticular formation make up a complex set of networks in the core of the brainstem that stretches from the upper part of the midbrain to the lower part of the medulla oblongata. The reticular formation includes ascending pathways to the cortex in the ascending reticular activating system (ARAS) and descending pathways to the spinal cord via the reticulospinal tracts of the descending reticular formation.

Neurons of the reticular formation, particularly those of the ascending reticular activating system, play a crucial role in maintaining behavioural arousal and consciousness. The functions of the reticular formation are modulatory and premotor. The modulatory functions are primarily found in the rostral sector of the reticular formation and the premotor functions are localized in the neurons in more caudal regions.

The reticular formation is divided into three columns: raphe nuclei (median), gigantocellular reticular nuclei (medial zone), and parvocellular reticular nuclei (lateral zone). The raphe nuclei are the place of synthesis of the neurotransmitter serotonin, which plays an important role in mood regulation. The gigantocellular nuclei are involved in motor coordination. The parvocellular nuclei regulate exhalation. The reticular formation is essential for governing some of the basic functions of higher organisms and is one of the phylogenetically oldest portions of the brain.

The human reticular formation is composed of almost 100 brain nuclei and contains many projections into the forebrain, brainstem, and cerebellum, among other regions. It includes the reticular nuclei, reticulothalamic projection fibers, diffuse thalamo-cortical projections, ascending cholinergic projections, descending non-cholinergic projections, and descending reticulospinal projections. The reticular formation also contains two major neural subsystems, the ascending reticular activating system and descending reticulospinal tracts, which mediate distinct cognitive and physiological processes. It has been functionally cleaved both sagittally and coronally.

Sagittal division reveals more morphological distinctions. The raphe nuclei form a ridge in the middle of the reticular formation, and, directly to its periphery, there is a division called the medial reticular formation. The medial RF is large and has long ascending and descending fibers, and is surrounded by the lateral reticular formation. The lateral RF is close to the motor nuclei of the cranial nerves, and mostly mediates their function.

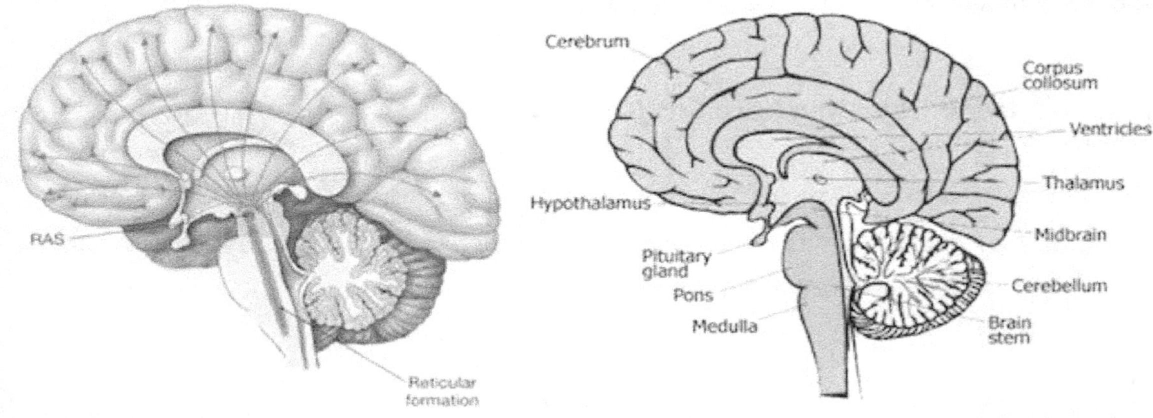

(Fig – 55) Medial and lateral reticular formation

The medial reticular formation and lateral reticular formation are two columns of neuronal nuclei with ill-defined boundaries that send projections through the medulla and into the mesencephalon (midbrain). The nuclei can be differentiated by function, cell type, and projections of efferent or afferent nerves. Moving caudally from the rostral midbrain, at the site of the rostral pons and the midbrain, the medial RF becomes less prominent, and the lateral RF becomes more prominent.

The reticular formation consists of more than 100 small neural networks, with varied functions including the following:

1. Somatic motor control – Some motor neurons send their axons to the reticular formation nuclei, giving rise to the reticulospinal tracts of the spinal cord. These tracts function in maintaining tone, balance, and posture—especially during body movements. The reticular formation also relays eye and ear signals to the cerebellum so that the cerebellum can integrate visual, auditory, and vestibular stimuli in motor coordination. Other motor nuclei include gaze centers, which enable the eyes to track and fixate objects, and central pattern generators, which produce rhythmic signals of breathing with swallowing, and with dedication and urination.

2. Cardiovascular control – The reticular formation includes the cardiac and vasomotor centers of the medulla oblongata.

3. Pain modulation – The reticular formation is one means by which pain signals from the lower body reach the cerebral cortex. It is also the origin of the descending analgesic pathways. The nerve fibers in these pathways act in the spinal cord to block the transmission of some pain signals to the brain.

4. Sleep and consciousness – The reticular formation has projections to the thalamus and cerebral cortex that allow it to exert some control over which sensory signals reach the cerebrum and come to our conscious attention. It plays a central role in states of consciousness like alertness and sleep. Injury to the reticular formation can result in irreversible coma.

5. Habituation – This is a process in which the brain learns to ignore repetitive, meaningless stimuli while remaining sensitive to others. A good example of this is a person who can sleep through loud traffic in a large city, but is awakened promptly due to the sound of an alarm or crying baby. Reticular formation nuclei that modulate activity of the cerebral cortex are part of the ascending reticular activating system.

Role of corticotropin-releasing hormone (CRH) systems in fear and anxiety

There is increasing evidence to suggest that extrahypothalamic corticotropin-releasing hormone (CRH) systems play an important role in the onset of fear and anxiety. Cells in the central nucleus contain CRH. Axons of central nucleus cells target locus coeruleus neurons which have CRH receptors and contain NE (Norepinephrine). In animals, administration of CRH into the cerebral ventricles so as to eventually reach receptors on amygdala and LC (Locus Coeruleus) cells effectively induces anxiety responses, including hypervigilance, enhancement of the freezing posture, and decreased exploration in unfamiliar situations. Furthermore, in anxiety-provoking situations that typically elicit these behavioural responses, administration of a CRH antagonist produces a reduction in the occurrence of these reactions. In rats, infusion of a CRH antagonist into the central nucleus reduces expression of fear behaviour ("freezing" in an environment where the animal had been previously shocked) suggesting that blockade of CRH receptors in the central nucleus has an antianxiety effect. In addition, stimulation of the central nucleus with microinfusions of CRH increases the release of norepinephrine and epinephrine from the adrenal medulla (via the sympathetic outflow). It is hypothesized that dysregulation of CRH systems may underlie or contribute to a state of chronic fear or anxiety by affecting behavioural and autonomic activity.

Autonomic response

The Autonomic Nervous System (ANS) is the portion of our nervous system that requires no conscious thought and functions automatically throughout the day. Balance of the body is controlled by two portions of the ANS the first being the Sympathetic Nervous System (SNS) which is the nervous system that is dominant during times of stress (mental, physical, and chemical). The second part of the ANS is known as the Parasympathetic Nervous System (PNS) which is dominant during times of relaxation or deep altered states. We need both of them working equally to maintain a proper tone within the body. The ANS helps to control the beating of our hearts; the rise and fall of blood pressure; the detoxification of the body's poisons; the digestion, assimilation, and elimination of our foods; the balancing of all our hormones; proper immune system responses; proper blood sugar levels; maximum brain function; and every automatic function of the body's organs and glands.   The ANS receives information from our biofields. Our body's biofield is an accumulation of electromagnetic energies emitted from all of our cells, tissues, organs, and glands. Although the body's biofield (infrared spectrum of light) is not visible with the human eye, it is detectable with some very sophisticated and sensitive equipment. This biofield, or light field, is produced and emitted by the body and through some very peculiar properties of light; it is also carrying information from our surroundings, in the form of electromagnetic signals, back into the physical body. The ANS then has an opportunity of responding to that electromagnetic/stress signal.   The body produces photons of light called biophotons. These biophotons are stored and released from the nucleus of our body's 70 trillion cells and these biophotons carry information within and between cells.

Autonomic specificity refers to the notion that emotions can be distinguished in terms of their associated patterns of autonomic nervous system activity. The idea that emotions are likely to have different patterns of autonomic nervous system activity is grounded in an evolutionary view of emotion that suggests that emotions were selected for their ability to help the organism deal effectively and efficiently with a small set of problems that were critical for the species survival . Viewed from this perspective, emotions can be seen as time-tested solutions to timeless problems and challenges, such as defending what is ours, avoiding harm, attracting potential mates, regulating social distance, soothing and restoring equilibrium, and engendering help from conspecifics. With our emotions, evolution has provided us with at least one generalized response to these problems that has a high likelihood of being successful most of the time. In humans this emotional response encompasses multiple psychological and physiological systems, some of which serve to prepare the organism for action, some of which serve to regulate the behaviour of conspecifics, and some of which do both. Emotions 'are short-lived psychological and physiological phenomena that represent efficient modes of adaptation to changing environmental demands. Psychologically, emotions alter attention, shift certain behaviours upward in response hierarchies, and activate relevant associative networks in memory. Physiologically, emotions rapidly organize the response of disparate biological systems including facial expression, somatic muscular tonus, voice tone, autonomic nervous system activity, and endocrine activity to produce a bodily milieu that is optimal for effective response. Emotions serve to establish our position vis-a.-vis our environment, pulling us toward certain people, objects, actions and ideas, and pushing us away from others. Emotions also serve as a repository for innate and learned influences, possessing certain invariant features, and others that show considerable variation across individuals, groups, and cultures. Learning more about how the autonomic nervous system is organized in emotion would be of value in much the same way as would learning whether there are differences in patterns of regional brain activation or in patterns of facial muscle action in different emotions.

FACIAL EXPRESSION AND RECOGNITION OF EMOTIONS

A cultural display rule is one of a collection of culturally specific standards that govern the types and frequencies of displays of emotions that are acceptable. Therefore, people from varying cultural backgrounds can have very different cultural display rules of emotion. For example, research has shown that individuals from the United States express negative emotions like fear, anger, and disgust both alone and in the presence of others, while Japanese individuals only do so while alone. Furthermore, individuals from cultures that tend to emphasize social cohesion are more likely to engage in suppression of emotional reaction so they can evaluate which response is most appropriate in a given context. There may be gender differences involved in emotional processing. While research into gender differences in emotional display is equivocal, there is some evidence that men and women may differ in regulation of emotions.

Despite different emotional display rules, our ability to recognize and produce facial expressions of emotion appears to be universal. In fact, even congenitally blind individuals produce the same facial expression of emotions, despite their never having the opportunity to observe these facial displays of emotion in other people. This would seem to suggest that the pattern of activity in facial muscles involved in generating emotional expressions is universal, and indeed, this idea was suggested in the late 19th century in Charles Darwin's book *The Expression of Emotions in Man and Animals* (1872). In fact, there is substantial evidence for seven universal emotions that are each associated with distinct facial expressions. These include: happiness, surprise, sadness, fright, disgust, contempt, and anger.

Clinical aspects of emotion

Emotional breakdown: Nervous breakdown or emotional breakdown is not an actual medical term or a mental illness, but it could indicate a serious health problem like anxiety or depression. The Mayo Clinic defines a nervous breakdown, or mental/emotional breakdown, as a situation in which someone cannot function normally because of overwhelming stress. There are physical, mental, and emotional warning signs for these episodes.

In the short term, stress can boost your brainpower by releasing hormones that enhance memory storage and improve concentration. But chronic stress fries your attention span—affecting your ability to focus on work projects (bad) or your surroundings while driving (really, really bad). In extreme cases, excessive amounts of the stress hormone cortisol can deteriorate your memory, according to the University of Maryland Medical Center.

Stress causes the brain to release hormones, including adrenaline, which energizes your muscles for a "fight or flight" response. Once the adrenaline wears off, cortisol tells the body to replenish its lost energy stores with food. The problem is, when you're stressed for reasons that don't involve crazy levels of physical activity (say, running from a saber-toothed tiger), you are biologically wired to eat when you don't really need to. High-fat and high-sugar comfort foods increase pleasure chemicals in the brain to trick you into temporarily feeling better. An American Psychological Association survey found that among 3,000 adults, 40 percent deal with stress through emotional eating. Psychosis is possible when a person has a nervous breakdown. Psychosis is a break with reality and can cause a number of different symptoms. Psychosis during a breakdown can lead to a feeling of detachment or depersonalization, not feeling like oneself, or feeling detached from situations. It can also cause paranoia or delusions, a sense that someone is watching or causing harm.

Psychotic breakdown symptoms may even include hallucinations or flashbacks that feel very real, especially in people who have experienced some type of trauma. Any signs of psychosis should be taken very seriously should be evaluated by a mental health professional.

Causes of breakdowns are varied which include problems with intimate relationships, such as divorce or marital separation, contributed to 24% of nervous breakdowns. Problems at work and school accounted for 17% of cases, and financial problems for 11%. A nervous breakdown is very similar to a panic attack. Stress is a major cause in both cases and they are both temporary. During a nervous breakdown, a person's emotional state of being shifts from an ability to cope with life stresses to a state of being totally overwhelmed to a point that normal functioning is disrupted. Excessive worry, nervousness, fear, anxiety are symptomatic. These states of being are accompanied by a variety of uncomfortable feelings often summarized as bad or sad. If these feelings become so intense they are perceived as life-threatening, the defense system blocks awareness. These mechanisms while protective can also be limiting to successful living. Overwhelming stress, therefore, is causative. Whether that stress is self-created or external requires different approaches and has different implications to the individual. A nervous breakdown is not limited to any one type of person: anyone can have this breakdown, but if someone is under a lot of stress and has a family background of mental disorders, they can be more likely to have one.

The most common signs of a nervous breakdown are depressive symptoms, such as loss of hope and thoughts of suicide or self-harm, anxiety with high blood pressure, tense muscles, clammy hands, dizziness, upset stomach, and trembling or shaking, insomnia, hallucinations, extreme mood swings or unexplained outbursts, panic attacks (chest pain), detachment from reality and self, extreme fear, difficulty breathing, paranoia, such as believing someone is watching you or stalking you, flashbacks of a traumatic event, which can suggest undiagnosed post-traumatic stress disorder (PTSD). People experiencing a nervous breakdown may also withdraw from family, friends, and co-workers. Signs of such withdrawal include avoiding social functions and engagements, eating and sleeping poorly, maintaining poor hygiene, calling in sick to work for days or not showing up to work at all, isolating yourself in your home.

The medication that may be prescribed to someone who has a mental breakdown is based upon the underlying causes, which are sometimes more serious mental disorders. Antidepressants are given to treat depression. Anxiolytics are used for those with anxiety disorders. Antipsychotics are used for schizophrenia and mood stabilizers help with bipolar disorder. Depending upon what caused a person's mental breakdown, any of these treatments can be helpful for them.

There are several different kinds of therapy that a patient can receive. The most common type of therapy is counselling. This is where the patient is able to talk about whatever is on their mind without worrying about any judgments. Psychotherapy is a very common type of therapy that addresses the current problems in someone's life and helps them to deal with them. Past experiences may also be explored in this type of therapy. In psychoanalysis therapy, the main focus is a patient's past experiences so that they can confront these issues and prevent breakdowns in the future. Cognitive behavioural therapy explores how a person behaves and what they are thinking and feeling. If there is anything negative in these three different categories, then this therapy will try to turn them around into more balanced alternatives. Hypnotherapy is where hypnosis is performed and used to help the patient relax. Hypnosis can also be used to figure out why a person acts or feels a certain way, by examining past events that may have caused the breakdown. Expressive therapy focuses on how the patient is able to express their feelings. If the patient has a hard time doing this, expression through the arts is highly recommended. There is also aromatherapy, which consists of herbs to help the patient relax and to try to relieve stress. Yoga and massage may also be included in this therapy that will help the muscles to relax. Meditation is also often recommended. All of these therapies help a person to relax and de-stress and also help to prevent future breakdowns.

Visceral breakdown

Stomach aches and cramps are often physical manifestations of stress and anxiety. Try using these natural home remedies to soothe your upset stomach. But if you notice a cluster of symptoms that includes abdominal pain, constipation, bloating, gas, and diarrhoea, you could have irritable bowel syndrome, which research suggests is linked with, but not solely caused by, anxiety. IBS(Irritable Bowel Syndrome) could be triggered by the immune system's response to stress, though researchers are still studying this. According to the Anxiety and Depression Association of America, anywhere from 50 to 90 percent of those suffering from IBS have a mental health condition, like generalized anxiety disorder or depression. If you suspect you have IBS, talk to your doctor about options for physical and emotional relief. The stress from IBS changes your hormone production, alters your immune system, and in some cases, upsets your digestive tract. So it comes as little surprise that anxiety has been linked to contributing to the development of irritable bowel syndrome (IBS), also known as "spastic colon" - a chronic condition that causes bloating, gastrointestinal discomforts, erratic bowel movements, chronic abdominal pain, diarrhoea, and constipation. IBS is diagnosed when these symptoms are present without a medical cause, and while scientists believe that there are likely other factors that go into IBS, most agree that anxiety and stress contribute to its development.

An important aspect of IBS, patients exhibit visceral hypersensitivity characterized by hyperalgesia and allodynia. Although the cause of visceral hypersensitivity is unknown, clinical studies have shown that chronic stress serves as a risk factor for IBS. The sympatho-medullary and the HPA (hypothalamic–pituitary–adrenal axis) axis are activated by exposure to stress. The sympatho-medullary axis releases epinephrine from the adrenal medulla, to allow the organism to "fight" or "flee" from a threat, whilst activation of the HPA axis releases cortisol (or corticosterone [CORT] in rodents) from the adrenal cortex to mobilize reserves of glucose with the goal of replenishing the expended sympatho-medullary system. Activation of the HPA axis by stress releases CRH (Corticotropin-Releasing Hormone)from the paraventricular nucleus of the hypothalamus into the hypophyseal portal circulation. CRH then binds to a CRH type-1 receptor in the anterior pituitary stimulating the production and the release of adrenocorticotropic hormone (ACTH) from the pituitary gland into the systemic circulation. The circulating ACTH binds to receptors in the adrenal cortex to stimulate production of CORT, which binds to a cortisol binding globulin, prior to being released at target organs throughout the body. A pivotal role for CORT release from the HPA axis in response to stress is the initiation of feedback-inhibition through binding to the mineralocorticoid receptor (MR) and the GR at multiple nuclei, such as the hippocampus, the paraventricular nucleus of the hypothalamus, and anterior pituitary. In contrast to the feedback-inhibition, when CORT binds at the amygdala there is an increase in CRH release and the subsequent facilitation of the stress axis.

Cognitive breakdown

Mood disorders are common psychiatric illnesses that represent a major cause of disability and mortality worldwide. It is estimated that 8% to 20% of the population will experience a depressive episode at some point in their lives. Mood disorders are characterized by conspicuous disturbances in emotional disposition (ie, extreme lows [depression] or highs [mania]). The lack of inability to enjoy what once was pleasurable (anhedonia) is also a primary symptom and may occur during major depression in place of depressed mood. Expansive mood can present in bipolar disorder, often accompanied or replaced by irritability.

Other symptoms accompany these mood disturbances, such as disruptions in normal sleep, appetite, and psychomotor functions. Delusions and hallucinations may be present, especially in relation to depressive thoughts (eg, pertaining to worthlessness or excessive guilt). Measurable decreases in attention, executive function, and recall memory have been observed in patients with mood disorders. In major depression, cognitive impairment can be severe and global, sometimes meeting criteria for dementia. In the acute phase of bipolar disorder, impairment of cognition may progress to a stuporous state. Other symptoms include motor impairments, which cover a wide range of symptoms. They can manifest themselves as abnormal involuntary disturbances that interrupt a patient's daily activities. They can escalate to a level of extreme psychomotor retardation (retarded catatonia) or, alternatively, agitation (agitated catatonia). The latter can be life-threatening if not treated in time because of elevated creatinine levels (secondary to muscle breakdown) and subsequent acute renal failure. Within these broad descriptions of deficits, symptoms of mood disorders can be divided into three primary domains: psychological and vegetative signs and symptoms, neurocognitive deficits, and neurological abnormalities.

Research has shown that the relationships between mood and cognition, as that between mood and movement, are dynamic ones, with components that are trait-dependent and others that are state-dependent. Because of their relatively static nature, trait characteristics of cognitive and neurological manifestations may provide insights into core brain abnormalities that give rise to severe mood disorders. Cognitive deficits within mood disorders have been studied extensively. Although results have not always been consistent, an overall pattern of specific impairments has become evident. In general, unipolar and bipolar patients have shown impaired performance in tests of attention, executive function, and memory. Increased cognitive dysfunction often is associated with greater symptom severity. Nevertheless, cognitive deficits persist during the euthymic/remitted states, indicating that some types of cognitive processing deficits represent fundamental trait characteristics. Examining deficits during remission allows researchers to better characterize the nature and course of nonaffective symptoms associated with mood disorders. Evidence that cognitive decline might develop in conjunction with mood disorders recently has been confirmed.

Clinical correlates of emotion

Panic attacks are an example of pathophysiology in the neural systems underlying fear and anxiety. These systems are integral to the original "fight/flight" concepts and appear to be evolutionarily important in protecting the organism from a wide variety of threats, particularly predators. Panic disorder is a prevalent and well-studied psychiatric disorder that consists of multiple disabling panic attacks. Between 2–3 % of people experience an episode of panic disorder in their lifetime and twice as many women as men suffer from the disorder. These panic attacks are characterized by extreme fear and an urge to flee as well as intense autonomic arousal involving a wide variety of symptoms. The symptoms originally occur spontaneously and unpredictably, and vary in length from several minutes to upwards of 60 minutes. If they continue for prolonged periods of time, they can be very disabling. Evidence suggests that panic attacks may be due to a hypersensitive autonomic nervous system involving an overly reactive LC-NE (locus coeruleus-noradrenergic) system. Agoraphobia is the most common complication of panic disorder. It is defined as a fear of being in places or situations from which escape might be difficult or embarrassing, or in which help might not be available in the event of a panic attack.

There are a number of naturalistic observations and research investigations that support the view that panic attacks occur as a result of hypersensitive alarm systems. For example, studies demonstrate that acute panic attacks are generated by abnormal neural activity in the brain stem. Clinical observations indicate that attacks are largely experienced by patients as "storms" of autonomic nervous activity. Patients frequently are fearful of the multiple physical symptoms associated with an attack, including light-headedness, a racing heart, difficulty breathing, chest discomfort, generalized sweating, or weakness. Research investigations indicate that administration of various doses of pharmacological agents can produce panic attacks in panic-prone, but not in normal individuals. In these studies, the physical symptoms of panic attacks can be reproduced, albeit in varying degrees, by carbon dioxide, yohimbine, and caffeine and epinephrine administration. Yohimbine (a mild hallucinogen/stimulant extracted from South African tree bark) is an alpha 2-noradrenergic receptor antagonist. The majority of alpha 2 receptors act as autoreceptors. Normally, release of endogenous NE from the LC cell will modulate its own release by binding to its autoreceptor,this in turn prevents the release of NE. Thus, alpha 2- noradrenergic receptor agonists act as a negative feedback signal to reduce the release of NE. Antagonists, like yohimbine, that bind to the alpha 2 receptor, block this negative feedback signal. Consequently, the LC cell continues to release NE. In the laboratory, administration of yohimbine to panic-prone patients reproduces many of the symptoms of a panic attack including dizziness, sweating, respiratory distress, light headedness, palpitations, and fear. Results of these clinical studies suggest that the NE system may be overly sensitive or hyperactive in individuals predisposed to develop panic disorder. Further evidence to support the involvement of the LC-NE system in panic disorder is obtained from studies showing that administration of clonidine has transient antipanic effects. Clonidine is an alpha2 noradrenergic receptor agonist that effectively reduces the firing of LC neurons. Thus, pharmacological agents that increase LC-NE activity produce panic attack symptoms, whereas agents that reduce LC-NE firing rates appear to reduce panic attacks.

Carbon dioxide inhalation is capable of inducing panic symptoms in patients with panic disorder but not in normal subjects. In the clinical laboratory, inhalation of 5% carbon dioxide was found to potentiate a rapid increase in ventilation before the panic state (ventilation is mediated by receptors that sense carbon dioxide in the lungs, heart, and brain stem medulla). These results have suggested that patients with panic disorder may have very sensitive brain stem carbon dioxide receptors, i.e., "suffocation alarm mechanisms." Of potential relevance to the NE system, animal studies demonstrate that carbon dioxide produces a dose-dependent increase in LC firing rates. This effect of carbon dioxide on LC discharge rates is probably influenced by medullary (nucleus solitarius-remember, it receives visceral afferent information) projections to the LC. However, it appears that some factors are involved in acting centrally upon vulnerable brain stem regions to provoke panic attacks. For example, physiological functions and metabolic demands occurring in the periphery are closely regulated by cells in the brain stem. Information from the cardiovascular and respiratory system reaches the solitary complex and are relayed to, and activate, the LC-NE system. Fearful perceptions and thoughts emanating from the cerebral cortex may also contribute by further lowering the threshold in brain stem systems, and thereby potentiate the production of panic symptoms (one pathway underlying this would be from cortex to amygdala to LC). Some individuals are more likely to experience panic attacks after exposure to stress associated with losses (i.e., death of loved ones, divorce) or certain situations (i.e., exams, near fatal accidents, trapped in a highly confined place).

Recently it has been observed that the neuropeptide cholecystokinin (CCK) is involved in panic disorders. Some investigators have hypothesized that panic attacks start with an excitation of the CCK neurons in the brain stem. Such CCK neurons stimulate the noradrenergic neurons of locus coeruleus and the panic attack begins. Negative emotions and sadness are commonly elicited by situations associated with the loss of an important social relationship (death of a spouse) or object (loss of a home due to fire). Sadness is an internal state that signals the need for affiliation and functions to motivate individuals to seek supportive social relationships. As with fear and anxiety, this emotion is present from birth and when expressed early in life alerts the care giver to meet the infant's needs. Many years ago, Harry Harlow at the University of Wisconsin observed that when infant monkeys were separated from their mothers, they emitted a high-pitched vocalization (coo call) which alerted the mothers to retrieve the infant. Infant monkeys subjected to prolonged maternal separation frequently succumbed to a state characterized by loss of interest in the environment, a reduction in food intake and huddling in the corner. Harlow drew parallels between this emotional state and that reported in institutionalized human infants undergoing prolonged maternal separation. Prolonged disruption of the maternal-infant bond can also have a profound impact on subsequent behaviour. Newborn monkeys socially isolated from an early age would not interact with other monkeys. They would not play, fight, or show any sexual interest. Older monkeys subjected to comparable periods of social isolation failed to develop these behavioural alterations. It appears that developmental, environmental, and biological interactions are important factors in determining the individual's emotional patterns of behaviour. Alterations in brain monoamines are associated with depression. Although sadness is a transient emotional state, depression is a mood or syndrome characterized by thoughts of self-worthlessness, excessive guilt, death and/or suicide. Physiological systems are also dramatically altered during depression. Patients with depression may have difficulty concentrating on tasks and may suffer from insomnia, altered appetite, decreased interest in pleasurable activities, and fatigue. An important clinical observation was made in the 1950's when the antihypertensive agent reserpine was prominently used. Clinicians noted that some individuals became markedly depressed after taking this drug, which produces a long-lasting depletion of monoamines (norepinephrine, serotonin and dopamine). Other work demonstrated that drugs that increased the level of monoamines were effective in the treatment of depression. Together, these observations led to the monoamine hypothesis of depression. According to this hypothesis, depression results from a deficit in brain norepinephrine or serotonin, or both.

The amino acid tryptophan is the substrate for the synthesis of serotonin. Tryptophan hydroxylase is the enzyme responsible for the hydroxylation of tryptophan to form 5- hydroxytryptophan. Once synthesized, 5-hydroxytryptophan is rapidly decarboxylated to form serotonin. After release from presynaptic terminals, the deamination of serotonin occurs following reuptake of serotonin and metabolism by monoamine oxidase (MAO) to yield 5-hydroxyindoleacetic acid (5 –HIAA). Additional support for the monoamine hypothesis of depression came from an examination of norepinephrine and serotonin metabolites in depressed patients. In some depressed patients, concentrations of a major metabolite of norepinephrine, 3-methoxy-4-hydroxyphenylglycol (MHPG), were found to be reduced in the cerebrospinal fluid. Similarly, some depressed patients have reduced concentrations of a major serotonin metabolite, 5-hydroxyindoleacetic acid (5-HIAA). Other work demonstrated that rapid dietary depletion of tryptophan, the precursor of serotonin synthesis, produces a rapid return to depression in patients with successful antidepressant treatment. Together, these results suggest that availability of brain monoamines is reduced in depressed patients.

Lowered brain serotonin is associated with suicide Monoamine oxidase inhibitors (MAOI), tricyclic antidepressants, and selective serotonin reuptake inhibitors (SSRIs) are effective antidepressants that share the pharmacological property of increasing the level of biogenic amines (dopamine (*DA*), norepinephrine (*NE*), epineph serotonin, histamine) but in different ways. MAOIs are a class of drugs that block MAO, the major enzyme responsible for the oxidation of monoamines. The tricyclic drugs work by blocking the reuptake (keep it around longer) of NE and serotonin into the presynaptic terminal resulting in a net increase in neurotransmitter availability. Consequently, there is an increase in postsynaptic receptor activity. Serotonin Reuptake Inhibitors (SSRIs) work by selectively blocking the reuptake of serotonin. SSRIs are as effective as the tricycylic compounds but without some of the sedating and cardiovascular side effects of tricyclic antidepressants. As a result, SSRIs (e.g., Prozac, Zoloft) are now used widely and underscore the importance of serotonergic systems in regulating mood. Reboxetine (mesylate), is the first of a novel class of drugs called selective norepinephrine reuptake inhibitors (SNRIs). As the name implies, they specifically boost levels of the neurotransmitter norepinephrine, which is thought to be associated with increased drive. With a unique mechanism of action and a relatively benign side-effect profile, reboxetine promises to give doctors new options for patients who are either treatment-refractory or unable to tolerate other antidepressants.

Although the concept is controversial, some researchers believe that reboxetine's specific effect on norepinephrine will make it particularly useful in the subset of depressed patients with decreased energy. To summarize, disruption of brain serotonin (5-HT) and NE concentrations appear to contribute to the depressive syndrome. The hypothesis that depression is caused entirely by a reduction in monoamines is somewhat simplistic but provides a reasonable account of the pharmacological efficacy of antidepressants. Suicide is a complex human behaviour and remains a significant source of mortality with approximately 30,000 people taking their lives annually. Although suicide is generally thought to be the result of stress or depression, there is little information to distinguish who may successfully take their life by an act of suicide. For example, the majority of patients faced with painful life ending illnesses do not commit suicide. In addition, a number of individuals have taken their own life when it appears that stress was relatively minor, if not absent. Recent research efforts have broadened our understanding of the underlying neurochemistry of suicide. Postmortem studies done a number of years ago revealed that brain stem levels (raphe nuclei; remember nucleus raphe magnus for SPA) of serotonin and its metabolite 5-HIAA are consistently reduced in suicide victims. More recent studies confirm a link between depression and low serotonin activity. These studies have shown that in depressed patients that have attempted or committed suicide, 5-HIAA levels in the cerebrospinal fluid are considerably lower than in nonsuicidal depressed patients. This association between CSF 5-HIAA levels and suicidal behaviour is especially strong in those with violent suicidal attempts. It should be noted that although depression and suicide risk are both linked to disturbances in brain serotonin activity, evidence suggests that serotonin concentrations normalize after mood improvement in depressed patients.

Mehanisms dealing with stress

Coping mechanisms are the strategies people often use in the face of stress and trauma to help to manage difficult or painful emotions. Coping mechanisms can help people adjust to stressful events while maintaining their emotional well-being. Significant life events, whether positive or negative, can cause psychological stress. Difficult events, such as divorce, the death of a loved one, or the loss of a job, often cause distressing emotions in most individuals. But even events that are considered positive by many getting married, having a child, and buying a home can lead to a significant amount of stress. To adjust to this stress, people may utilize some combination of behaviour, thought, and emotion, depending on the situation. Coping mechanisms are used to manage an external situation that is creating problems for an individual. Defence mechanisms can change a person's internal psychological state.

Coping Styles and Mechanisms

Coping styles can be problem-focused—also called instrumental—or emotion-focused. Problem-focused coping strategies are typically associated with methods of dealing with the problem in order to reduce stress, while emotion-focused mechanisms can help people handle any feelings of distress that result from the problem. Further, coping mechanisms can be broadly categorized as active or avoidant. Active coping mechanisms usually involve an awareness of the stressor and conscious attempts to reduce stress. Avoidant coping mechanisms, on the other hand, are characterized by ignoring or otherwise avoiding the problem.

Some coping methods, though they work for a time, are not effective for a long-term period. These ineffective coping mechanisms, which can often be counter productive or have unintended negative consequences, are known as "maladaptive coping." Adaptive coping mechanisms are those generally considered to be healthy and effective ways of managing stressful situations.

Commonly used coping mechanisms are:

- ❖ **Support-** Talking about a stressful event with a supportive person can be an effective way to manage stress. Seeking external support instead of self-isolating and internalizing the effects of stress can often greatly reduce the negative effects of a difficult situation.
- ❖ **Relaxation-** Any number of relaxing activities can help people cope with stressful situations. Relaxing activities may include practicing meditation, progressive muscle relaxation, or calming techniques, sitting in nature, or listening to soft music etc.
- ❖ **Problem-solving-** This coping mechanism involves identifying a problem that is causing stress and then developing and putting into action some potential solutions for effectively managing it.
- ❖ **Humor-** Making light of a stressful situation may help people maintain perspective and prevent the situation from becoming overwhelming.

- ❖ **Physical activity-** Exercise can serve, for many people, as a natural and healthy form of stress relief. Running, yoga, swimming, walking, dance, team sports, and many other types of physical activity can help people cope with stressful situations and the after effects of traumatic events.
- ❖ **Defense-** the unconscious ways of coping stress. Examples: reaction formation, regression
- ❖ **Adaptive-** tolerates the stress. Examples: altruism, symbolization
- ❖ **Avoidance** -keeps self away from the stress. Examples: denial, dissociation, fantasy, passive aggression, reaction formation.
- ❖ **Attack-** diverts one's consciousness to a person or group of individuals other than the stressor or the stressful situation. Examples: displacement, emotionality, projection.
- ❖ **Behavioural-** modifies the way we act in order to minimize or eradicate the stress. Examples: compensation, sublimation, undoing.
- ❖ **Cognitive-** alters the way we think so that stress is reduced or removed. Examples: compartmentalization, intellectualization, rationalization, repression, suppression.
- ❖ **Self-harm-** intends to harm self as a response to stress. Examples: introjection, self-harming
- ❖ **Conversion-** changes one thought, behaviour or emotion into another. Example: somatisation.

Coping mechanisms and Mental Health

The use of effective coping skills can often help improve mental and emotional well-being. People who are able to adjust to stressful or traumatic situations through productive coping mechanisms may be less likely to experience anxiety, depression, and other mental health concerns as a result of painful or challenging events. People who find themselves defaulting to maladaptive coping mechanisms or experience difficulty utilizing effective coping strategies may eventually see a negative impact on mental and emotional well-being. Consuming alcohol can often help people feel less stressed in the immediate moment, for example, but if a person comes to rely on alcohol, or any other substance, in the face of challenging situations, they may eventually become dependent on the substance over time.

A therapist or other mental health professional can often help people develop and improve their coping skills. Therapists can provide support and information about coping skills, and therapy sessions can be a safe, nonjudgmental environment for people to explore the coping methods they rely on and determine how they help or hinder stress management.

Types of Coping Strategies

Over the years, psychologists and researchers have identified about 400 to 600 coping strategies, and yet there are so many other potential coping strategies that are still under research. One of the recognized groupings of coping strategies includes the appraisal-focused or adaptive cognitive, the problem-focused or adaptive behavioural, and the emotion-focused.

The appraisal-focused strategies are those coping mechanisms which involve the change of mindset or a revision of thoughts. Denial is the most common coping mechanism under this category. The problem-focused strategies are those that modify the behaviour of the person. A good example of this is learning how to cook a family dinner upon knowing that your spouse's family would come over your house this weekend. The emotion-focused strategies include the alteration of one's emotions to tolerate or eliminate the stress. Examples include distraction, meditation, and relaxation techniques.

Healthy techniques of psychological research to help to reduce stress on a short- and long-term basis.

Take a break from the stressor - It may seem difficult to get away from a big work project, a crying baby or a growing credit card bill. But when you give yourself permission to step away from it, you let yourself have time to do something else, which can help you have a new perspective or practice techniques to feel less overwhelmed. It's important to not avoid your stress (those bills have to be paid sometime), but even just 20-minutes to take care of yourself is helpful.

Exercise - The research keeps growing — exercise benefits your mind just as well as your body. We keep hearing about the long-term benefits of a regular routine exercise. But even a 20-minute walk, run, swim or dance session in the midst of a stressful time can give an immediate effect that can last for several hours.

Smile and laugh - Our brains are interconnected with our emotions and facial expressions. When people are stressed, they often hold a lot of the stress in their face. So laughs or smiles can help relieve some of that tension and improve the situation.

Get social support - Call a friend, send an email. When you share your concerns or feelings with another person, it does help relieve stress. But it's important that the person whom you talk to is someone whom you trust and whom you feel can understand and validate you. If your family is a stressor, for example, it may not alleviate your stress if you share your works woes with one of them.

Meditate - Meditation and mindful prayer help the mind and body to relax and focus. Mindfulness can help people see new perspectives, develop self-compassion and forgiveness. When practicing a form of mindfulness, people can release emotions that may have been causing the body physical stress. Much like exercise, research has shown that even meditating briefly can reap immediate benefits.

Affective disorders

Affective disorders are a set of psychiatric diseases, also called mood disorders. The main types of affective disorders are depression, bipolar disorder, and anxiety disorder. Symptoms vary by individual, and can range from mild to severe. A psychiatrist or other trained mental health professional can diagnose an affective disorder. This is done with a psychiatric evaluation. Affective disorders can be disruptive to your life. However, there are effective treatments available, including both medication and psychotherapy.

Depression

Depression, or major depressive disorder, is characterized by feelings of extreme sadness and hopelessness. It is more than simply feeling down for a day or two. If you have depression, you may experience episodes that last for several days or even weeks. A milder form of depression is called dysthymia.

BIPOLAR DISORDER

Bipolar disorder means having periods of depression, and periods of mania. Mania is when you feel extremely positive and active. This may sound good, but mania also makes you feel irritable, aggressive, impulsive, and even delusional. There are different types of bipolar. They are classified by the severity of depression and mania, as well as by how often mood swings occur,exaggerated self-confidence, irritability, aggression, self-importance, impulsiveness, recklessness, or in severe cases delusions or hallucinations. They are as follows

❖ Bipolar I Disorder— defined by manic episodes that last at least 7 days, or by manic symptoms that are so severe that the person needs immediate hospital care. Usually, depressive episodes occur as well, typically lasting at least 2 weeks. Episodes of depression with mixed features (having depression and manic symptoms at the same time) are also possible.

❖ Bipolar II Disorder— defined by a pattern of depressive episodes and hypomanic episodes, but not the full-blown manic episodes described above.

❖ Cyclothymic Disorder (also called cyclothymia)— defined by numerous periods of hypomanic symptoms as well numerous periods of depressive symptoms lasting for at least 2 years (1 year in children and adolescents). However, the symptoms do not meet the diagnostic requirements for a hypomanic episode and a depressive episode.

❖ Other Specified and Unspecified Bipolar and Related Disorders— defined by bipolar disorder symptoms that do not match the three categories listed above.

People with bipolar disorder experience periods of unusually intense emotion, changes in sleep patterns and activity levels, and unusual behaviors. These distinct periods are called "mood episodes." Mood episodes are drastically different from the moods and behaviors that are typical for the person.

Anxiety disorders

There are several different types of anxiety disorders. All are characterized by feelings of nervousness, anxiety, and even fear. The classification include:

Social anxiety: Anxiety caused by social situations. People with social anxiety disorder (sometimes called "social phobia") have a marked fear of social or performance situations in which they expect to feel embarrassed, judged, rejected, or fearful of offending others.

The symptoms of the disorder include:

- ❖ Feeling highly anxious about being with other people and having a hard time talking to them
- ❖ Feeling very self-conscious in front of other people and worried about feeling humiliated, embarrassed, or rejected, or fearful of offending others
- ❖ Being very afraid that other people will judge them
- ❖ Worrying for days or weeks before an event where other people will be
- ❖ Staying away from places where there are other people
- ❖ Having a hard time making friends and keeping friends
- ❖ Blushing, sweating, or trembling around other people
- ❖ Feeling nauseous or sick to your stomach when other people are around

Post-traumatic stress disorder: Anxiety, fear, and flashbacks caused by a traumatic event. It is a serious potentially debilitating condition that can occur in people who have experienced or witnessed a natural disaster, serious accident, terrorist incident, sudden death of a loved one, war, violent personal assault such as rape, or other life-threatening events.

Generalized anxiety disorder: Anxiousness and fear in general, with no particular cause. People with generalized anxiety disorder display excessive anxiety or worry for months and face several anxiety-related symptoms. Generalized anxiety disorder symptoms include:

- ❖ Restlessness or feeling wound-up or on edge
- ❖ Being easily fatigued
- ❖ Difficulty concentrating or having their minds go blank
- ❖ Irritability
- ❖ Muscle tension
- ❖ Difficulty controlling the worry
- ❖ Sleep problems (difficulty falling or staying asleep or restless, unsatisfying sleep)

Panic disorder: People with panic disorder have recurrent unexpected panic attacks, which are sudden periods of intense fear that may include palpitations, pounding heart, or accelerated heart rate; sweating; trembling or shaking; sensations of shortness of breath, smothering, or choking; and feeling of impending doom. Panic disorder symptoms include:

- ❖ Sudden and repeated attacks of intense fear
- ❖ Feelings of being out of control during a panic attack
- ❖ Intense worries about when the next attack will happen
- ❖ Fear or avoidance of places where panic attacks have occurred in the past

Obsessive-compulsive disorder: Obsessive thoughts that cause anxiety and compulsive actions. Obsessive compulsive disorder (OCD) affects millions of people from all walks of life. People with OCD experiences obsessions and compulsions. Obsessions are intrusive and unwanted thoughts, images, or urge that cause distress or anxiety. Compulsions are behaviours that the person feels compelled to perform in order to ease their distress or anxiety or suppress the thoughts. Some of these behaviours are visible actions while others are mental behaviours. Common obsessions include concerns about contamination, cleanliness, aggressive impulses, or the need for symmetry. Common compulsions include checking, washing/cleaning, and arranging. There isn't always a logical connection between obsessions and compulsions. Often people with OCD experiences a variety of obsessions and compulsions.

Many people with OCD recognize that their obsessions and compulsions are not rational. Nevertheless, they still feel a strong need to perform the repetitive behavior or mental compulsions. They may spend several hours every day focusing on their obsessions, performing seemingly senseless rituals. If left untreated, OCD can be chronic and can interfere with a person's normal routine, schoolwork, job, family, or social activities. Proper treatment can help sufferers regain control over the illness and feel relief from the symptoms.

Physiology of learning

Learning is the process of acquiring new or modifying existing knowledge, behaviours, skills, values, or preferences. The ability to learn is possessed by humans, animals, and some machines, and there is also evidence for some kind of learning in some plants. Some learning is immediate, induced by a single event (e.g. being burned by a hot stove), but much skill and knowledge accumulates from repeated experiences. The changes induced by learning often last a lifetime, and it is hard to distinguish learned material that seems to be "lost" from that which cannot be retrieved. Human learning begins before birth and continues until death as a consequence of ongoing interactions between person and environment. The nature and processes involved in learning are studied in many fields, including educational psychology, neuropsychology, experimental psychology, and pedagogy. Research in such fields has led to the identification of various sorts of learning. For example, learning may occur as a result of habituation, or classical conditioning, operant conditioning or as a result of more complex activities such as play, seen only in relatively intelligent animals. Learning may occur consciously or without conscious awareness. Learning that an aversive event cannot be avoided nor escaped may result in a condition called learned helplessness. There is evidence for human behavioural learning prenatally, in which habituation has been observed as early as 32 weeks of a gestation, indicating that the central nervous system is sufficiently developed and primed for learning and memory to occur very early on in development.

Play has been approached by several theorists as the first form of learning. Children experiment with the world, learn the rules, and learn to interact through play. Lev Vygotsky agrees that play is pivotal for children's development, since they make meaning of their environment through playing educational games.

Learning and nervous system

Neuroscience is the study of the human nervous system, the brain, and the biological basis of consciousness, perception, memory, and learning. The nervous system and the brain are the physical foundation of the human learning process. Neuroscience links our observations about cognitive behaviour with the actual physical processes that support such behaviour. The brain is not a computer. The structure of the brain's neuron connections is loose, flexible, "webbed," overlapping, and redundant. It's impossible for such a system to function like a linear or parallel-processing computer. Instead, the brain is better described as a self-organizing system. The brain changes with use, throughout our lifetime. Mental concentration and effort alters the physical structure of the brain. Our nerve cells (neurons) are connected by branches called dendrites. There are about 10 billion neurons in the brain and about 1,000 trillion connections. The possible combinations of connections is about ten to the one-millionth power. As we use the brain, we strengthen certain patterns of connection, making each connection easier to create next time. This is how memory develops.

Cortex and learning

Central nervous system is a primitive structure running along the length of body. As evolution proceeds, brain enlargement directed towards the head end of the animal in a process called cephalization. The most recent structure to appear in the brain is thin layer of the tissue that covers most of the brain called neocortex. The curving in and out (gyri and sulci) of human neocortex produces convolutions. The brain regions are involved in learning in everyday life. The organization of neocortex into layers is one of its most salient anatomical features. These layers include circuits that form functional columns in cortical maps.

The cerebral cortex is the seat of our highest forms of intelligence, and its understanding is thus a goal for all students of mind and brain. Neocortex has an intricate design which exhibits a characteristic organization into six distinct cortical layers. Differences in the thickness of these layers and the sizes and shapes of neurons led to identify more than fifty divisions, or areas, of neocortex. This classification has been invaluable to later scientists as a basis for discerning different functional roles for different parts of the brain. On the other hand, why the neocortex has six layers, or indeed a laminar design, has remained a mystery from a functional point of view.

Cerebral cortex can be classified in to two parts, the large area of neocortex and a small area of allocortex. Neocortex also called as neopallium is a part of the mammalian brain. Neocortex is the largest part of the cerebral cortex which covers the two cerebral hemispheres. The neocortex is made up of six layers from the outer in I to VI. In humans, neocortex is involved in higher functions such as sensory perception, generation of motor commands, spatial reasoning, conscious thought and language. There are two types of cortex in the neocortex namely the true cortex and pro isocortex. The proisocortex is atranstional area between the true isocortex and periallocortex. It is found in cingulate gyrus, a part of the limbic system, in Broadmann's areas 24,25,30,32, the insula and parahippocampal gyrus. Neocortex contain two primary types of neurons, excitatory pyrimidal neurons and inhibitory interneurons. Neurons of intercortex also arranged in vertical structures called cortical columns and minicolumns. Minicolums are basic functional unit of cortex. In humans, neocortex consists of half a millions of these columns, each of which contains approxiametely 70,000 neurons. The neocortex is divided in to frontal, parietal and occipital and temporal areas, which perform different functions. The occipital area contains the primary visual cortex, temporal lobe contain primary auditory cortex. Frontal lobe contains complex language processing area localized to ventrolateral prefrontal cortex (Broca's area). Social and emotional processing localized to the orbitofrontal cortex. The neocortex have an influential role in sleep, memory, learning process and instrumental conditioning.

During learning nervous system gets altered in some way or other. This change is mainly depends on capability of animal to hold the new informaiton acquired during learning experience. Learning and memory are thought to occur through a brain process called long term potentiation (LTP). LTP produce changes in the connections (syanpses) between brain cells (neuron), that are necessary to store new information. Higher forms of learning occur in cerebral cortex. LTP is a system in which synapses become increasingly sensitive so that a steady level of pre synaptic stimulus become converted in to a large post synaptic output.

Lashey'work

Karl Spencer Lashley (June 7,1890 – August 7,1958) was a psychologist and behaviourist remembered for his contributions to the study of learning and memory. His most influential research centered around the cortical basis of learning and discrimination. He trained rats to perform specific tasks (seeking a food reward), then lesioned specific areas of the rats' cortex, either before or after the animals received the training. The cortical lesions had specific effects on acquisition and retention of knowledge, but the location of the removed cortex had no effect on the rats' performance in the maze. This led Lashley to conclude that memories are not localized, but that they are widely distibuted across the cortex. His study of V1 (primary visual cortex) led him to believe that it was a site of learning and memory storage (i.e. an engram) in the brain. He reached this erroneous conclusion due to imperfect lesioning methods.

By the 1950s two separate principles had grown out of Lashley's research: mass action and equipotentiality. "Mass action" refers to the idea that the rate, efficacy and accuracy of learning depend on the amount of cortex available. If cortical tissue is destroyed following the learning of a complex task, deterioration of performance on the task is determined more by the amount of tissue destroyed than by its location. "Equipotentiality" refers to the idea that one part of the cortex can take over the function of another part; within a functional area of the brain, any tissue within that area can perform its associated function. Therefore, to destroy a function, all the tissue within a functional area must be destroyed. If the area is not destroyed then the cortex can take over another part. These two principles grew out of Lashley's research on the cortical basis of learning and discrimination. Lashley was a pioneer of neuroscience before the term existed, and seeking to understand the connection between the physical structures of the brain and psychological processes of learning, memory, and planning.

Subcortical regions of the brain may be necessary and sufficient for the acquisition of the simple conditioned responses, but when dealing with more complicated, more intellectual learning tasks, it is understandable that the neocortex is critically important. Karl Lashley who spend more than 30 years investigating the role of cortex with visual discriminations and complex mazes. One of the issue addressed by him was the role of visual cortex for learning and retaining brightness-discrimination responses. Lashley found that if the entire visual cortex was removed the rats fail to demonstrate a previously learned discrimination response. However, they could relearn the tasks in as few trails as they had originally learned the task before the surgery. The brightness discrimination could be acquired by a process in the subcortex, the tectum. The relationship of cortex to tectum was further clarified when the tectum alone was leisonied. If the tectum was removed, leaving the visual cortex intact there was no effect on previously learned discriminations. When both tectum and visual cortex are removed, no relearning of tasks was possible, since the combined leisions produce complete blindness. It is interesting that only a small portion of intact visual cortex was needed for a retention of responses.

Long term potentiation

In neuroscience, long-term potentiation (LTP) is a persistent strengthening of synapses based on recent patterns of activity. These are patterns of synaptic activity that produce a long-lasting increase in signal transmission between two neurons. The opposite of LTP is long-term depression, which produces a long-lasting decrease in synaptic strength. It is one of several phenomena underlying synaptic plasticity, the ability of chemical synapses to change their strength. As memories are thought to be encoded by modification of synaptic strength,LTP is widely considered one of the major cellular mechanisms that underlies learning and memory. Many modern LTP studies seek to better understand its basic biology, while others aim to draw a causal link between LTP and behavioural learning. Still others try to develop methods, pharmacologic or otherwise, of enhancing LTP to improve learning and memory. LTP is also a subject of clinical research, for example, in the areas of Alzheimer's disease and addiction medicine. When a single electrical shock is applied to axon leading to hippocampus, a potential is evoked from hippocampal tissue as a result of stimulation. This is called extra cellular population spike. This potential activates the reaction of entire population of hippocampal neurons. When a series of hundred pulses of elctrical stimulation is administrated within one seconds of original shock, the amplitude of extracellular population spike increased. This phenomenon is called long term potentiation. This procedure makes the hippocampus highly reactive for quite a long time. It is possible to store new information in the hippocampus and can last for several months. The opposite of LTP is long term depression which produces a long lasting decrease in synaptic strength.

Different areas of the brain exhibit different forms of LTP. The specific type of LTP exhibited between neurons depends on a number of factors. One such factor is the age of the organism when

LTP is observed. For example, the molecular mechanisms of LTP in the immature hippocampus differ from those mechanisms that underlie LTP of the adult hippocampus. The signalling pathways used by a particular cell also contribute to the specific type of LTP present. For example, some types of hippocampal LTP depend on the NMDA (N-methyl D-aspartate) receptor, others may depend upon the metabotropic glutamate receptor (mGluR), while still others depend upon another molecule altogether. The variety of signaling pathways that contribute to LTP and the wide distribution of these various pathways in the brain are reasons that the type of LTP exhibited between neurons depends in part upon the anatomic location in which LTP is observed. For example, LTP in the Schaffer collateral pathway of the hippocampus is NMDA receptor-dependent, whereas LTP in the mossy fiber pathway is NMDA receptor-independent.

NMDA receptor-dependent LTP exhibits several properties, including input specificity, associativity, cooperativity, and persistence.

Input specificity

Once induced, LTP at one synapse does not spread to other synapses due to its input specificity. Long-term potentiation is only propagated to those synapses according to the rules of associativity and cooperativity. However, the input specificity of LTP may be incomplete at short distances.

Associativity

Associativity refers to the observation that when weak stimulation of a single pathway is insufficient for the induction of LTP, simultaneous strong stimulation of another pathway will induce LTP at both pathways.

Cooperativity

LTP can be induced either by strong tetanic stimulation of a single pathway to a synapse, or cooperatively via the weaker stimulation of many. When one pathway into a synapse is stimulated weakly, it produces insufficient postsynaptic depolarization to induce LTP. In contrast, when weak stimuli are applied to many pathways that converge on a single patch of postsynaptic membrane, the individual postsynaptic depolarizations generated may collectively depolarize the postsynaptic cell enough to induce LTP cooperatively.

Persistence

LTP is persistent, lasting from several minutes to many months, and it is this persistence that separates LTP from other forms of synaptic plasticity.

TYPES OF LEARNING

Simple non-associative learning

Learning involving exposure usually to a single event, and that is presumed not to reflect learning of a relationship between multiple events. Most animals show some degree of non-associative learning. This means they change their response to a stimuli without association with a positive or negative reinforcement. Animals frequently subjected to a stimulus will often become habituated to that stimulus. They will show a reduction or total elimination of response to a stimulus without positive or negative reinforcement.

Habituation

Habituation is an example of non-associative learning in which there is a progressive diminution of behavioural response probability with repetition stimulus. An animal first responds to a stimulus, but if it is neither rewarding nor harmful the animal reduces subsequent responses. One example of this can be seen in small song birds. If a stuffed owl (or similar predator) is put into the cage, the birds initially react to it as though it were a real predator. Soon the birds react less, showing habituation. If another stuffed owl is introduced (or the same one removed and reintroduced), the birds react to it again as though it were a predator, demonstrating that it is only a very specific stimulus that is habituated to (namely, one particular unmoving owl in one place).

Habituation has been shown in essentially every species of animal, including the large protozoan *Stentor coeruleus*.

Habituation is not a motor fatigue or sensory adaptation. Stimulus specific habituation shows how a decline in responsiveness cannot be due to motor fatigue, however, the phenomenon of dishabituation shows how a decline in responsiveness cannot be due to either motor fatigue or sensory adaptation. Therefore, the decline in responsiveness that we call habituation must have been due to a change in the central processes that intervene between sensory and motor neurons (this is usually thought to occur in the central nervous system). In other words, habituation refers to the reduced processing of information that accompanies repeated stimulation in the circuit that relates sensory input to motor output.

Habituation is sensitive to the ISI (inter-stimulus-interval). Short ISIs are better than long ISIs at promoting short term habituation, but that long ISIs are better than short ISIs at promoting long term habituation. In Short-term habituation rapid presentations of a stimulus with a short interval between presentations, results in habituation quickly but see spontaneous recovery . The degree of spontaneous recovery depends on length of rest interval. In long-term habituation there is one stimulus presentation in a day produce more long-term effects and less spontaneous recovery.

Sensitization

Sensitization is an example of non-associative learning in which the progressive amplification of a response follows repeated administrations of a stimulus. Sensitization is usually temporary and can last for up to a week but not generally a long-term effect with a stronger stimulus, the effects last longer. An everyday example of this mechanism is the repeated tonic stimulation of peripheral nerves that will occur if a person rubs his arm continuously. After a while, this stimulation will create a warm sensation that will eventually turn painful. The pain is the result of the progressively amplified synaptic response of the peripheral nerves warning the person that the stimulation is harmful. Sensitization is thought to underlie both adaptive as well as maladaptive learning processes in the organism.

Associative learning

Associative learning is the process by which an element is learned through association with a separate, pre-occurring element. It is also referred to as classical conditioning. In otherwards **a**ssociative learning is any learning process in which a new response becomes associated with a particular stimulus. Associative learning is a form of conditioning, a theory that states behaviour can be modified or learned based on a stimulus and a response. This means that behaviour can be learned or unlearned based on the response it generates.

Operant conditioning

Operant conditioning is the use of consequences to modify the occurrence and form of behaviour. Operant conditioning is distinguished from Pavlovian conditioning in that operant conditioning deals with the modification of voluntary behaviour. Discrimination learning is a major form of operant conditioning. One form of it is called Errorless learning.

Skinner is regarded as the father of Operant Conditioning. Skinner introduced a new term into the Law of Effect - Reinforcement. Behaviour which is reinforced tends to be repeated (i.e., strengthened); behaviour which is not reinforced tends to die out-or be extinguished (i.e., weakened). Skinner (1948) studied operant conditioning by conducting experiments using animals which he placed in a 'Skinner Box'. Operant conditioning can be described as a process that attempts to modify behaviour through the use of positive and negative reinforcement. Through operant conditioning, an individual makes an association between a particular behaviour and a consequence. Skinner identified three types of responses, or operant, that can follow behaviour.

Neutral operants: Responses from the environment that neither increase nor decrease the probability of a behaviour being repeated.

Reinforcers: Responses from the environment that increase the probability of a behaviour being repeated. Reinforcers can be either positive or negative.

Punishers: Responses from the environment that decrease the likelihood of a behaviour being repeated. Punishment weakens behaviour.

Positive and negative reinforcement

Skinner showed how positive reinforcement worked by placing a hungry rat in his Skinner box. The box contained a lever on the side, and as the rat moved about the box, it would accidentally knock the lever. Immediately it did so a food pellet would drop into a container next to the lever.

The rats quickly learned to go straight to the lever after a few times of being put in the box. The consequence of receiving food if they pressed the lever ensured that they would repeat the action again and again. The removal of an unpleasant reinforcer can also strengthen behaviour. This is known as negative reinforcement because it is the removal of an adverse stimulus which is 'rewarding' to the animal or person. Negative reinforcement strengthens behaviour because it stops or removes an unpleasant experience.

Skinner showed how negative reinforcement worked by placing a rat in his Skinner box and then subjecting it to an unpleasant electric current which caused it some discomfort. As the rat moved about the box it would accidentally knock the lever. Immediately it did so the electric current would be switched off. The rats quickly learned to go straight to the lever after a few times of being put in the box. The consequence of escaping the electric current ensured that they would repeat the action again and again.

In fact Skinner even taught the rats to avoid the electric current by turning on a light just before the electric current came on. The rats soon learned to press the lever when the light came on because they knew that this would stop the electric current being switched on. These two learned responses are known as Escape Learning and Avoidance Learning.

Punishment (weakens behaviour)

Punishment is defined as the opposite of reinforcement since it is designed to weaken or eliminate a response rather than increase it. It is an aversive event that decreases the behaviour that it follows. Like reinforcement, punishment can work either by directly applying an unpleasant stimulus like a shock after a response or by removing a potentially rewarding stimulus, for instance, deducting someone's pocket money to punish undesirable behaviour.

Classical conditioning

The typical paradigm for classical conditioning involves repeatedly pairing an unconditioned stimulus (which unfailingly evokes a reflexive response) with another previously neutral stimulus (which does not normally evoke the response). Following conditioning, the response occurs both to the unconditioned stimulus and to the other, unrelated stimulus (now referred to as the "conditioned stimulus"). The response to the conditioned stimulus is termed a conditioned response. The classic example is Pavlov and his dogs. Meat powder naturally will make a dog salivate when it is put into a dog's mouth; salivating is a reflexive response to the meat powder. Meat powder is the unconditioned stimulus (US) and the salivation is the unconditioned response (UR). Then Pavlov rang a bell before presenting the meat powder. The first time Pavlov rang the bell, the neutral stimulus, the dogs did not salivate, but once he put the meat powder in their mouths they began to salivate. After numerous pairings of the bell, and then food the dogs learned that the bell was a signal that the food was about to come and began to salivate just when the bell was rang. Once this occurs the bell becomes the conditioned stimulus (CS) and the salivation to the bell is the conditioned response (CR).

Imprinting

Imprinting is the term used in psychology and ethology to describe any kind of phase-sensitive learning (learning occurring at a particular age or a particular life stage) that is rapid and apparently independent of the consequences of behaviour. It was first used to describe situations in which an animal or person learns the characteristics of some stimulus, which is therefore said to be "imprinted" onto the subject. The best-known form of imprinting is filial imprinting, in which a young animal acquires several of its behavioural characteristics from its parent. It is most obvious in nidifugous birds, which imprint on their parents and then follow them around. It was first reported in domestic chickens. Sexual imprinting is the process by which a young animal learns the characteristics of a desirable mate. It is a process whereby mate preferences are affected by learning at a very young age, usually using a parent as the model.

Observational learning

Observational learning is learning that occurs through observing the behaviour of others. It is a form of social learning which takes various forms, based on various processes. In humans, this form of learning seems to not need reinforcement to occur, but instead, requires a social model such as a parent, sibling, friend, or teacher with surroundings. The most characteristic of this learnng process is imitation, one's personal repetition of an observed behaviour, such as a dance. Humans can copy three types of information simultaneously: the demonstrator's goals, actions and environmental outcomes (observational learning). Through copying these types of information, (most) infants will tune in to their surrounding culture.

Play

Play generally describes behaviour which has no particular end in itself, but improves performance in similar situations in the future. This is seen in a wide variety of vertebrates besides humans, but is mostly limited to mammals and birds. Cats are known to play with a ball of string when young, which gives them experience with catching prey. Besides inanimate objects, animals may play with other members of their own species or other animals, such as orcas playing with seals they have caught. Play involves a significant cost to animals, such as increased vulnerability to predators and the risk of injury and possibly infection. It also consumes energy, so there must be significant benefits associated with play for it to have evolved. Play is generally seen in younger animals, suggesting a link with learning. However, it may also have other benefits not associated directly with learning, for example improving physical fitness.

Enculturation

Enculturation is the process by which a person learns the requirements of their native culture by which he or she is surrounded, and acquires values and behaviours that are appropriate or necessary in that culture. The influences which as part of this process limit, direct or shape the individual, whether deliberately or not, include parents, other adults, and peers. If successful, enculturation results in competence in the language, values and rituals of the culture (compare acculturation, where a person is within a culture different to their normal culture, and learns the requirements of this different culture).

Multimedia learning

It is the learning where learner uses multimedia learning environments. This type of learning relies on dual-coding theory . Dual-coding theory is a theory of cognition, was hypothesized by Allan Paivio of the University of Western Ontario in 1971. According to Paivio, there are two ways a person could expand on learned material: verbal associations and visual imagery. Dual-coding theory postulates that both visual and verbal information is used to represent information. Visual and verbal information are processed differently and along distinct channels in the human mind, creating separate representations for information processed in each channel. The mental codes corresponding to these representations are used to organize incoming information that can be acted upon, stored, and retrieved for subsequent use. Both visual and verbal codes can be used when recalling information. For example, say a person has stored the stimulus concept "dog" as both the word 'dog' and as the image of a dog. When asked to recall the stimulus, the person can retrieve either the word or the image individually, or both simultaneously. If the word is recalled, the image of the dog is not lost and can still be retrieved at a later point in time. The ability to code a stimulus two different ways increases the chance of remembering that item compared to if the stimulus was only coded one way.

E-learning and augmented learning

Electronic learning or e-learning is a general term used to refer to Internet-based networked computer-enhanced learning. A specific and always more diffused e-learning is mobile learning (m- Learning), it uses different mobile telecommunication equipments, such as cellular phones. When a learner interacts with the e-learning environment, it is called augmented learning. By adapting to the needs of individuals, the context-driven instruction can be dynamically tailored to the learner's natural environment. Augmented digital content may include text, images, video, audio (music and voice). By personalizing instruction, augmented learning has been shown to improve learning performance for a lifetime.

ROTE LEARNING

Rote learning is a technique which avoids understanding the inner complexities and inferences of the subject that is being learned and instead focuses on memorizing the material so that it can be recalled by the learner exactly the way it was read or heard. The major practice involved in rote learning techniques is learning by repetition, based on the idea that one will be able to quickly recall the meaning of the material the more it is repeated. Rote learning is used in diverse areas, from mathematics to music to religion. Although it has been criticized by some schools of thought, rote learning is a necessity in many situations.

Informal learning

Informal learning occurs through the experience of day-to-day situations (for example, one would learn to look ahead while walking because of the danger inherent in not paying attention to where one is going). It is learning from life, during a meal at table with parents, play, exploring.

Formal learning

Formal learning is learning that takes place within a teacher-student relationship, such as in a school system.

Nonformal learning

Nonformal learning is organized learning outside the formal learning system. For example: learning by coming together with people with similar interests and exchanging viewpoints, in clubs or in (international) youth organizations, workshops.

Tangential learning

Tangential learning is the process by which some portion of people will self-educate if a topic is exposed to them in something that they already enjoy such as playing a musical instrument.

Dialogic learning

Dialogic learning is a type of learning based on dialogue. It is typically the result of egalitarian dialogue; in other words, the consequence of a dialogue in which different people provide arguments based on validity claims and not on power claims. The concept of dialogic learning is not a new one. Within the Western tradition, it is frequently linked to the Socratic dialogues. It is also found in many other traditions.

Environmental complexity and the brain

Environmental restriction or deprivation early in development can induce social, cognitive, affective, and motor abnormalities. Rearing animals in larger, more complex environments results in enhanced brain structure and function, including increased brain weight, dendritic branching, neurogenesis, gene expression, and improved learning and memory. The brain of the individual can change as a result of experiences that have encountered by the individual from the enviornment in which it lives.

A multidisciplinary team of researchers at University of California proved the biochemical and neuronal changes in the rat's brain exposed to different levels of environmental complexities. They took almost 30 years for the final conclusion. Littermates from a standard rat colony were assigned to one of the two environmental conditions at weaning stage of approximately 25 days of age. In one condition called the enriched condition or EC, the rats were housed in groups of ten to twelve in a large cage equipped with platforms wheels and other exploratory objects. These animals were also exposed in groups of five or six to a nine square feet field where there is a series of barriers forming a pattern that changed each day. The other conception called the impoverished or IC, rats were housed singly in cages where there is no possibility of seeing or touching another animals. Exposure of either of two environments in many of this studies contiuned for 80 days. At the end of experimental exposure period, series of anatomical and biochemical measurements were made. One of the major anatomical differences observed was the weight of the cortex. An average percentage difference of 4% in the weight of the cortex and in particular an average percentage difference of 6% in the weight of occipital or visual cortex observed. In both cases the average percentage difference was in the forebrain, it is heavier in EC rats over IC rats. In the rest of the brain-mid brain, cerebellum, medulla, there were no significant difference between EC and IC animals. The occipital cortex in EC rat brain is become more thicker than IC. Comparable differences in brain weights were observed in EC rats.

The neuronal advantage of EC rat over IC rat were established in terms of biochemical analysis. The quantity of acetylcholine esterase, an enzyme involved in breaking down acetylcholine, measured with particular interest because it may provide an indirect clue as to the changes in neurons using acetylcholine as a neuro transmitter. It was found that acetylcholine esterase level were greater in EC brains than in IC brains, but the difference was smaller than in difference seen in cortex weights. However measuements of the quantity of choline esterase, an enzyme less specific to acetylcholine and found principly in glial cells showed much greater difference in EC and IC groups. The implications that the EC versus IC differences in brain structure involved in glial population rather than the neuronal population. Glial involvment in the effect of envionmental exposure can be explained in two basic ways. The first is that neurons might be under a greater functional load in enriched condition, require more glia to nourish them and support a higher metabolic rate. The second is that neurons might branch off to a greater degree as a result of complex environment and require a greater number of glia to form the myelin sheath around the new branches.

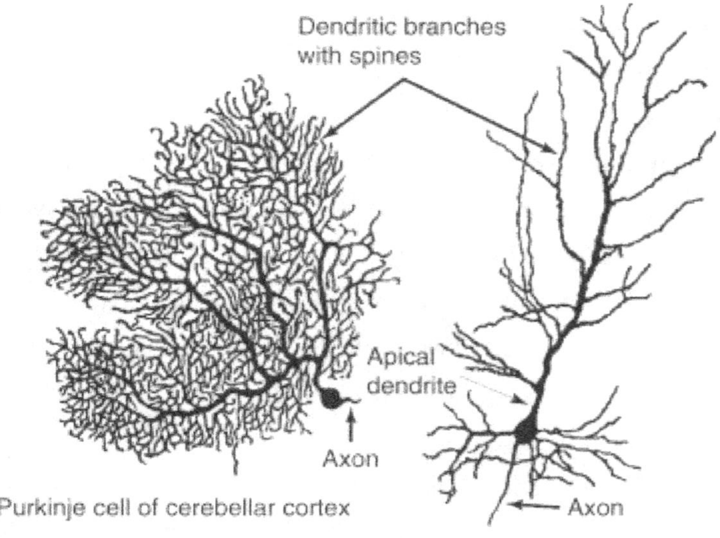

(Fig – 56) Pyramidal cells of cerebral cortex

Examination of large pyramidal neurons in the cortex of EC and IC rats gain attention with particular reference to dendritic spines (Fig – 56). The EC rat neuron had about a 10% greater number of basal dendritic spines, 3% greater number of oblique and terminal spine than IC rat neurons. Apical dendrite which form the main trunk of the dendritic branch showed no differnce in their spine count nor the measures of the neurons lateral width. The increase in certain types of dendrites indicates a greater number of synapse for inerneuronal communication. It is interesting that the greater differences seen in the basal dendrite since it is this dendrites that receive their input from other cortical cells. The apical dendrite carry information from the ascending sensory fibres in the thalamus. On a behavioural point of view, EC rats tend to perform better than IC rats in complex mazes.

EARLY LEARNING DISCOVERIES

Early learning discoveries is an effort to introduce ealry childhood learning activities in young children. Early learning activity of an individual influences variety of factors like social conditions, his or her work or activities, notions of cognition, language, imagination, learning and behavioural problems, childhood education, teaching and learning in early childhood class rooms etc. According to various research and studies, language act as a critical link between the social and psychological planes of human functioning. Early childhood learning often focuses on learning through play formally and informally up until the age of eight. Infant learning activity is from the birth to age of two. The first two years of child's life are spend in the creation of a child's first sense of self. Most children are able to differentaite themselves and others by their second year. The differentiation is critical to the child's ability to determine how they should function in relation to other people. Parents are child's first teacher and therefore the integral part of the early learning process. Children's natural curiosity and imagination evoke learning. Children learn more efficiently and gain knowledge through activities such as dramatic play, art and social games. Tassoi suggests that some play oppurnities will develop specific individual areas of developments. It is important that practioners promote children's development through play by using various types of play on a daily basis. This is called play based learning. Davy states that learning through play has been seen regularly in practice as the most versatile way a child can learn. Margaret Mc Millan suggested that children should be given free school meals, fruit and milk, plenty of exercise to keep them physically and emotionally healthy. Rudolf Steiner believed that play allows children to talk, socially interact, used their imagination and intellectual skills. Marie Montessori believed that children learn through movement and their senses. There are five areas of child development

1. Physical health, Well being and Movement Skills: These activities are designed to help develop your child's large and small muscle control, her coordination, and her overall physical fitness.

2. Social and Emotional Development: Activities in this area target your child's ability to make and keep social relationships, both with adults and with other children. He will learn to recognize and express his own feelings more effectively. He will gain experience understanding and responding to the emotions of others.

3. Approches to learning: Children differ in how they approach new tasks, difficult problems, or challenges. These activities will spark your child's curiosity, interest, and attention and the ability to stay on task. Research suggests strong links between positive approaches to learning and success in school.

4. Thinking abilities and General knowledge: The suggestions in this area help your child figure out how the world works and how things are organized. Your child will experience "learning how to learn," improving problem-solving ability and abstract thinking.

5. Comminication, Language and Literacy: These activities will help your child learn to express himself and to understand what others say. Early reading and writing skills are also targeted.

The developmental domain of childhood - Theories: Vygotsky's socio cultural learning theory

Vygotsky was a Russian theorist, who proposed the socio-cultural theory. During the 1920s–1930s while Piaget was developing his own theory, Vygotsky was an active scholar and at that time his theory was said to be "recent" because it was translated out of Russian language and began influencing western thinking.

He posited that children learn through hands-on experience, as Piaget suggested. However, unlike Piaget, he claimed that timely and sensitive intervention by adults when a child is on the edge of learning a new task (called the zone of proximal development) could help children learn new tasks. This technique is called "scaffolding," because it builds upon knowledge children already have with new knowledge that adults can help the child learn. An example of this might be when a parent "helps" an infant clap or roll her hands to the pat-a-cake rhyme, until she can clap and roll her hands herself.

Vygotsky was strongly focused on the role of culture in determining the child's pattern of development. He argued that "Every function in the child's cultural development appears twice: first, on the social level, and later, on the individual level; first, between people (inter-psychological) and then inside the child (intra-psychological). This applies equally to voluntary attention, to logical memory, and to the formation of concepts. All the higher functions originate as actual relationships between individuals."

Vygotsky felt that development was a process and saw periods of crisis in child development during which there was a qualitative transformation in the child's mental functioning.

Piagets Constructivist theory

Jean piaget theory gained influence 1970's and 1980's. Jean Piaget was a philosopher from Switzerland. He believed that learning comes from within – children construct their own knowledge of world through experience and reflection. Piaget's theory of constructivism impacts learning curriculum because teachers have to make a curriculum plan which enhances their students' logical and conceptual growth. Teacher must put emphasis on the significant role that experiences-or connections with the adjoining atmosphere-play in student education. For example, teachers must bear in mind the role of those fundamental concepts, such as the permanence of objects, plays when it comes to establishing cognitive structures. Piaget's theory of constructivism argues that people produce knowledge and form meaning based upon their experiences. Piaget's theory covered learning theories, teaching methods, and education reform. Two of the key components which create the construction of an individual's new knowledge are accommodation and assimilation. Assimilation causes an individual to incorporate new experiences into the old experiences. This causes the individual to develop new outlooks, rethink what were once misunderstandings, and evaluate what is important, ultimately altering their perceptions. Accommodation, on the other hand, is reframing the world and new experiences into the mental capacity already present. Individuals conceive a particular fashion in which the world operates. When things do not operate within that context, they must accommodate and reframing the expectations with the outcomes. Apart from learning theories, Piaget's theory of constructivism addresses how learning actually occurs, not focusing on what influences learning. The role of teachers are very important. Instead of giving a lecture the teachers in this theory function as facilitators whose role is to aid the student when it comes to their own understanding. This takes away focus from the teacher and lecture and puts it upon the student and their learning. The resources and lesson plans that must be initiated for this learning theory take a very different approach toward traditional learning as well. Instead of telling, the teacher must begin asking. Instead of answering questions that only align with their curriculum, the facilitator in this case must make it so that the student comes to the conclusions on their own instead of being told. Also, teachers are continually in conversation with the students, creating the learning experience that is open to new directions depending upon the needs of the student as the learning progresses. Teachers following Piaget's theory of constructivism must challenge the student by making them effective critical thinkers and not being merely a "teacher" but also a mentor, a consultant, and a coach. Some strategies for teacher include having students working together and aiding to answer one another's questions. Another strategy includes designating one student as the "expert" on a subject and having them teach the class. Finally, allowing students to work in groups or pairs and research controversial topics which they must then present to the class.

Kolb's Experimental learning theory

According to him children need to experience things in order to learn. Knowledge is created through the transformation of experiences. Knowledge results from combinations of grasping and transferring experience. According to Kolb, the learning cycle basically involves four stages namely: concrete learning, reflective observation, abstract conceptualization and active experimentation. Effective learning can be seen when the learner progress through the cycle. The learner can also enter the cycle at any stage of the cycle with logical sequence.

The first stage is concrete learning, where there is encounter of a new experience or reinterpretation of existing experience. Then it is followed by next stage, reflective observation, where one reflects on the experience on personal basis. After this is abstract conceptualization, where new ideas are formed based on the reflection or could be modifications of the existing abstract ideas. Lastly, active experimentation stage is where a learner will apply the ideas to his surroundings to see if there are any modifications in the next appearance of the experience. All this will lead to the next concrete experience. This can happen over a short duration or over a long duration of time.

Kolb's learning style is explained on the basis of two dimensions: they are how a person understands and processes the information. This perceived information is then classified as concrete experience or abstract conceptualization, and processed information as active experimentation or reflective observation.

Role of hippocampus in learning

When we are dealing with situations that are highly relavant to the well being of an animal-the avoidance of shock or the learning of maze inorder to find food, the process of learning cannot be properly understood without considering the emotional components of the behaviour. The systems in the brain that are linked to emotionality are also involved in the learning of shock avoidance and other conditioned responses. Lesions in the amygdala make it more difficult for animal to learn an association based upon odours or it to make a visual discrimination between two objects based upon an association with a reward of food.

The hippocampus is a very large area in the limbic system with overall curving shape that resembles a seahorse. The top portion of the hippocampus lies in the medial portion of subcortex just underneath the cingulate gyrus. It swings laterally and downward in a gentle arc until it ends near the amygdala. One effect of hippocampal lesion observed in rats is the diminished tendency for spontaneous alternation. Generally rats tend not to approach the same goal box on consecutive trails when placed in a T-maze and when both goal boxes in the maze are unrewarded. The deficit in spontaneous alternation following a hippocampal lesion might reflect a general deficit in the ability to use spatial information in behaviour.

Hippocampal lesion also produce a change in the performance of shock avoidance, but the direction of change depends upon the specific arrangement of tasks. If the animal run from one compartment to another as the avoidance response on one trail and run back to the first compartment as the avoidance response on the next, it is called two-way active avoidance, hippocampal lesion seems to provide the animal with an acquired advantage. Learning of this task is faster for operated animals than for controlled subjects. The same lesions produce slower learning of an avoidance task in which the animal runs always in one direction from a danger compartment to a safe compartment, is the one way active avoidance.

The spatial difference between the two way active avoidance task, on one hand and the one way active and passive avoidance task on the other have been used as a central element in theorizing the role of the hippocampus in the animal behaviour. The two way avoidance task produces a great deal of spatial conflict in normal animals because neither of the two compartment is consistently safe. If hippocampal lesion produce a deficit in processing spatial informaiton, animals with such lesions now be at an advantage. Likewise operated upon animals should be at a disadvantage when spatial information is consistent, as in the other two avoidance procedures. The interpretion is consistent with other studies that show the importance of hippocampus in spatial memory, that is the ability to remember where an animal has been and where the critical events have occurred.

Note: Lesioned animal are impaired in spatial memory therefore if one compartment is hot they run to the next compartment and if the second compartment is cold they run back to the first compartment, because they do not remember that the first compartment is hot which is the two way avoidance. However for unleisonied animal spatial memory ability is available hence from the first (hot compartment) they run to second (cold compartment). They do not run back to the first compartment because they remember the first is not safe.

Role of cerebellum in classical conditioning

Cerebellum is associated with motor control and equillibrium rather than on the learning process. However it is now considered to be the critical system for the acquisition of the classically conditioned response according to Thompson and his associates in 1987. The specific behaviour that they have studied is the movement of the rabbits nictitating membrane located in the medial corner of each eye. In the rabbit as well as in a number of other species the nictitating membrane sweeps across the cornea like a third eyelid. This movement is a part of defensive reflex, to prevent injury to the eye. In the experiment, a tone (the conditioned stimulus) was presented from 250–800 milliseconds prior to the presentation of an air puff to the cornea (the unconditioned stimulus). Movements of the nictitating membranes were observed reliably to the air puff and, through a series of paired tone-air puff trails and to the tone as well. The conditioned response was the nictitating membrane movement to the tone prior to the presentation of the air puff. Research showing that rabbit could still acquire nictitating membrane conditioning even after the removal of thalamus led the investigators to consider the cerebellum as a possible focus for this response. They found that localized lesions in the two deep nuclei in the cerebellum, the interpositus and dentate nuclei, produced a complete and permenant inability to emit conditioned responses, eventhough the animal have been trained to do so prior to the surgery and could still respond appropriately to air puff alone. It suggests that this nuclei are necessary components for the process of classical conditioning generally.

Role of prefrontal cortex in information processing

The prefrontal cortex is a region at the extreme anterior tip of the frontal lobe. Jacobsen and its associates in 1935 were among the first to report learning deficits in monkeys and chimpanzees following bilateral removal of the prefrontal cortex. The particular task performance that was found to be affected by lesion was the delayed response. In the delayed response task, the subject was first shown two identical cups. One of the cup is baited with a piece of banana placed in full sight of the animal. A delay interval of few seconds follows, with an opaque screen between the subject and cups. When the screen is lifted, the animal is permitted to choose a cup, and is rewarded with food, if a correct choice is made. The standard apparatus called Wisconsin General Testing Apparatus (WGTA) used for delayed response trainning as well as for a variety of other trainning procedures associated with the study primate learning.

Another task affected by prefrontal lesion is the delayed alternation task in which the baited cup alternate from trial to trail. The requirement for delayed response learning is that some representation of the information (about which cup has the food) be held for the duration of the delay period. The fact that the prefrontal lesions disrupt this kind of performance has led to the natural conclusion that this region of the brain is critical for short term memory. If the animal is in the dark during the delay interval or is sedated during the testing section, then the effects of prefrontal lesions are reduced. The implication from these studies is that an attentional process is disrupted by these lesions and that operated animals are more distractible. It was found that monkeys with prefrontal lesions has the increased tendency to react to novel situations and to switch their attention to novel cues that might appear during testing.

The effect of prefrontal damage in monkeys are quiet specific whereas effect of prefrontal damage in humans seemed for a time to be much more subtle. Extensive studies conducted with more than 200 brain injured men to examine a number of previously held ideas about human brain function. In the case of 20 men injury to the prefrontal cortex, the result in testing were striking. The intelligence of this men as measured in a standarised test was not different from intelligence prior to the injury. The conclusion that had to be drawn was that the frontal lobe did not appear to be especially singled out as the lobe containing the seat of intellect. The general intellectual functioning was unimpaired, however, other cognitive problems have been identified that are tied to the performance of the sepcific tasks. One task in which prefronal lobe injured individuals show deficits is the Wisconsin Card Sorting Test. This test consists of 128 cards with symbols differing in number, form and colour. There are four sample cards also, each variying along all three dimensions. Subjects have to sort the cards in to piles below the sample cards according to a single dimension, with responses guided by the experimenter saying right or wrong. Once 10 cards has been successfully sorted, the experimenter without warning switches the relevant dimension. Normal subjects would switch to the appriopriate dimension, but prefrontal lobe injured subjects tend to preservate with the previously correct dimension.

A deficiency is also seen in the Stroop's test, a procedure in which subjects are presented with colour words printed in a colour different in a word eg. the word yellow printed in green, subjects have to name the colour in which each word is printed as quickly as possible. Prefrontal lobe injured subjects perform this task at a slower pace than do normal individuals.

The deficit observed in the card sorting and stroop tests illustrate the difficulties that prefrontal lobe injured individuals have in either changing an attential set or else maintaining that set in the face of interference. Reviews on the neurophysiological effects of prefrontal injuries, have also pointed out, difficulties in seperating action from knowledge, that is being able to understand action expected of them but not being able to execute the behaviour corresponding to this knowledge. There is also and impairment in ability to monitor one's personal behaviour.

Synaptic basis of learning

The adult human brain contains over 100 billion neurons, with each interconnected by thousands of synapses. Synapses are crucial for brain function including cognition. Without well formed and well running synapses, learning, memory, planning and reasoning become slower or even imposible. Learning results from changes in the strength of the synapse was first suggested by Santiago Ramon in 1894 based on his anatomical studies. Electrophysiological recordings from experimental individuals neurons showed that change in synaptic strength is brought about by modulating the realease of transmitters. A single experience may therefore be translated into the activation of a nearly infinitely large diversity of possible neuronal circuits. Experiences can modify synapses, favouring some neuronal pathways within a circuit and weakening others. Plasticity at synapses can be regulated at the presynaptic site by changing the release of neurotransmitter molecules or postsynaptically by changing the number, types, or properties of neurotransmitter receptors. Studies using in vitro synaptic plasticity models have identified the regulated trafficking of postsynaptic AMPA-type glutamate receptors as a prevalent mechanism underlying activity-induced changes in synaptic transmission. Excitatory synapses contain AMPA-type receptors (AMPAR) to transmit signals and NMDA-type receptors (NMDAR) to trigger long-term changes in synaptic transmission: long-term potentiation (LTP) and long-term depression (LTD).

Opening of NMDA channel leads to a rise in post synaptic Ca^{2+} concentration and this is linked to LTP, as well as protein kinase activation. Strong depolarization of post synaptic cells completely displaces the Mg^{2+} that block the NMDA ion channels and allows Ca^{2+} enter a cell probably causing LTP. While weaker deporization displaces Mg^{2+} ions resulting in less Ca^{2+} entering the post synaptic neuron and lower intracellular Ca^{2+} concentration, which activate phosphatse and induced long term depression or LTD. This activated protein kinases, phosphorylate post synaptic excitatory recptors AMPA, for improving cation conduction, and there by potentaiting synapse, there by facilitating an influx of calcium. This in turn increases post synaptic excitation by a given presynaptic stimulus. When there is high frequency of NMDA receptors, there is an increase in the expression of protein PSD-95 (Post Synaptic Density protein 95) that increases synaptic capacity for AMPA receptors. This leads to synaptic strength and plasticity. Short term synaptic plasticity lasts for few milliseconds whereas longterm synaptic plasticity lasts from minutes to hours. Long term depression and long term potentiation are two terms of plasticity.

Four different genes (*GluR1*, *GluR2*, *GluR3*, and *GluR4*) encode AMPAR subunits. GluR1, GluR4, and GluR2L (a long splice form of GluR2) have a long cytoplasmic carboxy-terminal tail (c-tail), while GluR2, GluR3, and GluR4c (a short splice form of GluR4) have short and structurally similar c-tails. The rules for synaptic AMPAR trafficking are hypothesized to depend on subunit composition: (1) synaptic strengthening involves activity-dependent addition of long-tailed (e.g., GluR1-containing) AMPARs to synapses; (2) synaptic weakening occurs through activity-dependent endocytosis of either long-tailed or short-tailed AMPAR from synapses; (3) short-tailed AMPARs constitutively traffic into synapses independent of activity and without changing synaptic strength.

Cell biological studies between sensory and motor neurons revealed biochemical mechanism for the short term increase in transmitter release produced by sensitization. A decrease in transmitter realease is associated with short term habituation where as increase in transmitter subsatance realease occurs during short term dishabituation. The most important release of serotonin, which acts to increase the level of cAMP (Cyclic Adenosine Monophosphate), in the sensory neuron. This inturn activates the cyclic AMP – dependent protein kinase (PKA), which enhances synaptic transmission. Injecting cyclic AMP or catalytic subunit of PKA directly in the sensory neurons to enhance learning related transmitter release. Short term and long term sensitization involves post translational modifications and alterations in protein synthesis. A tactile stimulus can cause a sensory neuron to release glutamate to excite a motor neuron. Seratonin release from interneuron can activate a stimulatory G protein, which activates adenyl cyclase (AC), leading to the production of c AMP and PKA dependent phosphorylation of different substrates, K^+ and Ca^{2+} channels, which enhances glutamate release from the sensory neuron terminals. This will enhance protein synthesis leads to the growth of new synapses. Both increase and decrease in the synaptic strength can contribute to behavioural plasticity. Synaptic plasicity have temporal and molecular properties to behavioural learning-example short and long phases dependent on discrete signalling pathways. Different forms of learning use similar underlying cellular and molecular mechanism. Synaptic plasticity differ in their mechanisms of induction, time of persistence and synaptic locus. Synaptic plasticity is the ability of synapses for strengthen or weaken over time, in response to increase or decrease in their activity. Plastic change also results from the alternation of the number of neurotransmitter receptors located on a synapse. There are several mechanisms that cooperate to achieve synaptic plasticity, changes in the quantity of neurotransmitters relased in to a synapse and how effectively the cells responds to these neurotransmitters. Synaptic plasticity in both excitatory and inhibitory synapses has been found to be depend upon post synaptic calcium release. Synaptic plasticity is one of the importnat neurochemical foundations of learning and memory.

Coordination of cerebral hemispheres

The vertebrate cerebrum (brain) is formed by two cerebral hemispheres that are separated by a groove, the longitudinal fissure. The brain can thus be described as being divided into left and right cerebral hemispheres. Each of these hemispheres has an outer layer of grey matter, the cerebral cortex, that is supported by an inner layer of white matter. The interior portion of the hemispheres of the cerebrum includes the lateral ventricles, the basal nuclei, and the white matter. In eutherian (placental) mammals, the hemispheres are linked by the corpus callosum, a very large bundle of nerve fibers. Smaller commissures, including the anterior commissure, the posterior commissure and the fornix, also join the hemispheres and these are also present in other vertebrates. These commissures transfer information between the two hemispheres to coordinate localized functions. There are three known poles of the cerebral hemispheres named : the occipital pole, the frontal pole, and the temporal pole. The central sulcus is a prominent fissure which separates the parietal lobe from the frontal lobe and the primary motor cortex from the primary somatosensory cortex. Macroscopically the hemispheres are roughly mirror images of each other, with only subtle differences, such as the Yakovlevian torque seen in the human brain, which is a slight warping of the right side, bringing it just forward of the left side. On a microscopic level, the cytoarchitecture of the cerebral cortex, shows the functions of cells, quantities of neurotransmitter levels and receptor subtypes to be markedly asymmetrical between the hemispheres. However, while some of these hemispheric distribution differences are consistent across human beings, or even across some species, many observable distribution differences vary from individual to individual within a given species.

If the upper portions of the hemispheres be slightly drawn apart a broad band of white substance, the corpus callosum, will be observed, connecting them at the bottom of the longitudinal fissure; the margins of the hemispheres which overlap the corpus callosum are called the labia cerebri. Each labium is part of the cingulate gyrus and the slit-like interval between it and the upper surface of the corpus callosum is termed the callosal sulcus. If the hemispheres be sliced off to a level with the upper surface of the corpus callosum, the white substance of that structure will be seen connecting the two hemispheres. The large expanse of medullary matter now exposed, surrounded by the convoluted margin of gray substance, is called the centrum ovale majus. The blood supply to the centrum ovale is from the superficial middle cerebral artery. The cortical branches of this artery descend to provide blood to the centrum ovale.

Broad generalizations are often made in popular psychology about certain functions (e.g. logic, creativity) being lateralized, that is, located in the right or left side of the brain. These claims are often inaccurate, as most brain functions are actually distributed across both hemispheres. Most scientific evidence for asymmetry relates to low-level perceptual functions rather than the higher-level functions popularly discussed (e.g. subconscious processing of grammar, not "logical thinking" in general). In addition to this lateralization of some functions, the low-level representations also tend to represent the contralateral side of the body.

The best example of an established lateralization is that of Broca's and Wernicke's Areas (language) where both are often found exclusively on the left hemisphere. These areas frequently correspond to handedness however, meaning the localization of these areas is regularly found on the hemisphere opposite to the dominant hand. Function lateralization such as semantics, prosodic, intonation, accentuation, etc. has since been called into question and largely been found to have a neuronal basis in both hemispheres.

Perceptual information is processed in both hemispheres, but is laterally partitioned: information from each side of the body is sent to the opposite hemisphere (visual information is partitioned somewhat differently, but still lateralized). Similarly, motor control signals sent out to the body also come from the hemisphere on the opposite side. Thus, hand preference (which hand someone prefers to use) is also related to hemisphere lateralization.

In some aspects, the hemispheres are asymmetrical; one side is slightly bigger. There are higher levels of the neurotransmitter norepinephrine on the right and higher levels of dopamine on the left. There is more white matter (longer axons) on right and more grey matter (cell bodies) on the left. Linear reasoning functions of language such as grammar and word production are often lateralized to the left hemisphere of the brain. In contrast, holistic reasoning functions of language such as intonation and emphasis are often lateralized to the right hemisphere of the brain. Other integrative functions such as intuitive or heuristic arithmetic, binaural sound localization, etc. seem to be more bilaterally controlled.

FUNTIONS OF CORPUS CALLOSUM

The corpus callosum is a Latin word means "tough body", also called as callosal commissure, is a wide commissure, a flat bundle of commissural fibers, about 10 cm longbeneath the cerebral cortex in the brains of placental mammals. It is a part of the longitudinal fissure, connects the left and right cerebral hemispheres, and enables communication between the hemispheres. It is the largest white matter structure in the human brain, consisting of 200–250 million axonal projections. It has a high myelin content. Myelin is a fatty protective coating around the nerves that facilates quicker transmission of information. The brain uses grey matter for computation, thinking and memory storage. White matter like corpus callosum allows different parts of the brain to communicate each other. It is involved in several functions of the body including communication between brain hemispheres, eye movement, tactile localization and maintaining balance of arousal and attention. The corpus callosum can be divided to regions known as rostrum, genu, body and splenium. The rostrum and genu connect the left and right frontal lobes of the brain. The body and the splenium connects the hemispheres of the temporal and occipital lobes.

PHYSIOLOGY OF MEMORY

Memory is the faculty of the mind by which information is encoded, stored, and retrieved. Memory is vital to experiences and related to limbic systems, it is the retention of information over time for the purpose of influencing future action. Often memory is understood as an informational processing system with explicit and implicit functioning that is made up of a sensory processor. The sensory processor allows information from the outside world to be sensed in the form of chemical and physical stimuli and attended to with various levels of focus and intent. Working memory serves as an encoding and retrieval processor. The working memory also retrieves information from previously stored material. Finally, the function of long-term memory is to store data through various categorical models or systems. Explicit and implicit functions of memory are also known as declarative and non-declarative systems. These systems involve the purposeful intention of memory retrieval and storage.

Declarative, or explicit, memory is the conscious storage and recollection of data. Under declarative memory resides semantic and episodic memory. Semantic memory refers to memory that is encoded with specific meaning, while episodic memory refers to information that is encoded along a spatial and temporal plane.

Non-declarative, or implicit, memory is the unconscious storage and recollection of information. An example of a non-declarative process would be the unconscious learning or retrieval of information by way of procedural memory, or a priming phenomenon. Priming is the process of subliminally arousing specific responses from memory and shows that not all memory is consciously activated, whereas procedural memory is the slow and gradual learning of skills that often occurs without conscious attention to learning.

There are three stages in memory namely electrical,short term and long term. The physiological mechanisms are found involved in memory include transfer of neuronal excitation depends upon tranfer of transmitter. During this process the vesicle attaches, to presynaptic vesicle release sites, contraction at dithiolate structures of these sites, exocytosis of transmitter, movement of transmitter across synaptic cleft and reception at post synaptic site. Disulphate formation from dithiolates (calcium dithiolate salt) occurs during excitation and can represent a short term alteration in properties of vesicle release sites and thus short term memory established. Repaired by one mechanism of altered vesicle-release sites through reduction of the disulphide bond returns the system to its original state or by a second mechanism, enlarges the presynaptic area covered by these sites. Such enlargement is stable, permanent mode, which enhances long term memory. Suitable concentrations of transmitter at post synaptic receptor sites will help the mobilization of additional receptor sites through polymerization of monomeric receptor units.

Memory is not a perfect processor, and is affected by many factors. The manner information is encoded, stored, and retrieved can all be corrupted. The amount of attention given new stimuli can diminish the amount of information that becomes encoded for storage. Also, the storage process can become corrupted by physical damage to areas of the brain that are associated with memory storage, such as the hippocampus. Finally, the retrieval of information from long-term memory can be disrupted because of decay within long-term memory. Normal functioning, decay over time, and brain damage all affect the accuracy and capacity of memory. Memory loss is usually described as forgetfulness or amnesia.

Short term memory and Long term memory

Short-term memory is also known as working memory. Short-term memory allows recall for a period of several seconds to a minute without rehearsal. Its capacity is also very limited. Short-term memory is believed to rely mostly on an acoustic code for storing information, and to a lesser extent a visual code.

The storage in sensory memory and short-term memory generally has a strictly limited capacity and duration, which means that information is not retained indefinitely. By contrast, long-term memory can store much larger quantities of information for potentially unlimited duration (sometimes a whole life span). Its capacity is immeasurable. For example, given a random seven-digit number we may remember it for only a few seconds before forgetting, suggesting it was stored in our short-term memory. On the other hand, we can remember telephone numbers for many years through repetition; this information is said to be stored in long-term memory.

While short-term memory encodes information acoustically, long-term memory encodes it semantically: discovered that, after 20 minutes, test subjects had the most difficulty recalling a collection of words that had similar meanings (e.g. big, large, great, huge) long-term. Another part of long-term memory is episodic memory, "which attempts to capture information such as 'what', 'when' and 'where'" with episodic memory, individuals are able to recall specific events such as birthday parties and weddings.

Short-term memory is supported by transient patterns of neuronal communication, dependent on regions of the frontal lobe (especially dorsolateral prefrontal cortex) and the parietal lobe. Long-term memory, on the other hand, is maintained by more stable and permanent changes in neural connections widely spread throughout the brain. The hippocampus is essential (for learning new information) to the consolidation of information from short-term to long-term memory, although it does not seem to store information itself. It was thought that without the hippocampus new memories were unable to be stored into long-term memory. The hippocampus may be involved in changing neural connections for a period of three months or more after the initial learning.

Research has shown that some memory is stored throughout the body. So every thought you have is "felt" throughout your entire body because the receptors for the chemicals in your brain are found on the surfaces of cells throughout your body. Thus when the chemicals are activated across synapses in the brain, the message is communicated to every part of your body by chemotaxis, a process that allows cells to communicate by "neurotransmitters" or remote travel using blood and cerebrospinal fluid. The storage of information in LTM is a function of new interconnections and synapses and the production of new protein molecules. Research has also shown that short-term memory involves chemical modifications that strengthen existing connections, called synapses, between neurons.

Recognition and recall memory

Recognition memory tasks require individuals to indicate whether they have encountered a stimulus (such as a picture or a word) before. Recall memory tasks require participants to retrieve previously learned information. For example, individuals might be asked to produce a series of actions they have seen before or to say a list of words they have heard before.

Topographic memory

It involves the ability to orient oneself in space, to recognize and follow an itinerary, or to recognize familiar places. Getting lost when travelling alone is an example of the failure of topographic memory.

Flashbulb memories

They are clear episodic memories of unique and highly emotional events. People remembering where they were or what they were doing when they first heard the news.

RETROSPECTIVE AND PROSPECTIVE MEMORY

Retrospective memory or the past memory includes semantic, episodic and autobiographical memory. In contrast, prospective memory is memory for future intentions, or remembering to remember. Prospective memory can be further broken down into event- and time-based prospective remembering. Time-based prospective memories are triggered by a time-cue, such as going to the doctor (action) at 4pm (cue). Event-based prospective memories are intentions triggered by cues, such as remembering to post a letter (action) after seeing a mailbox (cue). Cues do not need to be related to the action (as the mailbox/letter example), and lists, sticky-notes, knotted handkerchiefs, or string around the finger all exemplify cues that people use as strategies to enhance prospective memory.

Memory consolidation

Memory Consolidation is the process of stabilizing a memory trace after the initial acquisition. It may perhaps be thought of part of the process of encoding or of storage, or it may be considered as a memory process in its own right(Fig – 57). It is usually considered to consist of two specific processes, synaptic consolidation, which occurs within the first few hours after learning or encoding. System consolidation,where hippocampus-dependent memories become independent of the hippocampus over a period of weeks to years. Neurologically, the process of consolidation utilizes a phenomenon called long-term potentiation, which allows a synapse to increase in strength as increasing numbers of signals are transmitted between the two neurons. Potentiation is the process by which synchronous firing of neurons makes those neurons more inclined to fire together in the future. Long-term potentiation occurs when the same group of neurons fire together so often that they become permanently sensitized to each other. As new experiences accumulate, the brain creates more and more connections and pathways, and may "re-wire" itself by re-routing connections and re-arranging its organization.

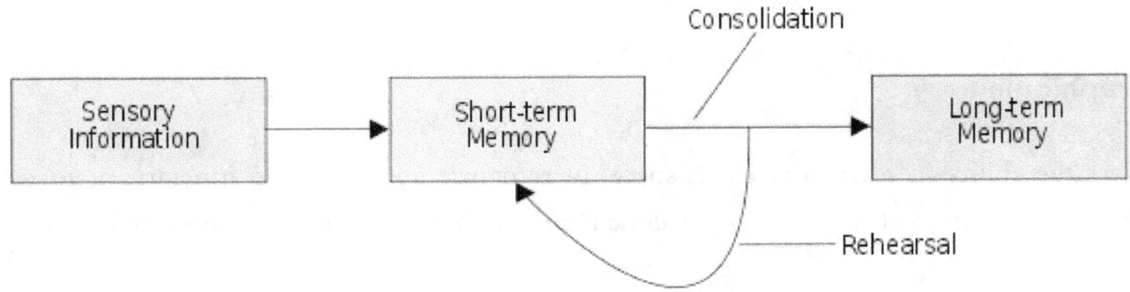

(Fig – 57) The line processes to make information memory.

As such a neuronal pathway, or neural network, is traversed over and over again, an enduring pattern is engraved and neural messages are more likely to flow along such familiar paths of least resistance. This process is achieved by the production of new proteins to rebuild the synapses in the new shape, without which the memory remains fragile and easily eroded with time. For example, if a piece of music is played over and over, the repeated firing of certain synapses in a certain order in your brain makes it easier to repeat this firing later on, with the result that the musician becomes better at playing the music, and can play it faster, with fewer mistakes.

In this way, the brain organizes and reorganizes itself in response to experiences, creating new memories prompted by experience, education or training. The ability of the connection, or synapse, between two neurons to change in strength, and for lasting changes to occur in the efficiency of synaptic transmission, is known as synaptic plasticity or neural plasticity, and it is one of the important neurochemical foundations of memory and learning.

It should be remembered that each neuron makes thousands of connections with other neurons, and memories and neural connections are mutually interconnected in extremely complex ways. Unlike the functioning of a computer, each memory is embedded in many connections, and each connection is involved in several memories. Thus, multiple memories may be encoded within a single neural network, by different patterns of synaptic connections. Conversely, a single memory may involve simultaneously activating several different groups of neurons in completely different parts of the brain.

The inverse of long-term potentiation, known as long-term depression, can also take place, whereby the neural networks involved in erroneous movements are inhibited by the silencing of their synaptic connections. This can occur in the cerebellum, which is located towards the back of the brain, in order to correct our motor procedures when learning how to perform a task (procedural memory), but also in the synapses of the cortex, the hippocampus, the striatum and other memory-related structures.

Contrary to long-term potentiation, which is triggered by high-frequency stimulation of the synapses, long-term depression is produced by nerve impulses reaching the synapses at very low frequencies, leading them to undergo the reverse transformation from long-term potentiation, and, instead of becoming more efficient, the synaptic connections are weakened. It is still not clear whether long-term depression contributes directly to the storage of memories in some way, or whether it simply makes us forget the traces of some things learned long ago so that new things can be learned.

Sleep (particularly slow-wave, or deep, sleep, during the first few hours) is also thought to be important in improving the consolidation of information in memory, and activation patterns in the sleeping brain, which mirror those recorded during the learning of tasks from the previous day, suggest that new memories may be solidified through such reactivation and rehearsal.

Memory re-consolidation is the process of previously consolidated memories being recalled and then actively consolidated all over again, in order to maintain, strengthen and modify memories that are already stored in the long-term memory. Several retrievals of memory (either naturally through reflection, or through deliberate recall) may be needed for long-term memories to last for many years, depending on the depth of the initial processing. However, these individual retrievals can take place at increasing intervals, in accordance with the principle of spaced repetition (this is familiar to us in the way that "cramming" the night before an exam is not as effective as studying at intervals over a much longer span of time).

The very act of re-consolidation, though, may change the intial memory. As a particular memory trace is reactivated, the strengths of the neural connections may change, the memory may become associated with new emotional or environmental conditions or subsequently acquired knowledge, expectations rather than actual events may become incorporated into the memory, etc.

CHEMICAL BASIS OF LONG TERM MEMORY

Vertebrate memory mechanisms generally assume that learning and memory are part of the same phenomenon viewed from a different perspective — memory being a means to achieve a learned response. Measures of memory generally involve behavioural outputs that depend on prior learning. When a rat learns where to swim to find a safe platform, he must remember where the platform is located. Intrinsic, procedural memories such as muscle memory can be viewed as a product of learning. After one learns to ride a bike, one always remembers how to ride a bike. Explicit, declarative memories, like remembered strings of numbers, could be viewed as learned responses. Few would argue with the idea that one can learn to remember or that one remembers what is learned.

The molecular substrates of memory in vertebrates, research has largely focused on mechanisms responsible for neuronal plasticity. The idea is that memory, like learning, derives in large part from altered synaptic connections between neurons that result from prior neuronal activities. Stronger and more synaptic connections lead to long-term potentiation (LTP) and weaker and fewer synaptic connections lead to long-term depression (LTD). These changes cause altered neuronal network circuitries that affect subsequent responses, i.e. learning.

There are numerous molecular mechanisms that serve to modulate synaptic connections in response to prior neuronal activities. Some of these are autonomous consequences of synaptic activation that involve mechanisms more or less contained within and intrinsic to a given activated synapse. Chemical synapses are organized around a synaptic cleft formed from the closely apposed, highly differentiated pre-synaptic axonal and post-synaptic dendritic membranes of two neurons. The pre-synaptic membrane is studded with synaptic vesicles filled with various neurotransmitters ready to be released into the cleft in response to the arrival of an action potential with its associated wave of elevated calcium. Glutamate is the principal excitatory neurotransmitter in the brain, and the generation of post-synaptic action potentials depends on the membrane depolarization produced by glutamate-induced opening of ionotropic glutamate receptors. Glutamate-induced opening of one of the most abundant glutamate receptors, the NMDA receptor, requires coordinate depolarization of the post-synaptic membrane. Action potentials that release sufficient glutamate to activate alternative post-synaptic glutamate channels such as AMPA-type receptors can depolarize post-synaptic membranes so as to subsequently allow NMDA-mediated glutamate signaling. This provides a mechanism for LTP at glutamatergic synapses and helps explain why NMDA receptors play a central role in learning. NMDA receptor activation is only one of many intrinsic control mechanisms associated with synaptic function, however. For instance, elevations in calcium associated with neurotransmission activate protein kinases and phosphatases that regulate a number of target activities associated with LTP and LTD.

In addition to ligand-gated ion channels, neurotransmitters generally interact with metabotropic G-protein coupled receptors, or GPCRs. Numerous different GPCRs clustered within synaptic membranes provide a sort of sensory cortex attuned to a wide range of neurotransmitter inputs. Different receptors modulate different signaling networks in response to different sets of agonists and antagonists. Clearly, metabotropic receptor signaling plays an important and pervasive role in the modulation of synaptic strength in response to previous neuronal activity. There are, for instance, at least three different metabotropic dopamine receptors that interact with heterotrimeric G-proteins that generally promote increased synapse strength, and there are at least two other dopamine receptors that activate other G-proteins that generally promote decreased synaptic strength. The ensemble of GPCRs, G-proteins and cellular signal transduction components at a particular synapse varies with genetic background, epigenetic status, age and history. GPCR regulatory outputs primarily act to control the network of interacting protein kinases that catalyze the transfer of phosphoryl groups from ATP to specific serine and threonine residues in regulatory targets.

Receptor-mediated signaling mechanisms that act locally to modulate synaptic strength are thought to account for short-term memories. Stronger and more persistent receptor activation can result in the activation of signal transduction networks that extend beyond individual synapses to effect changes in nuclear kinase activities that lead to changes in epigenetic modifications and alterations in gene expression. Processes that lead to changes in gene expression are thought to be responsible for long-term memories. There are numerous different protein kinases in a given neuron, each responsible for the phosphorylation of a specific set of cellular targets. Moreover, protein kinases are themselves targets of kinase-mediated phosphorylation. This extensive regulatory network of receptors, G-proteins, kinases and their regulatory targets ensures that the dynamic functional connectivity between neurons is continuously evolving so that LTP and LTD would be expected to be the rule rather than the exception, with every train of action potentials potentially triggering both short and long-term changes in neuronal function. Neurologic processes ranging from associative learning to addiction clearly depend on metabotropic signaling mechanisms. In a sense, all of these cognitive phenomena have an important memory component.

MEMORY IN BRAIN DAMAGED INDIVIDUALS

Object recognition is thought to be the canonical test of declarative memory, the type of memory putatively impaired after damage to the temporal lobes. Studies of object recognition memory have helped elucidate the anatomical structures involved in declarative memory, indicating a critical role for perirhinal cortex. We offer a mechanistic account of the effects of perirhinal cortex damage on object recognition memory, based on the assumption that perirhinal cortex stores representations of the conjunctions of visual features possessed by complex objects. Such representations are proposed to play an important role in memory when it is difficult to solve a task using representations of only individual visual features of stimuli, thought to be stored in regions of the ventral visual stream caudal to perirhinal cortex. The account is instantiated in a connectionist model, in which development of object representations with visual experience provides a mechanism for judgment of previous occurrence. We present simulations addressing the following empirical findings: (1) that impairments after damage to perirhinal cortex (modeled by removing the "perirhinal cortex" layer of the network) are exacerbated by lengthening the delay between presentation of to-be-remembered items and test, (2) that such impairments are also exacerbated by lengthening the list of to-be-remembered items, and (3) that impairments are revealed only when stimuli are trial unique rather than repeatedly presented. This study shows that it may be possible to account for object recognition impairments after damage to perirhinal cortex within a hierarchical, representational framework, in which complex conjunctive representations in perirhinal cortex play a critical role. Any brain function can be disrupted by brain trauma resulting in inattention, difficulty concentrating, excessive sleepiness, faulty judgment, depression, irritability, emotional outbursts, and slowed thinking. However, memory loss is one of the most common cognitive side effects of traumatic brain injury (TBI). Even in mild TBI, memory loss is still very common. The more severe the victim's memory loss after the TBI, the more significant the brain damage will most likely be. Some TBI-related amnesia such as patients unable to recall what happened just before, during and after the head injury is temporary. Temporary memory loss is often caused by swelling of the brain in response to the damage it sustained. But because the brain is pressed against the skull, even parts that were not injured are still not able to work. The patient's memory typically returns as the swelling goes down over a period of weeks or even months.

Temporary memory loss may also bean emotional response to the stressful events surrounding a TBI. Damage to the nerves and axons (connection between nerves) of the brain may also result in memory loss. The brain cannot heal itself like an arm or a leg, so any function that is damaged during a TBI is permanently impaired unless the brain learns how to perform that function differently. Fixed amnesia may include the loss of meanings of certain common, everyday objects or words, or a person may not remember skills he had before the TBI. A different kind of memory loss is called anteretrograde amnesia, which is an inability to form memories of events that happened after the injury. Doctors are not sure, exactly, why this happens, but some research has shown that it may have something to do with the fact that TBI's reduce the levels of a protein in the brain that helps the brain balance its activity. Without enough of that particular protein,the brain can easily overload and memory formation is affected. In general, symptoms of brain injury should lessen over time as the brain heals but sometimes the symptoms worsen because the patient's inability to adapt to the brain injury. It is not uncommon for psychological symptoms to arise and worsen after a brain injury.

At the current time, there is no treatment for memory loss following TBI; if the memory does not come back on its own, it will be lost permanently. There is a great deal of research in the field of TBI and memory loss, but, sadly, there are no cures for TBI-related amnesia at this time.

ANATOMICAL STRESS

The effects of stress on memory include interference with a person's capacity to encode memory and the ability to retrieve information. During times of, the body reacts by secreting stress hormones into the bloodstream. Stress can cause acute and chronic changes in certain brain areas which can cause long-term damage. Over-secretion of stress hormones most frequently impairs long-term delayed recall memory, but can enhance short-term, immediate recall memory. This enhancement is particularly relative in emotional memory. In particular, the hippocampus, prefrontal cortex and the amygdala are affected. One class of stress hormone responsible for negatively affecting long-term, delayed recall memory is the glucocorticoids (GCs), the most notable of which is cortisol. Glucocorticoids facilitate and impair the actions of stress in the brain memory process. Cortisol is a known biomarker for stress. Under normal circumstances, the hippocampus regulates the production of cortisol through negative feedback because it has many receptors that are sensitive to these stress hormones. However, an excess of cortisol can impair the ability of the hippocampus to both encode and recall memories. These stress hormones are also hindering the hippocampus from receiving enough energy by diverting glucose levels to surrounding muscles.

Stress affects many memory functions and cognitive functioning of the brain. There are different levels of stress and the high levels can be intrinsic or extrinsic. Intrinsic stress level is triggered by a cognitive challenge whereas extrinsic can be triggered by a condition not related to a cognitive task. Intrinsic stress can be acutely and chronically experienced by a person. The varying effects of stress on performance or stress hormones are often compared to or known as "inverted-u" which induce areas in learning, memory and plasticity. Chronic stress can affect the brain structure and cognition.

Studies considered the effects of stress on both intrinsic and extrinsic memory functions, using for both of them Pavlovian conditioning and spatial learning. In regard to intrinsic memory functions, the study evaluated how stress affected memory functions that was triggered by a learning challenge. In regard to extrinsic stress, the study focused on stress that was not related to cognitive task but was elicited by other situations. The results determined that intrinsic stress was facilitated by memory consolidation process and extrinsic stress was determined to be heterogeneous in regard to memory consolidation. Researchers found that high stress conditions were a good representative of the effect that extrinsic stress can cause on memory functioning. It was also proven that extrinsic stress does affect spatial learning whereas acute extrinsic stress does not affect the spatial learning.

PHYSIOLOGY OF STRESS

When a stressful situation is encountered, stress hormones are released into the blood stream. Adrenaline is released by the adrenal glands to begin the response in the body. Adrenaline acts as a catalyst for the fight-or-flight response,which is a response of the sympathetic nervous system to encourage the body to react to the apparent stressor. This response causes an increase in heart-rate, blood pressure, and accelerated breathing. The kidneys release glucose, providing energy to combat or flee the stressor. Blood is redirected to the brain and major muscle groups, diverted away from energy consuming bodily functions unrelated to survival at the present time. There are three important axes, the adrenocorticotropic axis, the vasopressin axis and the thyroxine axis, which are responsible for the physiologic response to stress.

(Fig – 58) Cortisol

ADRENOCORTICOTROPIC HORMONE AXIS

When a receptor within the body senses a stressor, a signal is sent to the anterior hypothalamus. At the reception of the signal, corticotrophin-releasing factor (CRF) acts on the anterior pituitary. The anterior pituitary in turn releases adrenocorticotropic hormone (ACTH). ACTH induces the release of corticosteriods and aldosterone from the adrenal gland. These substances are the main factors responsible for the stress response in humans. Cortisol (Fig – 58) for example stimulates the mobilization of free fatty acids and proteins and the breakdown of amino acids, and increases serum glucose level and blood pressure, among other effects. On the other hand, aldosterone is responsible for water retention associated with stress. As a result of cells retaining sodium and eliminating potassium, water is retained and blood pressure is increased by increasing the blood volume.

Vasopressin axis

A second physiological response in relation to stress occurs via the vasopressin axis. Vasopressin, also known as antidiuretic hormone (ADH), is synthesized and regulates fluid loss by manipulating the urinary tract. This pathway allows water reabsorption within the body and decreases the amount of water loss through perspiration. ADH has the greatest effect on blood pressure within the body. Under normal circumstances, ADH will regulate the blood pressure and increase or decrease the blood volume when needed. However, when stress becomes chronic, homeostatic regulation of blood pressure is lost. Vasopressin is released and causes a static increase in blood pressure. This increase in blood pressure under stressful conditions ensures that muscles receive the oxygen that they need to be active and respond accordingly. If these stressful conditions remain elevated, muscles will become fatigued, resulting in hypertension and in extreme cases can result in death.

Thyroxine axis

The third physiological response results in the release of thyrotropic hormone-release factor (TRF) which results in the release of thyrotropic hormone (TTH). TTH stimulates the release of thyroxine and triiodothyronine from the thyroid. This results in an increased basal metabolic rate (BMR). This effect is not as immediate as the other two, and can take days to weeks to become prevalent.

Chronic stress

Chronic stress is a stressor that is ongoing for a long period of time. When chronic stress is experienced, our body is in a state of continuous physiological arousal. When chronic stress is perceived, however, the body is in a continuous state of fight-or-flight response and never reaches a state of homeostasis. The physiological effects of chronic stress can negatively affect memory and learning. One study used rats to show the effects of chronic stress on memory by exposing them to a cat for five weeks and being randomly assigned to a different group each day. Their stress was measured in a naturalistic setting by observing their open field behaviour, and the effect on memory was estimated using the radial arm water maze (RAWM). In the RAWM, rats are taught the place of a platform that is placed below the surface of the water. They must recall this later to discover the platform to exit the water. It was found that the rats exposed to chronic psychosocial stress could not learn to adapt to new situations and environments, and had impaired memory on the RAM.

Chronic stress affects a person's cognitive functioning differently for normal subjects versus subjects with mild cognitive impairment. Chronic stress and elevated cortisol (a biomarker for stress) has been known to lead to dementia in elderly people. A longitudinal study was performed which included 61 cognitively normal people and 41 people who suffered from mild cognitive impairment. The participants were between 65 and 97 years old. 52 of the participants were followed for three years and repeatedly received stress and cognitive test assessments. Any patient that suffered from signs or conditions that would affect their cortisol level or cognitive functioning was exempt from participating.

In general, higher event based stress was associated with more rapid cognitive impairment. However, participants with greater cortisol levels showed signs of slower decline. Neither of these effects held for the non-cognitively-impaired group.

Acute stress

Acute stress is a stressor that is an immediate perceived threat. Unlike chronic stress, acute stress is not ongoing and the physiological arousal associated with acute stress is not nearly as demanding. There are mixed findings on the effects of acute stress on memory. One view is that acute stress can impair memory, while others believe that acute stress can actually enhance memory. Several studies have shown that stress and glucocorticoids enhance memory formation while they impair memory retrieval. First, the context in which the stress is being perceived must match the context of the information or material being encoded. Second, the brain regions involved in the retrieval of the memory must match the regions targeted by glucocorticoids. There are also differences in the type of information being remembered or being forgotten while being exposed to acute stress. In some cases neutral stimuli tend to be remembered, while emotionally charged stimuli tend to be forgotten. In other cases the opposite effect is obtained. What seems to be an important factor in determining what will be impaired and what will be enhanced is the timing of the perceived stressful exposure and the timing of the retrieval. For emotionally salient information to be remembered, the perceived stress must be induced before encoding, and retrieval must follow shortly afterwards. In contrast, for emotionally charged stimuli to be forgotten, the stressful exposure must be after encoding and retrieval must follow after a longer delay.

A study published in 2009 tested eighteen young healthy males between 19 and 31 years old. All participants were right-handed and had no history of a head injury, or of any medication that could affect a person central nervous system or endocrine system. All of the volunteers participated in two different sessions a month apart. The study consisted on the participants viewing movie clips and pictures that belonged to two different categories: neutral or negative. The participants had to memorize then rate each movie clip or picture by pressing a button with their right hand. They were also monitored in other areas such as their heart rate, pupil diameter, and stress measures by collection of saliva throughout the experiment. The participants mood was assessed by using the Positive and Negative Affect Schedule.

The results from the study confirmed that there were physiological measures in regard to stress induction. The participant's heart rate was elevated and pupil dilation was decreased when viewing the pictures. The study also showed psychological measures that proved that stress induction did cause an increase in subjective stress. In regard to memory enhancement, participants that were shown a stressful picture, often remembered them a day later, which is in accordance with the theory that negative incidents have lasting effects on our memory.

Acute stress can also affect a person's neural correlates which interfere with the memory formation. During a stressful time, a person's attention and emotional state may be affected, which could hinder the ability to focus while processing an image. Stress can also enhance the neural state of memory formation.

Arousal hypothesis

Arousal is the physiological and psychological state of being awoken or of sense organs stimulated to a point of perception. It involves activation of the ascending reticular activating system (ARAS) in the brain, which mediates wakefulness, the autonomic nervous system, and the endocrine system, leading to increased heart rate and blood pressure and a condition of sensory alertness, mobility, and readiness to respond.

Arousal is important in regulating consciousness, attention, alertness, and information processing. It is crucial for motivating certain behaviours, such as mobility, the pursuit of nutrition, the fight-or-flight response and sexual activity.

Physiology of arousal

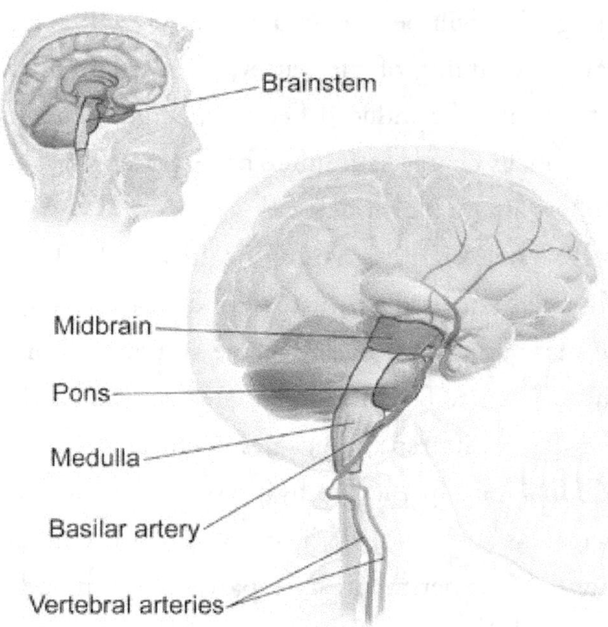

(Fig – 59) Structures of the brainstem, the origin of the arousal system, viewed along the sagittal plane

Wakefulness is regulated by the ascending reticular activating system, which is composed of five major neurotransmitter systems – the acetylcholine, norepinephrine, dopamine, histamine, and serotonin systems – that originate in the brainstem and form connections which extend throughout the cerebral cortex (Fig – 59). When stimulated, these systems produce cortical activity and alertness. The noradrenergic system is a bundle of axons that originate in the locus coeruleus and ascends up into the neocortex, limbic system, and basal forebrain. Most of the neurons are projected to the posterior cortex which is important with sensory information, and alertness. The activation of the locus coeruleus and release of norepinephrine causes wakefulness and increases vigilance. The neurons that project into the basal forebrain impact cholinergic neurons that results in a flood of acetylcholine into the cerebral cortex. The acetylcholinergic system has its neurons located in the pons and in the basal forebrain. Stimulation of these neurons result in cortical activity, shown from EEG records, and alertness. All of the other four neurotransmitters play a role in activating the acetylcholine neurons.

Another arousal system, the dopaminergic system, releases dopamine produced by the substantia nigra. The neurons arise in the ventral tegmental area in the midbrain, and projects to the nucleus accumbens, the striatum forebrain, limbic system, and prefrontal cortex. The limbic system is important for control of mood, and the nucleus accumbens signal excitement and arousal. The path terminating in the prefrontal cortex is important in regulating motor movements, especially reward oriented movements. The serotonergic system has almost all of its serotonergic neurons originating in the raphe nuclei. This system projects to the limbic system and the prefrontal cortex. Stimulation of these axons and release of serotonin causes cortical arousal and impacts locomotion and mood. The neurons of the histamergenic system are in the tuberomammillary nucleus of the hypothalamus. These neurons send pathways to the cerebral cortex, thalamus, and the basal forebrain, where they stimulate the release of acetylcholine into the cerebral cortex.

All of these systems are linked and show similar redundancy. The pathways described are ascending pathways, but there also arousal pathways that descend. One example is the ventrolateral preoptic area, which release GABA reuptake inhibitors, which interrupt wakefulness and arousal. Neurotransmitters of the arousal system, such as acetylcholine and norepinephrine, work to inhibit the ventrolateral preoptic area.

Arousal is important in regulating consciousness, attention, and information processing. It is crucial for motivating certain behaviours, such as mobility, the pursuit of nutrition, the fight-or-flight response and sexual activity.

The Yerkes–Dodson law states that there is a relationship between arousal and task performance, essentially arguing that there is an optimal level of arousal for performance, and too little or too much arousal can adversely affect task performance. One interpretation of the Yerkes–Dodson law is the Easterbrook cue-utilisation theory. It predicted that high levels of arousal will lead to attention narrowing, during which the range of cues from the stimulus and the environment decreases. According to this hypothesis, attention will be focused primarily on the arousing details (cues) of the stimulus, so that information central to the source of the emotional arousal will be encoded while peripheral details will not. In positive psychology, arousal is described as a response to a difficult challenge for which the subject has moderate skills.

EMOTIONAL AROUSAL

Emotional arousal is a process, which means it happens as a sequence over time. It is a state of heightened physiological activity. This includes having strong emotions like anger and fear and we go to the emotional arousal state in response to our daily experiences. For example the fight, flight or freeze response is a state of emotional arousal. Some people come into this world with their emotional arousal response on high alert. For others it takes a lot to trigger their emotional arousal response. Arousal starts with a nature component as a hardwired response to our experiences. That emotional arousal then develops over time as a reaction to a lifetime of experiences. Arousal often happens through a trigger, which appears through one of our senses. Thus, for example, arousal can happen through:

❖ Touch: A punch, kiss or caress

❖ Vision: Seeing something shocking or desirable

❖ Hearing: A sudden noise or somebody saying something

❖ Smell: An evocative odour that triggers powerful memories

❖ Taste: Of wonderful or disgusting food

Arousal typically happens when the body releases chemicals into the brain that act to stimulate emotions, reduce cortical functioning and hence conscious control, and create physical agitation and 'readiness for action'. Emotions can be classified in terms of how arousing or not. They are arousing emotions like joy, happiness, anger, frustration, hate, excitement and calming emotions such as contentment, sadness, confusion, shame, guilt, satisfaction etc. Arousal is sometimes talked of with the metaphor of heat, reflecting the energy created, with arousing emotions described as 'hot' or 'warm; and calmer emotions as 'cold' or 'cool'. Higher arousal tends to make people want to talk and communicate more. Hence people talk more when they are joyful and less when they are just contented.

There are a number of factors that influence the development of our emotional arousal, including Attachment Styles and Relational Feedback Loops. Everyone has an attachment style that affects the way we interact with others. As parents our attachment styles influence every interaction we have with our children. Our children then take all their interactions with us, combine them with their predisposed genetic temperament and develop their own attachment style. Attachment styles typically fall in one of four categories: secure, anxious, avoidant or anxious-avoidant. Attachment style is rarely an exclusive form of secure, avoidant or anxious. Relational Feedback Loops says that Infants and parents can go through what we call a bidirectional feedback loop. One loop looks like this:Infants with a higher temperamental baseline of arousal may be fussy and difficult. This may also be a result of physiological difficulties such as trouble digesting,this fussiness leads to parents becoming tired, frustrated, and less responsive,as parents become less responsive to the infant's needs the infant will likely become more anxious manifesting in more fussing and so on. The inverse is also true. If we are able to remain highly responsive the infant learns to trust this responsiveness. The baby knows it will have her needs met on a consistent basis. Levels of arousal can be conditioned and reconditioned, meaning that if we are anxious in relationships we can be reconditioned through consistency, validation, and love. We can help our daughters to have less anxiety in their relationships by forming a more secure attachment style.

There is some evidence that emotional arousal enhances memory for generalized forms of information that lack detail, a type of memory known as 'gist' memory, whereas other studies show that emotional arousal enhances memory for the specific perceptual details of an item.

Neuroscience is witnessing growing interest in understanding brain mechanisms of memory formation for emotionally arousing events, a development closely related to renewed interest in the concept of memory consolidation. Extensive research in animals implicates stress hormones and the amygdaloid complex as key, interacting modulators of memory consolidation for emotional events. Considerable evidence suggests that the amygdala is not a site of long-term explicit or declarative memory storage, but serves to influence memory-storage processes in other brain regions, such as the hippocampus, striatum and neocortex. Human-subject studies confirm the prediction of animal work that the amygdala is involved with the formation of enhanced declarative memory for emotionally arousing events.

Human studies suggest that prior emotional responses are stored within the brain as associations called somatic markers and are recalled to inform rapid decision-making. Consequently, behavioural and physiological indicators of arousal are detectable in humans when making decisions, and influence decision outcomes. The physical and physiological factors which activate and suppress behavioural arousal. Important activators include: rising blood oestrogen concentrations just before birth; physical stimuli during delivery; exposure to cold on delivery, and; elevation in blood oxygen levels following the onset of pulmonary respiration. Suppressors of behavioural arousal and awareness are low oxygen levels and high concentrations of progesterone and its metabolites.

SEXUAL AROUSAL

Sexual arousal (also sexual excitement) is the arousal of sexual desire, during or in anticipation of sexual activity. A number of physiological responses occur in the body and mind as preparation for sexual activity and continue during it. Genital responses are not the only changes, but noticeable and necessary for consensual and comfortable intercourse. Male arousal will lead to an erection, and in female arousal the body's response is engorged sexual tissues such as nipples, vulva, clitoris, vaginal walls and vaginal lubrication. Mental stimuli and physical stimuli such as touch, and the internal fluctuation of hormones, can influence sexual arousal.

Sexual arousal has several stages and may not lead to any actual sexual activity, beyond a mental arousal and the physiological changes that accompany it. Given sufficient sexual stimulation, sexual arousal in humans reaches its climax during an orgasm. It may also be pursued for its own sake, even in the absence of an orgasm.

Depending on the situation, a person can be sexually aroused by a variety of factors, both physical and mental. A person may be sexually aroused by another person or by particular aspects of that person, or by a non-human object. Physical stimulation of an erogenous zone or acts of foreplay can result in arousal, especially if it is accompanied with the anticipation of imminent sexual activity. Sexual arousal may be assisted by a romantic setting, music or other soothing situation. The potential stimuli for sexual arousal vary from person to person, and from one time to another, as does the level of arousal.

Stimuli can be classified according to the sense involved: somatosensory (touch), visual, and olfactory (scent). Auditory stimuli are also possible, though they are generally considered secondary in role to the other three. Erotic stimuli which can result in sexual arousal can include conversation, reading, films or images, or a smell or setting, any of which can generate erotic thoughts and memories in a person. Given the right context, these may lead to the person desiring physical contact, including kissing, cuddling, and petting of an erogenous zone. This may in turn make the person desire direct sexual stimulation of the breasts, nipples, buttocks and/or genitals, and further sexual activity. When sexual arousal is achieved by or dependent on the use of objects, it is referred to as sexual fetishism, or in some instances a paraphilia.

There is a common belief that women need more time to achieve arousal. However, recent scientific research has shown that there is no considerable difference for the time men and women require to become fully aroused. Scientists from McGill University Health Centre in Montreal (in Canada) used the method of thermal imaging to record baseline temperature change in genital area to define the time necessary for sexual arousal. Researchers studied the time required for an individual to reach the peak of sexual arousal while watching sexually explicit movies or pictures and came to the conclusion that on average women and men took almost the same time for sexual arousal — around 10 minutes. The time needed for foreplay is very individualistic and varies from one time to the next depending on many circumstances.

Unlike many other animals, humans do not have a mating season, and both sexes are potentially capable of sexual arousal throughout the year.

SEXUAL AROUSAL IN WOMAN

Stage 1: sexual excitement or arousal

When a woman becomes aroused (turned on), the blood vessels in her genitals dilate. There is increased blood flow in the vaginal walls, which causes fluid to pass through them. This is the main source of lubrication, which makes the vagina wet. The external genitalia or vulva (including the clitoris, vaginal opening, and inner and outer lips or labia) become engorged (swollen) due to the increased blood supply. Inside the body, the top of the vagina expands. The pulse and breathing quicken, and blood pressure rises. A woman may become flushed, especially on the chest and neck, due to the blood vessels dilating.

Stage 2: sexual plateau

Blood flow to the lower third of the vagina reaches its limit, and causes the lower area of the vagina to become swollen and firm. This is called the introitus, sometimes known as the orgasmic platform, and undergoes rhythmic contractions during orgasm. A woman's breasts may increase in size by up to 25%, and blood flow to the area around the nipple (the areola) increases, making the nipples look less erect. As a woman gets closer to orgasm, her clitoris pulls back against the pubic bone and seems to disappear. Continuous stimulation is needed in this phase to build up enough sexual excitement for orgasm.

Stage 3: orgasm

Orgasm is the intense and pleasurable release of sexual tension that has built up in the earlier stages, characterised by contractions (0.8 seconds apart) of the genital muscles, including the introitus. Most women don't experience the recovery period that men do after an orgasm. A woman may have another orgasm if she's stimulated again. Not all women have an orgasm every time they have sex. For most women, foreplay is an important role in an orgasm occurring. This can include stroking erogenous zones and stimulating the clitoris.

Stage 4: sexual resolution

This is when the woman's body slowly returns to its normal state. Swelling reduces, and breathing and heart rate slow down.

SEXUAL AROUSAL IN MEN

Stage 1: sexual excitement or arousal

A man gets an erection with physical or psychological stimulation, or both. This causes more blood to flow into three spongy areas called corpora that run along the length of his penis. The skin is loose and mobile, allowing his penis to grow. His scrotum – the bag of skin holding the testicles – becomes tighter, so his testicles are drawn up towards the body.

Stage 2: sexual plateau

The head (glans) of his penis gets wider, and the blood vessels in and around the penis fill with blood. This causes the colour to deepen and his testicles to grow up to 50% larger. His testicles continue to rise, and a warm feeling around the area between the testicles and anus (perineum) develops. His heart rate increases, blood pressure rises, breathing becomes quicker, and his thighs and buttocks tighten.

Stage 3: orgasm and ejaculation

A series of contractions force semen into the urethra, the tube along which urine and semen come out of the penis. These contractions occur in the pelvic floor muscles, in the tube that carries sperm from the testicles to the penis (vas deferens). They also occur in the seminal vesicles and the prostate gland, which both add fluid to the sperm. This mix of sperm (5%) and fluid (95%) is called semen. These contractions are part of orgasm, and the man reaches a point where he can't stop ejaculation happening. Contractions of the prostate gland and the pelvic floor muscles then lead to ejaculation, when semen is forced out of the penis.

Stage 4: resolution phase of sex

The man now has a recovery phase, when the penis and testicles shrink back to their normal size. He is breathing heavily and fast, his heart is beating rapidly, and he might be sweating. There's a period of time after ejaculation when another orgasm is not possible. This varies between men, from a few minutes to a few hours, or even days. The time generally gets longer as men get older. If a man gets aroused but does not ejaculate, this resolution stage can take longer, and his testicles and pelvis might ache.

PERCEPTUAL AROUSAL

Perceptual arousal is the state of arousal caused by direct sensory stimuli and our reactions to these. The main use of perceptual arousal is to grab attention that has been either lost or not yet gained. This gives the opportunity to continue communicating about the real point of interest.

Attention may be gained through novelty (something new and outside current models), surprise (something that contradicts expectation),contrast (with marked change in sensory levels),concretization (making abstract ideas more real), fun (making things enjoyable), and change (changing tempo, actions, context).

One of the first and biggest problems of attention is getting it. In a world full of noise it is difficult to stand out. Perceptual arousal is an approach that seeks to do this. An evolutionary force behind perceptual arousal is the way we constantly monitor our environment for opportunities and, especially, threats that leads us to pay attention to things which are different. When you want to get attention, rather than talking about interesting detail, start with something that purely gains attention. Then follow it up quickly with more subtle information that keeps them paying attention until you have got the agreement you need.

YERKES-DODSON LAW (THE INVERTED-U HYPOTHESIS)

The Yerkes–Dodson law is an empirical relationship between arousal and performance, originally developed by psychologists Robert M. Yerkes and John Dillingham Dodson in 1908. The law dictates that performance increases with physiological or mental arousal, but only up to a point. When levels of arousal become too high, performance decreases. The process is often illustrated graphically as a bell-shaped curve which increases and then decreases with higher levels of arousal.

Research has found that different tasks require different levels of arousal for optimal performance. For example, difficult or intellectually demanding tasks may require a lower level of arousal (to facilitate concentration), whereas tasks demanding stamina or persistence may be performed better with higher levels of arousal (to increase motivation).

Because of task differences, the shape of the curve can be highly variable. For simple or well-learned tasks, the relationship is monotonic, and performance improves as arousal increases. For complex, unfamiliar, or difficult tasks, the relationship between arousal and performance reverses after a point, and performance thereafter declines as arousal increases.

The effect of task difficulty led to the hypothesis that the Yerkes–Dodson Law can be decomposed into two distinct factors as in a bathtub curve. The upward part of the inverted U can be thought of as the energizing effect of arousal. The downward part is caused by negative effects of arousal (or stress) on cognitive processes like attention (e.g., "tunnel vision"), memory, and problem-solving.

PARADOXICAL SLEEP

The REM phase is also known as paradoxical sleep. REM sleep may favour the preservation of certain types of memories: specifically, procedural memory, spatial memory, and emotional memory. In rats, REM sleep increases following intensive learning, especially several hours after, and sometimes for multiple nights. Experimental REM sleep deprivation has sometimes inhibited memory consolidation, especially regarding complex processes (e.g., how to escape from an elabourate maze). In humans, the best evidence for REM's improvement of memory pertains to learning of procedures—new ways of moving the body (such as trampoline jumping), and new techniques of problem solving. REM deprivation seemed to impair declarative (i.e., factual) memory only in more complex cases, such as memories of longer stories. REM sleep apparently counteracts attempts to suppress certain thoughts.

According to the dual-process hypothesis of sleep and memory, the two major phases of sleep correspond to different types of memory. "Night half" studies have tested this hypothesis with memory tasks either begun before sleep and assessed in the middle of the night, or begun in the middle of the night and assessed in the morning. Slow-wave sleep, part of non-REM sleep, appears to be important for declarative memory. Artificial enhancement of the non-REM sleep improves the next-day recall of memorized pairs of words.

Graeme Mitchison and Francis Crick proposed in 1983 that by virtue of its inherent spontaneous activity, the function of REM sleep "is to remove certain undesirable modes of interaction in networks of cells in the cerebral cortex", which process they characterize as "unlearning". As a result, those memories which are relevant (whose underlying neuronal substrate is strong enough to withstand such spontaneous, chaotic activation) are further strengthened, whilst weaker, transient, "noise" memory traces disintegrate. Memory consolidation during paradoxical sleep is specifically correlated with the periods of rapid eye movement, which do not occur continuously. One explanation for this correlation is that the Ponto-geniculo-occipital waves (PGO electrical waves) which precede the eye movements, also influence memory. REM sleep could provide a unique opportunity for "unlearning" to occur in the basic neural networks involved in homeostasis, which are protected from this "synaptic downscaling" effect during deep sleep.

FORGETTING

Forgetting (retention loss) refers to apparent loss of information already encoded and stored in an individual's long term memory. It is a spontaneous or gradual process in which old memories are unable to be recalled from memory storage. It is subject to delicately balanced optimization that ensures that relevant memories are recalled. Forgetting can be reduced by repetition and/or more elaborate cognitive processing of information. Reviewing information in ways that involve active retrieval seems to slow the rate of forgetting.

DECAY THEORY

Decay theory proposes that memory fades due to the mere passage of time. Information is therefore less available for later retrieval as time passes and memory, as well as memory strength, wears away. When we learn something new, a neurochemical "memory trace" is created. However, over time this trace slowly disintegrates. Actively rehearsing information is believed to be a major factor counteracting this temporal decline. It is widely believed that neurons dies off gradually as we age, yet some older memories can be stronger than most recent memories. Thus, decay theory mostly affects the short-term memory system, meaning that older memories (in long-term memory) are often more resistant to shocks or physical attacks on the brain. The term decay theory was first coined by Edward Thorndike. This simply states that if a person does not access and use the memory representation they have formed the memory trace will fade or decay over time. This theory was based on the early memory work by Hermann Ebbinghaus in the late 1800s. The decay theory proposed by Thorndike was heavily criticized by McGeoch and his interference theory. This led to the abandoning of the decay theory, until the late 1950s when studies by John Brown and the Petersons showed evidence of time based decay by filling the retention period by counting backwards in threes from a given number. This led to what is known as the Brown-Peterson Paradigm. The theory was again challenged, this time a paper by Keppel and Underwood who attributed the findings to proactive interference. Studies in the 1970s by Reitmantried reviving the decay theory by accounting for certain confounds criticized by Keppel and Underwood. Roediger quickly found problems with these studies and their methods. Harris made an attempt to make a case for decay theory by using tones instead of word lists and his results are congruent making a case for decay theory. In addition, McKone used implicit memory tasks as opposed to explicit tasks to address the confound problems. They provided evidence for decay theory, however, the results also interacted with interference effects. One of the biggest criticisms of decay theory is that it can't be explained as a mechanism and that is the direction that the research is headed. Revisions in Decay Theory are being made in research today. The theory is simple and intuitive, but also problematic. Decay theory has long been rejected as a mechanism of long term forgetting. Now, its place in short term forgetting is being questioned. The simplicity of the theory works against it in that supporting evidence always leaves room for alternative explanations. Researchers have had much difficulty creating experiments that can pinpoint decay as a definitive mechanism of forgetting. Current studies have always been limited in their abilities to establish decay due to confounding evidence such as attention effects or the operation of interference.

INTERFERENCE THEORY

Interference theory states that interference occurs when the learning of something new causes forgetting of older material on the basis of competition between the two. There are 3 main kinds of Interference theory: Proactive, Retroactive and Output. The main assumption of Interference theory is that the stored memory is intact but unable to be retrieved due to competition created by newly acquired information.

The History of Interference Theory

Bergström, a German psychologist, is credited as conducting the first study regarding interference in 1892. His experiment was similar to the Stroop task and consisted of subjects to sort two decks of card with words into two piles. When the location was changed for the second pile sorting was lower showing that the first sorting rules interfered with the learning of the new sorting rules. German psychologists continued in the field with Georg Elias Müller and Pilzeker in 1900 studying Retroactive Interference. To the confusion of Americans at a later date Georg Elias Müller used associative hemming (inhibition) as a blanket term for retroactive and proactive inhibition. The next major progression came from an American psychologist by the name of Benton J. Underwood in 1915. Underwood found that the more lists that were learned, the less the last-learned list was retained after 24 hours. These results were controversial because of the well known effect of the learning theory at the time. In 1924, James J. Jenkins and Dallenback showed that everyday experiences can interfere with memory with an experiment that resulted in retention being better over a period of sleep than over the same amount of time devoted to activity. The United States again made headway in 1932 with John A. McGeoch suggesting that decay theory should be replaced by an Interference Theory. The most recent major paradigm shift came when Underwood proposed that proactive inhibition is more important or meaningful than retroactive inhibition in accounting for forgetting.

Proactive Interference

Proactive Interference is the "forgetting [of information] due to interference from the traces of events or learning that occurred prior to the materials to be remembered". Proactive Interference occurs when in any given context, past memories inhibit an individual's full potential to retain new memories. It has been hypothesized that forgetting from working memory would be non-existent if not for proactive interference. A real life example of Proactive Interference is if a person had the same credit card number for a number of years and memorized that number over time. Then if the credit card was compromised, and a new card dispensed to the client, the person would then have great difficulty memorizing the new credit card number as the old credit card number is so ingrained in their minds. The competition between the new and old credit card numbers cause Proactive Interference.

The leading experimental technique for studying Proactive Interference in the brain is the "Recent-Probes" Task, in which participants must commit a given set of items to memory and they are asked to recall a specific item which is indicated by a probe. Using the "Recent-Probes" Task, the brain mechanisms involved in the resolution of Proactive Interference have been identified as the ventrolateral prefrontal cortex and the left anterior prefrontal cortex. These influential areas of the brain have been identified through functional magnetic resonance imaging (fMRI).

Retroactive Interference

Retroactive Interference impedes the retrieval and performance of previously learned informationdue to newly acquired and practiced information. An example of Retroactive Interference would be if one was to memorize a phone number and then after a few moments memorize another phone number, practicing the second phone number more. When the recall of the first phone number is needed, the recollection will be poor because the last phone number was the item practiced the most. This Retroactive Interference is found because as the second phone number was practiced more, the retention for the first phone number decreases.

Retroactive Interference has been localized to the left anterior ventral prefrontal cortex by magnetoencephalography (MEG) studies investigating Retroactive Interference and working memory in elderly adults. The study found that adults 55–67 years of age showed less magnetic activity in their prefrontal cortices than the control group. Executive control mechanisms are located in the frontal cortex and deficits in working memory show changes in the functioning of this brain area.

Output Interference

Output Interference occurs when the initial act of recalling specific information interferes with the retrieval of the original information. Output Interference occurs if one had created a list of items that were to be purchased at a grocery store, which had been forgotten home. The act of remembering a couple items on that list decreases the probability of remembering the other items on that list.

Retrieval of Memory

Recall or retrieval of memory refers to the subsequent re-accessing of events or information from the past, which have been previously encoded and stored in the brain. During recall, the brain "replays" a pattern of neural activity that was originally generated in response to a particular event, echoing the brain's perception of the real event. In fact, there is no real solid distinction between the act of remembering and the act of thinking.

Memories are not stored in our brains like books on library shelves, or even as a collection of self-contained recordings or pictures or video clips, but may be better thought of as a kind of collage or a jigsaw puzzle, involving different elements stored in disparate parts of the brain linked together by associations and neural networks. Memory retrieval therefore requires re-visiting the nerve pathways the brain formed when encoding the memory, and the strength of those pathways determines how quickly the memory can be recalled. Recall effectively returns a memory from long-term storage to short-term or working memory, where it can be accessed, in a kind of mirror image of the encoding process. It is then re-stored back in long-term memory, thus re-consolidating and strengthening it.

The efficiency of human memory recall is astounding. Most of what we remember is by direct retrieval, where items of information are linked directly a question or cue, rather than by the kind of sequential scan a computer might use (which would require a systematic search through the entire contents of memory until a match is found). Other memories are retrieved quickly and efficiently by hierarchical inference, where a specific question is linked to a class or subset of information about which certain facts are known.

There are two main methods of accessing memory: recognition and recall. Recognition is the association of an event or physical object with one previously experienced or encountered, and involves a process of comparison of information with memory, e.g. recognizing a known face, true/false or multiple choice questions, etc. Recognition is a largely unconscious process, and the brain even has a dedicated face-recognition area, which passes information directly through the limbic areas to generate a sense of familiarity, before linking up with the cortical path, where data about the person's movements and intentions are processed. Recall involves remembering a fact, event or object that is not currently physically present (in the sense of retrieving a representation, mental image or concept), and requires the direct uncovering of information from memory, e.g. remembering the name of a recognized person, fill-in the blank questions, etc.

Recognition is usually considered to be "superior" to recall (in the sense of being more effective), in that it requires just a single process rather than two processes. Recognition requires only a simple familiarity decision, whereas a full recall of an item from memory requires a two-stage process (indeed, this is often referred to as the two-stage theory of memory) in which the search and retrieval of candidate items from memory is followed by a familiarity decision where the correct information is chosen from the candidates retrieved. Thus, recall involves actively reconstructing the information and requires the activation of all the neurons involved in the memory. Whereas recognition only requires a relatively simple decision as to whether one thing among others has been encountered before. However, even if a part of an object initially activates only a part of the neural network concerned, recognition may then suffice to activate the entire network.

There are three main types of recall:

❖ Free recall is the process in which a person is given a list of items to remember and then is asked to recall them in any order (hence the name "free"). This type of recall often displays evidence of either the primacy effect (when the person recalls items presented at the beginning of the list earlier and more often) or the recency effect (when the person recalls items presented at the end of the list earlier and more often), and also of the contiguity effect (the marked tendency for items from neighbouring positions in the list to be recalled successively).

❖ Cued recall is the process in which a person is given a list of items to remember and is then tested with the use of cues or guides. When cues are provided to a person, they tend to remember items on the list that they did not originally recall without a cue, and which were thought to be lost to memory. This can also take the form of stimulus-response recall, as when words, pictures and numbers are presented together in a pair, and the resulting associations between the two items cues the recall of the second item in the pair.

❖ Serial recall refers to our ability to recall items or events in the order in which they occurred, whether chronological events in our autobiographical memories, or the order of the different parts of a sentence (or phonemes in a word) in order to make sense of them. Serial recall in long-term memory appears to differ from serial recall in short-term memory, in that a sequence in long-term memory is represented in memory as a whole, rather than as a series of discrete items. If we assume that the "purpose" of human memory is to use past events to guide future actions, then keeping a perfect and complete record of every past event is not necessarily a useful or efficient way of achieving this. So, in most people, some specific memories may be given up or converted into general knowledge (i.e. converted from episodic to semantic memories) as part of the ongoing recall/re-consolidation process, so that we are able to generalize from experience.

RETRIEVAL THEORY

Memory retreival is not a random process. Cues can help with retrieval. It is the process of actually remembering something when you want to. If you encoded something visually, but are trying to retrieve it acoustically, you will have difficulty in remembering. Like encoding, information can be retrieved through visualizing it, thinking about the meaning or imaging the sound etc. The more ways information has been encoded, the more ways there are for retrieving it. Thus memory is aided by encoding and retreiving information in multiple ways.

According to the retrieval model, predictions for priming effects can be deduced from the contents of short term memory. The items of short term memory are used to form a compound cue and the familiarity of this cue determines accuracy and response time. The value of similiarity for any compound depends on the retrieval structure in memory.

RETRIEVAL FAILURE THEORY

Retrieval failure theory proposes that forgetting occurs because of breakdown in retrieval. Inconsistency between how we encode and retrieval cues negatively affects recall. This can be explained by the encoding specificity principle. The encoding specificity principle states that the value of a retrieval cue depends on how well it corresponds to the original memory code. Transfer appropriate processing is an example of encoding specificity. This process occurs when the initial processing of information is similar to the type of processing required by the subsequent measure of retention (Retrieve the months of the year alphabetically). Retrieval failure can occur for at least four reasons. Interference Theory which states that we forget not because memories are lost from storage but because other information gets in the way of what we want to remember. Decay Theory states that when something new is learned, a neurochemical memory trace is formed, but over time this chemical trail tends to disintegrate; the term for the phenomenon of memories fading with the passage of time is transience. Motivated forgetting, which occurs when people want to forget something is common when a memory becomes painful or anxiety laden, as in the case of emotional traumas such as rape and physical abuse. Amnesia the physiologically based loss of memory; can be anterograde, affecting the retention of new information or events; retrograde, affecting memories of the past but not new events; or both.

WEAK STORAGE THEORY

Poor memory can occur for many different reasons. Lack of concentration may be a reason for poor memory. For people whose memory are very poor and notable changes in personality and behaviour may be suffering from a form of brain disease, dementia. It seriously affects a person's ability to carry out daily activities. This theory suggest that overcome, memory traces begin to fade and disappear. If information is not retrieved and rehearsed, it will eventually be lost. Causes of weak memory include ageing, lack of concentration, depression, anxiety, alcoholism, drug abuse, brain tumors, medications, seizures etc.

MOTIVATED FORGETTING

Motivated forgetting is a debated concept referring to a psychological defence mechanism in which people forget unwanted memories, either consciously or unconsciously. There are times when memories are reminders of unpleasant experiences that make people angry, sad, anxious, ashamed or afraid. Motivated forgetting is a method in which people protect themselves by blocking there call of these anxiety-arousing memories. For example, if every time you see something or someone that reminds you of an unpleasant event, your mind will tend to steer towards topics which are unrelated to the event; this could induce forgetting without being generated by an intention to forget, making it a motivated action. There are two main classes of motivated forgetting which include: repression and suppression. Repression is an unconscious act, while suppression a conscious form of excluding thoughts and memories from awareness.

HISTORY

Neurologist Jean-Martin Charcot was the first to do research into hysteria as a psychological disorder in the late 19th century. Sigmund Freud, Joseph Breuer, and Pierre Janet continued with the research that

Charcot began on hysteria. These three psychologists determined that hysteria was an intense emotional reaction to some form of severe psychological disturbance, and they proposed that incest and other sexual traumas were the most likely cause of hysteria. The treatment that Freud, Breuer, and Pierre agreed upon was named the "talking cure" and was a method of encouraging patients to recover and discuss their painful memories. During this time, Janet created the term dissociation which is referred to as a lack of integration amongst various memories. He used dissociation to describe the way in which traumatizing memories are stored separately from other memories.

The publication of Freud's famous paper, "the Aetiology of Hysteria" in 1896 lead to much controversy regarding the topic of these traumatic memories. Freud stated that neuroses were caused by repressed sexual memories, which suggested that incest and sexual abuse must be common throughout upper and middle class Europe. The psychological community did not accept Freud's ideas, and years past without further research on the topic. It was during World War I and World War II that interest in memory disturbances was peaked again. During this time, many cases of memory loss appeared among war veterans, especially those who had experienced shell shock. Hypnosis and drugs became popular for the treatment of hysteria during the war. The term post traumatic stress disorder (PTSD) was introduced upon the appearance of similar cases of memory disturbances from veterans of the Korean War. Forgetting, or the inability to recall a portion of a traumatic event, was considered a key factor for the diagnosis of PTSD. Ann Burgess and Lynda Holmstrom looked into trauma related memory loss in rape victims during the 1970s. This began a large outpouring of stories related to childhood sexual abuse. It took until1980 to determine that memory loss due to all severe traumas was the same set of processes. The idea of motivated forgetting began with the philosopher Friedrich Nietzsche in 1994. Nietzsheand Sigmund Freud had similar views on the idea of repression of memories as a form of self preservation. Nietzsche wrote that man must forget in able to move forward. He stated that this process is active, in that we forget specific events as a defense mechanism. The False Memory Syndrome Foundation (FMSF) was created in 1992 as a response to the large number of memories claimed to be recovered. The FMSF was created to oppose the idea that memories could be recoverd using specific techniques; instead, its members believed that the "memories" were actually confabulations created through the inappropriate use of techniques such as hypnosis.

AMNESIA

Amnesia is a condition in which memory is disturbed or lost. Memory in this context refers either to stored memories or to the process of committing something to memory. The causes of amnesia have traditionally been divided into the "organic" or the "functional". Organic causes include damage to the brain, through physical injury, neurological disease or the use of certain (generally sedative) drugs. Functional causes are psychological factors, such as mental disorder, posttraumatic stress or, in psychoanalytic terms, defense mechanisms. Amnesia may also appear as spontaneous episodes, in the case of transient global amnesia.

Forms of amnesia

In anterograde amnesia, the ability to memorize new things is impaired or lost. A person may find themselves constantly forgetting information, people or events after a few seconds or minutes, because the data does not transfer successfully from their conscious short-term memory into permanent long-term memory (or possibly vice versa).

In retrograde amnesia, a person's pre-existing memories are lost to conscious recollection,beyond an ordinary degree of forgetfulness. The person may be able to memorize new things that occur after the onset of amnesia (unlike in anterograde amnesia), but is unable to recall some or all of their life or identity prior to the onset. It should be noted, however, that there are different types of memory, for example procedural memory (i.e. automated skills) declarative memory (personal episodes or abstract facts), and often only one type is impaired. For example, a person may forget the details of personal identity, but still retain a learned skill such as the ability to play the piano. In addition, the terms are used to categorize patterns of symptoms rather than to indicate a particular cause (etiology). Both categories of amnesia can occur together in the same patient, and commonly result from drug effects or damage to the brain regions most closely associated with episodic memory: the medial temporal lobes and especially the hippocampus. An example of mixed retrograde and anterograde amnesia may be a motorcyclist unable to recall driving his motorbike prior to his head injury (retrograde amnesia), nor can he recall the hospital ward where he is told he had conversations with family over the next two days (anterograde amnesia).

The effects of amnesia can last long after the condition has passed. Some sufferers claim that their amnesia changes from a neurological condition to also being a psychological condition, whereby they lose confidence and faith in their own memory and accounts of past events. Another effect of some forms of amnesia may be impaired ability to imagine future events. A 2006 study showed that future experiences imagined by amnesiacs with bilaterall damaged hippocampus lacked spatial coherence, and the authors speculated that the hippocampus may be responsible for binding different elements of experience together when re-experiencing the past or imagining the future.

TYPES AND CAUSES OF AMNESIA

Post-traumatic amnesia is generally due to a head injury (e.g. a fall, a knock on the head). Traumatic amnesia is often transient, but may be permanent of either anterograde, retrograde, or mixed type. The extent of the period covered by the amnesia is related to the degree of injury and may give an indication of the prognosis for recovery of other functions. Mild trauma, such as a car accident that results in no more than mild whiplash, might cause the occupant of a car to have no memory of the moments just before the accident due to a brief interruption in the short/long-term memory transfer mechanism. The sufferer may also lose knowledge of who people are, they may remember events, but will not remember faces of them.

Dissociative amnesia results from a psychological cause as opposed to direct damage to the brain caused by head injury, physical trauma or disease, which is known as organic amnesia. Dissociative amnesia can include:

Repressed memory refers to the inability to recall information, usually about stressful or traumatic events in persons' lives, such as a violent attack or rape. The memory is stored in long term memory, but access to it is impaired because of psychological defense mechanisms. Persons retain the capacity to learn new information and there may be some later partial or complete recovery of memory. This contrasts with e.g. anterograde amnesia caused by amnestics such as benzodiazepines or alcohol, where an experience was prevented from being transferred from temporary to permanent memory storage: it will never be recovered, because it was never stored in the first place. Formerly known as "Psychogenic Amnesia".

Dissociative Fugue (formerly Psychogenic Fugue) is also known as fugue state. It is caused by psychological trauma and is usually temporary, unresolved and therefore may return. The Merck Manual defines it as "one or more episodes of amnesia in which the inability to recall some or all of one's past and either the loss of one's identity or the formation of a new identity occur with sudden, unexpected, purposeful travel away from home."

Posthypnotic amnesia is where events during hypnosis are forgotten, or where past memories are unable to be recalled.

Lacunar amnesia is the loss of memory about one specific event.

Childhood amnesia (also known as infantile amnesia) is the common inability to remember events from one's own childhood. Sigmund Freud notoriously attributed this to sexual repression, while modern scientific approaches generally attribute it to aspects of brain development or developmental psychology, including language development.

Transient global amnesia is a well-described medical and clinical phenomenon. This form of amnesia is distinct in that abnormalities in the hippocampus can sometimes be visualized using a special form of magnetic resonance imaging of the brain known as diffusion-weighted imaging (DWI). Symptoms typically last for less than a day and there is often no clear precipitating factor nor any other neurological deficits. The cause of this syndrome is not clear, hypothesis include transient reduced blood flow, possible seizure or a typical type of migraine. Patients are typically amnestic of events more than a few minutes in the past, though immediate recall is usually preserved.

Source amnesia is a memory disorderin which someone can recall certain information, but they donot know where or how they obtained the information.

Memory distrust syndrome is a term invented by the psychologist Gisli Gudjonsson to describe a situation where someone is unable to trust their own memory.

Blackout phenomenon can be caused by excessive short-term alcohol consumption, with the amnesia being of the anterograde type.

Korsakoff's syndrome can result from long-term alcoholism or malnutrition. It is caused by brain damage due to a vitamin B1 deficiency and will be progressive if alcohol intake and nutrition pattern are not modified. Other neurological problems are likely to be present in combination with this type of Amnesia. Korsakoff's syndrome is also known to be connected with confabulation.

Drug-induced amnesia is intentionally caused by injection of an amnesiac drug to help a patient forget surgery or medical procedures, particularly those not performed under full anesthesia, or likely to be particularly traumatic. Such drugs are also referred to as "premedicants". Most commonly a 2'-halogenated benzodiazepine such as midazolam or flunitrazepam is the drug of choice, although other strongly amnestic drugs such as propofol or scopolamine may also be used for this application. Memories of the short time frame in which the procedure was performed are permanently lost or at least substantially reduced, but once the drug wears off, memory is no longer affected.

Electroconvulsive therapy in which seizures are electrically induced in patients for therapeutic effect can have acute effects including both retrograde and anterograde amnesia.

Prosopamnesia is the inability to remember faces, even in the presence of intact facial recognition capabilities. Both acquired and inborn cases have been documented.

Situation-Specific amnesia can arise in a variety of circumstances (e.g., committing an offence, child sexual abuse) resulting in PTSD. It has been claimed that it involves a narrowing of consciousness with attention focused on central perceptual details and/or that the emotional or traumatic events are processed differently from ordinary memories.

TECHNIQUES TO IMPROVE RETENTION AND RETRIEVAL PROCESS

There are several methods that can be employed to improve one's memory skills. Recall that the decay theory states that as time passes with a memory trace not being used, it becomes increasingly difficult for that pattern of neural activity to become reactivated, or in other words to retrieve that memory. The key is that information must be retrieved and rehearsed or it will eventually be lost. In remembering new information, the brain goes through three stages: registration, retention, and retrieval. It is only in the retention process that one is able to influence the retention rate if the information is properly organized in your brain. This can be done using these techniques:

1. Recall using cues- Connecting a piece of unfamiliar information with, say, a visual cue can help in remembering that piece of information much more easily.
2. Teach it- This is another way to speed up the process of learning new information.
3. Use mnemonic devices and acronyms- This is a preferable method to memorize lists and increase chances of long-term memory storage.

GENERAL TECHNIQUES TO IMPROVE MEMORY

In addition to exercising your brain, there are some basic things you can do to improve your ability to retain and retrieve memories:

1. **Pay attention:** You can't remember something if you never learned it, and you can't learn something — that is, encode it into your brain — if you don't pay enough attention to it. It takes about eight seconds of intent focus to process a piece of information through your hippocampus and into the appropriate memory center. So, no multitasking when you need to concentrate. If you distract easily, try to receive information in a quiet place where you won't be interrupted.

2. **Tailor information acquisition to your learning style:** Most people are visual learners; they learn best by reading or otherwise seeing what it is they have to know. But some are auditory learners who learn better by listening. They might benefit by recording information they need and listening to it until they remember it.

3. **Involve as many senses as possible:** Even if you are a visual learner, read out loud what you want to remember. If you can recite it rhythmically, even better. Try to relate information to colours, textures, smells and tastes. The physical act of rewriting information can help imprint it on to your brain.

4. **Relate information to what you already know:** Connect new data to information you already remember, whether it is new material that builds on previous knowledge, or something as simple as an address of someone who lives on a street where you already know someone.

5. **Organize information:** Write things down in address books, datebooks and on calendars; take notes on more complex material and reorganize the notes into categories later. Use both words and pictures in learning information.

6. **Understand and be able to interpret complex material**: For more complex material, focus on understanding basic ideas rather than memorizing isolated details. Be able to explain it to someone else in your own words.

7. **Rehearse information frequently and "over-learn":** Review what you have learned the same day you learn it, and at intervals thereafter. What researchers call "spaced rehearsal" is more effective than "cramming." If you are able to "over-learn" information so that recalling it becomes second nature, so much the better.

8. **Be motivated and keep a positive attitude:** Tell yourself that you want to learn what you need to remember, and that you can learn and remember it. Telling yourself you have a bad memory actually hampers the ability of your brain to remember, while positive mental feedback sets up an expectation of success.

HEALTHY HABITS THAT IMPROVE MEMORY

Regular Exercise- Increases oxygen to your brain and reduces the risk for disorders that lead to memory loss, such as diabetes and cardiovascular disease. It may enhance the effects of helpful brain chemicals and protect brain cells.

Managing stress- Cortisol, the stress hormone, can damage the hippocampus if the stress is unrelieved, stress makes it difficult to concentrate.

Good sleep habits- Sleep is necessary for memory consolidation. Sleep disorders like insomnia and sleep apnea leave you tired and unable to concentrate during the day.

Not smoking- Smoking heightens the risk of vascular disorders that can cause stroke and constrict arteries that deliver oxygen to the brain.

REFERENCES

American Psychiatric Association (APA). (1994), Diagnostic and statistical manual of mental disorders. 4th edition (DSM-IV). Washington (DC): American Psychiatric Association;

Andreasen N, Black D (1995). Introductory textbook of psychiatry. Washington (DC): American Psychiatric Press;

Antoni F. Hypothalamic control of adrenocorticotropin secretion: advances since the discovery of 41-residue corticotropin-releasing factor Endo Rev 1986; 7: 351 – 378.

Baddeley, A. D. (1966). "The influence of acoustic and semantic similarity on long-term memory for word sequences". Quart. J. Exp. Psychol. 18 (4): 302–9.

Baron, R.A.(2002). Psychology (5th ed), India Pearson Education, Asia

Bogousslavsky, J; Regli, F (1992). "Centrum ovale infarcts: subcortical infarction in the superficial territory of the middle cerebral artery". Neurology. 42 (10): 1992–8.

Bradley, M. M.; Greenwald, M. K.; Petry, M. C.; Lang, P. J. (1992). "Remembering pictures: Pleasure and arousal in memory". Journal of Experimental Psychology: Learning, Memory, & Cognition. 18 (2): 379–390.

Burke, A.; Heuer, F.; Reisberg, D. (1992). "Remembering emotional events". Memory & Cognition. 20 (3): 277–290.

Cahill, L.; McGaugh, J. L. (1995). "A novel demonstration of enhanced memory associated with emotional arousal". Consciousness and Cognition. 4 (4): 410–421.

Carlson, Neil R. (2010), Psychology: the science of behavior. Boston, Mass: Allyn & Bacon.

Cavanagh, J. F.; Frank, M. J.; Allen, J. J. B. (2010), "Social stress reactivity alters reward and punishment learning". Social Cognitive and Affective Neuroscience. 6(3): 311–320.

Charles F Levinthal (2005), Introduction to Physiological Psychology, Prentice Hall of India

Christianson, S. A. (1992). "Emotional stress and eyewitness memory: A critical review". Psychological Bulletin. 112 (2): 284–309.

Christianson, S.A.; Loftus, E. (1990). "Some characteristics of people's traumatic memories". Bulletin of the Psychonomic Society. 28: 195–198.

Clayton, N.S.; Dickinson, A. (1998). "Episodic-like memory during cache recovery by scrub jays". *Nature*. 395 (6699): 272–4.

Conrad, R (1964). "Acoustic Confusions in Immediate Memory". *British Journal of Psychology*. 55: 75–84.

Conway, M. A.; Anderson, S. J.; Larsen, S. F.; Donnelly, C. M.; McDaniel, M. A.; McClelland, A.G.R.; Rawls, R.E.; Logie, R.H. (1994). "The formation of flash bulb memories". *Memory and Cognition*. 22 (3): 326–343. doi:10.3758/BF03200860. PMID 8007835.

David Healy (2013), Pharmageddon, University of California Press

Easterbrook, J. A. (1959). "The effect of emotion on cue utilization and the organization of behaviour". *Psychological Review*. 66 (3): 183–201.

Edward Shorter (2013), How Everyone Became Depressed: The Rise and Fall of the Nervous Breakdown, Oxford University Press

Francis Leukel (1976), Introduction to Physiological Psychology, CBS publishers and distributors , India.

Freud, Siegmund (1950), Beyond the pleasure principle. New York: Liveright.

Hallowell, Edward M & John Ratey. (2005), Delivered from Distraction: Getting the Most out of Life with Attention Deficit Disorder. Ballantine Books.

Hamann, S.B. (2001). "Cognitive and neural mechanisms of emotional memory". *Trends in Cognitive Sciences*. 5 (9): 394–400.

Henckens, M. J. A. G.; Hermans, E. J.; Pu, Z.; Joels, M.; Fernandez, G. (2009). "Stressed Memories: How Acute Stress Affects Memory Formation in Humans". *Journal of Neuroscience*. 29 (32): 10111–10119.

Hulse, L. M.; Memon, A. (2006). "Fatal impact? The effects of emotional arousal and weapon presence on police officers' memories for a simulated crime". *Legal and Criminological Psychology*. 11 (2): 313–325.

Hutsler, J.; Galuske, R.A.W. (2003). "Hemispheric asymmetries in cerebral cortical networks". *Trends in Neurosciences*. 26 (8): 429–435.

Immelmann, Klaus (1972). "Sexual and other long-term aspects of imprinting in birds and other species". *Advances in the Study of Behavior*. Advances in the Study of Behavior. New York: Academic Press. 4: 147–174.

Kensinger EA, Corkin S. (2003), Memory enhancement for emotional words: Are emotional words more vividly remembered than neutral words? Memory and Cognition; 31:1169–1180.

Kensinger, E. A. (2004). "Remembering emotional experiences: The contribution of valence and arousal". *Reviews in the Neurosciences*. 15 (4): 241–251.

Kringelbach, Morten L.; Berridge, Kent C. (2010), "The Neuroscience of Happiness and Pleasure". Soc Res.

Kuhlmann, S.; Piel, M.; Wolf, O.T. (2005). "Impaired Memory Retrieval after Psychosocial Stress in Healthy Young Men". *Journal of Neuroscience*. 25 (11): 2977 2982.

LaBar, K. S.; Phelps, E. A. (1998). "Arousal-mediated memory consolidation: Role of the medial temporal lobe in humans". *Psychological Science*. 9 (6): 490–493.

Lang PJ, Greenwald MK, Bradley MM, Hamm AO. Looking at pictures: affective, facial, visceral and behavioral reactions Psychophysiology 1993; 30: 261–273.

Lefton, L.A. (1985), Psychology, Boston: Allyn & Bacon.

Loftus, E. F. (1979). "The malleability of human memory". American Scientist. 67 (3): 312–320.

Meng Y, Zhang Y, Jia Z (2003), Synaptic transmission and plasticity in the absence of AMPA glutamate receptor GluR2 and GluR3. Neuron; 39:163–176

Miller, G.A (1956). "The magical number seven plus or minus two: some limits on our capacity for processing information". Psychol Rev. 63 (2): 81–97.

Ochsner, K. N. (2000). "Are affective events richly recollected or simply familiar? The experience and process of recognizing feelings past". Journal of Experimental Psychology. General. 129 (2): 242–261

Rabins PV, Merchant A. (1984), Criteria for diagnosing reversible dementia caused by depression: validation by 2-year follow-up. Br J Psychiatry. 144:488–92.

Reisel D, Bannerman DM, Schmitt WB, Deacon RM, Flint J, Borchardt T, Seeburg PH, Rawlins JN(2003), Spatial memory dissociations in mice lacking GluR1. Nat. Neurosci. ;5:868–873.

Repa JC, Muller J, Apergis J, Desrochers T M, Zhou Y, LeDoux J E (2001), Two different lateral amygdala cell populations contribute to the initiation and storage of memory. Nat. Neurosci. ;4:724–731.

Rial Verde E M, Lee-Osbourne J, Worley PF, Malinow R, Cline H T (2006), Increased expression of the immediate-early gene arc/arg3.1 reduces AMPA receptor-mediated synaptic transmission. Neuron; 52:461–474.

Richter-Levin G, Akirav I. (2003), Emotional tagging of memory formation–in the search for neural mechanisms. Brain Res. Brain Res. Rev.; 43:247–256.

Rogan MT, Staubli UV, LeDoux JE. (1997), Fear conditioning induces associative long-term potentiation in the amygdala. Nature.; 390:604–607.

Russell, J. A. (1980). "A circumplex model of affect". Journal of Personality and Social Psychology. 39 (6): 1161–1178.

Sandi, Carmen; Pinelo-Nava, M. Teresa (2007). "Stress and Memory: Behavioral Effects and Neurobiological Mechanisms". Neural Plasticity: 1–20.

Schacter, D. L. (1996). Searching for memory. New York: Basic Books.

Schultz W (2015), "Neuronal reward and decision signals: from theories to data". Physiological Reviews. 95 (3): 853–951.

Scoville W.B.; Milner B. (1957). "Loss of Recent Memory After Bilateral Hippocampal Lesions" (PDF). Journal of Neurology, Neurosurgery, and Psychiatry. 20: 11–21.

Sebastian M M (1966), Animal Physiology, Madonna Books, India.

Sharot, T; Phelps, E A (2004). "How arousal modulates memory: Disentangling the effects of attention and retention". Cognitive, Affective, & Behavioral Neuroscience. 4 (3): 294–306.

T.L. Brink. (2008), Psychology: A Student Friendly Approach. "Unit 12: Developmental Psychology." pp. 268 [1]

Talbott, S. (2007). The cortisol connection. Alameda, CA: Hunter House Inc.

Viau, V.; Soriano, L.; Dallman, M (2001). "Androgens alter corticotropin releasing hormone and arginine vasopressin mrna within forebrain sites known to regulate activity in the hypothalamic-pituitary-adrenal axis". Journal of Neuroendocrinology. 13 (5): 442–452.

Wilson RS, Barnes LL, Mendes de Leon CF, (2002),Depressive symptoms, cognitive decline and risk of AD in older persons. Neurology; 59(3):364–70.

Ziegler, D; Herman, J (2002). "Neurocircuitry of stress integration: anatomical pathways regulating the hypothalamo-pituitary-adrenocortical axis of the rat". Integrative and Comparative Biology. 42 (3): 541–551.

Zimbardo, P.G. & Weber, A.L. (1997), Psychology, Harper Collins, N.Y.

Learn
C PROGRAMMING
with 500 Programs

Only Learning & Algorithm based Programs with Source Code

1st Edition (Jan-2024)

by Atul Soni

Copyright © 2024 by Atul Soni

Cover design by: Atul Soni

For my wonderful family.   For all your love and support.

- Atul Soni

Introduction

This book covers all the concepts that the programmers need to develop their skills:

- ➢ Contains 500 learning and algorithm based programs with source code.
- ➢ Contains only programs source code and output snapshots (it doesn't contain any theory, for theory there are many books available).
- ➢ We use MinGW compiler for C Programming.
- ➢ We use text editor VS Code, which is popular among beginner and professional programmers and works well on all operating systems.
- ➢ Each chapter contains well planned and organized collection of programs.
- ➢ This book will also be very helpful for beginners, teachers and trainers of C programming language.
- ➢ We use small variable or identifier names for better readability in digital media like kindle, ipad, tab and mobile.
- ➢ This book contains much simpler approach to coding.
- ➢ A simpler approach is used to organize the programs for beginners as well as professional.

About the Author

Atul Soni

is an engineer whose main interests and expertise are programming languages, algorithms, data structure, data analytics, web technologies and android mobile application development. He writes many programming tutorials. He has extensive experience in teaching programming languages to engineers and software developers.

He is a programmer, writer and android app developer. He develops many tutorial app of different programming languages like, C, C++, Java, Python, Android, VB.Net, C#, PHP, HTML5, CSS3, SQL & PL/SQL, JavaScript, jQuery etc. When he's not writing or programming, he enjoys reading books, touring by car and spending time with his family.

Table of Contents

****

Chapter – 1
C - Introduction

****

Program No. - 1 :
Program to display a String Literal in C using **printf()** function.

Code :
```c
#include <stdio.h>

int  main()
{
    printf( " Let\'s learn C Programming Language." );
    return 0;
}
```

Output :

Program No. - 2 :
Program to use **system("cls")** to clear output screen in Terminal of VSCode and use **system("pause")** to pause output screen in VSCode (It implicitly shows **"Press any key to continue . . ."** in Visual Studio Code).

Code :
```c
#include <stdio.h>

int  main()
{
    system( "cls" );
    printf( "Let\'s learn C Programming Language.\n" );
    system( "pause" );
    return 0;
}
```

Output :

Program No. - 3 :
Program to define comments in C programming.

Code :
```c
/* Linking section.  */
#include <stdio.h>

/*  program starts from main function.  */
int  main()
{
    system( "cls" );         /*  to clear output screen.  */
    /*  Output. */
    printf( "Let\'s learn C  Programming.\n" );
    system("pause");     /* to hold output screen.  */
    return 0;
}    /* end of main  */
```

Output :

Program No. - 4 :
Program to explain that the C is a **Free-form Language**.

Code :
```c
#include <stdio.h>

int  main() { system( "cls" ); printf(
"Let\'s learn C Programming.\n" );
system( "pause" ); return 0; }
```

Output :

```
TERMINAL

Let's learn C Programming.
Press any key to continue . . .|
```

____________ **** ____________

Program No. - 5 :
Program to display single line using multiple **printf()** statements.

Code :
```c
#include <stdio.h>

int  main()
{
    system( "cls" );

    printf( "Let\'s learn " );
    printf( "C Programming.\n" );

    system( "pause" );
    return 0;
}
```

Output :
```
TERMINAL

Let's learn C Programming
Press any key to continue . . .|
```

____________ **** ____________

Program No. - 6 :
Program to display multiple lines using single **printf()** statement.

Code :
```c
#include <stdio.h>

int  main()
{
    system( "cls" );

    printf( "Let\'s \nlearn \nC.\n" );

    system( "pause" );
```

```
    return 0;
}
```

Output :
```
TERMINAL

Let's
learn
C.
Press any key to continue . . .|
```

____________ **** ____________

Program No. - 7 :
Program to explain that you can skip **return 0;** statement from **int main()** function in Visual Studio Code.

Code :
```c
#include <stdio.h>

int  main()
{
    system( "cls" );

    printf( "Let\'s learn C Programming.\n" );

    system( "pause" );
}
```

Output :
```
TERMINAL

Let's learn C Programming.
Press any key to continue . . .|
```

____________ **** ____________

Program No. - 8 :
Program to explain variable declaration and assignment.

Code :
```c
#include <stdio.h>

int  main()
{
    int  n1, n2, s;              /* Variable declaration */
    system( "cls" );
```

```
    n1 = 10;           /*  Variable assignment  */
    n2 = 20;

    s = n1 + n2;

    printf( "Sum = " );
    printf( "%d\n", s );

    system( "pause" );
    return 0;
}
```

Output :

```
TERMINAL

Sum = 30
Press any key to continue . . . |
```

---- ******** ----

Program No. - 9 :
Program to read data from keyboard using **scanf** statement.

Code :
```
#include <stdio.h>

int  main()
{
    int n1, n2, s;
    system( "cls" );

    printf( "Enter First Number: " );
    scanf( "%d", &n1 );
    printf( "Enter Second Number: " );
    scanf( "%d", &n2 );

    s = n1 + n2;

    printf( "Sum = " );
    printf( "%d\n", s );

    system( "pause" );
    return 0;
}
```

Output :

```
TERMINAL

Enter First Number: 100
Enter Second Number: 200
Sum = 300
Press any key to continue . . . |
```

---- ******** ----

Program No. - 10 :
Program to explain input and display multiple values in single **printf** and **scanf** statement..

Code :
```
#include <stdio.h>

int  main()
{
    int  n1, n2, s;
    system( "cls" );

    printf( "Enter Two Numbers: " );
    scanf( "%d %d", &n1, &n2 );

    s = n1 + n2;

    printf( "%d + %d = %d\n", n1, n2,  s );

    system( "pause" );
    return 0;
}
```

Output :

```
TERMINAL

Enter Two Numbers: 100 200
100 + 200 = 300
Press any key to continue . . . |
```

---- ******** ----

Program No. - 11 :
Program to calculate Volume of Cylinder.

Code :
```
/*
This program is used to explain Multiple line
```

```
  comment and Single line comment.
  */
  #include <stdio.h>

  int  main()
  {
      float  r, h, v;              /* Variable Declaration.  */
      system( "cls" );

      printf( "Enter Radius & Height of Cylinder : " );
      scanf( "%f %f", &r, &h );  /* Reading data from KB. */

      v = 3.14 * r * r * h ;       /* Calculation of volume. */

      printf( "\nVolume of Cylinder  = %f\n", v );

      system( "pause" );
      return 0;
  }
```

Output :

```
TERMINAL
Enter Radius & Height of Cylinder : 10 10

Volume of Cylinder  = 3140.000000
Press any key to continue . . . |
```

———————————— **** ————————————

Program No. - 12 :
Program to find the Area and Circumference of Circle.

Code :
```
#include <stdio.h>

int  main()
{
    float radius, area, circum;
    system( "cls" );

    printf( "Enter Radius : " );
    scanf( "%f", &radius );

    area = 3.14 * radius * radius;
    circum = 2 * 3.14 * radius;

    printf( "\nArea of Circle = %f\n", area );
```

```
    printf( "Circumference of Circle = %f\n", circum );

    system( "pause" );
    return 0;
}
```

Output :

```
TERMINAL
Enter Radius : 10

Area of Circle = 314.000000
Circumference of Circle = 62.799999
Press any key to continue . . . |
```

———————————— **** ————————————

Program No. - 13 :
Program to Swap two numbers using Third Variable.

Code :
```
#include <stdio.h>

int  main()
{
    int  n1, n2, t;
    system( "cls" );

    printf( "Enter Two Numbers : " );
    scanf( "%d %d", &n1, &n2 );

    printf( "\nn1 = %d, n2 = %d\n", n1, n2 );

    t = n1;
    n1 = n2;
    n2 = t;

    printf( "n1 = %d, n2 = %d\n", n1, n2 );

    system( "pause" );
    return 0;
}
```

Output :

```
TERMINAL

Enter Two Numbers : 10 20

n1 = 10, n2 = 20
n1 = 20, n2 = 10
Press any key to continue . . .
```

****

Program No. - 14 :
Program to Swap two numbers without using Third Variable.

Code :

```c
#include <stdio.h>

int  main()
{
    int  n1, n2;
    system( "cls" );

    printf( "Enter Two Numbers : " );
    scanf( "%d %d", &n1, &n2 );

    printf( "\nn1 = %d, n2 = %d\n", n1, n2 );

    n1 = n1 + n2;
    n2 = n1 − n2;
    n1 = n1 − n2;

    printf( "n1 = %d, n2 = %d\n", n1, n2 );

    system( "pause" );
    return 0;
}
```

Output :

```
TERMINAL

Enter Two Numbers : 100 200

n1 = 100, n2 = 200
n1 = 200, n2 = 100
Press any key to continue . . .
```

****

Program No. - 15 :
Program to show output in required format.

Code :

```c
#include <stdio.h>

int  main()
{
    int a = 12, b = 123, c = 1234;
    system( "cls" );

    printf( "Without formatting : \n" );
    printf( "%d\n", a );
    printf( "%d\n", b );
    printf( "%d\n", c );

    printf( "\nWith formatting : \n" );
    printf( "%7d\n", a );
    printf( "%7d\n", b );
    printf( "%7d\n", c );

    system( "pause" );
    return 0;
}
```

Output :

```
TERMINAL

Without formatting :
12
123
1234

With formatting :
     12
    123
   1234
Press any key to continue . . .
```

****

Program No. - 16 :
Program to calculate Simple Interest.

Code :

```c
#include <stdio.h>

int  main( )
{
```

```c
    system( "cls" );
    float p, r, t, si ;

    printf( "Enter Principal, Rate & Time : " ) ;
    scanf( "%f %f %f", &p, &r, &t ) ;

    si = ( p * r * t ) / 100;

    printf( "\nSimple Interest = %.2f\n", si ) ;

    system( "pause" );
    return 0;
}
```

Output :

```
TERMINAL

Enter Principal, Rate & Time : 1000 10 3

Simple Interest = 300.00
Press any key to continue . . . |
```

—————————— **** ——————————

Program No. - 17 :
Program to convert Upper-case letter to Lower-case letter.

Code :

```c
#include <stdio.h>

int  main()
{
    char ch;
    system( "cls" );

    printf( "Enter a Capital / Upper case Letter : " );
    scanf( "%c", &ch );

    printf( "\nLower case Equivalent : %c\n",
                                    ( ch + 32 ) );

    system( "pause" );
    return 0;
}
```

Output :

```
TERMINAL

Enter a Capital / Upper case Letter : C

Lower case Equivalent : c
Press any key to continue . . . |
```

```
TERMINAL

Enter a Capital / Upper case Letter : A

Lower case Equivalent : a
Press any key to continue . . . |
```

```
TERMINAL

Enter a Capital / Upper case Letter : a

Lower case Equivalent : ü
Press any key to continue . . . |
```

—————————— **** ——————————

Program No. - 18 :
Program to calculate the Car's average from the given total distance travelled (in kms) and fuel consumed (in litres).

Code :

```c
#include <stdio.h>

int  main()
{
    float km, ltr, avg;
    system( "cls" );

    printf( "Enter Total Distance in km : " );
    scanf( "%f", &km );
    printf( "Enter Total Fuel consumed in litres : " );
    scanf( "%f", &ltr );

    avg = km / ltr;

    printf( "\nCar's Average (km/ltr) %.2f\n", avg );

    system( "pause" );
    return 0;
}
```

Output :

```
TERMINAL

Enter Total Distance in km : 495
Enter Total Fuel consumed in litres : 30

Car's Average (km/ltr) 16.50
Press any key to continue . . . []
```

———————— **** ————————

Program No. - 19 :
Program to compute the Perimeter and Area of a
rectangle with a length and width.

Code :
```c
#include <stdio.h>

int  main()
{
    float l = 10.0, w = 5.0;
    float peri, area;

    system( "cls" );

    peri = 2 * ( l + w );
    printf( "Perimeter of Rectangle : %f\n", peri );

    area = l * w;
    printf( "Area of Rectangle : %f\n", area );

    system( "pause" );
    return 0;
}
```

Output :

```
TERMINAL

Perimeter of Rectangle : 30.000000
Area of Rectangle : 50.000000
Press any key to continue . . . []
```

———————— **** ————————

Program No. - 20 :
Program to accepts two item's weight and number of
each items and calculate the average weight per item.

Code :
```c
#include <stdio.h>

int  main()
{
    float wt1, wt2, n1, n2, avg;
    system( "cls" );

    printf( "Weight of Item1 : " );
    scanf( "%f", &wt1 );
    printf( "No. of Item1 : ");
    scanf( "%f", &n1 );
    printf( "Weight of Item2 : " );
    scanf( "%f", &wt2 );
    printf( "No. of Item2 : " );
    scanf( "%f", &n2);

    avg = ((wt1 * n1) + (wt2 * n2)) / (n1 + n2);

    printf( "Average Weight per Item : %f\n", avg );

    system( "pause" );
    return 0;
}
```

Output :

```
TERMINAL

Weight of Item1 : 2.5
No. of Item1 : 20
Weight of Item2 : 5.0
No. of Item2 : 10
Average Weight per Item : 3.333333
Press any key to continue . . . []
```

———————— **** ————————

Program No. - 21 :
Program to calculate the Total Surface Area of Sphere.

Code :
```c
#include <stdio.h>

int main()
{
    system( "cls" );
    double radius, tsa;
```

```c
    printf( "Enter Radius : " );
    scanf( "%lf", &radius );

    tsa =  4.0 * 3.14 * radius * radius ;
    printf( "\nTotal Surface Area of Sphere : %lf\n", tsa );

    system( "pause" );
    return 0;
}
```

Output :

```
TERMINAL

Enter Radius : 10

Total Surface Area of Sphere : 1256.000000
Press any key to continue . . .
```

---- **** ----

Program No. - 22 :
Program to calculate the area of Triangle.

Code :
```c
#include <stdio.h>

int main()
{
    system( "cls" );
    double base = 5.0, height = 4.0, area;

    area = 0.5 * base * height;
    printf( "Area of Triangle : %lf\n", area );

    system( "pause" );
    return 0;
}
```

Output :

```
TERMINAL

Area of Triangle : 10.000000
Press any key to continue . . .
```

---- **** ----

Program No. - 23 :

Program to calculate Total Surface Area of Cuboid.

Code :
```c
#include <stdio.h>

int  main()
{
    float l, b, h, tsa;
    system( "cls" );

    printf( "Enter Length, Breath and Height : " );
    scanf("%f %f %f",&l,&b,&h);

    tsa = 2 * ((l*b) + (b*h) + (h*l));

    printf( "\nTotal Surface Area of cuboid = %f\n", tsa );

    system( "pause" );
    return 0;
}
```

Output :

```
TERMINAL

Enter Length, Breath and Height : 10 8 5

Total Surface Area of cuboid = 340.000000
Press any key to continue . . .
```

---- **** ----

Program No. - 24 :
Program to calculate Area of Trapezium.

Code :
```c
#include <stdio.h>

int  main()
{
    float area, h, b1, b2;
    system( "cls" );

    printf( "Enter Two Parallel Sides of Trapezium : " );
    scanf( "%f %f", &b1, &b2 );
    printf( "Enter Height of Trapezium : " );
    scanf( "%f",&h );

    area = (1.0 / 2.0) * h * (b1 + b2);
```

```c
printf( "\nArea of Trapezium = %f\n", area );
system( "pause" );
return 0;
}
```

Output :

```
TERMINAL

Enter Two Parallel Sides of Trapezium : 10 8
Enter Height of Trapezium : 5

Area of Trapezium = 45.000000
Press any key to continue . . . ▯
```

———————————— **** ————————————

Program No. - 25 :
Program to input Basic Monthly Salary and calculate HRA, DA and Gross Monthly Salary.

Code :

```c
#include <stdio.h>

int main()
{
    float bs, gs, da, hra ;
    system( "cls" );

    printf ( "Enter Basic Monthly Salary : " ) ;
    scanf ( "%f", &bs ) ;

    hra = bs * 20 / 100 ;
    da = bs * 45 / 100 ;
    gs = bs + hra + da ;

    printf ( "\nBasic Monthly Salary : Rs. %f\n", bs ) ;
    printf ( "HRA............................ : Rs. %f\n", hra ) ;
    printf ( "DA................................ : Rs. %f\n", da ) ;
    printf ( "Gross Monthly Salary.. : Rs. %f\n", gs ) ;

    system( "pause" );
    return 0;
}
```

Output :

```
TERMINAL

Enter Basic Monthly Salary : 25000

Basic Monthly Salary : Rs. 25000.000000
HRA.................. : Rs. 5000.000000
DA................... : Rs. 11250.000000
Gross Monthly Salary : Rs. 41250.000000
Press any key to continue . . . ▯
```

———————————— **** ————————————

Program No. - 26 :
Program to explain Simple **C Program Structure**.

Code :

```c
// File Inclusion Section
#include <stdio.h>

// Global Declaration & Definition Section
int  x, y = 20;
void  show();

// main Function
int  main()
{
    int  a, b = 40;
    system( "cls" );

    x = 10;
    a = 30;

    printf( "a = %d, b = %d\n", a, b );
    show();

    system( "pause" );
    return 0;
}

// Function Definition
void  show()
{
    printf( "x = %d, y = %d\n", x, y );
}
```

Output :

```
TERMINAL

a   = 30, b = 40
x   = 10, y = 20
Press any key to continue . . .
```

****

****

Chapter – 2
Variables, Constants & Data Types

****

Program No. - 27 :
Program to explain **Variable Declaration** and **Assignment**.

Code :
```c
#include <stdio.h>

int  main()
{
    int length;                 // Variable Declaration.
    system( "cls" );

    length = 10;                // Assignment.

    printf( "The length is " );
    printf( "%d\n", length );

    system( "pause" );
    return 0;
}
```

Output :

```
TERMINAL

The length is 10
Press any key to continue . . . |
```

―――――――― **** ――――――――

Program No. - 28 :
Program to explain Variable **Initialization**.

Code :
```c
#include <stdio.h>

int  main()
{
    float radius = 10.0, height = 10.0;
    float volume;
    system( "cls" );

    volume = 3.1416 * radius * radius * height;

    printf( "Volume is : %f\n", volume );

    system( "pause" );
    return 0;
```

```c
}
```

Output :

```
TERMINAL

Volume is : 3141.600098
Press any key to continue . . . |
```

―――――――― **** ――――――――

Program No. - 29 :
Program to define and use Constants using const keyword.

Code :
```c
#include <stdio.h>

int main()
{
    const int MAX = 100;
    const float PI = 3.14159;
    system( "cls" );

    printf( "SIZE : %d\n", MAX );
    printf( "PI   : %f\n", PI );

    system( "pause" );
    return 0;
}
```

Output :

```
TERMINAL

SIZE : 100
PI   : 3.141590
Press any key to continue . . . []
```

―――――――― **** ――――――――

Program No. - 30 :
Program to explain **Constant** definition.

Code :
```c
#include <stdio.h>

int  main()
{
```

```c
    float  rad, vol;
    const  float  PI = 3.14159;
    system( "cls" );

    printf( "Enter Radius of Sphere : " );
    scanf( "%f", &rad );

    vol = ( 4.0 / 3.0 ) * PI * rad * rad * rad;

    printf( "\nVolume of Sphere is = %f\n", vol );

    system( "pause" );
    return 0;
}
```

Output :

```
TERMINAL

Enter Radius of Sphere : 10.0

Volume of Sphere is = 4188.786621
Press any key to continue . . .
```

———————— **** ————————

Program No. - 31 :
Program to define and use Constants using #define preprocessor.

Code :
```c
#include <stdio.h>

#define MAX 100
#define PI 3.14159

int main()
{
    system( "cls" );

    printf( "SIZE : %d\n", MAX );
    printf( "PI   : %f\n", PI );

    system( "pause" );
    return 0;
}
```

Output :

```
TERMINAL

SIZE : 100
PI   : 3.141590
Press any key to continue . . .
```

———————— **** ————————

Program No. - 32 :
Program to create constant using **#define** preprocessor.

Code :
```c
#include <stdio.h>

#define   PI   3.14159

int  main()
{
    float   r, vol;
    system( "cls" );

    printf( "Enter Radius of Hemi-Sphere : " );
    scanf( "%f", &r );

    vol = ( 2.0 / 3.0 ) * PI * r * r * r;

    printf( "\nVolume of Hemi-Sphere = %f\n", vol );

    system( "pause" );
    return 0;
}
```

Output :

```
TERMINAL

Enter Radius of Hemi-Sphere : 10.0

Volume of Hemi-Sphere = 2094.393311
Press any key to continue . . .
```

———————— **** ————————

Program No. - 33 :
Program to explain Variable definition and use.

Code :
```c
#include <stdio.h>
```

```c
int  main()
{
    float  rad, area;
    system( "cls" );

    printf( "Enter Radius of Circle : " );
    scanf( "%f", &rad );

    area = 3.14 * rad * rad;

    printf( "\nArea of Circle is = %f\n", area );

    system( "pause" );
    return 0;
}
```

Output :

```
TERMINAL

Enter Radius of Circle : 10.0

Area of Circle is = 314.000000
Press any key to continue . . .
```

———————————— **** ————————————

Program No. - 34 :
Program to explain **Global & Local Variable**.

Code :
```c
#include <stdio.h>

int  x = 10;            /*   Global Variable */

int  main()
{
    int  y = 20;        /*   Local Variable   */
    system( "cls" );

    printf( "x = %d, y = %d\n", x,  y );

    system( "pause" );
    return 0;
}
```

Output :

```
TERMINAL

x = 10, y = 20
Press any key to continue . . .
```

———————————— **** ————————————

Program No. - 35 :
Program to use Character Data Type.

Code :
```c
#include <stdio.h>

int  main()
{
    char  ch;
    system( "cls" );

    ch = 'A';
    printf( "ch = %c\n", ch );

    ch = 97;                    /* ASCII value of a */
    printf( "ch = %c\n", ch );

    system( "pause" );
    return 0;
}
```

Output :

```
TERMINAL

ch = A
ch = a
Press any key to continue . . .
```

———————————— **** ————————————

Program No. - 36 :
Program to print **ASCII value** of given Character.

Code :
```c
#include <stdio.h>

int  main()
{
    char ch;
    system( "cls" );
```

```c
    printf( "Enter a Character : " );
    scanf( "%c", &ch );

    printf( "\nThe ASCII value of \'%c\' is : %d\n", ch, ch
);

    system( "pause" );
    return 0;
}
```

Output :

```
TERMINAL

Enter a Character : A

The ASCII value of 'A' is : 65
Press any key to continue . . .
```

---- **** ----

Program No. - 37 :
Program to use **Escape Sequence / Back-Slash**
character.

Code :
```c
#include <stdio.h>

int  main()
{
    system( "cls" );

    printf( "A\nB \n" );
    printf( "A\tB \n" );
    printf( "\"ATUL\" \n" );
    printf( "\'ATUL\' \n" );

    system( "pause" );
    return 0;
}
```

Output :

```
TERMINAL

A
B
A       B
"ATUL"
'ATUL'
Press any key to continue . . .
```

---- **** ----

Program No. - 38 :
Program to explain the input of single character using
getchar() function.

Code :
```c
#include <stdio.h>

int  main()
{
    char ch;
    system( "cls" );

    printf( "Enter a Character : " );
    ch = getchar();
    printf( "ch = %c\n", ch );

    system( "pause" );
    return 0;
}
```

Output :

```
TERMINAL

Enter a Character : C
ch = C
Press any key to continue . . .
```

---- **** ----

Program No. - 39 :
Program to use User-defined Type declaration (**typedef**
).

Code :
```c
#include <stdio.h>

typedef  int  integer;
```

```c
typedef float real;

int  main()
{
    integer  a = 100;
    real  b = 12.345;
    system( "cls" );

    printf( "a = %d, b = %f\n", a, b );

    system( "pause" );
    return 0;
}
```

Output :

```
TERMINAL

a = 100, b = 12.345000
Press any key to continue . . .
```

****

Program No. - 40 :
Program to calculate Compound Interest by using Math library function **pow()**.

Code :
```c
#include <stdio.h>
#include <math.h>

int  main()
{
    float  ci, p, r, n, a;
    system( "cls" );

    printf( "Enter Principal, Rate & Time : " );
    scanf( "%f %f %f", &p, &r, &n );

    a = p * pow( ( 1 + ( r / 100 ) ), n ) ;
    ci = a - p ;

    printf( "\nCompound interest = Rs. %f\n", ci );

    system( "pause" );
    return 0;
}
```

Output :

```
TERMINAL

Enter Principal, Rate & Time : 1000 10 3

Compound interest = Rs. 331.000122
Press any key to continue . . .
```

****

Program No. - 41 :
Program to calculate Area of Triangle by using Math library function **sqrt()**.

Code :
```c
#include <stdio.h>
#include <math.h>

int  main()
{
    float  s, a, b, c, ar;
    system( "cls" );

    printf( "Enter the value a, b & c : " );
    scanf( "%f %f %f", &a, &b, &c );

    s = (a + b + c) / 2;
    ar = sqrt( s * (s – a) * (s – b) * (s – c) );

    printf( "\nArea of Triangle is = %f\n", ar );

    system( "pause" );
    return 0;
}
```

Output :

```
TERMINAL

Enter the value a, b & c : 3.0 4.0 5.0

Area of Triangle is = 6.000000
Press any key to continue . . .
```

****

Program No. - 42 :
Program to calculate the distance between the two points.

Code :
```c
#include <stdio.h>
#include <math.h>

int  main()
{
    float x1, y1, x2, y2, dist;
    system( "cls" );

    printf( "Enter value of x1 : " );
    scanf( "%f", &x1 );
    printf( "Enter value of y1 : " );
    scanf( "%f", &y1 );
    printf( "Enter value of x2 : " );
    scanf( "%f", &x2 );
    printf( "Enter value of y2 : ");
    scanf( "%f", &y2 );

    dist = sqrt(((x2 − x1) * (x2 − x1)) + ((y2 − y1)
                                    * (y2 − y1)));

    printf( "\nDistance between Two Points : %.4f\n",
                                    dist );

    system( "pause" );
    return 0;
}
```

Output :

```
TERMINAL

Enter value of x1 : 10
Enter value of y1 : 5
Enter value of x2 : 20
Enter value of y2 : 30

Distance between Two Points : 26.9258
Press any key to continue . . . []
```

****

Program No. - 43 :
Program to display the range of different character and integer data types using pre-defined constants.

Code :
```c
#include <stdio.h>
#include <limits.h>
```

```c
int  main()
{
    int i;
    system( "cls" );

    printf( "CHAR_MIN : %d\n", CHAR_MIN );
    printf( "CHAR_MAX : %d\n", CHAR_MAX );

    printf( "SHRT_MIN : %d\n", SHRT_MIN );
    printf( "SHRT_MAX : %d\n", SHRT_MAX );

    printf( "INT_MIN : %d\n", INT_MIN );
    printf( "INT_MAX : %d\n", INT_MAX );

    printf( "LONG_MIN : %ld\n", LONG_MIN );
    printf( "LONG_MAX : %ld\n", LONG_MAX );

    printf( "LLONG_MIN : %lld\n", LLONG_MIN );
    printf( "LLONG_MAX : %lld\n", LLONG_MAX );

    system( "pause" );
    return 0;
}
```

Output :

```
TERMINAL

CHAR_MIN  :  −128
CHAR_MAX  :  127
SHRT_MIN  :  −32768
SHRT_MAX  :  32767
INT_MIN  :  −2147483648
INT_MAX  :  2147483647
LONG_MIN  :  −2147483648
LONG_MAX  :  2147483647
LLONG_MIN  :  −9223372036854775808
LLONG_MAX  :  9223372036854775807
Press any key to continue . . . |
```

****

Program No. - 44 :
Program to display the upper limit of different unsigned character and integer data types using pre-defined constants.

Code :
```c
#include <stdio.h>
```

```c
#include <limits.h>

int  main()
{
    int i;
    system( "cls" );

    printf( "UCHAR_MAX : %d\n", UCHAR_MAX );
    printf( "USHRT_MAX : %d\n", USHRT_MAX );
    printf( "UINT_MAX : %u\n", UINT_MAX );
    printf( "ULONG_MAX : %lu\n", ULONG_MAX );
    printf( "ULLONG_MAX : %llu\n", ULLONG_MAX );

    system( "pause" );
    return 0;
}
```

Output :

```
TERMINAL

UCHAR_MAX  :  255
USHRT_MAX  :  65535
UINT_MAX  :  4294967295
ULONG_MAX  :  4294967295
ULLONG_MAX  :  18446744073709551615
Press  any  key  to  continue . . .  |
```

———————————— **** ————————————

Program No. - 45 :
Program to explain **unsigned** modifier.

Code :
```c
#include <stdio.h>

int  main()
{
    int var1 = 1500000000;
    unsigned int var2 = 1500000000;
    system( "cls" );

    var1 = ( var1 * 2 ) / 3;
    var2 = ( var2 * 2 ) / 3;

    printf( "Signed variable = %d\n", var1 );
    printf( "Unsigned variable = %d\n", var2 );

    system( "pause" );
```

```c
    return 0;
}
```

Output :

```
TERMINAL

Signed variable = -431655765
Unsigned variable = 1000000000
Press  any  key  to  continue . . .  |
```

———————————— **** ————————————

****

Chapter – 3
Operators & Expressions

****

Program No. - 46 :
Program to explain all Unary Operators (+, −, !, ++, −−, ~).

Code :
```c
#include <stdio.h>

int  main()
{
    int a, b;
    system( "cls" );
    printf( "Unary Operators : \n" );

    a = +10;                    // Positive
    b = −10;                    // Negative
    printf( "a = %d \nb = %d\n", a, b );

    a = 1;
    b = !a;                     // Not
    printf( "\n!a = %d\n", b );

    a = 10;
    b = ++a;                    // Increment
    printf( "\n++a = %d\n", b );

    a = 10;
    b = −−a;                    // Decrement
    printf( "−−a = %d\n", b );

    a = 10;
    b = ~a;                     // Complement
    printf( "\n~a = %d\n", b );

    system( "pause" );
    return 0;
}
```

Output :

****

Program No. - 47 :
Program to use **Arithmetic operators** (+ − * / %).

Code :
```c
#include <stdio.h>

int  main()
{
    int  a = 20, b = 3;
    int  sum, sub, mul, rem, idiv ;
    float  rdiv;
    system( "cls" );

    sum = a + b;
    sub = a − b;
    mul = a * b;
    idiv = a / b;
    rem = a % b;
    rdiv = (float)a / (float)b;

    printf( "sum = %d\n", sum );
    printf( "sub = %d\n", sub );
    printf( "mul = %d\n", mul );
    printf( "idiv = %d\n", idiv );
    printf( "rem = %d\n", rem );
    printf( "\nrdiv = %f\n", rdiv );

    system( "pause" );
    return 0;
}
```

Output :

```
TERMINAL

sum = 23
sub = 17
mul = 60
idiv = 6
rem = 2

rdiv = 6.666667
Press any key to continue . . .
```

```
TERMINAL

Enter any Number : 20

(n < 10) is = 0
(n > 10) is = 1
(n <= 10) is = 0
(n >= 10) is = 1
(n == 10) is = 0
(n != 10) is = 1
Press any key to continue . . .
```

****

Program No. - 48 :
Program to explain **Relational** Operators (<, >, <=, >=, ==, !=).

Code :
```c
#include <stdio.h>

int  main()
{
    int n;
    system( "cls" );

    printf( "Enter any Number : " );
    scanf( "%d", &n );

    printf( "\n(n < 10) is = %d\n", ( n < 10 ) );
    printf( "(n > 10) is = %d\n", ( n > 10 ) );
    printf( "(n <= 10) is = %d\n", ( n <= 10 ) );
    printf( "(n >= 10) is = %d\n", ( n >= 10 ) );
    printf( "(n == 10) is = %d\n", ( n == 10 ) );
    printf( "(n != 10) is = %d\n", ( n != 10 ) );

    system( "pause" );
    return 0;
}
```

Output :

****

Program No. - 49 :
Program to explain the **Relational operator**.
(< > <= >= == !=).

Code :
```c
#include <stdio.h>

int  main()
{
    int a;
    system( "cls" );

    a = ( 10 < 20 );
    printf( "(10 < 20) = %d\n", a ) ;

    a = ( 10 > 20 );
    printf( "(10 > 20) = %d\n", a ) ;

    a = ( 10 <= 20 );
    printf( "(10 <= 20) = %d\n", a ) ;

    a = ( 10 >= 20 );
    printf( "(10 >= 20) = %d\n", a ) ;

    a = ( 20 == 20 );
    printf( "(20 == 20) = %d\n", a ) ;

    a = ( 20 != 20 );
    printf( "(20 != 20) = %d\n", a ) ;

    system( "pause" );
    return 0;
}
```

Output :

```
TERMINAL

(10 < 20) = 1
(10 > 20) = 0
(10 <= 20) = 1
(10 >= 20) = 0
(20 == 20) = 1
(20 != 20) = 0
Press any key to continue . . .
```

****

Program No. - 50 :
Program to explain Logical And (&&) operator.

Code :
```c
#include <stdio.h>

int  main()
{
    system( "cls" );

    printf( "0 && 0 = %d\n", (0 && 0) );
    printf( "0 && 1 = %d\n", (0 && 1) );
    printf( "1 && 0 = %d\n", (1 && 0) );
    printf( "1 && 1 = %d\n", (1 && 1) );

    system( "pause" );
    return 0;
}
```

Output :

```
TERMINAL

0 && 0 = 0
0 && 1 = 0
1 && 0 = 0
1 && 1 = 1
Press any key to continue . . .
```

****

Program No. - 51 :
Program to explain Logical Or (||) operator.

Code :
```c
#include <stdio.h>
```

```c
int  main()
{
    system( "cls" );

    printf( "0 || 0 = %d\n", (0 || 0) );
    printf( "0 || 1 = %d\n", (0 || 1) );
    printf( "1 || 0 = %d\n", (1 || 0) );
    printf( "1 || 1 = %d\n", (1 || 1) );

    system( "pause" );
    return 0;
}
```

Output :

```
TERMINAL

0 || 0 = 0
0 || 1 = 1
1 || 0 = 1
1 || 1 = 1
Press any key to continue . . .
```

****

Program No. - 52 :
Program to explain Logical Not (!) operator.

Code :
```c
#include <stdio.h>

int  main()
{
    system( "cls" );

    printf( "!0 = %d\n", (!0) );
    printf( "!1 = %d\n", (!1) );

    system( "pause" );
    return 0;
}
```

Output :

```
TERMINAL

!0 = 1
!1 = 0
Press any key to continue . . .
```

———————— **** ————————

Program No. - 53 :
Program to explain the **Logical AND (&&)** operator.

Code :
```c
#include <stdio.h>

int  main()
{
    int a;
    system( "cls" );

    a = ( 2< 1 ) && ( 4 < 3 );
    printf( "(2<1) && (4<3) = %d\n", a ) ;

    a = ( 2< 1 ) && ( 4 > 3 );
    printf( "(2<1) && (4>3) = %d\n", a ) ;

    a = ( 2> 1 ) && ( 4 < 3 );
    printf( "(2>1) && (4<3) = %d\n", a ) ;

    a = ( 2> 1 ) && ( 4 > 3 );
    printf( "(2>1) && (4>3) = %d\n", a ) ;

    system( "pause" );
    return 0;
}
```

Output :
```
TERMINAL

(2<1)  &&  (4<3)  =  0
(2<1)  &&  (4>3)  =  0
(2>1)  &&  (4<3)  =  0
(2>1)  &&  (4>3)  =  1
Press any key to continue . . .
```

———————— **** ————————

Program No. - 54 :
Program to explain the **Logical OR (||)** operator.

Code :
```c
#include <stdio.h>

int  main()
```

```c
{
    int a;
    system( "cls" );

    a = ( 2 < 1 ) || ( 4 < 3 );
    printf( "(2<1) || (4<3) = %d\n", a ) ;

    a = ( 2 < 1 ) || ( 4 > 3 );
    printf( "(2<1) || (4>3) = %d\n", a ) ;

    a = ( 2 > 1 ) || ( 4 < 3 );
    printf( "(2>1) || (4<3) = %d\n", a ) ;

    a = ( 2 > 1 ) || ( 4 > 3 );
    printf( "(2>1) || (4>3) = %d\n", a ) ;

    system( "pause" );
    return 0;
}
```

Output :
```
TERMINAL

(2<1)  ||  (4<3)  =  0
(2<1)  ||  (4>3)  =  1
(2>1)  ||  (4<3)  =  1
(2>1)  ||  (4>3)  =  1
Press any key to continue . . .
```

———————— **** ————————

Program No. - 55 :
Program to explain the **Logical NOT (!)** operator.

Code :
```c
#include <stdio.h>

int  main()
{
    int a;
    system( "cls" );

    a = !( 2 < 1 );
    printf( "!(2<1) = %d\n", a ) ;

    a = !( 2 > 1 );
    printf( "!(2>1) = %d\n", a ) ;
```

```c
    system( "pause" );
    return 0;
}
```

Output :

```
TERMINAL

!(2<1) = 1
!(2>1) = 0
Press any key to continue . . .
```

———————————— **** ————————————

Program No. - 56 :
Program to use **Assignment** Operator (**=**).

Code :
```c
#include <stdio.h>

int  main()
{
    int a, b, c, d;
    system( "cls" );

    a = 10;           /* 10 = a;    invalid */
    b = a;
    c = a + b;        /* a + b = c;     invalid */

        d = 10;
    d = d + 10;       /* equivalent to  d += 10; */

    printf( "a = %d, b = %d\n", a, b );
    printf( "c = %d, d = %d\n", c, d );

    system( "pause" );
    return 0;
}
```

Output :

```
TERMINAL

a = 10, b = 10
c = 20, d = 20
Press any key to continue . . .
```

———————————— **** ————————————

Program No. - 57 :
Program to use **Assignment** Operator (**=**).

Code :
```c
#include <stdio.h>

int  main()
{
    int a, b, c, d, e, f;
    system( "cls" );

    a = b = c = d = e = f = 10;

    printf( "a = %d, b = %d\n", a, b );
    printf( "c = %d, d = %d\n", c, d );
    printf( "e = %d, f = %d\n", e, f );

    system( "pause" );
    return 0;
}
```

Output :

```
TERMINAL

a = 10, b = 10
c = 10, d = 10
e = 10, f = 10
Press any key to continue . . .
```

———————————— **** ————————————

Program No. - 58 :
Program to explain **Short-hand Assignment(
Compound Assignment) Operator.**

Code :
```c
#include <stdio.h>

int  main()
{
    int num = 25;
    system( "cls" );

    printf( "Num : %d\n", num );
    num += 10;
    printf( "Num += 10 : %d\n", num );
    num -= 5;
```

```c
    printf( "Num -= 5 : %d\n", num );
    num *= 2;
    printf( "Num *= 2 : %d\n", num );
    num /= 3;
    printf( "Num /= 3 : %d\n", num );
    num %= 3;
    printf( "Num %= 3 : %d\n", num );

    system( "pause" );
    return 0;
}
```

Output :

```
TERMINAL

Num : 25
Num += 10 : 35
Num -= 5 : 30
Num *= 2 : 60
Num /= 3 : 20
Num %= 3 : 2
Press any key to continue . . .
```

****

Program No. - 59 :
Program to explain the Prefix and Postfix **Increment (
++)** operator.

Code :

```c
#include <stdio.h>

int  main( )
{
    int  a = 10, b;
    system( "cls" );

    b = ++a;
    printf( "After Prefix Increment  : " );
    printf( "a = %d and b = %d\n", a, b );

    a = 10;
    b = a++;
    printf( "After Postfix Increment : " );
    printf( "a = %d and b = %d\n", a, b );

    system( "pause" );
    return 0;
```

```c
}
```

Output :

```
TERMINAL

After Prefix Increment  : a = 11 and b = 11
After Postfix Increment : a = 11 and b = 10
Press any key to continue . . .
```

****

Program No. - 60 :
Program to explain the Prefix and Postfix **Decrement
(−−)** operator.

Code :

```c
#include <stdio.h>

int  main( )
{
    int  a = 10, b;
    system( "cls" );

    b = --a;
    printf( "After Prefix Decrement  : " );
    printf( "a = %d and b = %d\n", a, b );

    a = 10;
    b = a--;
    printf( "After Postfix Decrement : " );
    printf( "a = %d and b = %d\n", a, b );

    system( "pause" );
    return 0;
}
```

Output :

```
TERMINAL

After Prefix Decrement  : a = 9 and b = 9
After Postfix Decrement : a = 9 and b = 10
Press any key to continue . . .
```

****

Program No. - 61 :
Program to explain the use of **Prefix Increment(++)**
Operator.

Code :
```c
#include <stdio.h>

int  main()
{
    int a = 10, b = 20 ,c;
    system( "cls" );

    c = (++a) + (++b);

    printf( "Value of a = %d\n", a );
    printf( "Value of b = %d\n", b );
    printf( "Value of c = %d\n", c );

    system( "pause" );
    return 0;
}
```

Output :

```
TERMINAL

Value of a = 11
Value of b = 21
Value of c = 32
Press any key to continue . . .
```

—————————— **** ——————————

Program No. - 62 :
Program to explain the use of **Postfix Increment(++)** Operator.

Code :
```c
#include <stdio.h>

int  main()
{
    int a = 10, b = 20 ,c;
    system( "cls" );

    c = (a++) + (b++);

    printf( "Value of a = %d\n", a );
    printf( "Value of b = %d\n", b );
    printf( "Value of c = %d\n", c );
```

```c
    system( "pause" );
    return 0;
}
```

Output :

```
TERMINAL

Value of a = 11
Value of b = 21
Value of c = 30
Press any key to continue . . .
```

—————————— **** ——————————

Program No. - 63 :
Program to explain the use of **Prefix Decrement** Operator (--).

Code :
```c
#include <stdio.h>

int  main()
{
    int  a = 10, b = 20 ,c;
    system( "cls" );

    c = (--a) + (--b);

    printf( "Value of a = %d\n", a );
    printf( "Value of b = %d\n", b );
    printf( "Value of c = %d\n", c );

    system( "pause" );
    return 0;
}
```

Output :

```
TERMINAL

Value of a = 9
Value of b = 19
Value of c = 28
Press any key to continue . . .
```

—————————— **** ——————————

Program No. - 64 :

Program to explain the use of **Postfix Decrement** Operator (--).

Code :
```c
#include <stdio.h>

int main()
{
    int  a = 10, b = 20 ,c;
    system( "cls" );

    c = (a--) + (b--);

    printf( "Value of a = %d\n", a );
    printf( "Value of b = %d\n", b );
    printf( "Value of c = %d\n", c );

    system( "pause" );
    return 0;
}
```

Output :
```
TERMINAL

Value of a = 9
Value of b = 19
Value of c = 30
Press any key to continue . . .
```

———————— **** ————————

Program No. - 65 :
Program to explain the use of **Bitwise** Operators (&, |, ^, ~, <<, >>).

Code :
```c
#include <stdio.h>

int main()
{
    int a = 3, b = 6, c;
    system( "cls" );

    printf( "a = %d\n", a );
    printf( "b = %d\n", b );

    c = a & b;
    printf( "a & b = %d\n", c );

    c = a | b;
    printf( "a | b = %d\n", c );

    c = a ^ b;
    printf( "a ^ b = %d\n", c );

    c = ~a;
    printf( "~a = %d\n", c );

    c = a << 3;
    printf( "a << 3 = %d\n", c );

    c = b >> 2;
    printf( "b >> 2 = %d\n", c );

    system( "pause" );
    return 0;
}
```

Output :
```
TERMINAL

a = 3
b = 6
a & b = 2
a | b = 7
a ^ b = 5
~a = -4
a << 3 = 24
b >> 2 = 1
Press any key to continue . . .
```

———————— **** ————————

Program No. - 66 :
Program to use **sizeof()** operator.

Code :
```c
#include <stdio.h>

int main()
{
    int a = 100, b;
    system( "cls" );

    b = sizeof( a );
    printf( "The size of a : %d\n", b );
```

```c
    b = sizeof( double );
    printf( "The size of double : %d\n", b );

    b = sizeof( 123L );
    printf( "The size of 123L : %d\n", b );

    b = sizeof( 123.45 );
    printf( "The size of 123.45 : %d\n", b );

    b = sizeof( 123.45f );
    printf( "The size of 123.45f : %d\n", b );

    system( "pause" );
    return 0;
}
```

Output :

```
TERMINAL

The size of a : 4
The size of double : 8
The size of 123L : 4
The size of 123.45 : 8
The size of 123.45f : 4
Press any key to continue . . .
```

---- **** ----

Program No. - 67 :
Program to explain **sizeof()** operator.

Code :
```c
#include <stdio.h>

int  main()
{
    system( "cls" );
    printf( "The size of a char is:\t\t" );
    printf( "%d bytes.\n", sizeof( char ) );
    printf( "The size of a short int is:\t" );
    printf( "%d bytes.\n", sizeof( short ) );
    printf( "The size of an int is:\t\t" );
    printf( "%d bytes.\n", sizeof( int ) );
    printf( "The size of a long int is:\t" );;
    printf( "%d bytes.\n", sizeof( long ) );
    printf( "The size of a long long int is:\t" );;
    printf( "%d bytes.\n", sizeof( long long ) );
    printf( "The size of a float is:\t\t" );
    printf( "%d bytes.\n", sizeof( float ) );
    printf( "The size of a double is:\t" );
    printf( "%d bytes.\n", sizeof( double ) );
    printf( "The size of a long double is:\t" );
    printf( "%d bytes.\n", sizeof( long double ) );

    system( "pause" );
    return 0;
}
```

Output :

```
TERMINAL

The size of a char is:          1 bytes.
The size of a short int is:     2 bytes.
The size of an int is:          4 bytes.
The size of a long int is:      4 bytes.
The size of a long long int is: 8 bytes.
The size of a float is:         4 bytes.
The size of a double is:        8 bytes.
The size of a long double is:   16 bytes.
Press any key to continue . . .
```

---- **** ----

Program No. - 68 :
Program to explain the use **Comma(,)** Operator.

Code :
```c
#include <stdio.h>

int  main()
{
    int a, b, c;
    system( "cls" );

    c = ( a=10, b=20, a+b );

    printf( "a : %d\n", a );
    printf( "b : %d\n", b );
    printf( "c : %d\n", c );

    system( "pause" );
    return 0;
}
```

Output :

```
TERMINAL

a : 10
b : 20
c : 30
Press any key to continue . . . |
```

****

Program No. - 69 :
Program to use **Comma (,)** operator.

Code :
```c
#include <stdio.h>

int  main()
{
    int  num, sq, cube;
    system( "cls" );
    num = 10;

    sq = ( num * num ), cube = ( num * num * num );

    printf( "The square of %d is : %d\n", num, sq );
    printf( "The cube of %d is   : %d\n", num, cube );

    system( "pause" );
    return 0;
}
```

Output :
```
TERMINAL

The square of 10 is : 100
The cube of 10 is   : 1000
Press any key to continue . . . |
```

****

Program No. - 70 :
Program to explain the Comma Operator (,).

Code :
```c
#include <stdio.h>

int  main()
{
    int a = 10, b = 10;
```

```c
    system( "cls" );

    // Comma Operator ( L -> R )
    printf( "Value = %d\n", ( a *= 2, b ) );

    system( "pause" );
    return 0;
}
```

Output :
```
TERMINAL

Value = 10
Press any key to continue . . . |
```

****

Program No. - 71 :
Program to rotate values of three variables in single statement using comma operator.

Code :
```c
#include <stdio.h>

int  main()
{
    int a = 1, b = 2, c = 3, t;
    system( "cls" );
    printf( "a = %d, b = %d, c = %d", a, b, c );

    t=a, a=b, b=c, c=t;        /* comma operator */

    printf( "\nAfter Rotation : \n" );
    printf( "a = %d, b = %d, c = %d\n", a, b, c );

    system( "pause" );
    return 0;
}
```

Output :
```
TERMINAL

a = 1, b = 2, c = 3
After Rotation :
a = 2, b = 3, c = 1
Press any key to continue . . . . []
```

****

Program No. - 72 :
Program to explain the use **Conditional / Ternary Operator(? :).**

Code :
```c
#include <stdio.h>

int  main()
{
    int a, b, max;
    system( "cls" );

    printf( "Enter Two Numbers : " );
    scanf( "%d %d", &a, &b );

    max = ( (a > b) ? a : b );

    printf( "\nMaximum Value is : %d\n", max );

    system( "pause" );
    return 0;
}
```

Output :

```
TERMINAL

Enter Two Numbers : 10 20

Maximum Value is : 20
Press any key to continue . . .
```

****

Program No. - 73 :
Program to find biggest of three numbers using ternary operator / conditional operator (? :).

Code :
```c
#include <stdio.h>

int  main()
{
    int a, b, c, max;
    system( "cls" );

    printf( "Enter Three Numbers : " );
    scanf( "%d %d %d", &a ,&b, &c );
```

```c
    max = ( (a>b) ? ((a>c)?a:c) : ((b>c)?b:c) );

    printf( "\nMaximum = %d\n", max );

    system( "pause" );
    return 0;
}
```

Output :

```
TERMINAL

Enter Three Numbers : 20 30 10

Maximum = 30
Press any key to continue . . .
```

****

Program No. - 74 :
Program to check whether the given number is Positive or Negative number using Conditional Operator (**?:**) in puts() function.

Code :
```c
#include <stdio.h>

int  main()
{
    int n;
    system( "cls" );

    printf( "Enter a Number : " );
    scanf( "%d", &n );

    puts( (n >= 0) ? "\nPositive Number." :
                     "\nNegative Number." );

    system( "pause" );
    return 0;
}
```

Output :

```
TERMINAL

Enter a Number : 25

Positive Number.
Press any key to continue . . .
```

```
TERMINAL

Enter a Number : -5

Negative Number.
Press any key to continue . . .
```

****

Program No. - 75 :
Program to explain the **Expression**.

Code :
```c
#include <stdio.h>

int  main()
{
    int a, b, c, d, x;
    system( "cls" );

    printf( "Enter 4 Integers : " );
    scanf( "%d %d %d %d", &a, &b, &c, &c );

    x = ( a + b ) / ( c - d );

    printf( "Value = %d\n", x );

    system( "pause" );
    return 0;
}
```

Output :
```
TERMINAL

Enter 4 Integers : 6 3 5 2
Value = 4
Press any key to continue . . .
```

****

Program No. - 76 :

Program to explain **Operator Precedence**.

Code :
```c
#include <stdio.h>

int  main()
{
    float result;
    system( "cls" );

    result = 1.0 + 2.0 * 3.0 / 4.0;
    printf( "%f\n", result );

    result = 1.0 / 2.0 + 3.0;
    printf( "%f\n", result );

    result = (1.0 + 2.0) / 3.0;
    printf( "%f\n", result );

    result = (1.0 + 2.0 / 3.0) + 4.0;
    printf( "%f\n", result );

    system( "pause" );
    return 0;
}
```

Output :
```
TERMINAL

2.500000
3.500000
1.000000
5.666667
Press any key to continue . . .
```

****

Program No. - 77 :
Program to explain **Automatic or Implicit Type Conversion**.

Code :
```c
#include <stdio.h>

int  main()
{
    int  a = 10, b = 20;
    float c = 10.50;
```

```c
long d = 20L, e;
system( "cls" );

e = ( ( a + c ) * d ) + b;

printf( "Value of e : %ld\n", e );

system( "pause" );
return 0;
}
```

Output :

```
TERMINAL

Value of e : 430
Press any key to continue . . .
```

****

Program No. - 78 :
Program to use **Type Casting** or **Explicit Conversion**.

Code :
```c
#include <stdio.h>

int  main()
{
    int  a = 10, b = 20;
    float c = 10.50;
    long d = 20L, e;
    system( "cls" );

    e = ( ( ( ( (long)a + (long)c ) * d ) + (long)b );

    printf( "Value of e : %ld\n", e );

    system( "pause" );
    return 0;
}
```

Output :

```
TERMINAL

Value of e : 420
Press any key to continue . . .
```

****

Program No. - 79 :
Program to explain the **Type Casting**.

Code :
```c
#include <stdio.h>

int  main( )
{
    float  a ;
    int  x = 6, y = 4 ;
    system( "cls" );

    a = x / y ;
    printf( "Value of a (without casting ) = %f\n", a ) ;

    a = (float) x / y ;
    printf( "Value of a (with casting ) = %f\n", a ) ;

    system( "pause" );
    return 0;
}
```

Output :

```
TERMINAL

Value of a (without casting ) = 1.000000
Value of a (with casting ) = 1.500000
Press any key to continue . . .
```

****

Program No. - 80 :
Program to use **Explicit Conversion** or **Type Casting**.

Code :
```c
#include <stdio.h>

int  main()
{
    int  a = 2000000000, b = 2000000000;
    system( "cls" );

    a = ( (long long)a * 10 ) / 20;
    b = ( b * 10 ) / 20;

    printf( "a : %d\n", a );
    printf( "b : %d\n", b );
```

```
system( "pause" );
return 0;
}
```

Output :

```
TERMINAL

a : 1000000000
b : -73741824
Press any key to continue . . .
```

————————— **** —————————

Program No. - 81 :
Program to explain Automatic / Implicit type conversion.

Code :

```
#include <stdio.h>

// implicit conversion
int main()
{
    system( "cls" );
    long l = 100;           /* int -> long */
    double d = l;           /* long -> double */
    printf( "l = %ld\n", l );
    printf( "d = %lf\n", d );

    d = 25 + 10.5;          /* int -> double */
    printf( "d = %lf\n", d );

    /* double -> int (data loss possiblity) */
    int i = 325.5;

    /* int -> char (data loss possiblity)  */
    char c = i;
    printf( "i = %d\n", i );
    printf( "c = %c\n", c );

    system( "pause" );
}
```

Output :

```
TERMINAL

l = 100
d = 100.000000
d = 35.500000
i = 325
c = E
Press any key to continue . . .
```

————————— **** —————————

Program No. - 82 :
Program to explain Type Casting / Explicit type conversion.

Code :

```
#include <stdio.h>

// explicit conversion
int main()
{
    system( "cls" );
    int i = (int)12.5;          /* double -> int */
    char c = (char)65;          /* int -> char */
    printf( "i = %d\n", i );
    printf( "c = %c\n", c );

    i = 25 + (int)10.5;         /* double -> int */
    printf( "i = %d\n", i );

    /* double -> int (data loss possiblity) */
    i = (int)325.5;

    /* int -> char (data loss possiblity)  */
    c = (char)i;

    printf( "i = %d\n", i );
    printf( "c = %c\n", c );

    system( "pause" );
}
```

Output :

```
TERMINAL

i = 12
c = A
i = 35
i = 325
c = E
Press any key to continue . . . []
```

```
TERMINAL

Enter Total Number of Days : 1050
Years  = 2
Months = 10
Weeks  = 2
Days   = 6
Press any key to continue . . . |
```

****

Program No. - 83 :
Program to convert Total number of days into years, months, weeks and days.

Code :

```c
#include <stdio.h>

int  main()
{
    int  d, y, m, w;
    system( "cls" );

    printf( "Enter Total Number of Days : " );
    scanf( "%d", &d );

    y = d / 365;
    d = d % 365;
    m = d / 30;
    d = d % 30;
    w = d / 7;
    d = d % 7;

    printf( "Years  = %d\n", y );
    printf( "Months = %d\n", m );
    printf( "Weeks  = %d\n", w );
    printf( "Days   = %d\n", d );

    system( "pause" );
    return 0;
}
```

Output :

Program No. - 84 :
Program to find value of Hundred, Tens and Unit place of given Three Digit Number.

Code :

```c
#include <stdio.h>

int  main()
{
    int  n, u, t, h;
    system( "cls" );

    printf( "Enter a Three Digit Number : " );
    scanf( "%d", &n );

    u = n % 10;
    n = n / 10;
    t = n % 10;
    h = n / 10;

    printf( "Hundred Place = %d\n", h );
    printf( "Tens Place    = %d\n", t );
    printf( "Unit Place    = %d\n", u );

    system( "pause" );
    return 0;
}
```

Output :

```
TERMINAL

Enter a Three Digit Number : 123
Hundred Place = 1
Tens Place    = 2
Unit Place    = 3
Press any key to continue . . . |
```

———————— **** ————————

Program No. - 85 :
Program to Swap two numbers using Bitwise operator.

Code :

```c
#include <stdio.h>

int  main()
{
    int a, b;
    system( "cls" );

    printf( "Enter Two Numbers : " );
    scanf( "%d %d", &a, &b );

    printf( "\nBefore Swapping : a = %d, b = %d\n", a, b );

    a = a ^ b;
    b = a ^ b;
    a = a ^ b;

    printf( "After Swapping  : a = %d, b = %d\n", a, b );

    system( "pause" );
    return 0;
}
```

Output :

```
TERMINAL

Enter Two Numbers : 10 20

Before Swapping : a = 10, b = 10
After Swapping  : a = 20, b = 10
Press any key to continue . . . █
```

———————— **** ————————

****

Chapter – 4
Selection

****

Program No. - 86 :
Program to explain **Simple If** statement.

Code :
```c
#include <stdio.h>

int  main()
{
    int  n;
    system( "cls" );

    printf( "Enter a number : " );
    scanf( "%d", &n );

    if( n > 100 )
    {
        printf( "\nNumber is greater than 100.\n" );
    }

    system( "pause" );
    return 0;
}
```

Output :

```
TERMINAL

Enter a number : 200

Number is greater than 100.
Press any key to continue . . . |
```

```
TERMINAL

Enter a number : 50
Press any key to continue . . . |
```

———————————— **** ————————————

Program No. - 87 :
Program to explain **If-else** statement.

Code :
```c
#include <stdio.h>

int  main()
{
    int  n;
    system( "cls" );
```

```c
    printf( "Enter Number : " );
    scanf( "%d", &n );

    if( n > 100 )
    {
        printf( "\nNumber is greater than 100.\n" );
    }
    else
    {
        printf( "\nNumber is smaller than or equal
                                        to 100.\n" );
    }

    system( "pause" );
    return 0;
}
```

Output :

```
TERMINAL

Enter Number : 200

Number is greater than 100.
Press any key to continue . . . |
```

```
TERMINAL

Enter Number : 50

Number is smaller than or equal to 100.
Press any key to continue . . . |
```

———————————— **** ————————————

Program No. - 88 :
Program to find maximum of three numbers using simple if statement.

Code :
```c
#include <stdio.h>

int  main()
{
    int a, b, c, max = 0;
    system( "cls" );

    printf( "Enter Three Numbers : " );
```

```c
    scanf( "%d %d %d", &a, &b, &c );

    max = a;
    if( b > max )
        max = b;
    if( c > max )
        max = c;

    printf( "\nMaximum : %d\n", max );

    system( "pause" );
    return 0;
}
```

Output :

```
TERMINAL

Enter Three Numbers :  10 30 20

Maximum : 30
Press any key to continue . . .
```

――――――――――― **** ―――――――――――

Program No. - 89 :
Program to find Maximum of Two Numbers using **If-Else** statement.

Code :
```c
#include <stdio.h>

int  main()
{
    int  a, b, max;
    system( "cls" );

    printf( "Enter Two Numbers : " );
    scanf( "%d %d", &a, &b );

    if( a > b )
        max = a;
    else
        max = b;

    printf( "\nMaximum = %d\n", max );

    system( "pause" );
    return 0;
```

```c
}
```

Output :

```
TERMINAL

Enter Two Numbers :  20 10

Maximum = 20
Press any key to continue . . .
```

```
TERMINAL

Enter Two Numbers :  10 20

Maximum = 20
Press any key to continue . . .
```

――――――――――― **** ―――――――――――

Program No. - 90 :
Program to check whether the given number is Even or Odd ?

Code :
```c
#include <stdio.h>

int  main()
{
    int  n;
    system( "cls" );

    printf( "Enter a Number : " );
    scanf( "%d", &n );

    if( n % 2 == 0 )
        printf( "\n%d is an Even number.\n", n );
    else
        printf( "\n%d is an Odd number.\n", n );

    system( "pause" );
    return 0;
}
```

Output :

```
TERMINAL

Enter a Number : 20


20 is an Even number.
Press any key to continue . . .
```

```
TERMINAL

Enter a Number : 25


25 is an Odd number.
Press any key to continue . . .
```

———————————— **** ————————————

Program No. - 91 :
Program to check whether the given number is Positive
or Negative ?

Code :
```c
#include <stdio.h>

int  main()
{
    int  n;
    system( "cls" );

    printf( "Enter a Number : " );
    scanf( "%d", &n );

    if( n >= 0 )
        printf( "\n%d is a Positive number.\n", n );
    else
        printf( "\n%d is a Negative number.\n", n );

    system( "pause" );
    return 0;
}
```

Output :
```
TERMINAL

Enter a Number : 10


10 is a Positive number.
Press any key to continue . . .
```

```
TERMINAL

Enter a Number : -25


-25 is a Negative number.
Press any key to continue . . .
```

———————————— **** ————————————

Program No. - 92 :
Program to check whether the given character is
Alphanumeric or not.

Code :
```c
#include <stdio.h>
#include <ctype.h>

int  main()
{
    int  ch;
    system( "cls" );

    printf( "Enter a character : " );
    ch = getchar();

    if( isalnum( ch ) )
        printf( "\nIt is an alpha-numeric character.\n" );
    else
        printf( "\nThis is not an alpha-numeric
                                    character.\n" );

    system( "pause" );
    return 0;
}
```

Output :
```
TERMINAL

Enter a character : A


It is an alpha-numeric character.
Press any key to continue . . .
```

```
TERMINAL

Enter a character : $

This is not an alpha-numeric character.
Press any key to continue . . .
```

———————————— **** ————————————

Program No. - 93 :
Program to check whether the given year is Leap year or not.

Code :
```c
#include <stdio.h>

int main()
{
    int year;
    system( "cls" );

    printf( "Enter Year (yyyy) : " );
    scanf( "%d", &year );

    if( year % 4 == 0 )
        printf( "\n%d is Leap Year.\n", year );
    else
        printf( "\n%d is Not a Leap Year.\n", year );

    system( "pause" );
    return 0;
}
```

Output :
```
TERMINAL

Enter Year (yyyy) : 2024

2024 is Leap Year.
Press any key to continue . . .
```

```
TERMINAL

Enter Year (yyyy) : 2023

2023 is Not a Leap Year.
Press any key to continue . . .
```

———————————— **** ————————————

Program No. - 94 :
Program to find Maximum of Three Numbers using Nested If statement.

Code :
```c
#include <stdio.h>

int main()
{
    int a, b, c, g;
    system( "cls" );

    printf( "Enter Three Numbers : " );
    scanf( "%d %d %d", &a, &b, &c );

    if( a > b )
    {
        if( a > c )
            g = a;
        else
            g = c ;
    }
    else
    {
        if( b > c)
            g = b;
        else
            g = c;
    }

    printf( "\nGreatest Number is : %d\n", g );

    system( "pause" );
    return 0;
}
```

Output :
```
TERMINAL

Enter Three Numbers : 10 20 30

Greatest Number is : 30
Press any key to continue . . .
```

```
TERMINAL

Enter Three Numbers : 20 30 10

Greatest Number is : 30
Press any key to continue . . .
```

****

Program No. - 95 :
Program to find Grade using Nested If statement on the basis of Range of Marks.

Marks	Grade
80 to 100	A+
70 to 80	A
60 to 70	B
40 to 60	C
0 to 40	F

Code :

```c
#include <stdio.h>

int  main()
{
    int  m;
    system( "cls" );

    printf( "Enter the Marks : " );
    scanf( "%d", &m );

    if( m >= 80 )
    {
        printf( "\nGrade = A+ \n" );
    }
    else
    {
        if( m >= 70 )
        {
            printf( "\nGrade = A \n" );
        }
        else
        {
            if( m >= 60 )
            {
                printf( "\nGrade = B \n" );
            }
            else
            {
                if( m >= 40 )
                {
                    printf( "\nGrade = C \n" );
                }
                else
                {
                    printf( "\nGrade = F \n" );
                }
            }
        }
    }

    system( "pause" );
    return 0;
}
```

Output :

```
TERMINAL

Enter the Marks : 95

Grade = A+
Press any key to continue . . .
```

```
TERMINAL

Enter the Marks : 68

Grade = B
Press any key to continue . . .
```

```
TERMINAL

Enter the Marks : 35

Grade = F
Press any key to continue . . .
```

****

Program No. - 96 :
Program to check whether the given number is Positive, Negative or Zero.

Code :

```c
#include <stdio.h> >

int  main()
```

```c
{
    int n;
    system( "cls" );

    printf( "Enter a Number : " );
    scanf( "%d", &n );

    if( n > 0 )
            printf( "\nPositive Number.\n" );
    else if( n < 0 )
            printf( "\nNegative Number.\n" );
    else
            printf( "\nZero.\n" );

    system( "pause" );
    return 0;
}
```

Output :

```
TERMINAL

Enter a Number : -25

Negative Number.
Press any key to continue . . .
```

```
TERMINAL

Enter a Number : 10

Positive Number.
Press any key to continue . . .
```

```
TERMINAL

Enter a Number : 0

Zero.
Press any key to continue . . .
```

****

Program No. - 97 :
Program to find Maximum of three numbers using Nested If.

Code :

```c
#include <stdio.h>

int main()
{
    int n1, n2, n3;
    system( "cls" );

    printf( "Enter Three Numbers : " );
    scanf( "%d %d %d", &n1, &n2, &n3 );

    if( ( n1 > n2 ) && ( n1 > n3 ) )
        printf( "\nGreatest Number : %d\n", n1 );
    else
    {
        if( n2 > n3 )
            printf( "\nGreatest Number : %d\n", n2 );
        else
            printf( "\nGreatest Number : %d\n", n3 );
    }

    system( "pause" );
    return 0;
}
```

Output :

```
TERMINAL

Enter Three Numbers : 20 30 10

Greatest Number : 30
Press any key to continue . . .
```

****

Program No. - 98 :
Program to find Maximum of three numbers using Nested If.

Code :

```c
#include <stdio.h>

int main()
{
    int n1, n2, n3, n4;
    system( "cls" );

    printf( "Enter Four numbers : " );
```

```c
    scanf( "%d %d %d %d", &n1, &n2, &n3, &n4 );

    if( ( n1 > n2 ) && ( n1 > n3 ) && ( n1 > n4 ) )
        printf( "\nGreatest Number : %d\n", n1 );
    else
        if( ( n2 > n3 ) && ( n2 > n4 ) )
            printf( "\nGreatest Number : %d\n", n2 );
        else
            if( n3 > n4 )
                printf( "\nGreatest Number : %d\n", n3 );
            else
                printf( "\nGreatest Number : %d\n", n4 );


    system( "pause" );
    return 0;
}
```

Output :

```
TERMINAL

Enter Four numbers : 30 10 40 20

Greatest Number : 40
Press any key to continue . . . 
```

---- **** ----

Program No. - 99 :
Program to find Grade using Else If ladder statement on
the basis of Range of Marks.

Marks	Grade
80 to 100	A+
70 to 80	A
60 to 70	B
40 to 60	C
0 to 40	F

Code :
```c
#include <stdio.h>

int  main()
{
    int  m;
    system( "cls" );

    printf( "Enter the Marks : " );
    scanf( "%d", &m );

    if( m >= 80 )
    {
        printf( "\nGrade = A+ \n" );
    }
    else if( m >= 70 )
    {
        printf( "\nGrade = A \n" );
    }
    else if( m >= 60 )
    {
        printf( "\nGrade = B \n" );
    }
    else if( m >= 40 )
    {
        printf( "\nGrade = C \n" );
    }
    else
    {
        printf( "\nGrade = F \n" );
    }

    system( "pause" );
    return 0;
}
```

Output :

```
TERMINAL

Enter the Marks : 88

Grade = A+
Press any key to continue . . . 
```

```
TERMINAL

Enter the Marks : 72

Grade = A
Press any key to continue . . . 
```

```
TERMINAL

Enter the Marks : 55

Grade = C
Press any key to continue . . . 
```

———————— **** ————————

Program No. - 100 :
Program to check whether the Given Year is Leap or Not.

Code :

```c
#include <stdio.h>

int  main()
{
    int  y;
    system( "cls" );

    printf( "Enter the year (4-digit) : " );
    scanf( "%d", &y );

    if( y % 100 == 0 )
    {
        if( y % 400 == 0 )
            printf( "\nIt is a LEAP Year.\n" );
        else
            printf( "\nIt is NOT a LEAP Year.\n" );
    }
    else if( y % 4 == 0 )
        printf( "\nIt is a LEAP Year.\n" );
    else
        printf( "\nIt is NOT a LEAP Year.\n" );

    system( "pause" );
    return 0;
}
```

Output :

```
TERMINAL
Enter the year (4-digit) : 2022

It is NOT a LEAP Year.
Press any key to continue . . .
```

```
TERMINAL
Enter the year (4-digit) : 2024

It is a LEAP Year.
Press any key to continue . . .
```

```
TERMINAL
Enter the year (4-digit) : 1900

It is NOT a LEAP Year.
Press any key to continue . . .
```

```
TERMINAL
Enter the year (4-digit) : 2000

It is a LEAP Year.
Press any key to continue . . .
```

———————— **** ————————

Program No. - 101 :
Program to create Menu Based (Choice Based) Program for Temperature Conversion.

Code :

```c
#include <stdio.h>

int  main()
{
    int choice;
    float temp, cnvtemp;
    system( "cls" );

    printf( "Temp. conversation menu : \n" );
    printf( "1. Fahrenheit to Celsius.\n" );
    printf( "2. Celsius to Fahrenheit.\n" );
    printf( "Enter your choice  : " );
    scanf( "%d", &choice );

    if( choice == 1 )
    {
        printf( "\nEnter temp. in Fahrenheit : " );
        scanf( "%f", &temp );
        cnvtemp = ( temp − 32 ) / 1.8;
        printf( "\nThe temp in Celsius is = %f \n",
                                            cnvtemp );
    }
    else
    {
        printf( "\nEnter temp in Celsius : " );
        scanf( "%f", &temp );
```

```c
            cnvtemp = ( 1.8 * temp ) + 32;
            printf( "\nThe temp in Fahrenheit is = %f \n",
                                              cnvtemp );

        }

    system( "pause" );
    return 0;
}
```

Output :

```
TERMINAL

Temp. conversation menu :
1. Fahrenheit to Celsius.
2. Celsius to Fahrenheit.
Enter your choice  : 1

Enter temp. in Fahrenheit : 100.0

The temp in Celsius is = 37.777779
Press any key to continue . . .
```

```
TERMINAL

Temp. conversation menu :
1. Fahrenheit to Celsius.
2. Celsius to Fahrenheit.
Enter your choice  : 2

Enter temp in Celsius : 37.8

The temp in Fahrenheit is = 100.040001
Press any key to continue . . .
```

____________ **** ____________

Program No. - 101 :
Program to use Arithmetic Operators.

Code :
```c
#include <stdio.h>

int  main()
{
    char op;
    int a, b, res;
    system( "cls" );

    printf( "Enter Two Numbers : " );
    scanf( "%d %d", &a, &b );
```

```c
    printf( "Enter the Operator (+, −, *, /, %) : " );
    fflush( stdin );
    scanf( "%c", &op );

    if( op == '+' )
    {
        res = a + b;
    }
    else if( op == '−' )
    {
        res = a − b;
    }
    else if( op == '*' )
    {
        res = a * b;
    }
    else if( op == '/' )
    {
        res = a / b;
    }
    else if( op == '%' )
    {
        res = a % b;
    }
    else
    {
        printf( "Invalid operator.\n" );
    }

    printf( "\n%d %c %d = %d\n", a, op, b, res );

    system( "pause" );
    return 0;
}
```

Output :
```
TERMINAL

Enter Two Numbers : 10 20
Enter the Operator (+, -, *, /, %) : +

10 + 20 = 30
Press any key to continue . . .
```

```
TERMINAL

Enter Two Numbers : 20 3
Enter the Operator (+, -, *, /, %) : %

20 % 3 = 2
Press any key to continue . . .
```

```
TERMINAL

Enter Two Numbers : 20 5
Enter the Operator (+, -, *, /, %) : #
Invalid operator.

20 # 5 = 0
Press any key to continue . . .
```

______________ **** ______________

Program No. - 103 :
Program to display the name of the week day on the
basis of Week Day Number (1 to 7).

Code :
```c
#include <stdio.h>

int  main()
{
    int d;
    system( "cls" );

    printf( "Enter Day Number(1-7) : " );
    scanf( "%d", &d );

    if( d == 1 )
    {
        printf( "\nMonday.\n" );
    }
    else if( d == 2 )
    {
        printf( "\nTuesday.\n" );
    }
    else if( d == 3 )
    {
        printf( "\nWednesday.\n" );
    }
    else if( d == 4 )
    {
        printf( "\nThursday.\n" );
    }
    else if( d == 5 )
    {
        printf( "\nFriday.\n" );
    }
    else if( d == 6 )
    {
        printf( "\nSaturday.\n" );
    }
    else if( d == 7 )
    {
        printf( "\nSunday.\n" );
    }
    else
    {
        printf( "\nInvalid Day Number.\n" );
    }

    system( "pause" );
    return 0;
}
```

Output :
```
TERMINAL

Enter Day Number(1-7) : 7

Sunday.
Press any key to continue . . .
```

```
TERMINAL

Enter Day Number(1-7) : 9

Invalid Day Number.
Press any key to continue . . .
```

______________ **** ______________

Program No. - 104 :
Program to display the name of the week day on the
basis of Week Day Number (1 to 7).

Code :
```c
#include <stdio.h>

int  main()
{
```

```c
int  d;
system( "cls" );

printf( "Enter Day Number (1-7): " );
scanf( "%d", &d );

switch( d )
{
    case 1:
        printf( "\nMonday\n" );
        break;
    case 2:
        printf( "\nTuesday\n" );
        break;
    case 3:
        printf( "\nWednesday\n" );
        break;
    case 4:
        printf( "\nThursday\n" );
        break;
    case 5:
        printf( "\nFriday\n" );
        break;
    case 6:
        printf( "\nSaturday\n" );
        break;
    case 7:
        printf( "\nSunday\n" );
        break;
    default :
        printf( "\nWrong Day Number.\n" );
}

system( "pause" );
return 0;
}
```

Output :

```
TERMINAL

Enter Day Number (1-7): 1

Monday
Press any key to continue . . .
```

```
TERMINAL

Enter Day Number (1-7): 9

Wrong Day Number.
Press any key to continue . . .
```

——————————————— **** ———————————————

Program No. - 105 :
Program to use Elseif ladder for multiple values of single variable.

Code :
```c
#include <stdio.h>

int main()
{
    int a = 3;
    system( "cls" );

    if( a == 1 )
    {
        printf( "One.\n" );
    }
    else if( a == 2 )
    {
        printf( "Two.\n" );
    }
    else if( a == 3 )
    {
        printf( "Three.\n" );
    }
    else
    {
        printf( "Other Number.\n" );
    }

    system( "pause" );
    return 0;
}
```

Output :

```
TERMINAL

Three.
Press any key to continue . . .
```

———————— **** ————————

Program No. - 106 :
Program to use switch-case for multiple values of single variable.

Code :

```c
#include <stdio.h>

int main()
{
    int a = 3;
    system( "cls" );

    switch( a )
    {
            case 1:
            printf( "One.\n" );
            break;
            case 2:
            printf( "Two.\n" );
            break;
            case 3:
            printf( "Three.\n" );
            break;
            default:
            printf( "Other Number.\n" );
            break;
    }

    system( "pause" );
    return 0;
}
```

Output :

```
TERMINAL

Three.
Press any key to continue . . .
```

———————— **** ————————

Program No. - 107 :
Program to perform Arithmatic Operation using **Switch-case** statement.

Code :

```c
#include <stdio.h>

int main()
{
    char op;
    int a, b, res;
    system( "cls" );

    printf( "Enter Two Numbers : " );
    scanf( "%d %d", &a, &b );
    printf( "Enter the operator (+, −, *, /, %) : " );
    fflush( stdin );
    scanf( "%c", &op );

    switch( op )
    {
        case '+':
            res = a + b;
            break;
        case '−':
            res = a − b;
            break;
        case '*':
            res = a * b;
            break;
        case '/':
            res = a / b;
            break;
        case '%':
            res = a % b;
            break;
        default:
            printf( "\nInvalid operator.\n" );
            break;
    }

    printf( "\n%d %c %d = %d\n", a, op, b, res );

    system( "pause" );
    return 0;
}
```

Output :

```
TERMINAL

Enter Two Numbers : 100 200
Enter the operator (+, -, *, /, %) : *

100 * 200 = 20000
Press any key to continue . . .|
```

```
TERMINAL

Enter Two Numbers : 100 30
Enter the operator (+, -, *, /, %) : %

100 % 30 = 10
Press any key to continue . . .|
```

****

Program No. - 108 :
Program to use char datatype in switch-case statement.

Code :
```c
#include <stdio.h>

int main()
{
    char chart;
    system( "cls" );

    printf( "Chart : Bar/Scatter/Line/Pie/Exit.\n" );
    printf( "Press first letter of the chart you want : " );
    chart = toupper( getchar() );

    switch( chart )
    {
            case 'B':
            printf( "\nDrawing Bar Chart.\n" );
            break;
            case 'S':
            printf( "\nDrawing Scatter Chart.\n" );
            break;
            case 'L':
            printf( "\nDrawing Line Chart.\n" );
            break;
            case 'P':
            printf( "\nDrawing Pie Chart.\n" );
            break;
            default:
            printf( "\nWrorng Choice.\n" );
            break;
    }

    system( "pause" );
    return 0;
}
```

Output :
```
TERMINAL

Chart : Bar/Scatter/Line/Pie/Exit.
Press first letter of the chart you want : p

Drawing Pie Chart.
Press any key to continue . . .
```

****

Program No. - 109 :
Program to explain Nested Switch-Case Statement.

Code :
```c
#include <stdio.h>

int  main()
{
    int a = 100;
    int b = 200;
    system( "cls" );

    switch( a )
    {
        case 100:
            printf( "In Outer Switch.\n" );
            switch( b )
            {
                case 200:
                    printf( "In Inner Switch.\n" );
            }
    }
    printf( "Value of a is : %d \n", a );
    printf( "Value of b is : %d \n", b );

    system( "pause" );
    return 0;
}
```

Output :

```
TERMINAL

In Outer Switch.
In Inner Switch.
Value of a is : 100
Value of b is : 200
Press any key to continue . . .|
```

________________ **** ________________

Program No. - 110 :
Program to check whether the given character is Vowel
or not.

Code :
```c
#include <stdio.h>

int  main()
{
    char ch;
    system( "cls" );

    printf( "Enter an Alphabet : " );
    scanf( "%c", &ch );

    switch( ch )
    {
        case 'a':
        case 'A':
        case 'e':
        case 'E':
        case 'i':
        case 'I':
        case 'o':
        case 'O':
        case 'u':
        case 'U':
            printf( "\n%c is a Vowel.\n", ch );
            break;
        default :
            printf( "\n%c is not a Vowel.\n", ch );
            break;
    }

    system( "pause" );
    return 0;
}
```

Output :

```
TERMINAL

Enter an Alphabet : u

u is a Vowel.
Press any key to continue . . .|
```

```
TERMINAL

Enter an Alphabet : C

C is not a Vowel.
Press any key to continue . . .|
```

________________ **** ________________

Program No. - 111 :
Program to check whether the given character is Vowel
or not.

Code :
```c
#include <stdio.h>

int  main()
{
    char ch;
    system( "cls" );

    printf( "Enter an Alphabet : " );
    scanf( "%c", &ch );

    if( (ch == 'a' ) || ( ch == 'e' ) || ( ch == 'i' )
            || ( ch == 'o' ) || ( ch == 'u' ) || ( ch == 'A' )
            || ( ch == 'E' ) || ( ch == 'I' ) || ( ch == 'O' )
            || ( ch == 'U' ) )
    {
        printf( "\n%c is a Vowel.\n", ch );
    }
    else
    {
        printf( "\n%c is not a Vowel.\n", ch );
    }

    system( "pause" );
    return 0;
}
```

Output :

```
TERMINAL

Enter an Alphabet : a

a is a Vowel.
Press any key to continue . . .
```

```
TERMINAL

Enter an Alphabet : x

x is not a Vowel.
Press any key to continue . . .
```

———————————— **** ————————————

Program No. - 112 :
Program to test whether a particular bit in a given
number is ON or OFF using **Bitwise AND** operator.

Code :
```c
#include <stdio.h>

int  main()
{
    int  a = 45, b ;
    system( "cls" ) ;

    printf( "Value of a = %d", a ) ;
    b = a & 32 ;

    if( b == 0 )
        printf( " and its fifth bit is OFF.\n" ) ;
    else
        printf( " and its fifth bit is ON.\n" ) ;

    system( "pause" );
    return 0;
}
```

Output :

```
TERMINAL

Value of a = 45 and its fifth bit is ON.
Press any key to continue . . .
```

———————————— **** ————————————

Program No. - 113 :
Program to check whether the given character is
Uppercase, Lowercase , Digits or Special Symbols.

Code :
```c
#include <stdio.h>

int  main()
{
    char ch;
    system( "cls" );

    printf( "Enter any Character : " );
    scanf( "%c", &ch );

    if( ch >= 65 && ch <= 90 )
        printf( "\nUpper Case Letter.\n" );
    else if( ch >= 97 && ch <= 122 )
        printf( "\nLower Case Letter.\n" );
    else if( ch >= 48 && ch <= 57 )
        printf( "\nDigit.\n" );
    else
        printf( "\nSpecial Symbol.\n" );

    system( "pause" );
    return 0;
}
```

Output :

```
TERMINAL

Enter any Character : A

Upper Case Letter.
Press any key to continue . . .
```

———————————— **** ————————————

Program No. - 114 :
Program to check whether the given character is
Uppercase, Lowercase , Digits or Special Symbols.

Code :
```c
#include <stdio.h>
```

```c
int  main()
{
    char ch;
    system( "cls" );

    printf( "Enter any Character : " );
    scanf( "%c", &ch );

    if( ch >= 'A' && ch <= 'Z' )
        printf( "\nUpper Case Letter.\n" );
    else if( ch >= 'a' && ch <= 'z' )
        printf( "\nLower Case Letter.\n" );
    else if( ch >= '0' && ch <= '9' )
        printf( "\nDigit.\n" );
    else
        printf( "\nSpecial Symbol.\n" );

    system( "pause" );
    return 0;
}
```

Output :

```
TERMINAL

Enter any Character : s

Lower Case Letter.
Press any key to continue . . .  |
```

****

Program No. - 115 :
Program to check whether the given character is Uppercase, Lowercase , Digits or Special Symbols.

Code :
```c
#include <stdio.h>
#include <ctype.h>

int  main()
{
    char ch;
    system( "cls" );

    printf( "Enter any Character : " );
    scanf( "%c", &ch );

    if( isupper( ch ) )
```

```c
        printf( "\nUpper Case Letter.\n" );
    else if( islower( ch ) )
        printf( "\nLower Case Letter.\n" );
    else if( isdigit( ch ) )
        printf( "\nDigit.\n" );
    else
        printf( "\nSpecial Symbol.\n" );

    system( "pause" );
    return 0;
}
```

Output :

```
TERMINAL

Enter any Character : 5

Digit.
Press any key to continue . . .  |
```

****

Program No. - 116 :
Program to change the Case of a character (upper to lower or lower to upper).

Code :
```c
#include <stdio.h>

int  main()
{
    char ch;
    system( "cls" );

    printf( "Enter any Alphabet : " );
    scanf( "%c", &ch );

    if( ch >= 'A' && ch <= 'Z' )
        printf( "\nLower Case : %c\n", ( ch + 32 ) );
    else if( ch >= 'a' && ch <= 'z' )
        printf( "\nUpper Case : %c\n", ( ch - 32 ) );
    else
        printf( "\nNon-alphabet : %c\n", ch );

    system( "pause" );
    return 0;
}
```

Output :

```
TERMINAL

Enter any Alphabet : A

Lower Case : a
Press any key to continue . . .
```

```
TERMINAL

Enter any Alphabet : c

Upper Case : C
Press any key to continue . . .
```

```
TERMINAL

Enter any Alphabet : $

Non-alphabet : $
Press any key to continue . . .
```

****

Program No. - 117 :
Program to calculate Net Price after Discount on the basis of quantity purchase using Conditional Operator (?:).

Quantity	Discount (%)
> 10	5 %
> 25	10 %
> 50	15 %

Code :
```c
#include <stdio.h>

int main()
{
    const float price = 250.0;
    const float discount1 = 0.05;
    const float discount2 = 0.1;
    const float discount3 = 0.15;
    float total_price = 0.0;
    int quantity = 25;
    system( "cls" );

    total_price = quantity * price * ( 1.0 -
            ( quantity>50 ? discount3 : (
                quantity>20 ? discount2 : (
```

quantity>10 ? discount1 : 0.0))));

```c
    printf( "The price for %d is Rs. %.2f\n", quantity,
                                            total_price );

    system( "pause" );
    return 0;
}
```

Output :

```
TERMINAL

The price for 25 is Rs. 5625.00
Press any key to continue . . .
```

****

Program No. - 118 :
Program to find Smallest value of 4 numbers using conditional operators (?:).

Code :
```c
#include <stdio.h>

int main()
{
    Int a ,b, c, d, small;
    system( "cls" );

    printf( "Enter 4 Numbers : " );
    scanf( "%d %d %d %d", &a, &b, &c, &d );

    small = ( (a<b) ? ((a<c)?((a<d)?a:d):((c<d)?c:d)) :
                ((b<c)?((b<d)?b:d):((c<d)?c:d)) );

    printf( "\nSmallest Number : %d\n", small );

    system( "pause" );
    return 0;
}
```

Output :

```
TERMINAL

Enter 4 Numbers : 20 40 10 30

Smallest Number : 10
Press any key to continue . . .
```

****

****

Chapter − 5
Iteration

****

Program No. - 119 :
Program to display first N natural number using for loop.

Code :

```c
#include <stdio.h>

int  main()
{
    int i, n;
    system( "cls" );

    printf( "Enter Number : " );
    scanf( "%d", &n );

    for( i=1 ; i<= n ; i++ )
    {
        printf( "  %d", i );
    }
    printf( "\n" );

    system( "pause" );
    return 0;
}
```

Output :

```
TERMINAL

Enter Number : 10
   1  2  3  4  5  6  7  8  9  10
Press any key to continue . . . |
```

———————— **** ————————

Program No. - 120 :
Program to explain Simple **While** Loop.

Code :

```c
#include <stdio.h>

int  main()
{
    int n = 1;
    system( "cls" );

    while( n != 0 )
    {
        printf( "Enter No.( 0 for exit) : " );
        scanf( "%d", &n );
    }

    system( "pause" );
    return 0;
}
```

Output :

```
TERMINAL

Enter No.( 0 for exit) : 10
Enter No.( 0 for exit) : 20
Enter No.( 0 for exit) : 30
Enter No.( 0 for exit) : 0
Press any key to continue . . . |
```

———————— **** ————————

Program No. - 121 :
Program to display first N natural number using while loop.

Code :

```c
#include <stdio.h>

int  main()
{
    int  i, n;
    system( "cls" );

    printf( "Enter Number : " );
    scanf( "%d", &n );

    i = 1;
    while( i <= n  )
    {
        printf( "  %d", i );
        i++;
    }

    printf( "\n" );
    system( "pause" );
    return 0;
}
```

Output :

```
TERMINAL

Enter Number : 10
   1  2  3  4  5  6  7  8  9  10
Press any key to continue . . . |
```

---- **** ----

Program No. - 122 :
Program to explain Simple **Do-While** Loop.

Code :
```c
#include <stdio.h>

int  main()
{
    int n = 0;
    system( "cls" );

    do
    {
        printf( "Enter No.( 0 for exit) : " );
        scanf( "%d", &n );
    }while( n != 0 );

    system( "pause" );
    return 0;
}
```

Output :
```
TERMINAL

Enter No.( 0 for exit) : 30
Enter No.( 0 for exit) : 20
Enter No.( 0 for exit) : 10
Enter No.( 0 for exit) : 0
Press any key to continue . . . . |
```

---- **** ----

Program No. - 123 :
Program to display first N natural number using do-while loop.

Code :
```c
#include <stdio.h>
```

```c
int  main()
{
    int  i, n;
    system( "cls" );

    printf( "Enter Number : " );
    scanf( "%d", &n );

    i = 1;
    do
    {
        printf( " %d", i );
        i++;
    }while( i <= n  );

    printf( "\n" );
    system( "pause" );
    return 0;
}
```

Output :
```
TERMINAL

Enter Number : 10
   1  2  3  4  5  6  7  8  9  10
Press any key to continue . . . |
```

---- **** ----

Program No. - 124 :
Program to display series 1 to 10 using for loop.

Code :
```c
#include <stdio.h>

int  main()
{
    int  i;
    system( "cls" );

    for( i=1 ; i<=10 ; i++ )
    {
        printf( "%d  ", i );
    }

    printf( "\n" );
    system( "pause" );
```

```c
    return 0;
}
```

Output :

```
TERMINAL

1  2  3  4  5  6  7  8  9  10
Press any key to continue . . . ▯
```

****

Program No. - 125 :
Program to display series 1 to 10 using for loop (in for loop initialization part is optional).

Code :

```c
#include <stdio.h>

int  main()
{
    int  i;
    system( "cls" );

    i = 1;
    for( ; i<=10 ; i++ )
    {
        printf( "%d  ", i );
    }

    printf( "\n" );
    system( "pause" );
    return 0;
}
```

Output :

```
TERMINAL

1  2  3  4  5  6  7  8  9  10
Press any key to continue . . . ▯
```

****

Program No. - 126 :
Program to display series 1 to 10 using for loop (in for loop increment part is optional).

Code :

```c
#include <stdio.h>

int  main()
{
    int  i;
    system( "cls" );

    i = 1;
    for( ; i<=10 ; )
    {
        printf( "%d  ", i );
        i++;
    }

    printf( "\n" );
    system( "pause" );
    return 0;
}
```

Output :

```
TERMINAL

1  2  3  4  5  6  7  8  9  10
Press any key to continue . . . ▯
```

****

Program No. - 127 :
Program to display series 1 to 10 using for loop (in for loop condition part is optional).

Code :

```c
#include <stdio.h>

int  main()
{
    int  i;
    system( "cls" );

    i = 1;
    for( ; ; )
    {
        if( i > 10 )
        {
            break;
        }
        printf( "%d  ", i );
```

```
        i++;
    }


    printf( "\n" );
    system( "pause" );
    return 0;
}
```

Output :

```
TERMINAL

1  2  3  4  5  6  7  8  9  10
Press any key to continue . . . []
```

---- **** ----

Program No. - 128 :
Program to initialize and increment multiple variables in
for loop.

Code :
```
#include <stdio.h>

int  main()
{
    int  i, j;
    system( "cls" );

    for( i=1, j=10 ; i<j ; i++, j-- )
    {
        printf( "i : %d, j : %d\n", i, j );
    }

    system( "pause" );
    return 0;
}
```

Output :

```
TERMINAL

i : 1, j : 10
i : 2, j : 9
i : 3, j : 8
i : 4, j : 7
i : 5, j : 6
Press any key to continue . . . []
```

---- **** ----

Program No. - 129 :
Program to use Character variable in for loop.

Code :
```
#include <stdio.h>

int main()
{
    char ch;
    system( "cls" );

    for( ch='A' ; ch<='E' ; ch++ )
    {
        printf( "...%c", ch );
    }

    printf( "\n"  );

    system( "pause" );
    return 0;
}
```

Output :

```
TERMINAL

...A...B...C...D...E
Press any key to continue . . . []
```

---- **** ----

Program No. - 130 :
Program to calculate the **Factorial** of given Number.

Code :
```
#include <stdio.h>

int  main()
{
    long int n, f, i;
    system( "cls" );

    printf( "Enter a Number : " );
    scanf( "%ld", &n );

    f = 1;
    for( i=1 ; i<=n ; i++ )
```

```c
    {
        f = f * i;
    }

    printf( "\nFactorial of %ld = %ld\n", n, f );

    system( "pause" );
    return 0;
}
```

Output :

```
TERMINAL

Enter a Number : 5

Factorial of 5 = 120
Press any key to continue . . .|
```

——————————— **** ———————————

Program No. - 131 :
Program to calculate x raise to the power n using while loop.

Code :
```c
#include <stdio.h>

int  main()
{
    int x, n, p, i;
    system( "cls" );

    printf( "%s", "Enter Base: " );
    scanf( "%d", &x );
    printf( "%s", "Enter Power: " );
    scanf( "%d", &n );

    i = 1;
    p = 1;
    while( i <= n )
    {
        p *= x;
        i++;
    }

    printf( "\nPower : %d\n", p );

    system( "pause" );
```

```c
    return 0;
}
```

Output :

```
TERMINAL

Enter Base: 5
Enter Power: 3

Power : 125
Press any key to continue . . . []
```

——————————— **** ———————————

Program No. - 132 :
Program to calculate x raise to the power n using for loop.

Code :
```c
#include <stdio.h>

int  main()
{
    int x, n, p, i;
    system( "cls" );

    printf( "%s", "Enter Base: " );
    scanf( "%d", &x );
    printf( "%s", "Enter Power: " );
    scanf( "%d", &n );

    p = 1;
    for( i=1 ; i<=n ; i++ )
    {
        p *= x;
    }

    printf( "\nPower : %d\n", p );

    system( "pause" );
    return 0;
}
```

Output :

```
TERMINAL

Enter Base: 5
Enter Power: 3


Power : 125
Press any key to continue . . . ▯
```

****

Program No. - 133 :
Program to **Count Number of Digits** in a given Number.

Code :

```c
#include <stdio.h>

int  main()
{
    long int  n, c;
    system( "cls" );

    printf( "Enter a Positive number : " );
    scanf( "%ld", &n );

    c = 0;
    while( n != 0 )
    {
        n = n / 10;
        c = c + 1;              /*   c++;     */
    }

    printf( "\nThe number of the digits = %ld\n", c );

    system( "pause" );
    return 0;
}
```

Output :

```
TERMINAL

Enter a Positive number : 123456

The number of the digits = 6
Press any key to continue . . . |
```

****

Program No. - 134 :

Program to find **Sum of Digits** of given Number.

Code :

```c
#include <stdio.h>

int  main()
{
    long int  n, r, s;
    system( "cls" );

    printf( "Enter any Number : " );
    scanf( "%ld", &n );

    s = 0;
    while( n != 0 )
    {
        r = n % 10;
        s = s + r;
        n = n / 10;
    }

    printf( "\nThe Sum of the Digits = %ld\n", s );

    system( "pause" );
    return 0;
}
```

Output :

```
TERMINAL

Enter any Number : 123456

The Sum of the Digits = 21
Press any key to continue . . . |
```

****

Program No. - 135 :
Program to find **Reverse** of given Number.

Code :

```c
#include <stdio.h>

int  main()
{
    long int n, r, rev;
    system( "cls" );
```

```c
    printf( "Enter any number : " );
    scanf( "%ld", &n );

    rev = 0;
    while( n != 0 )
    {
        r = n % 10;
        rev = ( rev * 10 ) + r;
        n = n / 10;
    }

    printf( "\nReversed number is = %ld\n", rev );

    system( "pause" );
    return 0;
}
```

Output :

```
TERMINAL

Enter any number : 123456

Reversed number is = 654321
Press any key to continue . . .
```

———————————— **** ————————————

Program No. - 136 :
Program to chech whether the given Number is
Palindrome Number or not.

Code :
```c
#include <stdio.h>

int  main()
{
    long int n, r, x, rev;
    system( "cls" );

    printf( "Enter any number : " );
    scanf( "%ld", &n );

    x = n;
    rev = 0;
    while( n != 0 )
    {
        r = n % 10;
        rev = ( rev * 10 ) + r;
```

```c
        n = n / 10;
    }

    printf( "\nReversed number is = %ld\n", rev );

    if( rev == x )
        printf( "It is a Palindrome Number.\n" );
    else
        printf( "It is Not a Palindrome Number.\n" );

    system( "pause" );
    return 0;
}
```

Output :

```
TERMINAL

Enter any number : 1234321

Reversed number is = 1234321
It is a Palindrome Number.
Press any key to continue . . .
```

```
TERMINAL

Enter any number : 123456

Reversed number is = 654321
It is Not a Palindrome Number.
Press any key to continue . . .
```

———————————— **** ————————————

Program No. - 137 :
Program to check whether the given number is **Perfect
Number** or not.
(e.g. : 6 = 1 + 2 +3)

Code :
```c
#include <stdio.h>

int  main()
{
    int  i, n, s;
    system( "cls" );

    printf( "Enter a number : " );
    scanf( "%d", &n );
```

```c
    s = 0;
    for( i=1 ; i<=n/2 ; i++ )
    {
        if( n % i == 0 )
        {
            s = s + i;
        }
    }

    if( s == n )
    {
        printf( "It is a PERFECT Number.\n" );
    }
    else
    {
        printf( "It is NOT a PERFECT Number.\n" );
    }

    system( "pause" );
    return 0;
}
```

Output :

```
TERMINAL

Enter a number : 28
It is a PERFECT Number.
Press any key to continue . . .|
```

```
TERMINAL

Enter a number : 25
It is NOT a PERFECT Number.
Press any key to continue . . .|
```

****

Program No. - 138 :
Program to check whether the given number is **Prime Number** or not.

Code :
```c
#include <stdio.h>

int main()
{
    int  n, i, flag;
    system( "cls" );
```

```c
    printf( "Enter the Number : " );
    scanf( "%d", &n );

    flag = 1;
    for( i=2 ; i<=n/2 ; i++ )
    {
        if( n % i == 0 )
        {
            flag = 0;
            break;
        }
    }
    if( flag == 1 )                    /*    if( flag ) */
        printf( "%d is a Prime Number.\n", n );
    else
        printf( "%d is not a Prime Number.\n", n );

    system( "pause" );
    return 0;
}
```

Output :

```
TERMINAL

Enter the Number : 13
13 is a Prime Number.
Press any key to continue . . .|
```

```
TERMINAL

Enter the Number : 15
15 is not a Prime Number.
Press any key to continue . . .|
```

****

Program No. - 139 :
Program to check whether the given three digit number is **Armstrong Number** or Not.
(e.g. : $153 = 1^3 + 5^3 + 3^3$)

Code :
```c
#include <stdio.h>

int main()
{
    int x, n, r, s;
```

```c
    system( "cls" );

    printf( "Enter any Number : " );
    scanf( "%d", &n );

    x = n;
    s = 0;
    while( n != 0 )
    {
        r = n % 10;
        s = s + ( r * r * r );
        n = n / 10;
    }

    if( s == x )
        printf("\n%d is a Armstrong Number.\n", x );
    else
        printf( "\n%d is not a Armstrong Number.\n", x );

    system( "pause" );
    return 0;
}
```

Output :

```
TERMINAL

Enter any Number : 153

153 is a Armstrong Number.
Press any key to continue . . . |
```

```
TERMINAL

Enter any Number : 150

150 is not a Armstrong Number.
Press any key to continue . . . |
```

****

Program No. - 140 :
Program to check whether the given number is **Strong
Number** or Not.
(e.g. : 145 = 1! + 4! + 5!)

Code :
```c
#include <stdio.h>
```

```c
int  main()
{
    int n, x, r, s, i, f;
    system( "cls" );

    printf( "Enter any Number : " );
    scanf( "%d", &n );

    x = n;
    s = 0;
    while( n != 0 )
    {
        r = n % 10;
        f = 1;
        for( i=1 ; i<=r ; i++ )
        {
            f = f * i;
        }
        s = s + f;
        n = n / 10;
    }

    if( s == x )
        printf( "\n%d is a STRONG Number.\n", x );
    else
        printf( "\n%d is not a STRONG Number.\n", x );

    system( "pause" );
    return 0;
}
```

Output :

```
TERMINAL

Enter any Number : 145

145 is a STRONG Number.
Press any key to continue . . . |
```

```
TERMINAL

Enter any Number : 100

100 is not a STRONG Number.
Press any key to continue . . . |
```

****

Program No. - 141 :
Program to find **HCF** and **LCM** of Two Number.

Code :
```c
#include <stdio.h>

int  main()
{
    int a, b, s, hcf, i, lcm;
    system( "cls" );

    printf( "Enter Two Numbers : " );
    scanf( "%d %d", &a, &b );

    if( a< b )
        s = a;
    else
        s = b;

    for( i=1 ; i<=s ; i++ )
    {
        if( ( a % i == 0 ) && ( b % i == 0 ) )
        {
            hcf = i;
        }
    }

    printf( "\nThe HCF of given Numbers = %d\n", hcf );
    lcm = ( a * b ) / hcf;
    printf( "The LCM of given Numbers = %d\n", lcm );

    system( "pause" );
    return 0;
}
```

Output :
```
TERMINAL

Enter Two Numbers : 12 18

The HCF of given Numbers = 6
The LCM of given Numbers = 36
Press any key to continue . . . |
```

****

Program No. - 142 :
Program to find **LCM** and **HCF** of Two Number.

Code :
```c
#include <stdio.h>

int  main()
{
    int a, b, g, hcf, i, lcm;
    system( "cls" );

    printf( "Enter Two Numbers : " );
    scanf( "%d %d", &a, &b );

    if( a > b )
        g = a;
    else
        g = b;

    for( i=g ; i<=(a*b) ; i++ )
    {
        if( ( i % a == 0 ) && ( i % b == 0 ) )
        {
            lcm = i;
            break;
        }
    }

    printf( "\nThe LCM of given Numbers = %d\n", lcm );
    hcf = ( a * b ) / lcm;
    printf( "The HCF of given Numbers = %d\n", hcf );

    system( "pause" );
    return 0;
}
```

Output :
```
TERMINAL

Enter Two Numbers : 12 18

The LCM of given Numbers = 36
The HCF of given Numbers = 6
Press any key to continue . . . |
```

****

Program No. - 143 :
Program to find HCF and LCM of two given numbers.

Code :

```c
#include <stdio.h>

int main()
{
    int  x, y, a, b, hcf, lcm, t;
    system( "cls" );

    printf( "Enter two Numbers : " );
    scanf( "%d %d", &x, &y );
    if( x > y )
    {
        a = x;
        b = y;
    }
    else
    {
        a = y;
        b = x;
    }

    while( b != 0 )
    {
        t = b;
        b = a % b;
        a = t;
    }
    hcf = a;

    printf( "\nHCF of %d & %d : %d\n", x, y, hcf );

    lcm = (x * y) / hcf;
    printf( "LCM of %d & %d : %d\n", x, y, lcm );

    system( "pause" );
    return 0;
}
```

Output :

```
TERMINAL

Enter two Numbers : 12 18

HCF of 12 & 18 : 6
LCM of 12 & 18 : 36
Press any key to continue . . .
```

****

Program No. - 144 :
Program to convert Binary number to Decimal number.

Code :

```c
#include <stdio.h>
#include <math.h>

int  main()
{
    long i, n, r, num = 0;
    system( "cls" );

    printf( "Enter a Binary Number : " );
    scanf( "%d", &n );

    i = 0;
    while( n != 0 )
    {
        r = n % 10;
        num = num + ( r * pow( 2, i ) );
        n = n / 10;
        i++;
    }

    printf( "\nDecimal Equivalent : %d\n", num ) ;

    system( "pause" );
    return 0;
}
```

Output :

```
TERMINAL

Enter a Binary Number : 11011

Decimal Equivalent : 27
Press any key to continue . . .
```

****

Program No. - 145 :
Program to convert Octal number to Decimal number.

Code :

```c
#include <stdio.h>
#include <math.h>
```

```c
int  main()
{
    long i, n, r, num = 0;
    system( "cls" );

    printf( "Enter a Octal Number : " );
    scanf( "%d", &n );

    i = 0;
    while( n != 0 )
    {
        r = n % 10;
        num = num + ( r * pow( 8, i ) );
        n = n / 10;
        i++;
    }

    printf( "\nDecimal Equivalent : %d\n", num ) ;

    system( "pause" );
    return 0;
}
```

Output :

```
TERMINAL

Enter a Octal Number : 36

Decimal Equivalent : 30
Press any key to continue . . .
```

---- **** ----

Program No. - 146 :
Program to convert Decimal number to Binary number.

Code :
```c
#include <stdio.h>
#include <math.h>

int  main()
{
    long i, n, r, num = 0;
    system( "cls" );

    printf( "Enter a Decimal Number : " );
    scanf( "%ld", &n );
```

```c
    i = 0;
    while( n > 0 )
    {
        r = n % 2;
        num = num + ( r * pow( 10, i ) );
        n = n / 2;
        i++;
    }

    printf( "\nBinary Equivalent : %ld\n", num );

    system( "pause" );
    return 0;
}
```

Output :

```
TERMINAL

Enter a Decimal Number : 27

Binary Equivalent : 11011
Press any key to continue . . .
```

---- **** ----

Program No. - 147 :
Program to convert Decimal number to Octal number.

Code :
```c
#include <stdio.h>
#include <math.h>

int  main()
{
    long i, n, r, num = 0;
    system( "cls" );

    printf( "Enter a Decimal Number : " );
    scanf( "%d", &n );

    i = 0;
    while( n != 0 )
    {
        r = n % 8;
        num = num + ( r * pow( 10, i ) );
        n = n / 8;
        i++;
```

```
    }

    printf( "\nOctal Equivalent : %d\n", num );

    system( "pause" );
    return 0;
}
```

Output :

```
TERMINAL

Enter a Decimal Number : 30

Octal Equivalent : 36
Press any key to continue . . .
```

****

Program No. - 148 :
Program to Display **Multiplication Table** of given number.

Code :
```
#include <stdio.h>

int  main()
{
    int  n, i, a;
    system( "cls" );

    printf( "Enter a Number : " );
    scanf( "%d", &n );

    for( i=1 ; i<=10 ; i++ )
    {
        a = i * n;
        printf( "\n%2d * %2d = %2d", n, i, a );
    }

    printf( "\n" );
    system( "pause" );
    return 0;
}
```

Output :

```
TERMINAL

Enter  a  Number : 5

    5 *   1 =   5
    5 *   2 = 10
    5 *   3 = 15
    5 *   4 = 20
    5 *   5 = 25
    5 *   6 = 30
    5 *   7 = 35
    5 *   8 = 40
    5 *   9 = 45
    5 * 10 = 50
Press  any  key  to  continue . . .
```

****

Program No. - 149 :
Program to Display Multiplication Table from 1 to 10.

Code :
```
#include <stdio.h>

int  main()
{
    int n, i, j, a;
    system( "cls" );

    printf( " No|" );
    for( i=1 ; i<=10 ; i++ )
    {
        printf( " %3d", i );
    }
    printf( "\n_____________________________\n" );
    for( i=1 ; i<=10 ; i++ )
    {
        printf( "%2d |", i );
        for( j=1 ; j<=10 ; j++ )
        {
            a = i * j;
            printf( " %3d", a );
        }
        printf( "\n" );
    }

    system( "pause" );
    return 0;
}
```

Output :

```
TERMINAL

No|   1    2    3    4    5    6    7    8    9   10

1 |   1    2    3    4    5    6    7    8    9   10
2 |   2    4    6    8   10   12   14   16   18   20
3 |   3    6    9   12   15   18   21   24   27   30
4 |   4    8   12   16   20   24   28   32   36   40
5 |   5   10   15   20   25   30   35   40   45   50
6 |   6   12   18   24   30   36   42   48   54   60
7 |   7   14   21   28   35   42   49   56   63   70
8 |   8   16   24   32   40   48   56   64   72   80
9 |   9   18   27   36   45   54   63   72   81   90
10|  10   20   30   40   50   60   70   80   90  100
Press  any  key  to  continue . . . |
```

———————————— ******** ————————————

Program No. - 150 :

Program to find Largest value in "n" number of given numbers.

Code :

```c
#include <stdio.h>

int  main()
{
    int i, n, x, large = −2147483648;
    system( "cls" );

    printf( "Enter No. of Values : " );
    scanf( "%d", &n );

    for( i=0 ; i<n ; i++ )
    {
        printf( "Enter Number-%d : ", i+1 );
        scanf( "%d", &x );
        if( x > large )
            large = x;
    }

    printf( "\nLargest Value : %d\n", large );

    system( "pause" );
    return 0;
}
```

Output :

```
TERMINAL

Enter No. of Values : 5
Enter Number-1 : 30
Enter Number-2 : 20
Enter Number-3 : 40
Enter Number-4 : 50
Enter Number-5 : 10


Largest Value : 50
Press  any  key  to  continue . . . |
```

———————————— ******** ————————————

Program No. - 151 :

Program to find Largest value & Smallest value in "n" number of given numbers.

Code :

```c
#include <stdio.h>

int  main()
{
    int i, n, x, large = −2147483648;
    int small = 2147483647;
    system( "cls" );

    printf( "Enter No. of Values : " );
    scanf( "%d", &n );

    for( i=0 ; i<n ; i++ )
    {
        printf( "Enter Number-%d : ", i+1 );
        scanf( "%d", &x );
        if( x > large )
            large = x;
        if( x < small )
            small = x;
    }

    printf( "\nLargest Value : %d\n", large );
    printf( "Smallest Value : %d\n", small );

    system( "pause" );
    return 0;
}
```

Output :

```
TERMINAL

Enter No. of Values : 5
Enter Number-1 : 20
Enter Number-2 : 50
Enter Number-3 : 40
Enter Number-4 : 10
Enter Number-5 : 30

Largest Value : 50
Smallest Value : 10
Press any key to continue . . .
```

———————————— ******** ————————————

Program No. - 152 :
Program to display all Leap years between two given years.

Code :
```c
#include <stdio.h>

int main()
{
    int y1, y2;
    system( "cls" );

    printf( "Enter Year Range : " );
    scanf( "%d %d", &y1, &y2 );

    while( y1 <= y2 )
    {
        if( (y1 % 400 == 0) ||
                ( y1 % 100 != 0 && y1 % 4 == 0 ) )
        {
            printf( "\nLeap Year : %d", y1 );
        }
        y1++;
    }
    printf( "\n" );

    system( "pause" );
    return 0;
}
```

Output :

```
TERMINAL

Enter Year Range : 2000 2024

Leap Year : 2000
Leap Year : 2004
Leap Year : 2008
Leap Year : 2012
Leap Year : 2016
Leap Year : 2020
Leap Year : 2024
Press any key to continue . . .
```

———————————— ******** ————————————

Program No. - 153 :
Program to show Cube Table of 1 to 10.

Code :
```c
#include <stdio.h>

int main()
{
    int pow = 1;
    int num = 1;
    system( "cls" );

    printf( "1 to 10 Cube Table : \n" );
    while( pow <= 1000 )
    {
        pow = num * num * num;
        printf( "%3d :%5d\n", num, pow );
        num++;
    }

    system( "pause" );
    return 0;
}
```

Output :

```
TERMINAL

1 to 10 Cube Table :
   1 :     1
   2 :     8
   3 :    27
   4 :    64
   5 :   125
   6 :   216
   7 :   343
   8 :   512
   9 :   729
  10 :  1000
  11 :  1331
Press any key to continue . . . []
```

```
TERMINAL

Enter a number : 25
Square of 25 : 625
Want to enter another number (y/n) : y
Enter a number : 9
Square of 9 : 81
Want to enter another number (y/n) : y
Enter a number : 13
Square of 13 : 169
Want to enter another number (y/n) : n

Press any key to continue . . . []
```

****

Program No. - 154 :
Program to calculate Squares of given values.

Code :

```c
#include <stdio.h>

int main()
{
    char  another = 'y' ;
    int  num ;
    system( "cls" );

    while ( another == 'y' )
    {
        printf ( "Enter a number : " ) ;
        scanf ( "%d", &num ) ;
        printf ( "Square of %d : %d", num, (num * num) )
;

        printf ( "\nWant to enter another
                            number (y/n) : " ) ;
        scanf ( " %c", &another ) ;
    }

    printf( "\n" );
    system( "pause" );
    return 0;
}
```

Output :

Program No. - 155 :
Program to display all Pythogorus Triplets from 2 to N.

Code :

```c
#include <stdio.h>

int main()
{
    int i, j, k;
    int num;
    system( "cls" );

    printf( "Enter Upper limit for Pythogorus Triplet : " );
    scanf( "%d", &num );

    for( i=2 ; i<=num ; i++ )
    {
        for( j=i ; j<=num ; j++ )
        {
            for( k=j ; k<=num ; k++ )
            {
                if( ( i * i ) + ( j * j ) == ( k * k ) )
                {
                    printf( "\nSq(%d) + Sq(%d)\t=
                            sq(%d)", i, j, k );
                }
            }
        }
    }

    printf( "\n" );
    system( "pause" );
    return 0;
```

```
}
```

Output :

```
TERMINAL

Enter Upper limit for Pythogorus Triplet : 15

Sq(3) + Sq(4)    = sq(5)
Sq(5) + Sq(12)   = sq(13)
Sq(6) + Sq(8)    = sq(10)
Sq(9) + Sq(12)   = sq(15)
Press any key to continue . . . []
```

****

Program No. - 156 :
Program to explain **break** statement.

Code :

```c
#include <stdio.h>

int  main()
{
    int  i;
    system( "cls" );

    for( i=1 ; i<=10 ; i++ )
    {
        if( i == 5 )
        {
            break;
        }
        printf( "  %d", i );
    }

    printf( "\n" );
    system( "pause" );
    return 0;
}
```

Output :

```
TERMINAL

  1  2  3  4
Press any key to continue . . . |
```

****

Program No. - 157 :

Program to explain **continue** statement.

Code :

```c
#include <stdio.h>

int  main()
{
    int  i;
    system( "cls" );

    for( i=1 ; i<=10 ; i++ )
    {
        if( i == 5 )
        {
            continue;
        }
        printf( "  %d", i );
    }

    printf( "\n" );
    system( "pause" );
    return 0;
}
```

Output :

```
TERMINAL

  1  2  3  4  6  7  8  9  10
Press any key to continue . . . |
```

****

Program No. - 158 :
Program to explain the break and continue Jump
statements.

Code :

```c
#include <stdio.h>

int  main()
{
    int i;
    system( "cls" );

    for( i=1 ; i<=20 ; i++ )
    {
        if( i % 2 )
```

```c
        continue;        /* start next iteration */
    else if ( i == 16 )
        break;           /* end the loop */
    printf( "%d  ", i );
    }

    printf( "\n" );
    system( "pause" );
    return 0;
}
```

Output :

```
TERMINAL

2  4  6  8  10  12  14
Press any key to continue . . .
```

****

Program No. - 159 :
Program to explain **goto** statement with forward jump.

Code :
```c
#include <stdio.h>

int  main()
{
    int a = 10;
    system( "cls" );

    printf( "AAA\n" );
    printf( "BBB\n" );

    if( a == 10 )
    {
        goto LBL;
    }

    printf( "CCC\n" );
    printf( "DDD\n" );

LBL:
    printf( "EEE\n" );
    printf( "FFF\n" );

    system( "pause" );
    return 0;
}
```

Output :

```
TERMINAL

AAA
BBB
EEE
FFF
Press any key to continue . . .
```

****

Program No. - 160 :
Program to explain **goto** statement with backward jump.

Code :
```c
#include <stdio.h>

int  main()
{
    int i;
    system( "cls" );

    i = 1;

LABEL1:
    printf( " %d", i );
    i++;
    if( i <= 10 )
    {
        goto  LABEL1;
    }

    printf( "\n" );
    system( "pause" );
    return 0;
}
```

Output :

```
TERMINAL

  1  2  3  4  5  6  7  8  9  10
Press any key to continue . . .
```

****

Program No. - 161 :
Program to display **Even** numbers and using **continue**.

Code :

```c
#include <stdio.h>

int  main()
{
    int i, n;
    system( "cls" );

    printf( "Enter Number of Terms : " );
    scanf( "%d", &n );

    for( i=1 ; i<= (2 * n) ; i++ )
    {
        if( i % 2 != 0 )
        {
            continue;
        }
        printf( "  %d", i );
    }

    printf( "\n" );
    system( "pause" );
    return 0;
}
```

Output :

```
TERMINAL

Enter Number of Terms : 10
   2  4  6  8  10  12  14  16  18  20
Press any key to continue . . .
```

---- **** ----

Program No. - 162 :

Program to use **continue** statement.

Code :

```c
#include <stdio.h>

int  main()
{
    long dividend, divisor;
    char ch;
    system( "cls" );

    do
```

```c
    {
        printf( "Enter Dividend : " );
        scanf( "%ld", &dividend );
        printf( "Enter Divisor : " );
        scanf( "%ld", &divisor );
        if( divisor == 0 )
        {
            printf( "\nILLEGAL Divisor.\n" );
            continue;
        }
        printf( "\nQuotient = %d\n",
                            ( dividend / divisor ) );
        printf( "Remainder = %d\n",
                            ( dividend % divisor ) );
        printf( "Do another ? (y/n) : " );
        fflush( stdin );
        scanf( "%c", &ch );
    }while( ch != 'n' );

    system( "pause" );
    return 0;
}
```

Output :

```
TERMINAL

Enter Dividend : 20
Enter Divisor : 3

Quotient = 6
Remainder = 2
Do another ? (y/n) : y
Enter Dividend : 10
Enter Divisor : 0

ILLEGAL Divisor.
Enter Dividend : 50
Enter Divisor : 7

Quotient = 7
Remainder = 1
Do another ? (y/n) : n
Press any key to continue . . .
```

---- **** ----

Program No. - 163 :

Program to use **exit()** function to check whether the given Number is **Prime Number** or Not.

Code :

```c
#include <stdio.h>
#include <stdlib.h>        /*  #include <process.h> */

int  main()
{
    int n, i;
    system( "cls" );

    printf( "Enter the Number : " );
    scanf( "%d", &n );

    for( i=2 ; i<=n/2 ; i++ )
    {
        if( n % i == 0 )
        {
            printf( "\n%d is not a Prime Number.\n", n );
            system( "pause" );
            exit( 0 );
        }
    }
    printf( "\n%d is a Prime Number.\n", n );

    system( "pause" );
    return 0;
}
```

Output :

```
TERMINAL

Enter the Number : 13

13 is a Prime Number.
Press any key to continue . . . |
```

```
TERMINAL

Enter the Number : 20

20 is not a Prime Number.
Press any key to continue . . . |
```

****

Program No. - 164 :
Program to display all Perfect number between 1 to 100.

Code :
```c
#include <stdio.h>
```

```c
int main()
{
    int  n, i, sum;
    system( "cls" );

    printf( "Perfect Numbers between 1 to 100 : \n" );
    for( n=1 ; n<=100 ; n++ )
    {
        sum = 0;
        i = 1;
        while( i <= (n/2) )
        {
            if( n % i == 0 )
                sum = sum + i;
            i++;
        }
        if( sum == n )
            printf( "Perfect Number : %d\n", n );
    }

    system( "pause" );
    return 0;
}
```

Output :

```
TERMINAL

Perfect Numbers between 1 to 100 :
Perfect Number : 6
Perfect Number : 28
Press any key to continue . . . []
```

****

Program No. - 165 :
Program to display all Prime numbers from 2 to 100 and count it.

Code :
```c
#include <stdio.h>
#include <math.h>

int main()
{
    int i, x, n, r, flag, cnt=0;
    system( "cls" );
```

```c
    printf( "Enter Date of Birth (DDMMYYYY) : " );
    scanf( "%d", &num );


    while( num > 10 )
    {
        sum = 0;
        while( num != 0 )
        {
            r = num % 10;
            sum += r;
            num = num / 10;
        }
        if( sum > 10 )
            num = sum;
    }
    printf( "\nYour Lucky Number : %d\n", sum );

    system( "pause" );
    return 0;
}
```

Output :

```
TERMINAL

Enter Date of Birth (DDMMYYYY) : 24052005

Your Lucky Number : 9
Press any key to continue . . .
```

****

Program No. - 170 :
Program to find Prime Factors of given number.

Code :
```c
#include <stdio.h>

int main()
{
    int num, i=1, j, cnt;
    system( "cls" );

    printf( "Enter a Number : " );
    scanf( "%d", &num );

    printf( "\nPrime Factors of %d are : ", num );
```

```c
    while( i <= num )
    {
        cnt = 0;
        if( num % i == 0 )
        {
            j = 2;
            while( j <= i )
            {
                if( i % j == 0 )
                    cnt++;
                j++;
            }
            if( cnt == 1 )
                printf( "%3d", i );
        }
        i++;
    }

    printf( "\n" );
    system( "pause" );
    return 0;
}
```

Output :

```
TERMINAL

Enter a Number : 27

Prime Factors of 27 are :    3
Press any key to continue . . .
```

```
TERMINAL

Enter a Number : 84

Prime Factors of 84 are :    2  3  7
Press any key to continue . . .
```

****

****

Chapter – 6
Series

****

Program No. - 171 :
Program to display first n natural numbers.
    1 2 3 4 5 ... ... n terms

Code :
```c
#include <stdio.h>

int  main()
{
    int i, n;
    system( "cls" );

    printf( "Enter Number of Terms : " );
    scanf( "%d", &n );

    printf( "\n" );
    for( i=1 ; i<=n ; i++ )
    {
        printf( "%d  ", i );
    }

    printf( "\n" );
    system( "pause" );
    return 0;
}
```

Output :
```
TERMINAL

Enter Number of Terms : 10

1  2  3  4  5  6  7  8  9  10
Press any key to continue . . . |
```

****

Program No. - 172 :
Program to find sum of first n natural numbers.
    1 + 2 + 3 + ... + n terms

Code :
```c
#include <stdio.h>

int  main()
{
    int i, n, s;
    system( "cls" );
```

```c
    printf( "Enter Number of Terms : " );
    scanf( "%d", &n );

    s = 0;
    for( i=1 ; i<=n ; i++ )
    {
        s = s + i;
    }
    printf( "\nSum of Series = %d\n", s );

    system( "pause" );
    return 0;
}
```

Output :
```
TERMINAL

Enter Number of Terms : 10

Sum of Series = 55
Press any key to continue . . . |
```

****

Program No. - 173 :
Program to find sum of first n natural numbers.
    1 + 2 + 3 + ... + n terms

Code :
```c
#include <stdio.h>

int  main()
{
    int i, n, s;
    system( "cls" );

    printf( "Enter Number of Terms : " );
    scanf( "%d", &n );
    printf( "\n" );

    s = 0;
    for( i=1 ; i<=n ; i++ )
    {
        if( i == 1 )
            printf( "%d", i );
        else
```

```c
        printf( " + %d", i );
    s = s + i;
}
printf( " = %d\n", s );

system( "pause" );
return 0;
}
```

Output :

```
TERMINAL

Enter Number of Terms : 10

1 + 2 + 3 + 4 + 5 + 6 + 7 + 8 + 9 + 10 = 55
Press any key to continue . . .
```

****

Program No. - 174 :
Program to display first n terms of given series :
    2 4 6 8 ... ... n terms

Code :
```c
#include <stdio.h>

int  main()
{
    int i, n;
    system( "cls" );

    printf( "Enter Number of Terms : " );
    scanf( "%d", &n );

    printf( "\n" );
    for( i=2 ; i<=(2*n) ; i+=2 )
    {
        printf( "%d ", i );
    }

    printf( "\n" );
    system( "pause" );
    return 0;
}
```

Output :

```
TERMINAL

Enter Number of Terms : 10

2  4  6  8  10  12  14  16  18  20
Press any key to continue . . .
```

****

Program No. - 175 :
Program to display first n terms of given series :
    2 4 6 8 ... ... n terms

Code :
```c
#include <stdio.h>

int main()
{
    int i, n;
    system( "cls" );

    printf( "Enter Number of Terms : " );
    scanf( "%d", &n );

    printf( "\n" );
    for( i=1 ; i<=(2*n) ; i++ )
    {
        if( i % 2 == 0 )
        {
            printf( "%d  ", i );
        }
    }

    printf( "\n" );
    system( "pause" );
    return 0;
}
```

Output :

```
TERMINAL

Enter Number of Terms : 10

2   4   6   8   10   12   14   16   18   20
Press any key to continue . . .
```

****

Program No. - 176 :

Program to display first n terms of given series :
    2 4 6 8 ... ... n terms

Code :
```c
#include <stdio.h>

int  main()
{
    int i, n, t;
    system( "cls" );

    printf( "Enter Number of Terms : " );
    scanf( "%d", &n );

    printf( "\n" );
    for( i=1 ; i<=n ; i++ )
    {
        t = 2 * i;
        printf( "%d  ", t );
    }

    printf( "\n" );
    system( "pause" );
    return 0;
}
```

Output :

```
TERMINAL

Enter Number of Terms : 10

2  4  6  8  10  12  14  16  18  20
Press any key to continue . . .
```

****

Program No. - 177 :
Program to display first n terms of given series :
    1 3 5 7 ... ... n terms

Code :
```c
#include <stdio.h>

int  main()
{
    int i, n;
    system( "cls" );
```

```c
    printf( "Enter Number of Terms : " );
    scanf( "%d", &n );

    printf( "\n" );
    for( i=1 ; i<=(2*n) ; i+=2 )
    {
        printf( "%d  ", i );
    }

    printf( "\n" );
    system( "pause" );
    return 0;
}
```

Output :

```
TERMINAL

Enter Number of Terms : 10

1  3  5  7  9  11  13  15  17  19
Press any key to continue . . .
```

****

Program No. - 178 :
Program to display first n terms of given series :
    1 3 5 7 ... ... n terms

Code :
```c
#include <stdio.h>

int  main()
{
    int i, n;
    system( "cls" );

    printf( "Enter Number of Terms : " );
    scanf( "%d", &n );

    printf( "\n" );
    for( i=1 ; i<=(2*n) ; i++ )
    {
        if( i % 2 == 1 )        /*  if( i % 2 != 0 )  */
        {
            printf( "%d  ", i );
        }
    }

    printf( "\n" );
```

```
    system( "pause" );
    return 0;
}
```

Output :

```
TERMINAL

Enter Number of Terms : 10


1   3   5   7   9   11   13   15   17   19
Press any key to continue . . .
```

———————— ******** ————————

Program No. - 179 :
Program to display first n terms of given series :
    1 3 5 7 ... ... n terms

Code :
```c
#include <stdio.h>

int  main()
{
    int i, n, t;
    system( "cls" );

    printf( "Enter Number of Terms : " );
    scanf( "%d", &n );

    printf( "\n" );
    for( i=1 ; i<=n ; i++ )
    {
        t = 2 * i - 1;
        printf( "%d  ", t );
    }

    printf( "\n" );
    system( "pause" );
    return 0;
}
```

Output :

```
TERMINAL

Enter Number of Terms : 10


1   3   5   7   9   11   13   15   17   19
Press any key to continue . . .
```

———————— ******** ————————

Program No. - 180 :
Program to display first n terms of given series :
    −1 2 −3 4 −5 ... ... n terms.

Code :
```c
#include <stdio.h>
#include <math.h>

int  main()
{
    int i, n, t;
    system( "cls" );

    printf( "Enter Number of Terms : " );
    scanf( "%d", &n );

    printf( "\n" );
    for( i=1 ; i<=n ; i++ )
    {
        t = i * pow( (−1), i );
        printf( "%d  ", t );
    }

    printf( "\n" );
    system( "pause" );
    return 0;
}
```

Output :

```
TERMINAL

Enter Number of Terms : 10


-1   2   -3   4   -5   6   -7   8   -9   10
Press any key to continue . . .
```

———————— ******** ————————

Program No. - 181 :
Program to display first n terms of given series :
    1 −2 3 −4 5 ... ... n terms.

Code :
```c
#include <stdio.h>
#include <math.h>
```

```c
int  main()
{
    int i, n, t;
    system( "cls" );

    printf( "Enter Number of Terms : " );
    scanf( "%d", &n );

    printf( "\n" );
    for( i=1 ; i<=n ; i++ )
    {
        t = i * pow( (-1), (i + 1) );
        printf( "%d  ", t );
    }

    printf( "\n" );
    system( "pause" );
    return 0;
}
```

Output :

```
TERMINAL

Enter Number of Terms : 10

1   -2  3   -4  5   -6  7   -8  9   -10
Press any key to continue . . . |
```

****

Program No. - 182 :
Program to find the sum of all Even values & all Odd
values in "n" number of terms of natural number series.

Code :
```c
#include <stdio.h>

int  main()
{
    int n, i, esum = 0, osum = 00;
    system( "cls" );

    printf( "Enter No. of Terms : " );
    scanf( "%d", &n );

    for( i=1 ; i<=n ; i++ )
```

```c
    {
        printf( " %d", i );
        if( i % 2 == 0 )
            esum += i;
        else
            osum += i;
    }

    printf( "\nSum of Even Numbers : %d\n", esum );
    printf( "Sum of Odd Numbers  : %d\n", osum );

    system( "pause" );
    return 0;
}
```

Output :

```
TERMINAL

Enter No. of Terms : 10
 1 2 3 4 5 6 7 8 9 10
Sum of Even Numbers : 30
Sum of Odd Numbers  : 25
Press any key to continue . . . |
```

****

Program No. - 183 :
Program to display the squares of "n" number of terms of
natural number series and also find the sum.
    1 4 9 16 25 36 ... n terms

Code :
```c
#include <stdio.h>

int  main()
{
    int i, t, s, n;
    system( "cls" );

    printf( "Enter Number of Terms : " );
    scanf( "%d", &n );

    s = 0;
    for( i=1 ; i<=n ; i++ )
    {
        t = i * i;
        printf( " %d", t );
        s = s + t;
```

```
    }

    printf( "\nSum of Series : %d\n", s );

    system( "pause" );
    return 0;
}
```

Output :

```
TERMINAL

Enter Number of Terms : 10
 1 4 9 16 25 36 49 64 81 100
Sum of Series : 385
Press any key to continue . . .
```

---- **** ----

Program No. - 184 :
Program to display "n" terms of given series.
    1 2 4 8 16 32 ... n terms

Code :
```
#include <stdio.h>
#include <math.h>

int  main()
{
    int i, t, n;
    system( "cls" );

    printf( "Enter Number of Terms : " );
    scanf( "%d", &n );

    for( i=0 ; i<n ; i++ )
    {
        t = pow( 2, i );
        printf( " %d", t );
    }

    printf( "\n" );
    system( "pause" );
    return 0;
}
```

Output :

```
TERMINAL

Enter Number of Terms : 10
 1 2 4 8 16 32 64 128 256 512
Press any key to continue . . .
```

---- **** ----

Program No. - 185 :
Program to find the sum of "n" number of terms of Sine series.

Code :
```
#include <stdio.h>
#include <math.h>

int  main()
{
    int i, j, n, f;
    float x, t, s;
    system( "cls" );

    printf( "Enter Number of Terms : " );
    scanf( "%d", &n );
    printf( "Enter Degree for Sine Series : " );
    scanf( "%f", &x );

    x = x * ( 3.14159 / 180 );

    s = 0;
    for( i=1 ; i<=n ; i++ )
    {
        f = 1;
        for( j=1 ; j<=(2*i-1) ; j++ )
        {
            f = f * j;
        }
        t = ( pow( x, (2*i-1) ) * pow( -1, (i+1) ) ) / f;
        s = s + t;
    }

    printf( "\nSum of Sine Series : %f\n", s );

    system( "pause" );
    return 0;
}
```

Output :

```
TERMINAL

Enter Number of Terms : 10
Enter Degree for Sine Series : 60

Sum of Sine Series : 0.866025
Press any key to continue . . .
```

——————————————— **** ———————————————

Program No. - 186 :
Program to find sum of "n" number of terms of Cosine series.

Code :
```c
#include <stdio.h>
#include <math.h>

int  main()
{
    int i, j, n, f;
    float x, t, s;
    system( "cls" );

    printf( "Enter Number of Terms : " );
    scanf( "%d", &n );
    printf( "Enter Degree for Cosine Series : " );
    scanf( "%f", &x );

    x = x * ( 3.14159 / 180 );

    s = 1;
    for( i=1 ; i<n ; i++ )
    {
        f = 1;
        for( j=1 ; j<=(2*i) ; j++ )
        {
            f = f * j;
        }
        t = ( pow( x, (2*i) ) * pow( −1, i ) ) / f;
        s = s + t;
    }

    printf( "\nSum of Cosine Series : %f\n", s );

    system( "pause" );
    return 0;
```

}

Output :

```
TERMINAL

Enter Number of Terms : 10
Enter Degree for Cosine Series : 60

Sum of Cosine Series : 0.500001
Press any key to continue . . .
```

——————————————— **** ———————————————

Program No. - 187 :
Program to find the sum first n terms of given series :
$$x + 2x^2 + 3x^3 + 4x^4 + \ldots \ldots \; n \text{ terms}$$

Code :
```c
#include <stdio.h>
#include <math.h>

int  main()
{
    int i, n, x, t, s;
    system( "cls" );

    printf( "Enter Number of Terms : " );
    scanf( "%d", &n );
    printf( "Enter Value of x : " );
    scanf( "%d", &x );

    s = 0;
    for( i=1 ; i<=n ; i++ )
    {
        t = i * pow( x, i );
        s = s + t;
    }
    printf( "\nSum of Series = %d\n", s );

    system( "pause" );
    return 0;
}
```

Output :

```
TERMINAL

Enter Number of Terms : 5
Enter Value of x : 2

Sum of Series = 258
Press any key to continue . . .
```

****

Program No. - 188 :
Program to find the sum first n terms of given series :
    1 + 1/2 + 1/3 + 1/4 + ... n terms

Code :
```c
#include <stdio.h>

int  main()
{
    int i, n;
    float t, s;
    system( "cls" );

    printf( "Enter Number of Terms : " );
    scanf( "%d", &n );

    s = 0.0;
    for( i=1 ; i<=n ; i++ )
    {
        t = 1.0 / i;
        s = s + t;
    }
    printf( "\nSum of Series = %f\n", s );

    system( "pause" );
    return 0;
}
```

Output :
```
TERMINAL

Enter Number of Terms : 3

Sum of Series = 1.833333
Press any key to continue . . .
```

****

Program No. - 189 :
Program to find the sum first n terms of given series :
    1/2 + 2/3 + 3/4 + ... n terms

Code :
```c
#include <stdio.h>

int  main()
{
    int i, n;
    float t, s;
    system( "cls" );

    printf( "Enter Number of Terms : " );
    scanf( "%d", &n );

    s = 0.0;
    for( i=1 ; i<=n ; i++ )
    {
        t = (float) i / ( i + 1 );
        s = s + t;
    }
    printf( "\nSum of Series = %f\n", s );

    system( "pause" );
    return 0;
}
```

Output :
```
TERMINAL

Enter Number of Terms : 5

Sum of Series = 3.550000
Press any key to continue . . .
```

****

Program No. - 190 :
Program to find the sum first n terms of given series :
    1/(2*3) + 2/(3*4) + 3/(4*5) + ... n terms

Code :
```c
#include <stdio.h>

int  main()
{
    int i, n;
```

```c
    float t, s;
    system( "cls" );

    printf( "Enter Number of Terms : " );
    scanf( "%d", &n );

    s = 0.0;
    for( i=1 ; i<=n ; i++ )
    {
        t = (float) i / ( ( i + 1 ) * ( i + 2 ) );
        s = s + t;
    }
    printf( "\nSum of Series = %f\n", s );

    system( "pause" );
    return 0;
}
```

Output :

```
TERMINAL

Enter Number of Terms : 5

Sum of Series = 0.735714
Press any key to continue . . .
```

****

Program No. - 191 :
Program to find the sum first n terms of given series :
   1/1! + 1/2! + 1/3! + ... n terms

Code :
```c
#include <stdio.h>

int  main()
{
    int i, n, j, f;
    float t, s;
    system( "cls" );

    printf( "Enter Number of Terms : " );
    scanf( "%d", &n );

    s = 0.0;
    for( i=1 ; i<=n ; i++ )
    {
        f = 1;
```

```c
        for( j=1 ; j<=i ; j++ )
        {
            f = f * j;
        }
        t = 1.0 / f;
        s = s + t;
    }
    printf( "\nSum of Series = %f\n", s );

    system( "pause" );
    return 0;
}
```

Output :

```
TERMINAL

Enter Number of Terms : 5

Sum of Series = 1.716667
Press any key to continue . . .
```

****

Program No. - 192 :
Program to find the sum first n terms of given series :
   $-(2x^1)/1! + (3x^2)/2! - (4x^3)/3! + ...$ n terms

Code :
```c
#include <stdio.h>
#include <math.h>

int  main()
{
    int i, n, x, j, f;
    float t, s;
    system( "cls" );

    printf( "Enter Number of Terms : " );
    scanf( "%d", &n );

    printf( "Enter Value of x : " );
    scanf( "%d", &x );

    s = 0.0;
    for( i=1 ; i<=n ; i++ )
    {
        f = 1;
```

```c
    for( j=1 ; j<=i ; j++ )
    {
        f = f * j;
    }
    t = ( ( i+1 ) * pow( x, i ) * pow( -1, i ) ) / f;
    s = s + t;
}
printf( "\nSum of Series = %f\n", s );

system( "pause" );
return 0;
}
```

Output :

```
TERMINAL

Enter Number of Terms : 3
Enter Value of x : 2

Sum of Series = -3.333333
Press any key to continue . . . |
```

---- **** ----

Program No. - 193 :
Program to find the sum first n terms of given series :
    1 + (1+2) + (1+2+3) + ... + n terms

Code :
```c
#include <stdio.h>

int  main()
{
    int i, n, j, t, s;
    system( "cls" );

    printf( "Enter Number of Terms : " );
    scanf( "%d", &n );

    s = 0;
    for( i=1 ; i<=n ; i++ )
    {
        t = 0;
        for( j=1 ; j<=i ; j++ )
        {
            t = t + j;
        }
        s = s + t;
```

```c
    }
    printf( "\nSum of Series = %d\n", s );

    system( "pause" );
    return 0;
}
```

Output :

```
TERMINAL

Enter Number of Terms : 5

Sum of Series = 35
Press any key to continue . . . |
```

---- **** ----

Program No. - 194 :
Program to display first n terms of Fibonacci Series.
    0   1   1   2   3   5 ... ... n terms

Code :
```c
#include <stdio.h>

int  main()
{
    int i, n, a, b, c;
    system( "cls" );

    printf( "Enter Number of Terms : " );
    scanf( "%d", &n );

    a = 0;
    b = 1;
    printf( "%d  %d  ", a, b );
    for( i=1 ; i<=(n-2) ; i++ )
    {
        c = a + b;
        printf( "%d  ", c );
        a = b;
        b = c;
    }

    printf( "\n" );
    system( "pause" );
    return 0;
}
```

Output :

```
TERMINAL

Enter Number of Terms : 10
0  1  1  2  3  5  8  13  21  34
Press any key to continue . . . |
```

****

Program No. - 195 :
Program to display first n terms of Lucas Series.
1   1   1   3   5   9 ... ... n terms

Code :
```c
#include <stdio.h>

int  main()
{
    int i, n, a, b, c, d;
    system( "cls" );

    printf( "Enter Number of Terms : " );
    scanf( "%d", &n );

    a = 1;
    b = 1;
    c = 1;
    printf( "%d  %d  %d  ", a, b, c );
    for( i=1 ; i<=(n-3) ; i++ )
    {
        d = a + b + c;
        printf( "%d  ", d );
        a = b;
        b = c;
        c = d;
    }

    printf( "\n" );
    system( "pause" );
    return 0;
}
```

Output :

```
TERMINAL

Enter Number of Terms : 10
1  1  1  3  5  9  17  31  57  105
Press any key to continue . . . |
```

****

Program No. - 196 :
Program to display first n terms of following Series.
1   11   111   1111 ... ... n terms

Code :
```c
#include <stdio.h>

int  main()
{
    int i, n, t;
    system( "cls" );

    printf( "Enter Number of Terms : " );
    scanf( "%d", &n );

    t = 0;
    for( i=0 ; i<n ; i++ )
    {
        t = t * 10 + 1;
        printf( "%d  ", t );
    }

    printf( "\n" );
    system( "pause" );
    return 0;
}
```

Output :

```
TERMINAL

Enter Number of Terms : 6
1  11  111  1111  11111  111111
Press any key to continue . . . |
```

****

Program No. - 197 :
Program to display first n terms of following Series.
1   11   111   1111 ... ... n terms

Code :
```c
#include <stdio.h>
#include <math.h>
```

```c
int  main()
{
    int i, n, t;
    system( "cls" );

    printf( "Enter Number of Terms : " );
    scanf( "%d", &n );

    t = 0;
    for( i=0 ; i<n ; i++ )
    {
        t = t + pow( 10, i );
        printf( "%d  ", t );
    }

    printf( "\n" );
    system( "pause" );
    return 0;
}
```

Output :

```
TERMINAL

Enter Number of Terms : 6
1   11   111   1111   11111   111111
Press any key to continue . . . |
```

———————————— **** ————————————

Program No. - 198 :
Program to display first n terms of given Series.
    −1   4   −7   10 ... ... n terms

Code :
```c
#include <stdio.h>
#include <math.h>

int  main()
{

    int  i, t, n;
    system( "cls" );

    printf( "Enter Number of Terms : " );
    scanf( "%d", &n );

    for( i=0 ; i<n ; i++ )
```

```c
    {
        t = ( 3 * i + 1 ) * pow( (−1), ( i + 1 ) );
        printf( "%d  ", t );
    }

    printf( "\n" );
    system( "pause" );
    return 0;
}
```

Output :

```
TERMINAL

Enter Number of Terms : 10
-1   4   -7   10   -13   16   -19   22   -25   28
Press any key to continue . . . |
```

———————————— **** ————————————

Program No. - 199 :
Program to find sum of first n terms of given series :
    $x - 2x^2 + 3x^3 - $ ... ... n terms

Code :
```c
#include <stdio.h>
#include <math.h>

int  main()
{
    int n, i, x, t, sum;
    system( "cls" );

    printf( " Enter Number of Terms : " );
    scanf( "%d", &n );
    printf( " Enter a Value x : " );
    scanf( "%d", &x );

    sum = 0;
    for( i=1 ; i<=n ; i++ )
    {
        t = i * pow( (−1), ( i + 1 ) ) * pow( x, i );
        sum = sum + t;
    }

    printf( "\n Sum of Series = %d" , sum );

    system( "pause" );
```

```c
    return 0;
}
```

Output :

```
TERMINAL

Enter Number of Terms : 5
Enter a Value x : 2

Sum of Series = 114
Press any key to continue . . .
```

****

Program No. - 200 :
Program to display first n terms of given Series.
    1   4   9   16 ... ... n terms

Code :

```c
#include <stdio.h>

int  main()
{
    int n, i, t;
    system( "cls" );

    printf( "Enter Number of Terms : " );
    scanf( "%d", &n );

    for( i=1 ; i<=n ; i++ )
    {
        t = ( i * i );
        printf( "%d  ", t );
    }

    printf( "\n" );
    system( "pause" );
    return 0;
}
```

Output :

```
TERMINAL

Enter Number of Terms : 10
1  4  9  16  25  36  49  64  81  100
Press any key to continue . . .
```

****

****

Chapter - 7
Patterns

****

Program No. - 201 :
Program to display the following design pattern :

```
1
1 2
1 2 3
1 2 3 4
```

Code :

```c
#include <stdio.h>

int  main()
{
    int i, j, n;
    system( "cls" );

    printf( "Enter Number of Rows : " );
    scanf( "%d", &n );

    for( i=1 ; i<=n ; i++ )
    {
        for( j=1 ; j<=i ; j++ )
        {
            printf( " %d", j );
        }
        printf( "\n" );
    }

    system( "pause" );
    return 0;
}
```

Output :

```
TERMINAL

Enter Number of Rows : 5
 1
 1 2
 1 2 3
 1 2 3 4
 1 2 3 4 5
Press any key to continue . . .
```

———————————— **** ————————————

Program No. - 202 :
Program to display the following design pattern :

```
1
2 2
```

```
3 3 3
4 4 4 4
```

Code :

```c
#include <stdio.h>

int  main()
{
    int i, j, n;
    system( "cls" );

    printf( "Enter Number of Rows : " );
    scanf( "%d", &n );

    for( i=1 ; i<=n ; i++ )
    {
        for( j=1 ; j<=i ; j++ )
        {
            printf( " %d", i );
        }
        printf( "\n" );
    }

    system( "pause" );
    return 0;
}
```

Output :

```
TERMINAL

Enter Number of Rows : 5
 1
 2 2
 3 3 3
 4 4 4 4
 5 5 5 5 5
Press any key to continue . . .
```

———————————— **** ————————————

Program No. - 203 :
Program to display the following design pattern :

```
*
* *
* * *
* * * *
```

Code :

```c
#include <stdio.h>
#include <conio.h>

int  main()
{
    int i, j, n;
    system( "cls" );

    printf( "Enter Number of Rows : " );
    scanf( "%d", &n );

    for( i=1 ; i<=n ; i++ )
    {
        for( j=1 ; j<=i ; j++ )
        {
            printf( " *" );
        }
        printf( "\n" );
    }

    system( "pause" );
    return 0;
}
```

Output :

```
TERMINAL

Enter Number of Rows : 5
 *
 * *
 * * *
 * * * *
 * * * * *
Press any key to continue . . . |
```

———————————— **** ————————————

Program No. - 204 :
Program to display the following design pattern :
    A
    A B
    A B C
    A B C D

Code :
```c
#include <stdio.h>

int  main()
```

```c
{
    int i, j, n;
    system( "cls" );

    printf( "Enter Number of Rows : " );
    scanf( "%d", &n );

    for( i=1 ; i<=n ; i++ )
    {
        for( j=1 ; j<=i ; j++ )
        {
            printf( " %c", ( j + 64 ) );
        }
        printf( "\n" );
    }

    system( "pause" );
    return 0;
}
```

Output :

```
TERMINAL

Enter Number of Rows : 5
 A
 A B
 A B C
 A B C D
 A B C D E
Press any key to continue . . . |
```

———————————— **** ————————————

Program No. - 205 :
Program to display the following design pattern :
    a
    a b
    a b c
    a b c d

Code :
```c
#include <stdio.h>

int  main()
{
    int i, j, n;
    system( "cls" );
```

```c
    printf( "Enter Number of Rows : " );
    scanf( "%d", &n );

    for( i=1 ; i<=n ; i++ )
    {
        for( j=1 ; j<=i ; j++ )
        {
            printf( " %c", ( j + 96 ) );
        }
        printf( "\n" );
    }

    system( "pause" );
    return 0;
}
```

Output :

```
TERMINAL

Enter Number of Rows : 5
 a
 a b
 a b c
 a b c d
 a b c d e
Press any key to continue . . . |
```

———————————— **** ————————————

Program No. - 206 :
Program to display the following design pattern :
    A
    B B
    C C C
    D D D D

Code :
```c
#include <stdio.h>

int  main()
{
    int i, j, n;
    system( "cls" );

    printf( "Enter Number of Rows : " );
    scanf( "%d", &n );

    for( i=1 ; i<=n ; i++ )
```

```c
    {
        for( j=1 ; j<=i ; j++ )
        {
            printf( " %c", ( i + 64 ) );
        }
        printf( "\n" );
    }

    system( "pause" );
    return 0;
}
```

Output :

```
TERMINAL

Enter Number of Rows : 5
 A
 B B
 C C C
 D D D D
 E E E E E
Press any key to continue . . . |
```

———————————— **** ————————————

Program No. - 207 :
Program to display the following design pattern :
    a
    b b
    c c c
    d d d d

Code :
```c
#include <stdio.h>

int  main()
{
    int i, j, n;
    system( "cls" );

    printf( "Enter Number of Rows : " );
    scanf( "%d", &n );

    for( i=1 ; i<=n ; i++ )
    {
        for( j=1 ; j<=i ; j++ )
        {
            printf( " %c", ( i + 96 ) );
```

```c
        }
        printf( "\n" );
    }

    system( "pause" );
    return 0;
}
```

Output :

```
TERMINAL

Enter Number of Rows : 5
 a
 b b
 c c c
 d d d d
 e e e e
Press any key to continue . . . |
```

---- **** ----

Program No. - 208 :

Program to display the following design pattern :

```
    1
    1 2
    1 2 3
    1 2 3 4
```

Code :

```c
#include <stdio.h>

int  main()
{
    int i, j, k, n;
    system( "cls" );

    printf( "Enter Number of Rows : " );
    scanf( "%d", &n );

    for( i=1 ; i<=n ; i++ )
    {
        for( k=1 ; k<=(n-i) ; k++ )
        {
            printf( " " );
        }
        for( j=1 ; j<=i ; j++ )
        {
            printf( " %d", j );
```

```c
        }
        printf( "\n" );
    }

    system( "pause" );
    return 0;
}
```

Output :

```
TERMINAL

Enter Number of Rows : 5
        1
       1 2
      1 2 3
     1 2 3 4
    1 2 3 4 5
Press any key to continue . . . |
```

---- **** ----

Program No. - 209 :

Program to display the following design pattern :

```
    1
    1 2 1
    1 2 3 2 1
    1 2 3 4 3 2 1
```

Code :

```c
#include <stdio.h>

int  main()
{
    int i, j, k, l, n;
    system( "cls" );

    printf( "Enter Number of Rows : " );
    scanf( "%d", &n );

    for( i=1 ; i<=n ; i++ )
    {
        for( k=1 ; k<=(n-i) ; k++ )
        {
            printf( " " );
        }
        for( j=1 ; j<=i ; j++ )
        {
            printf( " %d", j );
```

```
        }
        for( l=i-1 ; l>=1 ; l-- )
        {
            printf( " %d", l );
        }
        printf( "\n" );
    }

    system( "pause" );
    return 0;
}
```

Output :

```
TERMINAL

Enter Number of Rows : 5
            1
          1 2 1
        1 2 3 2 1
      1 2 3 4 3 2 1
    1 2 3 4 5 4 3 2 1
Press any key to continue . . .|
```

****

Program No. - 210 :
Program to display the following design pattern :
```
        1
       1 2 1
      1 2 3 2 1
     1 2 3 4 3 2 1
      1 2 3 2 1
       1 2 1
        1
```

Code :
```c
#include <stdio.h>

int  main()
{
    int i, j, k, l, n;
    system( "cls" );

    printf( "Enter Number of Rows : " );
    scanf( "%d", &n );

    for( i=1 ; i<=n ; i++ )
    {
        for( k=1 ; k<=(n-i) ; k++ )
        {
            printf( " " );
        }
        for( j=1 ; j<=i ; j++ )
        {
            printf( " %d", j );
        }
        for( l=i-1 ; l>=1 ; l-- )
        {
            printf( " %d", l );
        }
        printf( "\n" );
    }

    for( i=n-1 ; i>=1 ; i-- )
    {
        for( k=1 ; k<=(n-i) ; k++ )
        {
            printf( " " );
        }
        for( j=1 ; j<=i ; j++ )
        {
            printf( " %d", j );
        }
        for( l=i-1 ; l>=1 ; l-- )
        {
            printf( " %d", l );
        }
        printf( "\n" );
    }

    system( "pause" );
    return 0;
}
```

Output :

```
TERMINAL

Enter Number of Rows : 5
          1
        1 2 1
      1 2 3 2 1
    1 2 3 4 3 2 1
  1 2 3 4 5 4 3 2 1
    1 2 3 4 3 2 1
      1 2 3 2 1
        1 2 1
          1
Press any key to continue . . .|
```

****

Program No. - 211 :
Program to display the following design pattern :
```
          1
        1   1
      1       1
    1           1
      1       1
        1   1
          1
```

Code :
```c
#include <stdio.h>

int  main()
{
    int i, j, k, l, n;
    system( "cls" );

    printf( "Enter Number of Rows : " );
    scanf( "%d", &n );

    for( i=1 ; i<=n ; i++ )
    {
        for( k=1 ; k<=(n-i) ; k++ )
        {
            printf( " " );
        }
        for( j=1 ; j<=i ; j++ )
        {
            if( j == 1 )
                printf( " %d", j );
            else
                printf( " " );
        }
        for( l=i-1 ; l>=1 ; l-- )
        {
            if( l == 1 )
                printf( " %d", l );
            else
                printf( " " );
        }
        printf( "\n" );
    }

    for( i=n-1 ; i>=1 ; i-- )
    {
        for( k=1 ; k<=(n-i) ; k++ )
        {
            printf( " " );
        }
        for( j=1 ; j<=i ; j++ )
        {
            if( j == 1 )
                printf( " %d", j );
            else
                printf( " " );
        }
        for( l=i-1 ; l>=1 ; l-- )
        {
            if( l == 1 )
                printf( " %d", l );
            else
                printf( " " );
        }
        printf( "\n" );
    }

    system( "pause" );
    return 0;
}
```

Output :

```
TERMINAL

Enter Number of Rows : 5
            1
         1     1
       1         1
     1             1
   1                 1
     1             1
       1         1
         1     1
            1
Press any key to continue . . . |
```

****

Program No. - 212 :

Program to display the following design pattern :

```
        1
      1   1
    1       1
  1     4     1
    1       1
      1   1
        1
```

Code :

```c
#include <stdio.h>

int  main()
{
    int i, j, k, l, n;
    system( "cls" );

    printf( "Enter Number of Rows : " );
    scanf( "%d", &n );

    for( i=1 ; i<=n ; i++ )
    {
        for( k=1 ; k<=(n-i) ; k++ )
        {
            printf( " " );
        }
        for( j=1 ; j<=i ; j++ )
        {
            if( j == 1 || j == n )
                printf( " %d", j );
            else
                printf( " " );
        }
        for( l=i-1 ; l>=1 ; l-- )
        {
            if( l == 1 )
                printf( " %d", l );
            else
                printf( " " );
        }
        printf( "\n" );
    }

    for( i=n-1 ; i>=1 ; i-- )
    {
        for( k=1 ; k<=(n-i) ; k++ )
        {
            printf( " " );
        }
        for( j=1 ; j<=i ; j++ )
        {
            if( j == 1 )
                printf( " %d", j );
            else
                printf( " " );
        }
        for( l=i-1 ; l>=1 ; l-- )
        {
            if( l == 1 )
                printf( " %d", l );
            else
                printf( " " );
        }
        printf( "\n" );
    }

    system( "pause" );
    return 0;
}
```

Output :

```
TERMINAL

Enter Number of Rows : 5
            1
         1     1
      1           1
   1                 1
1           5           1
   1                 1
      1           1
         1     1
            1

Press any key to continue . . . |
```

———————————— **** ————————————

Program No. - 213 :
Program to display the following design pattern :

```
      1
    1   1
  1       1
1 2 3 4 3 2 1
  1       1
    1   1
      1
```

Code :
```c
#include <stdio.h>

int  main()
{
    int i, j, k, l, n;
    system( "cls" );

    printf( "Enter Number of Rows : " );
    scanf( "%d", &n );

    for( i=1 ; i<=n ; i++ )
    {
        for( k=1 ; k<=(n-i) ; k++ )
        {
            printf( " " );
        }
        for( j=1 ; j<=i ; j++ )
        {
            if( j == 1 || i == n )
                printf( " %d", j );
            else
                printf( "  " );
        }
        for( l=i-1 ; l>=1 ; l-- )
        {
            if( l == 1 || i == n )
                printf( " %d", l );
            else
                printf( "  " );
        }
        printf( "\n" );
    }

    for( i=n-1 ; i>=1 ; i-- )
    {
        for( k=1 ; k<=(n-i) ; k++ )
        {
            printf( " " );
        }
        for( j=1 ; j<=i ; j++ )
        {
            if( j == 1 )
                printf( " %d", j );
            else
                printf( "  " );
        }
        for( l=i-1 ; l>=1 ; l-- )
        {
            if( l == 1 )
                printf( " %d", l );
            else
                printf( "  " );
        }
        printf( "\n" );
    }

    system( "pause" );
    return 0;
}
```

Output :

```
TERMINAL

Enter Number of Rows : 5
            1
         1     1
      1              1
    1                    1
 1 2 3 4 5 4 3 2 1
    1                    1
      1              1
         1     1
            1
Press any key to continue . . . |
```

****

Program No. - 214 :
Program to display the following design pattern :

```
        1
      1 2 1
    1   3   1
  1     4     1
    1   3   1
      1 2 1
        1
```

Code :
```c
#include <stdio.h>

int  main()
{
    int i, j, k, l, n;
    system( "cls" );

    printf( "Enter Number of Rows : " );
    scanf( "%d", &n );

    for( i=1 ; i<=n ; i++ )
    {
        for( k=1 ; k<=(n-i) ; k++ )
        {
            printf( " " );
        }
        for( j=1 ; j<=i ; j++ )
        {
            if( j == 1 || j == i )
                printf( " %d", j );
            else
                printf( "  " );
        }
        for( l=i-1 ; l>=1 ; l-- )
        {
            if( l == 1 )
                printf( " %d", l );
            else
                printf( "  " );
        }
        printf( "\n" );
    }

    for( i=n-1 ; i>=1 ; i-- )
    {
        for( k=1 ; k<=(n-i) ; k++ )
        {
            printf( " " );
        }
        for( j=1 ; j<=i ; j++ )
        {
            if( j == 1 || j == i )
                printf( " %d", j );
            else
                printf( "  " );
        }
        for( l=i-1 ; l>=1 ; l-- )
        {
            if( l == 1 )
                printf( " %d", l );
            else
                printf( "  " );
        }
        printf( "\n" );
    }

    system( "pause" );
    return 0;
}
```

Output :

```
TERMINAL

Enter Number of Rows : 5
            1
          1 2 1
        1   3   1
      1     4     1
    1       5       1
      1     4     1
        1   3   1
          1 2 1
            1
Press any key to continue . . .|
```

———————————— **** ————————————

Program No. - 215 :

Program to display the following design pattern (Floyd's Triangle) :

```
1
2 3
4 5 6
7 8 9 10
```

Code :

```c
#include <stdio.h>

int  main()
{
    int i, j, n, a;
    system( "cls" );

    printf( "Enter Number of Rows : " );
    scanf( "%d", &n );

    a = 1;
    for( i=1 ; i<=n ; i++ )
    {
        for( j=1 ; j<=i ; j++ )
        {
            printf( "%3d", a );
            a++;
        }
        printf( "\n" );
    }

    system( "pause" );
    return 0;
```

```
}
```

Output :

```
TERMINAL

Enter Number of Rows : 5
   1
   2  3
   4  5  6
   7  8  9 10
  11 12 13 14 15
Press any key to continue . . .|
```

———————————— **** ————————————

Program No. - 216 :

Program to display the following design pattern :

```
1
0 0
1 1 1
0 0 0 0
```

Code :

```c
#include <stdio.h>

int  main()
{
    int i, j, n;
    system( "cls" );

    printf( "Enter Number of Rows : " );
    scanf( "%d", &n );

    for( i=1 ; i<=n ; i++ )
    {
        for( j=1 ; j<=i ; j++ )
        {
            if( i % 2 == 0 )
                printf( "%2d", 0 );
            else
                printf( "%2d", 1 );
        }
        printf( "\n" );
    }

    system( "pause" );
    return 0;
}
```

Output :

```
TERMINAL

Enter Number of Rows : 5
 1
 0 0
 1 1 1
 0 0 0 0
 1 1 1 1 1
Press any key to continue . . . |
```

——————————— **** ———————————

Program No. - 217 :
Program to display the following design pattern :
```
    1
    0 0
    1 1 1
    0 0 0 0
```

Code :
```c
#include <stdio.h>

int  main()
{
    int i, j, n;
    system( "cls" );

    printf( "Enter Number of Rows : " );
    scanf( "%d", &n );

    for( i=1 ; i<=n ; i++ )
    {
        for( j=1 ; j<=i ; j++ )
        {
            printf( "%2d", ( i % 2 ) );
        }
        printf( "\n" );
    }

    system( "pause" );
    return 0;
}
```

Output :

```
TERMINAL

Enter Number of Rows : 5
 1
 0 0
 1 1 1
 0 0 0 0
 1 1 1 1 1
Press any key to continue . . . |
```

——————————— **** ———————————

Program No. - 218 :
Program to display the following design pattern :
```
    1
    1 0
    1 0 1
    1 0 1 0
```

Code :
```c
#include <stdio.h>

int  main()
{
    int i, j, n;
    system( "cls" );

    printf( "Enter Number of Rows : " );
    scanf( "%d", &n );

    for( i=1 ; i<=n ; i++ )
    {
        for( j=1 ; j<=i ; j++ )
        {
            if( j % 2 == 0 )
                printf( "%2d", 0 );
            else
                printf( "%2d", 1 );
        }
        printf( "\n" );
    }

    system( "pause" );
    return 0;
}
```

Output :

```
TERMINAL

Enter Number of Rows : 5
 1
 1 0
 1 0 1
 1 0 1 0
 1 0 1 0 1
Press any key to continue . . .|
```

```
TERMINAL

Enter Number of Rows : 5
 1
 1 0
 1 0 1
 1 0 1 0
 1 0 1 0 1
Press any key to continue . . .|
```

****

Program No. - 219 :
Program to display the following design pattern :

```
1
1 0
1 0 1
1 0 1 0
```

Code :
```c
#include <stdio.h>

int  main()
{
    int i, j, n;
    system( "cls" );

    printf( "Enter Number of Rows : " );
    scanf( "%d", &n );

    for( i=1 ; i<=n ; i++ )
    {
        for( j=1 ; j<=i ; j++ )
        {
            printf( "%2d", ( j % 2 ) );
        }
        printf( "\n" );
    }

    system( "pause" );
    return 0;
}
```

Output :

Program No. - 220 :
Program to display the following design pattern :

```
*   *   *   *   *
*   *   *   *   *
*   *   *   *   *
*   *   *   *   *
*   *   *   *   *
```

Code :
```c
#include <stdio.h>

int  main()
{
    int i, j, n;
    system( "cls" );

    printf( "Enter Number of Rows : " );
    scanf( "%d", &n );

    printf( "\n" );
    for( i=1 ; i<=n ; i++ )
    {
        for( j=1 ; j<=n ; j++ )
        {
            printf( " *" );
        }
        printf( "\n" );
    }

    system( "pause" );
    return 0;
}
```

Output :

```
TERMINAL

Enter Number of Rows : 5

   * * * * *
   * * * * *
   * * * * *
   * * * * *
   * * * * *
Press any key to continue . . .
```

****

Program No. - 221 :

Program to display the following design pattern :

```
*   *   *   *   *
*               *
*               *
*               *
*   *   *   *   *
```

Code :

```c
#include <stdio.h>

int  main()
{
    int i, j, n;
    system( "cls" );

    printf( "Enter Number of Rows : " );
    scanf( "%d", &n );

    printf( "\n" );
    for( i=1 ; i<=n ; i++ )
    {
        for( j=1 ; j<=n ; j++ )
        {
            if( i == 1 || i == n || j == 1 || j == n )
                printf( " *" );
            else
                printf( "  " );
        }
        printf( "\n" );
    }

    system( "pause" );
    return 0;
```

```
}
```

Output :

```
TERMINAL

Enter Number of Rows : 5

   * * * * *
   *       *
   *       *
   *       *
   * * * * *
Press any key to continue . . .
```

****

Program No. - 222 :

Program to display the following design pattern :

```
*   *   *   *   *
*   *       *   *
*       *       *
*   *       *   *
*   *   *   *   *
```

Code :

```c
#include <stdio.h>

int  main()
{
    int i, j, n;
    system( "cls" );

    printf( "Enter Number of Rows : " );
    scanf( "%d", &n );

    printf( "\n" );
    for( i=1 ; i<=n ; i++ )
    {
        for( j=1 ; j<=n ; j++ )
        {
            if( i == 1 || i == n || j == 1 || j == n || i == j
                                    || ( i+j ) == (n+1) )
                printf( " *" );
            else
                printf( "  " );
        }
        printf( "\n" );
```

```
    }

    system( "pause" );
    return 0;
}
```

Output :

```
TERMINAL

Enter Number of Rows : 7

 * * * * * * *
 * *       * *
 *   *   *   *
 *     *     *
 *   *   *   *
 * *       * *
 * * * * * * *

Press any key to continue . . .
```

****

Program No. - 223 :
Program to display the following design pattern :

```
       1
      1 2 3
     1 2 3 4 5
    1 2 3 4 5 6 7
```

Code :

```c
#include <stdio.h>

int  main()
{
    int i, j, k, n;
    system( "cls" );

    printf( "Enter Number of Rows : " );
    scanf( "%d", &n );

    for( i=1 ; i<2*n ; i+=2 )
    {
        for( k=1 ; k<=(2*n-i) ; k++ )
        {
            printf( " " );
        }
        for( j=1 ; j<=i ; j++ )
        {
            printf( " %d", j );
```

```
        }
        printf( "\n" );
    }

    system( "pause" );
    return 0;
}
```

Output :

```
TERMINAL

Enter Number of Rows : 5
            1
          1 2 3
        1 2 3 4 5
      1 2 3 4 5 6 7
    1 2 3 4 5 6 7 8 9
Press any key to continue . . .
```

****

Program No. - 224 :
Program to display the following design pattern :

```
    C
    C O
    C O M
    C O M P
    C O M P U
    C O M P U T
    C O M P U T E
    C O M P U T E R
```

Code :

```c
#include <stdio.h>
#include <string.h>

int  main()
{
    int i, j, k;
    char str[25];
    system( "cls" );

    printf( "Enter a String : " );
    scanf( "%s", str );

    k = strlen( str );
    for( i=0 ; i< k ; i++ )
    {
```

```c
        for( j=0 ; j <= i ; j++ )
        {
            printf( " %c", str[ j ] );
        }
        printf( "\n" );
    }

    system( "pause" );
    return 0;
}
```

Output :

```
TERMINAL

Enter a String : COMPUTER
 C
 C O
 C O M
 C O M P
 C O M P U
 C O M P U T
 C O M P U T E
 C O M P U T E R
Press any key to continue . . .
```

——————— ******** ———————

Program No. - 225 :
Program to display the following design pattern :
```
    C O M P U T E R
      O M P U T E R
        M P U T E R
          P U T E R
            U T E R
              T E R
                E R
                  R
```

Code :
```c
#include <stdio.h>
#include <string.h>

int  main()
{
    int i, j, k, l;
    char str[25];
    system( "cls" );

    printf( "Enter a String : " );
```

```c
    scanf( "%s", str );

    l = strlen( str );
    for( i=0 ; i< l ; i++ )
    {
        for( k=0 ; k <i ; k++ )
        {
            printf( "  " );
        }
        for( j=i ; j < l ; j++ )
        {
            printf( " %c", str[ j ] );
        }
        printf( "\n" );
    }

    system( "pause" );
    return 0;
}
```

Output :

```
TERMINAL

Enter a String : COMPUTER
 C O M P U T E R
   O M P U T E R
     M P U T E R
       P U T E R
         U T E R
           T E R
             E R
               R
Press any key to continue . . .
```

——————— ******** ———————

Program No. - 226 :
Program to display the following design pattern :
```
        I
      I N I
    I N D N I
  I N D I D N I
I N D I A I D N I
```

Code :
```c
#include <stdio.h>
#include <string.h>
```

```c
int main()
{
    int i, j, k, l, len;
    char str[25];
    system( "cls" );

    printf( "Enter a String : " );
    scanf( "%s", str );

    len = strlen( str );
    for( i=0 ; i<len ; i++ )
    {
        for( k=0 ; k<( len – i ) ; k++ )
        {
            printf( " " );
        }
        for( j=0 ; j<i ; j++ )
        {
            printf( " %c", str[ j ] );
        }
        for( l=i; l>=0 ; l-- )
        {
            printf( " %c", str[ l ] );
        }
        printf( "\n" );
    }

    system( "pause" );
    return 0;
}
```

Output :

```
TERMINAL

Enter a String : INDIA
            I
          I N I
        I N D N I
      I N D I D N I
    I N D I A I D N I
Press any key to continue . . .
```

****

Program No. - 227 :
Program to display the Pascal Triangle :
```
             1
           1   1
          1   2   1
         1   3   3   1
```

Code :
```c
#include <stdio.h>

int main()
{
    int n, i, j, k, t;
    system( "cls" );

    printf( "Enter Number of Rows : " );
    scanf( "%d", &n );

    for( i=0 ; i<n ; i++ )
    {
        for( k=0 ; k<(n–i) ; k++ )
        {
            printf( " " );
        }
        for( j=0 ; j<=i ; j++ )
        {
            if( j == 0 || i == 0 )
                t = 1;
            else
                t = ( t * ( i – j + 1 ) ) / j ;
            printf( "   %d", t );
        }
        printf( "\n" );
    }

    system( "pause" );
    return 0;
}
```

Output :

```
TERMINAL

Enter Number of Rows : 5
            1
          1   1
        1   2   1
      1   3   3   1
    1   4   6   4   1
Press any key to continue . . .
```

****

Program No. - 228 :
Program to display following pattern using break :
```
1
2 4
3 6 9
4 8 12 16
```

Code :
```c
#include <stdio.h>

int  main()
{
    int i, j, n;
    system( "cls" );

    printf( "Enter Number of Rows : " );
    scanf( "%d", &n );

    printf( "\n" );
    for( i=1 ; i<=n ; i++ )
    {
        for( j=1 ; j<=n ; j++ )
        {
            printf( "%3d", ( i * j ) );
            if( i == j )
                    break;
        }
        printf( "\n" );
    }

    system( "pause" );
    return 0;
}
```

Output :
```
TERMINAL

Enter Number of Rows : 5

1
2  4
3  6  9
4  8 12 16
5 10 15 20 25
Press any key to continue . . .
```

________________ **** ________________

Program No. - 229 :
Program to explain use of break statement with following pattern :
```
1
1 2
1 2 3
1 2 3 4
1 2 3 4 5
```

Code :
```c
#include <stdio.h>

int main()
{
    int  i, j;
    system( "cls" );

    for( i=1 ; i<=5 ; i++ )
    {
        for( j=1 ; j<=10 ; j++ )
        {
            printf ( " %d", j ) ;
            if ( i == j )
                    break ;
        }
        printf( "\n" );
    }

    system( "pause" );
    return 0;
}
```

Output :
```
TERMINAL

1
1 2
1 2 3
1 2 3 4
1 2 3 4 5
Press any key to continue . . .
```

________________ **** ________________

Program No. - 230 :
Program to explain use of break statement with following pattern :
```
1
```

```
1 2
1 2 3
1 2 3 4
1 2 3 4 5
```

Code :
```c
#include <stdio.h>

int main()
{
    int  i, j;
    system( "cls" );

    for( i=1 ; i<=10 ; i++ )
    {
        for( j=1 ; j<=10 ; j++ )
        {
            printf ( " %d", j ) ;
            if ( i == j )
                break ;
        }
        printf( "\n" );
        if( i == 5 )
            break;
    }

    system( "pause" );
    return 0;
}
```

Output :

```
TERMINAL

1
1 2
1 2 3
1 2 3 4
1 2 3 4 5
Press any key to continue . . . 
```

———————— **** ————————

Program No. - 231 :
Program to explain use of break statement with following pattern :
```
1 2 3 4 5
1 2 3 4
```

```
1 2 3
1 2
1
```

Code :
```c
#include <stdio.h>

int main()
{
    int i, j;
    system( "cls" );

    for( i=1 ; i<=5 ; i++ )
    {
        for( j=1 ; j<=5 ; j++ )
        {
            if ( i > j )
                continue ;
            printf( " %d", j );
        }
        printf( "\n" );
    }

    system( "pause" );
    return 0;
}
```

Output :

```
TERMINAL

1 2 3 4 5
2 3 4 5
3 4 5
4 5
5
Press any key to continue . . . 
```

———————— **** ————————

****

Chapter − 8
Arrays

****

Program No. - 232 :
Program to use Simple Array.

Code :
```c
#include <stdio.h>

int  main()
{
    int  num[5];
    int  i;
    system( "cls" );

    for( i=0 ; i<5 ; i++ )
    {
        printf( "Enter value %d : ", (i + 1) );
        scanf( "%d", &num[ i ] );
    }

    printf( "\nThe elements are : " );
    for( i=0 ; i<5 ; i++ )
    {
        printf( " %d", num[ i ] );
    }

    printf( "\n" );
    system( "pause" );
    return 0;
}
```

Output :

```
TERMINAL

Enter value 1 : 10
Enter value 2 : 20
Enter value 3 : 30
Enter value 4 : 40
Enter value 5 : 50

The elements are :    10  20  30  40  50
Press any key to continue . . .
```

———————— **** ————————

Program No. - 233 :
Program to explain **Initialization** of an Array.

Code :
```c
#include <stdio.h>
```

```c
int  main()
{
    int  i;
    int  num[10] = { 10, 20, 30, 40, 50, 60, 70, 80,
                                        90, 100 };
    system( "cls" );

    for( i=0 ; i<10 ; i++ )
    {
        printf( " %d : %d\n", (i + 1), num[ i ] );
    }

    system( "pause" );
    return 0;
}
```

Output :

```
TERMINAL

 1  :  10
 2  :  20
 3  :  30
 4  :  40
 5  :  50
 6  :  60
 7  :  70
 8  :  80
 9  :  90
 10 : 100
Press any key to continue . . .
```

———————— **** ————————

Program No. - 234 :
Program to find **Average** of an Array.

Code :
```c
#include <stdio.h>

int  main()
{
    float a[5];
    float s, avg;
    int i;
    system( "cls" );

    for ( i=0 ; i<5 ; i++ )
```

```c
    {
        printf( "Enter Value : " );
        scanf( "%f", &a[ i ] );
    }

    s = 0.0;
    for( i=0 ; i<5 ; i++ )
    {
        s = s + a[ i ];
    }

    avg = s / 5;
    printf( "\nSum    : %f\n", s );
    printf( "Average : %f\n", avg );

    system( "pause" );
    return 0;
}
```

Output :

```
TERMINAL

Enter Value : 10
Enter Value : 20
Enter Value : 30
Enter Value : 40
Enter Value : 50

Sum     : 150.000000
Average : 30.000000
Press any key to continue . . . |
```

****

Program No. - 235 :
Program to twice the value of all elements of Array.

Code :
```c
#include <stdio.h>

int main()
{
    int ar[50], n,i;
    system( "cls" );

    printf(   "Enter No. of Array Elements : " );
    scanf( "%d", &n );
```

```c
    for( i=0 ; i<n ; i++ )
    {
        printf( "Enter [%d] element : ", i+1 );
        scanf( "%d", &ar[ i ] );
    }

    printf( "\nArray with doubled elements : " );
    for( i=0 ; i<n ; i++ )
    {
        ar[ i ] *= 2;
        printf( "%d  ", ar[ i ] );
    }

    printf( "\n" );
    system( "pause" );
    return 0;
}
```

Output :

```
TERMINAL

Enter No. of Array Elements : 5
Enter [1] element : 10
Enter [2] element : 20
Enter [3] element : 30
Enter [4] element : 40
Enter [5] element : 50

Array with doubled elements : 20  40  60  80  100
Press any key to continue . . . []
```

****

Program No. - 236 :
Program to find **Maximum** and **Minimum** of Array elements.

Code :
```c
#include <stdio.h>

int main()
{
    int  i, arr[5], min, max;
    system( "cls" );

    printf( "Enter Five Numbers : " );
    for( i=0 ; i<5 ; i++ )
    {
        scanf( "%d", &arr[ i ] );
```

```
}

    min = arr[0];
    max = arr[0];
    for( i=1 ; i<5 ; i++ )
    {
        if( min > arr[ i ] )
            min = arr[ i ];
        if( max < arr[ i ] )
            max = arr[ i ];
    }

    printf( "\nMinimum value = %d\n", min );
    printf( "Maximum value = %d\n",  max );

    system( "pause" );
    return 0;
}
```

Output :

```
TERMINAL

Enter Five Numbers : 30 20 40 50 10

Minimum value = 10
Maximum value = 50
Press any key to continue . . .
```

—————————— **** ——————————

Program No. - 237 :
Program to search an element in array using **Linear Search**.

Code :

```
#include <stdio.h>

int  main()
{
    int  num[10], i, pos = -1, value;
    system( "cls" );

    printf( "Enter Ten Numbers : " );
    for( i=0 ; i<10 ; i++ )
    {
        scanf( "%d", &num[ i ] );
    }
```

```
    printf( "Enter the number to be searched : " );
    scanf( "%d", &value );

    for( i=0 ; i<10 ; i++ )
    {
        if( value == num[ i ] )
        {
            pos = i + 1;
            break;
        }
    }

    if( pos == -1 )
        printf( "\nThe element %d not found.\n", value );
    else
        printf( "\nThe position of %d : %d\n", value,
                                                pos );

    system( "pause" );
    return 0;
}
```

Output :

```
TERMINAL

Enter Ten Numbers : 1 2 3 4 5 6 7 8 9 10
Enter the number to be searched :  7

The position of 7 : 7
Press any key to continue . . .
```

```
TERMINAL

Enter Ten Numbers : 1 2 3 4 5 6 7 8 9 10
Enter the number to be searched :  15

The element 15 not found.
Press any key to continue . . .
```

—————————— **** ——————————

Program No. - 238 :
Program to search an element in array using **Binary Search**.

Code :

```
#include <stdio.h>
```

```c
int  main()
{
    int num[10], i, beg, end, mid, pos = -1, value;
    system( "cls" );

    printf( "Enter Ten Numbers in Ascending Order: " );
    for( i=0 ; i<10 ; i++ )
    {
        scanf( "%d", &num[ i ] );
    }

    printf( "Enter the number to be searched : " );
    scanf( "%d", &value );

    beg = 0;
    end = 10 − 1;
    while( beg<= end )
    {
        mid = ( beg + end ) / 2;
        if( value == num[mid] )
        {
            pos = mid + 1;
            break;
        }
        else if( value > num[mid] )
            beg = mid + 1;
        else
            end = mid − 1;
    }

    if( pos == −1 )
        printf( "\nThe element %d not found.\n", value );
    else
        printf( "\nThe position of %d : %d\n" , value,
                                                pos );

    system( "pause" );
    return 0;
}
```

Output :

```
TERMINAL

Enter Ten Numbers in Ascending Order: 1 2 3 4 5 6 7 8 9 10
Enter the number to be searched : 6

The position of 6 : 6
Press any key to continue . . .
```

```
TERMINAL

Enter Ten Numbers in Ascending Order: 1 2 3 4 5 6 7 8 9 10
Enter the number to be searched : 20

The element 20 not found.
Press any key to continue . . .
```

****

Program No. - 239 :
Program to **Reverse an Array** elements without using Second Array.

Code :

```c
#include <stdio.h>

int  main()
{
    int  arr[5];
    int  i, j, t;
    system( "cls" );

    for( i=0 ; i<5 ; i++ )
    {
        printf( "Enter Value %d : ", (i + 1) );
        scanf( "%d", &arr[ i ] );
    }

    printf( "\nArray before reversing are : " );
    for( i=0 ; i<5 ; i++ )
    {
        printf( "  %d", arr[ i ] );
    }

    for( i=0, j=5−1 ; i<5/2 ; i++, j-- )
    {
        t = arr[ i ];
        arr[ i ] = arr[ j ];
        arr[ j ] = t;
    }

    printf( "\nArray after reversing are  : " );
    for( i=0 ; i<5 ; i++ )
    {
        printf( "  %d", arr[ i ] );
    }

    printf( "\n" );
```

```
    system( "pause" );
    return 0;
}
```

Output :

```
TERMINAL

Enter Value 1 : 10
Enter Value 2 : 20
Enter Value 3 : 30
Enter Value 4 : 40
Enter Value 5 : 50


Array before reversing are :   10  20  30  40  50
Array after reversing are  :   50  40  30  20  10
Press any key to continue . . .
```

****

Program No. - 240 :
Program to Sort elements of array using **Bubble Sort**.

Code :
```c
#include <stdio.h>

int  main()
{
    int  i, j, t;
    int  n[ ] = { 30, 40, 50, 10, 20 };
    system( "cls" );

    printf( "Before Sorting :" );
    for( i=0 ; i<5 ; i++ )
    {
        printf( " %d", n[ i ] );
    }

    for( i=0 ; i<5-1 ; i++ )
    {
        for( j=0 ; j<5-1-i ; j++ )
        {
            if( n[ j ] > n[ j+1] )
            {
                t = n[ j ];
                n[ j ] = n[ j+1];
                n[ j+1] = t;
            }
        }
    }
```

```c
    printf( "\n\nAfter Sorting  :" );
    for( i=0 ; i<5 ; i++ )
    {
        printf( " %d", n[ i ] );
    }

    printf( "\n" );
    system( "pause" );
    return 0;
}
```

Output :

```
TERMINAL

Before Sorting :   30  40  50  10  20

After Sorting  :   10  20  30  40  50
Press any key to continue . . .
```

****

Program No. - 241 :
Program to Sort elements of array using **Selection Sort**.

Code :
```c
#include <stdio.h>

int  main()
{
    int  i, j, small, pos, tmp ;
    int  n[ ] = { 30, 40, 50, 10, 20 };
    system( "cls" );

    printf( "Before Sorting :" );
    for( i=0 ; i<5 ; i++ )
    {
        printf( " %d", n[ i ] );
    }

    for( i=0 ; i<5 ; i++ )
    {
        small = n[ i ];
        pos = i;
        for( j=i+1 ; j<5 ; j++ )
        {
            if( n[ j ] < small )
            {
```

```c
                small = n[ j ];
                pos = j;
            }
        }
        tmp = n[ i ];
        n[ i ] = n[pos];
        n[pos] = tmp;
    }

    printf( "\n\nAfter Sorting  :" );
    for( i=0 ; i<5 ; i++ )
    {
        printf( "  %d", n[ i ] );
    }

    printf( "\n" );
    system( "pause" );
    return 0;
}
```

Output :

```
TERMINAL

Before Sorting :   30  40  50  10  20

After Sorting  :   10  20  30  40  50
Press any key to continue . . .
```

————————— **** —————————

Program No. - 242 :
Program to Sort elements of array using **Insertion Sort**.

Code :
```c
#include <stdio.h>

int  main()
{
    int  i, j, tmp;
    int  n[ ] = { 0, 30, 40, 50, 10, 20 };
    system( "cls" );

    printf( "Before Sorting :" );
    for( i=1 ; i<=5 ; i++ )
    {
        printf( "  %d", n[ i ] );
    }
```

```c
    n[0] = -2147483648;
    for( i=1 ; i<=5 ; i++ )
    {
        tmp = n[ i ];
        j = i - 1;
        while( tmp < n[ j ] )
        {
            n[ j + 1 ] = n[ j ];
            j--;
        }
        n[ j + 1 ] = tmp;
    }

    printf( "\n\nAfter Sorting  :" );
    for( i=1 ; i<=5 ; i++ )
    {
        printf( "  %d", n[ i ] );
    }

    printf( "\n" );
    system( "pause" );
    return 0;
}
```

Output :

```
TERMINAL

Before Sorting :   30  40  50  10  20

After Sorting  :   10  20  30  40  50
Press any key to continue . . .
```

————————— **** —————————

Program No. - 243 :
Program to create **Fibonacci Series** in an Array.

Code :
```c
#include <stdio.h>

int  main()
{
    int  i, n, a[50];
    system( "cls" );

    printf( "Enter the Number of Terms : " );
    scanf( "%d", &n );
```

```c
    a[0] = 0;
    a[1] = 1;

    for( i=2 ; i<n ; i++ )
    {
        a[ i ] = a[ i – 1 ] + a[ i – 2 ];
    }

    printf( "\n" );
    for( i=0 ; i<n ; i++ )
    {
        printf( "  %d", a[ i ] );
    }

    printf( "\n" );
    system( "pause" );
    return 0;
}
```

Output :

```
TERMINAL

Enter the Number of Terms : 10

  0  1  1  2  3  5  8  13  21  34
Press any key to continue . . .
```

———————————— **** ————————————

Program No. - 244 :
Program to check whether the given number is Unique
Number or Not.

Code :
```c
#include <stdio.h>

int main()
{
    int i, t, n, x, r, flag;
    int a[10] = {0};
    system( "cls" );

    printf( "Enter a Number : " );
    scanf( "%d", &n );

    x = n;
    while( n != 0 )
    {
```

```c
        r = n % 10;
        a[ r ]++;
        n = n / 10;
    }

    flag = 1;
    for( i=0 ; i<10 ; i++ )
    {
        if( a[ i ] > 1 )
        {
            flag = 0;
            break;
        }
    }
    if( flag )          //  if( flag == 1 )
        printf( "\n%d is a Unique Number.\n", x );
    else
        printf( "\n%d is not a Unique Number.\n", x );

    system( "pause" );
    return 0;
}
```

Output :

```
TERMINAL

Enter a Number : 123456

123456 is a Unique Number.
Press any key to continue . . .
```

```
TERMINAL

Enter a Number : 1234321

1234321 is not a Unique Number.
Press any key to continue . . .
```

———————————— **** ————————————

Program No. - 245 :
Program to Swap two one dimensional array of same
size.

Code :
```c
#include <stdio.h>

int main()
```

```c
{
    int a[5], b[5];
    int i, t;
    system( "cls" );

    printf( "Enter Values of Array-1 : \n" );
    for( i=0 ; i<5 ; i++ )
    {
        scanf( "%d", &a[ i ] );
    }

    printf( "Enter Values of Array-2 : \n" );
    for( i=0 ; i<5 ; i++ )
    {
        scanf( "%d", &b[ i ] );
    }

    printf( "\nArrays before Swapping : " );
    printf( "\nArray-1 : " );
    for( i=0 ; i<5 ; i++ )
    {
        printf( "%d ", a[ i ] );
    }

    printf( "\nArray-2 : " );
    for( i=0 ; i<5 ; i++ )
    {
        printf( "%d ", b[ i ] );
    }

    for( i=0 ; i<5 ; i++ )
    {
        t = a[ i ];
        a[ i ] = b[ i ];
        b[ i ] = t;
    }

    printf( "\n\nArrays After Swapping : " );
    printf( "\nArray-1 : " );
    for( i=0 ; i<5 ; i++ )
    {
        printf( "%d ", a[ i ] );
    }

    printf( "\nArray-2 : " );
    for( i=0 ; i<5 ; i++ )
    {
        printf( "%d ", b[ i ] );
    }

    printf( "\n" );
    system( "pause" );
    return 0;
}
```

Output :

```
TERMINAL

Enter Values of Array-1 :
10 20 30 40 50
Enter Values of Array-2 :
50 40 30 20 10

Arrays before Swapping :
Array-1 : 10 20 30 40 50
Array-2 : 50 40 30 20 10

Arrays After Swapping :
Array-1 : 50 40 30 20 10
Array-2 : 10 20 30 40 50
Press any key to continue . . .
```

****

Program No. - 246 :
Program to find First Biggest and Second Biggest of array elements.

Code :
```c
#include <stdio.h>
#include <limits.h>

int main()
{
    int a[5];
    int i, t, big, sbig;
    system( "cls" );

    printf( "Enter Values of Array : \n" );
    for( i=0 ; i<5 ; i++ )
    {
        scanf( "%d", &a[ i ] );
    }

    printf( "\nArray : " );
    for( i=0 ; i<5 ; i++ )
```

```
    {
        printf( "%d ", a[ i ] );
    }


    big = a[0];
    for( i=1 ; i<5 ; i++ )
    {
        if( big < a[ i ] )
            big = a[ i ];
    }

    sbig = INT_MIN;        // -2147483648
    for( i=0 ; i<5 ; i++ )
    {
        if( ( sbig < a[ i ] ) && ( a[ i ] != big ) )
            sbig = a[ i ];
    }

    printf( "\nFirst Biggest  : %d\n", big );
    printf( "Second Biggest : %d\n", sbig );

    printf( "\n" );
    system( "pause" );
    return 0;
}
```

Output :

```
TERMINAL

Enter Values of Array :
40 20 10 50 30

Array : 40 20 10 50 30
First Biggest  : 50
Second Biggest : 40

Press any key to continue . . . 
```

---- **** ----

Program No. - 247 :
Program to Insert an element in given array at specific location.

Code :
```
#include <stdio.h>
```

```
int main()
{
    int ar[25], pos, i, n, value;
    system( "cls" );

    printf( "Enter number of elements in array : " );
    scanf( "%d", &n );
    printf( "Enter %d elements :\n", n );
    for( i=0 ; i<n ; i++ )
    {
        scanf( "%d", &ar[ i ] );
    }
    printf( "Enter the Location to Insert : " );
    scanf( "%d", &pos );
    printf( "Enter the Value to Insert : " );
    scanf( "%d", &value );

    printf( "\nArray before Insertion : \n" );
    for( i=0 ; i<n ; i++ )
    {
        printf( "%d ", ar[ i ] );
    }

    for( i=n-1 ; i>=pos-1; i-- )
    {
        ar[ i+1] = ar[ i ];
    }
    ar[pos-1] = value;
    n++;

    printf( "\n\nArray after Insertion : \n" );
    for( i=0 ; i<n ; i++ )
    {
        printf( "%d ", ar[ i ] );
    }

    printf( "\n" );
    system( "pause" );
    return 0;
}
```

Output :

```
TERMINAL

Enter number of elements in array : 5
Enter 5 elements :
10 20 30 40 50
Enter the Location to Insert : 3
Enter the Value to Insert : 25

Array before Insertion :
10 20 30 40 50

Array after Insertion :
10 20 25 30 40 50
Press any key to continue . . . []
```

****

Program No. - 248 :
Program to Delete an element from given array.

Code :
```c
#include <stdio.h>

int main()
{
    int ar[25], pos, i, j, n, value, flag;
    system( "cls" );

    printf( "Enter number of elements in array : " );
    scanf( "%d", &n );
    printf( "Enter %d elements :\n", n );
    for( i=0 ; i<n ; i++ )
    {
        scanf( "%d", &ar[ i ] );
    }
    printf( "Enter the Value to Delete : " );
    scanf( "%d", &value );

    printf( "\nArray before Deletion : \n" );
    for( i=0 ; i<n ; i++ )
    {
        printf( "%d ", ar[ i ] );
    }

    flag = 0;
    for( i=0 ; i<n; i++ )
    {
        if( value == ar[ i ] )
        {
            for( j=i ; j<n-1 ; j++ )
            {
                ar[ j ] = ar[ j+1];
            }
            n--;
            flag = 1;
        }
    }

    if( !flag )                 // (flag == 0)
    {
        printf( "\n\nValue %d not in Array.", value );
    }
    else
    {
        printf( "\n\nArray after Deletion : \n" );
        for( i=0 ; i<n ; i++ )
        {
            printf( "%d ", ar[ i ] );
        }
    }

    printf( "\n" );
    system( "pause" );
    return 0;
}
```

Output :

```
TERMINAL


Enter number of elements in array : 5
Enter 5 elements :
10 20 30 40 50
Enter the Value to Delete : 30

Array before Deletion :
10 20 30 40 50

Array after Deletion :
10 20 40 50
Press any key to continue . . . []
```

```
TERMINAL


Enter number of elements in array : 5
Enter 5 elements :
10 20 30 40 50
Enter the Value to Delete : 25

Array before Deletion :
10 20 30 40 50

Value 25 not in Array.
Press any key to continue . . .
```

****

Program No. - 249 :
Program to remove all duplicate elements from array.

Code :

```c
#include <stdio.h>

int main()
{
    int ar[25], pos, i, j, k, n, flag;
    system( "cls" );

    printf( "Enter number of elements in array : " );
    scanf( "%d", &n);
    printf("Enter %d elements :\n", n );
    for( i=0 ; i<n ; i++ )
    {
        scanf( "%d", &ar[ i ] );
    }

    printf( "\nOriginal Array : \n" );
    for( i=0 ; i<n ; i++ )
    {
        printf( "%d ", ar[ i ] );
    }

    flag = 0;
    for( i=0 ; i<n; i++ )
    {
        for( j=i+1 ; j<n ; j++ )
        {
            if( ar[ j ] == ar[ i ] )
            {
                for( k=j ; k<(n−1) ; k++ )
                {
                    ar[k] = ar[k+1];
                }
                n--;
                flag = 1;
            }
        }
    }

    if( ! flag )              // (flag == 0)
    {
        printf( "\n\nNo Duplicates in Array." );
    }
    else
    {
        printf( "\n\nArray without Duplicates : \n" );
        for( i=0 ; i<n ; i++ )
        {
            printf( "%d ", ar[ i ] );
        }
    }

    printf( "\n" );
    system( "pause" );
    return 0;
}
```

Output :

```
TERMINAL


Enter number of elements in array : 7
Enter 7 elements :
10 20 30 20 40 30 50

Original Array :
10 20 30 20 40 30 50

Array without Duplicates :
10 20 30 40 50
Press any key to continue . . .
```

```
TERMINAL

Enter number of elements in array : 7
Enter 7 elements :
10 20 30 40 50 60 70

Original Array :
10 20 30 40 50 60 70

No Duplicates in Array.
Press any key to continue . . .
```

****

Program No. - 250 :
Program to Delete an element at specific location in array.

Code :

```c
#include <stdio.h>

int main()
{
    int ar[25], pos, i, n;
    system( "cls" );

    printf( "Enter number of elements in array : " );
    scanf( "%d", &n );
    printf( "Enter %d elements :\n", n );
    for( i=0 ; i<n ; i++ )
    {
        scanf( "%d", &ar[ i ] );
    }
    printf( "Enter the Location of element to Delete : " );

    scanf( "%d", &pos );

    printf( "\nArray before Deletion : \n" );
    for( i=0 ; i<n ; i++ )
    {
        printf( "%d ", ar[ i ] );
    }

    if( (pos < 1) || (pos > n) )
    {
        printf( "\n\nLocation %d is out of Range.", pos );
    }
    else
    {
        for( i=pos-1 ; i<n-1; i++ )
        {
            ar[ i ] = ar[ i+1];
        }
        n--;

        printf( "\n\nArray after Deletion : \n" );
        for( i=0 ; i<n ; i++ )
        {
            printf( "%d ", ar[ i ] );
        }
    }

    printf( "\n" );
    system( "pause" );
    return 0;
}
```

Output :

```
TERMINAL

Enter number of elements in array : 5
Enter 5 elements :
10 20 30 40 50
Enter the Location of element to Delete : 3

Array before Deletion :
10 20 30 40 50

Array after Deletion :
10 20 40 50
Press any key to continue . . .
```

```
TERMINAL

Enter number of elements in array : 5
Enter 5 elements :
10 20 30 40 50
Enter the Location of element to Delete : 10

Array before Deletion :
10 20 30 40 50

Location 10 is out of Range.
Press any key to continue . . .
```

****

Program No. - 251 :
Program to Input and display a Matrix (2-D Array).

Code :
```c
#include <stdio.h>

int  main()
{
    int  a[2][3];
    int  i, j;
    system( "cls" );

    for( i=0 ; i<2 ; i++ )
    {
        for( j=0 ; j<3 ; j++ )
        {
            printf( "Enter value : " );
            scanf( "%d", &a[ i ][ j ] );
        }
    }

    printf( "\nThe Matrix is : \n" );
    for( i=0 ; i<2 ; i++ )
    {
        for( j=0 ; j<3 ; j++ )
        {
            printf( "%d     ", a[ i ][ j ] );
        }
        printf( "\n" );
    }

    system( "pause" );
    return 0;
}
```

Output :
```
TERMINAL

Enter value : 10
Enter value : 20
Enter value : 30
Enter value : 40
Enter value : 50
Enter value : 60

The Matrix is :
10       20       30
40       50       60
Press any key to continue . . .
```

****

Program No. - 252 :
Program to **Initialize** a Matrix (2-D Array).

Code :
```c
#include <stdio.h>

int  main()
{
    int a[2][3] = { { 10, 20, 30 },
            { 40, 50, 50 } };
    int i, j;
    system( "cls" );

    printf( "Matrix A : \n" );
    for( i=0 ; i<2 ; i++ )
    {
        for( j=0 ; j<3 ; j++ )
        {
            printf( " %d", a[ i ][ j ] );
        }
        printf( "\n" );
    }

    system( "pause" );
    return 0;
}
```

Output :
```
TERMINAL

Matrix A :
  10   20   30
  40   50   50
Press any key to continue . . .
```

****

Program No. - 253 :
Program for **Addition** of Two Matrices.

Code :
```c
#include <stdio.h>

int  main()
```

```c
{
    int  a[2][3], b[2][3], c[2][3];
    int  i, j;
    system( "cls" );

    for( i=0 ; i<2 ; i++ )
    {
        for( j=0 ; j<3 ; j++ )
        {
            printf( "Enter value of A : " );
            scanf( "%d", &a[ i ][ j ] );
        }
    }

    for( i=0 ; i<2 ; i++ )
    {
        for( j=0 ; j<3 ; j++ )
        {
            printf( "Enter value of B : " );
            scanf( "%d", &b[ i ][ j ] );
        }
    }

    for( i=0 ; i<2 ; i++ )
    {
        for( j=0 ; j<3 ; j++ )
        {
            c[ i ][ j ] = a[ i ][ j ] + b[ i ][ j ];
        }
    }

    printf( "\nMatrix A is :\n" );
    for( i=0 ; i<2 ; i++ )
    {
        for( j=0 ; j<3 ; j++ )
        {
            printf( " %d", a[ i ][ j ] );
        }
        printf( "\n" );
    }

    printf( "Matrix B is :\n" );
    for( i=0 ; i<2 ; i++ )
    {
        for( j=0 ; j<3 ; j++ )
        {
            printf( " %d", b[ i ][ j ] );
        }
        printf( "\n" );
    }

    printf( "Matrix C is ::: \n" );
    for( i=0 ; i<2 ; i++ )
    {
        for( j=0 ; j<3 ; j++ )
        {
            printf( " %d", c[ i ][ j ] );
        }
        printf( "\n" );
    }

    system( "pause" );
    return 0;
}
```

Output :

```
TERMINAL

Enter value of A : 2
Enter value of A : 3
Enter value of A : 4
Enter value of A : 5
Enter value of A : 6
Enter value of B : 6
Enter value of B : 5
Enter value of B : 4
Enter value of B : 3
Enter value of B : 2
Enter value of B : 1

Matrix A is :
  1   2   3
  4   5   6
Matrix B is :
  6   5   4
  3   2   1
Matrix C is :::
  7   7   7
  7   7   7
Press any key to continue . . .
```

****

Program No. - 254 :
Program to find Transpose of given Matrix.

Code :
```c
#include <stdio.h>
```

```c
int  main()
{
    int  a[2][3], b[3][2];
    int  i, j;
    system( "cls" );

    for( i=0 ; i<2 ; i++ )
    {
        for( j=0 ; j<3 ; j++ )
        {
            printf( "Enter Value : " );
            scanf( "%d", &a[ i ][ j ] );
        }
    }

    for( i=0 ; i<2 ; i++ )
    {
        for( j=0 ; j<3 ; j++ )
        {
            b[ j ][ i ] = a[ i ][ j ] ;
        }
    }

    printf( "\nMatrix A is :\n" );
    for( i=0 ; i<2 ; i++ )
    {
        for( j=0 ; j<3 ; j++ )
        {
            printf( " %d", a[ i ][ j ] );
        }
        printf( "\n" );
    }

    printf( "Matrix B is :\n" );
    for( i=0 ; i<3 ; i++ )
    {
        for( j=0 ; j<2 ; j++ )
        {
            printf( " %d", b[ i ][ j ] );
        }
        printf( "\n" );
    }

    system( "pause" );
    return 0;
}
```

Output :

```
TERMINAL

Enter Value : 1
Enter Value : 2
Enter Value : 3
Enter Value : 4
Enter Value : 5
Enter Value : 6

Matrix A is :
  1   2   3
  4   5   6
Matrix B is :
  1   4
  2   5
  3   6
Press any key to continue . . .
```

———————————— ******** ————————————

Program No. - 255 :
Program to Transpose a Square Matrix without using
Second matrix.

Code :

```c
#include <stdio.h>

int  main()
{
    int  a[10][10];
    int  n, i, j, temp;
    system( "cls" );

    printf( "Enter order of matrix (n x n) : " );
    scanf( "%d", &n );

    printf( "Enter the elements of Matrix :\n" );
    for( i=0 ; i<n ; i++ )
    {
        for( j=0 ; j<n ; j++ )
        {
            printf( "Enter element : " );
            scanf( "%d", &a[ i ][ j ] );
        }
    }

    printf( "\nThe Original matrix is :\n" );
```

```c
    for( i=0 ; i<n ; i++ )
    {
        for( j=0 ; j<n ; j++ )
        {
            printf( " %d", a[ i ][ j ] );
        }
        printf( "\n" );
    }

    for( i=0 ; i<n ; i++ )
    {
        for( j=0 ; j<n ; j++ )
        {
            if( i < j )
            {
                temp = a[ i ][ j ];
                a[ i ][ j ] = a[ j ][ i ];
                a[ j ][ i ] = temp;
            }
        }
    }

    printf( "\nThe Transposed matrix is :\n" );
    for( i=0 ; i<n ; i++ )
    {
        for( j=0 ; j<n ; j++ )
        {
            printf( " %d", a[ i ][ j ] );
        }
        printf( "\n" );
    }

    system( "pause" );
    return 0;
}
```

Output :

```
TERMINAL

Enter order of matrix (n x n) : 3
Enter the elements of Matrix :
Enter element : 1
Enter element : 2
Enter element : 3
Enter element : 4
Enter element : 5
Enter element : 6
Enter element : 7
Enter element : 8
Enter element : 9

The Original matrix is :
   1   2   3
   4   5   6
   7   8   9

The Transposed matrix is :
   1   4   7
   2   5   8
   3   6   9
Press any key to continue . . .
```

****

Program No. - 256 :
Program to Multiply Two Matrices.

Code :

```c
#include <stdio.h>

int  main()
{
    int a[2][3], b[3][2], c[2][2];
    int i, j, k;
    system( "cls" );

    for( i=0 ; i<2 ; i++ )
    {
        for( j=0 ; j<3 ; j++ )
        {
            printf( "Enter Value of A : " );
            scanf( "%d", &a[ i ][ j ] );
        }
    }

    for( i=0 ; i<3 ; i++ )
    {
```

```c
    for( j=0 ; j<2 ; j++ )
    {
        printf( "Enter Value of B : " );
        scanf( "%d", &b[ i ][ j ] );
    }
}

for( i=0 ; i<2 ; i++ )
{
    for( j=0 ; j<2 ; j++ )
    {
        c[ i ][ j ] = 0;
        for( k=0 ; k<3 ; k++ )
        {
            c[ i ][ j ] = c[ i ][ j ] + (a[ i ][ k ] * b[ k ][ j ]);
        }
    }
}

printf( "\nMatrix A : \n" );
for( i=0 ; i<2 ; i++ )
{
    for( j=0 ; j<3 ; j++ )
    {
        printf( " %d", a[ i ][ j ] );
    }
    printf( "\n" );
}

printf( "Matrix B : \n" );
for( i=0 ; i<3 ; i++ )
{
    for( j=0 ; j<2 ; j++ )
    {
        printf( " %d", b[ i ][ j ] );
    }
    printf( "\n" );
}

printf( "Matrix C : \n" );
for( i=0 ; i<2 ; i++ )
{
    for( j=0 ; j<2 ; j++ )
    {
        printf( " %d",  c[ i ][ j ] );
    }
    printf( "\n" );
```

```c
    }
    system( "pause" );
    return 0;
}
```

Output :

```
TERMINAL

Enter Value of A : 2
Enter Value of A : 3
Enter Value of A : 4
Enter Value of A : 5
Enter Value of A : 6
Enter Value of B : 1
Enter Value of B : 4
Enter Value of B : 2
Enter Value of B : 5
Enter Value of B : 3
Enter Value of B : 6

Matrix A :
  1  2  3
  4  5  6
Matrix B :
  1  4
  2  5
  3  6
Matrix C :
  14  32
  32  77
Press any key to continue . . .
```

****

Program No. - 257 :
Program to find Sum of Principle Diagonal, Other Diagonal, Upper Triangle, Lower Triangle and All elements of Square Matrix.

Code :
```c
#include <stdio.h>

int  main()
{
    int a[3][3];
    int i, j, spd=0, sod=0, sut=0, slt=0, sa=0;
    system( "cls" );

    for( i=0 ; i<3 ; i++ )
    {
```

```c
        for( j=0 ; j<3 ; j++ )
        {
            printf( "Enter Value of A : " );
            scanf( "%d", &a[ i ][ j ] );
        }
    }

    for( i=0 ; i<3 ; i++ )
    {
        for( j=0 ; j<3 ; j++ )
        {
            if( i == j )
                spd = spd + a[ i ][ j ];
            if( ( i + j ) == 2 )
                sod = sod + a[ i ][ j ];
            if( i <= j )
                sut = sut + a[ i ][ j ];
            if( i >= j )
                slt = slt + a[ i ][ j ];
            sa = sa + a[ i ][ j ];
        }
    }

    printf( "\nMatrix A : \n" );
    for( i=0 ; i<3 ; i++ )
    {
        for( j=0 ; j<3 ; j++ )
        {
            printf( "  %d", a[ i ][ j ] );
        }
        printf( "\n" );
    }

    printf( "Sum of All elements      : %d\n", sa );
    printf( "Sum of Principal Diagonal: %d\n", spd );
    printf( "Sum of Other Diagonal    : %d\n", sod );
    printf( "Sum of Upper Triangle    : %d\n", sut );
    printf( "Sum of Lower Triangle    : %d\n", slt );

    system( "pause" );
    return 0;
}
```

Output :

```
TERMINAL

Enter Value of A : 1
Enter Value of A : 2
Enter Value of A : 3
Enter Value of A : 4
Enter Value of A : 5
Enter Value of A : 6
Enter Value of A : 7
Enter Value of A : 8
Enter Value of A : 9

Matrix A :
   1   2   3
   4   5   6
   7   8   9
Sum of All elements       : 45
Sum of Principal Diagonal: 15
Sum of Other Diagonal     : 15
Sum of Upper Triangle     : 26
Sum of Lower Triangle     : 34
Press any key to continue . . .
```

****

Program No. - 258 :
Program to find Row-wise Sum and Column-wise Sum and Sum of all elements of Matrix.

Code :
```c
#include <stdio.h>

int  main()
{
    int a[3][3];
    int  i, j, gt=0;
    int  rs[3] = {0}, cs[3] = {0};
    system( "cls" );

    for( i=0 ; i<3 ; i++ )
    {
        for( j=0 ; j<3 ; j++ )
        {
            printf( "Enter Value of A : " );
            scanf( "%d", &a[ i ][ j ] );
        }
    }

    for( i=0 ; i<3 ; i++ )
    {
        for( j=0 ; j<3 ; j++ )
```

```c
        {
            rs[ i ] = rs[ i ] + a[ i ][ j ];
            cs[ j ] = cs[ j ] + a[ i ][ j ];
            gt = gt + a[ i ][ j ];
        }
    }

    printf( "\nMatrix A : \n" );
    for( i=0 ; i<3 ; i++ )
    {
        for( j=0 ; j<3 ; j++ )
        {
            printf( "%4d", a[ i ][ j ] );
        }
        printf( " | %d \n", rs[ i ] );
    }

    printf( " _______________________\n" );
    for( i=0 ; i<3 ; i++ )
    {
        printf( "%4d",  cs[ i ] );
    }
    printf( " | %d \n", gt );

    system( "pause" );
    return 0;
}
```

Output :

```
TERMINAL

Enter Value of A : 1
Enter Value of A : 2
Enter Value of A : 3
Enter Value of A : 4
Enter Value of A : 5
Enter Value of A : 6
Enter Value of A : 7
Enter Value of A : 8
Enter Value of A : 9

Matrix A :
   1    2    3 | 6
   4    5    6 | 15
   7    8    9 | 24
  _______________________
  12   15   18 | 45
Press any key to continue . . . |
```

****

Program No. - 259 :
Program to check whether the Two Matrices are Equal or not.

Code :

```c
#include <stdio.h>

int  main()
{
    int  n1[5][5], n2[5][5];
    int  i, j, r, c, flag;
    system( "cls" );

    printf( "Enter Order of Matrices : " );
    scanf( "%d %d", &r, &c );

    printf( "Enter Values of Matrix A : \n " );
    for( i=0 ; i<r ; i++ )
    {
        for( j=0 ; j<c ; j++ )
        {
            scanf( "%d", &n1[ i ][ j ] );
        }
    }

    printf( "Enter Values of Matrix B : \n " );
    for( i=0 ; i<r ; i++ )
    {
        for( j=0 ; j<c ; j++ )
        {
            scanf( "%d", &n2[ i ][ j ] );
        }
    }

    flag = 0;
    for( i=0 ; i<r ; i++ )
    {
        for( j=0 ; j<c ; j++ )
        {
            if( n1[ i ][ j ] != n2[ i ][ j ] )
            {
                flag = 1;
                break;
            }
        }
    }
    if( flag == 1 )             /* if( flag )  */
```

```
            break;
    }

    if( flag == 1 )                    /*  if( flag )  */
        printf( "\nBoth Matrices are Unequal.\n" );
    else
        printf( "\nBoth Matrices are Equal.\n" );

    system( "pause" );
    return 0;
}
```

Output :

```
TERMINAL
Enter Order of Matrices : 2 3
Enter Values of Matrix A :
 1 2 3 4 5 6
Enter Values of Matrix B :
 1 2 3 4 4 6

Both Matrices are Unequal.
Press any key to continue . . . |
```

```
TERMINAL
Enter Order of Matrices : 3 2
Enter Values of Matrix A :
 1 2 3 4 5 6
Enter Values of Matrix B :
 1 2 3 4 5 6

Both Matrices are Equal.
Press any key to continue . . . |
```

****

Program No. - 260 :
Program to check whether the given matrix is Identity
Matrix or Not.

Code :
```c
#include <stdio.h>
#include <stdlib.h>

int  main()
{
    int  a[5][5];
    int  i, j, r, c, flag;
    system( "cls" );

    printf( "Enter Order of Matrices : " );
    scanf( "%d %d", &r, &c );

    if( r != c )
    {
            printf("\nNot an Identity Matrix
                            (rows!=columns).\n" );
            exit(0);
    }

    printf( "Enter Values of Matrix : \n" );
    for( i=0 ; i<r ; i++ )
    {
        for( j=0 ; j<c ; j++ )
        {
            scanf( "%d", &a[ i ][ j ] );
        }
    }

    printf( "\nMatrix-A : \n" );
    for( i=0 ; i<r ; i++ )
    {
        for( j=0 ; j<c ; j++ )
        {
            printf( " %d", a[ i ][ j ] );
        }
        printf( "\n" );
    }

    flag = 1;
    for( i=0 ; i<r ; i++ )
    {
        for( j=0 ; j<c ; j++ )
        {
            if( ( i == j && a[ i ][ j ] != 1 )
                            || ( i != j && a[ i ][ j ] != 0 ) )
            {
                flag = 0;
                break;
            }
        }
        if( flag == 0 )            /*  if( ! flag )  */
            break;
    }

    if( flag == 1 )                /*  if( flag )  */
```

```c
        printf( "\nMatrix is an Identity Matrix.\n" );
    else
        printf( "\nMatrix is not an Identity Matrix.\n" );

    system( "pause" );
    return 0;
}
```

Output :

```
TERMINAL

Enter Order of Matrices : 3 3
Enter Values of Matrix :
1 0 0 0 1 0 0 0 1

Matrix-A :
  1  0  0
  0  1  0
  0  0  1

Matrix is an Identity Matrix.
Press any key to continue . . . 
```

```
TERMINAL

Enter Order of Matrices : 2 3

Not an Identity Matrix (rows!=columns).
PS D:\C> 
```

```
TERMINAL

Enter Order of Matrices : 2 2
Enter Values of Matrix :
1 2 3 4

Matrix-A :
  1  2
  3  4

Matrix is not an Identity Matrix.
Press any key to continue . . . 
```

****

Program No. - 261 :
Program to check whether the given matrix is Sparse
Matrix or Not.

Code :
```c
#include <stdio.h>
```

```c
int  main()
{
    int  a[5][5];
    int  i, j, r, c, zcnt=0;
    system( "cls" );

    printf( "Enter Order of Matrices : " );
    scanf( "%d %d", &r, &c );

    printf( "Enter Values of Matrix : \n" );
    for( i=0 ; i<r ; i++ )
    {
        for( j=0 ; j<c ; j++ )
        {
            scanf( "%d", &a[ i ][ j ] );
            if( a[ i ][ j ] == 0 )
                zcnt++;
        }
    }

    printf( "\nMatrix-A : \n" );
    for( i=0 ; i<r ; i++ )
    {
        for( j=0 ; j<c ; j++ )
        {
            printf( " %d", a[ i ][ j ] );
        }
        printf( "\n" );
    }

    if( zcnt > ((r * c) / 2) )
        printf( "\nMatrix is a Sparse Matrix.\n" );
    else
        printf( "\nMatrix is not a Sparse Matrix
                                    (Dense).\n" );

    system( "pause" );
    return 0;
}
```

Output :

```
TERMINAL

Enter Order of Matrices : 3 3
Enter Values of Matrix :
1 0 0 1 1 0 0 0 1

Matrix-A :
   1   0   0
   1   1   0
   0   0   1

Matrix is a Sparse Matrix.
Press any key to continue . . . █
```

```
TERMINAL

Enter Order of Matrices : 2 2
Enter Values of Matrix :
1 0 1 1

Matrix-A :
   1   0
   1   1

Matrix is not a Sparse Matrix (Dense).
Press any key to continue . . . █
```

****

Program No. - 262 :
Program to find No. of even values and No. of odd
values in given matrix.

Code :
```c
#include <stdio.h>

int main()
{
    int a[5][5];
    int i, j, r, c, ecnt, ocnt;
    system( "cls" );

    printf( "Enter Order of Matrices : " );
    scanf( "%d %d", &r, &c );

    printf( "Enter Values of Matrix : \n" );
    for( i=0 ; i<r ; i++ )
    {
        for( j=0 ; j<c ; j++ )
        {
            scanf( "%d", &a[ i ][ j ] );
        }
    }

    ecnt = ocnt = 0;
    for( i=0 ; i<r ; i++ )
    {
        for( j=0 ; j<c ; j++ )
        {
            if( a[ i ][ j ] % 2 == 0 )
                ecnt++;
            if( a[ i ][ j ] % 2 != 0 )
                ocnt++;
        }
    }

    printf( "\nMatrix-A : \n" );
    for( i=0 ; i<r ; i++ )
    {
        for( j=0 ; j<c ; j++)
        {
            printf( " %d", a[ i ][ j ] );
        }
        printf( "\n" );
    }

    printf( "\nNo. of Even Values : %d\n", ecnt );
    printf( "No. of Odd Values  : %d\n", ocnt );

    system( "pause" );
    return 0;
}
```

Output :
```
TERMINAL

Enter Order of Matrices : 3 3
Enter Values of Matrix :
1 2 3 4 5 6 7 8 9

Matrix-A :
   1   2   3
   4   5   6
   7   8   9

No. of Even Values : 4
No. of Odd Values  : 5
Press any key to continue . . . █
```

———————— **** ————————

Program No. - 263 :
Program to display Upper-Trianglar matrix of given
Square matrix.

Code :
```c
#include <stdio.h>

int main()
{
    int a[3][3];
    int i, j;
    system( "cls" );

    printf( "Enter Values of Matrix : \n" );
    for( i=0 ; i<3 ; i++ )
    {
        for( j=0 ; j<3 ; j++ )
        {
            scanf( "%d", &a[ i ][ j ] );
        }
    }

    printf( "\nGiven Matrix-A : \n" );
    for( i=0 ; i<3 ; i++ )
    {
        for( j=0 ; j<3 ; j++ )
        {
            printf( "  %d", a[ i ][ j ] );
        }
        printf( "\n" );
    }

    printf( "\nUpper Triangular Matrix-A : \n" );
    for( i=0 ; i<3 ; i++ )
    {
        for( j=0 ; j<3 ; j++ )
        {
            if( i <= j )
                printf( "  %d", a[ i ][ j ] );
            else
                printf( "  0" );
        }
        printf( "\n" );
    }
```

```c
        system( "pause" );
        return 0;
}
```

Output :

```
TERMINAL

Enter Values of Matrix :
1 2 3 4 5 6 7 8 9

Given Matrix-A :
   1   2   3
   4   5   6
   7   8   9

Upper Triangular Matrix-A :
   1   2   3
   0   5   6
   0   0   9
Press any key to continue . . . ▯
```

———————— **** ————————

Program No. - 264 :
Program to display Lower-Trianglar matrix of given
Square matrix.

Code :
```c
#include <stdio.h>

int main()
{
    int a[3][3];
    int i, j;
    system( "cls" );

    printf( "Enter Values of Matrix : \n" );
    for( i=0 ; i<3 ; i++ )
    {
        for( j=0 ; j<3 ; j++ )
        {
            scanf( "%d", &a[ i ][ j ] );
        }
    }

    printf( "\nGiven Matrix-A : \n" );
    for( i=0 ; i<3 ; i++ )
    {
```

```c
        for( j=0 ; j<3 ; j++ )
        {
            printf( " %d", a[ i ][ j ] );
        }
        printf( "\n" );
    }

    printf( "\nLower Triangular Matrix-A : \n" );
    for( i=0 ; i<3 ; i++ )
    {
        for( j=0 ; j<3 ; j++ )
        {
            if( i >= j )
                printf( " %d", a[ i ][ j ] );
            else
                printf( " 0" );
        }
        printf( "\n" );
    }

    system( "pause" );
    return 0;
}
```

Output :

```
TERMINAL

Enter Values of Matrix :
1 2 3 4 5 6 7 8 9

Given Matrix-A :
  1  2  3
  4  5  6
  7  8  9

Lower Triangular Matrix-A :
  1  0  0
  4  5  0
  7  8  9
Press any key to continue . . . 
```

****

****

Chapter – 9
Strings

****

Program No. - 265 :
Program to Input and Display String.

Code :
```c
#include <stdio.h>

int  main()
{
    char str[25];
    system( "cls" );

    printf( "Enter Name : " );
    scanf( "%s", str );

    printf( "\nName = %s\n",  str );
    printf( "Name = " );
    puts( str );

    system( "pause" );
    return 0;
}
```

Output :

```
TERMINAL

Enter Name : Atul

Name = Atul
Name = Atul
Press any key to continue . . .
```

——————————— ******** ———————————

Program No. - 266 :
Program to Input Multiple Words String (Embedded
Blanks) using **gets()** function.

Code :
```c
#include <stdio.h>

int  main()
{
    char str[50];
    system( "cls" );

    printf( "Enter a String : " );
    gets( str );
```

```c
    printf( "\nString = %s\n", str );

    system( "pause" );
    return 0;
}
```

Output :

```
TERMINAL

Enter a String : Atul Kumar Soni

String = Atul Kumar Soni
Press any key to continue . . .
```

——————————— ******** ———————————

Program No. - 267 :
Program to Initialize a String.

Code :
```c
#include <stdio.h>

int  main()
{
    char  s1[ ] = "Atul";
    char  s2[ ] = { 'A', 't', 'u', 'l', '\0' };
    char  s3[5];
    system( "cls" );

    s3[0] = 'A';
    s3[1] = 't';
    s3[2] = 'u';
    s3[3] = 'l';
    s3[4] = '\0';

    printf( "s1 = %s\n", s1 );
    printf( "s2 = %s\n", s2 );
    printf( "s3 = %s\n", s3 );

    system( "pause" );
    return 0;
}
```

Output :

```
TERMINAL

s1 = Atul
s2 = Atul
s3 = Atul
Press any key to continue . . .
```

****

Program No. - 268 :
Program to display a string character-wise.

Code :
```c
#include <stdio.h>

int  main()
{
    char  name[ ] = "ATUL" ;
    int  i = 0 ;
    system( "cls" );

    while( name[ i ] != '\0' )
    {
        printf( " %c\n", name[ i ] ) ;
        i++ ;
    }

    system( "pause" );
    return 0;
}
```

Output :
```
TERMINAL

A
T
U
L
Press any key to continue . . .
```

****

Program No. - 269 :
Program to explain that multiple strings are cancatenated.

Code :
```c
#include <stdio.h>
```

```c
int  main()
{
    char s1[25] = "Atul" "Kumar" "Soni";
    system( "cls" );

    puts( s1 );

    system( "pause" );
    return 0;
}
```

Output :
```
TERMINAL

AtulKumarSoni
Press any key to continue . . .
```

****

Program No. - 270 :
Program to find the length of string using strlen( ) function.

Code :
```c
#include <stdio.h>
#include <string.h>

int  main()
{
    char  str[ ] = "Atul Kumar Soni" ;
    int  len ;
    system( "cls" ) ;

    len = strlen( str ) ;

    printf( "String = %s \nLength = %d\n", str, len ) ;

    system( "pause" );
    return 0;
}
```

Output :
```
TERMINAL

String = Atul Kumar Soni
Length = 15
Press any key to continue . . .
```

---- ******** ----

Program No. - 271 :
Program to copy a string using strcpy( ) function.

Code :
```c
#include <stdio.h>
#include <string.h>

int  main()
{
    char  str1[ ] = "INDIA" ;
    char  str2[25] ;
    system( "cls" );

    strcpy( str2, str1 ) ;

    printf( "String-1 = %s\n", str1 ) ;
    printf( "String-2 = %s\n", str2 ) ;

    system( "pause" );
    return 0;
}
```

Output :

```
TERMINAL

String-1 = INDIA
String-2 = INDIA
Press any key to continue . . .
```

---- ******** ----

Program No. - 272 :
Program to Concat string using strcat( ) function.

Code :
```c
#include <stdio.h>
#include <string.h>

int  main()
{
    char name[50] = "Atul";
    system( "cls" );

    strcat( name, " Kumar" );
```

strcat(name, " Soni");

```c
    printf( "Full Name : %s\n", name );

    system( "pause" );
    return 0;
}
```

Output :

```
TERMINAL

Full Name : Atul Kumar Soni
Press any key to continue . . .
```

---- ******** ----

Program No. - 273 :
Program to Concat Strings using strcat() function.

Code :
```c
#include <stdio.h>
#include <string.h>

int  main()
{
    char name[50];
    system( "cls" );

    strcpy( name, "Atul" );
    strcat( name, " " );
    strcat( name, "Kumar" );
    strcat( name, " " );
    strcat( name, "Soni" );

    printf( "Full Name : %s\n", name );

    system( "pause" );
    return 0;
}
```

Output :

```
TERMINAL

Full Name : Atul Kumar Soni
Press any key to continue . . .
```

---- ******** ----

Program No. - 274 :
Program to use **strcmp()** function to Compare String.

Code :
```c
#include <stdio.h>
#include <string.h>

int  main()
{
    char str1[25] = "ATUL";
    char str2[25] = "ATul";
    int d = 0;
    system( "cls" );

    d = strcmp( str1, str2 );

    printf( "str1 : %s\n", str1 );
    printf( "str2 : %s\n", str2 );
    printf( "\nDifference = %d\n", d );

    if( d == 0 )
        printf( "Strings are same.\n" );
    else
        printf( "Strings are different.\n" );

    system( "pause" );
    return 0;
}
```

Output :
```
TERMINAL
str1 : ATUL
str2 : ATul

Difference = -1
Strings are different.
Press any key to continue . . .
```

---- **** ----

Program No. - 275 :
Program to use **strcmpi()** function to Compare String.

Code :
```c
#include <stdio.h>
#include <string.h>
```

```c
int  main()
{
    char pass[20] = "INDIA", ps[20];
    int ctr = 0;
    system( "cls" );

    printf( "Enter Your Password : " );
    scanf( "%s", ps );

    ctr = strcmpi( pass, ps );

    if( ctr == 0 )
        printf( "\nCorrect password!!!\n" );
    else
        printf( "\nWrong password!!!\n" );

    system( "pause" );
    return 0;
}
```

Output :
```
TERMINAL
Enter Your Password : India

Correct password!!!
Press any key to continue . . .
```

```
TERMINAL
Enter Your Password : Delhi

Wrong password!!!
Press any key to continue . . .
```

---- **** ----

Program No. - 276 :
Program to Swap Two Strings.

Code :
```c
#include <stdio.h>
#include <string.h>

int  main()
{
    char str1[25], str2[25], t[25];
```

```c
system( "cls" );

printf( "Enter Two Strings : " );
scanf( "%s %s", str1, str2 );

printf( "\nStrings Before Swapping are : \n" );
printf( " 1. %s \t 2. %s\n", str1, str2 );

strcpy( t, str1 );
strcpy( str1, str2 );
strcpy( str2, t );

printf( "\nStrings After Swapping are : \n" );
printf( " 1. %s \t 2. %s\n", str1, str2 );

system( "pause" );
return 0;
}
```

Output :

```
TERMINAL

Enter Two Strings : DELHI MUMBAI

Strings Before Swapping are :
 1. DELHI          2. MUMBAI

Strings After Swapping are :
 1. MUMBAI         2. DELHI
Press any key to continue . . .
```

---- **** ----

Program No. - 277 :
Program to explain the use of strrev() string library
function .

Code :
```c
#include <stdio.h>
#include <string.h>

int main()
{
    char s1[25] = "GREEN";
    system( "cls" );

    printf( "Original String : %s\n", s1 );
```

```c
    strrev( s1 );

    printf( "Reversed String : %s\n", s1 );

    system( "pause" );
    return 0;
}
```

Output :

```
TERMINAL

Original String : GREEN
Reversed String : NEERG
Press any key to continue . . .
```

---- **** ----

Program No. - 278 :
Program to check whether the given string is
Palindrome or Not using string library functions.

Code :
```c
#include <stdio.h>
#include <string.h>

int main()
{
    char s1[25] = "RADAR";
    //  char s1[25] = "INDIA";
    char s2[25];
    system( "cls" );

    printf( "Original String : %s\n", s1 );

    strcpy( s2, s1 );
    strrev( s2 );

    printf( "Reversed String : %s\n", s2 );

    if( strcmp(s1, s2) == 0 )
        printf( "%s is a Palindrome.\n", s1 );
    else
        printf( "%s is not a Palindrome.\n", s1 );

    system( "pause" );
    return 0;
}
```

Output :

```
TERMINAL

Original String : RADAR
Reversed String : RADAR
RADAR is a Palindrome.
Press any key to continue . . . _
```

```
TERMINAL

Original String : INDIA
Reversed String : AIDNI
INDIA is not a Palindrome.
Press any key to continue . . . _
```

****

Program No. - 279 :
Program to Remove all Vowels from given string.

Code :
```c
#include <stdio.h>
#include <string.h>

int main()
{
    char s1[25] = "INDIA";
    char s2[25];
    int i, j;
    system( "cls" );

    printf( "Original String : %s\n", s1 );

    j = 0;
    for( i=0 ; s1[ i ]!='\0' ; i++ )
    {
        if( s1[ i ]!='A' && s1[ i ]!='a' && s1[ i ]!='E'
                && s1[ i ]!='e' && s1[ i ]!='I' && s1[ i ]!='i'
                && s1[ i ]!='O' && s1[ i ]!='o'
                && s1[ i ]!='U' && s1[ i ]!='u' )
        {
            s2[ j ] = s1[ i ];
            j++;
        }
    }
    s2[ j ] = '\0';
```

```c
    printf( "String without Vowels : %s\n", s2 );

    system( "pause" );
    return 0;
}
```

Output :

```
TERMINAL

Original String : INDIA
String without Vowels : ND
Press any key to continue . . . _
```

****

Program No. - 280 :
Program to Remove all Vowels from the given string without using second string.

Code :
```c
#include <stdio.h>

int main()
{
    char s1[25] = "INDIA";
    int i, j;
    system( "cls" );

    printf( "Original String : %s\n", s1 );

    i = 0;
    while( s1[ i ] != '\0' )
    {
        if( s1[ i ]=='A' || s1[ i ]=='a' || s1[ i ]=='E'
                || s1[ i ]=='e' || s1[ i ]=='I' || s1[ i ]=='i'
                || s1[ i ]=='O' || s1[ i ]=='o' || s1[ i ]=='U'
                || s1[ i ]=='u' )
        {
            for( j=i ; s1[ j ]!='\0' ; j++ )
                s1[ j ] = s1[ j+1];
        }
        else
            i++;
    }

    printf( "String without Vowels : %s\n", s1 );

    system( "pause" );
```

```
    return 0;
}
```

Output :

```
TERMINAL

Original String : INDIA
String without Vowels : ND
Press any key to continue . . . []
```

****

Program No. - 281 :
Program to find Length of String without using strlen() function.

Code :
```c
#include <stdio.h>

int  main()
{
    char str[50];
    int  i, len;
    system( "cls" );

    printf( "Enter String : " );
    gets( str );

    for( i=0 ; str[ i ] != '\0' ; i++ );

    len = i;

    printf( "\nLength of String : %d\n",  len );

    system( "pause" );
    return 0;
}
```

Output :

```
TERMINAL

Enter String : ATUL

Length of String : 4
Press any key to continue . . . |
```

****

Program No. - 282 :
Program to copy String without using strcpy() function.

Code :
```c
#include <stdio.h>

int  main()
{
    char str1[25] = "Atul Kumar Soni";
    char str2[25];
    int i;
    system( "cls" );

    for ( i=0 ; str1[ i ] != '\0' ; i++ )
    {
        str2[ i ] = str1[ i ];
    }
    str2[ i ] = '\0';

    printf( "str1 = %s\n", str1 );
    printf( "str2 = %s\n", str2 );

    system( "pause" );
    return 0;
}
```

Output :

```
TERMINAL

str1 = Atul Kumar Soni
str2 = Atul Kumar Soni
Press any key to continue . . . |
```

****

Program No. - 283 :
Program to concat String without using strcat() function.

Code :
```c
#include <stdio.h>

int  main()
{
    char str1[50] = "Atul";
    char str2[ ] = " Soni";
    int  i, l;
    system( "cls" );
```

```c
    for ( i=0 ; str1[ i ] != '\0' ; i++ );
    l = i;

    for ( i=0 ; str2[ i ] != '\0' ; i++)
    {
        str1[ l + i ] = str2[ i ];
    }
    str1[ l + i ] = '\0';

    printf( "str1 = %s\n", str1 );
    printf( "str2 = %s\n", str2 );

    system( "pause" );
    return 0;
}
```

Output :

```
TERMINAL

str1 = Atul Soni
str2 =  Soni
Press any key to continue . . .
```

---- **** ----

Program No. - 284 :
Program to Reverse a String without using String function.

Code :
```c
#include <stdio.h>

int  main()
{
    char str1[25], str2[25];
    int i, j, l;
    system( "cls" );

    printf( "Enter a string : " );
    gets( str1 );

    for( i=0 ; str1[ i ] != '\0' ; i++ ) ;
    l = i;

    for( i=0, j=l-1 ; j >= 0 ; j--, i++ )
    {
```

```c
        str2[ i ] = str1[ j ];
    }
    str2[ i ] = '\0';

    printf( "\nReverse : %s\n", str2 );

    system( "pause" );
    return 0;
}
```

Output :

```
TERMINAL

Enter a string : DELHI

Reverse : IHLED
Press any key to continue . . .
```

---- **** ----

Program No. - 285 :
Program to check whether the Input String is Palindrome or not.

Code :
```c
#include <stdio.h>

int  main()
{
    char str[26];
    int i, j, len, flag;

    system( "cls" );

    printf( "Enter the string : " );
    gets( str );

    for( len=0 ; str[len] != '\0' ; len++ ) ;

    flag = 1;
    for( i=0, j=len-1 ; i<len/2 ; i++, j-- )
    {
        if( str[ i ] != str[ j ] )
        {
            flag = 0;
            break;
        }
```

```c
    }

    if( flag == 1 )                    /*  if( flag )  */
        printf( "\nIt is Palindrome.\n" );
    else
        printf( "\nIt is not a Palindrome.\n" );

    system( "pause" );
    return 0;
}
```

Output :

```
TERMINAL

Enter the string : RADAR

It is Palindrome.
Press any key to continue . . .
```

```
TERMINAL

Enter the string : INDIA

It is not a Palindrome.
Press any key to continue . . .
```

****

Program No. - 286 :
Program to Reverse a String without using String functions and Second String.

Code :
```c
#include <stdio.h>

int  main()
{
    int  i, j, len;
    char  ch, str[50];
    system( "cls" );

    printf( "Enter a String : " );
    gets( str );

    printf( "\nGiven String = %s\n", str );

    for( len=0 ; str[ len ] != '\0' ; len++ ) ;
```

```c
    for( i=0, j=len-1 ; i<len/2 ; i++, j-- )
    {
        ch = str[ i ];
        str[ i ] = str[ j ];
        str[ j ] = ch;
    }

    printf( "\nReversed String = %s\n", str );

    system( "pause" );
    return 0;
}
```

Output :

```
TERMINAL

Enter a String : MUMBAI

Given String = MUMBAI
Reversed String = IABMUM
Press any key to continue . . .
```

****

Program No. - 287 :
Program to Count the Number of Vowels in the Sentence.

Code :
```c
#include <conio.h>

int  main()
{
    int  i, j, c;
    char  str[50];
    system( "cls" );

    printf( "Enter String : " );
    gets( str );

    c = 0;
    for( i=0 ; str[ i ] != '\0' ; i++ )
    {
        if( ( str[ i ]=='a' ) || ( str[ i ]=='e' ) || ( str[ i ]=='i' )
                || ( str[ i ]=='o' ) || ( str[ i ]=='u' )
                || ( str[ i ]=='A' ) || ( str[ i ]=='E' )
                || ( str[ i ]=='I' ) || ( str[ i ]=='O' )
                || ( str[ i ]=='U' ) )
```

```
        {
            c++;
        }
    }

    printf( "\nNumber of Vowels = %d\n", c );

    system( "pause" );
    return 0;
}
```

Output :

```
TERMINAL

Enter String : Atul Kumar Soni

Number of Vowels = 6
Press any key to continue . . .
```

———————————— **** ————————————

Program No. - 288 :
Program to convert lowercase characters of string to
uppercase characters.

Code :

```
#include <stdio.h>
#include <ctype.h>

int  main()
{
    char s1[ ] = "india";
    int i;
    system( "cls" );

    printf( "s1 : %s \n", s1 );

    for( i=0 ; s1[ i ] != '\0' ; i++ )
        if( (s1[ i ] >= 97) && (s1[ i ] <= 122) )
            s1[ i ] = toupper( s1[ i ] );

    printf( "s1 : %s \n", s1 );

    system( "pause" );
    return 0;
}
```

Output :

```
TERMINAL

s1 : india
s1 : INDIA
Press any key to continue . . .
```

———————————— **** ————————————

Program No. - 289 :
Program to convert uppercase characters of string to
lowercase characters.

Code :

```
#include <stdio.h>
#include <ctype.h>

int  main()
{
    char s1[ ] = "INDIA";
    int i;
    system( "cls" );

    for( i=0 ; s1[ i ] != '\0' ; i++ )
        if( (s1[ i ] >= 65) && (s1[ i ] <= 90) )
            s1[ i ] = tolower( s1[ i ] );

    printf( "s1 : %s \n", s1 );

    system( "pause" );
    return 0;
}
```

Output :

```
TERMINAL

s1 : india
Press any key to continue . . .
```

———————————— **** ————————————

Program No. - 290 :
Program to Count the Number of Vowels in the
Sentence.

Code :

```
#include <stdio.h>
```

```c
int  main()
{
    int  c, i;
    char  str[50];
    system( "cls" );

    printf( "Enter String : " );
    gets( str );

    c = 0;
    for( i=0 ; str[ i ] != '\0' ; i++ )
    {
        switch( str[ i ] )
        {
            case 'a':
            case 'A':
            case 'e':
            case 'E':
            case 'i':
            case 'I':
            case 'o':
            case 'O':
            case 'u':
            case 'U':
                c++;
        }
    }

    printf( "\nNumber of Vowels = %d\n", c );

    system( "pause" );
    return 0;
}
```

Output :

```
TERMINAL

Enter String : Atul Kumar Soni

Number of Vowels = 6
Press any key to continue . . .|
```

——————————— **** ———————————

Program No. - 291 :
Program to count Number of Words and Number of
Characters in Given String.

Code :
```c
#include <stdio.h>

int  main()
{
    char str[25];
    int  i, c = 0, w = 1;
    system( "cls" );

    printf( "Enter String : " );
    gets( str );

    for( i=0 ; str[ i ] != '\0' ; i++ )
    {
        if( ( str[ i ] == ' ' ) && ( str[ i−1 ] != ' ' ) )
            w++;
        else if( str[ i ] != '.' )
            c++;
    }

    printf( "\nNumber of words : %d\n", w );
    printf( "Number of characters : %d\n", c );

    system( "pause" );
    return 0;
}
```

Output :

```
TERMINAL

Enter String : Atul Kumar Soni

Number of words : 3
Number of characters : 13
Press any key to continue . . .|
```

——————————— **** ———————————

Program No.- 292 :
Program to show the use of while loop in string.

Code :
```c
#include <stdio.h>

int  main()
{
    char  name[ ] = "Atul Kumar Soni" ;
```

```c
    int  i = 0 ;
    system( "cls" );

    while( name[ i ] != '\0' )        /* while( name[ i ] ) */
    {
        printf( "%c", name[ i ] );
        i++ ;
    }

    printf( "\n" );
    system( "pause" );
    return 0;
}
```

Output :

```
TERMINAL
Atul Kumar Soni
Press any key to continue . . . |
```

____________ **** ____________

Program No. - 293 :
Program to use pointer to access string character-wise.

Code :
```c
#include <stdio.h>

int  main()
{
    char  name[ ] = "Atul Kumar Soni" ;
    char  *ptr ;
    system( "cls" );

    ptr = name ;      /* store base address of string */

    while( *ptr != '\0' )
    {
        printf( "%c", *ptr ) ;
        ptr++ ;
    }

    printf( "\n" );
    system( "pause" );
    return 0;
}
```

Output :

```
TERMINAL
Atul Kumar Soni
Press any key to continue . . . |
```

____________ **** ____________

Program No. - 294 :
Program to Sort all characters of string in Ascending Order.

Code :
```c
#include <stdio.h>
#include <string.h>

int main()
{
    char s1[25] = "INDIA", ch;
    int i, j, l;
    system( "cls" );

    printf( "Original String : %s\n", s1 );

    len = strlen( s1 );
    for( i=0 ; i<len-1 ; i++ )
    {
        for( j=0 ; j<len−1−i ; j++ )
        {
            if( s1[ j ] > s1[ j+1] )
            {
                ch = s1[ j ];
                s1[ j ] = s1[ j+1];
                s1[ j+1] = ch;
            }
        }
    }

    printf( "Sorted String : %s\n", s1 );

    system( "pause" );
    return 0;
}
```

Output :

```
TERMINAL

Original String : INDIA
Sorted String : ADIIN
Press any key to continue . . . []
```

****

Program No. - 295 :
Program to check whether input character is Capital letter, Small letter, Digit or Special Symbol.

Code :
```c
#include <stdio.h>
#include <ctype.h>

int  main()
{
    char ch;
    system( "cls" );

    printf( "Enter a character : " );
    scanf( "%c", &ch );

    if( isupper( ch ) )
        printf( "\nCharacter %c is in Upper Case.\n",
                                                ch );
    else if( islower( ch ) )
        printf( "\nCharacter %c is in Lower Case.\n",
                                                ch );
    else if( isdigit( ch ) )
        printf( "\nCharacter %c is a Digit.\n", ch );
    else
        printf( "\nCharacter %c is a Special Symbol.\n",
                                                ch );

    system( "pause" );
    return 0;
}
```

Output :
```
TERMINAL

Enter a character : A

Character A is in Upper Case.
Press any key to continue . . . |
```

```
TERMINAL

Enter a character : b

Character b is in Lower Case.
Press any key to continue . . . |
```

```
TERMINAL

Enter a character : 5

Character 5 is a Digit.
Press any key to continue . . . |
```

```
TERMINAL

Enter a character : @

Character @ is a Special Symbol.
Press any key to continue . . . |
```

****

Program No. - 296 :
Program to count number of Capital letters, Small letters, Digits and Special Symbols.

Code :
```c
#include <stdio.h>

int  main()
{
    int i, c = 0, sm = 0, d = 0, ss = 0;
    char s[50];
    system( "cls" );

    printf( "Enter a String : " );
    gets( s );

    for( i=0 ; s[ i ] != '\0' ; i++ )
    {
        if( s[ i ] >= 65 && s[ i ] <= 90 )
            c++;
        else if( s[ i ] >= 97 && s[ i ] <= 122 )
            sm++;
        else if( s[ i ] >= 48 && s[ i ] <= 57 )
            d++;
        else
```

```
        ss++;
    }

    printf( "\nNumber of Capital Letters : %d\n", c );
    printf( "Number of Small Letters   : %d\n", sm );
    printf( "Number of Digits          : %d\n", d );
    printf( "Number of Special Symbols : %d\n", ss );

    system( "pause" );
    return 0;
}
```

Output :

```
TERMINAL

Enter a String : INdiaDeLHi$@$125

Number of Capital Letters : 5
Number of Small Letters   : 5
Number of Digits          : 3
Number of Special Symbols : 3
Press any key to continue . . .
```

---- **** ----

Program No. - 297 :
Program to count number of Capital letters, Small letters, Digits and Special Symbols.

Code :
```c
#include <stdio.h>

int  main()
{
    int i, c = 0, sm = 0, d = 0, ss = 0;
    char s[50];
    system( "cls" );

    printf( "Enter a String : " );
    gets( s );

    for( i=0 ; s[ i ] != '\0' ; i++ )
    {
        if( s[ i ] >= 'A' && s[ i ] <= 'Z' )
            c++;
        else if( s[ i ] >= 'a' && s[ i ] <= 'z' )
            sm++;
        else if( s[ i ] >= '0' && s[ i ] <= '9' )
```

```
            d++;
        else
            ss++;
    }

    printf( "\nNumber of Capital Letters : %d\n", c );
    printf( "Number of Small Letters   : %d\n", sm );
    printf( "Number of Digits          : %d\n", d );
    printf( "Number of Special Symbols : %d\n", ss );

    system( "pause" );
    return 0;
}
```

Output :

```
TERMINAL

Enter a String : 12345***ATULsoni$#$

Number of Capital Letters : 4
Number of Small Letters   : 4
Number of Digits          : 5
Number of Special Symbols : 6
Press any key to continue . . .
```

---- **** ----

Program No. - 298 :
Program to count number of Capital letters, Small letters, Digits and Special Symbols.

Code :
```c
#include <stdio.h>
#include <ctype.h>

int  main()
{
    int i, c = 0, sm = 0, d = 0, ss = 0;
    char s[50];
    system( "cls" );

    printf( "Enter a String : " );
    gets( s );

    for( i=0 ; s[ i ] != '\0' ; i++ )
    {
        if( isupper( s[ i ] ) )
            c++;
```

```c
        else if( islower( s[ i ] ) )
            sm++;
        else if( isdigit( s[ i ] ) )
            d++;
        else
            ss++;
    }

    printf( "\nNumber of Capital Letters : %d\n", c );
    printf( "Number of Small Letters   : %d\n", sm );
    printf( "Number of Digits          : %d\n", d );
    printf( "Number of Special Symbols : %d\n", ss );

    system( "pause" );
    return 0;
}
```

Output :

```
TERMINAL

Enter a String : DELHI123456india***$$$***

Number of Capital Letters : 5
Number of Small Letters   : 5
Number of Digits          : 6
Number of Special Symbols : 9
Press any key to continue . . .
```

****

Program No. - 299 :
Program to explain the array of strings.

Code :
```c
#include <stdio.h>

int  main()
{
    char str[ ][15] = { "RED", "GREEN", "BLUE" };
    int i;
    system( "cls" );

    for( i = 0 ; i<3 ; i++ )
    {
        printf( " %s\n", str[ i ] );
    }

    system( "pause" );
```

```c
    return 0;
}
```

Output :

```
TERMINAL

 RED
 GREEN
 BLUE
Press any key to continue . . .
```

****

Program No. - 300 :
Program to sort array of strings (two dimensional char array).

Code :
```c
#include <stdio.h>
#include <string.h>

int  main()
{
    char  colors[5][10] = {    "RED",
                               "GREEN",
                               "BLUE",
                               "ORANGE",
                               "YELLOW"
                          };
    int  i, j;
    char  temp[10];
    system( "cls" );

    printf( "Colors before Sorting :\n" );
    for( i = 0 ; i<5 ; i++ )
    {
        printf( " %s\n", colors[ i ] );
    }

    for( i=0 ; i<5-1 ; i++ )
    {
        for( j=0 ; j<5-1-i ; j++ )
        {
            if( strcmp( colors[ j ], colors[ j + 1 ] ) > 0 )
            {
                strcpy( temp, colors[ j ] );
                strcpy( colors[ j ], colors[ j + 1 ] );
```

```c
            strcpy( colors[ j + 1 ], temp );
        }
    }
}

    printf( "\nColors after Sorting :\n" );
    for( i = 0 ; i<5 ; i++ )
    {
        printf( " %s\n", colors[ i ] );
    }

    system( "pause" );
    return 0;
}
```

Output :

```
TERMINAL

Colors before Sorting :
 RED
 GREEN
 BLUE
 ORANGE
 YELLOW

Colors after Sorting :
 BLUE
 GREEN
 ORANGE
 RED
 YELLOW
Press any key to continue . . . |
```

****

Program No. - 301 :
Program to convert each digits of a number in English word.

Code :
```c
#include <stdio.h>

int main()
{
    int num, i=0, j, dig;
    char *word[10] = { "Zero", "One", "Two", "Three",
                       "Four", "Five", "Six", "Seven",
                       "Eight", "Nine" };
    char *num_names[10];
```

```c
    system( "cls" );

    printf( "Enter any Number : " );
    scanf( "%d", &num );

    i = 0;
    while( num )
    {
        dig = num % 10;
        num_names[ i++ ] = word[ dig ];
        num = num / 10;
    }

    for( j=i-1 ; j>=0 ; j-- )
    {
        printf( "%s ", num_names[ j ] );
    }

    printf( "\n" );
    system( "pause" );
    return 0;
}
```

Output :

```
TERMINAL

Enter any Number : 123456
One Two Three Four Five Six
Press any key to continue . . . []
```

****

Program No. - 302 :
Program to convert each digits of a number in English word.

Code :
```c
#include <stdio.h>

int main()
{
    int num, i=0, j, dig;
    char *num_names[10];
    system( "cls" );

    printf( "Enter any Number : " );
    scanf( "%d", &num );
```

```c
    i = 0;
    while( num )
    {
        dig = num % 10;
        num = num / 10;

        switch( dig )
        {
            case 0: num_names[ i ] = "Zero"; break;
            case 1: num_names[ i ] = "One"; break;
            case 2: num_names[ i ] = "Two"; break;
            case 3: num_names[ i ] = "Three"; break;
            case 4: num_names[ i ] = "Four"; break;
            case 5: num_names[ i ] = "Five"; break;
            case 6: num_names[ i ] = "Six"; break;
            case 7: num_names[ i ] = "Seven"; break;
            case 8: num_names[ i ] = "Eight"; break;
            case 9: num_names[ i ] = "Nine"; break;
        }
        i++;
    }

    for( j=i-1 ; j>=0 ; j-- )
    {
        printf( "%s ", num_names[ j ] );
    }

    printf( "\n" );
    system( "pause" );
    return 0;
}
```

Output :

```
TERMINAL

Enter any Number : 13579246
One Three Five Seven Nine Two Four Six
Press any key to continue . . .
```

****

****

Chapter – 10
Functions

****

Program No. - 303 :
Program to Simple Function.

Code :
```c
#include <stdio.h>

void  show( int x );              // Function
Declaration/Prototype

int  main()
{
    int a = 10;
    system( "cls" );

    show( a );                    // Calling of Function

    system( "pause" );
    return 0;
}

void  show( int x )               // Function Definition
{
    printf( "x = %d\n", x );
}
```

Output :

```
TERMINAL

x = 10
Press any key to continue . . . |
```

****

Program No. - 304 :
Program to Eliminate Function Declaration with Function Definition at Top.

Code :
```c
#include <stdio.h>

// Eliminating declaration.
void  show( int x )
{
    printf( "x = %d\n", x );
}

int  main()
```

{
```c
    int a = 10;
    system( "cls" );

    show( a );

    system( "pause" );
    return 0;
}
```

Output :

```
TERMINAL

x = 10
Press any key to continue . . . |
```

****

Program No. - 305 :
Program to explain returning value from function.

Code :
```c
// returning value
#include <stdio.h> >

int sum( int, int );

int  main( void )
{
    int s1;
    system( "cls" );

    s1 = sum( 10, 20 );

    printf( "Sum : %d\n", s1 );

    system( "pause" );
    return 0;
}

int sum( int x, int y )
{
    return (x + y);
}
```

Output :

```
TERMINAL

Sum : 30
Press any key to continue . . .
```

****

Program No. - 306 :
Program to explain the calling of function from printf() statement.

Code :
```c
// calling in printf()
#include <stdio.h>

int sum( int, int );

int  main( void )
{
    system( "cls" );

    printf( "\nSum : %d\n", sum( 10, 20 ) );

    system( "pause" );
    return 0;
}

int sum( int x, int y )
{
    return (x + y);
}
```

Output :
```
TERMINAL

Sum : 30
Press any key to continue . . .
```

****

Program No. - 307 :
Program to calculate Simple Interest using Function (**No Argument and No Return Value**).

Code :
```c
#include <stdio.h>
```

```c
void  Simp_Int();

int  main()
{
    system( "cls" );

    Simp_Int();

    system( "pause" );
    return 0;
}

void  Simp_Int()
{
    float p, r, t, si;
    printf( "Enter Principal, Rate and Time : " );
    scanf( "%f %f %f", &p, &r, &t );

    si = ( p * r * t ) / 100;

    printf( "\nSimple Interest = %f\n", si );
}
```

Output :
```
TERMINAL

Enter Principal, Rate and Time : 1000 10 3

Simple Interest = 300.000000
Press any key to continue . . .
```

****

Program No. - 308 :
Program to calculate Simple Interest using Function (**No Argument but Return Value**).

Code :
```c
#include <stdio.h>

float  Simp_Int();

int  main()
{
    float si1;
    system( "cls" );
```

```c
    si1 = Simp_Int();

    printf( "\nSimple Interest = %f\n", si1 );

    system( "pause" );
    return 0;
}

float  Simp_Int()
{
    float p, r, t, si;
    printf( "Enter Principal, Rate and Time : " );
    scanf( "%f %f %f", &p, &r, &t );

    si = ( p * r * t ) / 100;

    return si;
}
```

Output :

```
TERMINAL

Enter Principal, Rate and Time : 1000 10 3

Simple Interest = 300.000000
Press any key to continue . . .
```

——————————— **** ———————————

Program No. - 309 :
Program to calculate Simple Interest using Function (
Argument but No Return Value).

Code :
```c
#include <stdio.h>

void  Simp_Int( float, float, float );

int  main()
{
    float p1, r1, t1;
    system( "cls" );

    printf( "Enter Principal, Rate and Time : " );
    scanf( "%f %f %f", &p1, &r1, &t1 );

    Simp_Int( p1, r1, t1 );
```

```c
    system( "pause" );
    return 0;
}

void  Simp_Int( float p, float r, float t )
{
    float si;

    si = ( p * r * t ) / 100;

    printf( "\nSimple Interest = %f\n", si );
}
```

Output :

```
TERMINAL

Enter Principal, Rate and Time : 2000 10 3

Simple Interest = 600.000000
Press any key to continue . . .
```

——————————— **** ———————————

Program No. - 310 :
Program to calculate Simple Interest using Function (
Argument and Return Value).

Code :
```c
#include <stdio.h>

float  Simp_Int( float, float, float );

int  main()
{
    float p1, r1, t1, si1;
    system( "cls" );

    printf( "Enter Principal, Rate and Time : " );
    scanf( "%f %f %f", &p1, &r1, &t1 );

    si1 = Simp_Int( p1, r1, t1 );

    printf( "\nSimple Interest = %f\n", si1 );

    system( "pause" );
    return 0;
}
```

```
float  Simp_Int( float p, float r, float t )
{
    float si;

    si = ( p * r * t ) / 100;

    return si;
}
```

Output :

```
TERMINAL

Enter Principal, Rate and Time : 2000 10 3

Simple Interest = 600.000000
Press any key to continue . . .
```

____________________ **** ____________________

Program No. - 311 :
Program to use return statement in void function to
terminate the function.

Code :
```
#include <stdio.h>

void show();

int  main()
{
    system( "cls" );
    printf( "Red\n" );
    show();
    printf( "Blue\n" );
    system( "pause" );
    return 0;
}

void show()
{
    printf( "Green\n" );
    return;
    printf( "Orange\n" );
}
```

Output :

```
TERMINAL

Red
Green
Blue
Press any key to continue . . .
```

____________________ **** ____________________

Program No. - 312 :
Program to explain **Call By Value**.

Code :
```
#include <stdio.h>

void  cube( int );

int  main()
{
    int a = 10;
    system( "cls" );

    cube( a );

    printf( "a = %d\n", a );

    system( "pause" );
    return 0;
}

void  cube( int  x )
{
    x = x * x * x;
    printf( "x = %d\n", x );
}
```

Output :

```
TERMINAL

x = 1000
a = 10
Press any key to continue . . .
```

____________________ **** ____________________

Program No. - 313 :
Program to explain **Call By Address / Pointer**.

Code :

```c
#include <stdio.h>

void  cube( int* );

int  main()
{
    int a = 10;
    system( "cls" );

    cube( &a );

    printf( "a = %d\n", a );

    system( "pause" );
    return 0;
}

void  cube( int *pa )
{
    *pa = (*pa) * (*pa) * (*pa);
    printf( "*pa = %d\n", *pa );
}
```

Output :

```
TERMINAL

*pa = 1000
a = 1000
Press any key to continue . . .
```

———————————— **** ————————————

Program No. - 314 :
Program to Swap two numbers using **Call By Value**.

Code :

```c
#include <stdio.h>

void  swap( int, int );

int  main()
{
    int a = 10, b = 20;
    system( "cls" );

    printf( "Before Swapping (in main) : a = %d,
                             b = %d\n", a, b );

    swap( a, b );

    printf( "After Swapping (in main)  : a = %d,
                             b = %d\n", a, b );

    system( "pause" );
    return 0;
}

void  swap( int x, int y )
{
    int t;
    printf( "Before Swapping (in swap) : x = %d,
                             y = %d\n", x, y );

    t = x;
    x = y;
    y = t;

    printf( "After Swapping (in swap)  : x = %d,
                             y = %d\n", x, y );
}
```

Output :

```
TERMINAL

Before Swapping (in main) : a = 10, b = 20
Before Swapping (in swap) : x = 10, y = 20
After Swapping (in swap)   : x = 20, y = 10
After Swapping (in main)   : a = 10, b = 20
Press any key to continue . . .
```

———————————— **** ————————————

Program No. - 315 :
Program to Swap two numbers using **Call By Reference / Address / Pointer**.

Code :

```c
#include <stdio.h>

void  swap( int*, int* );

int  main()
{
    int a = 10, b = 20;
    system( "cls" );
```

```c
    printf( "Before Swapping (in main) : a = %d,
                                    b = %d\n", a, b );

    swap( &a, &b );

    printf( "After Swapping (in main)  : a = %d,
                                    b = %d\n", a, b );

    system( "pause" );
    return 0;
}

void  swap( int *pa, int *pb )
{
    int t;
    printf( "Before Swapping (in swap) : *pa = %d,
                                    *pb = %d\n", *pa, *pb );

    t = *pa;
    *pa = *pb;
    *pb = t;

    printf( "After Swapping (in swap)  : *pa = %d,
                                    *pb = %d\n", *pa, *pb );
}
```

Output :

```
TERMINAL

Before Swapping (in main) : a = 10, b = 20
Before Swapping (in swap) : *pa = 10, *pb = 20
After Swapping (in swap)  : *pa = 20, *pb = 10
After Swapping (in main)  : a = 20, b = 10
Press any key to continue . . .
```

------------------------- **** -------------------------

Program No. - 316 :
Program to explain **Returning By Reference / Address / Pointer**.

Code :
```c
#include <stdio.h>

int*  max( int*, int* );

int  main()
```

```c
{
    int a = 10, b = 20, *p;
    system( "cls" );

    p = max( &a, &b );

    printf( "Maximum = %d\n", *p );

    system( "pause" );
    return 0;
}

int*  max( int *pa, int *pb )
{
    if( *pa > *pb )
        return pa;
    else
        return pb;
}
```

Output :

```
TERMINAL

Maximum = 20
Press any key to continue . . .
```

Program No. - 317 :
Program for passing Array to function.

Code :
```c
#include <stdio.h>

/* void  display( int* );     */
void  display( int[ ] );

int  main()
{
    int a[ ] = { 10, 20, 30, 40, 50 };
    system( "cls" );

    display( a );

    printf( "\n" );
    system( "pause" );
    return 0;
}
```

```c
/* void  display( int *x )   */
void  display( int x[ ] )
{
    int i;
    for( i=0 ; i<5 ; i++ )
    {
        printf( " %d", x[ i ] );      /*  *( x + i )  */
    }
}
```

Output :

```
TERMINAL

 10   20   30   40   50
Press  any  key  to  continue  .  .  .  |
```

――――――――― **** ―――――――――

Program No. - 318 :
Program for passing 2D Array to function.

Code :
```c
#include <stdio.h>

void  display( int[ ][3] );

int  main()
{
    int a[ ][3] = { { 10, 20, 30 },
              { 40, 50, 60 } };
    system( "cls" );

    display( a );

    system( "pause" );
    return 0;
}

void  display( int x[ ][3] )
{
    int i, j;
    printf( "Matrix-A : \n" );
    for( i=0 ; i<2 ; i++ )
    {
        for( j=0 ; j<3 ; j++ )
        {
            printf( " %d", x[ i ][ j ] );
```

```c
        }
        printf( "\n" );
    }
}
```

Output :

```
TERMINAL

Matrix-A :
  10   20   30
  40   50   60
Press  any  key  to  continue  .  .  .  |
```

――――――――― **** ―――――――――

Program No. - 319 :
Program for passing String to function.

Code :
```c
#include <stdio.h>

/* void  display( char* );  */
void  display( char[ ] );

int  main()
{
    char s[ ] = "ATUL";
    system( "cls" );

    display( s );

    system( "pause" );
    return 0;
}

/* void  display( char *s1 )    */
void  display( char s1[ ] )
{
    int i;
    printf( "%s\n", s1 );
    for( i=0 ; s1[ i ] != '\0' ; i++ )
    {
        printf( "%c\n", s1[ i ] );        /*  *( s1 + i )  */
    }
}
```

Output :

```
TERMINAL

ATUL
A
T
U
L
Press any key to continue . . . |
```

———————— **** ————————

Program No. - 320 :
Program for passing Array of Strings to function.

Code :
```c
#include <stdio.h>

void  display( char[ ][10] );

int  main()
{
    char s[ ][10] = { "Red", "Green", "Blue" };
    system( "cls" );

    display( s );

    printf( "\n" );
    system( "pause" );
    return 0;
}

void  display( char s1[ ][10] )
{
    int i;
    printf( "Colors are :" );
    for( i=0 ; i<3 ; i++ )
    {
        printf( " %s", s1[ i ] );
    }
}
```

Output :
```
TERMINAL

Colors are : Red Green Blue
Press any key to continue . . . |
```

———————— **** ————————

Program No. - 321 :
Program for passing Array Elements by value to function.

Code :
```c
#include <stdio.h>

void  display( int );

int  main( )
{
    int  i ;
    int  a[ ] = { 10, 20, 30, 40, 50 } ;
    system( "cls" );

    for ( i = 0 ; i< 5 ; i++ )
    {
        display( a[ i ] ) ;
    }

    printf( "\n" );
    system( "pause" );
    return 0;
}

void  display( int n )
{
    printf( "  %d", n ) ;
}
```

Output :
```
TERMINAL

 10   20   30   40   50
Press  any  key  to  continue  . . . |
```

———————— **** ————————

Program No. - 322 :
Program for passing array elements by reference to function.

Code :
```c
#include <stdio.h>

void  display( int* );
```

```c
int  main( )
{
    int  i ;
    int  a[ ] = { 10, 20, 30, 40, 50 } ;
    system( "cls" );

    for ( i = 0 ; i< 5 ; i++ )
    {
        display( &a[ i ] ) ;
    }

    printf( "\n" );
    system( "pause" );
    return 0;
}

void  display( int *p )
{
    printf( " %d", *p ) ;
}
```

Output :

```
TERMINAL

    10   20   30   40   50
Press any key to continue . . . |
```

——————————— **** ———————————

Program No. - 323 :
Program to find Factorial of given Number without
Recursion.

Code :
```c
#include <stdio.h>

long  fact( long );

int  main()
{
    long n, f;
    system( "cls" );

    printf( "Enter the Number : " );
    scanf( "%ld", &n );
```

```c
    f = fact( n );
    printf( "\nFactorial = %ld\n", f );

    system( "pause" );
    return 0;
}

long  fact( long a )
{
    long f = 1;
    int i;
    for( i=1 ; i<= a ; i++ )
    {
        f = f * i;
    }
    return f;
}
```

Output :

```
TERMINAL

Enter the Number : 5

Factorial = 120
Press any key to continue . . . |
```

```
TERMINAL

Enter the Number : 12

Factorial = 479001600
Press any key to continue . . . |
```

——————————— **** ———————————

Program No. - 324 :
Program to calculate Factorial using Recursion.

Code :
```c
#include <stdio.h>

long  fact( long );

int  main()
{
    long n, f;
    system( "cls" );
```

```c
    printf( "Enter any Number : " );
    scanf( "%ld", &n );

    f = fact( n );

    printf( "\nFactorial = %ld\n", f );

    system( "pause" );
    return 0;
}

long  fact( long a )
{
    if( a == 1 )
        return 1;
    else
        return  a * fact( a - 1 );
}
```

Output :

```
TERMINAL

Enter any Number : 5

Factorial = 120
Press any key to continue . . . |
```

———————————— **** ————————————

Program No. - 325 :
Program to find the sum of first n Natural number by recursive function.

Code :
```c
#include <stdio.h>

int  sum( int );

int  main()
{
    int num, s;
    system( "cls" );

    printf( "Enter a Number : " );
    scanf( "%d", &num );

    s = sum( num );
    printf( "\nSum of %d Natural Number = %d\n",
```

```c
                                        num, s );

    system( "pause" );
    return 0;
}

int  sum( int n )
{
    if( n == 1 )
        return 1;
    else
        return  n + sum( n - 1 );
}
```

Output :

```
TERMINAL

Enter a Number : 10

Sum of 10 Natural Number = 55
Press any key to continue . . . |
```

———————————— **** ————————————

Program No. - 326 :
Program to find nth power of x using Recursion.

Code :
```c
#include <stdio.h>

int  power( int, int );

int  main()
{
    int  x, n, p;
    system( "cls" );

    printf( "Enter the Base : " );
    scanf( "%d", &x );
    printf( "Enter the Exponent/Power : " );
    scanf( "%d", &n );

    p = power( x, n );

    printf( "\nPower = %d\n", p );

    system( "pause" );
    return 0;
```

```c
}

int  power( int x, int n )
{
    if( n == 0 )
        return 1;
    else
        return  x * power( x, n − 1 );
}
```

Output :

```
TERMINAL

Enter the Base : 5
Enter the Exponent/Power : 3

Power = 125
Press any key to continue . . . |
```

****

Program No. - 327 :
Program to find nth term of Fibonacci Series using
Recursion.

Code :
```c
#include <stdio.h>

int  fibo( int );

int  main()
{
    int n, t;
    system( "cls" );

    printf( "Enter Term Position : " );
    scanf( "%d", &n );

    t = fibo( n );

    printf( "\n%dth term of Fibonacci series = %d\n",
                                                n, t );

    system( "pause" );
    return 0;
}

int  fibo( int n )
```

```c
{
    if( n == 0 || n == 1 )
        return n;
    else
        return  fibo( n − 1 ) + fibo( n − 2 );
}
```

Output :

```
TERMINAL

Enter Term Position : 5

5th term of Fibonacci series = 5
Press any key to continue . . . |
```

****

Program No. - 328 :
Program to find nth term of Lucas Series using
Recursion.

Code :
```c
#include <stdio.h>

int  lucas( int );

int  main()
{
    int n, t;
    system( "cls" );

    printf( "Enter Term Position : " );
    scanf( "%d", &n );

    t = lucas( n );

    printf( "\n%dth term of Lucas series is = %d\n", n, t );

    system( "pause" );
    return 0;
}

int  lucas( int n )
{
    if( n == 0 || n == 1 || n == 2 )
        return 1;
    else
        return  lucas(n − 1) + lucas(n − 2) + lucas(n − 3);
```

```
}
```

Output :

```
TERMINAL

Enter Term Position : 5

5th term of Lucas series is = 9
Press any key to continue . . .
```

———————————— ******** ————————————

Program No. - 329 :
Program to find Length of String using function (Passing String).

Code :
```c
#include <stdio.h>

int  length( char s[ ] )
{
    int i, l = 0;

    for( i=0 ; s[ i ] != '\0' ; i++ );
    l = i;

    return l;
}

int  main()
{
    int  len = 0;
    char str[50];
    system( "cls" );

    printf( "Enter a String : " );
    gets( str );

    len = length( str );

    printf( "\nLength of the String = %d\n", len );

    system( "pause" );
    return 0;
}
```

Output :

```
TERMINAL

Enter a String : Atul Kumar Soni

Length of the String = 15
Press any key to continue . . .
```

———————————— ******** ————————————

Program No. - 330 :
Program to explain **Constant Argument** to function.

Code :
```c
#include <stdio.h>

void  show( const int );

int  main()
{
    int a = 10;
    system( "cls" );

    show( a );

    printf( "a = %d\n",  a );

    system( "pause" );
    return 0;
}

void  show( const int b )
{
    /*  b = 20;   */        /*  can't be changed.   */
    printf( "b = %d\n", b );
}
```

Output :

```
TERMINAL

b = 10
a = 10
Press any key to continue . . .
```

———————————— ******** ————————————

Program No. - 331 :
Program to explain Function with Constant Argument.

Code :
```c
#include <stdio.h>

const  float  PI = 3.1415926;

float  area( const float r )
{
    return ( PI * r * r );
}

int  main()
{
    float radius, ar;
    system( "cls" );

    printf( "Enter the radius of a Circle : " );
    scanf( "%f", &radius );

    ar = area( radius );

    printf( "\nThe area of circle is %f\n", ar );

    system( "pause" );
    return 0;
}
```

Output :

```
TERMINAL
Enter the radius of a Circle : 10.0

The area of circle is 314.159241
Press any key to continue . . .
```

****

Program No. - 332 :
Program to Return Multiple Values from Function using
Reference.

Code :
```c
#include <stdio.h>

void  AreaCircum( float, float*, float* );

int  main()
{
    float radius, area, circum;
```

```c
    system( "cls" );

    printf( "Enter a Radius : " );
    scanf( "%f", &radius );

    AreaCircum( radius, &area, &circum );

    printf( "\nArea of Circle = %f\n", area );
    printf( "Circumference of Circle = %f\n", circum );

    system( "pause" );
    return 0;
}

void  AreaCircum( float r, float *par, float *pcir )
{
    *par = 3.14 * r * r;
    *pcir = 2 * 3.14 * r;
}
```

Output :

```
TERMINAL
Enter a Radius : 10

Area of Circle = 314.000000
Circumference of Circle = 62.799999
Press any key to continue . . .
```

****

Program No. - 333 :
Program to Return Multiple Values from Function using
call by reference.

Code :
```c
#include <stdio.h>

int  main()
{
    void intfrac( float, float*, float* );
    float number, intpart, fracpart;
    system( "cls" );

    printf( "Enter a Real Number : " );
    scanf( "%f", &number );

    intfrac( number, &intpart, &fracpart );
```

```c
    printf( "\nInteger part  = %.0f\n", intpart );
    printf( "Fraction part = %f\n", fracpart );

    system( "pause" );
    return 0;
}

void  intfrac( float n, float *intp, float *fracp )
{
    *intp = (float)( (long)n ) ;
    *fracp = n - *intp;
}
```

Output :

```
TERMINAL
Enter a Real Number : 12.345

Integer part  = 12
Fraction part = 0.345000
Press any key to continue . . .
```

---- **** ----

Program No. - 334 :
Program to explain Nesting of Functions.

Code :

```c
#include <stdio.h>

void  func2();

void  func1()
{
    printf( "function1-1 \n" );
    func2();
    printf( "function1-2 \n" );
}

void  func2()
{
    printf( "function2-1 \n" );
}

int  main()
{
    system( "cls" );
```

```c
    printf( "main-1 \n" );
    func1();
    printf( "main-2 \n" );

    system( "pause" );
    return 0;
}
```

Output :

```
TERMINAL
main-1
function1-1
function2-1
function1-2
main-2
Press any key to continue . . .
```

---- **** ----

Program No. - 335 :
Program to explain Nested function call.

Code :

```c
#include <stdio.h>

int main()
{
    int add( int, int );
    int a = 10, b = 15, s;
    system( "cls" );

    s = add( add(a, b), add(a, b) );
    printf( "Result : %d \n", s );

    system( "pause" );
    return 0;
}

int add( int a, int b )
{
    return ( a + b );
}
```

Output :

```
TERMINAL

Result : 50
Press any key to continue . . . []
```

****

Program No. - 336 :
Program to Find the Number of Permutations without repeatation.
(i.e., nPr = n! / (n−r)!.

Code :
```c
#include <stdio.h>

int  fact( int );

int  main()
{
    int n, r, p;
    system( "cls" );

    printf( "Enter Value of n and r : " );
    scanf( "%d %d", &n, &r );

    p = fact( n ) / fact( n − r );

    printf( "\nnPr : %d\n", p );

    system( "pause" );
    return 0;
}

int  fact( int a )
{
    int  i, f=1;
    for( i=1 ; i<=a ; i++ )
    {
        f = f * i;
    }
    return  f;
}
```

Output :

```
TERMINAL

Enter Value of n and r : 3 2

nPr : 6
Press any key to continue . . . |
```

****

Program No. - 337 :
Program to Find the Number of Combinations without repeatation.
(i.e., nCr = n! / (r! * (n−r)!).

Code :
```c
#include <stdio.h>

int  fact( int );

int  main()
{
    int n, r, p;
    system( "cls" );

    printf( "Enter Value of n and r : " );
    scanf( "%d %d", &n, &r );

    p = fact( n ) / ( fact( r ) * fact( n − r ) );

    printf( "\nnCr : %d\n", p );

    system( "pause" );
    return 0;
}

int  fact( int a )
{
    int  i, f=1;
    for( i=1 ; i<=a ; i++ )
    {
        f = f * i;
    }
    return  f;
}
```

Output :

```
TERMINAL

Enter Value of n and r : 3 2

nCr : 3
Press any key to continue . . .
```

****

Program No. - 338 :
Program to check   whether a number can be
expressed as sum of two prime numbers or not.

Code :

```c
#include <stdio.h>

int main()
{
    int n, i, flag=0;
    system( "cls" );

    printf( "Enter a Number : " );
    scanf( "%d", &n );

    for( i=2 ; i<=n/2 ; i++ )
    {
        if( ( isprime( i ) != 0 ) && ( isprime( n-i ) != 0 ) )
        {
            printf( "%2d = %2d + %2d\n", n, i, (n-i) );
            flag = 1;
        }
    }

    if( flag == 0 )
        printf( "%d can not be expressed as sum of
                            two Prime Numbers.\n", n );

    system( "pause" );
    return 0;
}

int  isprime( int n )
{
    int i, flag=1;
    for( i=2 ; i<=n/2 ; i++ )
    {
        if( n % i == 0 )
            flag = 0;
```

```
    }
    return flag;
}
```

Output :

```
TERMINAL

Enter a Number : 22
22 =   3 + 19
22 =   5 + 17
22 = 11 + 11
Press any key to continue . . .
```

```
TERMINAL

Enter a Number : 34
34 =   3 + 31
34 =   5 + 29
34 = 11 + 23
34 = 17 + 17
Press any key to continue . . .
```

```
TERMINAL

Enter a Number : 29
29 can not be expressed as sum of two Prime Numbers.
Press any key to continue . . .
```

****

Program No. - 339 :
Program to display Pascal Triangle.

```
        1
      1   1
    1   2   1
  1   3   3   1
1   4   6   4   1
```

Code :

```c
#include <stdio.h>

int fact( int );

int main()
{
    int n, i, j, k, t;
    system( "cls" );

    printf( "Enter Number of Rows : " );
```

```c
    scanf( "%d", &n );

    for( i=0 ; i<n ; i++ )
    {
        for( k=0 ; k<(n-i) ; k++ )
        {
            printf( " " );
        }
        for( j=0 ; j<=i ; j++ )
        {
            t = fact( i ) / ( fact( j ) * fact( i - j ) );
            printf( "  %d", t );
        }
        printf( "\n" );
    }
    system( "pause" );
    return 0;
}

int fact( int n )
{
    int i, f;
    f = 1;
    for( i=1 ; i<=n ; i++ )
    {
        f *= i;
    }
    return f;
}
```

Output :

```
TERMINAL

Enter Number of Rows : 5
            1
         1     1
       1    2    1
     1    3    3    1
   1    4    6    4    1
Press any key to continue . . . _
```

________________   ****   ________________

Program No. - 340 :
Program to check whether the given two strings are
Anagram Strings or Not.

Code :

```c
#include <stdio.h>
#include <string.h>

void sort_string( char s1[ ] );

int main()
{
    char s1[25] = "silent";
    char s2[25] = "listen";
    int i, j, l;
    system( "cls" );

    printf( "Original String-1 : %s\n", s1 );
    printf( "Original String-2 : %s\n", s2 );

    sort_string( s1 );
    sort_string( s2 );

    if( strcmp(s1, s2) == 0 )
        printf( "\nStrings are Anagram strings.\n" );
    else
        printf( "\nStrings are not Anagram strings.\n" );

    system( "pause" );
    return 0;
}

void sort_string( char s1[ ] )
{
    int i, j, len;
    char ch;
    len = strlen( s1 );
    for( i=0 ; i<len-1 ; i++ )
    {
        for( j=0 ; j<len-1-i ; j++ )
        {
            if( s1[ j ] > s1[ j+1] )
            {
                ch = s1[ j ];
                s1[ j ] = s1[ j+1];
                s1[ j+1] = ch;
            }
        }
    }
}
```

Output :

```
TERMINAL

Original String-1 : silent
Original String-2 : listen

Strings are Anagram strings.
Press any key to continue . . . 
```

```
TERMINAL

Original String-1 : silent
Original String-2 : listener

Strings are not Anagram strings.
Press any key to continue . . . 
```

____________ **** ____________

Program No. - 341 :
Program to check whether the given two strings are
Anagram Strings or Not.

Code :
```c
#include <stdio.h>
#include <string.h>

int is_anagram( char s1[ ], char s2[ ] );

int main()
{
    char s1[25] = "silent";
    char s2[25] = "listen";
    int i, j, l;
    system( "cls" );

    printf( "Original String-1 : %s\n", s1 );
    printf( "Original String-2 : %s\n", s2 );


    if( is_anagram(s1, s2) )
        printf( "\nStrings are Anagram strings.\n" );
    else
        printf( "\nStrings are not Anagram strings.\n" );

    system( "pause" );
    return 0;
}

int is_anagram( char s1[ ], char s2[ ] )
{
    char chars1[256] = {0}, chars2[256] = {0};
    int i;
    for( i=0 ; s1[ i ] && s2[ i ] ; i++ )
    {
        chars1[ i ]++;
        chars2[ i ]++;
    }
    if( s1[ i ] || s2[ i ] )
        return 0;
    for( i=0 ; i<256 ; i++ )
    {
        if( chars1[ i ] != chars2[ i ] )
            return 0;
    }
    return 1;
}
```

Output :
```
TERMINAL

Original String-1 : silent
Original String-2 : listen

Strings are Anagram strings.
Press any key to continue . . . 
```

```
TERMINAL

Original String-1 : slent
Original String-2 : listen

Strings are not Anagram strings.
Press any key to continue . . . 
```

____________ **** ____________

Program No. - 342 :
Program to explain **Linear Search** using Function.

Code :
```c
#include <stdio.h>

int  Lsearch( int ar[ ], int size, int item );

int  main()
{
    int  ar[50], item, n, index, i;
```

```c
    system( "cls" );

    printf( "Enter Desired Array Size(max. 50) : " );
    scanf( "%d", &n );

    printf( "Enter Array Elements : " );
    for( i=0 ; i<n ; i++)
    {
        scanf( "%d", &ar[ i ] );
    }
    printf( "Enter Element to be searched for : " );
    scanf( "%d", &item );

    index = Lsearch( ar, n, item );

    if( index == -1 )
        printf( "\nSorry!! Element not found.\n" );
    else
    {
        printf( "\nElement found at index : %d", index );
        printf( ", Position : %d\n", ( index + 1 ) );
    }

    system( "pause" );
    return 0;
}

int  Lsearch( int ar[ ], int size, int item )
{
    int  i;

    for( i=0 ; i<size ; i++ )
    {
        if( item == ar[ i ] )
            return  i;
    }
    return  -1;
}
```

Output :

```
TERMINAL

Enter Desired Array Size(max. 50) : 5
Enter Array Elements : 10 20 30 40 50
Enter Element to be searched for : 30

Element found at index : 2, Position : 3
Press any key to continue . . .
```

```
TERMINAL

Enter Desired Array Size(max. 50) : 4
Enter Array Elements : 10 20 30 40
Enter Element to be searched for : 80

Sorry!! Element not found.
Press any key to continue . . .
```

****

Program No. - 343 :
Write a program to SORT a given element of an array in
Ascending order using **Bubble Sort**?

Code :
```c
#include <stdio.h>
#include <conio.h>

void  bubble_sort( int*, int );

int  main()
{
    int a[5] = { 30, 50, 40, 20, 10 };
    int i;
    system( "cls" );

    printf( "Before Sorting : " );
    for( i=0 ; i<5 ; i++ )
    {
        printf( "  %d", a[ i ] );
    }

    bubble_sort( a, 5 );

    printf( "\nAfter Sorting  : " );
    for( i=0 ; i<5 ; i++ )
    {
        printf( "  %d", a[ i ] );
    }

    printf( "\n" );
    system( "pause" );
    return 0;
}

void  bubble_sort( int *p, int n )
```

```c
{
    int i, j, t;
    for( i=0 ; i<n-1 ; i++ )
    {
        for( j=0 ; j<n-i-1 ; j++ )
        {
            if( *(p+j) > *(p+j+1) )    /* if( p[ j ] > p[ j+1 ] ) */
            {
                t = *(p+j);                /* t = p[ j ];    */
                *(p+j) = *(p+j+1);     /* p[ j ] = p[ j+1 ]; */
                *(p+j+1) = t;            /*  p[ j+1 ] = t;       */
            }
        }
    }
}
```

Output :

```
TERMINAL

Before Sorting :    30  50  40  20  10
After Sorting  :    10  20  30  40  50
Press any key to continue . . . |
```

****

Program No. - 344 :
Program to Merge Two Array using Function.

Code :

```c
#include <stdio.h>

void  Merge( int [ ], int, int[ ], int, int[ ] );

int  main()
{
    int A[50], B[50], C[100], MN = 0, M, N, i;
    system( "cls" );

    printf( "Enter Number of Elements in First Array : " );
    scanf( "%d", &M );
    printf( "Enter First Array elements
                            [ASCENDING]: " );
    for( i=0 ; i<M ; i++ )
    {
        scanf( "%d", &A[ i ] );
    }
    printf( "\nEnter Number of Elements in Second
                            Array : " );
    scanf( "%d", &N );
    printf( "Enter Second Array elements
                            [ASCENDING]: " );
    for( i=0 ; i<N ; i++ )
    {
        scanf( "%d", &B[ i ] );
    }

    MN = M + N;

    Merge( A, M, B, N, C );

    printf( "\nThe Sorted Array After Merging = \n" );
    for( i=0 ; i<MN ; i++ )
    {
        printf( "%d  ", C[ i ] );
    }

    printf( "\n" );
    system( "pause" );
    return 0;
}

void  Merge( int A[ ], int M, int B[ ], int N, int C[ ] )
{
    int a, b, c;
    for( a=0, b=0, c=0 ; a<M && b<N ; )
    {
        if( A[a] < B[b] )
            C[c++] = A[a++];
        else
            C[c++] = B[b++];
    }
    if( a < M )
    {
        while( a < M )
            C[c++] = A[a++];
    }
    else
    {
        while( b < N )
            C[c++] = B[b++];
    }
}
```

Output :

```
TERMINAL
Enter Number of Elements in First Array : 4
Enter First Array elements [ASCENDING]: 10 40 50 70

Enter Number of Elements in Second Array : 3
Enter Second Array elements [ASCENDING]: 20 30 60

The Sorted Array After Merging =
10  20  30  40  50  60  70
Press any key to continue . . .
```

****

Program No. - 345 :
Program to explain Local Variable.

Code :
```c
#include <stdio.h>

void localVar();

int main()
{
    system( "cls" );
    int x = 10;

    printf( "x in main() : %d\n", x );
    for( int i=1 ; i<=3 ; i++ )
    {
        localVar();
    }
    printf( "x in main() : %d\n", x );

    system( "pause" );
    return 0;
}

void localVar()
{
    int x = 20;
    printf( "x in localVar() : %d\n", x );
    x++;
    printf( "x in localVar() : %d\n", x );
}
```

Output :

```
TERMINAL
x in main() : 10
x in localVar() : 20
x in localVar() : 21
x in localVar() : 20
x in localVar() : 21
x in localVar() : 20
x in localVar() : 21
x in main() : 10
Press any key to continue . . .
```

****

Program No. - 346 :
Program to explain Global Variable.

Code :
```c
#include <stdio.h>

void globalVar();

int x = 10;

int main()
{
    system( "cls" );

    printf( "x in main() : %d\n", x );
    x++;
    for( int i=1 ; i<=3 ; i++ )
    {
        globalVar();
    }
    x++;
    printf( "x in main() : %d\n", x );

    system( "pause" );
    return 0;
}

void globalVar()
{
    x++;
    printf( "x in globalVar() : %d\n", x );
}
```

Output :

```
TERMINAL

x in main() : 10
x in globalVar() : 12
x in globalVar() : 13
x in globalVar() : 14
x in main() : 15
Press any key to continue . . .
```

****

Program No. - 347 :
Program to explain Static Variable.

Code :
```c
#include <stdio.h>

void staticVar();

int main()
{
    system( "cls" );
    int x = 10;

    printf( "x in main() : %d\n", x );
    for( int i=1 ; i<=3 ; i++ )
    {
        staticVar();
    }
    printf( "x in main() : %d\n", x );

    system( "pause" );
    return 0;
}

void staticVar()
{
    static int x = 20;
    printf( "x in staticVar() : %d\n", x );
    x++;
}
```

Output :

```
TERMINAL

x in main() : 10
x in staticVar() : 20
x in staticVar() : 21
x in staticVar() : 22
x in main() : 10
Press any key to continue . . .
```

****

Program No. - 348 :
Program to explain Local variables.

Code :
```c
#include <stdio.h>

int main()
{
    system( "cls" );
    int a = 10, i;
    printf( "%d ", a );
    {
        int a = 200;
        for( i=0 ; i<3 ; i++ )
        {
            printf( "%d ", a );
        }
    }
    printf( "%d\n", a );

    system( "pause" );
    return 0;
}
```

Output :

```
TERMINAL

10 200 200 200 10
Press any key to continue . . .
```

****

Program No. - 349 :
Program to input multiptle numbers and find average
after each input.

Code :

```c
#include <stdio.h>

float avg( float );

int main()
{
    float val = 1, av, i;
    system( "cls" );

    while( val != 0 )
    {
        printf( "Enter a Value ( 0 to exit) : ");
        scanf( "%f", &val );
        if( val == 0 )
            break;
        av = avg( val );
        printf( "New average : %f\n",av );
    }

    system( "pause" );
    return 0;
}

float avg( float value )
{
    static float sum = 0;
    static int count = 0;
    count++;
    sum += value;
    return (sum / count);
}
```

Output :

```
TERMINAL

Enter a Value ( 0 to exit) : 10
New average : 10.000000
Enter a Value ( 0 to exit) : 20
New average : 15.000000
Enter a Value ( 0 to exit) : 30
New average : 20.000000
Enter a Value ( 0 to exit) : 0
Press any key to continue . . .
```

_______________ **** _______________

Program No. - 350 :

Program to explain Register variable with it default value.

Code :
```c
#include <stdio.h>

int main()
{
    system( "cls" );
    // Memory : CPU register
    register int a;

    // Default value : 0
    printf( "a = %d\n", a );

    system( "pause" );
    return 0;
}
```

Output :

```
TERMINAL

a = 0
Press any key to continue . . .
```

_______________ **** _______________

Program No. - 351 :
Program to explain External variable.

Code :
```c
#include <stdio.h>

int a;

int main()
{
    system( "cls" );
    extern int a;

    // Default value : 0
    printf( "a = %d\n", a );

    system( "pause" );
    return 0;
}
```

Output :

```
TERMINAL

a = 0
Press any key to continue . . .
```

****

****

Chapter – 11
Structure, Union & Enum

****

Program No. - 352 :
Program to explain Simple Structure.

Code :
```c
#include <stdio.h>

/* Global Structure  */
struct  Distance
{
    int feet;
    float inches;
};

int  main()
{
    struct Distance d1;
    system( "cls" );

    d1.feet = 12;
    d1.inches = 9.5;

    printf( "Feet   : %d\n", d1.feet );
    printf( "Inches : %f\n", d1.inches );

    system( "pause" );
    return 0;
}
```

Output :

```
TERMINAL

Feet    : 12
Inches : 9.500000
Press any key to continue . . .
```

________________ **** ________________

Program No. - 353 :
Program to input Structure elements.

Code :
```c
#include <stdio.h>

struct  Distance
{
    int feet;
    float inches;
};
```

```c
int  main()
{
    struct Distance d1;
    system( "cls" );

    printf( "Enter feet : " );
    scanf( "%d", &d1.feet );
    printf( "Enter inches : " );
    scanf( "%f", &d1.inches );

    printf( "\nFeet   : %d\n",  d1.feet );
    printf( "Inches : %f\n",  d1.inches );

    system( "pause" );
    return 0;
}
```

Output :

```
TERMINAL

Enter feet : 15
Enter inches : 6.5


Feet    : 15
Inches : 6.500000
Press any key to continue . . .
```

________________ **** ________________

Program No. - 354 :
Program to explain Global Structure with Global and Local structure variable.

Code :
```c
#include <stdio.h>

/*   Global Structure*/
struct  Distance
{
    int feet;
    float inches;
};

struct  Distance d1;         /*   Global variable   */

int  main()
{
```

```c
    struct Distance d2;        /*  Local variable  */
    system( "cls" );

    d1.feet = 12;
    d1.inches = 9.5;

    d2.feet = 15;
    d2.inches = 3.5;

    printf( "%d\'-%f\" \n", d1.feet, d1.inches );
    printf( "%d\'-%f\" \n", d2.feet, d2.inches );

    system( "pause" );
    return 0;
}
```

Output :

```
TERMINAL

12'-9.500000"
15'-3.500000"
Press any key to continue . . .
```

——————————— **** ———————————

Program No. - 355 :
Program to explain Local Structure with Local structure variable.

Code :
```c
#include <stdio.h>

int  main()
{
    /*  Local Structure    */
    struct  Distance
    {
        int feet;
        float inches;
    }d1;

    struct  Distance d2;        /*  Local variable  */
    system( "cls" );

    d1.feet = 12;
    d1.inches = 9.5;

    d2.feet = 15;
```

```c
    d2.inches = 3.5;

    printf( "%d\'-%f\" \n", d1.feet, d1.inches );
    printf( "%d\'-%f\" \n", d2.feet, d2.inches );

    system( "pause" );
    return 0;
}
```

Output :

```
TERMINAL

12'-9.500000"
15'-3.500000"
Press any key to continue . . .
```

——————————— **** ———————————

Program No. - 356 :
Program to use Multiple Structure Variables.

Code :
```c
struct  Distance
{
    int feet;
    float inches;
};

int  main()
{
    struct  Distance d1, d2;
    system( "cls" );

    d1.feet = 12;
    d1.inches = 9.5;

    /*   Reading Distance from Keyboard.      */
    printf( "Enter feet : " );
    scanf( "%d", &d2.feet );
    printf( "Enter inches : " );
    scanf( "%f", &d2.inches );

    printf( "%d\'-%f\" \n", d1.feet, d1.inches );
    printf( "%d\'-%f\" \n", d2.feet, d2.inches );

    system( "pause" );
    return 0;
```

```
}
```

Output :

```
TERMINAL

Enter feet : 15
Enter inches : 6.5
12'-9.500000"
15'-6.500000"
Press any key to continue . . .
```

———————————— ******** ————————————

Program No. - 357 :
Program to Initialize Structure Variable and expain Structure Assignment.

Code :
```c
#include <stdio.h>

struct  Distance
{
    int feet;
    float inches;
};

int  main()
{
    struct Distance d1 = { 15, 6.5 };
    struct Distance d2, d3;
    system( "cls" );

    /*  Element-wise Assignment.    */
    d2.feet = d1.feet;
    d2.inches = d1.inches;

    /*  Structure Variable Assignment.  */
    d3 = d1;

    printf( "d1 = %d\'-%f\" \n", d1.feet, d1.inches );
    printf( "d2 = %d\'-%f\" \n", d2.feet, d2.inches );
    printf( "d3 = %d\'-%f\" \n", d3.feet, d3.inches );

    system( "pause" );
    return 0;
}
```

Output :

```
TERMINAL

d1 = 15'-6.500000"
d2 = 15'-6.500000"
d3 = 15'-6.500000"
Press any key to continue . . .
```

———————————— ******** ————————————

Program No. - 358 :
Program to explain the Anonymous Structure(without tagname).

Code :
```c
#include <stdio.h>

//  Structure without Tag name
struct
{
    int feet;
    float inches;
}d1, d2 = { 15, 6.5 };

int  main()
{
    system( "cls" );

    d1.feet = 12;
    d1.inches = 9.5;

    printf( "d1 : %d\'-%.1f\" \n", d1.feet, d1.inches );
    printf( "d2 : %d\'-%.1f\" \n", d2.feet, d2.inches );

    system( "pause" );
    return 0;
}
```

Output :

```
TERMINAL

d1 : 12'-9.5"
d2 : 15'-6.5"
Press any key to continue . . .
```

———————————— ******** ————————————

Program No. - 359 :

Program to explain the element-wise comparison of structure variable.

Code :

```c
#include <stdio.h>

struct  Distance
{
    int feet;
    float inches;
} d1, d2 = { 15, 6.5 };

int  main()
{
    system( "cls" );

    d1.feet = 15;
    d1.inches = 6.5;

    if( ( d1.feet == d2.feet ) &&
                    ( d1.inches == d2.inches ) )
        printf( "(d1 == d2)\n" );
    else
        printf( "(d1 != d2)\n" );

    system( "pause" );
    return 0;
}
```

Output :

```
TERMINAL
(d1 == d2)
Press any key to continue . . .
```

****

Program No. - 360 :
Program to.create and use a simple rectangle structure.

Code :

```c
#include <stdio.h>

struct rectangle
{
    int l, b;
};
```

```c
int main()
{
    system( "cls" );
    struct rectangle r1;

    r1.l = 10;
    r1.b = 5;

    printf( "length = %d\n", r1.l );
    printf( "breadth = %d\n", r1.b );
    system( "pause" );
}
```

Output :

```
TERMINAL

length = 10
breadth = 5
Press any key to continue . . .
```

****

Program No. - 361 :
Program to.input data of rectangle structure.

Code :

```c
#include <stdio.h>

struct rectangle
{
    int l, b;
};

int main()
{
    system( "cls" );
    struct rectangle r1;

    printf( "Enter length & breadth : " );
    scanf( "%d %d", &r1.l, &r1.b );

    printf( "length = %d\n", r1.l );
    printf( "breadth = %d\n", r1.b );
    system( "pause" );
}
```

Output :

```
TERMINAL

Enter length & breadth : 20 10
length = 20
breadth = 10
Press any key to continue . . . _
```

---- **** ----

Program No. - 362 :
Program to.initialize rectangle structure.

Code :
```c
#include <stdio.h>

struct rectangle
{
    int l, b;
};

int main()
{
    system( "cls" );
    struct rectangle r1 = { 10, 8 };

    printf( "length = %d\n", r1.l );
    printf( "breadth = %d\n", r1.b );
    system( "pause" );
}
```

Output :

```
TERMINAL

length = 10
breadth = 8
Press any key to continue . . . _
```

---- **** ----

Program No. - 363 :
Program to.create structure variables with rectangle structure definition.

Code :
```c
#include <stdio.h>
```

```c
struct rectangle
{
    int l, b;
} r1, r2;

int main()
{
    system( "cls" );
    r1.l = 10;
    r1.b = 5;

    printf( "length = %d\n", r1.l );
    printf( "breadth = %d\n", r1.b );
    system( "pause" );
}
```

Output :

```
TERMINAL

length = 10
breadth = 5
Press any key to continue . . . _
```

---- **** ----

Program No. - 364 :
Program to.create structure variables with nameless structure definition.

Code :
```c
#include <stdio.h>

/* nameless structure */
struct
{
    int l, b;
} r1, r2;

int main()
{
    system( "cls" );
    r1.l = 10;
    r1.b = 5;

    printf( "length = %d\n", r1.l );
    printf( "breadth = %d\n", r1.b );
```

```
    system( "pause" );
}
```

Output :

```
TERMINAL


length = 10
breadth = 5
Press any key to continue . . . []
```

****

Program No. - 365 :
Program to use typedef for alias to the rectangle
structure.

Code :

```c
#include <stdio.h>

struct rectangle
{
    int l, b;
};

typedef struct rectangle rect;

int main()
{
    system( "cls" );
    rect r1;
    r1.l = 10;
    r1.b = 5;

    printf( "length = %d\n", r1.l );
    printf( "breadth = %d\n", r1.b );
    system( "pause" );
}
```

Output :

```
TERMINAL


length = 10
breadth = 5
Press any key to continue . . . []
```

****

Program No. - 366 :
Program to typedef for alias with rectangle structure
definition.

Code :

```c
#include <stdio.h>

typedef struct rectangle
{
    int l, b;
} rect;

int main()
{
    system( "cls" );
    rect r1;
    r1.l = 10;
    r1.b = 5;

    printf( "length = %d\n", r1.l );
    printf( "breadth = %d\n", r1.b );
    system( "pause" );
}
```

Output :

```
TERMINAL


length = 10
breadth = 5
Press any key to continue . . . []
```

****

Program No. - 367 :
Program to initialize structure variable with rectangle
structure definition.

Code :

```c
#include <stdio.h>

struct rectangle
{
    int l, b;
} r1 = { 20, 10 };

int main()
```

```
{
    system( "cls" );

    printf( "length = %d\n", r1.l );
    printf( "breadth = %d\n", r1.b );
    system( "pause" );
}
```

Output :

```
TERMINAL


length = 20
breadth = 10
Press any key to continue . . . 
```

****

Program No. - 368 :
Program to explain named initialization of structure variable.

Code :
```
#include <stdio.h>

struct rectangle
{
    int l, b;
};

int main()
{
    system( "cls" );
    struct rectangle r1 = { .b = 10, .l = 20 };

    printf( "length = %d\n", r1.l );
    printf( "breadth = %d\n", r1.b );
    system( "pause" );
}
```

Output :

```
TERMINAL


length = 20
breadth = 10
Press any key to continue . . . 
```

****

Program No. - 369 :
Program to initialize a structure variable with another structure variable.

Code :
```
#include <stdio.h>

struct rectangle
{
    int l, b;
};

int main()
{
    system( "cls" );
    struct rectangle r1 = { 20, 10 };
    struct rectangle r2 = r1;

    printf( "length = %d\n", r2.l );
    printf( "breadth = %d\n", r2.b );
    system( "pause" );
}
```

Output :

```
TERMINAL


length = 20
breadth = 10
Press any key to continue . . . 
```

****

Program No. - 370 :
Program to assign a structure variable to another structure variable.

Code :
```
#include <stdio.h>

struct rectangle
{
    int l, b;
};

int main()
{
```

```c
    system( "cls" );
    struct rectangle r1 = { 20, 10 };
    struct rectangle r2;

    r2 = r1;

    printf( "length = %d\n", r2.l );
    printf( "breadth = %d\n", r2.b );
    system( "pause" );
}
```

Output :

```
TERMINAL


length = 20
breadth = 10
Press any key to continue . . . []
```

____________ **** ____________

Program No. - 371 :
Program to Add Two Structure Variables.

Code :
```c
#include <stdio.h>

struct  Distance
{
    int feet;
    float inches;
};

int  main()
{
    struct Distance d1, d3;
    struct Distance d2 = { 12, 6.5 };
    system( "cls" );

    printf( "Enter feet   : " );
    scanf( "%d", &d1.feet );
    printf( "Enter inches : " );
    scanf( "%f", &d1.inches );

    d3.feet = d1.feet + d2.feet;
    d3.inches = d1.inches + d2.inches;
    if( d3.inches >= 12.0 )
    {
```

```c
        d3.inches -= 12.0;
        d3.feet++;
    }

    printf( "\n%d\'-%.2f\"", d1.feet, d1.inches );
    printf( " + %d\'-%.2f\"", d2.feet, d2.inches );
    printf( " = %d\'-%.2f\" \n", d3.feet, d3.inches );

    system( "pause" );
    return 0;
}
```

Output :

```
TERMINAL

Enter feet   : 15
Enter inches : 9.5

15'-9.50" + 12'-6.50" = 28'-4.00"
Press any key to continue . . . |
```

____________ **** ____________

Program No. - 372 :
Program to explain Array of Structure.

Code :
```c
#include <stdio.h>

struct  Distance
{
    int feet;
    float inches;
};

int  main()
{
    struct  Distance d[5];
    int i;
    system( "cls" );

    for( i=0 ; i<5 ; i++ )
    {
        printf( "Enter Feet & Inches : " );
        scanf( "%d %f", &d[ i ].feet, &d[ i ].inches );
    }

    for( i=0 ; i<5 ; i++ )
```

```
    {
        printf( "%d\'-%f\" \n", d[ i ].feet, d[ i ].inches );
    }

    system( "pause" );
    return 0;
}
```

Output :

```
TERMINAL

Enter Feet & Inches : 11 2.5
Enter Feet & Inches : 12 3.5
Enter Feet & Inches : 13 4.5
Enter Feet & Inches : 14 5.5
Enter Feet & Inches : 15 6.5
11'-2.500000"
12'-3.500000"
13'-4.500000"
14'-5.500000"
15'-6.500000"
Press any key to continue . . .
```

****

Program No. - 373 :
Program to explain Array within Structure.

Code :
```c
#include <stdio.h>

struct  Student
{
    int rno;
    char name[25];
    float marks[5];
};

int  main()
{
    int i;
    struct  Student s;
    system( "cls" );

    printf( "Enter Roll Number : " );
    scanf( "%d", &s.rno );
    printf( "Enter Name : " );
    fflush( stdin );
    gets( s.name );
    for( i=0 ; i<5 ; i++ )
    {
        printf( "Enter Marks-%d : ", ( i+1 ) );
        scanf( "%f", &s.marks[ i ] );
    }

    printf( "\nRoll Number : %d\n", s.rno );
    printf( "Name : %s\n", s.name );
    for( i=0 ; i<5 ; i++ )
    {
        printf( "Marks-%d : %f\n", (i+1), s.marks[ i ] );
    }

    system( "pause" );
    return 0;
}
```

Output :

```
TERMINAL

Enter Roll Number : 101
Enter Name : Aman
Enter Marks-1 : 88
Enter Marks-2 : 94
Enter Marks-3 : 92
Enter Marks-4 : 78
Enter Marks-5 : 91

Roll Number : 101
Name : Aman
Marks-1 : 88.000000
Marks-2 : 94.000000
Marks-3 : 92.000000
Marks-4 : 78.000000
Marks-5 : 91.000000
Press any key to continue . . .
```

****

Program No. - 374 :
Program to explain the concept of Array within Structure
& Array of Structure.

Code :
```c
#include <stdio.h>

struct  Student
{
```

```c
    int rno;
    char name[25];
    float marks[5];
};

int  main()
{
    struct  Student s[10];
    int i, j, n;
    system( "cls" );

    printf( "Enter Number of student : " );
    scanf( "%d", &n );

    for( i=0 ; i<n ; i++ )
    {
        printf( "Enter Roll Number : " );
        scanf( "%d", &s[ i ].rno );
        fflush( stdin );
        printf( "Enter Name : " );
        gets( s[ i ].name );
        for( j=0 ; j<5 ; j++ )
        {
            printf( "Enter marks-%d : ", (j+1) );
            scanf( "%f", &s[ i ].marks[ j ] );
        }
    }

    printf( "\n%5s %-15s %7s %7s %7s %7s %7s",
                "R.No.", "Name", "M-1","M-2","M-3",
                "M-4", "M-5" );
    for( i=0 ; i<n ; i++ )
    {
        printf( "\n%-5d", s[ i ].rno );
        printf( " %-15s", s[ i ].name );
        for( j=0 ; j<5 ; j++ )
        {
            printf( " %7.2f", s[ i ].marks[ j ] );
        }
    }

    printf( "\n" );
    system( "pause" );
    return 0;
}
```

Output :

```
TERMINAL
Enter Number of student : 2
Enter Roll Number : 101
Enter Name : Prateek
Enter marks-1 : 86
Enter marks-2 : 92
Enter marks-3 : 88
Enter marks-4 : 79
Enter marks-5 : 91
Enter Roll Number : 102
Enter Name : Harsh
Enter marks-1 : 92
Enter marks-2 : 90
Enter marks-3 : 85
Enter marks-4 : 83
Enter marks-5 : 95

R.No. Name          M-1     M-2     M-3     M-4     M-5
101   Prateek       86.00   92.00   88.00   79.00   91.00
102   Harsh         92.00   90.00   85.00   83.00   95.00
Press any key to continue . . .
```

****

Program No. - 375 :
Program to pass a structure variable to function as pass by value.

Code :
```c
#include <stdio.h>

struct rectangle
{
    int l, b;
};

void show( struct rectangle );

int main()
{
    system( "cls" );
    struct rectangle r1 = { 20, 10 };

    show( r1 );

    system( "pause" );
}

void show( struct rectangle r )
{
    printf( "length = %d\n", r.l );
    printf( "breadth = %d\n", r.b );
}
```

Output :

```
TERMINAL


length = 20
breadth = 10
Press any key to continue . . .
```

———————— **** ————————

Program No. - 376 :
Program to pass a structure variable to function as pass by address/pointer.

Code :
```c
#include <stdio.h>

struct rectangle
{
    int l, b;
};

void show( struct rectangle* );

int main()
{
    system( "cls" );
    struct rectangle r1 = { 20, 10 };

    show( &r1 );

    system( "pause" );
}

void show( struct rectangle *p )
{
    printf( "length = %d\n", p->l );
    printf( "breadth = %d\n", p->b );
}
```

Output :

```
TERMINAL


length = 20
breadth = 10
Press any key to continue . . .
```

———————— **** ————————

Program No. - 377 :
Program to pass a structure variable to function as pass by address/pointer.

Code :
```c
#include <stdio.h>

struct rectangle
{
    int l, b;
};

void show( struct rectangle* );

int main()
{
    system( "cls" );
    struct rectangle r1 = { 20, 10 };

    show( &r1 );

    system( "pause" );
}

void show( struct rectangle *p )
{
    printf( "length = %d\n", (*p).l );
    printf( "breadth = %d\n", (*p).b );
}
```

Output :

```
TERMINAL


length = 20
breadth = 10
Press any key to continue . . .
```

———————— **** ————————

Program No. - 378 :
Program to initialize structure variable using function.

Code :
```c
#include <stdio.h>
```

```c
struct rectangle
{
    int l, b;
};

void init( struct rectangle* );

int main()
{
    system( "cls" );
    struct rectangle r1;

    init( &r1 );

    printf( "length = %d\n", r1.l );
    printf( "breadth = %d\n", r1.b );
    system( "pause" );
}

void init( struct rectangle *p )
{
    p->l = 10;
    p->b = 5;
}
```

Output :

```
TERMINAL


 length = 10
 breadth = 5
 Press any key to continue . . . 
```

---- **** ----

Program No. - 379 :
Program to input structure variable using function.

Code :
```c
#include <stdio.h>

struct rectangle
{
    int l, b;
};

void init( struct rectangle* );
```

```c
int main()
{
    system( "cls" );
    struct rectangle r1;

    init( &r1 );

    printf( "length = %d\n", r1.l );
    printf( "breadth = %d\n", r1.b );
    system( "pause" );
}

void init( struct rectangle *p )
{
    printf( "Enter length & breadth : " );
    scanf( "%d %d", &p->l, &p->b );;
}
```

Output :

```
TERMINAL


 Enter length & breadth : 8 5
 length = 8
 breadth = 5
 Press any key to continue . . . 
```

---- **** ----

Program No. - 380 :
Program to pass Structure Variable to Function.

Code :
```c
#include <stdio.h>

struct  Distance
{
    int feet;
    float inches;
};

void  display( struct Distance d )
{
    printf( "Distance = %d\'-%f\" \n", d.feet, d.inches );
}

int  main()
{
```

```c
    struct  Distance d1;
    struct  Distance d2;
    system( "cls" );

    printf( "Enter feet and inches : " );
    scanf( "%d %f", &d1.feet, &d1.inches );

    // Structure Variable Assignment.
    d2 = d1;

    display( d1 );
    display( d2 );

    system( "pause" );
    return 0;
}
```

Output :

```
TERMINAL

Enter feet and inches : 15 9.5
Distance = 15'-9.500000"
Distance = 15'-9.500000"
Press any key to continue . . .
```

—————————— **** ——————————

Program No. - 381 :
Program to Pass Structure Variable to Function.

Code :
```c
#include <stdio.h>

struct  Distance
{
    int feet;
    float inches;
};

void  display( struct Distance d )
{
    printf( "Distance = %d\'-%f\" \n", d.feet, d.inches );
}

void  add_dist( struct Distance, struct Distance );

int  main()
{
```

```c
    struct Distance d1;
    struct Distance d2;
    system( "cls" );

    printf( "Enter feet and inches : " );
    scanf( "%d %f", &d1.feet, &d1.inches );

    printf( "Enter feet and inches : " );
    scanf( "%d %f", &d2.feet, &d2.inches );

    display( d1 );
    display( d2 );

    add_dist( d1, d2 );

    system( "pause" );
    return 0;
}

void  add_dist( struct Distance dd1, struct Distance dd2 )
{
    struct Distance dd3;
    dd3.feet = dd1.feet + dd2.feet;
    dd3.inches = dd1.inches + dd2.inches;
    if( dd3.inches >= 12.0 )
    {
        dd3.inches -= 12.0;
        dd3.feet++;
    }
    display( dd3 );
}
```

Output :

```
TERMINAL

Enter feet and inches : 12 9.5
Enter feet and inches : 16 6.5
Distance = 12'-9.500000"
Distance = 16'-6.500000"
Distance = 29'-4.000000"
Press any key to continue . . .
```

—————————— **** ——————————

Program No. - 382 :
Program to Return Structure Variable from Function.

Code :

```c
#include <stdio.h>

struct  Distance
{
    int feet;
    float inches;
};

void  display( struct Distance d )
{
    printf( "Distance = %d\'-%f\" \n", d.feet, d.inches );
}

struct Distance  add_dist( struct Distance,
                                    struct Distance );

int  main()
{
    struct Distance d1, d2, d3;
    system( "cls" );

    printf( "Enter feet and inches : " );
    scanf( "%d %f", &d1.feet, &d1.inches );

    printf( "Enter feet and inches : " );
    scanf( "%d %f", &d2.feet, &d2.inches );

    display( d1 );
    display( d2 );

    d3 = add_dist( d1, d2 );

    display( d3 );

    system( "pause" );
    return 0;
}

struct Distance  add_dist( struct Distance dd1,
                                    struct Distance dd2 )
{
    struct  Distance dd3;
    dd3.feet = dd1.feet + dd2.feet;
    dd3.inches = dd1.inches + dd2.inches;
    if( dd3.inches >= 12.0 )
    {
        dd3.inches -= 12.0;
        dd3.feet++;
    }
    return  dd3;
}
```



```
TERMINAL

Enter feet and inches : 16 2.5
Enter feet and inches : 14 10.5
Distance = 16'-2.500000"
Distance = 14'-10.500000"
Distance = 31'-1.000000"
Press any key to continue . . .
```

****

Program No. - 383 :
Program to explain Nested Structure.

Code :
```c
#include <stdio.h>

struct  Distance
{
    int feet;
    float inches;
};

struct  Room
{
    struct Distance length;
    struct Distance width;
};

int  main()
{
    float  l, w, a;
    struct  Room drawing = { { 15, 6.0 }, { 12, 9.0 } };
    system( "cls" );

    l = drawing.length.feet +
                    drawing.length.inches / 12.0;
    w = drawing.width.feet +
                    drawing.width.inches / 12.0;

    a = l * w;
```

```
    printf( "Area of Drawing Room = %.2f square
                                      feet.\n", a );

    system( "pause" );
    return 0;
}
```

Output :

```
TERMINAL

Area of Drawing Room = 197.62 square feet.
Press any key to continue . . .
```

―――――― ******** ――――――

Program No. - 384 :
Program to explain the concept of **Nested Structure (** Structure within Structure **).**

Code :
```
#include <stdio.h>

struct  Room
{
    struct  Dist
    {
        int feet;
        float inches;
    }l, b;
};

int  main()
{
    struct  Room  dr;
    float l1, b1, a;
    system( "cls" );

    dr.l.feet = 15;
    dr.l.inches = 6.0;
    dr.b.feet = 12;
    dr.b.inches = 9.0;

    l1 = dr.l.feet + ( dr.l.inches / 12.0 );
    b1 = dr.b.feet + ( dr.b.inches / 12.0 );

    a = l1 * b1;
```

```
    printf( "Area of Drawing Room = %.3f sq. ft.\n", a );

    system( "pause" );
    return 0;
}
```

Output :

```
TERMINAL

Area of Drawing Room = 197.625 sq. ft.
Press any key to continue . . .
```

―――――― ******** ――――――

Program No. - 385 :
Program to create Book Structure.

Code :
```
#include <stdio.h>

struct  Book
{
    char name[25];
    char author[20];
    float price;
};

int  main()
{
    struct  Book b;
    system( "cls" );

    printf( "Enter the Name of Book : " );
    gets( b.name );
    printf( "Enter the Author's Name : " );
    gets( b.author );
    printf( "Enter the Price of the book : " );
    scanf( "%f", &b.price );

    printf( "\nName of the Book   : %s\n", b.name );
    printf( "Author of the Book : %s\n", b.author );
    printf( "Price of the Book  : %f\n", b.price );

    system( "pause" );
    return 0;
}
```

Output :

```
TERMINAL

Enter the Name of Book : C App
Enter the Author's Name : Atul Soni
Enter the Price of the book : 450

Name of the Book    : C App
Author of the Book : Atul Soni
Price of the Book   : 450.000000
Press any key to continue . . .
```

———————— **** ————————

Program No. - 386 :
Program to explain String within Structure.

Code :
```c
#include <stdio.h>

struct  Book
{
    char name[25];
    int page;
    int price;
};

int  main()
{
    int i;
    struct  Book b1[3];
    system( "cls" );

    for( i=0 ; i<3 ; i++ )
    {
        printf( "Enter Name of Book : " );
        fflush( stdin );
        gets( b1[ i ].name );
        printf( "Enter Number of Pages : " );
        scanf( "%d", &b1[ i ].page );
        printf( "Enter Price of Book : " );
        scanf( "%d", &b1[ i ].price );
    }

    for( i=0 ; i<3 ; i++ )
    {
        printf( "\nName of Book  = %s\n", b1[ i ].name );
```

```c
        printf( "Number of Page = %d\n", b1[ i ].page );
        printf( "Price of Book  = %d\n",  b1[ i ].price );
    }

    system( "pause" );
    return 0;
}
```

Output :

```
TERMINAL

Enter Name of Book : C App
Enter Number of Pages : 225
Enter Price of Book : 450
Enter Name of Book : C++ App
Enter Number of Pages : 250
Enter Price of Book : 450
Enter Name of Book : JAVA App
Enter Number of Pages : 300
Enter Price of Book : 500

Name of Book    = C App
Number of Page = 225
Price of Book  = 450

Name of Book    = C++ App
Number of Page = 250
Price of Book  = 450

Name of Book    = JAVA App
Number of Page = 300
Price of Book  = 500
Press any key to continue . . .
```

———————— **** ————————

Program No. - 387 :
Program to Pass Structure Variable to Function by Reference / Address / Pointer.

Code :
```c
#include <stdio.h>

struct  Distance
{
    int feet;
    float inches;
};

void  scale( struct Distance*, float );
```

```c
void  display( struct Distance );

int  main()
{
    struct Distance d1 = { 12, 6.0 };
    struct Distance d2 = { 10, 6.0 };
    system( "cls" );

    printf( "Dist1 = " );
    display( d1 );

    printf( "Dist2 = " );
    display( d2 );

    scale( &d1, 0.5 );
    scale( &d2, 0.25 );

    printf( "\nDist1 = " );
    display( d1 );

    printf( "Dist2 = " );
    display( d2 );

    system( "pause" );
    return 0;
}

void  scale( struct Distance *p, float factor )
{
    float inches = ( p->feet * 12 + p->inches ) * factor;
    p->feet = inches / 12;
    p->inches = inches - ( p->feet * 12 );
}

void  display( struct Distance dd )
{
    printf( "%d\'-%.2f\"\n", dd.feet, dd.inches );
}
```

Output :

```
TERMINAL

Dist1 = 12'-6.00"
Dist2 = 10'-6.00"

Dist1 = 6'-3.00"
Dist2 = 2'-7.50"
Press any key to continue . . .
```

****

Program No. - 388 :
Program to explain bit-field with structure.

Code :

```c
#include <stdio.h>

/* bit field*/
struct test
{
    unsigned int a : 4;
    unsigned int b : 4;
    unsigned int c : 10;
} t1;

int main()
{
    system( "cls" );
    struct test t2;

    t1.a = 5;
    t1.b = 10;
    t1.c = 200;

    printf( "t1.a = %d\n", t1.a );
    printf( "t1.b = %d\n", t1.b );
    printf( "t1.c = %d\n", t1.c );
    printf( "sizeof(t1) = %d\n", sizeof(t1) );

    system( "pause" );
}
```

Output :

```
TERMINAL

t1.a = 5
t1.b = 10
t1.c = 200
sizeof(t1) = 4
Press any key to continue . . .
```

****

Program No. - 389 :
Program to explain Enum.

Code :
```c
#include <stdio.h>

enum  days_of_week { SUN, MON, TUE, WED, THU,
                     FRI, SAT };

int  main()
{
    enumdays_of_week day1, day2;
    int diff;
    system( "cls" );

    day1 = MON;
    day2 = THU;

    diff = day2 - day1;

    printf( "Days between day1 & day2 = %d\n", diff );

    if( day1 < day2 )
        printf( "Day1 comes before Day2.\n" );

    system( "pause" );
    return 0;
}
```

Output :

```
TERMINAL

Days between day1 & day2 = 3
Day1 comes before Day2.
Press any key to continue . . .
```

——————————— **** ———————————

Program No. - 390 :
Program to show an Enumeration type (**enum**).

Code :
```c
#include <stdio.h>

enum  Colors { Red, Green, Blue };

int  main()
{
    enum  Colors c1, c2;
```

```c
    int d;
    system( "cls" );

    c1 = Red;
    c2 = Green;

    d = c2 - c1;
    printf( "Difference = %d\n", d );

    if( c1 < c2 )
        printf( "RED comes before GREEN.\n" );
    else
        printf( "GREEN comes before RED.\n" );

    system( "pause" );
    return 0;
}
```

Output :

```
TERMINAL

Difference = 1
RED comes before GREEN.
Press any key to continue . . .
```

——————————— **** ———————————

Program No. - 391 :
Program to show an Enumeration type (**enum**).

Code :
```c
#include <stdio.h>

enum  Colors { Red=10, Green, Blue };

int  main()
{
    enum  Colors c1, c2;
    int d;
    system( "cls" );

    c1 = Red;
    c2 = Blue;

    printf( "c1 = %d\n", c1 );
    printf( "c2 = %d\n", c2 );
```

```c
    d = c2 - c1;
    printf( "Difference = %d\n", d );

    if( c1 < c2 )
        printf( "RED comes before GREEN.\n" );
    else
        printf( "GREEN comes before RED.\n" );

    system( "pause" );
    return 0;
}
```

Output :

```
TERMINAL

c1 = 10
c2 = 12
Difference = 2
RED comes before GREEN.
Press any key to continue . . .
```

–––––––––––––––––– **** ––––––––––––––––––

Program No. - 392 :
Program to show an Enumeration type (**enum**).

Code :
```c
#include <stdio.h>

enum  Colors { Red=10, Green=20, Blue=30 };

int  main()
{
    enum  Colors c1, c2;
    int d;
    system( "cls" );

    c1 = Red;
    c2 = Blue;

    printf( "c1 = %d\n", c1 );
    printf( "c2 = %d\n", c2 );

    d = c2 - c1;
    printf( "Difference = %d\n", d );

    if( c1 < c2 )
```

```c
        printf( "RED comes before GREEN.\n" );
    else
        printf( "GREEN comes before RED.\n" );

    system( "pause" );
    return 0;
}
```

Output :

```
TERMINAL

c1 = 10
c2 = 30
Difference = 20
RED comes before GREEN.
Press any key to continue . . .
```

–––––––––––––––––– **** ––––––––––––––––––

Program No. - 393 :
Program to explain **Union**.

Code :
```c
#include <stdio.h>

union  Abc
{
    char c;
    int i;
    float f;
};

int  main()
{
    union Abc x;
    system( "cls" );

    x.c = 'A';
    printf( "x.c = %c\n", x.c );

    x.i = 100;
    printf( "x.i = %d\n", x.i );

    x.f = 123.45;
    printf( "x.f = %f\n", x.f );

    system( "pause" );
```

```
}
```

Output :

```
TERMINAL

x.c = A
x.i = 100
x.f = 123.449997
Press any key to continue . . .
```

****

Program No. - 394 :
Program to differentiate **Structure and Union**.

Code :
```
#include <stdio.h>

union  ABC
{
    char a;
    int b;
    float c;
};

struct  XYZ
{
    char x;
    int y;
    float z;
};

int  main()
{
    union  ABC p;
    struct  XYZ q;
    system( "cls" );

    printf( "Size of Structure : %d\n",
                        sizeof( struct XYZ ) );
    q.x = 'A';
    q.y = 100;
    q.z = 12.345;
    printf( "q.x = %c\nq.y = %d\nq.z = %f\n", q.x,
                                    q.y, q.z );

    printf( "\nSize of Union : %d\n",
```

```
                        sizeof( union ABC ) );
    p.a = 'C';
    printf( "p.a : %c\n", p.a );
    p.b = 100;
    printf( "p.b : %d\n", p.b );
    p.c = 12.345;
    printf( "p.c : %f\n", p.c );

    system( "pause" );
    return 0;
}
```

Output :

```
TERMINAL

Size of Structure : 12
q.x = A
q.y = 100
q.z = 12.345000

Size of Union : 4
p.a : C
p.b : 100
p.c : 12.345000
Press any key to continue . . .
```

****

Program No. - 395 :
Program to explain the use of pointer to structure.

Code :
```
#include <stdio.h>

int  main()
{
    struct  date
    {
        int dd, mm, yy;
    }dt = { 22, 1, 2024 };

    struct  date *ptr;
    system( "cls" );

    ptr = &dt;

    printf( "Using Structure Variable :\n" );
    printf( "dd = %d, mm = %d, yy = %d\n", dt.dd,
```

```
                                    dt.mm, dt.yy );
    printf( "\nUsing Structure Pointer  :\n" );
    printf( "dd = %d, mm = %d, yy = %d\n", ptr->dd,
                                    ptr->mm,  ptr->yy );

    system( "pause" );
    return 0;
}
```

Output :

```
TERMINAL

Using Structure Variable :
dd = 22, mm = 1, yy = 2024

Using Structure Pointer  :
dd = 22, mm = 1, yy = 2024
Press any key to continue . . .
```

****

Program No. - 396 :
Program to explain **Nested Structure** by employee structure.

Code :

```
#include <stdio.h>

struct address
{
    char  phone[15] ;
    char  city[25] ;
    long  pin ;
};

struct  emp
{
    char  name[25] ;
    struct  addressadr ;
};

int  main()
{
    struct  emp  e = { "Harsh", "099999888888",
                                "Bhilai", 490006 };
    system( "cls" ) ;

    printf( "Name = %s  \nPhone = %s\n", e.name,
```

```
                                    e.adr.phone ) ;
    printf( "City = %s \nPin = %ld\n", e.adr.city,
                                    e.adr.pin ) ;

    system( "pause" );
    return 0;
}
```

Output :

```
TERMINAL

Name = Harsh
Phone = 099999888888
City = Bhilai
Pin = 490006
Press any key to continue . . .
```

****

Program No. - 397 :
Program to explain the concept of Passing Structure by Reference to function by Book Structure example.

Code :

```
#include <stdio.h>

struct  book
{
    char  name[25] ;
    char  author[25] ;
    float  price;
};

void  display( struct book  *b );

int  main()
{
    struct  book  b1 = { "C Programming", "Atul",
                                        500.00 };
    system( "cls" );

    display ( &b1 ) ;

    system( "pause" );
    return 0;
}

void  display( struct book  *b )
```

```
{
    printf( "Book Name: %s\n", b->name );
    printf( "Author   : %s\n", b->author );
    printf( "Price    : %.2f\n", b->price ) ;
}
```

Output :

```
TERMINAL

Book Name: C Programming
Author   : Atul
Price    : 500.00
Press any key to continue . . .
```

———————————— **** ————————————

Program No. - 398 :
Program to explain the use of user-defined Type
Declaration (**typedef**).

Code :
```c
#include <stdio.h>

struct book
{
    char name[25];
    char author[25];
    float price;
};

typedef struct book BOOK;

void display( BOOK *b );

int main()
{
    BOOK b1 = { "C Programming", "Atul", 500.00 } ;
    system( "cls" );

    display( &b1 ) ;

    system( "pause" );
    return 0;
}

void display( BOOK *b )
{
    printf( "Book Name: %s\n", b->name );
```

```
    printf( "Author   : %s\n", b->author );
    printf( "Price    : %.2f\n", b->price ) ;
}
```

Output :

```
TERMINAL

Book Name: C Programming
Author   : Atul
Price    : 500.00
Press any key to continue . . .
```

———————————— **** ————————————

****

Chapter – 12
Pointers

****

Program No. - 399 :
Program to explain simple use of Pointer.

Code :
```c
#include <stdio.h>

int  main()
{
    int a = 10;
    int * p;
    system( "cls" );

    p = &a;

    printf( "a = %d\n", a );
    printf( "&a = %u\n", &a );
    printf( "p = %u\n", p );
    printf( "*p = %d\n", *p );
    printf( "&p = %u\n", &p );

    system( "pause" );
    return 0;
}
```

Output :

```
TERMINAL

a = 10
&a = 3638557436
p = 3638557436
*p = 10
&p = 3638557424
Press any key to continue . . .
```

****

Program No. - 400 :
Program to explain that a pointer can point differnt
variable at different point of time.

Code :
```c
#include <stdio.h>

int  main()
{
    int a = 10, b = 20, c = 30;
    int * p;
    system( "cls" );
```

    p = &a;
    printf("*p = %d\n", *p);

    p = &b;
    printf("*p = %d\n", *p);

    p = &c;
    printf("*p = %d\n", *p);

    system("pause");
    return 0;
}
```

Output :

```
TERMINAL

*p = 10
*p = 20
*p = 30
Press any key to continue . . .
```

****

Program No. - 401 :
Program to explain that a pointer can point differnt
variable at different point of time.

Code :
```c
#include <stdio.h>

int  main()
{
    int a = 10;
    int *p1, *p2, *p3;
    system( "cls" );

    p1 = &a;
    p2 = &a;
    p3 = &a;

    printf( "*p1 = %d\n", *p1 );
    printf( "*p2 = %d\n", *p2 );
    printf( "*p3 = %d\n", *p3 );

    *p2 = 50;

    printf( "*p1 = %d\n", *p1 );
```
```

```c
printf( "*p2 = %d\n", *p2 );
printf( "*p3 = %d\n", *p3 );

*p3 = *p1 + *p2;

printf( "*p1 = %d\n", *p1 );
printf( "*p2 = %d\n", *p2 );
printf( "*p3 = %d\n", *p3 );

system( "pause" );
return 0;
}
```

Output :

```
TERMINAL

*p1 = 10
*p2 = 10
*p3 = 10
*p1 = 50
*p2 = 50
*p3 = 50
*p1 = 100
*p2 = 100
*p3 = 100
Press any key to continue . . .
```

****

Program No. - 402 :
Program to explain new format spacifier %p for address of variable, i.e. pointer.

Code :
```c
#include <stdio.h>

int  main()
{
    int a = 10;
    int *ptr = &a;
    system( "cls" );

    printf( "a : %d\n", *ptr );
    printf( "&a : %p\n", ptr );
    printf( "&a : %u\n", ptr );

    system( "pause" );
    return 0;
}
```

Output :

```
TERMINAL

a : 10
&a :  0061FF18
&a :  6422296
Press any key to continue . . .
```

****

Program No. - 403 :
Program to calculate Volume of cylinder by using pointer.

Code :
```c
#include <stdio.h>

int  main()
{
    float r, h, v;
    float *pr, *ph, *pv;
    const float PI = 3.14;
    system( "cls" );


    pr = &r;
    ph = &h;
    pv = &v;

    printf( "Enter Radius & Height : " );
    scanf( "%f %f", pr, ph );

    *pv = PI * (*pr) * (*pr) * (*ph);
    printf( "\nVolume of Cylinder = %f\n", *pv );

    system( "pause" );
    return 0;
}
```

Output :

```
TERMINAL

Enter Radius & Height : 10 10

Volume of Cylinder = 3140.000000
Press any key to continue . . .
```

———————— **** ————————   ———————— **** ————————

Program No. - 404 :
Program to explain array of pointers.

Code :
```c
#include <stdio.h>

int  main()
{
    int a = 10, b = 20, c = 30;
    int *p[3], *t;
    int i;
    system( "cls" );

    p[0] = &a;
    p[1] = &b;
    p[2] = &c;

    printf( "Values are : " );
    for( i=0 ; i<3 ; i++ )
    {
        printf( " %d", *p[ i ] );
    }

    t = p[0];
    p[0] = p[2];
    p[2] = t;

    printf( "\nValues are : " );
    for( i=0 ; i<3 ; i++ )
    {
        printf( " %d", *p[ i ] );
    }

    printf( "\n" );
    system( "pause" );
    return 0;
}
```

Output :
```
TERMINAL

Values are :    10  20  30
Values are :    30  20  10
Press any key to continue . . . |
```

Program No. - 405 :
Program to explain array and pointers.

Code :
```c
#include <stdio.h>

int  main()
{
    int a[ ] = { 10, 20, 30, 40, 50 };
    int *p;
    int i;
    system( "cls" );

    p = &a[0];                    /*  p = a; */

    printf( "Array Elements are (a[i])  :" );
    for( i=0 ; i<5 ; i++ )
    {
        printf( " %d", a[ i ] );
    }

    printf( "\nArray Elements are (i[a])  :" );
    for( i=0 ; i<5 ; i++ )
    {
        printf( " %d", i[a] );
    }

    printf( "\nArray Elements are (*(a+i)):" );
    for( i=0 ; i<5 ; i++ )
    {
        printf( " %d", *( a + i ) );
    }

    printf( "\nArray Elements are (*(p+i)):" );
    for( i=0 ; i<5 ; i++ )
    {
        printf( " %d", *( p + i ) );
    }

    printf( "\nArray Elements are (p[i])  :" );
    for( i=0 ; i<5 ; i++ )
    {
        printf( " %d", p[ i ] );
    }
```

```
    printf( "\nArray Elements are (*p++)  :" );
    for( i=0 ; i<5 ; i++ )
    {
        printf( "  %d", *p++ );
    }

    printf( "\n" );
    system( "pause" );
    return 0;
}
```

Output :

```
TERMINAL

Array Elements are (a[i])   :  10  20  30  40  50
Array Elements are (i[a])   :  10  20  30  40  50
Array Elements are (*(a+i)):  10  20  30  40  50
Array Elements are (*(p+i)):  10  20  30  40  50
Array Elements are (p[i])   :  10  20  30  40  50
Array Elements are (*p++)   :  10  20  30  40  50
Press any key to continue . . .
```

———————— **** ————————

Program No. - 406 :
Program to pass Array to Function using Pass by Pointer.

Code :
```
#include <stdio.h>

void  display( int* );

int  main()
{
    int a[ ] = { 10, 20, 30, 40, 50 };
    system( "cls" );

    display( a );

    printf( "\n" );
    system( "pause" );
    return 0;
}

void  display( int *p )
{
    int i;
    printf( "Array Elements are :" );
```

```
    for( i=0 ; i<5 ; i++ )
    {
        printf( "  %d", *( p + i ) );
    }
}
```

Output :

```
TERMINAL

Array Elements are :  10  20  30  40  50
Press any key to continue . . .
```

———————— **** ————————

Program No. - 407 :
Program to pass a Character Array (String) by Pointer.

Code :
```
#include <stdio.h>

void  display( char* );

int  main()
{
    char s[ ] = "Atul Kumar Soni";
    system( "cls" );

    display( s );

    system( "pause" );
    return 0;
}

void  display( char *ps )
{
    printf( "String : %s\n", ps );
}
```

Output :

```
TERMINAL

String : Atul Kumar Soni
Press any key to continue . . .
```

———————— **** ————————

Program No. - 408 :
Program to explain **Pass by Value**.

Code :
```c
#include <stdio.h>

void  square( int  );

int  main()
{
    int a = 10;
    system( "cls" );

    square( a );

    printf( "a = %d\n", a );

    system( "pause" );
    return 0;
}

void  square( int  x )
{
    x = x * x;
    printf( "x = %d\n", x );
}
```

Output :
```
TERMINAL

x = 100
a = 10
Press any key to continue . . . |
```

———————— **** ————————

Program No. - 409 :
Program to explain **Pass by Reference / Address / Pointer**.

Code :
```c
#include <stdio.h>

void  square( int* );

int  main()
{
    int a = 10;
    system( "cls" );
```

```c
    square( &a );

    printf( "a = %d\n", a );

    system( "pause" );
    return 0;
}

void  square( int *pa )
{
    *pa = *pa * *pa;
    printf( "*pa = %d\n", *pa );
}
```

Output :
```
TERMINAL

*pa = 100
a = 100
Press any key to continue . . . |
```

———————— **** ————————

Program No. - 410 :
Program to explain Returning by reference (returning by pointer).

Code :
```c
#include <stdio.h>

int*  max( int*, int* );

int  main()
{
    int a = 10, b = 20, *p;
    system( "cls" );

    p = max( &a, &b );

    printf( "Maximum = %d\n", *p );

    system( "pause" );
    return 0;
}

int*  max( int *pa, int *pb )
```

```c
{
    if( *pa > *pb )
        return pa;
    else
        return pb;
}
```

Output :

```
TERMINAL

Maximum = 20
Press any key to continue . . . |
```

———————————— **** ————————————

Program No. - 411 :
Program to pass a string by pointer.

Code :
```c
#include <stdio.h>

void  display( char* );

int  main()
{
    char a[ ] = "INDIA";
    system( "cls" );

    display( a );

    printf( "\n" );
    system( "pause" );
    return 0;
}

void  display( char *p )
{
    int i;
    printf( "String : " );
    for( i=0 ; *(p+i) != '\0' ; i++ )
    {
        printf( " %c", *( p + i ) );
    }
}
```

Output :

```
TERMINAL

String :  I N D I A
Press any key to continue . . . |
```

———————————— **** ————————————

Program No. - 412 :
Program to explain **Pointer and 2-D Array**.

Code :
```c
#include <stdio.h>

int  main()
{
    int a[2][3] = { { 10, 20, 30 },
                    { 40, 50, 60 } };
    int *p;
    int i, j;
    system( "cls" );

    printf( "Matrix-A : \n" );
    for( i=0 ; i<2 ; i++ )
    {
        for( j=0 ; j<3 ; j++ )
        {
            printf( " %d", *( *( a + i ) + j ) );
        }
        printf( "\n" );
    }

    printf( "\nMatrix-A : \n" );
    for( i=0 ; i<2 ; i++ )
    {
        for( j=0 ; j<3 ; j++ )
        {
            printf( " %d", *( a[ i ] + j ) );
        }
        printf( "\n" );
    }

    p = &a[0][0];

    printf( "\nMatrix-A : \n" );
    for( i=0 ; i<2 ; i++ )
    {
        for( j=0 ; j<3 ; j++ )
```

```
        {
            printf( "  %d", *( p + 3 * i + j ) );
        }
        printf( "\n" );
    }

    system( "pause" );
    return 0;
}
```

Output :

```
TERMINAL

Matrix-A :
  10  20  30
  40  50  60

Matrix-A :
  10  20  30
  40  50  60

Matrix-A :
  10  20  30
  40  50  60
Press any key to continue . . .
```

——————————— ******** ———————————

Program No. - 413 :
Program to explain **Pointer to Function**.

Code :
```
#include <stdio.h>

void  Add( int, int );
void  Sub( int, int );

int  main()
{
    int a = 10, b = 20;
    void (*pf)( int, int );
    system( "cls" );

    pf = Add;

    (*pf)( a, b );            /*  Add( a, b );  */

    pf = Sub;
```

```
    (*pf)( a, b );            /*  Sub( a, b );  */

    system( "pause" );
    return 0;
}

void  Add( int x, int y )
{
    int s;
    s = x + y;
    printf( "Sum = %d\n", s );
}

void  Sub( int x, int y )
{
    int d;
    d = x - y;
    printf( "Difference = %d\n", d );
}
```

Output :

```
TERMINAL

Sum = 30
Difference = -10
Press any key to continue . . .
```

——————————— ******** ———————————

Program No. - 414 :
Program to explain **Chain of Pointers**.

Code :
```
#include <stdio.h>

int  main()
{
    int a = 10;
    int *p, **pp, ***ppp, ****pppp;
    system( "cls" );

    p = &a;

    printf( "p = %u\n", p );
    printf( "*p = %d\n", *p );

    pp = &p;
```

```c
printf( "\npp = %u\n", pp );
printf( "*pp = %u\n", *pp );
printf( "**pp = %d\n", **pp);

ppp = &pp;

printf( "\nppp = %u\n", ppp );
printf( "*ppp = %u\n", *ppp );
printf( "**ppp = %u\n", **ppp );
printf( "***ppp = %d\n", ***ppp );

pppp = &ppp;

printf( "\npppp = %u\n", pppp );
printf( "*pppp = %u\n", *pppp );
printf( "**pppp = %u\n", **pppp );
printf( "***pppp = %u\n", ***pppp );
printf( "****pppp = %d\n", ****pppp );

system( "pause" );
return 0;
}
```

Output :

```
TERMINAL

p = 3101686836
*p = 10

pp = 3101686824
*pp = 3101686836
**pp = 10

ppp = 3101686816
*ppp = 3101686824
**ppp = 3101686836
***ppp = 10

pppp = 3101686808
*pppp = 3101686816
**pppp = 3101686824
***pppp = 3101686836
****pppp = 10
Press any key to continue . . . |
```

****

Program No. - 415 :
Program to explain Pointer to structure.

Code :

```c
#include <stdio.h>

struct rectangle
{
    int l, b;
};

int main()
{
    system( "cls" );
    struct rectangle r1;
    struct rectangle *p;

    p = &r1;

    p->l = 10;
    p->b = 5;

    printf( "length = %d\n", r1.l );
    printf( "breadth = %d\n", r1.b );
    system( "pause" );
}
```

Output :

```
TERMINAL

length = 10
breadth = 5
Press any key to continue . . . []
```

****

Program No. - 416 :
Write a program to SORT a given element of an array in Ascending order using **Bubble Sort**?

Code :

```c
#include <stdio.h>

int  main()
{
    int a[5] = { 30, 50, 40, 20, 10 };
    int i, j, t;
    int *p;
    system( "cls" );
```

```c
    p = a;                          /* p = &p[0];   */

    printf( "Before Sorting :" );
    for( i=0 ; i<5 ; i++ )
    {
        printf( " %d", *( p + i ) );
    }

    for( i=0 ; i<5-1 ; i++ )
    {
        for( j=0 ; j<5-1-i ; j++ )
        {
            if( *( p + j ) > *( p + j + 1 ) )
            {
                t = *( p + j );
                *( p + j ) = *( p + j + 1 );
                *( p + j + 1 ) = t;
            }
        }
    }

    printf( "\n\nAfter Sorting  :" );
    for( i=0 ; i<5 ; i++ )
    {
        printf( " %d", *( p + i ) );
    }

    printf( "\n" );
    system( "pause" );
    return 0;
}
```

Output :

```
TERMINAL

Before Sorting :  30  50  40  20  10

After Sorting  :  10  20  30  40  50
Press any key to continue . . .
```

****

****

Chapter – 13
Dynamic Memory Allocation

****

Program No. - 417 :
Program to explain Dynamic Memory Management.

Code :
```c
#include <stdio.h>
#include <stdlib.h>

int  main()
{
    int *p;
    system( "cls" );

    p = ( int* ) malloc( 1 * sizeof( int ) );
    *p = 10;

    printf( "Value : %d\n",  *p );
    free( p );

    system( "pause" );
    return 0;
}
```

Output :
```
TERMINAL

Value : 10
Press any key to continue . . .
```

———————— ******** ————————

Program No. - 418 :
Program to explain Dynamic Memory Management.

Code :
```c
#include <stdio.h>
#include <stdlib.h>

int  main()
{
    int *p;
    system( "cls" );

    p = ( int* ) calloc( 1,  sizeof( int ) );
    *p = 10;

    printf( "Value : %d\n",  *p );
    free( p );
```

```c
    system( "pause" );
    return 0;
}
```

Output :
```
TERMINAL

Value : 10
Press any key to continue . . .
```

———————— ******** ————————

Program No. - 419 :
Program to explain Dynamic Memory Allocation for String.

Code :
```c
#include <stdio.h>
#include <stdlib.h>
#include <string.h>

int  main()
{
    char s1[25] = "Atul Kumar Soni";
    int len = strlen( s1 );
    char *ps;
    system( "cls" );

    ps = ( char* ) malloc( ( len + 1 ) * sizeof( char ) );
    strcpy( ps, s1 );

    printf( "ps = %s\n",  ps );
    free( ps );

    system( "pause" );
    return 0;
}
```

Output :
```
TERMINAL

ps = Atul Kumar Soni
Press any key to continue . . .
```

———————— ******** ————————

Program No. - 420 :
Program to explain Dynamic Memory Management for Array.

Code :
```c
#include <stdio.h>
#include <stdlib.h>

int  main()
{
    int *p;
    int i;
    system( "cls" );

    p = ( int* ) malloc( 5 * sizeof( int ) );

    for( i=0 ; i<5 ; i++ )
    {
        printf( "Enter Value : " );
        scanf( "%d", ( p + i ) );
    }

    printf( "\nValues are : " );
    for( i=0 ; i<5 ; i++ )
    {
        printf( " %d", *( p + i ) );
    }
    free( p );

    printf( "\n" );
    system( "pause" );
    return 0;
}
```

Output :

```
TERMINAL

Enter Value : 10
Enter Value : 20
Enter Value : 30
Enter Value : 40
Enter Value : 50

Values are :  10 20 30 40 50
Press any key to continue . . .
```

****

Program No. - 421 :
Program to use **malloc( )** function.

Code :
```c
#include <stdio.h>
#include <malloc.h>

int  main()
{
    int *p;
    int i, n, s;
    system( "cls" );

    printf( "Enter Number of Terms : " );
    scanf( "%d", &n );
    p = (int *) malloc( n * sizeof( int ) );

    if( !p )
        printf( "\nUnable to allocate size. \n" );
    else
    {
        for( i=0 ; i<n ; i++ )
        {
            printf( "Enter Value : " );
            scanf( "%d", ( p + i ) );
        }

        printf( "\nValues are : " );
        s = 0;
        for( i=0 ; i<n ; i++ )
        {
            printf( " %d", *( p + i ) );
            s = s + *( p + i );
        }
        printf( "\nSum of elements = %d\n", s );
    }

    free( p );

    system( "pause" );
    return 0;
}
```

Output :

```
TERMINAL

Enter Number of Terms : 5
Enter Value : 10
Enter Value : 20
Enter Value : 30
Enter Value : 40
Enter Value : 50

Values are :   10  20  30  40  50
Sum of elements = 150
Press any key to continue . . .
```

****

Program No. - 422 :
Program to use **calloc( )** function.

Code :
```c
#include <stdio.h>
#include <malloc.h>

int  main()
{
    int *p;
    int i, n, s;
    system( "cls" );

    printf( "Enter Number of Terms : " );
    scanf( "%d", &n );
    p = (int *)calloc( n, sizeof( int ) );

    if( ! p )
        printf( "\nUnable to allocate size.\n" );
    else
    {
        for( i=0 ; i<n ; i++ )
        {
            printf( "Enter Value : " );
            scanf( "%d", ( p + i ) );
        }

        printf( "\nValues are : " );
        s = 0;
        for( i=0 ; i<n ; i++ )
        {
            printf( " %d", *( p + i ) );
            s = s + *( p + i );
```

```c
        }
        printf( "\nSum of Elements = %d\n", s );
    }

    free( p );

    system( "pause" );
    return 0;
}
```

Output :

```
TERMINAL

Enter Number of Terms : 5
Enter Value : 10
Enter Value : 20
Enter Value : 30
Enter Value : 40
Enter Value : 50

Values are :   10  20  30  40  50
Sum of Elements = 150
Press any key to continue . . .
```

****

Program No. - 423 :
Program to use **realloc( )** function.

Code :
```c
#include <stdio.h>
#include <malloc.h>
#include <stdlib.h>         /*  #include <process.h> */

int  main()
{
    int *p;
    int i, x, n, s;
    system( "cls" );

    printf( "Enter Size of Dynamic Array : " );
    scanf( "%d", &n );
    p = (int *)malloc(n * sizeof( int ) );

    if( ! p )
        printf( "\nUnable to allocate size.\n" );
    else
    {
```

```c
    for( i=0 ; i<n ; i++ )
    {
        printf( "Enter Value : " );
        scanf( "%d", ( p + i ) );
    }

    printf( "\nValues are : " );
    s = 0;
    for( i=0 ; i<n ; i++ )
    {
        printf( " %d", *( p + i ) );
        s = s + *( p + i );
    }
    printf( "\nSum of Elements = %d", s );

    x = n;
    printf( "\n\nEnter New Size of Dynamic
                             Array : " );
    scanf( "%d", &n );

    realloc( p, n * sizeof( int ) );

    if( !p )
    {
        printf( "\nUnable to allocate size.\n" );
        exit( 1 );
    }

    for( i=x ; i<n ; i++ )
    {
        printf( "Enter Additional Value : " );
        scanf( "%d", ( p + i ) );
    }

    printf( "\nValues are : " );
    s = 0;
    for( i=0 ; i<n ; i++ )
    {
        printf( " %d", *( p + i ) );
        s = s + *( p + i );
    }
    printf( "\nSum of elements = %d\n", s );
}

free( p );

system( "pause" );
```

```c
    return 0;
}
```

Output :

```
TERMINAL

Enter Size of Dynamic Array : 3
Enter Value : 10
Enter Value : 20
Enter Value : 30

Values are :    10   20   30
Sum of Elements = 60

Enter New Size of Dynamic Array : 5
Enter Additional Value : 40
Enter Additional Value : 50

Values are :    10   20   30   40   50
Sum of elements = 150
Press any key to continue . . .
```

****

****

Chapter – 14
Preprocessors

****

Program No. - 424 :
Program to explain **Simple Macro Substitution(#define).**

Code :
```c
#include <stdio.h>

#define  PI 3.14159

int  main()
{
    system( "cls" );
    printf( "Value of PI : %f\n",  PI );
    system( "pause" );
    return 0;
}
```

Output :
```
TERMINAL
Value of PI : 3.141590
Press any key to continue . . .
```

---- **** ----

Program No. - 425 :
Program to explain **Simple Macro Substitution(#define).**

Code :
```c
#include <stdio.h>

#define  PI  3.14159

int  main()
{
    float r, a;
    system( "cls" );

    printf( "Enter Radius : " );
    scanf( "%f", &r );

    a = PI * r * r;

    printf( "Area of Circle : %f\n",  a );

    system( "pause" );
```

```c
    return 0;
}
```

Output :
```
TERMINAL
Enter Radius : 10.0
Area of Circle : 314.158997
Press any key to continue . . .
```

---- **** ----

Program No. - 426 :
Program to use **Macro Substitution with Arguments.**

Code :
```c
#include <stdio.h>

#define  MIN(a,b)  (((a)<(b))?a:b)

int  main()
{
    int x, y;
    system( "cls" );

    x = 10;
    y = 20;
    printf( "Minimum = %d\n",  MIN(x, y) );

    system( "pause" );
    return 0;
}
```

Output :
```
TERMINAL
Minimum = 10
Press any key to continue . . .
```

---- **** ----

Program No. - 427 :
Program to explain **Nested Macro Substitution.**

Code :
```c
#include <stdio.h>

#define  PI  3.14159
```

```c
#define   Volume(r)   (4.0/3.0)*PI*(r)*(r)*(r)

int  main()
{
    float r, v;
    system( "cls" );

    printf( "Enter Radius of Sphere : " );
    scanf( "%f", &r );

    v = Volume( r );

    printf( "\nVolume of Sphere : %f\n",  v );

    system( "pause" );
    return 0;
}
```

Output :

```
TERMINAL

Enter Radius of Sphere : 10

Volume of Sphere : 4188.786621
Press any key to continue . . .
```

——————————— **** ———————————

Program No. - 428 :
Program to Swap two numbers using #define preprocessor.

Code :

```c
#include <stdio.h>

#define  SWAP(a,b)  {int temp; temp=a; a=b; b=temp;}

int  main()
{
    int x, y;
    system( "cls" );

    printf( "Enter Two Numbers : " );
    scanf( "%d %d", &x, &y );

    printf( "x : %d, y : %d\n", x, y );
```

```c
    SWAP( x, y );

    printf( "x : %d, y : %d\n", x, y );

    system( "pause" );
    return 0;
}
```

Output :

```
TERMINAL

Enter Two Numbers : 10 20
x : 10, y : 20
x : 20, y : 10
Press any key to continue . . .
```

——————————— **** ———————————

Program No. - 429 :
Program to use **#include** Preprocessor.

Code-1 [myheader.h] :

```c
//  Save this file as "myheader.h" in current directory.
int  add( int x, int y)
{
    int s;
    s = x + y;
    return s;
}

int  sub( int x, int y)
{
    int d;
    d = x − y;
    return d;
}
```

Code-2 :

```c
//  Save this file with .cpp file extension.
#include <stdio.h>

#include "myheader.h"

int  main()
{
    int a = 20, b = 10, res;
    system( "cls" );
```

```c
    res = add( a, b );
    printf( "Sum = %d\n",  res );

    res = sub( a, b );
    printf( "Difference = %d\n",  res );

    system( "pause" );
    return 0;
}
```

Output :

```
TERMINAL

Sum = 30
Difference = 10
Press any key to continue . . . |
```

———————————— ******** ————————————

Program No. - 430 :
Program to create user-defined header file use it in the program.

Code-1 [myfile.h] :

```c
int square( int n )
{
    int r;
    r = n * n;
    return r;
}
```

Code-2 :

```c
#include <stdio.h>
#include "myfile.h"

int  main()
{
    int s, n = 10;
    system( "cls" );

    s = square( n );
    printf( "Square : %d\n", s );

    system( "pause" );
    return 0;
}
```

Output :

```
TERMINAL

Square : 100
Press any key to continue . . .
```

———————————— ******** ————————————

Program No. - 431 :
Program to include user-defined Header file using Absolute Path.

Code-1 [d:\myfile.h] :

```c
int square( int n )
{
    int r;
    r = n * n;
    return r;
}
```

Code-2 :

```c
#include <stdio.h>
#include "d:\myfile.h"              // absolute path

int  main()
{
    int s, n = 10;
    system( "cls" );

    s = square( n );
    printf( "Square : %d\n", s );

    system( "pause" );
    return 0;
}
```

Output :

```
TERMINAL

Square : 100
Press any key to continue . . . []
```

———————————— ******** ————————————

Program No. - 432 :
Program to include user-defined Header file using Relative Path.

Code-1 [.\CPrograms\myfile.h] :
```c
int square( int n )
{
    int r;
    r = n * n;
    return r;
}
```

Code-2 :
```c
#include <stdio.h>
#include ".\CPrograms\myfile.h"        // relative path

int  main()
{
    int s, n = 10;
    system( "cls" );

    s = square( n );
    printf( "Square : %d\n", s );

    system( "pause" );
    return 0;
}
```

Output :

```
TERMINAL

Square : 100
Press any key to continue . . . 
```

____________________ **** ____________________

Program No. - 433 :
Program to include user-defined Header file using Relative Path.

Code-1 [..\myfile.h] :
```c
int square( int n )
{
    int r;
    r = n * n;
    return r;
}
```

Code-2 :
```c
#include <stdio.h>
```

```c
#include "..\myfile.h "           // relative path

int  main()
{
    int s, n = 10;
    system( "cls" );

    s = square( n );
    printf( "Square : %d\n", s );

    system( "pause" );
    return 0;
}
```

Output :

```
TERMINAL

Square : 100
Press any key to continue . . . 
```

____________________ **** ____________________

Program No. - 434 :
Program to use Compiler Control Directives (**#if** and **#endif**).

Code :
```c
#include <stdio.h>

#define  INDIA  1

// #define  USA  1

#if( defined  INDIA )
    #define  PI  3.14159
#endif

#if( defined USA )
    #define  PI  3.14
#endif

int  main()
{
    float r, a;
    system( "cls" );

    printf( "Enter Radius : " );
```

```
    scanf( "%f", &r );

    a = PI * r * r;

    printf( "\nArea of Circle : %f\n",  a );

    system( "pause" );
    return 0;
}
```

Output (If INDIA defined):

```
TERMINAL

Enter Radius : 10


Area of Circle : 314.158997
Press any key to continue . . . |
```

Output (If USA defined):

```
TERMINAL

Enter Radius : 10


Area of Circle : 314.000000
Press any key to continue . . . |
```

———————————— ******** ————————————

Program No. - 435 :
Program to use Compiler Control Directives (**#ifdef** and **#endif**).

Code :
```
#include <stdio.h>

#define  INDIA  1

// #define  USA  1

#ifdef  INDIA
    #define  PI  3.14159
#endif

#ifdef  USA
    #define  PI  3.14
#endif

int  main()
```

```
{
    float r, a;
    system( "cls" );

    printf( "Enter Radius : " );
    scanf( "%f", &r );

    a = PI * r * r;

    printf( "\nArea of Circle : %f\n", a );

    system( "pause" );
    return 0;
}
```

Output (If INDIA defined):

```
TERMINAL

Enter Radius : 10


Area of Circle : 314.158997
Press any key to continue . . . |
```

Output (If USA defined):

```
TERMINAL

Enter Radius : 10


Area of Circle : 314.000000
Press any key to continue . . . |
```

———————————— ******** ————————————

Program No. - 436 :
Program to use Compiler Control Directives (**#ifndef** and **#endif**).

Code :
```
#include <stdio.h>

#define  INDIA  1

// #define  USA  1

#ifndef  USA
    #define  PI  3.14159
#endif
```

```c
#ifndef  INDIA
    #define  PI  3.14
#endif

int  main()
{
    float r, a;
    system( "cls" );

    printf( "Enter Radius : " );
    scanf( "%f", &r );

    a = PI * r * r;

    printf( "\nArea of Circle : %f\n",  a );

    system( "pause" );
    return 0;
}
```

Output (If USA not defined):

```
TERMINAL
Enter Radius : 10

Area of Circle : 314.158997
Press any key to continue . . .
```

Output (If INDIA not defined):

```
TERMINAL
Enter Radius : 10

Area of Circle : 314.000000
Press any key to continue . . .
```

_____________ **** _____________

Program No. - 437 :
Program to use **#define** Preprocessor.

Code :
```c
#include <stdio.h>

#define  pf  printf
#define  sf  scanf

int  main()
```

```c
{
    int a, b, s;
    system( "cls" );

    pf( "Enter Two Numbers : " );
    sf( "%d %d", &a, &b );

    s = a + b;

    pf( "\nSum = %d\n", s );

    system( "pause" );
    return 0;
}
```

Output :

```
TERMINAL
Enter Two Numbers : 100 200

Sum = 300
Press any key to continue . . .
```

_____________ **** _____________

Program No. - 438 :
Program to use Compiler Control Directives (**#undef**).

Code :
```c
#include <stdio.h>

#define  VAL 40

#ifdef  VAL
    #undef  VAL
#endif

#define  VAL 50

int  main()
{
    system( "cls" );

    printf( "Value = %d\n",  VAL );

    system( "pause" );
```

```
    return 0;
}
```

Output :

```
TERMINAL

Value = 50
Press any key to continue . . .
```

———————— **** ————————

Program No. - 439 :
Program to use Compiler Control Directives (**#if**).

Code :
```c
#include <stdio.h>

#define  MAX  1

int  main()
{
    int a = 10, b = 20;
    system( "cls" );

    #if  MAX == 1
        printf( "Maximum = %d\n",  (a>b?a:b) );
    #else
        printf( "Minimum = %d\n",  (a<b?a:b) );
    #endif

    system( "pause" );
    return 0;
}
```

Output :

```
TERMINAL

Maximum = 20
Press any key to continue . . .
```

———————— **** ————————

Program No. - 440 :
Program to use **#line** Preprocessor & __LINE__,
__DATE__, __TIME__.

Code :
```c
#include <stdio.h>
```

```c
int  main()
{
    system( "cls" );
    #line 101
    printf( "Line No.: %d\n", __LINE__ );

    #line 201
    printf( "Line No.: %d\n", __LINE__ );
    printf( "Current Date: %s\n", __DATE__ );
    printf( "Current Time: %s\n", __TIME__ );

    system( "pause" );
    return 0;
}
```

Output :

```
TERMINAL

Line No.: 101
Line No.: 201
Current Date: Jan 10 2024
Current Time: 01:11:02
Press any key to continue . . .
```

———————— **** ————————

Program No. - 441 :
Program to use **Macro Continuation Operator (\)** and
Stringizing Operator (#).

Code :
```c
#include <stdio.h>

#define  message(a, b) \
    printf( "Learn " #a " and " #b "\n")

int  main()
{
    system( "cls" );

    message( C, C++ );

    system( "pause" );
    return 0;
}
```

Output :

```
TERMINAL

Learn C and C++
Press any key to continue . . . []
```

———————————— **** ————————————

Program No. - 442 :
Program to use **Stringizing(#)** Operator.

Code :
```c
#include <stdio.h>

#define  MKSTR(x)  #x

int  main()
{
    system( "cls" );

    printf( "\n%s\n", MKSTR(Atul Kumar Soni) );

    system( "pause" );
    return 0;
}
```

Output :
```
TERMINAL

Atul Kumar Soni
Press any key to continue . . . |
```

———————————— **** ————————————

Program No. - 443 :
Program to use **Token Pasting(##)** Operator.

Code :
```c
#include <stdio.h>

#define  concat(a,b)  a##b

int  main()
{
    int  xy = 100;
    system( "cls" );

    printf( "Value : %d\n",  concat(x, y) );
```

```c
    system( "pause" );
    return 0;
}
```

Output :
```
TERMINAL

Value : 100
Press any key to continue . . . |
```

———————————— **** ————————————

****

Chapter – 15
Input / Output Formatting

****

Program No. - 444 :
Program to find ASCII value of given character.

Code :
```c
#include <stdio.h>

int  main()
{
    char ch;
    system( "cls" );

    printf( "Enter a Char : " );
    ch = getchar();
    printf( "\nASCII code of %c = %d\n", ch, ch );

    system( "pause" );
    return 0;
}
```

Output :
```
TERMINAL

Enter a Char : A

ASCII code of A = 65
Press any key to continue . . .
```

———————— **** ————————

Program No. - 445 :
Program to use getchar() and putchar() function.

Code :
```c
#include <stdio.h>

int  main()
{
    char ch;
    system( "cls" );

    printf( "Enter a Char : " );
    ch = getchar();
    putchar( ch );

    printf( "\n" );
    system( "pause" );
    return 0;
```

```c
}
```

Output :
```
TERMINAL

Enter a Char : C
C
Press any key to continue . . .
```

———————— **** ————————

Program No. - 446 :
Program to print integer value inside a string.

Code :
```c
#include <stdio.h>

int  main()
{
    int num;
    system( "cls" );

    num = 100;
    printf( "\nnum = %d\n", num );

    system( "pause" );
    return 0;
}
```

Output :
```
TERMINAL

num =  100
Press any key to continue . . .
```

———————— **** ————————

Program No. - 447 :
Program to use calculation inside the printf() statement.

Code :
```c
#include <stdio.h>

int  main()
{
    int length, width, height;
    system( "cls" );
```

```c
    printf( "Enter length : " );
    scanf( "%d", &length );

    printf( "Enter width : " );
    scanf( "%d", &width );

    printf( "Enter height : " );
    scanf( "%d", &height );

    printf( "\nVolume = %d\n",
                        ( length * width * height ) );

    system( "pause" );
    return 0;
}
```

Output :

```
TERMINAL

Enter length : 10
Enter width  : 10
Enter height : 5

Volume = 500
Press any key to continue . . .
```

****

Program No. - 448 :
Program to use integer literal inside printf() statement.

Code :
```c
#include <stdio.h>

int  main()
{
    system( "cls" );

    printf( "Integer Literal = %d\n", 100 );

    system( "pause" );
    return 0;
}
```

Output :

```
TERMINAL

Integer Literal = 100
Press any key to continue . . .
```

****

Program No. - 449 :
Program to input a integer using scanf().

Code :
```c
#include <stdio.h>

int  main()
{
    int n;
    system( "cls" );

    printf( "Enter a Number : ");
    scanf( "%d", &n );
    printf( "\nSquare of Number is = %d\n", (n * n) );

    system( "pause" );
    return 0;
}
```

Output :

```
TERMINAL

Enter a Number : 10

Square of Number is = 100
Press any key to continue . . .
```

****

Program No. - 450 :
Program to print literals of different data types using printf().

Code :
```c
#include <stdio.h>

int  main()
{
    char c;
    int i;
    long l;
```

```c
    long longll;
    float f;
    double d;
    long double ld;
    system( "cls" );

    c = 'A';
    i = 10;
    l = 100L;
    ll = 1000LL;
    f = 12.34f;
    d = 12.34;
    ld = 12.34;

    printf( "c = %c\n", c );
    printf( "i = %d\n", i );
    printf( "l = %ld\n", l );
    printf( "ll = %lld\n", ll );
    printf( "\nf = %f\n", f );
    printf( "d = %lf\n", d );
    printf( "ld = %Lf\n", ld );

    system( "pause" );
    return 0;
}
```

Output :

```
TERMINAL

c = A
i = 10
l = 100
ll = 1000

f = 12.340000
d = 12.340000
ld = 12.340000
Press any key to continue . . . |
```

————————————— **** —————————————

Program No. - 451 :
Program to use decimal, octal and hexadecimal integer
values in C program.

Code :
```c
#include <stdio.h>
```

```c
int  main()
{
    int dec = 12;
    int oct = 015;
    int hex = 0x2F;
    system( "cls" );

    printf( "dec : %d\n", dec );
    printf( "oct : %o\n", oct );
    printf( "dec(oct) : %d\n", oct );
    printf( "hex : %x\n", hex );
    printf( "dec(hex) : %d\n", hex );

    system( "pause" );
    return 0;
}
```

Output :

```
TERMINAL

dec : 12
oct : 15
dec(oct) : 13
hex : 2f
dec(hex) : 47
Press any key to continue . . . []
```

————————————— **** —————————————

Program No. - 452 :
Program to explain the use of escape sequence (\0) in
printf().

Code :
```c
#include <stdio.h>

int  main()
{
    system( "cls" );

    printf( "Atul\0 Kumar Soni" );

    printf( "\n" );
    system( "pause" );
    return 0;
}
```

Output :

```
TERMINAL

Atul
Press any key to continue . . .
```

****

Program No. - 453 :
Program to use escape sequences (backslash characters).

Code :
```c
#include <stdio.h>

int  main()
{
    system( "cls" );

    printf( "Red\nGreen\nBlue\n" );
    printf( "Red\tGreen\tBlue\n" );

    system( "pause" );
    return 0;
}
```

Output :

```
TERMINAL

Red
Green
Blue
Red      Green    Blue
Press any key to continue . . .
```

****

Program No. - 454 :
Program to input single word string using scanf().

Code :
```c
#include <stdio.h>

int  main()
{
    char str[25];
    system( "cls" );
```

```c
    printf( "Enter a String : " );
    scanf( "%s", str );
    printf( "\nString : %s\n", str );

    system( "pause" );
    return 0;
}
```

Output :

```
TERMINAL

Enter a String : Atul Kumar Soni

String : Atul
Press any key to continue . . .
```

****

Program No. - 455 :
Program to display string literal using puts().

Code :
```c
#include <stdio.h>

int  main()
{
    system( "cls" );

    puts( "Atul" );
    puts( "Kumar" );
    puts( "Soni" );

    system( "pause" );
    return 0;
}
```

Output :

```
TERMINAL

Atul
Kumar
Soni
Press any key to continue . . .
```

****

Program No. - 456 :
Program to display string variable using puts().

Code :
```c
#include <stdio.h>

int  main()
{
    char str[25] = "Atul Kumar Soni";
    system( "cls" );

    puts( str );

    system( "pause" );
    return 0;
}
```

Output :
```
TERMINAL

Atul Kumar Soni
Press any key to continue . . . |
```

****

Program No. - 457 :
Program to using getchar() and putchar() to input and display a single character.

Code :
```c
#include <stdio.h>

int  main()
{
    char ch;
    system( "cls" );

    ch = getchar();
    putchar( ch );

    system( "pause" );
    return 0;
}
```

Output :
```
TERMINAL

A
APress any key to continue . . . |
```

****

Program No. - 458 :
Program to input multiple integer using scanf().

Code :
```c
#include <stdio.h>

int  main()
{
    int a, b, c;
    system( "cls" );

    printf( "Enter Two Numbers : " );
    c = scanf( "%d%d", &a, &b );

    printf( "\nNumber of Inputs = %d\n", c );
    printf( "a = %d\nb = %d\n", a, b );

    system( "pause" );
    return 0;
}
```

Output :
```
TERMINAL

Enter Two Numbers : 10 20

Number of Inputs = 2
a = 10
b = 20
Press any key to continue . . . |
```

****

Program No. - 459 :
Program to input a integer in hexadecimal format using scanf().

Code :
```c
#include <stdio.h>

int  main()
{
    int n;
    system( "cls" );

    printf( "Enter a Hex Number : " );
```

```c
    scanf( "%x", &n );

    printf( "\nDecimal Equivalent = %d\n", n );

    system( "pause" );
    return 0;
}
```

Output :

```
TERMINAL
Enter a Hex Number : AB

Decimal Equivalent = 171
Press any key to continue . . . |
```

****

Program No. - 460 :
Program to input and display different types of integer values.

Code :
```c
#include <stdio.h>

int  main()
{
    unsigned int u;
    long l;
    short int s;
    system( "cls" );

    printf( "Enter an Unsigned : " );
    scanf( "%u", &u );

    printf( "Enter a Long : " );
    scanf( "%ld", &l );

    printf( "Enter a Short : " );
    scanf( "%hd", &s );

    printf( "\nUnsigned Number = %u\n", u );
    printf( "Long Number = %ld\n", l );
    printf( "Short Number = %hd\n", s );

    system( "pause" );
    return 0;
```

```c
}
```

Output :

```
TERMINAL
Enter an Unsigned : 80000
Enter a Long : 123456789
Enter a Short : 32767

Unsigned Number = 80000
Long Number = 123456789
Short Number = 32767
Press any key to continue . . . |
```

****

Program No. - 461 :
Program to input two three digits integer values using scanf().

Code :
```c
#include <stdio.h>

int  main()
{
    int a, b;
    system( "cls" );

    printf( "Enter Two 3-digit Numbers : " );
    scanf( "%3d %3d", &a, &b );

    printf( "\na = %d\n", a );
    printf( "b = %d\n", b );

    system( "pause" );
    return 0;
}
```

Output :

```
TERMINAL
Enter Two 3-digit Numbers : 123456

a = 123
b = 456
Press any key to continue . . . |
```

****

Program No. - 462 :
Program to input multiple word string using gets().

Code :
```c
#include <stdio.h>

int  main()
{
    char str[25];
    system( "cls" );

    printf( "Enter String : " );
    gets( str );

    printf( "\nString = %s\n", str );

    system( "pause" );
    return 0;
}
```

Output :

```
TERMINAL

Enter String : Atul Kumar Soni

String = Atul Kumar Soni
Press any key to continue . . .
```

****

Program No. - 463 :
Program to use gets() function in different way.

Code :
```c
#include <stdio.h>

int  main()
{
    char str[25], *p;
    system( "cls" );

    printf( "Enter a String : " );

    p = gets( str );

    if( p )                         /* if not null */
    {
```

        printf("\n%s\n", str);
        printf("%s\n", p);
    }

    system("pause");
    return 0;
}

Output :

```
TERMINAL

Enter a String : Atul Kumar Soni

Atul Kumar Soni
Atul Kumar Soni
Press any key to continue . . .
```

****

Program No. - 464 :
Program to input single word string using scanf().

Code :
```c
#include <stdio.h>

int  main()
{
    char str[25];
    system( "cls" );

    printf( "Enter a String : " );
    scanf( "%s", str );
    printf( "\nString = %s\n", str );

    system( "pause" );
    return 0;
}
```

Output :

```
TERMINAL

Enter a String : Atul

String = Atul
Press any key to continue . . .
```

****

Program No. - 465 :
Program to input a string maximum 15 characters.

Code :
```c
#include <stdio.h>

int  main()
{
    char str[25];
    system( "cls" );

    printf( "Enter a String : " );
    scanf( "%15s", str );
    printf( "\nString = %s\n", str );

    system( "pause" );
    return 0;
}
```

Output :

```
TERMINAL

Enter a String : ABCDEFGHIJKLMNOPQRST

String = ABCDEFGHIJKLMNO
Press any key to continue . . .
```

———————— **** ————————

Program No. - 466 :
Program to input a string that contain only Alphabets.

Code :
```c
#include <stdio.h>

int  main()
{
    char str[25];
    system( "cls" );

    printf( "Enter Letters only : " );
    scanf( "%[a-zA-Z]", str );

    printf( "\nString = %s\n", str );

    system( "pause" );
    return 0;
```

```c
}
```

Output :

```
TERMINAL

Enter Letters only : Atul Soni 12345

String = Atul
Press any key to continue . . .
```

———————— **** ————————

Program No. - 467 :
Program to input a string that contain Alphabets with space.

Code :
```c
#include <stdio.h>

int  main()
{
    char str[25];
    system( "cls" );

    printf( "Enter Letters and Space : " );
    scanf( "%[a-zA-Z ]", str );

    printf( "\nString = %s\n", str );

    system( "pause" );
    return 0;
}
```

Output :

```
TERMINAL

Enter Letters and Space : Atul Soni 12345

String = Atul Soni
Press any key to continue . . .
```

———————— **** ————————

Program No. - 468 :
Program to use expression directly in printf().

Code :
```c
#include <stdio.h>
```

```c
int  main()
{
    float radius = 10.0f;
    const float PI = 3.14159f;
    system( "cls" );

    printf( "Circumference = %.2f\n",
                            ( 2.0f * PI * radius ) );
    printf( "Area = %.2f\n", ( PI * radius * radius ) );

    system( "pause" );
    return 0;
}
```

Output :

```
TERMINAL

Circumference = 62.83
Area = 314.16
Press any key to continue . . . |
```

――――――――― **** ―――――――――

Program No. - 469 :
Program to use printf() for integer formatting.

Code :
```c
#include <stdio.h>

int  main()
{
    int a = 123;
    long b = 987654;
    system( "cls" );

    printf( "|%7d|\n", a );
    printf( "|%-7d|\n", a );
    printf( "|%07d|\n", a );
    printf( "|%2d|\n", a );

    printf( "\n|%10ld|\n", b );
    printf( "|%-10ld|\n", b );
    printf( "|%010ld|\n", b );
    printf( "|%3ld|\n", b );

    system( "pause" );
```

```c
    return 0;
}
```

Output :

```
TERMINAL

|     123|
|123     |
|0000123|
|123|

|      987654|
|987654      |
|0000987654|
|987654|
Press any key to continue . . . |
```

――――――――― **** ―――――――――

Program No. - 470 :
Program to use printf() for integer formatting.

Code :
```c
#include <stdio.h>

int main()
{
    system( "cls" );

    printf( "%4d\n", 1 );
    printf( "%4d\n", 12 );
    printf( "%4d\n", 123 );
    printf( "%4d\n", 1234 );
    printf( "%4d\n\n", 12345 );

    printf( "%4d\n", -1 );
    printf( "%4d\n", -12 );
    printf( "%4d\n", -123 );
    printf( "%4d\n", -1234 );
    printf( "%4d\n", -12345 );

    system( "pause" );
    return 0;
}
```

Output :

```
TERMINAL

     1
    12
   123
  1234
 12345

    -1
   -12
  -123
 -1234
-12345
Press any key to continue . . .
```

****

Program No. - 471 :

Program to use different format specifiers for floating-point values.

Code :

```c
#include <stdio.h>

int  main()
{
    float x = 123.45f;
    system( "cls" );

    printf( "x : %f", x );
    printf( "\nx : %g", x );
    printf( "\nx : %e\n", x );

    system( "pause" );
    return 0;
}
```

Output :

```
TERMINAL

x : 123.449997
x : 123.45
x : 1.234500e+002
Press any key to continue . . .
```

****

Program No. - 472 :

Program to use printf() for floating-point formatting.

Code :

```c
#include <stdio.h>

int  main()
{
    float a = 987.654;
    system( "cls" );

    printf( "|%12.4f|\n", a );
    printf( "|%12.2f|\n", a );
    printf( "|%-12.4f|\n", a );
    printf( "|%-12.2f|\n", a );
    printf( "|%f|\n", a );
    printf( "\n|%12.4e|\n", a );
    printf( "|%12.2e|\n", a );
    printf( "|%-12.4e|\n", a );
    printf( "|%-12.2e|\n", a );
    printf( "|%e|\n", a );

    system( "pause" );
    return 0;
}
```

Output :

```
TERMINAL

|    987.6540|
|      987.65|
|987.6540    |
|987.65      |
|987.653992|

|   9.8765e+02|
|     9.88e+02|
|9.8765e+02   |
|9.88e+02     |
|9.876540e+02|
Press any key to continue . . .
```

****

Program No. - 473 :

Program to use printf() for floating-point formatting.

Code :

```c
#include <stdio.h>
```

```c
int  main()
{
    float a = 987.654;
    system( "cls" );

    printf( "|%*.*f|\n", 12, 4, a );
    printf( "|%-*.*f|\n", 12, 4, a );

    printf( "\n|%*.*e|\n", 12, 4, a );
    printf( "|%-*.*e|\n", 12, 4, a );

    system( "pause" );
    return 0;
}
```

Output :

```
TERMINAL
|     987.6540|
|987.6540     |

|   9.8765e+02|
|9.8765e+02   |
Press any key to continue . . .
```

****

Program No. - 474 :
Program to explain Floating-point formatting.

Code :
```c
#include <stdio.h>

int  main()
{
    system( "cls" );

    printf( "%.2f\n", 123.2999353210643 );
    printf( "%.3f\n", 123.2999353210643 );
    printf( "%.4f\n", 123.2999353210643 );
    printf( "%.5f\n", 123.2999353210643 );
    printf( "%.10f\n", 123.2999353210643 );
    printf( "%.12f\n", 123.2999353210643 );

    system( "pause" );
    return 0;
}
```

Output :

```
TERMINAL
123.30
123.300
123.2999
123.29994
123.2999353211
123.299935321064
Press any key to continue . . .
```

****

Program No. - 475 :
Program to use printf() for string formatting.

Code :
```c
#include <stdio.h>

int  main()
{
    char str[25] = "Atul Kumar Soni";
    system( "cls" );

    printf( "|%25s|\n", str );
    printf( "|%-25s|\n", str );
    printf( "|%25.10s|\n", str );
    printf( "|%-25.10s|\n", str );
    printf( "|%.4s|\n", str );
    printf( "|%10s|\n", str );

    system( "pause" );
    return 0;
}
```

Output :

```
TERMINAL
|          Atul Kumar Soni|
|Atul Kumar Soni          |
|               Atul Kumar|
|Atul Kumar               |
|Atul|
|Atul Kumar Soni|
Press any key to continue . . .
```

****

****

Chapter – 16
File Handling

****

Program No. - 476 :
Program to write char values to File using **putc()** or **fputc()** function.

Code :
```c
#include <stdio.h>

int  main()
{
    FILE *fp;
    char ch;
    system( "cls" );
    fp = fopen( "demo", "w" );

    printf( "Enter String ( ctrl+z to end ) : " );
    ch = getchar();
    while( ch != EOF )
    {
        putc( ch, fp );          /*   fputc( ch, fp );   */
        ch = getchar();
    }

    fclose( fp );
    system( "pause" );
    return 0;
}
```

Output :

———————————— **** ————————————

Program No. - 477 :
Program to read char values from File using **getc()** or **fgetc()** function.

Code :
```c
#include <stdio.h>

int  main()
{
    FILE *fp;
    char ch;
    system( "cls" );
```

fp = fopen("demo", "r");

```c
    printf( "String : " );
    ch = getc( fp );          /*  ch = fgetc( fp );  */
    while( ch != EOF )
    {
        printf( "%c", ch );
        ch = getc( fp );   /*  ch = fgetc( fp );  */
    }

    fclose( fp );
    system( "pause" );
    return 0;
}
```

Output :

———————————— **** ————————————

Program No. - 478 :
Program to write integer values to File using **putw()** function.

Code :
```c
#include <stdio.h>

int  main()
{
    FILE *fp;
    int n;
    system( "cls" );
    fp = fopen( "demo1", "w" );

    while( 1 )
    {
        printf( "Enter Number ( -1 to end ) : " );
        scanf( "%d", &n );
        if( n == -1 )
            break;
        putw( n, fp );
    }
```

```
    fclose( fp );
    system( "pause" );
    return 0;
}
```

Output :

```
TERMINAL

Enter Number ( -1 to end ) : 10
Enter Number ( -1 to end ) : 20
Enter Number ( -1 to end ) : 30
Enter Number ( -1 to end ) : 40
Enter Number ( -1 to end ) : -1
Press any key to continue . . .
```

****

Program No. - 479 :
Program to read integer values from File using **getw()** function.

Code :
```
#include <stdio.h>

int  main()
{
    FILE *fp;
    int n;
    system( "cls" );

    fp = fopen( "demo1", "r" );

    printf( "Numbers are :" );
    n = getw( fp );
    while( n != EOF )
    {
        printf( "  %d", n );
        n = getw( fp );
    }

    fclose( fp );
    printf( "\n" );
    system( "pause" );
    return 0;
}
```

Output :

```
TERMINAL

Numbers are :   10  20  30  40
Press any key to continue . . .
```

****

Program No. - 480 :
Program to write string to File using **fputs()** function.

Code :
```
#include <stdio.h>

int  main()
{
    FILE *fp;
    char s[50];
    system( "cls" );

    fp = fopen( "demo2", "w" );

    printf( "Enter String : " );
    gets( s );

    fputs( s, fp );
    fputs( "\n", fp );

    fclose( fp );
    system( "pause" );
    return 0;
}
```

Output :

```
TERMINAL

Enter String : INDIA
Press any key to continue . . .
```

****

Program No. - 481 :
Program to read string values from File using **fgets()** function.

Code :
```
#include <stdio.h>

int  main()
{
```

```c
    FILE *fp;
    char s[50];
    system( "cls" );

    fp = fopen( "demo2", "r" );

    printf( "String = " );
    fgets( s, 50, fp );
    printf( "%s", s );

    fclose( fp );
    system( "pause" );
    return 0;
}
```

Output :

```
TERMINAL

String = INDIA
Press any key to continue . . .
```

****

Program No. - 482 :
Program to write multiple lines of text to File using
fputs() function..

Code :
```c
#include <stdio.h>

int  main()
{
    FILE *fp;
    char s[50];
    system( "cls" );

    fp = fopen( "demo2", "w" );

    printf( "Enter Lines of Text : \n" );
    gets( s );

    while( strlen( s ) > 0 )
    {
        fputs( s, fp );
        fputs( "\n", fp );
        gets( s );
    }
```

```c
    fclose( fp );
    system( "pause" );
    return 0;
}
```

Output :

```
TERMINAL

Enter Lines of Text :
Atul
Kumar
Soni

Press any key to continue . . .
```

****

Program No. - 483 :
Program to read multiple lines of text from file using
fgets() function.

Code :
```c
#include <stdio.h>

int  main()
{
    FILE *fp;
    char s[50];
    system( "cls" );

    fp = fopen( "demo2", "r" );

    printf( "Strings are : \n" );
    fgets( s, 50, fp );
    while( ! feof( fp ) )
    {
        printf( "%s", s );
        fgets( s, 50, fp );
    }

    fclose( fp );
    system( "pause" );
    return 0;
}
```

Output :

```
TERMINAL

Strings are :
Atul
Kumar
Soni
Press any key to continue . . . |
```

****

Program No. - 484 :
Program to write different types of values to File using **fprintf()** function.

Code :

```c
#include <stdio.h>

int  main()
{
    FILE *fp;
    int rno = 101;
    char name[50] = "Animesh";
    float marks = 92.5;
    system( "cls" );

    fp = fopen( "test", "w");
    fprintf( fp, "%d %s %f\n", rno, name, marks );
    printf( "Details saved in file.\n" );

    fclose( fp );
    system( "pause" );
    return 0;
}
```

Output :

```
TERMINAL

Details saved in file.
Press any key to continue . . . |
```

****

Program No. - 485 :
Program to read different types of values from File using **fscanf()** function.

Code :

```c
#include <stdio.h>
```

```c
int  main()
{
    FILE *fp;
    int rno;
    char name[50];
    float  marks;
    system( "cls" );

    fp = fopen( "test", "r" );
    fscanf( fp, "%d %s %f", &rno, name, &marks );

    printf( "Details from file : \n" );
    printf( "Roll No. : %d\n", rno );
    printf( "Name     : %s\n", name );
    printf( "Marks    : %.2f\n", marks );

    fclose( fp );
    system( "pause" );
    return 0;
}
```

Output :

```
TERMINAL

Details from file :
Roll No. : 101
Name      : Animesh
Marks     : 92.50
Press any key to continue . . . |
```

****

Program No. - 486 :
Program to use **getc()** & **putc()** function with console (**stdin & stdout**).

Code :

```c
#include <stdio.h>

int  main()
{
    char  ch ;
    system( "cls" ) ;

    printf( "Enter String( ctrl+z to end ):\n" );
    while( ( ch = getc ( stdin ) ) != EOF )
```

```
    {
        putc( ch, stdout ) ;
    }

    system( "pause" );
    return 0;
}
```

Output :

```
TERMINAL

Enter String( ctrl+z to end ):
Red
Red
Green
Green
Blue
Blue
^Z
Press any key to continue . . .
```

****

Program No. - 487 :
Program to write structure variable to File using **fwrite()** function.

Code :

```c
#include <stdio.h>

struct  student
{
    int rno;
    char name[50];
    float marks;
};

int  main()
{
    FILE *fp;
    struct student s;
    system( "cls" );

    fp = fopen( "students", "wb" );

    printf( "Enter Roll No. : " );
    scanf( "%d", &s.rno );
    printf( "Enter Name : " );
    fflush( stdin );
    gets( s.name );
    printf( "Enter Marks : " );
    scanf( "%f", &s.marks );

    fwrite( &s, sizeof( s ), 1, fp );

    fclose( fp ) ;
    system( "pause" );
    return 0;
}
```

Output :

```
TERMINAL

Enter Roll No.  : 101
Enter Name : Kritika
Enter Marks : 92.5
Press any key to continue . . .
```

****

Program No. - 488 :
Program to read structure variable from File using **fread()** function.

Code :

```c
#include <stdio.h>

struct  student
{
    int rno;
    char name[50];
    float marks;
};

int  main()
{
    FILE *fp;
    struct student s;
    system( "cls" );

    fp = fopen( "students", "rb" );
    fread( &s, sizeof( s ), 1, fp );

    printf( "Roll No.    : %d\n", s.rno );
    printf( "Enter Name  : %s\n", s.name );
    printf( "Enter Marks : %.2f\n", s.marks );
```

```
    fclose( fp ) ;
    system( "pause" );
    return 0;
}
```

Output :

```
TERMINAL

Roll No.     : 101
Enter Name   : Kritika
Enter Marks : 92.50
Press any key to continue . . .
```

———————————— ******** ————————————

Program No. - 489 :
Program to write structure variable to File using **fprintf()** function.

Code :

```
#include <stdio.h>

struct  student
{
    int rno;
    char name[50];
    float marks;
};

int  main()
{
    FILE *fp;
    struct student s;
    system( "cls" );

    fp = fopen( "students", "w" );

    printf( "Enter Roll No. : " );
    scanf( "%d", &s.rno );
    printf( "Enter Name : " );
    fflush( stdin );
    gets( s.name );
    printf( "Enter Marks : " );
    scanf( "%f", &s.marks );

    fprintf( fp, "%d %s %f\n", s.rno, s.name, s.marks );
```

```
    fclose( fp ) ;
    system( "pause" );
    return 0;
}
```

Output :

```
TERMINAL

Enter Roll No. : 101
Enter Name : Deepak
Enter Marks : 90.5
Press any key to continue . . .
```

———————————— ******** ————————————

Program No. - 490 :
Program to read structure variable from File using **fscanf()** function.

Code :

```
#include <stdio.h>

struct  student
{
    int rno;
    char name[50];
    float marks;
};

int  main()
{
    FILE *fp;
    struct student s;
    system( "cls" );

    fp = fopen( "students", "r" );
    fscanf( fp, "%d %s %f", &s.rno, s.name, &s.marks );

    printf( "Roll No.: %d\n", s.rno );
    printf( "Name : %s\n", s.name );
    printf( "Marks : %.2f\n", s.marks );

    fclose( fp ) ;
    system( "pause" );
    return 0;
}
```

Output :

```
TERMINAL

Roll No.: 101
Name   : Deepak
Marks  : 90.50
Press any key to continue . . .
```

****

Program No. - 491 :

Program to write structure variables to File using **fprintf()** function.

Code :

```c
#include <stdio.h>

struct  student
{
    int rno;
    char name[50];
    float marks;
};

int  main()
{
    FILE *fp;
    char another = 'Y';
    struct student s;
    system( "cls" );

    fp = fopen( "students", "w" ) ;

    while( another == 'Y' || another == 'y' )
    {
        printf( "Enter Roll No, Name & Marks : " );
        scanf( "%d %s %f", &s.rno, s.name, &s.marks );

        fprintf( fp, "%d %s %f\n", s.rno, s.name,
                                            s.marks );

        printf( "Add another record (Y/N) : " );
        fflush( stdin );
        another = getche( );
        printf( "\n" );
    }

    fclose( fp );
```

```c
    system( "pause" );
    return 0;
}
```

Output :

```
TERMINAL

Enter Roll No, Name & Marks : 101 Aman 88.25
Add another record (Y/N) : y
Enter Roll No, Name & Marks : 102 Deepak 95.0
Add another record (Y/N) : y
Enter Roll No, Name & Marks : 103 Prateek 92.5
Add another record (Y/N) : y
Enter Roll No, Name & Marks : 104 Preeti 90.75
Add another record (Y/N) : n
Press any key to continue . . .
```

****

Program No. - 492 :

Program to read structure variables from File using **fscanf()** function.

Code :

```c
#include <stdio.h>

struct  student
{
    int rno;
    char name[50];
    float marks;
};

int  main()
{
    FILE *fp;
    struct student s;
    system( "cls" );

    fp = fopen( "students", "r" );

    while( fscanf( fp, "%d %s %f", &s.rno, s.name,
                                    &s.marks ) != EOF )
    {
        printf( "\nRoll No.   : %d\n", s.rno );
        printf( "Enter Name  : %s\n", s.name );
        printf( "Enter Marks : %.2f\n", s.marks );
    }
```

```c
    fclose( fp );
    system( "pause" );
    return 0;
}
```

Output :

```
TERMINAL

Roll No.      : 101
Enter Name    : Aman
Enter Marks : 88.25

Roll No.      : 102
Enter Name    : Deepak
Enter Marks : 95.00

Roll No.      : 103
Enter Name    : Prateek
Enter Marks : 92.50

Roll No.      : 104
Enter Name    : Preeti
Enter Marks : 90.75
Press any key to continue . . . |
```

———————————— ******** ————————————

Program No. - 493 :
Program to write structure variables to File using **fwrite()** function.

Code :
```c
#include <stdio.h>

struct  student
{
    int rno;
    char name[50];
    float marks;
};

int  main()
{
    FILE *fp;
    char another = 'Y';
    struct student s;
    system( "cls" );

    fp = fopen( "students", "wb" ) ;
```

```c
    while( another == 'Y' || another == 'y' )
    {
        printf( "Enter Roll No, Name & Marks : " );
        scanf( "%d %s %f", &s.rno, s.name, &s.marks );

        fwrite( &s, sizeof( s ), 1, fp );

        printf( "Add another record (Y/N) : " );
        fflush( stdin );
        another = getche( );
        printf( "\n" );
    }

    fclose( fp );
    system( "pause" );
    return 0;
}
```

Output :

```
TERMINAL

Enter Roll No, Name & Marks : 101 Preeti 95.5
Add another record (Y/N) : y
Enter Roll No, Name & Marks : 102 Sourabh 90.25
Add another record (Y/N) : y
Enter Roll No, Name & Marks : 103 Kritika 92.75
Add another record (Y/N) : n
Press any key to continue . . . |
```

———————————— ******** ————————————

Program No. - 494 :
Program to read structure variables from File using **fread()** function.

Code :
```c
#include <stdio.h>

struct  student
{
    int rno;
    char name[50];
    float marks;
};

int  main( )
{
    FILE *fp;
```

```c
    struct student s;
    system( "cls" );

    fp = fopen( "students", "rb" );

    while( fread( &s, sizeof( s ), 1, fp ) == 1 )
    {
        printf( "\nRoll No.: %d\n", s.rno );
        printf( "Name  : %s\n", s.name );
        printf( "Marks : %.2f\n", s.marks );
    }

    fclose( fp );
    system( "pause" );
    return 0;
}
```

Output :

```
TERMINAL

Roll No.: 101
Name   : Preeti
Marks : 95.50

Roll No.: 102
Name   : Sourabh
Marks : 90.25

Roll No.: 103
Name   : Kritika
Marks : 92.75
Press any key to continue . . .
```

****

Program No. - 495 :
Program to use Error Handling function **fopen()**.

Code :

```c
#include <stdio.h>

int  main()
{
    FILE *fp;
    int n;
    system( "cls" );

    fp = fopen( "demo1", "r" );
```

```c
    if( fp == NULL )
    {
        printf( "File can not open.\n" );
    }
    else
    {
        printf( "File is opened.\n" );
    }

    fclose( fp );
    system( "pause" );
    return 0;
}
```

Output :

```
TERMINAL

File is opened.
Press any key to continue . . .
```

****

Program No. - 496 :
Program to use Error-handling function **fopen( )** to check whether the given file is open or not.

Code :

```c
#include <stdio.h>
#include <process.h>

int  main()
{
    FILE  *fp ;
    system( "cls" );

    fp = fopen( "text.txt", "r" ) ;
    if ( fp == NULL )
    {
        puts( "Unable to Open File." ) ;
        system( "pause" );
        exit( 1 ) ;
    }

    system( "pause" );
    return 0;
}
```

Output :

```
TERMINAL

Unable to Open File.
Press any key to continue . . .
```

****

Program No. - 497 :
Program to use Error-handling functions **feof( )** and **ferror( )** while reading data from file.

Code :
```c
#include <stdio.h>

int  main()
{
    FILE  *fp ;
    char  ch ;
    system( "cls" ) ;

    fp = fopen( "demo", "r" ) ;

    while( !feof ( fp ) )
    {
        ch = fgetc( fp ) ;
        if( ferror( fp ) )
        {
            printf( "Error in Reading File.\n" ) ;
            break ;
        }
        else
            printf( "%c", ch ) ;
    }

    fclose( fp ) ;

    system( "pause" );
    return 0;
}
```

Output :

```
TERMINAL

Atul Kumar Soni
 Press any key to continue . . .
```

****

Program No. - 498 :
Program to use Random access function **fseek( ), ftell( )** and **rewind( )** function.

Code :
```c
#include <stdio.h>

int  main()
{
    FILE *fp;
    char ch;
    long n;
    system( "cls" );

    fp = fopen( "demo", "w" );
    printf( "Enter String ( ctrl+z to end ) : " );
    ch = getchar();
    while( ch != EOF )
    {
        putc( ch, fp );
        ch = getchar();
    }
    fclose( fp );

    fp = fopen( "demo", "r" );
    printf( "\nChar - Pos" );

    n = 0L;
    while( feof( fp ) == 0 )
    {
        fseek( fp, n, 0 );
        printf( "\n%3c - %2d", fgetc( fp ), ftell( fp ) );
        n = n + 1L;
    }

    rewind( fp );
    printf( "\nString : " );
    ch = fgetc( fp );
    while( ch != EOF )
    {
        printf( "%c", ch );
        ch = fgetc( fp );
    }

    printf( "\n" );
```

```c
    fclose( fp );
    system( "pause" );
    return 0;
}
```

Output :

```
TERMINAL

Enter String ( ctrl+z to end ) : ATUL^Z
^Z

Char - Pos
  A -   0
  T -   1
  U -   2
  L -   3
    -   4
String : ATUL
Press any key to continue . . . |
```

______________ **** ______________

Program No. - 499 :
Program to show the use of **Command-line arguments**.

Code :
```c
#include <stdio.h>

int  main( int argc, char *argv[ ] )
{
    int i;
    system( "cls" );

    printf( "Program Name: %s\n", argv[0] );

    for( i=1 ; i<argc ; i++ )
    {
        printf( "Argument %d : %s\n", i, argv[ i ] );
    }

    system( "pause" );
    return 0;
}
```

Output :

```
TERMINAL

Program Name: D:\C\CApp261.exe
Press any key to continue . . . |
```

Command to run on Command Prompt :

```
D:\C>CApp261 Red Green Blue Orange Yellow
```

```
Program Name: CApp261
Argument 1 : Red
Argument 2 : Green
Argument 3 : Blue
Argument 4 : Orange
Argument 5 : Yellow
Press any key to continue . . . ▪
```

______________ **** ______________

Program No. - 500 :
Program to use command line argument to **copy** the content of source file to target file.

Code :
```c
#include <stdio.h>
#include <stdlib.h>            /* #include <process.h> */

int  main( int  argc, char  *argv[ ] )
{
    FILE  *fs, *ft;
    char  ch;
    system( "cls" );

    if( argc != 3 )
    {
        puts( "Improper Number of Arguments." );
        exit( 1 );
    }

    fs = fopen( argv[1], "r" );
    if( fs == NULL )
    {
        puts( "Unable to Open Source File." );
        exit( 1 ) ;
    }

    ft = fopen( argv[2], "w" );
    if( ft == NULL )
    {
        puts( "Unable to Open Target File." );
        fclose( fs );
        exit( 1 );
```

```c
    }

    while( 1 )
    {
        ch = fgetc( fs );

        if( ch == EOF )
            break;
        else
            fputc( ch, ft ) ;
    }

    fclose( fs ) ;
    fclose( ft ) ;

    system( "pause" );
    return 0;
}
```

Output :

```
TERMINAL

Improper Number of Arguments.
```

Command to run on Command Prompt :

```
D:\C>CApp262 test1.txt test2.txt_
```

```
Press any key to continue . . .
```

Source File (test1.txt) :

```
test1.txt

1     Atul Kumar Soni
2
```

Target File (test2.txt) :

```
test2.txt

1     Atul Kumar Soni
2
```

————————————— **** —————————————

————————————— **** —————————————

We Wish You All The Best ! ! !

————————————— **** —————————————